SPORTS
IN AMERICA
FROM COLONIAL TIMES TO THE
TWENTY-FIRST CENTURY

———

VOLUME 1

SPORTS IN AMERICA

FROM COLONIAL TIMES TO THE TWENTY-FIRST CENTURY

AN ENCYCLOPEDIA

VOLUME 1

STEVEN A. RIESS, EDITOR

SHARPE REFERENCE

an imprint of M.E. Sharpe, Inc.

SHARPE REFERENCE

Sharpe Reference is an imprint of M.E. Sharpe, Inc.

M.E. Sharpe, Inc.
80 Business Park Drive
Armonk, NY 10504

Cover images (clockwise, from top left) were provided by the following: AFP/Getty Images; Bob Martin/ Getty Images; Sports Illustrated/Getty Images; Otto Greule, Jr./Stringer/Getty Images; The Granger Collection, New York; Stephen Dunn/Getty Images.

Library of Congress Cataloging-in-Publication Data

Sports in America from colonial times to the twenty-first century: an encyclopedia / Steven A. Riess, editor.
   p. cm.
Includes bibliographical references and index.
ISBN 978-0-7656-1706-4 (hardcover: alk. paper)
1. Sports—United States—History. 2. Sports—Social aspects—United States—History.

GV583.S68588 2011
796.0973—dc22   2010050824

Printed and bound in the United States

The paper used in this publication meets the minimum requirements of American National Standard for Information Sciences—Permanence of Paper for Printed Library Materials, ANSI Z 39.48.1984.

CW (c) 10 9 8 7 6 5 4 3 2 1

Publisher: Myron E. Sharpe
Vice President and Director of New Product Development: Donna Sanzone
Vice President and Production Director: Carmen Chetti
Executive Development Editor: Jeff Hacker
Project Manager: Laura Brengelman
Program Coordinator: Cathleen Prisco
Editorial Assistant: Lauren LoPinto
Text Design and Cover Design: Jesse Sanchez

Contents

Volume 2

Volume 3

TOPIC FINDER

Business, Industry, and Labor

Events, Competitions, and Historical Incidents

Leagues, Conferences, and Circuits

Venues and Facilities

Russ Crawford
Ohio Northern University

Scott A.G.M. Crawford
Eastern Illinois University

Richard C. Crepeau
University of Central Florida

Carson J. Cunningham
DePaul University

Michael Dawson
St. Thomas University

Fernando Delgado
Hamline University

Paul J. DeLoca
North American Society for Sport History

Lane Demas
Central Michigan University

Élise Detellier
Université de Montréal

James I. Deutsch
Smithsonian Institute

Sundiata A. Djata
Northern Illinois University

Dan Drane
University of Southern Mississippi

Mark Dyreson
Pennsylvania State University

Jocelyn East
University of Ottawa

Anthony Edmonds
Ball State University

Jessie L. Embry
Charles Redd Center, Brigham Young University

Amy Essington
California State University, Long Beach

Michael Ezra
Sonoma State University

John D. Fair
Georgia College and State University

Merrie A. Fidler
Independent Scholar

Sarah K. Fields
The Ohio State University

Peter S. Finley
Nova Southeastern University

Donald M. Fisher
Niagara County Community College

Benjamin Franklin V
University of South Carolina

Joel S. Franks
San Jose State University

Jerry Garcia
Michigan State University

Gerald R. Gems
North Central College

Steven P. Gietschier
Lindenwood University

Aram Goudsouzian
University of Memphis

Mary Ellen Hanson
University of New Mexico

Marie Hardin
Pennsylvania State University

Robin Hardin
University of Tennessee

Michael J. Haupert
University of Wisconsin–La Crosse

Leslie Heaphy
Kent State University at Stark

Jenika Heim
San Diego State University

Benita Heiskanen
University of Southern Denmark

Annette R. Hofmann
Ludwigsburg University of Education

Deborah Beth Horn-Spiegel
Maine East High School

Thomas M. Hunt
University of Texas at Austin

Jorge Iber
Texas Tech University

Zachary Michael Jack
North Central College

Eliza L. Jacobs
Temple University

Michael D. Jacobs
University of Wisconsin–Baraboo

Duncan R. Jamieson
Ashland University

Christiane Job
University of British Columbia

Alan S. Katchen
Capital University

Richard Keller
Emporia State University

Kurt Edward Kemper
University of South Dakota

Kevin F. Kern
University of Akron

George B. Kirsch
Manhattan College

Alan S. Kornspan
University of Akron

Yasue Kuwahara
Northern Kentucky University

Joselyn K. Leimbach
San Diego State University

Robert F. Lewis, II
University of New Mexico

Richard C. Lindberg
Independent Scholar

Matthew P. Llewellyn
California State University, Fullerton

H. Matthew Loayza
Minnesota State University, Mankato

Gabe Logan
Northern Michigan University

David N. Lucsko
Auburn University

Ryan Madden
Sheldon Jackson College

Sean Malone
University of Kansas

Martin J. Manning
U.S. Department of State

Peter N. Marquis
*École des Hautes Études en Sciences
    Sociales, Centre D'Études
    Nord-Américaines*

Daniel S. Mason
University of Alberta

Fred Mason
University of New Brunswick

Erin McCarthy
Columbia College, Chicago

Keith McClellan
Independent Scholar

Ashley McGhee
University of British Columbia

Shelly McKenzie
George Washington University

Aaron W. Miller
Miami University

Andrew Miller
Sacred Heart University

John D. Miller
College of William and Mary

Andrew Milner
*Society for American Baseball
    Research*

Louis A. Moore
Grand Valley State University

Marilyn Morgan
Radcliff Institute, Harvard University

Lauren S. Morimoto
*California State University,
    East Bay*

Caroline C. Morris
College of William and Mary

Joseph C. Morton
Northeastern Illinois University

Morris Mott
Brandon University

Donald J. Mrozek
Kansas State University

William H. Mulligan, Jr.
Murray State University

Susan Nance
University of Guelph

Daniel A. Nathan
Skidmore College

Timothy B. Neary
Salve Regina University

Murry R. Nelson
Pennsylvania State University

Jim Nendel
Eastern Washington University

Caryn E. Neumann
Miami University Middletown

James E. Overmyer
*Society for American Baseball
    Research*

Dominique Padurano
Horace Mann School

Amanda L. Paule
Bowling Green State University

Sean Patrick Phelps
Auckland University of Technology

Darcy C. Plymire
Independent Scholar

Jerald Podair
Lawrence University

Megan Popovic
University of Western Ontario

Robert Pruter
Lewis University

Susan J. Rayl
*State University of New York,
    Cortland*

Elizabeth Redkey
State University of New York, Albany

Samuel O. Regalado
California State University, Stanislaus

Ron Reynolds
University of Saskatchewan

Chanelle Rose
Rowan University

Rob Ruck
University of Pittsburgh

Karen E. Sause
Independent Scholar

Gabriel Schechter
*National Baseball Hall of
Fame and Museum*

Raymond Schmidt
Independent Scholar

Brad Schultz
University of Mississippi

Ari Sclar
Hunter College

Mark Scott
Independent Scholar

Nigel Anthony Sellars
*Christopher Newport
University*

David A. Serafini
Western Kentucky University

Ameenah Shakir
University of Miami

Andrew Smith
Purdue University

Maureen Margaret Smith
*California State University,
Sacramento*

Ronald A. Smith
*Pennsylvania State
University*

Donald Spivey
University of Miami

David Stevens
Independent Scholar

Mark Storey
University of Nottingham

Richard A. Swanson
*University of North Carolina at
Greensboro*

Sarah Teetzel
University of Western Ontario

Holly Thorpe
University of Waikato

Elizabeth Tobey
National Sporting Library

Jan Todd
University of Texas at Austin

A. Bowdoin Van Riper
Southern Polytechnic State University

Travis Vogan
Indiana University

Kevin B. Wamsley
University of Western Ontario

Patricia Campbell Warner
University of Massachusetts Amherst

Stephan Wassong
Liverpool Hope University

John S. Watterson
James Madison University

Tim J. Watts
Kansas State University

David Welky
University of Central Arkansas

Erin Whiteside
Pennsylvania State University

Nathan Andrew Wilson
York University

Suzanne Wise
Appalachian State University

John Chi-Kit Wong
Washington State University

Ying Wushanley
Millersville University

Ben Wynne
Gainesville State College

Ronald Young
Canterbury School

Susan G. Zieff
*San Francisco State
University*

INTRODUCTION

Perhaps no country in the world has embraced sports—in both their spectatorial and their participatory forms—quite like the United States. Certainly, as the historical emphasis of this encyclopedia reveals, no other country has embraced sports so readily and so enthusiastically. Since colonial times, sports in America have been a major source of entertainment, a form of recreation, and a way of achieving physical fitness. Sports have helped define who Americans are, even as Americans have put their own stamp on sports.

Americans have participated in sports throughout the nation's history. Native Americans, of course, had their hunting- and war-related games in pre-Columbian times, while European colonists and African slaves brought their own forms of athletic diversion. However, the term "sport" has changed over time. In the seventeenth century, "sport" referred to virtually any diversion. Thus, for the Puritans, playing cards, bowling, and shooting at a target were all sports. By the eighteenth century, the term had narrowed to a more modern meaning: competitive athletic activities governed by a set of rules or customs.

By any definition, sports always have been interwoven into the fabric of American life, promoting traditional values among the well-established, aiding acculturation among newly arrived immigrants, and reinforcing pride in shared ethnic identity. In fact, sports have been, and continue to be, a source of local, regional, and national pride for many Americans.

Participation in sports has served as a means of certifying social status and as a venue for promoting manliness and fitness and, later, feminine skill and strength. Sports provide myriad business opportunities as well as occupations for athletes, coaches, and many others. Sports hold up a mirror to society, reflecting trends in ethnicity, race, class, and gender. In essence, sports have come to represent a virtual social institution, one shaped by forces such as bureaucratization, immigration, industrialization, and urbanization.

As of the early twenty-first century, interest in sports, both active and passive, is at an all-time high.

Sports are enjoyed by men and women, children and adults, and people of all ethnic, racial, and class backgrounds. Sports also are big business. According to publisher Street & Smith, spectatorial and participatory sports in America generated more than $200 billion in 2011—twice as much as the automobile industry.

Americans spend billions of dollars each year on sporting equipment alone. The two most popular participatory sports—fishing and hunting—lead the way: By the end of the first decade of the twenty-first century, some 30 million Americans spent more than $40 billion annually on fishing gear, while more than 12 million spent upwards of $25 billion on hunting equipment.

Spectator sports are bigger than ever. Americans devote more of their leisure time to watching sports—on television, in person, or through other forms of media such as the Internet—than they do taking part in them. American television networks produce some 2,100 hours of sports programming per year, with thousands more on cable; ESPN alone televises 24 hours a day, seven days a week, or about 8,500 hours each year. Americans are spending increasing sums of money on spectator sports—$22.4 billion in 2010.

As a result, professional sports franchises have become extremely valuable. The New York Yankees, for example, were worth a reported $1.7 billion in 2011, while the average Major League Baseball (MLB) team was valued at $523 million. The leader in the National Football League (NFL) in 2010 (the latest available data) was the Dallas Cowboys, valued at $1.8 billion, with a team average of $1.02 billion. The leading franchise in the National Basketball Association (NBA) in 2011 was the New York Knicks, worth a reported $655 million, while the NBA average was $369 million per team. And in the National Hockey League (NHL), the most valuable franchise was the Toronto Maple Leafs at $505 million, with a league average of $228 million per team. Major college athletic programs continue to expand as well, with budgets of $40 million to $75 million annually and attendance at football games sometimes exceeding 100,000. Meanwhile, to support growing fan interest, private investors, companies, universities, and municipalities have been building facilities for professional sports teams on a regular basis since the late nineteenth century.

Professional athletes, oppressed by management for decades, began to assert their rights in the 1970s. Today, the best athletes earn tens of millions of dollars annually, while even journeyman players in the top leagues can become millionaires. In the NBA, for example, players made an average of $5.85 million in 2010; in MLB, players earned an average of $3.3 million. In the NFL, players averaged $2.4 million, and in the NHL, they earned an average of $1.9 million (a median of $770,000). In individual sports, the stakes can be even higher. Golfer Tiger Woods, for instance, is estimated to have made more than $1 billion over the course of his career, largely through endorsements.

Purpose of this Encyclopedia

This encyclopedia is divided into three sections. A series of long essays covers the history of American sports from colonial times to the twenty-first century. An A-to-Z section—the bulk of the book—covers a wide array of topics, including major athletes, teams, and institutions; individual and team sports; and broader thematic topics, such as business, media, immigration, and diplomacy. The book also includes a variety of ancillary materials, such as a thematic topic finder, a directory of leading sports organizations and leagues, a general bibliography, and a detailed index. In addition, each article offers a specialized list of recommended further readings, and A-to-Z entries also include cross references to related entries.

Generally, this work serves two purposes: First, it provides a comprehensive history of American sports—both in their spectatorial and their participatory forms—from the nation's beginnings to the present day. This is not the kind of history that you will find in conventional sports reference works, such as those that fill the sports sections of local bookstores. Not every player and team is covered here—rather, this book focuses on those who have shaped their sport and American society in significant ways.

Second, this book provides in-depth analysis of how social forces have shaped American sports history, and, in turn, how sports have shaped American society—affecting such issues as integration, social policy, class, and gender—throughout the course of history. Thus,

this encyclopedia emphasizes analysis and interpretation, along with factual information. While critical statistical information can be found in abundance here, it is provided not as an end in itself, but as a means of assessing the significance of a team or an individual athlete's accomplishments so as to measure his or her impact on a specific sport and on the history of sports in general.

Curious fans, of course, can find more comprehensive statistical information in almanacs or, increasingly, on the Internet. But what they usually cannot find there is analysis and contextualization—what sports have meant to American history and society for the past 400 years—and an examination of how sports have evolved from a morally suspect form of fringe entertainment to become a treasured national institution and an integral part of our daily lives. For that, intellectually curious fans—as well as those who are not fans—can find much to explore in this work.

Acknowledgments

This project has truly been a marathon and not a sprint. The encyclopedia originated in 2005 under the sponsorship of James Ciment, a scholar and consulting editor for M.E. Sharpe. I began the endeavor with the close support and advice of Melvin Adelman and Patricia Vertinsky, who played a critical role in putting together our table of contents. I received wise suggestions from the distinguished editorial board of Allan Guttmann, Colin Howell, Michael Lomax, Michael Oriard, Roberta J. Park, and Benjamin G. Rader.

Once the project was under way, many people provided ideas and suggestions, ranging from potential topics to thoughts about particular themes such as nationalism and identity. I want to thank Richard C. Crepeau, Michael Doxtater, Jocelyn East, Gerald R. Gems, Greg Gillespie, Alan Gordon, Christopher Green, Andrew Holman, Bruce Kidd, John McClelland, Karen McGarry, Alan Metcalfe, Don Morrow, Robert Pruter, Andrew Ross, Ronald A. Smith, Michel Vigneault, Charlene Weaving, and John Chi-Kit Wong.

I also want to thank the many other contributors who did such a fine job researching, analyzing, and writing for the encyclopedia. In addition, I would like to apologize to those contributors whose essays could not be included in the final work. Late in the process, it became clear that the extensive amount of important information to be included required that we narrow the scope of the project from a broader discussion of North American sports to focus primarily on sports in the United States.

Due to the enormity of this endeavor, it required a steady hand to manage the operation, keep open lines to contributors, and maintain our records. I want to thank Jamie Riess, who is undoubtedly the most organized person I know, for a superb job as my editorial assistant. Here at Northeastern Illinois University in Chicago, I also received admirable assistance from the office manager of the Department of History, Christina Joe, as well as from our interlibrary loan department, led by Debbie Siegel.

This project benefited enormously from the outstanding team at M.E. Sharpe. Jeff Hacker, James Ciment, and Larry Lorimer helped shape and reshape the encyclopedia with great vision and tireless work in developing, editing, prodding, and finding contributors for some of the toughest assignments, particularly historian Christopher G. Bates, who at the last moment wrote or co-authored several challenging entries. Jeff Hacker also did a superb job collecting photographs and writing captions to complement the text. Project coordinator Cathy Prisco ably organized the many aspects of this complex project. The project manager was Laura Brengelman, who worked assiduously to get the final draft into shape; she has a remarkable ability to clarify authors' prose and analysis. And we had great work from our copy editor Deborah Ring. My hat's off to all of you.

Finally, I want to thank my wife Tobi, for her continued good spirits in supporting me throughout a project that took far more time to complete than anyone anticipated. My thanks also go out to my daughter Jennifer, who went away to college, graduated, and has moved on to the world of marketing in the years it has taken to bring this landmark encyclopedia to completion.

Steven A. Riess

ESSAYS

COLONIAL ERA

Sports were an important element of life in the American colonies from the earliest days. Colonists used the term "sport" to refer to any pastime or diversion, including traditional athletic contests encompassing tests of strength, skill, manliness, and honor.

During the seventeenth century, sporting options were restricted in New England because of stringent Puritan beliefs, which frowned on sports that promoted idleness, gambling, and the desecration of the Sabbath, although uplifting activities, such as marksmanship, were permitted. Farther south, Anglican Virginians enjoyed gambling and blood sports, though not on the Sabbath. In general, popular sports derived from the colonists' English heritage, the social class of the participants, and their proximity to woods for hunting, bodies of water for fishing, and the presence of deadly enemies, which required skills such as shooting.

In the eighteenth century, support for sports became more widespread, and colonists nearly everywhere enjoyed a varied sporting life made possible by greater security, a more cosmopolitan worldview, declining religious orthodoxy, commercialization, a changing social structure, and urbanization. Cities were disproportionately important sites of organized sporting competition, especially commercialized sport, even though 95 percent of the population lived in rural areas. Urban residents provided a substantial sporting audience for publicans, or tavern keepers, who were the earliest sports promoters.

The presence of concentrated populations facilitated the development of the first sports clubs, which promoted angling, horse racing, and other sports practiced by the English gentry and the well-to-do in London. These associations helped members of the colonial social and economic elite separate themselves from their social inferiors. Governments were drawn into the sporting nexus to protect community norms and morality, maintain order, and prevent the pleasure of the few from interfering with the business of the many—

developments that foreshadowed future trends in the history of American sports.

Seventeenth-Century Sports

British colonists began participating in sports as soon as they arrived in North America, playing the same games they had enjoyed in the villages and towns of England.

Virginia

One of the causes of early labor problems in the colony of Jamestown, Virginia, historians have noted, was that its first inhabitants often spent time bowling when they should have been working, or hunted game when they had been assigned to tend cattle. In 1611, Governor Thomas Dale found it necessary to impose laws forbidding hunting for pleasure on the Sabbath, and one year later, the "Lawes Divine, Morall and Martial" banned card playing and wasting gunpowder by shooting at game. In 1619, the Virginia House of Burgesses called for strict enforcement of the Sabbath and banned gambling; however, over time, these laws were laxly enforced.

The most important sport in Virginia, and eventually all of British North America, was horse racing, the favorite pastime of the English aristocracy. American racing originated in New York in 1665, a year after the British took over the colony of New Netherland. Governor Richard Nicolls organized annual races at the Newmarket Course in Hempstead, Long Island, named in honor of the home of English racing. By the end of the century, the sport was enjoyed in Boston and Philadelphia, despite the gambling, swearing, and wild riding in city streets that it engendered.

The "sport of kings" was dominated in the late seventeenth century by the wealthy planters of Virginia, who rode their own workhorses in short races of about a quarter mile (0.4 kilometers). As historian Timothy Breen has pointed out, the sport reflected their materialism, individuality, and competitiveness.

The livelihood of Virginia's tobacco growers was itself a high-risk venture, vulnerable to cold, frosts, plagues, cargo lost to shipwrecks, and the vagaries of the market. As a counterpoint to their volatile business, planters enjoyed racing and high-stakes gambling with their peers as forms of recreation, though arranged matches and wagers were taken very seriously and considered legally binding contracts.

Planters also took part in racing to demonstrate their courage, brawn, intelligence, and honor, and to promote a sense of shared values and consciousness among the racing and gambling gentry. Furthermore, the rituals of the contests encouraged a fellowship between the landed elite and mass spectators that reinforced traditional patterns of respect and deference.

New Netherland

Farther north, the Dutch burghers of New Amsterdam and Albany also enjoyed sports. By 1631, residents ventured outside the village walls on fishing and hunting parties. In addition, the townsfolk enjoyed traditional Dutch sports such as boat racing, bowling, golfing, skating, and sledding. But there were conflicts over the appropriateness of some sporting activities. In 1647, for example, Governor Peter Stuyvesant banned Sunday recreation.

Massachusetts Bay Colony

The Puritan Massachusetts Bay Colony was founded in 1629 as a homogeneous community of "visible saints" who shared strict Calvinist beliefs and values and expected to make their settlement a Christian role model. Thus, they strictly maintained the Sabbath and prohibited any entertainment that they viewed as a waste of time, that distracted people from their public responsibilities, or that encouraged sinful behavior. Animal baiting, fighting, Sunday sports, and all games associated with gambling were barred. Religious and civic leaders were particularly leery of amusements at inns and taverns because of their association with drunkenness and gambling, and so they regulated such pastimes closely from the start.

At mid-century, the colony banned bowling and shuffleboard because of their association with gambling. Gambling was a sin according to Puritan theology, for two reasons: 1) because bettors coveted their neighbor's

At A COUNCIL
Held at Boston the 9th. of April, 1677

THe COUNCIL being informed, that among other Evils that are prevailing among us, in this day of our Calamity, there is practised by some that vanity of Horse racing, for mony, or monyes worth, thereby occasioning much misspence of pretious time, and the drawing of many persons from the duty of their particular Callings, with the hazard of their Limbs and Lives.

It is hereby Ordered that henceforth it shall not be Lawful for any persons to do or practise in that kind, within *four miles* of any Town, or in any *Highway* or *Common Rode*, on penalty of forfeiting *twenty Shillings* apiece, nor shall any Game or run in that kind for any mony, or monyes worth upon penalty of forfeiting Treble the value thereof, one half to the *party informing*, and the other half to the *Treasury*, nor shall any accompany or abbett any in that practice on the like penalty, and this to continue til the General Courtt take further Order.

And all *Constables* respectively are hereby injoyned to present the Names of all such as shall be found transgressing, contrary to this Order to the *Magistrate*.

Dated the *ninth of April*, 1677.

By the Council
Edward Rawson Sec.

An order by the Boston council in 1677 prohibits horse racing and gambling within 4 miles of town. In Puritan Massachusetts, sports and recreation said to promote idleness, desecration of the Sabbath, or public disorder were banned by such "blue laws." *(MPI/Stringer/Getty Images)*

property, and 2) because making money without labor denied the godly obligation to work hard at one's "calling," the occupation that God ordained for each person.

Nonetheless, athletic activities were permitted if they were viewed as useful and productive, such as hunting game or dangerous animals like wolves or fishing (which, strictly speaking, was work and not leisure), or if the activities were self-improving. The Massachusetts Body of Liberties (1641) guaranteed all householders the right to hunt birds and fish on public land. Marksmanship was encouraged to develop skills needed for hunting, as well as for fighting Indians.

The principal site of public sports in Boston was the Common, which was established in 1634 for grazing cattle and military training, but also was used for executions, whippings, and burials. Martial arts such as archery and musketry were practiced when authorities required "military muster," an event called Training Day. By the late seventeenth century, Training Day was a time for a general town revel, a day when boys chased greased pigs, raced each other, and played ball games, or went ice-skating, depending on the season. On such days, militiamen engaged in contests of marksmanship, horse and foot races, and wrestling.

Urban Puritans also regulated sports that interfered with orderly town life. Town leaders believed that it was essential to maintain the safety of city streets in order to protect pedestrians and to keep thoroughfares open for traffic and commerce. Inconsiderate youths disrupted free movement with their games and made it dangerous to walk on Boston's narrow streets.

Indeed, so many Bostonians were injured by youths playing football that laws were passed in 1657, 1677, and 1701 banning the sport. In 1672, the Essex County Court also barred horse racing within 2 miles (3.2 kilometers) of any town meetinghouse, not only to prevent betting, but also to protect pedestrians from speeding horses. In 1710, the General Court of Massachusetts forbade shooting at pigeons or targets in Boston, in response to public concerns about guns being shot in crowded areas and stray bullets striking innocent bystanders.

Pennsylvania

In 1682, William Penn established Pennsylvania as a haven for dissenting English Quakers. Like the Puritans, Quakers believed that sports, games, and "loose behavior" diverted man from work, devotion to God, and the "First Day" (the Sabbath). Thus, the Pennsylvania Assembly prohibited "rude and riotous sports" such as bull baiting and cockfighting to better exercise social control over those outside the Society of Friends.

The Pennsylvania government also discouraged attendance at sporting contests for fear that excited crowds would detract from public discipline. Running races were opposed, because they stimulated such sins as the wish to excel (vanity) and gambling (coveting another's property). A 1705 provincial edict prohibited 14 different tavern games, including billiards, ninepins, and shuffleboard; however, as elsewhere, such laws were not always heeded.

Eighteenth-Century Sports

By the turn of the eighteenth century, third-generation Puritans were less committed than the early settlers to their creed, and they took a more liberal view of sports. The Reverend Cotton Mather, in his "Advice to a Young Man" (1709), promoted lawful and moderate sport under parental supervision to teach traditional values and to establish closer bonds between fathers and sons.

There was a notable increase in sporting activities during the eighteenth century throughout the colonies as communities became more developed and religious scruples less limiting, and as sports became more organized and commercialized. At the same time, social class became even more important, as members of the upper class sought to emulate the rustic pastimes of the English gentry.

Colonists took advantage of nearby waters to enjoy aquatic sports, particularly swimming, rowing, and boating in the summer and ice-skating in the winter. Philadelphians had a reputation as the best skaters in the world and as fine swimmers, many of whom were taught by Benjamin Franklin. Girls were not allowed to swim with men, but they did visit the New Jersey shore on family vacations and swam in the ocean there.

Taverns

Colonial cities had a sufficient number of residents who were interested in sports to encourage publicans to become the first sports promoters and to persuade businessmen to sell sporting equipment that was imported from England. Tavern keepers recognized that they could make substantial profits by promoting sports to thirsty men. They sponsored sporting contests by providing the necessary equipment, such as billiard tables, outdoor bowling lanes, or targets for marksmen, as well as prizes for competitors, whose contests drew spectators. Prizes for a target-shooting contest could be cash, a side of beef, a gold watch, furniture, or even a house. Taverns also sponsored cockfights and bull- and bear-baiting contests.

The masses engaged in tavern sports as a catharsis, as a means to win valuable prizes and gain respect and peer recognition, and as a vehicle for forming an independent community. Members of respectable society generally frowned on the plebeian tavern goers and their raucous public pastimes, yet often engaged in the same pastimes in more private settings.

By the 1720s, Philadelphians were unimpeded in their enjoyment of billiards, bowling, animal baiting, and cockfighting. Tavern culture flourished as the Quaker influence declined and as the city became more heterogeneous with the arrival of Palatine German and Scots-Irish immigrants, a growing gap in wealth between rich and poor, and the increasing political influence of English merchants. In the process, religious scruples against non-utilitarian sports gave way to the morality of a mercantile English elite that approved of sports.

Cockfighting

Cockfighting was a traditional rural amusement that pitted specially trained and bred roosters against one another in bouts, often fought to the death. In many colonies, the sport was declared illegal, not just for its bloodiness, but also because it encouraged gambling and diverted men from work. Bird owners took great pride in breeding fowl for speed and ferocity, and they tested the birds' prowess in individual matches or formal tournaments called mains.

Fights between male birds were a popular diversion on plantations, inns at rural crossroads, and urban taverns, where it became the most popular spectator sport. Cockfighting was second in popularity only to horse racing among Southern sportsmen. Matches often drew a socially mixed crowd, though the more fashionable folk avoided the riff-raff, preferring exclusive taverns such as New York's Sign of the Fighting Cocks.

Southern tavern keepers sponsored matches whenever there was a challenge, but the sport was most profitable during "public times," when the county court or provincial legislature was in session and people visited from out of town. Still, respectable society worried about riotous behavior among the working class at such matches.

Nevertheless, cockfighting remained a popular urban sport in the postrevolutionary period, although newspapers in New York and Philadelphia refused to advertise matches. Broadsides posted at public places and handbills distributed on street corners informed the sporting crowd about the location of mains, though most Northern contests were private affairs and fanciers were informed of matches by word of mouth.

Sports and the Elite

Elite urbanites, New York patroons who owned large Hudson River Valley manors, and Southern planters all had aristocratic pretensions and emulated the English gentry by establishing a wide-ranging club life and copying such country pleasures as hunting, riding and fishing. At the same time, wealth in cities was becoming increasingly concentrated in the hands of a few. In Boston, for instance, the wealthiest 10 percent of the population, mainly merchants, possessed 63 percent of the taxable wealth in 1771.

These high-status men had the time, discretionary income, and desire to participate in a leisurely lifestyle that provided a means of conspicuously displaying their achievements or inherited status. The gayest social life during the colonial era was to be had in cosmopolitan New York, which had originated as a Dutch community before it became a British royal colony led by men who identified with an aristocratic culture, and where religious scruples were less inhibiting than in other cities. Royal governors consistently sponsored and encouraged sports in emulation of English society. New York's sophisticated upper class enjoyed many pleasures that were available only in a big city, such as joining social clubs and attending the theater, but they also enjoyed many rural sports—still accessible because of the small size of the colonial city—such as horse racing, hunting, and sleighing, as well as the more elite sports of coaching (racing carriages) and yachting.

A new sport of the period was cricket. In 1751, Americans and Londoners participated in a cricket match that marked the first international sporting event in North America—to the surprise of many, the colonials won.

Golf also was introduced to America at this time. Before the Revolutionary War, Andrew Johnson of Charles Town, South Carolina, brought home golf clubs from Scotland, although he did not play until after the war. In 1786, Scottish merchants formed a golf society in South Carolina.

Meanwhile, hunting remained a sporting activity for the elite, rather than a way to put meat on the table or to bag skins for sale. The sport was so popular on Long Island that overhunting resulted in a scarcity of game. New York responded in 1706 by creating a closed hunting season from April through October. A generation later, conservation-minded Governor William Cosby helped establish game preserves and deer parks to protect wildlife.

Military leaders represented an important segment of the upper class. During the revolutionary era, British officers enjoyed their sporting pleasures. Officers stationed in New York played cricket, went fox hunting, and visited Thomas McMullan's tavern, the Sign of George III, to witness bull baiting, which they often followed up with a British-style roast beef dinner.

Elite Men's Clubs

Upper-class urbanites formed voluntary associations to promote sociability and to maintain ethnic and class distinctions, often by establishing private clubs. The most exclusive of these in Philadelphia was the Schuylkill Fishing Company of Pennsylvania (originally known as the Colony in Schuylkill) founded in 1732, possibly the first men's club in the English-speaking world, which fostered conviviality among gentlemen who enjoyed fishing, hunting, and dining. The club was a role model for subsequent colonial sports clubs, including four other fishing companies, which were created by 1767. Many members of the club also were patriots who, in November 1774, organized the Philadelphia Light Horse Troop, the oldest continuous military organization in the United States.

Upper-class Philadelphians further emulated the English gentry by engaging in fox hunting beginning in the 1730s. The sport provided excitement, romance, and a focal point for camaraderie. Fox hunting was an expensive undertaking—which assured its exclusivity—requiring extensive planning and organization, professional guides, and trained hounds. Again, such hunting by the elite was very different from the hunting of common folk, which often was a means to obtain food to eat or hides to sell.

The first organized formal fox hunt was held in 1747 in Virginia by Lord Thomas Fairfax. Nineteen years later, elite Philadelphians established the Gloucester Fox Hunting Club, probably the first of its kind in the world.

Horse Racing

Horse racing, the most popular sport of the English gentry, was equally popular in the colonies. Virginians still dominated with 12 tracks in 1700 and 24 in 1730. Shortly thereafter, racing underwent a big change as colonists began emulating the English style of long-distance racing instead of quarter-mile horse racing. In addition, the riders were no longer horse owners but slaves. The change in racing fashion led in the 1740s to the importing of expensive Arabian horses from England, bred for size, strength, and endurance.

Long-distance racing also became popular at urban racetracks established by voluntary elite organizations, known as jockey clubs, to promote the sport. The first organized races around a circular track were staged in New York's Bowery district in April 1735. The New York area had seven courses by the 1760s, most notably the Newmarket track, where the finest horses—owned by elite families such as the Morrisses, DeLanceys, and other members of the mercantile and landed elite—competed in high-stakes races.

The main Southern tracks were located in the colonial capitals of Annapolis (Maryland), Charles Town (later Charleston, South Carolina), and Williamsburg (Virginia). In 1734, Charles Town's first jockey club was formed; it raced at the York Course, which opened one year later. The York Course was the colony's main venue until the mid-1750s, but it was supplanted in 1760 by the Newmarket Course. Williamsburg opened a circular track for mile races in 1739, and six years later, the Annapolis elite formed their own jockey club. These races were well publicized in press advertisements and tavern broadsides. By the 1760s, the local press regularly published detailed postrace accounts. At times, gambling was so heavy that it threatened some family fortunes.

The races became a staple of the social calendar during public times, when weeklong meets were scheduled. All members of the community, including the esteemed military hero George Washington, attended the races, though there was little intermingling among the classes at the track. Afterward, the masses visited their favorite taverns to discuss the matches or entertained themselves with cudgeling contests, foot races, or chasing greased pigs, while the elite retired to the theater and to lavish balls. The Revolutionary War had a negative impact on the turf. In Philadelphia, radicals in the Provincial Assembly passed a bill in 1774 to discourage racing and other gambling sports in an effort to impose a more sober and patriotic value system on the community. A similar resolution was passed one month later by the Continental Congress as a statement against aristocratic social pretensions associated with England.

When the war broke out, elite loyalists continued to enjoy their exclusive pleasures, confirming for many patriots that the colonial upper class lacked republican virtue. When the Continental Congress returned to Philadelphia in 1778, a new resolution was approved encouraging each colony to suppress racing "and such other diversions as are productive of idleness and dissipation." Pennsylvania promptly banned Sunday activities and all gambling sports.

Women and Sports

Conventional wisdom has held that women were not interested in sports during the colonial era, but historian Nancy Struna has found evidence of women's participation in sports in that period. She attributes this involvement to the increase in family stability and decline in death rates, widespread access to sporting goods and horses, and a growing positive orientation to the human body among enlightened figures such as Benjamin Franklin and John Adams, who supported exercise and bodily development for both sexes. Adams argued that exercise made people happier, more satisfied, and ready for business and pleasure, and he recommended that his family attend to their own physical development.

By the 1720s, New England women were increasingly riding horses in saddle or in a chaise (a two- or four-wheeled carriage), and, by the 1740s, girls participated in running and horse races at local fairs. At mid-century, women were more commonly seen in public participating in such coeducational activities as fishing parties, sleigh rides, and sailing. Rich Southern women hunted foxes and raced horses. They also attended horse races, where they were welcomed by jockey clubs for the moral tone they set; the clubs initiated ladies' purses and designated seating areas for them.

In eastern Massachusetts, women in the 1760s transformed the work of spinning into a competition between teams divided by age, marital status, or location. Struna identifies this as the first feminine-defined sport form. Such contests represented attempts by women to establish their autonomy from men, although their very nature reinforced the traditional woman's sphere of domesticity and work inside the home.

Finally, well-to-do women enjoyed access to their husband's billiard tables, fowling pieces, and sleighs. By 1790, married or widowed women owned about 5 percent of inventoried sporting equipment in Boston and 11 percent in Baltimore.

Legacy

Sporting life in the colonial era set the stage for the activities that followed in the young republic. Sports were mainly male, participatory, and rural based; however, they generally were organized by publicans for the masses and by elite urban clubs for the rich. Sports were most appreciated in the South for providing a public display of manliness. They were least regarded in New England, where conservative religious and social values associated most sports with gambling, drinking, and other "vile" activities.

Steven A. Riess

Further Reading

Breen, T.H. "Horses and Gentlemen: The Cultural Significance of Gambling Among the Gentry of Virginia." *William and Mary Quarterly* 34:2 (April 1977): 239–257.

Bridenbaugh, Carl. *Cities in Revolt: Urban Life in America, 1743–1776.* New York: Alfred A. Knopf, 1955.

———. *Cities in the Wilderness: The First Century of Urban Life in America, 1625–1742.* New York: Ronald Press, 1938.

Carson, Jane. *Colonial Virginians at Play.* Charlottesville: University Press of Virginia, 1965.

Daniels, Bruce C. *Puritans at Play: Leisure and Recreation in Colonial New England.* New York: St. Martin's, 1995.

Ewing, William C. *The Sports of Colonial Williamsburg.* Richmond, VA: Dietz, 1937.

Jable, J. Thomas. "The Pennsylvania Sunday Blue Laws of 1779: A View of Pennsylvania Society and Politics During the American Revolution." *Pennsylvania History* 40:4 (October 1973): 413–426.

———. "Pennsylvania's Early Blue Laws: A Quaker Experiment in the Suppression of Sport and Amusements, 1682–1740." *Journal of Sport History* 1:2 (Fall 1974): 107–121.

Ledbetter, Bonnie S. "Sports and Games of the American Revolution." *Journal of Sport History* 6:3 (Winter 1979): 29–40.

Solberg, Winton U. *Redeem the Time: The Puritan Sabbath in Early America.* Cambridge, MA: Harvard University Press, 1977.

Stanard, William G. "Racing in Colonial Virginia." *Virginia Magazine of History and Biography* 2 (January 1895): 299–305.

Struna, Nancy L. *People of Prowess: Sport, Leisure, and Labor in Early Anglo-America.* Urbana: University of Illinois Press, 1996.

EARLY REPUBLIC, ANTEBELLUM, AND CIVIL WAR ERAS, 1790-1870

American sports underwent a significant transformation between 1790 and 1870. During these 80 years, sports were at first dominated by participatory pastimes rather than mass spectator sports. There was a lively male sporting subculture on the frontier that emphasized traditional pastimes such as hunting, fishing, fighting, and horse racing, and another in cities that was dominated by a sporting brotherhood of wealthy young men and athletic urban workers. The sporting life was a focal point of the bachelor subculture that dominated urban sports such as billiards, bowling, horse racing, and prizefighting, all of which were both participatory and spectatorial. The lifestyles of these two classes of men were abhorred by members of the "respectable" middle class, who saw nothing uplifting in a sporting life that glorified violence and gambling.

Beginning in the early republic period, however, a dramatic change took place in middle-class attitudes toward sport. A positive sports creed gradually developed, which held that participation in clean sports could improve the morality, character, and health of young people in dirty, crime- and vice-ridden cities. This change was encouraged by the positive example of immigrant sporting cultures and by the development of the new game of baseball, which seemed to epitomize the best attributes of sport.

Sports in the Early Republic

In 1800, 95 percent of the American population lived in rural areas and participated in sports that reflected their environment. Their principal sports involved contests of strength, skill, and courage staged in taverns or the nearby countryside. They fished, hunted, shot at targets, and rode horses, while spectators watched horse races and such blood sports as gouging, wrestling, and cockfighting.

The sporting culture in the Early Republic remained similar to that of the colonial era, in that it emulated the sports of Great Britain, the dominant sporting nation in Europe, and the main source of American culture. Horse racing was the main sport, but there was strong public opposition to horse racing in the Northeast, where it was decried as a reflection of the decadence of old loyalists during the Revolutionary War, encouraging lazy behavior on the part of spectators and sinful gambling. Thoroughbred racing, however, remained popular in the South, where there were formal tracks run by elite jockey clubs, and in the territories west of the Appalachian Mountains. In Lexington, Kentucky, the streets were converted into racetracks.

On the frontier, sporting life reflected the martial tradition of the region's many Scots-Irish inhabitants, the dangerous environment, and the lack of law and order. Young frontiersmen enjoyed wrestling, marksmanship contests, and the occasional festival at which they ran, jumped, and threw axes. Sport was enjoyed at Western military outposts such as Fort Dearborn (present-day Chicago), where soldiers, French Canadians, and Native Americans competed in hunting and running races.

The most violent frontier sport was the brutal, "rough and tumble" activity of gouging, a form of wrestling and fighting in which the only rule was that there were no rules. Such matches usually resulted from personal insults among poor backcountry folk or mountain men who possessed nothing but their honor, and they fought to defend that honor.

Sports in the Antebellum City

Less than 10 percent of the population lived in cities as late as 1820. Urban areas were physically small places, known as walking cities, because they were only a few miles in size, and people walked from place to place. They were located close to waterways and forests, and there often was sufficient vacant space in town or nearby for people to engage in rural sports. By 1860, 20 percent of Americans lived in cities, where growing populations provided both potential athletes and spectators.

WILD DUCK SHOOTING.

Wild duck hunting, as depicted in this 1840s Currier & Ives lithograph, was among the popular pastimes on the American frontier in the early nineteenth century. Fishing, shooting, and fighting were likewise part of the male sporting culture. *(Library of Congress)*

Young men drawn to the cities for jobs and pleasure had ample opportunities to engage in unsupervised activities and to live free from the social controls that regulated small-town life. Indeed, cities had large numbers of single men—more than 40 percent in New Orleans, for example. They made up a bachelor subculture that reveled in drinking, whoring, gambling, and sports—a preferable alternative to the dominant Victorian culture, which emphasized hard work, deferred gratification, accumulation of property, and domesticity. To these bachelors, manliness meant aggressiveness, courage, honor, strength, virility, and violence.

This subculture mainly comprised journeymen, apprentices, semiskilled and unskilled men, and members of urban street gangs and volunteer fire companies who were heavily involved in machine politics. These men had little control over their work, and instead turned to their leisure activities for fulfillment, identity, a sense of manliness, and fun. They represented the core of a pre-industrial sporting fraternity that centered on plebeian billiard halls, firehouses, gambling halls, and especially taverns.

In these establishments, spectators could watch and bet on such blood sports as cockfighting and animal baiting, activities that reformers worked to halt in the 1830s and 1840s. Another option was pugilism, a step up from knife fights or gouging, as a demonstration of courage and manliness, but it was universally illegal. Matches were held secretly in saloon backrooms or well out of town.

Technological Innovation and the Growth of Sports

The United States in the antebellum era underwent a revolution in communication that made sporting news more accessible, which, in turn, enhanced public interest in physical culture. Entrepreneurs created weeklies that focused on such rural sports as angling, hunting, and horse racing, beginning with John Stuart Skinner's *American Farmer,* established in 1819. It was followed 12 years later by William T. Porter's *The Spirit of the Times: A Chronicle of the Turf, Agriculture, Field Sports, Literature and the Stage,* which became the leading sporting periodical in the United States. *The Spirit of the Times* originally focused on horse and foot racing, fishing, and rowing, and later expanded its coverage to baseball, cricket, pugilism, and yachting.

There also were major developments in the daily newspapers, which before the 1830s were expensive and focused on business and politics. Mass-oriented penny newspapers such as the New York *Sun* and the *New York Herald* gave considerable coverage to horse racing and boxing. This, in turn, helped generate and sustain popular interest in sport. James G. Bennett's *New York Herald,* begun in 1835, became America's most popular newspaper by the Civil War, in large part because of its emphasis on sports. Bennett was particularly adept at employing the latest technology, such as telegraphy, which dramatically sped up reportage from distant places, and the rotary press (1846), which printed 20,000 sheets per hour.

There also was a great transportation revolution. Railroads began to have an impact on sport by the 1850s, helping participants and spectators travel to events. The railroad's potential to bolster interest in athletics was demonstrated in 1852, when the Boston, Concord, & Montreal Railroad sponsored the Harvard–Yale rowing race at Lake Winnipesaukee, New Hampshire, to encourage ridership.

Sports and Social Class

Social class was one of the prime determinants of the sporting interests of antebellum Americans, as different levels of income and family backgrounds often dictated the types of sports that people participated in and watched as spectators. Upper-class young men had the most money and time to engage in sports. They typically joined sports clubs that enhanced their social status, as in the colonial era, and occasionally sponsored public contests.

Wealthy financier John C. Stevens of New York was the preeminent antebellum sportsman, involved in horse racing, pedestrianism, and yachting. He was the leading Northern horseman, and in 1823, he organized the Great Match Race between the Northern stallion

Eclipse (also known as American Eclipse) and the top Southern horse, Sir Henry, at Long Island's Union Course. Reportedly, more than 50,000 people saw Eclipse capture two out of three 4-mile (6.4-kilometer) heats for the victory. Twelve years later, Stevens promoted the first major pedestrian race by offering $1,000 to any man who could run 10 miles (16 kilometers) in under an hour. The race was won by Connecticut farmer Henry Stannard, who came in just 12 seconds under an hour.

In 1844, Stevens organized the New York Yacht Club to promote upper-class leisure, sociability, and good health, as well as American naval architecture. Seven years later, his *America* won the Royal Yacht Squadron regatta. This victory over the British, considered the greatest sailors and ship builders in the world, was the first by American athletes over the mother country, and a moment of great national pride. The winning trophy became known as the America's Cup. Thereafter, the New York Yacht Club became the nation's preeminent athletic organization and one of New York's most prestigious men's clubs.

The antebellum middle class was composed of white Protestant shopkeepers, clerks, professionals, prosperous farm owners, and highly skilled workmen, who demonstrated their manliness through hard work, making the home the center of their lives, and maintaining Victorian standards of behavior. They disdained the lower-class sporting fraternity for turning the middle-class value system upside down with their urban counterculture, which denigrated hard work and glorified violence. Clergymen, journalists, physicians, and other middle-class social reformers condemned baiting sports, cockfighting, and boxing as time-wasting, immoral, cruel, and debilitating sports that undermined the social order, bringing together crowds of unruly and often drunken young men. State and local governments influenced by such reformers often passed laws against such activities.

The first sport identified with the middle class was harness racing, which gained popularity in the 1820s. Even though it usually involved gambling, by the 1850s, harness racing was the most popular spectator sport in the country. Trotting, as it also was called, was an exciting sport that gave owners a chance to show off their horses and demonstrate their prowess as drivers. Trotting originally was an urban sport centered in New York City, the Northern hub of the horse breeding and training industry. It was the first modern sport, organized in 1825 when the New York Trotting Association was formed to schedule meets on a semiannual basis at a racecourse, replacing the customary spontaneous races, known as brushes, on city streets.

Trotting was considered a more democratic sport than aristocratic horse racing, because it employed inexpensive standardbred horses, often used for transporting freight or passengers in wagons, instead of costly thoroughbreds, whose only use was for racing and breeding. However, by mid-century, members of the nouveaux riche, notably Cornelius Vanderbilt, head of the New York Central Railroad, and newspaper publisher Robert Bonner, got into the sport and bought up the best trotters.

Some of the most prominent antebellum sportsmen were members of the working class (wage workers), particularly well-paid artisans and food tradesmen, especially butchers, who were renowned for their strength. These traditionally minded men wanted to maintain customary values such as respect for physicality. They represented an oppositional culture to that of the middle class and were an integral segment of the bachelor subculture, even though they usually earned enough money to indulge themselves in sports, ranging from illegal blood and gambling contests to baseball. Working-class athletes often gravitated to sports in which money could be made, such as pedestrian races by the mid-1830s and the Scottish American Caledonian Games of the 1850s.

Old Immigrants

Some of the most important antebellum working-class athletes were immigrants from Western and Central Europe, including people from the British Isles and the German-speaking nations.

British immigrants, who typically were artisans, brought with them the most vigorous sporting tradition in the Western world and formed ethnic sports clubs such as the many Albion societies they established wherever they settled. Skilled textile workers brought cricket with them to Lawrence and Lowell, Massachusetts, and to Philadelphia, while English merchants and professionals established crickering "XIs" (so called because teams were made up of 11 players) in Boston, Brooklyn, and New York City. The most famous cricket team was that of the New York's St. George's Cricket Club, organized in 1840, which played the first international match against a Toronto team four years later in Hoboken, New Jersey. The game became popular in the United States, and at mid-century, cricket was the leading American ball sport.

America also attracted professional English boxers and pedestrians. One-fifth of New York City's boxers were English immigrants, including "Young Barney" Aaron, who became the American lightweight champion in 1857. English runners competed in long-distance races at Hoboken, New Jersey's Beacon Race Course, which reputedly drew up to 30,000 spectators for a single event.

Beginning in Boston in 1853, Scottish immigrants founded Caledonian societies, which provided them with a sense of community. Eventually, there were more than 100 such clubs, which sponsored athletic meets awarding monetary prizes to winners. Their contests emphasized traditional Scottish activities such as throwing the caber and pitching the heavy stone, along with sprint races and field events such as the hammer throw, shot put, and pole vault. Caledonian competitions dominated American track and field until the 1870s, with some events drawing paying crowds that surpassed 20,000.

The British migrants were surpassed by the 1.7 million unskilled and uneducated Irish who came to the United States during and after the potato famine of 1845–1846. They settled in urban slums and brought with them a male bachelor subculture that helped them fit into the underground American sports culture.

Irish immigrants mostly took part in American sports, particularly boxing, which they quickly dominated. Indeed, some 70 percent of New York's pugilists during this era were Irish or Irish Americans seeking to escape poverty. Because boxing was illegal, there were few formal matches. Boxers often depended on political sponsors for patronage jobs that required physical prowess, such as "shoulder hitters" (political intimidators). These boxers often were members of street gangs or fire companies closely tied to Tammany Hall, New York's Democratic political machine. They fought for side bets and to protect personal honor, ethnic pride, and the Democratic Party against English immigrants or native white Americans tied to the Whig or Know Nothing parties.

The most renowned Irish American boxer was John Morrissey, the American champion from 1853 to 1858, who, unlike his peers, became a wealthy man as New York City's most successful gambling hall proprietor; Morrissey would go on to help revitalize the sport of horse racing in the North during the Civil War, and he become a U.S. congressman.

In the mid-1850s, Germans replaced the Irish as the largest immigrant group, but they were quicker to succeed in American society, as about half were farmers and the rest were skilled and literate workmen. They brought their culture with them, including Turnverein, or gymnastic societies, begun in 1811 by Friedrich Jahn to promote German nationalism and physical fitness in preparation for future wars with France. Members of these societies, known as Turners, first arrived in America in the 1820s and taught college students gymnastics. In 1848, German political refugees brought the movement to the United States and established clubs in Louisville, Kentucky; Cincinnati, Ohio; and Newark, New Jersey, and then throughout all German communities in America. The clubs were open to all Germans and became community centers that promoted gymnastics, German culture, working-class interests, and liberal (mainly Republican) politics.

Making a New Sporting Culture

The American sporting culture underwent a dramatic change around the mid-nineteenth century, setting the stage for a sporting boom after the Civil War. Many factors contributed to this, including urbanization, industrialization, the revolution in transportation and communication, the example of English, Scottish, and German athletes, the development of new sports, the rise of broader social reforms, especially those concerned with public health and law and order, and the creation of a positive sports creed that promoted physical culture as a force for improving the American people.

Urban Reform and the Ideology of Sports

During the Jacksonian era of the 1830s and early 1840s, a new sports creed emerged that promoted athletic activity as a useful recreation with many social benefits, including character building, improving morality, and promoting public health for urbanites. This belief derived from several sources, including ancient Greek culture, which stressed the union of fitness and education; the rhetoric of eighteenth-century Enlightenment philosophers, which argued that man had the potential to improve himself by the dint of his own efforts; and the ideas of early nineteenth-century European educators, which emphasized physical activity in school. This led to the rise of a fitness movement that advocated physical activity and a sound diet, as well as a municipal park movement that sought to secure public space for outdoor recreation in fresh air, especially for the "toiling masses."

All of this occurred at a time when reformers were securing universal white male suffrage, encouraging more economic opportunity for the working class, and pushing for essential public services in growing cities, such as sanitation, compulsory education, and police protection. The impetus came from the Second Great Awakening, a rebirth of religious fervor and social awareness among evangelical Protestants, as well as from secular-minded physicians, journalists, statisticians, and other educated people who wanted to alleviate pressing social ills. These problems were largely the products of urbanization, including growing class divisions attributable to extremes of poverty and wealth, increased social conflict among people of different backgrounds and cultures resulting from mass immigration, the breakdown of law and order among transient urban populations, and poor public health, especially in overcrowded slums with inadequate sanitation and polluted water, that resulted in epidemics and high mortality rates.

The leading proponents of the new sports creed included liberal Unitarian clergymen such as the Reverend William Ellery Channing of Boston; scientists such as statistician Lemuel Shattuck, the founder of vital record keeping; journalists such as William Cullen Bryant of the *New York Evening Post*; physicians such as Bronson Alcott; and health faddists such as Sylvester Graham, inventor of the Graham cracker. They criticized urban men as unhealthy and unproductive, reserving special censure for sedentary middle-class office workers.

The antidote, these reformers believed, was clean, fresh-air sports and sound diets that would give urbanites a healthier lifestyle and the moral values of the yeoman farmer. In his essay "Autocrat of the Breakfast Table" in the *Atlantic Monthly* (1858), Oliver Wendell Holmes, Sr., chastised the American bourgeois lifestyle in comparison to the robust life of the English gentry: "Such a set of black-coated, stiff-jointed, soft-muscled, paste-complexioned youth as we can boast in our Atlantic cities never before sprang from loins of Anglo-Saxon lineage."

Catharine Beecher was a leading advocate of domesticity for women, but she also promoted women's fitness through sports, considered an entirely a male sphere at the time. In her *Course of Calisthenics for Young Ladies* (1832), she argued that women needed to be fit in order to combat chronic frailty; to prevent frequent illnesses such as nervousness, indigestion, palpitations, and headaches; and to prepare themselves for motherhood. Women were urged to ride horses, dance, and do calisthenics to enhance their femininity, beauty, and grace.

Besides improving health, the sports creed asserted that physical culture would benefit society by promoting traditional American values, such as hard work and self-discipline, develop higher standards of character, and provide a substitute for vile slum amusements, thereby protecting communities from criminality and immorality. Reformers such as Unitarian minister Edward Everett Hale urged a rational recreation movement consisting of wholesome and uplifting fun. They recognized that lower-class urbanites had a great need for leisure activities but were spending their time at diversions that hardened men's souls to brutality and offered instant gratification through gambling. Hale preferred that these men enjoy traditional rustic pleasures, such as fishing or hunting. Because those pastimes often were difficult for urban men to participate in, he encouraged such moral entertainments as legitimate theater, classical music, and physical culture.

Muscular Christianity

Hale became a leading advocate of "muscular Christianity," a mid-nineteenth-century English philosophy that advocated the practice of clean sport and physical culture to develop moral, devout, and physically fit men, thereby enhancing their mental, physical, and spiritual dimensions. Muscular Christians viewed sport as a way to promote manliness, check effeminacy, and provide an alternative to sexual expenditures of energy. Muscular Christians believed that religion and physical vigor, rather than being opposed to each other, went hand in hand. The philosophy was popularized by Thomas Hughes in his best seller *Tom Brown's School Days* (1857), a fictional account of Rugby, an English preparatory school that emphasized the use of athletics to build character.

Muscular Christianity provided the intellectual underpinnings for the growth of the Young Men's Christian Association (YMCA), an evangelical organization founded in London in 1844, which, in turn, became muscular Christianity's main institutional supporter. The YMCA came to America seven years later to help rural youth moving to cities adjust to urban life. By the 1860s, the organization was using moral athletics and gymnastics as an engaging alternative to vile amusements for young white-collar men. The YMCA sought to develop honorable Christian gentlemen who exercised self-control, abstained from sex outside of marriage, and used their strength to protect others, and the association promoted its philosophy that a strong mind, sound spirit, and healthy body worked hand in hand.

The positive sports creed struck a chord with the middle class, who became convinced of the power of sports to improve morality, character, and health. They also admired non-Irish immigrants as models of uplifting sports and turned to exciting team games, especially baseball, that were perceived as avenues for ameliorating the lives of participants and spectators.

Municipal Park Movement

As urban populations rose and land-use patterns in the walking city began to shift, traditional playing areas often were destroyed, and there were few public spaces where athletes could play. Empty lots that once had served as cricket pitches were developed for housing or factories. Nearby fields and streams became inaccessible as they were drained and cleared, requiring sportsmen to travel farther to reach wooded areas and unpolluted waterways. By the 1850s, New York's old cricket sites had been built up, and the roads formerly used for trotting horses were no longer available. New Yorkers, such as the Knickerbockers cricket team, increasingly relied on playing fields out of town in Brooklyn and in Hoboken, New Jersey.

One answer to the space problem was offered by the municipal park movement, which originated in overcrowded New York during the 1840s, led by journalist and poet William Cullen Bryant and landscape architect Andrew Jackson Downing. The movement was supported by a broad-based coalition of social reformers, physicians, labor leaders, businessmen, and professional politicians who wanted the city government to construct a public park. Their aim was to improve public health by providing access to fresh air and foster order by providing a venue for social classes to mingle and the lower classes to learn from their betters. They also believed that parks would aid the local economy by providing jobs, boost the city's public image, and raise property values on adjacent land. The project appealed to the Tammany Hall machine that controlled the city government because of the prospect of new construction contracts and patronage jobs.

The 843-acre (341-hectare) Central Park was built between 1858 and 1873 on the outskirts of town, where land was cheaper. The board of trustees held an open competition for the park's design, which required a wooded area, a formal English garden, and a parade ground for cricket. Frederick Law Olmsted and Calvert Vaux won the contract. The cricket field never was built, however, because Olmsted believed the park should be reserved for receptive recreation—pleasure derived from enjoying beautiful scenery—not active recreation that would destroy the grass.

Initially, Central Park was considered an "elite park" because of Olmsted's recreational philosophy and because its location was more accessible to wealthy owners of horses and carriages than to the working classes, who had to walk far uptown to get there. The completion of Central Park nevertheless demonstrated how an independent government agency could administer development projects and encouraged municipalities to get involved in urban planning. Central Park became the model for the many large suburban parks built after the Civil War by Olmsted, the nation's preeminent landscape architect, in Boston, Brooklyn, Chicago, Philadelphia, and San Francisco.

College Sports

Important sites for sports among the sons of the upper and upper-middle classes were Eastern colleges, where young men pursued boxing, fencing, football, handball, horseback riding, quoits (a game similar to horseshoes), running, and swimming. Interclass contests dated to the 1820s and 1830s. The games promoted class loyalty and served as a venue for initiation rites. The faculty and administration did not endorse such activities, but they preferred participation in sports to other rowdy youthful behavior.

The first intercollegiate sport was crew, popularized by professional boatmen, upper-middle-class rowing clubs, and the annual Oxford–Cambridge race in England, which began in 1829. Fifteen year later, a four-man team of seniors from Yale University raced lowerclassmen in the initial college rowing contest; this was followed in 1852 by the first intercollegiate race, a contest in which Harvard University beat Yale. There were just a few races thereafter, until students from four Eastern schools established the College Union Regatta in 1858, a contest that drew 15,000 to its inaugural race a year later.

In 1869, Harvard was invited to send its eight-man crew to a 2-mile (3.2-kilometer) race against England's Oxford University. Harvard lost by only six seconds—an achievement that was seen as evidence of America's advances in culture, manliness, and athletic prowess. The race helped increase interest in crew and led to the formation of the Rowing Association of American Colleges in 1871.

The second major intercollegiate sport was baseball. The first collegiate contest in 1859 was played under the "Massachusetts rules," which allowed for a more wide-open ball game than modern baseball. In that match, Amherst College defeated Williams College, 65–32. Baseball took off as a college game after the Civil War. Harvard's nine, organized in 1865, was the top college squad. In 1870, the team made a 44-game Western tour, playing amateurs and professionals and winning two-thirds of their games against the pros. Through the 1870s, baseball was the principal game on campus.

Baseball

The new game of baseball, which started out as a children's game, fit well with the emerging antebellum sports creed. The modern game was developed by Alexander Cartwright and his teammates on the New York Knickerbocker Base Ball Club in 1845. It was both an

Alexander Cartwright, a New York City bookstore owner and volunteer fireman, drafted the first rules of the modern game of baseball in 1845. He also established the first organized team, the Knickerbocker Base Ball Club, and set the dimensions of the field. *(Associated Press)*

athletic and a social organization of white-collar workers who took the game seriously and expected players to be disciplined, trained, and well drilled.

A baseball fraternity soon emerged, with dozens of clubs in the early 1850s composed mainly of young artisans, clerks, and small businessmen who shared the same Victorian work and leisure ethic and internalized the positive values of the new sports creed, such as self-control and cooperation. Few players were drawn from the lower classes.

Players looked to baseball as uplifting fun and a chance to display their athletic skills and form friendships. The game was considered less manly than cricket, whose batsmen needed bravery to stand up against hard-throwing bowlers and required balls to be caught on the fly, not on a bounce, as in early baseball. Soon, however, cricket was surpassed by baseball, which was easier to play, did not require a perfect playing field, did not take all day to play, and had American origins, a fact that appealed to patriotic sentiment.

The early ballplayers, who at first were located mainly in New York, Brooklyn, and the surrounding metropolitan area, played on clubs organized by occupation, ethnicity, or neighborhood. One of the first teams was the Brooklyn Eckfords, which consisted mainly of prosperous shipwrights and mechanics. The best working-class nine was the Brooklyn Atlantics, composed of Irish Catholic food industry employees with strong ties to the Democratic Party. In 1860, the Atlantics played a series against the middle-class Brooklyn Excelsiors, drawing enormous interest, because they represented opposing ethnic, political, and socioeconomic groups.

The fraternal aspect of baseball soon gave way to "playing for keeps," and a championship series emerged in metropolitan New York during the Civil War. Baseball quickly became commercialized as entrepreneurs took advantage of the public's growing willingness to pay for entertainment. Tickets first were sold for an 1858 all-star series between New York and Brooklyn, with the revenue used to defray expenses. Four years later, William Cammeyer made the game a business by enclosing his skating rink in the Williamsburg section of Brooklyn, renaming it the Union Grounds, and charging spectators 10 cents to watch baseball teams play.

The quest for victory led to the recruitment and payment of top players, a development that was opposed by the National Association of Base Ball Players,

founded in 1857. The association considered professionalization unfair to amateurs, who did not devote themselves full time to sport. In 1860, pitcher James Creighton of the Brooklyn Excelsiors was paid under the table, making him the first professional baseball player.

Baseball boomed in the aftermath of the Civil War, partly as a result of the increased national exposure it had received in army camps. There were more than 2,000 organized clubs by 1869, mostly in the Northeast, including 13 professional teams that played more than 50 games a year. The first openly all-salaried nine was the Cincinnati Red Stockings of 1869, organized by local boosters to promote their city.

Steven A. Riess

Further Reading

Adelman, Melvin L. *A Sporting Time: New York City and the Rise of Modern Athletics, 1820–70.* Urbana: University of Illinois Press, 1986.

Betts, John Rickards. "Mind and Body in Early American Thought." *Journal of American History* 54:4 (March 1968): 787–805.

———. "Sporting Journalism in Nineteenth-Century America." *American Quarterly* 5:1 (Spring 1953): 39–56.

———. "The Technological Revolution and the Rise of Sports, 1850–1900." *Mississippi Valley Historical Review* 40:2 (September 1953): 231–256.

Dizikes, John. *Sportsmen and Gamesmen.* Boston: Houghton Mifflin, 1981.

Goldstein, Warren. *Playing for Keeps: A History of Early Baseball.* Ithaca, NY: Cornell University Press, 1989.

Gorn, Elliott J. *The Manly Art: Bare-Knuckle Prize Fighting in America.* Ithaca, NY: Cornell University Pres, 1986.

Gorn, Elliott J., and Warren Goldstein. *A Brief History of American Sports.* New York: Hill and Wang, 1993.

Kirsch, George B. *The Creation of American Team Sports: Baseball and Cricket, 1838–72.* Urbana: University of Illinois Press, 1989.

Rader, Benjamin G. *American Sports: From the Age of Folk Games to the Age of Televised Sports.* 6th ed. Upper Saddle River, NJ: Prentice Hall, 2009.

Riess, Steven A. *City Games: The Evolution of American Urban Society and the Rise of Sports.* Urbana: University of Illinois Press, 1989.

Seymour, Harold. *Baseball.* 3 vols. New York: Oxford University Press, 1960–1989.

Somers, Dale A. *The Rise of Sports in New Orleans, 1850–1900.* Baton Rouge: Louisiana State University Press, 1972.

Whorton, James C. *Crusaders for Fitness: The History of American Health Reformers.* Princeton, NJ: Princeton University Press, 1982.

THE GILDED AGE, 1870-1900

Organized sports emerged on a popular scale in American cities before the Civil War, a result of immigrants bringing their sporting culture with them, changing attitudes among the middle class regarding the moral uplift provided by athletics, the rise of the municipal park movement, and the emergence of wholesome outdoor sports, most notably baseball. However, a real boom in sports took place after the Civil War, when organized sports emerged on a major scale. Sports became modernized in the period between the end of the Civil War and the end of the nineteenth century—the so-called Gilded Age—as new games were created, athletic stars became national heroes, and American sports, such as baseball, were exported across the globe as symbols of progress and freedom.

The rise of sport also was tied to developments in the broader society, particularly the quickening pace of urbanization and the growth of industrial capitalism. Cities provided sites for the sports boom, because they had the critical number of participants to play sports and sufficient spectators to make commercial sports profitable. Industrial capitalism influenced sports by reshaping the social structure, producing important technological innovations, and making possible the mass production of sporting goods in factories.

Technological Revolution and the Rise of Sports

The sports boom was facilitated by daily press coverage in new penny newspapers. Papers received instant reports of distant events by telegraphy (invented in 1842) and telephony (1876), as did poolrooms and saloons, which also served as illegal off-track betting parlors, facilitating wagering. In 1896, Joseph Pulitzer's New York *World* established the first sports department and the first distinctive sports page. Daily coverage was reinforced by weekly general-interest magazines and specialized periodicals such as *Wilkes' Spirit of the Times* (established in 1859 as the successor to William

T. Porter's earlier *Spirit of the Times,* a title publisher George Wilkes turned back to in 1868), which was renowned for its coverage of the turf and track and field, and Richard Kyle Fox's *National Police Gazette* (1845), which emphasized boxing. Meanwhile, baseball was the focus of *Sporting Life* (1883) and the *Sporting News* (1886).

Cheap mass transit boomed, advancing from horse-drawn streetcars to electrified trolleys, and even the first subway in Boston (1896), all of which made it easier for fans to get to sporting events, which often were sponsored by traction, or streetcar, firms. Traction companies even backed professional baseball leagues, including the New England Trolley League (1899). Intercity railroads shortened travel time for teams, making long-distance travel possible. In 1869, the Cincinnati Red Stockings, the first fully professional team, used trains to make a national tour, traveling from San Francisco to Boston.

Industrialization also facilitated the mass production of inexpensive sporting goods, including bats, gloves, and 5-cent baseballs, in factories owned by vertically integrated companies that controlled all stages of production, from raw materials to production to selling, such as A.G. Spalding & Brothers. The Spalding firm was also horizontally integrated, having bought up several other sporting goods companies.

Several new inventions were utilized for sporting needs, such as stopwatches to record race times and cameras to help determine the winners of close horse races. Illumination at indoor arenas was improved by using arc lighting and, later, Thomas Edison's incandescent lightbulb (1879). In 1897, Edison's new kinetoscope, the first practical motion picture, was used to film the James J. Corbett–Bob Fitzsimmons heavyweight championship fight.

New products also were invented specifically for sporting use. Crew was enhanced by the use of sliding seats (1870s) in racing shells, while streamlined horse racing sulkies with pneumatic tires (1888) cut the mile record by five seconds. Baseball was improved by the introduction of the catcher's mask and chest protector, and by vulcanized rubber, which made balls more elastic and resilient.

The bicycle was a major technological innovation, beginning with Pierre Lallement's velocipede, known as the "boneshaker," in 1866, which led to a brief bicycling fad. This model was supplanted in 1876 by the difficult-to-ride high wheeler (also known as an "ordinary" or "penny farthing"). It had a huge front wheel and a tiny rear wheel, which increased speed. In the late 1880s came the English safety bicycle, which was lighter in weight, easier to ride, and featured matched pneumatic tires and efficient coaster brakes. A new cycling fad emerged, and by the mid-1890s, there were 4 million cyclists in America.

Cycling became especially popular among women. The sport provided a socially acceptable form of exercise and independent travel, and it justified the wearing of less restrictive sports clothes, signifying women's growing liberation from the constraints of the Victorian era.

The bicycle era was short-lived, as many bicycles used for independent transportation were supplanted by automobiles powered by the internal combustion engine.

American manufacturers, many originally in the cycling business, tested the cars they built by racing them. In 1895, six cars contested the 53-mile (85-kilometer) round-trip race from Chicago's South Side to Evanston, Illinois, won by manufacturer Charles Duryea.

Sports and Public Space

Traditional playing areas in the industrial city often were destroyed by urban growth. City governments responded to the dearth of open breathing spaces by establishing public parks on the outskirts of town, modeled after New York City's 843-acre (341-hectare) Central Park.

Like Central Park, many such public spaces were designed as grand suburban parks, emphasizing receptive recreation—pleasure derived from enjoying beautiful scenery—rather than active games, which would harm the grass. However, by the 1880s, parks were reconfigured for more active middle-class use, with baseball fields and tennis courts. However, inner-city residents who most needed breathing spaces frequently had little access to distant parks.

Urban development in the late nineteenth century spawned public parks in many of the nation's cities and suburban areas, providing space for fresh-air recreation to the middle class. New York's Central Park, depicted here, was the model. (Hulton Archive/Getty Images)

Social Class

Industrial capitalism reshaped the urban social structure, creating unprecedented wealth for a small upper class, new opportunities for the growing middle class, and low-paying jobs for blue-collar workers, who made up the majority of the population. A person's social class had a big influence on sporting options in the Gilded Age.

The Upper Class

The top 5 percent of the population, with 30 percent of the national wealth, had the time and money to amuse themselves as they pleased, especially with costly sports at exclusive clubs where they could conspicuously display their affluence. These sport clubs not only facilitated athletic competition, they also fostered the formation of a community of like-minded people who shared the same social backgrounds, beliefs, values, customs, and lifestyles. Membership in these voluntary associations, which included athletic (track and field), hunting, jockey, polo, yacht, and country clubs, was highly selective.

The New York Athletic Club, founded in 1866, was one of the most important upper-class sports organizations. It also was the nation's preeminent track and field organization. The club sponsored the first national track and field championships in 1876 and set national standards for amateurism. It helped found the Amateur Athletic Union in 1888 to uphold strict amateur principles, barring anyone who pursued athletics as a career, had competed or coached athletes for money, or who had competed against professionals.

In 1882, proper Bostonians founded the Country Club in Brookline, Massachusetts. This prestigious suburban resort was modeled on the lifestyle of the English gentry, and members enjoyed exclusive sports, especially golf. Five years later, John Reed built St. Andrews, the first American golf course, in Yonkers, New York. Golf was very popular with older men, as it was not particularly strenuous. By 1900, there were about 1,000 golf courses in the country. Country club members also could play tennis, fish, hunt, ice-skate, ride sleighs, and socialize.

Upper-class young men preferred more vigorous sports through which they could prove their virility at a time when the upper classes feared that their culture and religion were being feminized, and when birthrates were declining. Playing football was seen as a moral equivalent of war, enabling participants to prove that they measured up to contemporary standards of masculinity. Future president Theodore Roosevelt exemplified an active lifestyle as a big-game hunter, boxer, cowboy, and "Rough Rider" in the Spanish-American War, and he wrote influential essays extolling the "strenuous life," an idea that took hold at colleges and elite Eastern prep schools.

Elite women gained access to athletic clubs as both spectators and competitors at a time when most people still considered sports a manly sphere, inappropriate for young ladies. However, their high status gave them the confidence to contest conventional perceptions of femininity. Women whose husbands belonged to athletic clubs had time set aside for them to play billiards, bowl, fence, or swim. Golf was considered appropriate for women, because it was not strenuous; women could play during off-peak hours at a father's or husband's country club. In the 1890s, women formed their own golf organizations; they held their first national championship in 1895, one year after the men.

Women also were active in the new sport of lawn tennis, invented in 1873 by Englishman John Wingfield and brought to America a year later by Mary Outerbridge, who laid out a court at the Staten Island Cricket and Baseball Club near New York City. Men played the game and organized the U.S. Lawn Tennis Association in 1881, but tennis was not considered a manly sport. Women enjoyed doubles matches and a sedate baseline game that did not require much strength or vigorous exertion, which was discouraged by their full-length skirts. The women's national championship began in 1887.

Elite athletic sportswomen provided a model for the "Gibson girl" of the 1890s—attractive, slim, and physically fit young ladies who did not wear restrictive corsets and participated in coed cycling, golf, tennis, and horseback riding.

The Middle Class

Middle-class participation in sports also skyrocketed during this era. This demographic grew and changed significantly after the Civil War. Many members of the middle class were office workers and small businessmen in sedentary jobs. They saw participation in sports as a way to certify their manliness, which they no longer proved through physical work. They also had the discretionary time and money to enjoy themselves at sports that built character, health, and morality. They joined the Young Men's Christian Association (YMCA), whose philosophy was to build "muscular Christians" by training the mind, body, and spirit. In addition, they organized or joined baseball, cycling, target-shooting, and track and field clubs to compete, make friends, and gain social status. They also were avid spectators, especially of baseball.

Middle-class Victorian women were expected to be physically inactive, because, it was believed, they were prone to physical, emotional, moral, and mental afflictions that could be exacerbated by athletic activity. Many people did not like the idea of women athletes, not only because they considered females unfit for vigorous physical activity, but also because they feared that such activities would make women too competitive and aggressive. Still, many physicians urged moderate exercise for women, and women educators promoted physical culture, contending that exercise actually enhanced women's health and attractiveness.

Appropriate activities included calisthenics, precision drills (Swedish gymnastics), and Dr. Diocletian Lewis's system of rhythmic exercises, which employed rings, wands, and wooden dumbbells to promote flexibility, agility, and grace. By the 1860s, middle-class young women participated in coeducational recreational sports, such as croquet, horseback riding, ice-skating, sledding, and later cycling, golf, and tennis. Some women utilized the Young Women's Christian Association (YWCA), founded in 1858, which began sponsoring women's sports in the 1880s.

Athletic college girls enjoyed some intercollegiate competition in sports such as basketball beginning in the 1890s, but there was strong opposition. Men were barred from viewing their games, and the rules were adapted to fit women's presumed limited capacities.

The Working Class

Working-class sport was hindered by urbanization, industrialization, and a civilizing process that tried to eliminate traditional gambling and violent sports. Before industrialization, artisans exercised considerable control over the workplace and were prominent sportsmen, with free time and resources to spend on recreation. They admired physicality and sought to maintain traditional masculine and working-class values. But the factory system and timework discipline led to the deskilling of workers (only 15 percent of factory workers were craftsmen), leaving them with little leisure time, low incomes, and living in crowded urban neighborhoods with few accessible sporting facilities. It was hard for them to go to baseball games because of work schedules, ticket prices, and the cost of travel, but they did live near saloons, where they could gamble, play billiards, throw darts, and watch boxing matches in backrooms.

Blue-collar sports got a boost from companies, political parties, ethnic organizations, and unions, all of whom sponsored picnic games that emphasized track and field contests. Winners received trophies and products—such as jewelry, furniture, and clothing—which could be pawned or sold for cash. The best working-class athletes were professionals, notably long-distance runners who raced in lucrative six-day events, such as the 1878–1879 International Astley Belt races for purses of up to $20,000. The winners routinely ran as far as 500 miles (805 kilometers) in a single event.

At first, businessmen believed that sports were a waste of time for workers, but in 1872, the railroads began supporting YMCA programs for their employees. A decade later, industrialists began setting up their own athletic programs as part of the new welfare capitalism intended to produce a contented, loyal, punctual, efficient, hardworking, and nonunion workforce and to attract new workers. Such sponsored athletic teams also served to advertise the company.

Ethnicity and Race

Ethnicity and race were critical factors in working-class sport. The old immigrants from Western Europe—notably the British and Germans—brought with them their athletic traditions. The Irish also brought a lively sporting tradition that was nationalistic, but also fit into the bachelor subculture that native middle-class people considered disreputable. In 1870, the secret revolutionary group Clan na Gael began sponsoring track and field meets to attract followers, and a decade later, the Gaelic Athletic Association reinvented the tradition of ancient Hibernian games such as hurling and Gaelic football.

However, the second generation of Irish Americans preferred mainstream sports, particularly prizefighting. Nine of 19 U.S. world pugilist champions in the 1890s were of Irish descent, most notably John L. Sullivan, the last bare-knuckle heavyweight champion, the idol of the shanty Irish, and the greatest sports hero of the century. The Irish also were active on the baseball diamond and were surpassed, in terms of numbers, only by native-born white Americans in professional baseball. In addition, the Irish became active in the business of sports as bookmakers, boxing promoters, and baseball team owners, which reflected the nexus of urban politics, illegal gambling, and sports, all areas in which the Irish figured prominently in the late nineteenth century.

The experience of new immigrants from Eastern and Southern Europe, who arrived near the end of the century, was very different, as they came without a sporting legacy and disdained American sports as a waste of time. However, their sons often circumvented parental disapproval and played sports for fun, hoping to prove that they were not "greenhorns" (unassimilated newcomers) and to dispel negative stereotypes about their ethnic community.

These youth did well in sports that suited their inner-city environment, especially boxing, a useful skill for boys who often got into street fights. Their role models included fighters such as Joe Choynski, the Jewish heavyweight who fought James J. Corbett three times. By contrast, these youth fared poorly in baseball, which required large fields that were not available in the inner city. Furthermore, many children of immigrants dropped out of school early and did not have the opportunity to play on high school teams.

The difference between old and new immigrants was reflected in the gap between German Jews, who arrived in the mid-nineteenth century, and Russian Jews, who came at the century's end. The former participated in mainstream American sports, producing some renowned track stars, football players, and sports entrepreneurs. In the 1880s, German Jews encountered growing anti-Semitism and could not get into many prestigious clubs, so they established their own athletic clubs and supported the Young Men's Hebrew Association, modeled after the YMCA. Philanthropic German Jews helped their coreligionists from Eastern Europe adapt to America and established settlement houses, such as the Educational Alliance (1893) on New York's Lower East Side, which offered civics classes, employment bureaus, as well as gymnasiums. German Jews believed that participating in sports would teach Russian Jewish boys American values and behavior, while at the same time countering negative stereotypes about Jewish manliness.

The African American sporting experience differed from that of European Americans. African Americans participated in many American sports in the antebellum South, as slaves or as free men, including boxing, cockfighting, and horse racing. However, after the Civil War, they faced extreme prejudice in sports, as the South, where 90 percent of blacks lived, was totally segregated, first by custom and later by law. African Americans relied on their own fraternal, church, political, and sporting groups to sponsor recreational and spectator sports, to promote a sense of community, and occasionally to gain recognition in white society through public or private contests with white teams.

Nevertheless, African Americans made notable achievements in sports. Marshall "Major" Taylor was the world champion sprint cyclist in 1899, and Isaac Murphy was a three-time (1884, 1890, and 1891) Kentucky Derby–winning jockey. There also were more than 70 blacks in organized baseball from 1878 to 1899. By the late 1890s, however, the only African Americans in professional baseball were members of all-black teams, notably the Acme Giants, who played in 1898 in the Iron and Oil League. Despite their ousting from professional baseball, blacks continued to play year-round with their own touring nines, most notably the Cuban Giants, established in 1885.

Sports and Education

A key development in sports during the industrial age was the blossoming of intercollegiate sports, based on the English model found at preparatory schools and Oxford and Cambridge universities. Sports gave college men a chance to demonstrate their manliness, and gave both men and women an opportunity to display their athletic prowess, organize their own extracurricular activities, and promote school spirit. Intercollegiate sports emerged first at elite Eastern institutions, whose student bodies belonged to the upper or upper-middle class, and then was emulated elsewhere, including at the more democratic state universities.

The first intercollegiate sporting event was a rowing race between Harvard and Yale universities in 1852, which inspired the establishment of the College Union Regatta in 1859. Intercollegiate baseball began with a game between Amherst and Williams colleges in 1859, and after the Civil War, baseball became the leading college sport. Harvard had the finest team, and in 1870, when its home games drew up to 10,000 spectators, its team took a 44-game Western tour. In 1879, the College Baseball Association was organized. However, its weak eligibility rules allowed some winning college teams to use professionals.

Track and field at American colleges was an outgrowth of the popularity of the Scottish American Caledonian Games, which began in the 1850s, and the Oxford–Cambridge competitions, first held in 1864. The first U.S. intercollegiate track and field meet was held in 1873, in conjunction with a college regatta in Saratoga, New York. Two years later, ten colleges established the Intercollegiate Association of Amateur Athletes of America to regulate track and field. Harvard and Yale dominated, winning all team titles between 1880 and 1897. In 1896, five Princeton and Harvard undergraduates and five Harvard alumni represented the United States at the first modern Olympics in Athens, Greece, and won nine of 12 track and field events.

Baseball was supplanted by football as the "big game" in college athletics during the 1880s. The first intercollegiate football game was played in 1869, when Rutgers University beat Princeton University, 6–4, using rules similar to soccer. In 1876, Harvard, Princeton, Columbia, and Yale formalized common rules, and all but Yale joined to establish the Intercollegiate Football Association (IFA); Yale joined the organization in 1879. Led by volunteer coach Walter Camp, Yale's team dominated the game, outscoring opponents 4,660–92 from 1883 to 1891. Camp proposed most of the major rule changes and tactical innovations during those years; he later would become known as the "Father of American Football."

The IFA teams and others that soon developed were run by student associations without official support from their colleges. They created highly commercialized intercollegiate sports programs, recruiting athletes and professional coaches to win at all costs, and bringing in large crowds of paying spectators. Students found sports much more fun and more exciting than traditional extracurricular activities, and they also liked how sports promoted school spirit and publicized their institutions.

College athletics were even more important for women. Women physical educators, many of whom were trained by Bostonians Amy Morris Homans and Dudley Sargent, exercised significant control over their students, supervising mainly noncompetitive interclass athletic programs in basketball, rowing, and tennis at elite Eastern women's colleges.

Opportunities to play organized sports before college emerged slowly. Physical education for boys was introduced to schools during the Civil War era by Dr. Diocletian Lewis, who stressed military drills and gymnastics. In the late 1880s, New England schools adopted the Swedish system of calisthenics, the Midwest favored gymnastics in the Turnverein tradition, and New York, Brooklyn, and Washington, D.C., implemented mixed systems. Girls' physical education was less rigorous, focusing on light gymnastics, dance, and exercise, activities that were supposed to help them avoid mental strain and become more attractive.

Interscholastic high school sports developed in the 1870s and 1880s, in emulation of college programs.

These events were operated by student-run athletic organizations, which financed teams, found playing sites, and booked games, independent of adult interference. The contests promoted school spirit and became a focal point for developing a sense of community among local residents.

Children relied on their own ingenuity when it came to playing sports, arranging their own pick-up ball games with their own rules in vacant fields and alleyways and swimming off city docks or in rural lakes. In the 1880s, Turnverein organizations introduced physical education to elementary schools, and the YMCA established junior departments (ages 10–16) for its middle-class clientele, supposedly to help prolong a needed childhood period of development and defer adolescence.

Inner-city institutional churches and new settlement houses that promoted the social gospel used sports such as baseball, basketball, bowling, boxing, and billiards to attract youth and pull them away from corrupting and dangerous street life. Reformers especially advocated adult-directed team sports to acculturate immigrant boys; elevate their morals, character, and health; build self-confidence; and teach cooperation.

Commercialized Sports

The rise of commercialized, professional spectator sports was the most significant development in post–Civil War athletics. It was facilitated by rapid urbanization, which created the necessary mass audiences, as well as by internal developments in sports, including the rise of entrepreneurs and outstanding athletes. However, prizefighting was barred virtually everywhere because of its brutality, while horse racing was widely banned because of the betting that accompanied it.

The other main professional sport was baseball, already the national pastime, which was considered uplifting, honest, and free of gambling (although there actually was a lot of betting on games). The leading sports promoters were professional politicians or their close associates, who used their connections to protect their investments with preferential treatment from city hall.

Early prizefights were arranged at saloons and staged in barns, on river barges, or in the backrooms of saloons to avoid the police. Fighters often were promoted and managed by big-city machine politicians. In the 1880s, the stature of the ring improved thanks to the adoption of the Marquis of Queensberry rules, which introduced boxing gloves and three-minute rounds, while banning wrestling and hugging holds. The change made boxing somewhat more humane, and, as a result, the "manly art" gained popularity among upper-class young men. However, the new rules actually had the effect of speeding up fights and made pugilism more dangerous, because fighters could hit harder and throw more punches with protected hands.

In 1890, wide-open New Orleans became the first major city to permit prizefights if they were arranged by an established athletic club. Two years later, the local boxing scene reached its peak with three consecutive days of world championships, culminating in James J. Corbett's knockout of John L. Sullivan for the heavyweight title.

Shortly thereafter, the center of boxing shifted to Brooklyn, where Coney Island machine politicians protected the sport. Then in 1896, Tammany Hall's number-two man, State Senator Tim Sullivan, secured passage of the Horton Act, which permitted sparring matches in buildings owned by athletic clubs. However, the new law was repealed by the state four years later in 1900.

Northern horse racing was revived in 1863 at Saratoga, New York, by elite turf men in cooperation with gambling kingpin and former boxing champion John Morrissey. Prestigious jockey clubs soon were formed that established prestigious racetracks, such as New York's Jerome Park (1866); Monmouth in Long Branch, New Jersey (1870); and Chicago's Washington Park (1884). The tracks featured rich stakes races to attract the top stables and elegant clubhouses for the pleasure of members.

New York was the national center of the turf, aided by the political clout of leading Democratic horsemen such as financier August Belmont, Sr., trolley magnate William C. Whitney, and Tammany Hall boss Richard Croker, who stood up for horse racing and on-track betting against widespread condemnation. But in Illinois, New Jersey, and several other states, reformers closed the tracks in the 1890s. Still, moralists could not halt illegal off-track betting, which flourished at downtown poolrooms run by organized crime figures and were protected through political connections and payoffs.

Baseball began to become professionalized in the early 1860s, when amateur teams recruited top players with financial incentives. The game became commercialized after William Cammeyer enclosed his Brooklyn skating rink in 1862, renamed it the Union Grounds, and began charging customers 10 cents to watch baseball teams play. In 1869, the Cincinnati Red Stockings, the

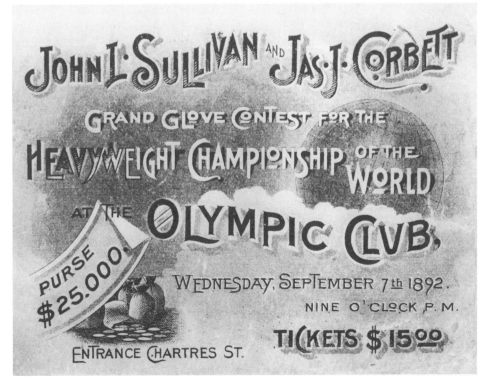

In a historic 1892 boxing match, James J. Corbett knocked out John L. Sullivan, the last bare-knuckle heavyweight champion. It was one of the first title bouts fought with gloves and under Marquis of Queensberry rules, which popularized commercial prizefighting. *(American Stock/Getty Images)*

first overtly professional squad, went 57–0–1 on a national tour, encouraging other teams to copy them. In 1871, the nine-team National Association of Professional Base Ball Players was established. It lasted only five years, however, because of such problems as players jumping teams, weak competition, and a small $10 franchise fee with no restrictions, which allowed teams from small cities that could not support them to join.

In 1876, the profit-oriented eight-team National League supplanted the National Association, operating on sounder business principles. It charged $100 to join and required member cities to have at least 75,000 residents. The National League sought middle-class fans by discouraging gambling, banning Sunday ball and liquor sales, and charging 50 cents for admission. The league struggled at first, but it soon became profitable. Its success led to the creation of the rival American Association in 1882, which appealed to working-class fans by charging 25 cents for tickets, permitting Sunday ball games, and selling liquor. The two leagues made peace in 1883, establishing a stranglehold over the professional sport.

The main expense for baseball teams was salaries. In order to increase profits and keep wages down, owners in 1879 added a reserve clause to players' contracts. The clause gave teams the right to renew a player's contract each year and prohibited other teams from employing that player. The players responded by forming the Brotherhood of Professional Baseball Players, baseball's first labor union, in 1885. Five years later, the Brotherhood established the Players' League, which outdrew both the American Association and National League.

All three leagues suffered large financial losses, however. The Players' League folded after one season, and the American Association and National League merged in 1892, leaving a single 12-team league called the National League, which quickly reduced salaries by more than 30 percent. The unwieldy league had too many underfunded teams, and in 1899, it dropped the four weakest clubs. Baseball fans were outraged, creating a window of opportunity for a new rival, the American League, which proclaimed itself a major league in 1901.

American Sports in 1900

Sports in America made enormous strides between 1870 and 1900, propelled by industrialization and urbanization, the emergence of new sports, and the flourishing of a positive sports creed. By the end of that era, the United States was one of the leading sporting nations in the world. Sports had become a major male participatory and spectator recreation; however, sports was not democratic, as options varied widely by social class and ethnicity. Professional sports had emerged, dominated by professional baseball. America had gone from a borrower of civilization to an exporter of culture, selling baseball to the Caribbean and Japan, and the new sports of basketball and volleyball (invented in 1891 and 1895, respectively) around the world.

Steven A. Riess

Further Reading

Betts, John Rickards. "The Technological Revolution and the Rise of Sport, 1850–1900." *Mississippi Valley Historical Review* 40:2 (March 1953): 231–256.

Gorn, Elliott J. *The Manly Art: Bare-Knuckle Prize Fighting in America.* Ithaca, NY: Cornell University Press, 1986.

Harmond, Richard. "Progress and Flight: An Interpretation of the American Cycling Craze of the 1890s." *Journal of Social History* 5:2 (Winter 1971): 235–257.

Lester, Robin. *Stagg's University: The Rise, Decline and Fall of Big-Time Football.* Urbana: University of Illinois Press, 1995.

Levine, Peter. *A.G. Spalding and the Rise of Baseball: The Promise of American Sport.* New York: Oxford University Press, 1985.

Lomax, Michael E. *Black Baseball Entrepreneurs, 1860–1901: Operating by Any Means Necessary.* Syracuse, NY: Syracuse University Press, 2003.

Mrozek, Donald J. *Sport and American Mentality, 1880–1910.* Knoxville: University of Tennessee Press, 1983.

Riess, Steven A. *City Games: The Evolution of American Urban Society and the Rise of Sports.* Urbana: University of Illinois Press, 1989.

Seymour, Harold. *Baseball.* 3 vols. New York: Oxford University Press, 1960–1989.

Smith, Ronald A. *Sports and Freedom: The Rise of Big-Time College Athletics.* New York: Oxford University Press, 1988.

Vincent, Ted. *Mudville's Revenge: The Rise and Fall of American Sport.* New York: Seaview, 1981.

PROGRESSIVE ERA, 1900-1920

The development of sports in the early twentieth century was influenced significantly by industrialization, urbanization, and Progressivism, a broad-based social movement that began in the late nineteenth century and continued through the onset of World War I. The Progressive movement originated as a response to the problems associated with rapid industrialization, urbanization, and immigration in the late nineteenth century. Its goals were to promote political democracy, social justice, economic opportunity, and efficiency through government and philanthropic institutions. It encompassed a wide array of contradictory influences, ranging from liberalism to religious fundamentalism.

Progressive reformers, who were mostly middle-class, white Anglo-Saxon Protestants, sought a more orderly society. They campaigned against widespread corruption in state and city governments and the capitalist excesses of the Gilded Age robber barons, who trampled on consumers, workers, the environment, and fair competition. In order to rectify such problems, reformers proposed more direct involvement of citizens in government through the exercise of new powers, including initiatives, referendums, direct recall of politicians and judges, and vigorous application of anti-trust laws to combat monopolies.

Social reformers in the early twentieth century looked to sports to ameliorate some of the era's social problems. The prevailing positive ideology of sports saw athletic activity as a way to promote good character, elevate morals, and enhance public health. Reformers saw sports as a means to socialize immigrant youths and make them into law-abiding, hardworking citizens. Sports also provided an uplifting option to such vile amusements as prostitution, drinking, and gambling. However, certain sports, particularly boxing, which was brutal, and horse racing, which was tied to gambling and corrupt politicians, were anything but elevating entertainment and received severe criticism and calls for their elimination.

Social Reform and Sport

Clergymen also emphasized the social value of sports. The puritanical idea of the body as a source of sinful temptation was rejected in favor of a theology that viewed the body as a physical housing for the soul, and exercise and sports as means of strengthening that shelter, honoring God in the process. This philosophy, known as "muscular Christianity," became the hallmark of programs developed by the Young Men's Christian Association (YMCA) through World War I. In addition to inventing the sports of basketball and volleyball in the 1890s as a means to enhance the body, physical education teachers promoted American sports throughout the world as part of their evangelical mission.

The social gospel movement, which sought to apply Christian ethics to the problems of the late nineteenth and early twentieth centuries, found sports to be a useful tool to draw inner-city youth to their churches, which often housed gymnasiums. Even more important was the role of settlement houses, which were established in the late 1880s and numbered more than 400 by 1913. They were set up by middle-class men and women who secured large old mansions in slums where they lived and set about studying the social issues of the neighborhood. Once they had identified the community's problems, they set about working with local residents to solve them.

The best-known settlement house was Hull House, founded on Chicago's Near West Side in 1889 by Jane Addams and Ellen Gates Starr. There, they fashioned a community institution that worked to Americanize immigrants by providing English-language lessons, cooking classes, and myriad programs to teach social and vocational skills. They also provided a gym and sponsored athletic teams for both boys and girls, both as part of the acculturation process and the broader goal of improving the social, mental, and physical well-being of

Spurred by the "muscular Christianity" movement at the turn of the twentieth century, YMCA facilities proliferated in urban neighborhoods. Sport was a primary means of acculturating immigrant youth. *(Library of Congress)*

inner city residents. The success of Hull House soon spawned similar institutions elsewhere.

Progressive reformers helped enact child labor laws to remove boys and girls from the workplace, despite the wishes of parents, who needed the children's wages to support their poor families. Reformers also pressed for mandatory education laws, providing a captive audience for teachers who instructed students in proper American middle-class values. At the same time, compulsory physical education classes instilled the traits and training desired by the philosophers and psychologists.

The Progressives sought to alter public space efficiently to promote public health. Architect Daniel Burnham unveiled his City Beautiful movement at the 1893 World's Fair in Chicago, and went on to develop city plans for Chicago, Cleveland, Ohio, and Washington, D.C. In Chicago, Burnham planned to provide orderly streets ringed by healthy forest preserves and public beaches, all of which were meant to encourage physical

activity and demonstrate that the physical environment could shape social behavior.

Even before Burnham's plan was initiated, Chicago's reformers developed new play sites throughout the city. Hull House provided a sandlot for young children to keep them safe from street traffic, an idea that had originated in Boston. Such sites grew into playgrounds to accommodate older children in urban neighborhoods. In the larger public parks, the city built field houses with gyms, swimming pools, and clubrooms to attract youth, even during the winter months.

Male and female supervisors in the parks and playgrounds, like teachers in public schools, taught children to play in a manner that was conducive to mainstream norms and standards of healthy competition and avoidance of vice. The field house concept soon was copied by other American cities as a means to alleviate delinquency and direct the leisure activities of the young. Teams that wished to use the facilities had to adhere to American norms by scheduling their practices, while officials affirmed respect for authority. By 1907, the Playground Association of America assumed national leadership of such adult-directed youth sports.

Educational Reform and Sport

The ideas of educational reformers had an important role in encouraging the use of sports in schools. John Dewey of the University of Chicago developed his pragmatic philosophy, which had a great influence on educational reforms throughout the twentieth century. Dewey's emphasis on learning by doing fit well with the belief that team sports developed the leadership abilities, cooperation, and self-sacrifice needed by both athletes and American democracy.

Another important theorist was G. Stanley Hall, the first president of the American Psychological Association, who theorized that societies progressed through stages—from savage to barbarian to civilized states—as evidenced by their methods of play. He reasoned that willpower could be trained, implying that less socially developed groups, such as the immigrants who were then flooding America's shores, could be taught the civilized values of mainstream American culture, in part through participation in sports.

As working-class and ethnic immigrant children began to attend schools after the turn of the century, they were exposed to American sports and games. Initially organized and administered by older students who formed baseball and football clubs, extracurricular activities increasingly came under adult supervision. Student teams in the late nineteenth century often recruited nonstudents for important games, which also involved wagering and had few regulations governing play. Games were arranged through challenges in the newspaper if local leagues did not exist. Even with abundant local competition, high school teams tended to travel widely to contest regional and even national championships.

Reformers sought to institutionalize athletic competition and rid contests of socially undesirable characteristics, such as gambling, drinking, and professionalism. Luther Gulick, formerly a superintendent of physical education at the YMCA and instrumental in the invention of basketball, established the privately funded Public Schools Athletic League (PSAL) in New York City in 1903.

The PSAL sponsored a host of competitive sports aimed at instilling proper values in participants. For children in grades five through eight who had at least a B average and a record of good behavior, it promoted participation in team sports, opportunities to compete for athletic badges in such events as running, jumping, and chinning (today known as chin-ups), and other activities aimed at promoting physical fitness. In addition, interscholastic competition was organized for high school students in most major sports. In 1905, a girls' program was initiated that included a dozen sports and stressed "Athletics for All Girls." Similar adult-controlled athletic associations soon governed interscholastic play in other American cities.

Sports and Higher Education

At the college level, too, healthy competition and the institutionalization of sports proceeded apace. Students in the late nineteenth organized their own sporting ventures, including regattas, track meets, and baseball and football contests.

By 1890, football overshadowed all other sports, and teams increasingly relied on professional coaches for leadership. The most influential figure in the sport was Walter Camp, a former team captain and later coach at Yale University who was a central figure in college football's influential rules committee from 1877 until his death in 1925. Football assumed a distinctly American character under Camp's guidance, and he became known as the "Father of American Football."

Football coaches at the turn of the century were among the most influential men on college campuses. For instance, Amos Alonzo Stagg at the University of Chicago was responsible for recruiting and retaining star players, planning practices, creating tactics for games, and scheduling opponents to make sure the team attracted the maximum number of paying fans. Winning was emphasized over sportsmanship.

Football was the "big game" on college campuses—so big that major contests often were played off campus. By the 1890s, big match-ups already were spectacles. The annual championship game between Yale and Princeton universities in New York was preceded by a four-hour parade and drew 40,000 spectators. Yale's success over the last quarter of the nineteenth century served as a model for other football programs, and many athletic clubs and colleges sought out former Yale players, such as Stagg, as coaches.

The growing interest in football led school administrations to take over the programs and create conferences to regulate athletics. Universities began to build new facilities to satisfy public interest in the big game. In 1903, Harvard University constructed Soldiers Field, a 40,000-seat concrete stadium, on its campus.

The stadium commemorated the sacrifice of soldiers, thereby linking the game to nationalism and military values, including self-sacrifice for the greater good. At the same time, the stadium brought profitable contests to the school.

The downsides of big college sports soon became apparent. As early as 1906, University of Michigan President James Angell complained that colleges were becoming hosts to public spectacles, undermining their primary mission of public service. Despite such qualms, colleges concentrated on the advantages of sports. In addition to revenues, football rivalries brought welcome attention—and generous contributions—from alumni.

Schools continued to build new stadiums. In 1914, Princeton University unveiled Palmer Stadium, which seated nearly 46,000, while Yale University surpassed that with the Yale Bowl, with seating for more than 70,000 spectators. Other schools and municipalities built even larger structures to host football games and other civic spectacles.

Another downside of football was the violence of the game. When the 1905 season resulted in at least 18 deaths and 159 serious injuries to players, some colleges dropped the sport in favor of rugby. President Theodore Roosevelt, an ardent advocate and practitioner of sports, called the coaches of Harvard, Princeton, and Yale universities to the White House to discuss reforms. Roosevelt and other national leaders believed that football and other martial sports were essential to building a strong and expansionist nation, an idea that was grounded in the social Darwinist belief in the "survival of the fittest."

When the coaches' efforts to modify the sport proved ineffective, college presidents formed a governing body, constituted in 1906 as the Intercollegiate Athletic Association of the United States, to enforce the necessary changes. It was renamed the National Collegiate Athletic Association in 1910.

Regulation of Sport

One of the most important goals for Progressive reformers was to rid sports of gambling, which they viewed as a corrupting influence, both on the individuals who gambled and on the sports they bet on. Particular attention was focused on prizefighting and thoroughbred racing. The so-called sport of kings was conducted at elite racetracks such as Sheepshead Bay in Brooklyn, New York, and Washington Park in Chicago, which featured elegant clubhouses for jockey club members and

their families, as well as more modest proprietary tracks such as Gravesend in Brooklyn. The prestigious tracks drew the rich and well born for classic events such as the American Derby at Washington Park, though some tracks also drew unsavory characters, including petty criminals and prostitutes.

Reformers in the late nineteenth century raged against gambling at tracks, and they had some success at halting racing, as occurred in New Jersey in 1893 and in Chicago in 1905. Racing in New York ceased in 1910 (though tracks reopened in 1913) as a result of laws passed at the behest of Progressive Governor Charles Evans Hughes. By 1910, the only major tracks in operation were located in Kentucky and Maryland. At the same time, reformers had little success in halting illegal off-track betting, which flourished at downtown poolrooms (betting parlors) or in the neighborhoods with bookmakers.

Baseball: The National Pastime

The institutionalization impulse of the Progressive Era also resulted in the consolidation of Major League Baseball. The National League, founded in 1876 as the first major league run on business principles, faced competition in 1901 from another self-proclaimed major league, the American League. In contrast to the National League, American League owners forbade the sale of alcohol at games to promote a more wholesome sporting experience. They undercut National League ticket prices and enticed dozens of National League stars to jump to American League teams. However, after two seasons of financial and legal warfare, the leagues agreed to end their costly competition by uniting to form a single umbrella organization, known as organized baseball, that extended its power to encompass the minor leagues as well. The American and National Leagues agreed to recognize each others' player contracts, and jointly created the National Commission (comprised of each league's president and a third party they chose) to mediate any disputes and stage a season-ending World Series between the pennant winners of each league.

Team owners had considerable political connections, which they used to get inside information about the best sites for ballparks, to prevent interlopers from invading their territory, and to obtain preferential treatment from local municipal governments. Baseball dominated the national sporting scene in the early 1900s, and star players became popular heroes. The major leagues were so profitable that by 1915 nearly all of the teams were playing in large new fire-resistant ballparks.

The boom in baseball extended to the minor leagues as well. In 1912, there were 46 leagues, and nearly every city had a professional team. Fan interest and profit-making potential spurred the emergence of a new rival, the Federal League, which proclaimed itself a major league in 1914, with four of its eight teams in major league cities. The new league tried to recruit established stars with high salaries; though it had little success, the result was significantly higher salaries for veteran players in the Major Leagues.

After the 1915 season, when the Kansas City Feds went bankrupt, organized baseball bought out the owners of the Brooklyn, Buffalo, Newark, and Pittsburgh Federal League teams. In addition, Phil Ball, owner of the St. Louis Terriers, was allowed to buy the St. Louis Browns of the American League, and Charles Weeghman, owner of the Chicago Whales, purchased the Chicago Cubs, and both merged their old and new teams. The Baltimore Terrapins rejected any offers and instead sued Major League Baseball for antitrust violations. The case was held up for several years, until 1922, when the U.S. Supreme Court ruled in favor of organized baseball and granted it an exemption from antitrust legislation.

Sports and Class

Social class was a big factor in determining the sporting options of Americans in an industrialized nation. White-collar workers had more free time and higher incomes than blue-collar workers, who worked, on average, nearly 60 hours a week in manufacturing and 50 hours in construction, typically earning about $438 a year (about $11,500 in 2011 dollars). Typically, Sunday was their only day off, and thus the only day they had free for recreation. However, in the East and the South, blue laws limited their sporting options by prohibiting games on Sundays.

Upper-class men had the most freedom and wealth, and typically engaged in the most expensive sports in the exclusive settings. They belonged to a variety of voluntary sports organizations, many of which required applicants to be approved by current members, such as country clubs, polo clubs, yacht clubs, jockey clubs, athletic clubs, and even selective hunting clubs, such as the 100-member Boone and Crockett Club. Participating in such organizations certified members' elite status. Playing expensive sports also gave athletes an opportunity to display their wealth, a theme of sociol-

ogist Thorstein Veblen in his famous book *Theory of the Leisure Class* (1899).

Elite and middle-class men also were drawn to sports by a need to prove their manliness. In the late nineteenth century, there was concern that men who held sedentary jobs were losing their virility, producing small families, and becoming feminized by religion and culture. Vice President Theodore Roosevelt gave a lecture in 1899, published a year later as the title essay in *The Strenuous Life,* in which he encouraged men to engage in physical activity. Psychologist William James gave a speech in 1906 called "The Moral Equivalent of War," which many interpreted as promoting football as a character-building sport that approximated the experience of going into combat. These views influenced a focus on a strenuous lifestyle at elite prep schools and college campuses; involvement in physical activity also became seen as an antidote to the debilitating effects of work in modern bureaucracies.

In the early twentieth century, sports flourished among members of the middle class. They took advantage of public facilities at large parks near their homes to play tennis and golf. They joined a variety of sports clubs, ranging from baseball to track and field, tennis, and cycling. Their sons played varsity sports in high schools. In addition, the middle class formed a large segment of spectators at professional baseball games.

Poorer workers mainly played sports that were inexpensive and accessible in neighborhood saloons, such as billiards or bowling (in basement alleys), or else attended boxing matches in a saloon backroom or a nearby gymnasium. Other working-class athletes saw sports such as baseball and boxing as a means of securing employment and achieving social mobility. They might participate in track and field events at a union picnic on Labor Day or an outing sponsored by a local machine boss.

A growing number of workers participated in industrial sports programs sponsored by companies such as the Ford Motor Company and Hershey's Chocolate, which aimed to promote teamwork and loyalty in their labor force. Some companies recruited the YMCA to dispense their particular brand of morality through sports. A number of firms, including the Pullman Palace Car Company and Bethlehem Steel, sponsored company teams that played baseball, football, soccer, or rowed against other companies. In 1920, the American Professional Football Association (which became the National Football League in 1922) was formed by several company squads, including Delco's Dayton Triangles and Green Bay's Indian Packing Company.

African Americans

Restrictions on participation in sports proved most severe for African Americans. They encountered Jim Crow laws in the South that barred them from most city parks and prevented interracial athletic competition. A few of the best black athletes in the South migrated north, but for the most part, programs at historically black colleges and universities offered the only opportunities to participate in sports. In 1910, about 10 percent of, or less than 1 million, African Americans lived in the North. That number increased dramatically following the Great Migration (1916–1919), as the urban black population in the North rose 500,000 by 1920 and another 1 million by 1930. Even in the North, African Americans often lived in impoverished ghettoes with inadequate recreation facilities and still faced segregation at YMCAs, parks, and beaches.

Many blacks in the late nineteenth century were highly skilled athletes, especially in baseball. However, they were banned from the major leagues after 1884, and from all professional baseball leagues after 1899. Consequently, black players sought employment on all-black teams that barnstormed much of the year. In 1920, the Negro National League was formed in the Midwest with eight franchises, seven of which were owned by African Americans.

African Americans were very successful as jockeys during the later decades of the nineteenth century. Their success, however, created a backlash, and white competitors forced them from the sport in the early 1900s.

A few African Americans achieved great success competing against white competitors. Marshall "Major" Taylor bested all others in the world sprint cycling championship in 1899. By 1900, he had set seven world records, but jealous white opponents obstructed his efforts thereafter, forcing him to compete in Europe and Australia. Meanwhile, George Poage won two bronze medals as a hurdler at the 1904 Olympic Games in St. Louis, Missouri.

African American basketball teams began to appear in New York, Chicago, and the Baltimore–Washington, D.C., areas. They formed a black basketball circuit. Teams such as the New York Renaissance, known as the Rens, would be fully professionalized in the 1920s.

Boxing offered blacks a venue for interracial competition in some parts of the North, though they were restricted to the less prestigious lower weight levels. Joe Gans reigned as the world lightweight champion from 1902 until 1908. While whites assumed that blacks lacked endurance and the competitive instinct, white heavyweight champions refused to fight blacks in title matches, as the crown symbolized white superiority. Then, in 1908, Canadian champion Tommy Burns agreed to fight Jack Johnson, a black contender, in Australia. Johnson's easy victory sparked an ongoing but unsuccessful search for the "Great White Hope" who might return the laurel to the white race.

With the heavyweight crown resting on Johnson's head, the prevailing belief in white superiority suffered a severe blow. In 1910, undefeated heavyweight champion Jim Jeffries came out of retirement to regain the title, only to be knocked out by the flamboyant Johnson. Johnson's triumph set off celebrations by jubilant blacks, though white retaliation resulted in several riots and deaths.

The black champion further provoked mainstream white society by challenging its mores, marrying a succession of white women. In 1913, Johnson was convicted for violating the Mann Act, which made it illegal to take a woman across state lines for sexual purposes. He fled the country and went to Europe. In 1915, Johnson lost his title in Havana, Cuba, to the white giant Jess Willard in 26 rounds.

White Ethnics

Immigrants from Central Europe came to the United States with a heritage of physical culture. Germans brought their Turner societies to America by 1848, and later in the century, Czech Sokols and Polish Falcons established gymnastic clubs to promote physical fitness and sustain their ethnic culture. However, the second generation—immigrant children born or raised in the United States—was more influenced by American sports played in schools, parks, and playgrounds, and they increasingly adopted baseball, basketball, and football.

German American youths from the Buffalo, New York, YMCA, for example, captured the Amateur Athletic Union basketball championship in 1901. Three years later, they won the basketball tournament at the Olympic Games in St. Louis and then became professional barnstormers. Their success inspired other ethnic teams, such as the Celtics (originally from New York), as well as numerous Jewish clubs.

New immigrants from Russia and Italy arrived with no sporting heritage. However, their sons wanted to acculturate and enjoy American pastimes. German Jews founded settlement houses during the Progressive Era to help their Eastern European brethren become Americanized. Settlement houses used adult-directed sports as a means to attract the interest of immigrant youths and help them adjust to life in the United States. Jewish youths became avid sports fans, but they succeeded mainly in sports that fit life in the crowded slums, such as boxing and basketball, rather than baseball or football, which required open spaces.

Women

Women's sports were advocated in the early twentieth century by feminists and other proponents who believed that sports improved young women's health and beauty, promoted self-confidence, and offered a source of enjoyment. Illustrator Charles Dana Gibson's iconic "Gibson Girl" was a beautiful young lady who often was drawn holding a tennis racket or a golf club.

At the same time, there was substantial opposition to women participating in sports, a legacy of the Victorian era, when "respectable" women were believed to have delicate constitutions and behave in a ladylike manner. Sports were exertive and competitive and traditionally a male sphere. Physicians worried that participation in sports might injure women's supposedly delicate bodies and damage their reproductive organs. Women physical educators opposed vigorous exercise and competitive sports, because they feared participants would become aggressive and manly.

A leading feminist who had a long history of supporting sports, Charlotte Perkins Gilman saw sports as a means for women to take control of their own bodies. She founded the Providence (Rhode Island) Ladies' Sanitary Gymnasium in 1881.

Around the turn of the century, wealthy women began to establish their own athletic clubs. The first was the Chicago Athletic Club in 1898, whose president was Belle Ogden Armour, wife of renowned meatpacker Philip Armour. The goal of the club was to provide women with the same opportunities for exercise,

The women's rights movement of the early twentieth century also gave rise to major competitive sports for women, especially tennis and golf. May Sutton (*left*) was one of America's first female champions, winning the U.S. Open (1904) and Wimbledon (1905, 1907). *(Hulton Archive/Stringer/Getty Images)*

relaxation, and sociability that were available in men's clubs; its elegant clubhouse had a marble swimming pool, gymnasium, bowling alley, and running track. As other clubs formed, the Federation of Women's Athletic Clubs was established in 1901 to advance their common concerns.

Upper-class and upper-middle-class women took up tennis and golf, often at country clubs where their fathers or husbands were members; cycling, which provided a degree of independence; or college sports such as basketball and rowing. An adventurous handful succeeded at male-dominated sports, such as mountain climbing. Such athletic activities called for reforms in dress, and bustled skirts and corsets gave way to shorter skirts and attire that permitted greater freedom of movement. Margaret Abbott, a Chicagoan on sojourn in Paris in 1900, became the first female Olympic golf champion when she won a tournament against opponents who played in high-heeled shoes.

On the tennis courts, May Sutton adopted short-sleeved blouses, which enabled her to hit powerful, overhead strokes, and shorter skirts that helped her move around the court like her male counterparts. She won the national women's singles championship in 1904. Sutton's contemporary, Eleanora Sears, further defied convention by wearing pants and challenging men in athletic pursuits. Sears played baseball, field hockey, and golf, and she won several national championships in tennis and squash. In 1912, she took up polo, not only playing against men, but also riding in the straddle position, a departure from the customary sidesaddle position deemed appropriate for women. Later, she took to racing cars and airplanes, further pushing the boundaries that restricted women's lives.

In addition to individual sports, there also was interest among colleges in team sports, particularly the new sport of basketball. James Naismith invented the game at the International YMCA Training School in Springfield, Massachusetts, in 1891. Shortly thereafter, Senda Berenson adapted the game for women at nearby Smith College in Northampton.

Berenson alleviated some of the concerns about women's participation in sports by dividing the basketball court into three segments, with two players from each team confined to a single zone, thus limiting the amount of running involved. To facilitate movement, the hemlines of the players' skirts were shortened to above the ankle, exposing flesh previously hidden from male view and thus necessitating a ban on most male spectators.

Women took readily to basketball, and it spread rapidly across the country. Intramural contests gave way to interscholastic and club competitions, although female physical educators discouraged unladylike competition by mixing players from different teams for contests. Games were followed by postgame refreshments, a means of further fostering noncompetitive camaraderie.

Female physical educators wanted their students to participate in sports that promoted sociability, like play days, when young women from different colleges would be mixed together to play recreational sports and make new friends. Women sports leaders successfully curtailed intercollegiate sports for female college students, because such contests stressed the undesirable attribute of being highly competitive and challenged gender boundaries. Meanwhile, working-class women, found greater opportunities for sports in the parks, playgrounds, settlement houses, and industrial recreation teams fostered by the Progressive movement.

The Military and World War I

The American military used sports a means of spreading American cultural hegemony. After the Spanish-American War in 1898, soldiers and marines introduced baseball and boxing to the residents of the newly acquired Philippines and competed against Caribbean teams. American military baseball teams competed with Japanese teams as early as the 1890s, and American college teams began traveling to Japan for international series in the next decade. In turn, Japanese teams toured the United States, Hawaii, and the Philippines, playing American sports rather than introducing Japanese ones. In the Philippines, the YMCA organized the Far East Games, an Asian Olympics, between Japan, China, and the Philippines in 1912, as Western sports spread across the Pacific.

The beginning of World War I hastened the Americanization process, as local and national governments issued propaganda against foreign cultures. Ethnic sports, in particular German gymnastic systems, were purged from school curricula. Participation in American sports became a badge of loyalty, and even German Turner societies fielded their own baseball and basketball teams.

The military had relied on sports in training programs in the late nineteenth century, and this became even more important during and after World War I. With the onset of war, fitness became essential for combat troops, and boxing was seen as a way to simulate bayonet training. The U.S. government employed Walter Camp, former football coach at Yale University, to develop the "Daily Dozen," a system of calisthenics for the U.S. Army. The YMCA was secured to provide services and moral guidance to American troops, and sports became a primary means of both training and recreation on military bases. During this time, the military produced some of the best football teams in the country, with the 1918 and 1919 Rose Bowl games featuring contingents from the U.S. Army, Navy, and Marines.

Limits of Progressive Reform

Despite their efforts to spread American sports and middle-class values of healthy competition and clean play, the Progressive reformers were not completely successful. While many ethnic immigrants moved closer to the mainstream sporting culture and women achieved increased but still limited opportunities on the playing field, sports could not ameliorate all urban problems. Despite the efforts of settlement house workers, youth gangs continued to operate, often with the blessing and sponsorship of powerful politicians, engaging in illicit activities and even using the parks and playgrounds as their headquarters.

Gender and class conceptions also thwarted the aims of reformers, as men clung to the bachelor subculture of the past. Working-class men met in saloons for gambling, drinking, and revelry that often revolved around sporting activities, such as boxing. The growth of pool halls and bowling alleys provided additional sites for the maintenance of the male sporting culture and the extension of gambling practices. The beginning of Prohibition actually led to a boom in poolrooms, as tavern keepers moved into the business, but shortly thereafter, cities such as Chicago introduced stricter regulations, and the number of poolrooms dropped from 2,244 in 1920 to 861 in 1922.

Perhaps the greatest symbolic failure of the Progressives' moral crusade was the infamous Black Sox scandal. Baseball, the national game, symbolized all that Americans believed to be good about their nation, standing for integrity, fair play, democracy, and meritocracy. It was the primary sport used to acculturate immigrant youth in parks and playgrounds, and ethnic stars in the major leagues reinforced the perception of baseball as a level playing field (though the game excluded African Americans) and a means to achieve social mobility and acceptance. In 1919, players on the Chicago White Sox—arguably the best team in baseball at the time—colluded with gamblers to lose the World Series against the Cincinnati Reds. Revelations of the subterfuge took almost a year to emerge and led to the reform of the major leagues under a powerful commissioner of baseball, former federal judge Kenesaw Mountain Landis. The authoritarian leader underscored the need to clean up baseball by imposing a lifetime ban on the eight White Sox players involved in the scandal.

With the rise of George Herman "Babe" Ruth and other athletic stars, a new era in American sports began. The so-called golden age of American sports—the 1920s and 1930s—would see spectator sports gain a vast new audience through the media of radio and film. Sports may have maintained an ideology that justified it as building character, improving morality, promoting good health, and epitomizing democracy, but increasingly the emphasis was on sports as a business.

Gerald R. Gems

Further Reading

Cavallo, Dominick. *Muscles and Morals: Organized Playgrounds and Urban Reform.* Philadelphia: University of Pennsylvania Press, 1981.

Gems, Gerald R. *Windy City Wars: Labor, Leisure, and Sport in the Making of Chicago.* Lanham, MD: Scarecrow, 1997.

Goodman, Cary. *Choosing Sides: Playground and Street Life on the Lower East Side.* New York: Schocken, 1979.

Hardy, Stephen. *How Boston Played: Sport, Recreation, and Community, 1865–1915.* Boston: Northeastern University Press, 1982.

Lears, T.J. Jackson. *No Place of Grace: Antimodernism and the Transformation of American Culture, 1880–1920.* New York: Pantheon, 1981.

Marks, Patricia. *Bicycles, Bangs, and Bloomers: The New Woman and the Popular Press.* Lexington: University Press of Kentucky, 1990.

Mrozek, Donald J. *Sport and American Mentality, 1880–1910.* Knoxville: University of Tennessee Press, 1983.

Nasaw, David. *Children of the City: At Work and At Play.* Garden City, NY: Anchor, 1985.

Oriard, Michael. *Reading Football: How the Popular Press Created an American Spectacle.* Chapel Hill: University of North Carolina Press, 1993.

Putney, Clifford. *Muscular Christianity: Manhood and Sports in Protestant America, 1880–1920.* Cambridge, MA: Harvard University Press, 2001.

Rader, Benjamin G. *American Sports: From the Age of Folk Games to the Age of Televised Sports.* 6th ed. Upper Saddle River, NJ: Prentice Hall, 2009.

Riess, Steven A. *City Games: The Evolution of American Urban Society and the Rise of Sports.* Urbana: University of Illinois Press, 1989.

———. *Sport in Industrial America, 1850–1920.* Wheeling, IL: Harlan Davidson, 1995.

———. *Touching Base: Professional Baseball and American Culture in the Progressive Era.* Westport, CT: Greenwood, 1980.

INTERWAR PERIOD AND WORLD WAR II, 1920-1945

Between the end of World War I and the end of the Second World War, the United States became the world's dominant power. During these decades, the nation proceeded to a new phase of the Industrial Revolution, with the focus shifting from the production of capital goods, such as factories, machinery, tools, and equipment used to make producer goods, to a greater emphasis on the making of consumer products. At the same time, America's centralized governmental structures evolved, from a vastly expanded Department of Commerce to the "alphabet" agencies of the New Deal, to better regulate much of the economy and society. These processes, paradoxically, made the United States both more homogenous and more diverse at the same time.

Amid these changes, sports expanded enormously, enjoying a "golden age" abetted by a 30 percent increase in per capita income between 1922 and 1929. Journalist Frederick Lewis Allen saw sports becoming the nation's most fervent passion. Even during the Great Depression, sports continued to flourish and helped forge cultural identities based on American pastimes. Class, gender, ethnic, and racial identities shaped and, in turn, were shaped by sports. Americans also used sports to create local, metropolitan, regional, and national identities. In most respects, sports survived the economic collapse in better condition than many rival industries and continued to be woven into the fabric of American life.

From 1920 to 1945, entrepreneurs developed a powerful industry that centered on professional baseball and college football, and took two old American pastimes, horse racing and prizefighting—both long tainted by connections with gambling and crime—and endeavored to transform them into respectable entertainments. New spectacles, ranging from airplane races to women's sports, expanded that business, a process facilitated by the proliferation of print media, radio, and newsreels, which engendered a sports celebrity culture.

Rise of Consumer Culture and the "Golden Age" of American Sport

During the 1920s, the manufacture of consumer goods expanded the nation's economy dramatically. Standards of living increased, as many Americans enjoyed more leisure time and higher salaries. The new economic order produced an increasingly homogeneous, consumer-oriented national society. And sports ranked high on the list of activities that consumers spent their money and time on.

Baseball and football enjoyed acclaim in almost all segments of American society. In fact, Americans viewed team sports as part of the cultural fabric that knit their society together. To accommodate the continuing interest in professional baseball and the burgeoning fascination with intercollegiate football, enormous stadiums, seating 50,000 or more fans, were constructed in cities with professional baseball teams and in major college football towns, from the Bronx's 58,000-seat Yankee Stadium (1923) to Ann Arbor's 84,500-seat University of Michigan Stadium (1927).

Baseball

In the 1920s, Major League Baseball underwent a fundamental reorganization to respond to changing market conditions, to develop centralized authority, and to systematize its player development system. The league also had to respond to the damaging Black Sox scandal of 1919, in which members of the Chicago White Sox colluded with gamblers to lose the World Series. The ensuing furor prompted baseball owners to hammer out the 1921 National Agreement, which created a commissioner's office to oversee the sport with Judge Kenesaw Mountain Landis as the all-powerful first commissioner. Led by Branch Rickey, then the general manager of the St. Louis Cardinals, Major League

Yankee Stadium opened in the Bronx, New York, on April 28, 1923. The first three-tiered outdoor sports venue in America, it was one of many stadiums built in the 1920s to accommodate the nation's burgeoning interest in spectator sports. *(MLB Photos/Getty Images)*

Baseball also created a "farm system" to develop minor league talent.

The game on the field underwent an offensive revolution, with livelier balls and the banning of trick pitches. Batting averages rose and scoring skyrocketed. The fan-pleasing home run increased ticket sales and made George Herman "Babe" Ruth the most famous American of the era. Ruth—whose penchant for the good life mirrored the hedonistic spirit of the times—slugged more home runs than most entire teams, setting a single-season record of 60 in 1927 and 714 over the course of his career. He earned fame and fortune by turning himself into a brand name, marketed by agent Christy Walsh.

Yet baseball suffered a relative decline during this period, as its market share slipped compared to other leisure pursuits. For example, Major League Baseball's growth lagged far behind the 75 percent rise in attendance at the movies. In fact, gross attendance at major league games rose by only 11.5 percent during the 1920s—less than the growth rate of the national population.

"King Football"

College football grew dramatically in popularity, and by several measures, "King Football" surpassed even baseball during the 1920s. Major League Baseball was played in only ten U.S. cities, whereas college football was a national phenomenon. Most Americans lived near one of the 400 colleges or universities that fielded a football squad. National powers sprang up in small towns as well as in metropolitan areas in the Midwest, South, and Far West. Millions of Americans identified with their local gridiron heroes as "our boys."

College football became big business, drawing millions of spectators and generating huge revenues. As baseball's relative market share declined, football's increased. Attendance doubled in the 1920s, from 5 million to 10 million, while ticket revenues tripled. Many universities built huge new stadiums during this decade to meet demand. In 1920, only the Yale Bowl seated more than 70,000 spectators, but by 1930, there were seven other facilities of similar size. College football attracted students, alumni, and the public to state

The "Four Horsemen" of Notre Dame—the 1924 backfield of (*left to right*) Don Miller, Elmer Layden, Jim Crowley, and Harry Stuhldreher—became part of the school's football lore. College football was king among American sports in the interwar period. *(The Granger Collection, New York)*

universities, providing institutions with important capital, both financial and political.

The game's popularity also was driven by new styles of play. Rule changes and tactical innovations opened up the game in the 1920s, putting more emphasis on speed, agility, and ball skills rather than on mass formations and brute strength. Offensive players who broke for dazzling runs or threw spectacular passes became national stars. The archetype of the speedy, elusive running back was Harold "Red" Grange, who played at the University of Illinois from 1923 to 1925 and was known as the "Galloping Ghost." In the 1930s, stellar passers, such as Texas Christian University's Sammy Baugh and Columbia University's Sid Luckman, thrilled fans with their deep, accurate throws.

The University of Notre Dame, a little-known Midwestern Catholic college, developed into a gridiron powerhouse. Charismatic coach Knute Rockne promoted his squads in the national press by traveling coast to coast to take on national competitors, and by allowing national radio networks to broadcast Notre Dame games for free. Rockne connected Notre Dame to the Catholic community by building a loyal group of "subway alumni" who had never even attended the school. He stocked his squad with the sons of European immigrants, exploiting the American melting pot to build ties to Irish, Italian, and other ethnic communities. Most important, the Notre Dame team won consistently against traditional powerhouses. From 1918 until Rockne's untimely demise in an airplane crash in 1931, his squads went 105–12–5.

Likewise, other major college programs built media allegiances, developed broadcasting contracts, played intersectional games against powerful opponents, and made coaches symbols of their institutions. Among these acclaimed coaches were Glenn "Pop" Warner at the University of Pittsburgh and Stanford University, and Amos Alonzo Stagg at the University of Chicago.

Horse Racing and Prizefighting

During the interwar period, more Americans attended horse races annually than any other sport's events, although a championship heavyweight prizefight in

1927 drew a crowd of more than 100,000, Chicago's 1937 Austin–Leo city high school football championship at Soldier Field was attended by more than 120,000, and the annual Indianapolis 500 drew more than 150,000. Race tracks thrived as the introduction of pari-mutuel gambling sparked a resurgence in racing, long a staple of American culture, which reform nearly had quashed in the early 1900s. As the era of Progressive reform faded, the public's appetite for gambling, always the central attraction of horse racing, returned.

Prizefighting had existed for more than a century as the province of working-class and wealthy men who were attracted to violence and gambling, but the sport was illegal in most states until the 1920s, when public opinion began to shift. By then, New York and other states had legalized boxing, at least in part due to a recognition of its value in training soldiers during World War I. A shrewd new cadre of promoters led by George "Tex" Rickard legitimized prizefighting. Rickard promoted fights as wholesome spectacles with million-dollar purses, mainstream press coverage, and the patronage of political, business, and social leaders. He transformed prizefights into cultural events that attracted an audience of both men and women for a glamorous night out.

Rickard's biggest draw was Jack Dempsey, who won the heavyweight championship in 1919 against the gargantuan Jess Willard. "Jack the Giant Killer" became an overnight celebrity, a true rags-to-riches tale. Rickard matched Dempsey against aging, overhyped contenders in million-dollar fights staged in huge venues. Dempsey fought sparingly, holding his title until 1926, when he was upset by Gene "The Fighting Marine" Tunney before 120,000 fans in Philadelphia. Rickard cleverly set up a rematch one year later before 104,000 spectators at Soldier Field in Chicago, while another 50 million listened to a national radio broadcast of the bout. Tunney won a controversial decision over the former champion in the infamous "long-count" fight, when Dempsey failed to go to a neutral corner after knocking down Tunney. The referee delayed starting the count for five seconds, giving Tunney extra time to recover.

Great Depression

In the 1930s, the thriving consumer culture began to unravel as the U.S. economy slid into financial collapse. By 1933, unemployment in the United States reached nearly 25 percent. President Franklin D. Roosevelt's New Deal programs promoted relief, recovery, and re-

form, but it was not until the end of the decade that Americans saw an upturn.

The Great Depression had a significant impact on American sports. Expenditures for sporting goods dropped, along with attendance at sporting events. Many minor league baseball teams folded, and nascent sports operations suffered, such as the American Basketball League, the American Soccer League, and the first Negro National League, all of which failed. Meanwhile, the National Hockey League and National Football League both lost a substantial number of franchises.

Baseball

The specter of bankruptcy even hovered over Major League Baseball. Attendance declined from 10 million in 1930 to 6 million by 1933. The floundering St. Louis Browns drew only 80,000 fans to their home games in 1933, and they joined other struggling franchises in pleading unsuccessfully with the league for a profit-sharing plan. Teams slashed player salaries from an average of $7,000 in 1933 to $4,500 in 1936, cut rosters, and downsized umpiring crews. By 1935, however, major league attendance was on the rise again, reaching its pre-Depression level by 1941.

The Depression produced some innovations in baseball. The Cincinnati Reds introduced night games, an idea borrowed from the Negro and minor leagues. Owners looked for new sources of revenue in radio and advertising. Major League Baseball initially resisted broadcasting games, fearing a decline in attendance, but in the 1930s, several teams developed regional radio networks. In 1934, Commissioner of Baseball Kenesaw Mountain Landis signed a $400,000 contract for a nationwide broadcast of the World Series, sponsored by Ford and Gillette. When Prohibition ended in 1933, teams rushed to ink deals with reopened breweries. By the beginning of World War II, Major League Baseball derived about 10 percent of its revenue from radio and commercial sponsorships.

Other Sports Industries

Certain segments of the sports industry actually grew during the Great Depression, as they offered a temporary escape for the masses. College football suffered initial losses at the turnstiles, leading a few schools to eliminate their football programs; however, the game soon rebounded. Most programs cut ticket prices, which helped double attendance from 10 million to 20 million between 1930 and 1937. College and high school administrators cut women's sports programs, but attendance at men's basketball games increased.

Public participation in golf, tennis, and bowling remained steady. In 1932, Lake Placid, New York, hosted the Winter Olympic Games, while Los Angeles put on the Summer Games. Prizefighting remained a popular and lucrative business, and attendance increased at the race track.

Seabiscuit, an unlikely thoroughbred with a strange gait, served during the Depression as an apt symbol of perseverance against great obstacles and became a beloved folk hero. As a two-year-old in 1935, he won only five of his first 35 races, and he did not begin to win regularly until late as a three-year-old. Then, as a four-year-old, he became the nation's leading money winner. As a five-year-old, Seabiscuit was named Horse of the Year, an accomplishment highlighted by his victory in a match race against War Admiral, winner of the Triple Crown in 1937.

New Deal for Sports

President Roosevelt appreciated the American public's appetite for sports. As governor of New York, he supported the Lake Placid Olympics as a linchpin of economic rejuvenation, and he used the winter carnival to garner attention for his presidential bid. Roosevelt peppered his famous "fireside chats" with sports analogies and urged Americans to enjoy the escape that sports provided.

Roosevelt made sports a key component of his New Deal. The Civilian Conservation Corps, Works Progress Administration, and other agencies put people to work by constructing a vast new system of recreational facilities. Federal workers erected parks, playgrounds, gymnasiums, and swimming pools. On federal lands, they constructed campgrounds and cut hiking trails through forests. Between 1935 and 1941, the federal government spent $941 million on sports venues and other recreational areas and an additional $229 million to finance community recreation.

The Fans

The Depression did not dampen the public's enthusiasm for sports as much as it reduced consumption in almost every other sector of the economy. Americans continued to buy tickets for games. Radio ratings rose for many sports. More people read the sports pages and watched sports segments on newsreels than in the prosperous 1920s.

"Golden Age" of Sportswriting

In the 1920s and 1930s, sports journalism in newspapers and magazines blossomed. Sports accounted for 5 percent of the average newspaper's volume in 1900, but an astounding 25 percent by 1925. Sportswriters became journalistic stars, earning higher salaries and greater editorial freedom than news or editorial writers. Journalism critics complained that readers cared more about sports than the leading civic issues of the day.

One group of reporters developed a style that turned sporting events into epics peopled by larger-than-life heroes. Grantland Rice, the most widely syndicated American columnist, made an art form of this style, crafting majestic poetry for athletic sagas. Lesser writers turned the "Gee Whiz" school into sappy hyperbole. Another school of reporting led by Paul Gallico, Ring Lardner, Damon Runyon, and John Tunis combined sports with social criticism, turning sports coverage into extended social commentary. Many of these writers went on to become accomplished essayists, novelists, and screenwriters.

Journalists even made news, creating new contests. The *Chicago Tribune* and *New York Daily News* invented the Golden Gloves boxing championship in the 1920s. Arch Ward of the *Chicago Tribune* devised the Major League Baseball All-Star Game (1933) and the College All-Star Football Game (1935). Local papers sponsored myriad contests, games, and teams.

Radio and Newsreels

Americans not only read about sports, they also listened to broadcasts of sporting events on the radio and watched sports replays on newsreels. Indeed, sports filled the radio waves even before the first for-profit stations existed. Stations carried prizefights, beginning with Dempsey's title defenses in 1920 and 1921.

Pittsburgh's KDKA, America's first commercial radio station, made sports a staple, airing Major League Baseball and college football games in 1921. A year later, New Jersey's WJZ broadcast the World Series. Other stations followed suit, and by the mid-1920s, broadcasts of the Indianapolis 500 and the Kentucky Derby also could be heard on the radio.

Coast-to-coast networks such as the National Broadcasting Corporation (NBC, 1926) and the Columbia Broadcasting System (CBS, 1927) made sports transmission a nationwide habit. Broadcasts bolstered fan devotion and spurred attendance, particularly for the top teams and important matches. The 1938 fight between Max Schmeling and Joe Louis, a rematch of the German's stunning 1936 upset of the African American star, drew the largest audience in the history of the medium to that time. Two-thirds of Americans tuned in to hear Louis knock out Schmeling in the first round.

Newsreels served as the precursor to televised sports, broadcasting a visual "magazine" of world and national news, human-interest features, and sports that became a template for later local television news programs. During the interwar era, 30 million to 100 million Americans watched newsreels every week. Athletic events from the Olympic Games to Alaskan dogsled races filled the newsreels.

Participants

Recreational opportunities for average Americans expanded dramatically during the prosperous 1920s. The Depression lowered standards of living, but most Americans still embraced the new recreations that emerged in the more affluent era. While some private recreational ventures and welfare capitalism programs failed, the federal government stepped in to boost participatory sports.

Golf, Tennis, Swimming, Bowling, Driving, and Cycling

In the 1920s, the middle class flocked to country club sports such as tennis, golf, and swimming, once the province of the elite. Cheaper, mass-produced sporting goods combined with the expansion of club facilities broadened the demographics of tennis and golf. Golf boomed among businessmen seeking to make valuable contacts. During the Depression, one-third of clubs went bankrupt; however, federal, state, and local public works programs built hundreds of municipal golf courses, as well as tennis courts and swimming pools.

Bowling in the 1920s boomed among the working class, becoming one of the most popular participatory sports. The number of American Bowling Congress–sanctioned bowling alleys grew from 450 to 2,000. They went "dry" during the 1920s because of Prohibition, helping to make bowling a family game. Most alleys weathered the downturn of the 1930s by providing inexpensive entertainment. In 1933, when Prohibition was repealed, breweries underwrote local bowling leagues, and alleys again thrived as male social centers. Bowling in the 1930s was the leading women's recreation as well. In 1939, the all-male American

Bowling Congress (founded in 1895) merged with the all-female Women's International Bowling Congress (founded in 1916) to form the International Bowling Association.

The automobile revolution had an enormous impact on American culture in the 1920s, vastly expanding public access to camping, hiking, skiing, and other outdoor pastimes, but nearly killing off cycling for transportation and recreation among adults. Bicycles became children's toys. In the 1930s, bicycle companies struggled to survive. Schwinn, for instance, focused on producing inexpensive bicycles. Its new Excelsior model, with fat tires, a spring fork, and a rugged frame, became a best seller for youths whose parents could afford it.

Youth Sports Explosion

American children and adolescents engaged in sports in ever-growing numbers during the interwar years. In the 1920s, elementary and secondary schools developed comprehensive programs for boys that typically included baseball, basketball, football, and track and field. Interscholastic sports became a hallmark of adolescent life. High school varsity squads shaped the identities of villages, towns, and urban neighborhoods. High school football in the interwar years became a Friday night staple in many areas.

High school basketball's growth symbolized the new importance of youth sports in American life. In basketball-obsessed Indiana, for example, many towns built gymnasiums with seating that exceeded their populations in order to draw fans from surrounding communities. Basketball, which required little space, also flourished in crowded metropolitan areas. By 1939, more than 95 percent of the nation's schools sponsored basketball teams.

Basketball fostered ethnic and religious as well as local and regional identities. Youth organizations, such as the Young Men's Christian Association and the Young Men's Hebrew Association, promoted it. Successful Jewish teams in New York City and other large metropolitan areas made basketball an important game for developing a Jewish American identity. In 1930, the Catholic Youth Organization developed leagues in Chicago, New York, and other cities to provide athletic competition for second-generation immigrant youths within a religious environment.

Other programs trained younger boys for high schools squads. In 1929, the Junior Football Conference was founded, later becoming known as the Pop Warner Conference, named for the renowned college coach. In

1939, Little League baseball was invented by Carl Stolz in Williamsport, Pennsylvania. Pop Warner football and Little League baseball created adult-supervised games that supplanted the child-centered and child-oriented sandlot experiences of earlier generations.

Women's Sport

From 1920 to 1945, women both gained and lost ground on American playing fields. The best American female athletes garnered more attention and had more opportunities than in past eras. The media celebrated new female sports stars as symbols of women's new political and social freedoms, but many women found their athletic horizons limited.

The Catholic Youth Organization, Young Women's Christian Association, and Young Women's Hebrew Association provided some opportunities, but a battle raged in coeducational public schools over the inclusion of girls in competitive sports. In the early 1920s, many schools fielded interscholastic girls' teams in basketball, volleyball, and track and field, but they came under fire from female physical education teachers and administrators who feared that competitive sports threatened femininity.

The Women's Division of the National Amateur Athletic Foundation, established in 1923, led the assault against competitive sports for women. By the early 1930s, members of the organization had closed most women's intercollegiate programs and led a campaign to end statewide high school basketball tournaments, succeeding in 14 states.

Women's sports continued to thrive at the highest competitive levels, however. The Amateur Athletic Union (AAU) established national championships for women's swimming and diving in 1916, and added track and field in 1924 and basketball in 1926. "Amateur" female athletes, such as tennis player Helen Wills Moody and golfer Glenna Collett Vare, became celebrities, earning substantial sums under the table.

American women had more opportunities in the Olympics as the International Olympic Committee added more women's sports, including figure skating, swimming and diving, tennis, and track and field. Medalists, such as diver Aileen Riggin, swimmers Sybil Bauer and Gertrude Ederle, and sprinter Elizabeth Robinson, became national heroines. In fact, the two Olympic swimmers pushed the boundaries of gender stereotypes by besting their male rivals. In 1924, Bauer set a world record in the backstroke, while Ederle became a celebrity in 1926 when she was the first woman to swim the English Channel, beating the prior record—set by a man—by more than two hours.

At the same time, athletic heroines became sex symbols for male audiences, reinforcing the old gender stereotypes. The media and fans were especially fond of "feminine" sports, particularly figure skating, tennis, swimming, diving, and golf. The media's increased coverage of female athletes provided opportunities for pictures of women in revealing swimsuits, short tennis skirts, and skating costumes.

Sex appeal also had an impact on other women's sports. Municipal and industrial basketball, volleyball, and softball leagues sprang up for working-class women; the leagues developed high-level competition and dominated the AAU championships. Their administrators, however, pointedly capitalized on the combination of athleticism and attractiveness, parading their athletes in beauty contests as well as in athletic competitions.

The greatest female athlete of the era was a working-class Texan, Mildred "Babe" Didrikson, who starred in AAU basketball tournaments and won the 1932 AAU track and field championship as a one-woman team. Limited to three events at the 1932 Olympic Games in Los Angeles, she won two gold medals and one silver medal. The press applauded her athleticism but questioned her femininity, viewing her as "mannish." In the mid-1930s, Didrikson took up golf, which was considered a more acceptable sport for women.

Sports Stars and American Identities

While new female athletes dramatized American debates over gender, both male and female athletes served as catalysts for the formation of ethnic, racial, and religious identities.

Ethnic and Religious Dimensions

Nativism, or anti-immigrant sentiment, was rife in the 1920s, as Americans responded to the waves of newcomers arriving in the United States in the late nineteenth and early twentieth centuries. Sports seemed to provide an outlet to counter nativism and to provide minorities a way to fit into American society. Social commentators claimed that for European Americans, sports represented a "melting pot."

Every major European ethnic group had major league stars to cheer. German Americans applauded English Channel swimmer Gertrude Ederle. Italian Americans identified with baseball star Joe DiMaggio.

College football rosters increasingly were dotted with the offspring of the "new immigration" from Southern and Eastern Europe, from the University of Notre Dame's Italian Joe Savoldi to the University of Minnesota's Polish-Ukrainian Bronko Nagurski to Columbia University's Jewish Sid Luckman. The Notre Dame squad represented the new multiethnic reality of American sports; the "Fighting Irish" were icons for the new European Americans who formed the bedrock of the nation's Catholic communities.

The ethnic and religious dimensions of American society also emerged in other sports, notably boxing and basketball. Jewish Americans dominated all levels of basketball, including urban professional leagues, serving simultaneously as symbols of cultural pride and successful assimilation. They also were very successful in prizefighting, where heroes such as champions Benny Leonard and Barney Ross disproved negative stereotypes about Jewish manliness.

Italians, Poles, and Jews only achieved major breakthroughs in baseball in the 1930s. Slugger Hank Greenberg of the Detroit Tigers became the new Jewish athletic hero for smashing home runs, standing up against anti-Semitism, and following his religious convictions by refusing to play in a game held on Yom Kippur, a Jewish holy day.

Race and Segregation

For non-European ethnic groups, sports also revealed the complex patterns of assimilation and identity. Native Americans took pride in the achievements of baseball and football star Jim Thorpe, one of the most accomplished athletes of the twentieth century. Native Hawaiian Duke Paoa Kahanamoku won Olympic swimming medals and introduced surfing to the mainland. These indigenous athletes provided white Americans with both exotic heroes and reassurance about the benefits of acculturation.

African American participation in sports presented a more mixed picture of inclusion and exclusion. Professional baseball kept an impermeable barrier in place, relegating black players to the Negro Leagues. Nonetheless, pitching star Satchel Paige led black all-stars against St. Louis Cardinals pitching ace Dizzy Dean and his major league all-stars in exhibitions during the 1930s. The National Football League included a few black stars, such as Fritz Pollard in the 1920s, but then it drew the color line in 1934.

Golf, tennis, and even bowling largely excluded black athletes. American Olympic teams included some blacks, particularly in track and field. At the 1932 Olympic Games, African American sprinters Eddie Tolan and Ralph Metcalfe dazzled the nation with their multiple-medal performances.

Football and other college sports provided a pastiche of semipermeable boundaries in an era of "gentlemen's agreements" that mostly excluded black athletes. Southern universities were rigidly segregated, but a few African Americans appeared on teams in the North and the West. Some Southern universities refused to play against integrated teams at home or on the road, while others would play integrated squads in major intersectional contests when they ventured north. Northern schools with black athletes generally adhered to Southern wishes, but by the early 1940s, New York University and Pennsylvania State University began challenging these pacts, demanding that their black athletes be allowed to play wherever their teams completed.

Top black college athletes became popular figures. Tolan and Metcalfe starred at the University of Michigan and Marquette University, respectively, and Jesse Owens became a track sensation at Ohio State University. The University of California, Los Angeles led the nation in recruiting black stars, such as quarterback Kenny Washington and running back Jackie Robinson.

Prizefighting drew a color line in the prestigious heavyweight division, fearing the rise of another Jack Johnson, although lower weight classes allowed black champions. In 1937, with the heavyweight crown tarnished by a series of white journeymen champions, the color barrier collapsed when Joe Louis earned a title shot and seized the champion's belt, which he wore until 1949.

In the late 1930s, as the world moved toward war once again, Louis and Owens turned in unforgettable performances on the international stage, making them the leading African American heroes of their era. Owens's triumphs at the Olympic Games in Berlin in 1936 and Louis's defeat of German boxer Schmeling in 1938 also made them the first African Americans to rank as interracial national heroes.

Louis in particular served as a powerful emblem of black identity, as African Americans listened to radio broadcasts of his bouts, celebrating his victories and mourning his only defeat back in 1936 to Schmeling. During World War II, Louis joined the government's war effort, serving in the military and fighting bouts to benefit war relief, while also allying with other African American leaders to fight economic and social discrimination.

American Identity in a Global Arena

As Owens and Louis illustrate, international sports had a tremendous impact on American society. The United States used sports to connect with allies, challenge rivals, and spread American culture and products. The country engaged the world in every imaginable contest, from Davis Cup tennis to World Cup soccer. In 1930 at the first World Cup, the United States came in third, its best finish ever.

The Olympic Games were the primary sites for international athletic clashes. American teams dominated competition at Antwerp (1920), Paris (1924), and Amsterdam (1928), more than doubling the medal counts of their nearest rivals. The press and the public read U.S. victories as proof of American hegemony.

To bolster its image as a world city, Los Angeles rigorously petitioned the International Olympic Committee, winning the right to host the 1932 Games. Then, in the depths of the Great Depression, the city put on a spectacle promoting Southern California while American athletes romped to a medal-count blowout. Although they were bested by Germany at the 1936 Berlin Games, Americans sought solace in Owens's victories on the field and against Nazi racial ideology, though some commentators responded by pointing out America's own racial hypocrisies.

World War II

World War II transformed the nation. Industrial production for the war effort ended the Great Depression and revitalized the economy, while the homogenizing, centralizing, and nationalizing tendencies of modern warfare altered American social patterns. The United

A capacity crowd of more than 100,000 attended the opening ceremonies of the 1932 Olympic Games in Los Angeles. Despite the Great Depression, it was the greatest series of athletic events in the United States to that time. *(Getty Images)*

States exited the war with a firmer commitment to live up to its professed ideals of equality, a political necessity in its new role as a world superpower.

On the home front, the military's needs thinned the ranks of college and professional athletes. College football teams struggled, except for those of the U.S. Military Academy and the U.S. Naval Academy; both schools enjoyed burgeoning enrollments and fielded powerful football squads. The U.S. Military Academy's team (known as Army) went undefeated and finished at the top of the college football polls in 1944 and 1945. The 1945 Army–Navy game was the first nationwide network football telecast.

Baseball also suffered manpower shortages. President Roosevelt chose not to close down the game, citing the national pastime's role in boosting morale. However, approximately 1,000 players enlisted in the war effort, causing the quality of play to decline markedly, as clubs scrambled to fill rosters with marginal talents, including youths and even a one-armed player.

Into the breach stepped Chicago Cubs owner Phillip K. Wrigley, who organized the Midwestern four-city All-American Girls Softball League in 1943, the first professional sports league for women in American history, which drew nearly 1 million fans annually. In 1945, the league switched to hardball rules and became the All-American Girls Baseball League. Girls' baseball worked as a wartime novelty, but it drifted into extinction in the postwar era.

The postwar era also produced more profound changes in racial relations. In October 1945, Jackie Robinson signed a minor league contract with the Brooklyn Dodgers, confronting head-on racial segregation in America's national pastime and American society in general. The connections between national and racial identities and American sports forged between 1920 and 1945 built toward this moment. American sports and society moved toward profound changes, with an athlete leading the way.

Mark Dyreson

Further Reading

Alexander, Charles C. *Breaking the Slump: Baseball in the Depression Era.* New York: Columbia University Press, 2002.

Baker, William J. *Jesse Owens: An American Life.* New York: Free Press, 1986.

Cahn, Susan K. *Coming on Strong: Gender and Sexuality in Twentieth-Century Women's Sport.* New York: Free Press, 1994.

Carroll, John M. *Red Grange and the Rise of Modern Football.* Urbana: University of Illinois Press, 1999.

Cayleff, Susan E. *Babe: The Life and Legend of Babe Didrikson Zaharias.* Urbana: University of Illinois Press, 1995.

Creamer, Robert W. *Babe: The Legend Comes to Life.* New York: Simon & Schuster, 1974.

Dyreson, Mark. *Crafting Patriotism for Global Domination: America at the Olympics.* London: Routledge, 2008.

———. "The Emergence of Consumer Culture and the Transformation of Physical Culture: American Sport in the 1920s." *Journal of Sport History* 16:3 (Winter 1989): 261–281.

———. "Icons of Liberty or Objects of Desire? American Women Olympians and the Politics of Consumption." *Journal of Contemporary History* 38:3 (July 2003): 435–460.

Levine, Peter. *Ellis Island to Ebbets Field: Sport and the American Jewish Experience.* New York: Oxford University Press, 1992.

Oriard, Michael. *King Football: Sport and Spectacle in the Golden Age of Radio and Newsreels, Movies and Magazines, the Weekly and the Daily Press.* Chapel Hill: University of North Carolina Press, 2001.

Riess, Steven A. "Power Without Authority: Los Angeles Elites and the Construction of the Coliseum." *Journal of Sport History* 8:2 (Spring 1981): 50–65.

Roberts, Randy. *Jack Dempsey: The Manassa Mauler.* Baton Rouge: Louisiana State University Press, 1979.

Seymour, Harold. *Baseball.* 3 vols. New York: Oxford University Press, 1960–1989.

Smith, Ronald A. *Play-by-Play: Radio, Television, and Big-Time College Sport.* Baltimore: Johns Hopkins University Press, 2001.

Watterson, John Sayle. *College Football: History, Spectacle, Controversy.* Baltimore: Johns Hopkins University Press, 2000.

Wong, John Chi-Kit. "FDR and the New Deal on Sport and Recreation." *Sport History Review* 29:2 (November 1998): 173–191.

POSTWAR ERA, 1946-1970

During the decades immediately following World War II, North American society and sports underwent massive changes. Opportunities opened up for those once excluded from the mainstream, either by race or by social class; international tensions were played out on the diamond, field, and court; and technological innovations became widespread, particularly television. Black athletes took their place in professional sports, the Cold War gave added significance to international competition and to the purpose of sports for young Americans, and television allowed fans across the nation to see their favorite teams without leaving home. While the games remained essentially the same, these developments transformed the landscape of sports—whom fans cheered for, what sports they followed, how sports were presented to fans, and how fans viewed athletes.

African Americans Gain a Place on the Team

One of the first and most significant changes of the postwar period was the opening of opportunities in professional sports to include African Americans, who had been barred from professional leagues and many college athletic contests, especially in the South, for most of the century. Sports provided the first chance for blacks to participate fully in American life. The long struggle to attain equality would be aided by such groundbreaking athletes as Nat "Sweetwater" Clifton, Larry Doby, Marion Motley, Jackie Robinson, and Kenny Washington.

The first breakthrough came in professional football, which was gaining in popularity but still had a long way to go to catch up with professional baseball and college football. In 1946, the Los Angeles Rams of the National Football League (NFL) signed Kenny Washington and Woody Strode, the first African Americans to play in any premier professional league since the NFL was segregated in the early 1930s. Washington and Strode, both talented athletes, benefited from the

efforts of Los Angeles politicians, who made the inclusion of African American players a requirement when the Rams moved from Cleveland to the city-owned Los Angeles Memorial Coliseum. Washington, an All-American halfback at the University of California, Los Angeles in the late 1930s, played for three seasons until bad knees ended his career. Strode played for one year before moving on to the Calgary Rough Riders of the Canadian Football League.

Marion Motley also entered professional football in 1946, when Paul Brown, coach of the Cleveland Browns of the All-America Football Conference (AAFC), convinced the star of the wartime Great Lakes Naval Training Station team to forgo finishing his college degree and play professional football instead. Motley and All-American lineman Bill Willis starred for the Browns from 1946 to 1953, helping the team win all four AAFC championships. Motley was the AAFC's leading rusher with 3,024 yards (2,765 meters), and Willis was named All-League three times. Injuries plagued Motley's later career, and in retirement, he faced discrimination when he attempted to become a coach, reflecting the still-limited opportunities for African Americans in professional football.

Jackie Robinson Breaks the Color Line in Baseball

Jackie Robinson's entry into professional baseball had a far greater impact on sports than the integration of professional football. Baseball was the unchallenged national pastime and seen as reflection of the core values of American culture.

The major leagues had been segregated since 1884, and the minor leagues since 1899. Politicians, social activists, and East Coast journalists already had been pressing for integration for a number of years. In the immediate postwar period, New York City Mayor Fiorello La Guardia hinted that if sports franchises did not integrate voluntarily, he might introduce bills in

Jackie Robinson, the first African American player admitted to Major League Baseball in the modern era, enters the Brooklyn Dodgers's clubhouse after the team announced the purchase of his contract from the minor league Montreal Royals in April 1947. *(New York Daily News/Getty Images)*

the city council to force them to do so. Politicians in Boston threatened to ban liquor sales at ballparks on Sundays, prompting the Red Sox to give Robinson a sham tryout in 1945.

Branch Rickey, president of the Brooklyn Dodgers, explored the idea of signing African Americans before the pressure began to mount and always denied that such threats ever played a role in his decision. However, he certainly was influenced by a desire to acquire better players and to improve the gate, along with the aim of doing justice to African American athletes. Despite the opposition of other team owners, Rickey signed Robinson in October 1945, and the following spring, he assigned Robinson to the Dodgers's top farm club in Montreal, where he would encounter less racial hostility than in the United States.

Robinson performed spectacularly in 1946, and the next season, he was called up to the majors, effectively breaking baseball's color line. He persevered in the face of enormous prejudice, earning Rookie of the Year honors and helping the Dodgers win the National League pennant. Robinson's integration of the major leagues may have been the greatest contribution of any sportsman to American history, serving as a major step toward desegregation of the broader society.

Larry Doby, signed by Bill Veeck of the Cleveland Indians 11 weeks after Robinson's debut, was the first black player in the American League. Like Robinson, he faced many obstacles, but received only a fraction of the press coverage. Other major league teams slowly began to integrate, but as late as September 1953, seven seasons after Robinson's appearance, only 6 of 16 major league teams had African Americans on their rosters. They were mainly in the National League, where African Americans won five straight Rookie of the Year awards (1949–1953) and seven straight Most Valuable Player titles (1953–1959). The last team to integrate was the Boston Red Sox, whose owner, Tom Yawkey, resisted hiring black players until 1959, when he signed infielder Elijah "Pumpsie" Green.

Professional Basketball

In 1946, the Basketball Association of America was formed—renamed the National Basketball Association (NBA) in 1949—and the following season, the league broke the color barrier when the New York Knicks signed Wataru Misaka, a Japanese American. In 1950, Earl Lloyd, Chuck Cooper, and Nat "Sweetwater" Clifton became the first African Americans in the NBA, when they signed with the Washington Capitols, Boston Celtics, and Knicks, respectively.

All-American Bill Russell signed with the Boston Celtics, becoming the first black basketball star in 1956. Three years later, Wilt Chamberlain joined the Philadelphia Warriors, engaging with Russell in one of the greatest personal rivalries in all of sport.

African American Women

Black women achieved success in track and field at historically black colleges during the postwar era. In 1948, Alice Coachman, formerly of the Tuskegee Institute, took first place in the high jump at the Olympic Games in London, capturing the only gold medal in track by an American woman. In the era before passage of Title IX, U.S. Olympic teams relied heavily on African American women. The brightest star was sprinter Wilma Rudolph, who in 1960 won three gold medals at the Olympic Games in Rome.

However, black women struggled to gain recognition in higher-status sports. Tennis star Althea Gibson, known as the Jackie Robinson of the women's professional tennis tour, won both Wimbledon and the U.S. championships in 1957–1958.

Sports and the Cold War

Viewed as an imperialistic affectation by Russian leaders such as Joseph Stalin, sports during the 1950s became a new front for the global competition between democratic capitalism and totalitarian communism. In 1952, the Soviets attended their first Olympic Games in Helsinki, Finland, and the quadrennial event increasingly focused on competition between the Soviet Union and the United States.

The Soviets posted impressive results, especially in women's events, at a time when athletic opportunities for American women were rare. The American press denigrated Soviet women athletes as "mannish." Ironically, this opened a cultural space for black women—whose participation in athletics was not seen as an affront to femininity to the same degree it still was for white women—and U.S. teams relied on them to bring home medals.

Soviet gains in the Olympics reflected their focus on events that offered many medals, such as gymnastics and wrestling. In 1956, the combined Soviet men's and women's medal totals surpassed that of the United States for the first time. In the eyes of American political leaders, the Olympics provided a chance for nonaligned nations to judge the relative merits of the two social systems by studying the medal results.

Professionalism was a constant subject of contention between the superpowers. Americans claimed that Soviet athletes, many of whom were employed by the army or the secret police, were subsidized, whereas American athletes were true amateurs, albeit often supported by college scholarships. Another concern was charges of mannishness among Soviet female athletes. Contrasts were drawn between Russian women's androgynous appearance and the more feminine American athletes. As a consequence, gender testing was introduced at the 1968 Mexico City Games.

There also were fears during the Cold War that young people in America were becoming too physically soft, a result of the postwar abundance and consumerism of the 1950s. When studies revealed that American children were in worse shape than their European counterparts—and, potentially, Soviet youths as well—President Dwight D. Eisenhower formed the Council on Physical Fitness in 1956. The council languished until the early 1960s, when President John F. Kennedy bolstered the body with a higher profile and a bigger budget.

As a candidate for the presidency in 1960, Kennedy penned an article for *Sports Illustrated* titled "The Soft American." He, like other Cold War politicians, believed that America's struggle against communism demanded a more vigorous citizenry. They believed that youths, in particular, needed to be physically fit in order to excel in life and strengthen the country. Failure to train physically fit youths was viewed as threatening America's future and undermining the nation's ability to fight communism around the world.

Even as the U.S. government was promoting physical fitness as a way to strengthen America's Cold War defenses, it was employing America's top athletic youths as propaganda tools across the globe. The U.S. Department of State, for example, sent African American athletes on tours of developing-world nations to spread goodwill toward America and to refute Soviet charges that minorities were ill treated in the United States.

Sports on Television

The advent of television had an enormous impact on postwar sports, and sports, in turn, helped popularize the new media. Boxing, wrestling, and roller derby were early staples of television in the late 1940s, as all took place in small spaces that were easy to televise. Viewers watched these events on small television screens, often in neighborhood bars, until they could afford the new technology at home. Other sports, including baseball, football, and golf, also were telecast, helping to increase public interest.

Baseball

Immediately following World War II, fans flocked to major and minor league ballparks, but by the 1950s, attendance was beginning to slump, especially in the minor leagues. The decline was attributable to several factors, including competition from other entertainment options, such as television. Baseball did not suit the new medium: There were long gaps between periods of brief action, and the small ball was hard to see on the television screen. In addition, the minor leagues were hit hard when the majors began televising games in their towns. Given the option of buying a ticket to see a team of relative unknowns play or going to a bar or staying home to watch Joe DiMaggio or Ted Williams for free, fans generally chose the latter.

Major League Baseball also was hurt by its inability to negotiate a unified television deal—a move that the federal government opposed on the grounds that it violated antitrust law. While some aspects of major league operations, particularly labor negotiations, were exempt from antitrust law, such exemptions did not necessarily apply to the negotiation of broadcasting contracts. Teams created their own local television packages, which allowed teams in major media markets such as Chicago, Los Angeles, and New York to negotiate lucrative deals, while small-market teams received far less for television coverage. Congress addressed the problem by passing the Sports Broadcasting Act of 1961, which allowed sports leagues to negotiate television contracts as a single unit.

Technological advances in the 1960s helped to make television coverage of spectator sports, and thus the sports themselves, more appealing to audiences. Particularly popular was the use of multiple lenses on television cameras—and later zoom lenses—allowing networks to vary their shots, from a close-up of a catcher giving signals to a wide-angle shot of the subsequent play. With the perfection of instant replay in 1963, networks assigned multiple cameras to cover the action. This allowed viewers to see a spectacular or controversial play from different angles, and helped fill some of the dead airtime during telecasts. Slow-motion technology allowed fans to second-guess umpires, who were handicapped by having to call balls, strikes, and tags in real time. Color television, introduced widely in the

1960s, brought the onscreen image much closer to what could be seen at the ballpark. Combined with other technological advances, this provided a spectacle that was superior in many ways to attendance at a live event.

National Football League

No sport benefited more from television than professional football. Still a relatively minor sport in 1945, by 1970, it would eclipse baseball as the public's favorite sport. Unlike baseball, the action of a football game lent itself to live broadcasts. The action took place in a relatively confined part of the field, so that one camera could focus effectively on the point of collision between the teams, and play followed play, punctuated only by brief pauses while the sides regrouped in huddles.

The 1958 NFL championship game between the New York Giants and the Baltimore Colts, the first season finale to be decided in dramatic sudden-death overtime, fired the public interest in professional football. In public opinion polls, the share of Americans who rated professional football as their favorite sport increased from 21 percent in 1961 to 36 percent in 1972, while the share of those naming baseball fell from 34 percent to 21 percent during the same period.

The NFL's cause was aided significantly by Pete Rozelle, who became NFL commissioner in 1959. Rozelle had risen from the business side of professional football, and he employed that expertise in his negotiations with the television networks. In 1960, the NFL's chief rival, the American Football League (AFL), signed a unified television contract with ABC, but when Rozelle signed a similar deal with CBS in 1962, the federal government declared the deal an infringement of antitrust law. Rozelle helped convince Congress to pass the Sports Broadcasting Act, bolstering the NFL's revenues. Rozelle's first contract with CBS was relatively modest— $4.65 million—but that figure rose dramatically to $14 million in 1964, while NBC signed a five-year deal with the AFL worth $42 million. After its merger with the AFL, the NFL's television deal rose to $50 million in 1970.

The NFL, unlike Major League Baseball, decided early on to share national television revenues equally with its constituent teams. Each team received 40 percent of the gate for road games and an equal share of revenues from the television contract. This enabled teams in smaller markets to make money, while spending enough to field competitive teams and sustain fan interest. Rozelle enjoyed much greater control over league policy than the contentious baseball owners ever surrendered to their commissioner.

The competition for talent between the rival NFL and AFL sparked enormous publicity, as teams threw money at players to lure them to their leagues. When the competition began to threaten the financial health of the leagues, Rozelle negotiated an agreement to merge the two in 1969 under his leadership. Two years earlier, the NFL and AFL already had begun playing a postseason championship, which later would become known as the Super Bowl. The powerful Green Bay Packers of the NFL, led by Coach Vince Lombardi and quarterback Bart Starr, easily won the first two contests in 1967 and 1968, but the American Football Conference (comprised mostly of former AFL teams) gained parity in 1969 when the New York Jets, led by quarterback Joe Namath, defeated the Baltimore Colts 16–7 in Super Bowl III.

National Basketball Association

As Major League Baseball declined and professional football rose in popularity, the National Basketball Association struggled to find its place in American professional sports. Early on, the NBA faced competition from other basketball circuits, such as college basketball, the Harlem Globetrotters, and the Amateur Athletic Union (AAU).

College basketball enjoyed great popularity in the immediate postwar period, and the NBA often was shut out of premier sporting venues such as New York's Madison Square Garden by college games. The all-black Harlem Globetrotters enjoyed phenomenal popularity after the war, entertaining fans with their showmanship and basketball skills, and even defeating the world champion Minnesota Lakers in 1948. The NBA hesitated to sign top black talent, in part because of a reluctance to compete for their services against Globetrotters owner Abraham "Abe" Saperstein, whose team often played games as part of NBA doubleheaders. The AAU also drained much of the top talent, as its company-sponsored teams arranged high-paying jobs for "amateur" players—often more than they could earn as a professional. Another problem for the NBA was that game scores typically were low and play was rough and tumble, which turned off many fans.

In the 1950s, as the league slowly integrated, the quality of play rose and the game became faster and more creative. Rising revenues enabled the NBA to outbid AAU teams for player talent. The rise of the first NBA dynasty, the Minneapolis Lakers, led by center

George Mikan, also helped promote interest in the game. Finally, rule changes, including the introduction of the 24-second shot clock in 1954, sped up the game and made it more television friendly.

The dominant team in the early NBA was the Boston Celtics. Bill Russell joined the club in 1956, teaming up with flashy point guard Bob Cousy under Coach Arnold Jacob "Red" Auerbach. They formed the nucleus of a team that went on to win nine titles between 1957 and 1966. The Celtics played a fast-paced style of basketball and helped attract fans to the sport with their fast breaks and sharp passing. Russell contributed two more titles as a player-coach before retiring in 1969, making the Celtics one of the most successful teams in any sport.

Despite the progress of the NBA, its popularity on television lagged far behind that of baseball and football, and in 1970, its contract with ABC brought in only $2 million. The NBA also had to contend with competition from the American Basketball Association (ABA), formed in 1967, which included several franchises in the Southeast, a hotbed of enthusiasm for college basketball. The ABA signed many top collegians, including Julius "Dr. J." Erving, and introduced such gimmicks as a red, white, and blue basketball and the 3-point shot. However, the ABA never succeeded in gaining a major television contract. In 1976, the league folded, and four of its teams joined the NBA.

College Sports

Unlike professional sports, American universities and the National Collegiate Athletic Association (NCAA) were slow to embrace television, fearing that it would cut into their gate receipts. The NCAA opposed the efforts of individual schools to cash in on the bonanza being reaped by the professionals, and, in response to declining attendance in the 1950s, it limited each region of the country to seven televised football games per season into the late 1960s.

Television money began pouring into college sports, but any suggestion of revenue sharing was put aside by pressure from the powerhouse schools. Individual conferences did create such revenue-sharing programs, but marginal schools and conferences missed the gravy train of televised sports. Fans of second-tier institutions had few chances to see their favorite teams play, except in person.

College sports experienced a drop-off in attendance during the 1950s, partly as a result of the college basketball scandal in 1951, when 32 players from seven schools were indicted for shaving points (purposely winning by less than the point spread established by gamblers). The scandal prompted many big basketball schools to deemphasize the sport, and conferences prohibited their teams from playing in venues such as Madison Square Garden, whose officials had been implicated in the scandal. In addition, respect for college sports also was hurt by the West Point cheating scandal of 1951 that resulted in 37 players being expelled. Meanwhile, the NCAA gained extensive powers to enforce rules against schools that broke intercollegiate rules.

Even as college basketball languished, college football came roaring back in the 1960s. Several factors—on and off the field—aided this comeback. Offensives became more exciting as the level of play improved when schools in the South, a region with several football powerhouses, dropped their policy of excluding black athletes. And, of course, television made the sport more accessible to millions of Americans who could not attend games in person. Television broadcasts enhanced fan interest in traditional school rivalries and made the postseason bowl games national events.

College basketball had a slower recovery. The NCAA Tournament expanded from 8 teams to 16 in 1951, and soon supplanted the National Invitation Tournament as the main postseason event. However, the NCAA Tournament was not broadcast on a major network until 1969.

ABC Sports

In addition to the major spectator sports, television programs such as *ABC's Wide World of Sports,* which debuted in 1961, brought sports with a marginal fan base, such as track and field and figure skating, to American viewers. Beginning with broadcaster Jim McKay's voiceover touting the "thrill of victory, and the agony of defeat," *Wide World of Sports* became an American institution, helping to propel the career of ABC news chairman Roone Arledge, who in 1970 brought the NFL to prime time with *Monday Night Football.*

Television would radically transform the world of American sports, changing the way fans watched sports, and the sports they watched. Now, ball games were accompanied by expert analysis from former players or coaches, which helped demystify the mayhem of football and made it the nation's favorite sport. Television also would transform sports, encouraging rule changes, such as lowering the Major League pitching mound by

5 inches (13 centimeters) to improve offense in 1969, providing a better spectacle for the audience.

Transportation innovations also had a significant impact on sports. The advent of jet travel made it practicable for teams to travel across the country to compete with one another. This had a particularly significant effect on baseball, with its game-heavy schedule. In 1958, just a few years after the introduction of jet travel, baseball became a truly transcontinental sport when the Brooklyn Dodgers and New York Giants—much to the chagrin of their local fans—relocated to Los Angeles and San Francisco, respectively.

Franchise Movements

Prior to 1953, Major League Baseball's geography had been stable for 50 years. The last franchise move had occurred in 1903, when the Baltimore Orioles franchise went to New York, becoming the Highlanders (later renamed Yankees). Since then, the 16 teams (eight in each league) had remained in the same cities in the Northeast and Midwest. St. Louis, Missouri, was both the westernmost and southernmost outpost.

The first change came in 1953, when the Boston Braves, which had struggled financially for years, relocated to Milwaukee and soon set franchise attendance records. Their success caught the attention of other owners of besieged franchises. In 1954, the St. Louis Browns moved to Baltimore, becoming the Orioles, and in 1955, the Philadelphia Athletics moved to Kansas City, Missouri.

The West and South were clamoring for new teams, but Major League Baseball's conservative leaders, who were worried about overexposure, looked suspiciously at expansion. This attitude contributed to the most significant team moves in the era. After the 1957 season, Brooklyn Dodgers owner Walter O'Malley announced that his highly profitable team would move to Los Angeles. The same day, New York Giants owner Horace Stoneham reported his team would move to San Francisco. For many fans in New York, the news was devastating—suddenly, they were losing two of their three major league teams. (O'Malley, the main instigator, never apologized.) Both teams desperately needed new stadiums, but the New York City government offered no help or encouragement. By contrast, city fathers in California were eager to cooperate. At the same time, millions of baseball fans in the West were overjoyed, clamoring for tickets and television coverage.

These dramatic changes in the National League pressured the American League to take similar action. In 1961, it was the first league to expand, adding teams in Minnesota (the Twins) and Los Angeles (the Angels). The following season, the National League added teams in Houston (the Colt 45s, later renamed the Astros) and, to address the continuing outrage of New Yorkers, in New York (the Mets). By the end of the 1960s, Major League Baseball had expanded to 12 teams in each league, adding National League teams in San Diego and Montreal and American League teams in Kansas City and Seattle.

Athletic Revolution

In the 1960s, American society was rocked by the rise of a youth counterculture that questioned prevailing values and norms. Athletes historically were among the most traditional young people and rarely challenged authority, but even they began to openly challenge some of the basic assumptions of the sports world and the larger society. As part of those challenges, athletes began questioning the authority of coaches, managers, and trainers.

The pioneer of this new spirit was American boxer Cassius Clay, who won a gold medal at the Summer Olympic Games in Rome in 1960 and became heavyweight champion of the world in 1964 after defeating Sonny Liston. Following his title fight, Clay announced that he had joined the Nation of Islam, a Muslim sect that preached Black Power and separatism, and that he was changing his name to Muhammad Ali. In the next few years, Ali turned against the war in Vietnam, one of the most contentious issues of the day. In 1967, he refused induction into the armed services, claiming religious objections to the war. He was convicted of draft evasion, and boxing authorities took away his championship and canceled his licenses to fight in the United States. Ali responded by continuing to box overseas, gaining a worldwide following. In June 1971, the U.S. Supreme Court overturned the draft evasion charges. By that time, Ali had been licensed to fight in the United States again but was defeated by Joe Frazier in Madison Square Garden in a bid to regain the heavyweight crown. As a majority of Americans came to oppose the war, opinions on Ali shifted in his favor.

In 1967, Harry Edwards, an assistant professor at San Jose State College, founded the Olympic Project for Human Rights, which sought to use sports to promote civil rights. Its goals included restoring Ali's title, im-

Reflecting the social and political upheaval of the times, U.S. track and field athletes Tommie Smith (*center*) and John Carlos raise their fists in protest of American racism after receiving their medals for the 200-meter event at the 1968 Mexico City Olympics. *(AFP/Stringer/Getty Images)*

proving opportunities for African American college athletes, and fighting racism in Rhodesia and South Africa. Edwards was especially critical of Avery Brundage, the American chairman of the International Olympic Committee, whom he branded a white supremacist.

At the 1968 Olympic Games in Mexico City, two of Edwards's followers, Tommie Smith and John Carlos, won the gold and bronze medals, respectively, in the 200-meter (219-yard) dash. At the medal ceremony, each wore black gloves and raised one fist in a Black Power salute to protest American racism. Brundage immediately suspended the two athletes and sent them home. Many sports fans condemned the protesters, believing that politics belonged on the sidelines; however, supporters saw the demonstration as an important political statement in a setting that already was thoroughly politicized.

Ball Four

In 1970, two former professional athletes published books that made public the manipulation of professional athletes by team owners and demythologized the private conduct of professional sportsmen. The first, former St. Louis Cardinals linebacker Dave Meggyesy, exposed the NFL's seamy underbelly, including violence, racism, and exploitation of players, in his book *Out of Their League.*

The same year, major league pitcher Jim Bouton, a star of the New York Yankees in the early 1960s, was struggling to stay in the big leagues. In *Ball Four: My Life and Hard Times Throwing the Knuckleball in the Big Leagues,* Bouton opened the locker room door, allowing fans to glimpse the private lives of their baseball heroes. The sight was not pretty, as Bouton chronicled the sexual exploits of major leaguers. He told readers of the stupidity of managers, the cupidity of general managers who tried to cheat players out of a fair salary, and asked whether the career of legendary Yankee Mickey Mantle might have lasted longer if he had not drunk so much.

Reaction against *Ball Four* was severe. Players were angry at Bouton for exposing their private lives. Sportswriter Dick Young called Bouton and co-author Leonard Schecter "social lepers," and Commissioner of Baseball Bowie Kuhn tried to force the author to admit that the book was fictional. Bouton retired midway through the 1970 season after the Houston Astros sent him down to the minors.

Athletes during the 1960s and 1970s began to reflect the attitudes of the counterculture, which overturned many social conventions. Some changes were superficial, as players began to sport longer hair, beards, and mustaches, while other behaviors, such as protesting the war and fighting for unions, directly challenged one of the tenets of American sports—that athletes remain above politics. These developments both reflected changes in the larger society and aided the transformation of that society.

Russ Crawford

Further Reading

Cahn, Susan K. *Coming on Strong: Gender and Sexuality in Twentieth-Century Women's Sport.* New York: Free Press, 1994.

Crawford, Russ. *The Use of Sports to Promote the American Way of Life During the Cold War: Cultural Propaganda, 1945–1963.* Lewiston, NY: Edwin Mellen, 1968.

Goodwin, Doris Kearns. *Wait Till Next Year: A Memoir.* New York: Simon & Schuster, 1997.

Grundy, Pamela. *Learning to Win: Sports, Education, and Social Change in Twentieth-Century North Carolina.* Chapel Hill: University of North Carolina Press, 2001.

Jay, Kathryn. *More than Just a Game: Sports in American Life Since 1945.* New York: Columbia University Press, 2004.

Moore, Joseph Thomas. *Pride Against Prejudice: The Biography of Larry Doby.* New York: Praeger, 1988.

Oriard, Michael. *King Football: Sport and Spectacle in the Golden Age of Radio and Newsreels, Movies and Magazines, the Weekly and the Daily Press.* Chapel Hill: University of North Carolina Press, 2001.

Rader, Benjamin G. *American Sports: From the Age of Folk Games to the Age of Televised Sports.* 6th edition. Upper Saddle River, NJ: Prentice Hall, 2009.

———. *Baseball: A History of America's Game.* 3rd ed. Urbana: University of Illinois Press, 2008.

———. *In Its Own Image: How Television Has Transformed Sports.* New York: Free Press, 1984.

Scott, Jack. *The Athletic Revolution.* New York: Free Press, 1971.

Tygiel, Jules. *Baseball's Great Experiment: Jackie Robinson and His Legacy.* New York: Oxford University Press, 1983.

Van Auken, Lance, and Robin Van Auken. *Play Ball! The Story of Little League Baseball.* University Park: Pennsylvania State University Press, 2001.

Wiggins, David K., ed. *Out of the Shadows: A Biographical History of African American Athletes.* Fayetteville: University of Arkansas Press, 2006.

Zang, David W. *Sports Wars: Athletes in the Age of Aquarius.* Fayetteville: University of Arkansas Press, 2001.

POSTWAR ERA, SINCE 1970

After 1970, sports in the United States enjoyed explosive growth, fueled largely by cultural and technological changes that helped sports become an international multibillion-dollar entertainment industry. With the shackles of segregation and racial prejudice released, African Americans became a dominant presence on many team sports and made significant inroads into sports management. Huge steps were taken toward gender equality, driven by the feminist movement and by the passage of Title IX in 1972. Professional athletes enjoyed enormous opportunities as the once-amateur Olympic sports opened to all competitors and as professionals in team sports secured free agency, leading to an extraordinary escalation in salaries. Sports remained an important arena of Cold War diplomacy through the early 1990s. A new development was the role of performance-enhancing drugs in athletic competition, which tainted the achievements of a number of high-profile athletes.

Financial Growth

No single enterprise demonstrated the growth of sports during this era better than the National Football League (NFL), which completed its merger with the American Football League in 1970. Paid attendance rose from 12.7 million in 1978 to 22.3 million in 2008. The NFL has become the most valuable and profitable team sport organization in the world. In 2009, the average team was worth just over $1 billion.

Developments in media and media technology played an essential role in the growth of all sports, but especially professional football. In 1962, the NFL sold the rights to televise its games to CBS for $4.65 million. By 1977 it was $656 million for four years with three major networks ($6 million annually per team), raised to $14.2 million per team in 1982. The escalation continued. The NFL's contract from 2004 through the 2011 season was worth $17.6 billion over eight years—

an average of $2.2 billion per season—paid by CBS, FOX, NBC, and ESPN. Television rights fees for the league increased 10,000 percent in 40 years, reflecting tremendous audience interest in NFL programming. From 1964 through early 2010, 21 of the 45 top-rated television shows (by percentage of households) in the United States were Super Bowl games. In 2011, Super Bowl XLV was seen by 111 million viewers, the most in history.

While in the shadow of the NFL, other team sports also saw substantial growth. Major League Baseball (MLB) continued the expansion begun in the 1960s, growing to 30 teams by 1998. League attendance increased steadily, from 28,747,333 in 1970 to a high of 79,502,524 in 2007. Television revenue also generated huge profits for major league clubs. In 2010, FOX was in the middle of a six-year, $2.5 billion deal, while ESPN was paying $851 million. In addition, major league teams reported large revenues from local television contracts, although there is a wide gap between major markets such as New York, where the Yankees made more than $80 million in 2009, compared to the league average of about $30 million. By 2010, the average MLB team was worth an estimated $491 million, led by the Yankees at $1.6 billion.

The popularity of the National Basketball Association (NBA) declined in the 1970s, but rebounded beginning in the 1980s. The average NBA team is worth $369 million at the start of 2011 (down from a record $379 million in 2009). The most valuable franchise in the NBA is the New York Knicks, whose value increased from $296 million in 1998 to $655 million in 2011, despite a series of losing seasons, abetted by the addition of Amar'e Stoudemire. Attendance at NBA games was 21,094,015 or 17,150 per game, down from an all-time high of 21,841,480 in 2006–2007. Fourteen of 30 operated at over 90 percent of capacity. In addition, the league has more than doubled its television rights revenue since 1994, reaching about $600 million a year by 2010 from ABC, ESPN, and Turner Sports.

Ideally suited to television, pro football emerged as a major media phenomenon during the postwar period—so much so that stadiums began installing large-screen video scoreboards to give spectators a clearer view of the action and instant replay. *(Sports Illustrated/Getty Images)*

Hockey and soccer struggled to gain a financial foothold. The National Hockey League (NHL) expanded several times, reaching 30 teams by the 2000–2001 season. Five of the teams are located in Canada, and the remainder are in the United States. Attendance grew from 7,257,670 in 1970–1971 to 20,907,061 in 2009–2010, and 19 of the 30 teams sold 90 percent or more of their capacities. The chief problem for the NHL has been the lack of a lucrative television contract in the United States. The league had a relatively small five-year, $600 million deal with ABC and ESPN, which expired in 2005. When ESPN decided not to renew the deal, the NHL signed with the Versus cable network, which reached far fewer homes. The league did have a small deal in place with NBC to televise select games. In 2007, the NHL signed an agreement to extend NHL coverage on Versus to the 2010–2011 season; Versus paid $72.5 million for the 2007–2008 season and inflationary increases over the next three years.

While youth soccer flourished in the United States, the same could not be said for the professional game.

Professional leagues generally suffered from lack of interest and attendance, despite the hiring of such world-class players as Pelé (Edison Arantes do Nascimento), Giorgio Chinaglia, and Franz Beckenbauer in the 1970s to play for the New York Cosmos in the North American Soccer League. (The league ceased operations in 1985.) The sport enjoyed a revival in 1994 when the United States hosted the World Cup. This led to the formation of Major League Soccer in 1996, which later landed a relatively small $160 million television contract with ESPN and ABC. The signing of British soccer superstar David Beckham by the Los Angeles Galaxy in 2007 increased the league's visibility and popularity. Attendance in 2010 was 4,002,053 or an average of 16,675 per game.

The Olympic Games grew substantially in stature as television made them more accessible, in turn, producing enormous revenue. In 1960, CBS spent only $50,000 to televise the Winter Games from Squaw Valley, California. By contrast, the 1984 Summer Games in Los Angeles brought in $225 million in television revenue. The event made $200 million, the first profitable Olympics since the 1932 Summer Games, also held in Los Angeles. NBC paid $894 million for rights to the 2008 Summer Games in China. Broadcast ratings fell, however, and future Olympics may see reduced offers from television networks.

Player Empowerment

As sports leagues grew in economic power and influence, some of that power shifted from team owners to athletes. Historically, professional athletes were bound in service to one team through a contractual agreement known as the reserve clause.

Baseball player Curt Flood challenged the legality of the reserve clause in 1970, when he was traded from the St. Louis Cardinals to the Philadelphia Phillies against his wishes. Although Flood lost his case before the U.S. Supreme Court, fighting the reserve clause became a major objective of the Major League Baseball Players Association (MLBPA). In 1975, arbitrator Peter Seitz effectively struck down the reserve clause when he ruled that players Dave McNally and Andy Messersmith could become free agents and sign with any team. Other professional leagues soon adopted similar policies that allowed for some degree of free agency.

The result was a staggering increase in player salaries. Under the reserve clause, owners could keep salaries low, because players could not change teams, but under free agency, owners had to bid against one another for the top players. In 1969, the average major leaguer made $24,909, which rose to $578,000 in 1990 and to $3,340,133 in 2010. Salaries in other major team sports experienced similar gains.

Unions such as the MLBPA were instrumental in giving players more freedom and financial gain. Most professional leagues in North America now have union representation—which was not the case before 1970—on such collective bargaining issues as salaries, arbitration, and grievances. As these unions became more vocal and powerful, work stoppages became more common. MLB has had eight such stoppages, the most notable a players strike in 1994 that canceled the end of the season and the World Series. NFL players went on strike in 1982 and again in 1987, and an owner lockout canceled the entire 2004–2005 NHL season. The NBA lost 32 games because of a lockout in 1998–1999.

Another by-product of player empowerment was the growing role of sports agents, who help players negotiate contracts and endorsement deals. Agents work on their own or as part of an agency such as IMG, which

has a staff of 2,200 in 30 countries. Agents such as Leigh Steinberg in football and Scott Boras in baseball not only helped players gain huge contracts, but they also influenced some teams' choices in the amateur draft for fear that their clients would not sign with them or would demand too much money.

Meanwhile, many professional athletes gained the opportunity to compete in amateur competitions, notably in the Olympics, as the International Olympic Committee gave more leeway to governing bodies and national Olympic committees to determine the eligibility of athletes. The most conspicuous result of this rule change was the formation of America's "Dream Team" of NBA players, who have dominated Olympic competition in that sport since the 1992 Barcelona Games.

Technology

The impact of technology in sports has accelerated over the past generation, dramatically increasing the reach and exposure of athletes and sporting events through the media. The major networks dominated the production and distribution of live sporting events through the 1970s, but such developments as satellite transmission, cable television, home satellite distribution, and the Internet all combined to erode network dominance. They also allowed new companies and content providers to satisfy the increasing demand for sports programming.

A key innovator was Ted Turner, whose WTCG-TV Channel 17 (now WTBS) in Atlanta was the first "superstation." The growth of cable television in the 1970s opened up new avenues for sports content, specifically through pay-per-view channels. Providers found that customers would pay extra fees, usually between $30 and $50, to see special events such as championship boxing fights. The match between Oscar De La Hoya and Floyd Mayweather in 2007 recorded 2.15 million pay-per-view purchases and earned $120 million, making it the most lucrative bout in history.

Pay-per-view also became popular with consumers who could not see certain games or teams in their local area. Most major sports leagues, including MLB, the NBA, the NFL, and the NHL, offered out-of-market programming for an additional fee. In 2007, the NFL had about 1.6 million subscribers to its Sunday Ticket programming, which allowed consumers to watch up to 14 games per weekend. The NFL earned around $400 million in gross revenues through its distribution on DirecTV satellite. In a similar way, sports leagues are using satellite radio to reach consumers.

Many individual sports franchises and leagues gained additional revenue and attention from their own media distribution outlets, relying mainly on cable television. Turner bought baseball's Atlanta Braves in 1976 and broadcast their games nationally on WTBS. In Chicago, WGN also became a superstation and broadcast most games of the Chicago Cubs and other Chicago sports franchises. More recently, such franchises as the New York Yankees and New York Mets established separate cable channels devoted to their teams' games and other sports programming. The NFL and MLB also launched their own networks over cable and satellite. At the same time, the vast broadcast offering made possible by cable television led to the development of channels dedicated to the two most widely followed individual sports, golf and tennis.

College sports, particularly football and basketball, also benefited from the exposure provided by regular broadcast and cable channels. Contracts between the National Collegiate Athletic Association (NCAA) and the major networks for college bowl games and the "March Madness" Division I men's basketball tournament—which came to boast a bigger audience for its final games than baseball's World Series—have gen-

erated hundreds of millions of dollars for the organization and participating schools.

The most powerful sports programmer by far, however, was ESPN (which originally stood for the Entertainment and Sports Programming Network). ESPN began as a small all-sports cable channel in 1979, showing programming that the major networks did not want, such as lacrosse and Australian rules football. It grew into the dominant provider of sports entertainment and programming in the world, with estimated revenues of more than $2 billion annually. In 2011, ESPN had at least seven domestic and 25 international television networks, five online entities, two magazines, ESPN Books, and ESPN Radio, and it also provided video on demand, broadband, merchandise sales, consumer products, and event management.

All of these technological developments have given sports fans many more choices in terms of channels, content, and opportunities for feedback. The most recent area of growth is the Internet. In 2007, ESPN launched ESPN360.com to deliver more than 2,500 live sporting events on a yearly basis via Internet broadband technology. As blogs of all descriptions proliferated, those concentrating on sports ranked third, behind politics and entertainment. In just a single month in

NBA stars take on a Chinese squad in a nationally televised game in Beijing in 2007. Professional basketball has led the way in the globalization of American sports. *(AFP/Getty Images)*

2007, Yahoo!Sports brought in more than 24.5 million unique visitors.

The impact that technology had on the games and events themselves is less obvious. Technology became an indispensable part of how games were played and sometimes decided. The most obvious example is the use of instant replay, particularly in the NFL. In 1986, the league approved using replay during games to re-visit referees' decisions, and it played a role in deciding some key games. Today, replay is used during games in the NHL, NBA, and NCAA. MLB traditionally opposed the use of replay, but implemented it late in 2008 for boundary calls and interference for home runs.

Globalization

Financial and technological growth have helped broaden the perspective of American sports to take in the rest of the world. An early focus was Canada. The NHL originated in Canada and had franchises there from the beginning, but other leagues began to catch up. MLB became international with the addition of the Montreal Expos in 1969 and the Toronto Blue Jays in 1977. In the 1990s, the NBA added teams in Vancouver (the Grizzlies) and Toronto (the Raptors). In both leagues, only the Toronto franchises survived.

Beginning in the 1980s, major sporting leagues stepped up efforts to move beyond North America. The NFL began playing exhibition games in Europe, and in 1991, it created the World League of American Football, a ten-team league that played in cities such as Amsterdam, Berlin, and London. The effort was handicapped by the wide popularity of soccer across Europe and the competition of other homegrown football varieties in Britain and Ireland. The league formally ended in 2007.

By contrast, basketball was rapidly becoming a popular game around the world. The NBA aggressively pursued a global strategy, beginning with the media distribution of NBA games, which in 2007–2008 were broadcast in 41 languages to 215 countries. The NBA encouraged the development of strong professional leagues in Europe, which soon were serving as a source of talent for the league.

The NBA also played games in China, which became a big market because of stars such as Yao Ming and Yi Jianlian. When the Houston Rockets with Yao played Milwaukee Bucks and Yi on November 9, 2007, more than 200 million people in China watched the game on 19 different networks, making it the most-viewed NBA game in history. In 2010–2011, the NBA

had 84 international players from 38 countries and territories.

In a similar way, MLB opened itself to more international opportunities. Baseball has a longer history of international relations, dating to a tour of Japan by teams in the 1920s. Baseball had become a popular spectator sport in Japan, Mexico, and the Caribbean region by the 1930s. Beginning in the 1990s, the league held occasional regular-season games in Mexico, Japan, and Puerto Rico. In 2010, the major leagues had 231 international players from 14 different countries and territories. In 2006, MLB organized and hosted the first World Baseball Classic, a 17-day tournament involving 16 teams.

Canadians dominated the early NHL. Then, in the late 1970s, the rival World Hockey Association, founded in 1972, began recruiting Europeans. The end of the Cold War substantially increased the Russian and Eastern European presence in the WHA, with star players including Pavel Bure from Russia and Jaromír Jágr from Czechoslovakia. The NHL played several exhibition games and series overseas, but the presence of strong professional leagues in Europe kept the focus on North America.

Other professional sports and leagues increased their international visibility. The biannual Ryder Cup, which began in the 1920s as a competition between the best professional U.S. and English golfers, evolved into a competition involving golfers from the United States and all of Europe and became popular and highly contested. The major championships in professional tennis, including the French Open, Australian Open, and Wimbledon, remained enormously popular international events.

Politics, Diplomacy, and Sport

Sports remained an important means for nations to define their ideological identity, and since the 1950s, the Olympics have been a scene of peaceful Cold War confrontation. The United States and the Soviet Union both worked hard to win the overall medal count to prove the superiority of their economic and political systems. The Soviets gained an edge in this regard at the 1972 Summer Games in Munich, Germany, winning 99 medals (50 gold) compared to the 94 won by the United States (33 gold). Then, in 1976, the Russians won 125 medals to the United States's 94, while tiny East Germany won more gold medals than the Americans, 40–34.

International conflict during the Cold War strongly influenced Olympic competition in the 1980s. U.S.

President Jimmy Carter pressured the American team to boycott the 1980 Summer Games in Moscow to protest the Soviet Union's invasion of Afghanistan; the Soviets responded by boycotting the 1984 Summer Games in Los Angeles. Without the two largest contestants present, the customary medal count had much less meaning. When both the United States and the Soviet Union returned to the 1988 Games, the Russians won 132 medals, East Germany won 102, and the United States won 94, in what would be the last Cold War Olympics. By 1992, the Soviet bloc countries had become independent, and the Soviet Union had dissolved.

Performance-Enhancing Drugs

Extraordinary advancements in pharmaceuticals, combined with the age-old search for a competitive edge and the huge sums of money involved in modern sports, led to a series of scandals concerning the use of performance-enhancing drugs in amateur and professional sports during the late twentieth and early twenty-first centuries. Among the most widely used drugs were various forms of steroid and hormone treatments, including human growth hormone. Such drugs can increase muscle mass and performance, but also can cause serious mental and physical problems.

The use of such substances emerged first in weightlifting, bodybuilding, and then football, but after 1990, their use was especially prevalent in track and field. Runner Marion Jones won five medals at the 2000 Olympic Games in Sydney, Australia. For years afterward, she denied allegations that she had used performance-enhancing drugs. However, in 2007, Jones admitted her guilt to federal investigators. She was stripped of her medals and sentenced to six months in prison. U.S. sprinter Tim Montgomery, former world record holder in the 100-meter (109-yard) dash, also was stripped of his record for his drug abuse.

Jones and Montgomery allegedly received the drugs from the Bay Area Laboratory Cooperative (BALCO) near San Francisco, California. A 2004 investigation— and a book based on that probe, *Game of Shadows,* by two *San Francisco Chronicle* reporters—linked BALCO with several other athletes, including baseball stars Barry Bonds and Jason Giambi. The revelations tainted Bonds's pursuit of the all-time major league home run record, which he broke in 2007, reaching 762.

A congressional hearing into steroid use in baseball was held in March 2005. Several major leaguers testified that they had never taken steroids, but investigators were not convinced. Afterward, MLB stiffened its penalties for steroid use and asked former Senator George Mitchell to lead an investigation into the issue. The Mitchell Report, released in December 2007, reported widespread steroid use in the major leagues for at least a decade. The report linked the use of steroids and human growth hormone to several big stars, including Bonds, Roger Clemens, and Andy Pettitte. A month earlier, on November 15, 2007, Bonds was indicted by a federal grand jury for lying to prosecutors about steroid use. His trial was postponed repeatedly until 2011.

Steroids and performance-enhancing drugs also created headlines in other sports. Former NFL player Lyle Alzado blamed steroid use for the brain cancer that took his life in 1992. Professional wrestling long has been subject to rumors about steroid use, which surfaced again in June 2007, when Chris Benoit of World Wrestling Entertainment killed his wife, son, and then himself in a murder-suicide. Benoit had steroids and other drugs in his system.

Race

Jackie Robinson breaking the color barrier in baseball in 1947 is considered the seminal moment in race and sports in American history, although further progress was slow at first. By the late 1950s, the proportion of African American players in the NFL and the NBA was much higher than their share of the national population. In 2010, African Americans made up 77 percent of NBA rosters and 67 percent of rosters in the NFL. In MLB, African American players made up 9 percent of the players in 2011, but international (primarily Latino) players accounted for 28 percent.

Today, more than 50 percent of collegiate scholarship athletes in men's football and basketball are African American. Furthermore, the problem of "stacking" players in certain positions, or keeping them out of key positions (such as quarterback), largely has dissipated. Nonetheless, there still is a wide gap in graduation rates between white and black college athletes.

The remaining inequalities are mainly in the management and ownership of teams. There were no black managers in MLB until 1975, when Frank Robinson became the first African American manager with the Cleveland Indians. In 2009, there were four African American managers, one Asian, and four Latino managers at the start of the season. In the NFL, a 2002 report found that 28 percent of the assistant coaches and 6 percent of the head coaches were African American.

In response, the NFL required that teams hiring new coaches must interview minority candidates. In 2010, six of the NFL's 32 coaches were African American, including the coaches of both Super Bowl teams. Blacks have been most successful in the NBA, where currently 40 percent of the coaches are African American, yet their average tenure is 1.6 seasons compared to 2.4 for white coaches.

Minorities are vastly underrepresented among owners. Former players Earvin "Magic" Johnson and Isiah Thomas were limited partners of NBA teams in the 1990s, and in 2004, television entrepreneur Robert Johnson became the first African American majority owner of a major sports franchise, the expansion Charlotte Bobcats in the NBA. In 2010, Johnson sold a majority interest in the club to former NBA superstar Michael Jordan. In baseball, businessman Artie Moreno bought the Los Angeles Angels of Anaheim in 2003, becoming the first Latino to own a major sports franchise.

The greatest confluence of race and sports in the modern era took place during the murder trial of former NFL star O.J. Simpson. In June 1994, Simpson was charged with the murders of two people, including his former wife, Nicole Brown Simpson. The subsequent trial gripped the nation, splitting public opinion along racial lines. After the trial, a CNN/USA Today/Gallup Poll reported that 20 percent of white Americans felt that Simpson was innocent, while 62 percent of black Americans expressed the opinion that he was innocent. Simpson was declared not guilty in criminal court on October 3, 1995, but a civil court jury found him liable for the deaths on February 4, 1997.

In the early part of the era, the dominant sports figure was Muhammad Ali, the world heavyweight champion, who previously had been stripped of his title and sentenced to prison for refusing to support the draft and the unpopular war in Vietnam. His vindication began in 1970 when his boxing license was restored, and it was completed when the U.S. Supreme Court overturned his conviction one year later. In 1974, Ali, by then an international hero, regained his championship by knocking out champion George Foreman in Zaire. Two years later, he successfully defended the title against Joe Frazier in a fight billed as the "Thrilla in Manila." Ali's rehabilitation was cemented in 1996 when he was chosen to light the Olympic Flame at the Atlanta Games.

The sports world in the 1990s and after was dominated by other African American athletes, including Michael Jordan, who helped turn the NBA into a major sports and business juggernaut; Tiger Woods, who dominated professional golf like no other golfer of his generation; and Barry Bonds, whose home run record became tainted by allegations of performance-enhancing drug use.

Gender

During the 1970s, there was an explosion in women's sports, a product of the feminist movement of the late 1960s that promoted opportunity and equality, the fitness craze of the 1970s that advocated health and beauty, the role model of Billie Jean King and other women athletes, and Title IX of the Education Amendments of 1972. Title IX stated that "no person in the United States shall, on the basis of sex, be excluded from participation in, be denied the benefits of, or be subject to discrimination under any programs or activity receiving federal financial assistance." Before Title IX, only one in 27 high school girls participated in sports. Thirty years later, it was almost one in three.

The fight for justice was led by tennis star Billie Jean King, who battled gendered pay inequities in tournaments such as the U.S. Open, helped start the Virginia Slims Tournament, and organized the Women's Tennis Association, a union of women players. In the "Tennis Battle of the Sexes" on September 20, 1973, Billie Jean King defeated hustler Bobby Riggs in straight sets at the Houston Astrodome before the largest crowd (30,492) ever to attend a tennis match; the match was seen by another 48 million on television. Later, she helped start the Women's Sports Foundation. King's successes helped expand the opportunities for female tennis players, who gained rough parity with their male counterparts in the amount of prize money they could win and whose World Tennis Association tour remains among the most-watched individual sports competitions in the United States.

In 1972, the Association for Intercollegiate Athletics for Women (AIAW) became the first national governing body for women's intercollegiate athletics. It supported an educational model for intercollegiate sports that, unlike the NCAA's commercial focus, barred athletic scholarships. The idealistic AIAW believed that it would protect young women from exploitative coaches or universities, especially as a backlash against Title IX developed. Because Title IX required parity in school spending on male and female sports, some of the former had to be cut in order to provide more funding for the latter. Male athletes in non-revenue-generating sports—such as gymnastics, swimming, and wrestling—resented the loss of program funding. Still, despite the frustration, women's sports parity had been established, a fact acknowledged by the NCAA, which began its own women's sports competitions in 1981, undercutting the AIAW and eventually driving it out of business.

Currently, there are professional leagues for women in tennis, golf, bowling, soccer, and a number of other sports. Women's golf and tennis, in particular, have generated as much revenues and popularity—or nearly so—as their male counterparts, and the Women's National Basketball Association has shown that there is a significant fan base for women's professional team sports. Despite such successes, women's sports generally did not achieve the general popularity or financial success of men's sports. This may be a result of men's greater interest in watching sports compared to women, as well as entrenched stereotyped attitudes about the dominance of men's athletics.

At the same time, the era saw an enormous improvement in U.S. women athletes' success in international competition beyond traditionally feminine sports, especially in soccer, as well as wrestling and the martial arts. The apex of U.S. women's achievement was the 1999 FIFA (Fédération Internationale de Football Association) Women's World Cup soccer final, in which the United States team defeated China 1–0 before 90,185 people at the Rose Bowl, the highest-attended women's athletic event in history. That victory also helped cement Mia Hamm's status as American women's soccer's first nationally known star.

Conclusion: Sports in a Postindustrial Era

The great boom in American sports since 1970 has been a product of many factors, such as the end of racial discrimination, the rise in women's sports, globalization, the expansion of television coverage, especially cable television, and the growth of the Internet. The end of racial discrimination has opened off-the-field opportunities for African Americans, while feminism and Title IX have broadened opportunities for female athletes. Sports now represents an international multibillion-dollar entertainment industry.

With the Olympic competitions open to professionals, amateurism has become largely an anachronism outside of the NCAA. At the same time, athletes in professional team sports have the freedom to negotiate huge salaries, comparable to those of other entertainers, even movie stars. However, sports also have been damaged by the specter of performance-enhancing drugs, resulting in unfairly achieved records, the loss of public confidence in sportsmanship, and the destruction of certain athletes' reputations and the negation of their accomplishments.

Brad Schultz

Further Reading

Bryant, Howard. *Juicing the Game: Drugs, Power, and the Fight for the Soul of Major League Baseball.* New York: Viking, 2005.

Daddario, Gina. *Women's Sport and Spectacle: Gendered Television Coverage and the Olympic Games.* Westport, CT: Praeger, 1998.

Davies, Richard O., and Richard G. Abram. *Betting the Line: Sports Wagering in American Life.* Columbus: Ohio State University Press, 2001.

Evey, Stuart. *Creating an Empire: ESPN—The No-Holds-Barred Story of Power, Ego, Money, and Vision That Transformed a Culture.* Chicago: Triumph, 2004.

Fainaru-Wada, Mark, and Lane Williams. *Game of Shadows: Barry Bonds, BALCO, and the Steroids Scandal That Rocked Professional Sports.* New York: Gotham, 2006.

Freeman, Michael. *ESPN: The Uncensored History.* Dallas, TX: Taylor, 2000.

King, Peter. *75 Seasons: The Complete Story of the National Football League, 1920–1995.* Atlanta, GA: Turner, 1994.

Miller, David. *Athens to Athens: The Official History of the Olympic Games and the IOC, 1894–2004.* Edinburgh, UK: Mainstream, 2005.

Miller, Patrick, and David K. Wiggins, eds. *Sport and the Color Line: Black Athletes and Race Relations in Twentieth-Century America.* New York: Routledge, 2004.

Snyder, Brad. *A Well-Paid Slave: Curt Flood's Fight for Free Agency in Professional Sports.* New York: Viking, 2006.

Zang, David W. *Sports Wars: Athletes in the Age of Aquarius.* Fayetteville: University of Arkansas Press, 2001.

A-Z Entries

Aaron, Hank
(1934–)

In 23 major league seasons (1954–1976), Henry Louis "Hank" Aaron became one of the greatest hitters in baseball history. Although he lacked the star qualities of contemporaries such as Mickey Mantle and Willie Mays, "Hammerin' Hank," as he was known, outlasted them both and surpassed every other major league hitter in career home runs and runs batted in (RBIs). In April 1974, as Aaron approached Babe Ruth's career mark for home runs, the games of his team, the Atlanta Braves, received national media coverage. Finally, on April 8, he hit number 715, becoming the new home run king.

Aaron was born in Mobile, Alabama, on February 5, 1934, one of six children of Herbert Aaron, a boilermaker's assistant who also ran a small tavern, and homemaker Estella Aaron. He grew up in Toulminville, a small village just outside the city, and attended Central High School before graduating from the private Josephine Allen Institute. His baseball skills were so advanced that by age 15, he already was playing semiprofessional ball with the Mobile Black Bears.

When he was 18, Aaron joined the Indianapolis Clowns of the Negro American League in the spring, and then was sold at the start of summer to the Boston Braves for $10,000. Assigned to the Class C Eau Claire (Wisconsin) Bears of the Northern League, where he played second base, he hit .336 and was named Rookie of the Year.

The next year, Aaron played for the Jacksonville (Florida) Tars of the Class A South Atlantic League, batting a league-leading .362 and earning Most Valuable Player (MVP) honors. He was one of only five African Americans playing in the league in the Deep South that season. Because public transportation and hotels were segregated, he often had to travel and live apart from his white teammates.

In 1954, Aaron went to spring training with the Braves, who had moved to Milwaukee the previous season. There, he became the starting left fielder for the Milwaukee Braves after veteran Bobby Thomson broke his ankle in an exhibition game. Aaron did well, batting .280 and hitting 13 homers, but he suffered a broken ankle in September, ending his season.

Aaron played at a consistently high level for nearly all his 23-year big league career. In 1955, he batted .314 and was named to the All-Star team for the first time. In the years to come, he would play in 24 All-Star games, a record shared by Willie Mays and Stan Musial. (From 1959 to 1962, two All-Star games were played each year.)

In 1956, he hit .328, leading the National League in batting, hits (200), and total bases (340). The Braves won the National League pennant in 1957, and Aaron was chosen as the league MVP, ranking first in runs (118), home runs (44), RBIs (132), and total bases (369). That year, he led the team to a World Series victory over the New York Yankees, batting .393 with three homers. He was almost as productive the following year, when the Braves again went to the series, though they lost in seven games to the Yankees.

In 1959, during the prime of his career, Aaron led the National League in batting average (.355) and hits (223). Four years later, he nearly won the Triple Crown (the league leader in home runs, RBIs, and batting average), finishing the season first in the National League in home runs (44), first in RBIs (130), and third in batting (.319). During his career, he led the National League twice in batting average, four times in homers and RBIs, and eight times in total bases, and he earned three Gold Glove Awards.

He broke the major league records for home runs (755), RBIs (2,297), total bases (6,856), and extra base hits (1,477), and finished with a lifetime .305 batting average. He averaged 143 games a season, almost 33 home runs (with a high of 47 in 1971), and nearly 100 runs. Despite his impressive statistics, Aaron was not a charismatic player, and he remained underappreciated for much of his remarkably steady career.

Once the Braves moved to Atlanta in 1966, Aaron seemed to focus more on power hitting than on his batting average. Fans viewed Mickey Mantle and Willie Mays as sluggers who could break Babe Ruth's home run record, but Aaron reached the 500 mark in 1968, and 600 in 1971. By the end of the 1973 season, he was approaching Ruth's total of 714 homers, one of the most famous—even hallowed—records in baseball history. Media focus on the Braves slugger, who was then in his twenty-first major league season, mounted. He finished the year with 713 home runs.

Aaron faced tremendous pressure as he approached Ruth's record. Some fans believed that Ruth's records should never be surpassed, while others were outraged that an African American would be the one to challenge Babe Ruth's performance. Some of the letters Aaron received contained death threats, which he understandably took seriously. He feared he might not live to set the record.

Excitement attended the start of the 1974 season. Aaron needed just one homer to tie Ruth and two to break the record. During the Braves' first series in Cincinnati, Aaron homered in his first at bat against Jack Billingham, tying Ruth. The Braves' second series was at home against the Los Angeles Dodgers. On April 8, the Braves drew a record crowd of 53,775. In the fourth inning, at bat against pitcher Al Downing, Aaron slammed homer number 715. The crowd went wild. A few fans even raced onto the field to congratulate him. He would hit 19 more home runs that season.

In 1975, Aaron was traded to the Milwaukee Brewers of the American League, putting him back in the city where he had started, now playing as a designated hitter. He retired after his second season with the Brewers, finishing his career with 755 home runs. (Aaron's record was broken in 2007 by Barry Bonds, who would set a new record of 762.)

Aaron was inducted into the National Baseball Hall of Fame in 1982, his first year of eligibility. In retirement, he returned to Atlanta and, in 1989, joined the Braves' front office as senior vice president and assistant to the president. In 1999, Major League Baseball established the Hank Aaron Award to honor the top hitters in each league. There are statues in his honor in front of both Atlanta's Turner Field and Milwaukee's Miller Park. In 2002, President George W. Bush awarded Aaron the Presidential Medal of Freedom, the nation's highest civilian award.

Benjamin Franklin V

See also: African American Baseball, Negro League Era; Baseball, Major League; Braves, Atlanta/Milwaukee/Boston.

Further Reading

Aaron, Hank, with Lonnie Wheeler. *I Had a Hammer: The Hank Aaron Story.* New York: HarperCollins, 1991.

Bryant, Howard. *The Last Hero: A Life of Henry Aaron.* New York: Pantheon, 2010.

Stanton, Tom. *Hank Aaron and the Home Run That Changed America.* New York: William Morrow, 2004.

Stewart, Mark, and Mike Kennedy. *Hammering Hank: How the Media Made Henry Aaron.* Guilford, CT: Lyons, 2006.

Abdul-Jabbar, Kareem (1947–)

Kareem Abdul-Jabbar was one of the most outstanding basketball players in the history of college hoops, leading the University of California, Los Angeles (UCLA) Bruins to an unprecedented three straight championship titles. In the National Basketball Association (NBA), he was one of the top players in basketball history and led his teams to six NBA titles. At 7 feet, 2 inches (2.18 meters), Abdul-Jabbar was the first graceful 7-plus-footer who played with finesse, rather than overpowering strength, and he displayed an impressive all-around floor game.

He was born Ferdinand Lewis Alcindor, Jr., on April 16, 1947, in Harlem, New York, the son of Ferdinand Lewis, a New York City transit police officer and jazz musician, and Cora Alcindor, a department store price checker. Both parents were immigrants from Trinidad and Tobago. In 1950, the family moved to Inwood in Upper Manhattan.

By the eighth grade, Alcindor stood 6 feet, 8 inches (about 2 meters), and already was a phenom on the playground. He grew at least 4 more inches (about 10 centimeters) while attending Power Memorial Academy, a Christian Brothers high school, where his skills attracted national attention and the team went 96–6 during his four years. Unlike most 7-footers to that time, he was a complete basketball player: He was athletic and agile, he could shoot from some distance, and he could dribble well enough to bring the ball up against a press. He scored 2,067 points and took down 2,002 rebounds, both New York City high school records.

Alcindor also was among the first high school basketball players to receive national attention. Power Memorial went undefeated during his sophomore and junior years, finally losing after 71 straight victories to

DeMatha Catholic of Hyattsville, Maryland, in his senior year. In those three years, his team won three straight city championships, and in 1963–1964, the squad was chosen by *USA Today* as the greatest high school team of all time.

The College Years

Heavily recruited by colleges across the country, Alcindor chose to attend UCLA to play for legendary coach John Wooden. UCLA had just won a second consecutive national championship, and college basketball was poised to emerge as a major national sport. He was a part of one of the first nationally prominent recruiting classes in college basketball, joining fellow high school stars Lucius Allen from Kansas City, Kansas, and Californians Lynn Shackleford and Kenny Heitz, among others. At a time when freshmen were ineligible to play varsity basketball, Alcindor's freshman team defeated the two-time defending national champions in a scrimmage. There were enormous expectations for his cohort's future—several sportswriters considered his freshman team the best college five in the United States.

In late fall 1966, Alcindor and his classmates joined the varsity squad. Wooden started four sophomores, and the team went 30–0 and won the National Collegiate Athletic Association (NCAA) championship. The following year, the Bruins lost to the University of Houston by 2 points in the first nationally televised regular season college basketball game, ending a record 47-game winning streak. However, in the NCAA finals, Alcindor recovered from a scratched eye that had hampered his play in the first game to lead UCLA to victory over Houston by 32 points in the semifinal game. The Bruins went on to defeat the University of North Carolina to win their second consecutive national championship, and their fourth in five years.

In Alcindor's senior year, UCLA lost only once, to the University of Southern California during the regular season, and won a third consecutive national championship, easily defeating Purdue University in the championship game. He finished his UCLA career with a record of 88–2, scoring 2,325 points in three years and taking down 1,367 rebounds. He was a three-time All-American, two-time Player of the Year, Most Outstanding Player in the NCAA tournament three times, and the first Naismith College Player of the Year awardee in 1969. He helped propel college basketball into the national spotlight.

"Lew," as he was known, converted from Roman Catholicism to Islam while in college. He adopted the name Kareem Abdul-Jabbar in 1971.

Abdul-Jabbar and the National Basketball Association

He was selected first overall in the 1969 NBA Draft, chosen by the Milwaukee Bucks. He enjoyed immediate success in the NBA, earning Rookie of the Year honors in 1969–1970.

With Bill Russell of the Boston Celtics having just retired and Wilt Chamberlain of the Los Angeles Lakers entering the twilight of his career, NBA fans were eager for a new star center, and Abdul-Jabbar filled the bill. The following season, he was named Most Valuable Player (MVP) in the league and led the Bucks to the NBA championship, sweeping the Baltimore Bullets in the finals. He won two more MVP awards with the Bucks, in 1972 and 1973, and led the team to four consecutive division titles from 1971 to 1974.

It was in Milwaukee that Abdul-Jabbar began to wear his trademark goggles, after receiving an eye injury during a preseason game in 1974. Though he was successful with the Bucks, Abdul-Jabbar did not feel at home in Milwaukee, and he requested a trade to either New York or Los Angeles, cities that he felt would better fit his social, cultural, and intellectual needs.

In 1975, the Bucks traded Abdul-Jabbar to the Los Angeles Lakers for four very talented players—center Elmore Smith, guard Brian Winters, and rookie stars Dave Meyers and Junior Bridgeman. With the Lakers, Abdul-Jabbar won three more MVP awards and five NBA championships, becoming a part of a legendary squad—together with point guard Earvin "Magic" Johnson, forward James Worthy, and coach Pat Riley—that would vie with the Boston Celtics for the NBA Championship throughout the 1980s, earning Abdul-Jabbar championship rings in 1980, 1982, 1985, 1987, and 1988. Even though he was nearing 40, Abdul-Jabbar was named the NBA Finals MVP in 1985.

A Life Well Lived

When he retired in 1989 after 20 seasons, he held records for all-time scoring (38,387 points), most minutes played (57,446), and most All-Star Game selections (19). He had been MVP six times and had played on six championship teams. Abdul-Jabbar was *Sports Illustrated*'s Sportsman of the Year in 1985, and he graced 29 of its covers over the years. In 1995, he was inducted into the Naismith Memorial Basketball Hall of Fame.

After leaving the NBA, Abdul-Jabbar pursued a diverse career. He completed a master's degree in Arabic studies at Harvard University and appeared as an actor in motion pictures and on television. He coached basketball as an assistant coach at several levels, even spending a season on an Indian reservation. He is the author or coauthor of several books on African American history, including *Black Profiles in Courage: A Legacy of African American Achievement* (1996) and *Brothers in Arms: The Epic Story of the 761st Tank Battalion, World War II's Forgotten Heroes* (2004), as well as a number of autobiographical volumes, including *A Season on the Reservation* (2000).

William H. Mulligan, Jr.

See also: Basketball, College; Basketball, Professional, NBA Era; Lakers, Los Angeles/Minneapolis; Wooden, John.

Further Reading

Abdul-Jabbar, Kareem, with Peter Knobler. *Giant Steps.* New York: Bantam, 1983.

Abdul-Jabbar, Kareem, with Mignon McCarthy. *Kareem.* New York: Random House, 1990.

Abdul-Jabbar, Kareem, with Steven Singular. *A Season on the Reservation: My Sojourn with the White Mountain Apache.* New York: William Morrow, 2000.

African American Baseball, Before 1920

African Americans and other athletes of African descent played amateur and professional baseball from its earliest days, but beginning in the late nineteenth century, they encountered pervasive discrimination as one organization after another disqualified black players. There was no question about black players' abilities—dozens played in white professional leagues, including two in the major leagues. Yet fans, team owners, and white players united to oppose black participants.

White teams stopped hiring black players altogether, putting them out of organized baseball. In response to this exclusion, African Americans began to organize all-black teams.

Early Black Ballplayers

In the early 1850s, many of baseball's first participants were former cricket players—some of them black, as cricket remained a vital sport in the British West In-

dies. The first recorded game involving blacks took place in fall 1859 between two New York City teams, the Unknowns of Weeksville and the Henson club of Jamaica, New York. Two black teams, the Unknowns and the Monitors of Brooklyn, played in 1862, but it was not until after the Civil War that black baseball began to take hold. Teams formed in Buffalo, New York, Chicago, Philadelphia, Washington, D.C., and a host of smaller cities. Players mainly came from the small black middle class, and they were strongly committed to amateurism.

Charles Douglass, a Civil War veteran, federal clerk, and son of African American leader Frederick Douglass, played for the Alert Club of Washington, D.C. His team often played the Pythians of Philadelphia, an athletic and social organization, much like many other baseball clubs of the day. Home teams often offered food and drink to visiting clubs, providing occasions for socializing and discussing political and economic matters.

Despite the end of slavery, African Americans faced increasing discrimination. In October 1867, the Pennsylvania Association of Amateur Base Ball Players refused to allow the Pythians to join, and two months later, the National Association of Amateur Base Ball Players also banned black teams. The exclusion of blacks from full participation in the national pastime had begun.

At the same time, the number of black baseball clubs continued to increase. In 1869, the Pythians became one of the first black teams to defeat a white squad, the Philadelphia City Items, in a series. However, the Pythians folded after the team's captain and founder Octavius Valentine Catto, principal of the Institute for Colored Youth, was assassinated during an election day riot in October 1871.

Black Players on White Teams

Although black teams officially were excluded from early white baseball leagues, individual players began to appear on amateur and professional teams. The first black player in professional ball was John "Bud" Fowler. An outstanding second baseman, Fowler first played for a white team in Lynn, Massachusetts, in 1878. He would play for 17 clubs in nine leagues, eventually joining the Binghamton, New York, franchise of the International League in 1887, which was just one level below the major leagues.

The first African American to play in the major leagues was Moses Fleetwood "Fleet" Walker, who had attended Oberlin College and the University of Michigan. An excellent catcher, he played for the Toledo Blue Stockings of the Northwestern League in 1883. One year later, that team joined the major league American Association, and Walker batted .263 in 42 games, missing most of the season because of injury. His younger brother, Welday "Weldy" Walker, played six games for Toledo, but both were released at the end of the season. The Walkers were the last African Americans to play in the majors until Jackie Robinson in 1947. Recent research suggests that William E. White, who played one game for the Providence Grays in 1879, was the mulatto son of a slave owner.

By 1887, there were 13 black players on 12 white teams scattered over five Eastern and Midwestern minor leagues. *Sporting Life* and *Sporting News,* leading baseball periodicals, criticized the presence of blacks in the International League, the highest-level minor league, despite their talent.

An exhibition game was scheduled that summer between the Chicago White Stockings, the defending National League champion, and the Newark Giants of the International League. But on July 14, the Chicago club manager Cap Anson, then an influential figure in baseball, demanded that George Stovey, Newark's outstanding black pitcher who had won an all-time International League record 34 games that season, be excluded. Anson's demands reflected the prevailing white view at that time that the sport should be segregated.

On the same day, International League owners, under pressure from their white players, made a "gentleman's agreement" to limit each team in the league to no more than two black players and to sign no new black players in the future. Two years later, there were no blacks in the International League. In all, about 70 men of color played in white professional leagues in the late nineteenth century. The last, Canadian Bill Galloway, played in the Canadian League in 1899.

Independent Black Teams

In the 1880s, as attempts at creating a black baseball league failed, independent teams began to form. The most important of these was the Cuban Giants, founded by waiter Frank Thompson at the Argyle Hotel in Babylon, New York, in 1885. Thompson chose the name "Cuban" because he believed it would be easier to attract white opponents to play against supposedly Latin American players, even if many of them had dark skin. The Cuban Giants set the standard for future independent black teams. They were a talented team that barn-stormed constantly, attracting both black and white fans. In 1889, the Cuban Giants and the New York Gorhams played in the otherwise all-white Middle States League.

Inspired by the success of the Cuban Giants, dozens of black teams formed across the United States in the 1890s, including the Cuban X-Giants (founded in 1896 by several former Cuban Giants), the New York Gorhams, the Chicago Unions, the Colored Monarchs of York (Pennsylvania), the St. Louis Black Stockings, the Norfolk (Virginia) Red Stockings, and the Lincoln (Nebraska) Giants.

In addition to the independent clubs, black colleges such as Hampton, Tuskegee, Howard, and Morehouse also fielded teams. In the North, black students played for Amherst and Oberlin colleges but often experienced discrimination on the road. On the Western frontier, black troops of the Ninth and Tenth cavalries and the Twenty-Fourth and Twenty-Fifth Infantry regiments competed against each other, as well as against white civilians and soldiers. After 1900, players from the Twenty-Fifth Infantry formed the nucleus of the famed Kansas City Monarchs.

Industrial teams also would enlist black players, most notably the Page Fence Giants, an all-black barn-storming team. The team was the brainchild of Bud Fowler, who had secured the backing of the Page Woven Wire Fence Company, which produced fencing for livestock. The team traveled in its own private railroad coach, which meant that players did not have to endure discrimination in restaurants and hotels.

Black baseball also had a visionary—"King" Solomon White, an infielder for both white and black teams in the late nineteenth century. He believed that although the game was segregated, baseball could become a lucrative black enterprise. In 1902, he joined with two white sportswriters, Harry Smith and H. Walter Schlichter, to form the Philadelphia Giants. The team dominated black baseball in the East for the rest of the decade, featuring such stars as pitcher Danny McClellan and two shortstops, Grant "Home Run" Johnson, a former Page Fence Giant, and John Henry "Pop" Lloyd, who was known as the "Black Honus Wagner." White managed the team, occasionally played the infield, and wrote the first history of black baseball.

In 1904, the Philadelphia Giants acquired southpaw pitcher Andrew "Rube" Foster from the Cuban X-Giants. An outstanding hurler who also batted .400, Foster played a crucial role in Philadelphia's domination of the Eastern black teams. Although segregation kept Foster out of the major leagues, New York Giants manager John McGraw hired him to instruct his pitchers in the off-season; it is said that Giants pitcher Christy Mathewson learned his "fadeaway" pitch (a screwball) from Foster. McGraw previously had attempted to bring black ballplayer Charlie Grant into the major leagues by claiming that he was a Cherokee named Tokohama.

Foster criticized white control of ticket sales and booking arrangements, and he departed for Chicago in 1907, taking with him several disgruntled Philadelphia Giants. There, they joined one of the Midwest's best black teams, the Leland Giants, which was partly owned by Frank Leland, the black commissioner of Cook County. The ambitious Foster became a player-manager, and the team went 110–10. In 1909, Foster and the team's treasurer, attorney Beauregard Mosley, one of the major stockholders, led a hostile takeover of the Leland Giants. Leland sued to regain his team but lost. He then organized the Chicago Giants.

In late 1910, Moseley attempted to form a professional black league, inviting team owners from New Orleans, Louisville, Memphis, St. Louis, and both Kansas Cities. High travel costs and lack of capital dampened his hopes, however, and plans for the new league were abandoned. Despite the disappointment, Foster and a few others believed that a black league was possible.

Foster organized a new team, the Chicago American Giants, and secured the use of Schorling Park, the former home of the Chicago White Sox, a few blocks from the growing Black Belt on Chicago's South Side. John Schorling, a white tavern owner who had been involved in semiprofessional baseball, was Foster's secret partner. The park seated about 9,000 and had locker rooms with hot showers at a time when most black teams played in substandard venues. The park was the key to the American Giants' success.

In the 1910s, new black teams sprang up across the country. The top semiprofessional teams played more than 100 games, typically on Sundays at home, and the rest of the week they barnstormed, challenging teams in outlying areas. Many of these teams were white owned, including the Indianapolis ABCs, the New York Lincoln Giants, and the Bacharach Giants of Atlantic City. Top players included John Henry Lloyd, shortstop for the Indianapolis ABCs, and "Smokey Joe" Williams of the Lincoln Giants.

White owners and booking agents understood that black baseball was becoming increasingly popular— and therefore increasingly lucrative. African American populations in the North were growing rapidly as migrants from the Deep South arrived, seeking better economic, political, and social conditions.

One team that benefited from the migration was the Hilldale Athletic Club, also known as the Hilldale Daisies, of Darby, Pennsylvania, near Philadelphia. Owned and managed by blacks, this sandlot team made the transition to professional ball in 1917. Hilldale's roster included two veteran outfielders—Otto Briggs and Spotswood Poles—and eventually became a major powerhouse of African American baseball.

Birth of the Negro Leagues

The United States' entrance into World War I in 1917 had profound implications for black baseball. Dozens of black players joined the military or worked in defense production to secure exemption from the draft. Black teams supplemented their depleted ranks by recruiting younger players and Cuban immigrants such as pitcher José Méndez and slugger Cristóbal Torriente. A few light-skinned Cubans recently had joined the major leagues, but they were excluded because of their racial origin and culture.

In the aftermath of the war, racial tension coupled with an economic downturn and fears of a Bolshevik-style revolution ignited a powder keg. In summer 1919, cities across the nation experienced race riots. The worst violence took place in Chicago, where 23 blacks and 15 whites died. Most of the destruction occurred on the city's South Side. The Illinois National Guard occupied Schorling Park, and a game against the Bacharach Giants had to be canceled. Following the riot, Foster convened a meeting with black owners in Indianapolis to discuss the future of black baseball.

For years, Foster had dreamed of building an independent black league. He believed that such a league could rival the majors and that, eventually, organized baseball would be integrated. In winter 1919–1920, he made his case in a *Chicago Defender* in a series of columns under the title "Pitfalls of Baseball." In it, Foster criticized players for jumping from team to team and owners for encouraging such behavior. He described a host of problems that plagued black baseball, from the condition of ballparks to the lack of cooperation between Eastern and Midwestern clubs. Foster was a strong proponent of black-owned businesses, but he conceded that white financial support would be needed. As the last column appeared, Foster and other baseball owners planned to meet in Kansas City in February 1920. The meeting would lay the groundwork for the formation of the Negro Leagues.

Stanley Keith Arnold

See also: African American Baseball, Negro League Era; African Americans; Giants, Cuban (Baseball); Race and Race Relations.

Further Reading

Arnold, Stanley. "The Rise of Black Professional Baseball in Philadelphia, 1850–1910." *Elysian Fields Quarterly* 22:3 (2005): 46–56.

Bruce, Janet. *The Kansas City Monarchs: Champions of Black Baseball.* Lawrence: University Press of Kansas, 1985.

Debono, Paul. *The Chicago American Giants.* Jefferson, NC: McFarland, 2007.

Heaphy, Leslie A. *The Negro Leagues, 1869–1960.* Jefferson, NC: McFarland, 2003.

Lanctot, Neil. *Fair Dealing and Clean Playing: The Hilldale Club and the Development of Black Professional Baseball, 1910–1932.* Syracuse, NY: Syracuse University Press, 2007.

Lomax, Michael E. *Black Baseball Entrepreneurs, 1860–1901: Operating by Any Means Necessary.* Syracuse, NY: Syracuse University Press, 2003.

African American Baseball, Negro League Era

The Negro Leagues, which began in 1920 and survived into the 1950s, were a major business and cultural venture in the African American community, providing entertainment for the masses and jobs for elite athletes and other African Americans. They were part of a parallel world created by African Americans in an era of racial prejudice, when they were barred from organized baseball because of the color of their skin.

Owners, who were among the wealthiest African Americans, saw baseball as a way to make money, provide a community service, and gain social prestige. Outstanding ballplayers such as Satchel Paige, James "Cool Papa" Bell, and Josh Gibson were proud to play in the Negro Leagues, making money, demonstrating their skills, and gaining respect from fans and their peers in the major leagues.

Rube Foster and the Rise of the Negro National League

If African American players could not get into the white leagues, the next best thing was to form their own organization and regularize their occupation. The driving force behind the formation of a Negro baseball league was Andrew "Rube" Foster, who, after pitching his way to fame in Texas in the early 1900s, went north to play for teams such as the Philadelphia Giants and the Leland Giants. Foster not only pitched for Leland, but he also managed and eventually took over ownership of the team, renaming his club the Chicago American Giants. It was the top black ball club in the 1910s.

Foster was an ardent "race man" and a capitalist who wanted to advance the interests of his people. In 1920, he believed the time had come for a league with black players, owners, umpires, and office staff. He called a meeting of interested owners, managers, newspaper reporters, and lawyers at the Kansas City Young Men's Christian Association in February 1920 to form the Negro National League.

Some of the best Midwestern teams in baseball joined the new venture under Foster's presidency. Along with his own Chicago American Giants, the league included J.L. Wilkinson's Kansas City Monarchs, C.I. Taylor's Indianapolis ABCs, Joe Green's Chicago Giants, Lorenzo Cobb's St. Louis Giants, and Tenny Blount's Detroit Stars. The Cuban Stars joined as a traveling club, and the Dayton Marcos made the league eight strong. All of the owners were African American, except for Wilkinson.

Foster received 5 percent of gate receipts for scheduling the games and sold the league its official equipment. He also helped keep competition strong between league teams, even trading some of his own top players to losing teams. The league suffered from instability, though, and several teams came and went. Foster's scheduling led to some dissatisfaction and a desire to create a second league.

In 1923, Ed Bolden of the Hilldale Daisies, of Darby, Pennsylvania, near Philadelphia, and Nat Strong, a white promoter from New York, created a rival organization, the Eastern Colored League, whose teams had the advantage of proximity to one another. The league included Hilldale, the Cuban Stars, the Brooklyn Royal Giants, the Bacharach Giants, the Lincoln Giants, and the Baltimore Black Sox.

The Negro National and Eastern Colored leagues began to cooperate, concerned about players jumping their contracts. In 1924, the leagues played the first Colored World Series, which lasted for four years. The Kansas City Monarchs beat Hilldale five games to four to win the first championship. The Monarchs relied on the arms of Wilber "Bullet Joe" Rogan, José Méndez, and Bill Drake to upset the Daisies.

Black professional teams followed their regular seasons with an extensive barnstorming schedule. The clubs played any opponents who were willing to take their challenge as they traveled across the United

States, playing teams such as the House of David (Benton Harbor, Michigan), the Monroe (Louisiana) Monarchs, the Dallas Giants, and the Zanesville (Ohio) Firefighters. These games introduced much of America to the Negro Leagues and provided many young black athletes with role models and a chance to play professionally.

Many ballplayers also continued to play outside the United States. Players found opportunities in Mexico, Cuba, the Dominican Republic, Venezuela, and even, on occasion, in Japan. In such places, they had the chance to compete against the best players in all of baseball, as many major leaguers also played outside the country in the winter.

Willie Wells, Ray Dandridge, Ray Brown, and others found that playing in other countries not only gave them higher salaries, but also a sense of belonging. At home in the United States, they were barred from hotels and many ballparks because of their race, but in the Caribbean and Latin America, they were welcome, often becoming fan favorites and heroes.

Collapse and Rebirth

Foster had a mental breakdown in 1926, forcing him to cede control of the Negro National League to William C. Hueston. The league floundered and then folded in 1931, as the country became mired in the Great Depression. Bolden also had a breakdown, and the Eastern Colored League collapsed in mid-1928. Some of the teams joined the Negro National League, while the rest formed the short-lived American Negro League in 1929. The only remaining league was the Negro Southern League, formed in 1920 as a minor league for the Negro National League.

In 1932, Cumberland Posey of the Homestead (Pennsylvania) Grays founded the East-West League, but it did not last the season. One year later, Gus Greenlee and the Pittsburgh Crawfords led a revival by creating a second Negro National League, made up of the Crawfords, the Columbus Blue Birds, the Indianapolis ABCs, the Baltimore Black Sox, the Brooklyn Royal Giants, Cole's American Giants, and the Nashville Elite Giants. Many of the team owners, including Greenlee, were in the numbers rackets, one of the few ways for African Americans to amass capital in the 1930s.

In 1937, the Negro American League was established. Taking in teams in the South and Midwest, many of which had played in earlier, now-defunct

leagues, the Negro American League became the most powerful Negro League and survived longer than any other. Among its strongest teams were the Kansas City Monarchs, the Birmingham Black Barons, and the Chicago American Giants.

The culmination of the season for black players was the East-West Classic, an annual all-star contest that began in 1933. It brought together the best players, chosen by fan votes, to play before sellout crowds at Chicago's Comiskey Park, home of the Chicago White Sox. In the inaugural contest, fans were treated to spectacular play, including a winning home run by future Hall of Famer George "Mule" Suttles and the outstanding pitching of lefthander Willie Foster. The East-West Classic proved that fans would come out in large numbers to watch African American ballplayers. The African American elite turned out for the event, as did many other fans who arranged their summer vacations around the game.

One of the leagues' biggest problems was that players jumped their contracts. For example, two of the greatest stars, pitcher Satchel Paige and catcher Josh Gibson, left their teams in 1937 to play for a team owned by Dominican Republic dictator Rafael Trujillo. Paige, who was one of the highest-paid ballplayers of the day, drew fans wherever he went. His dramatic pitching delivery and antics on and off the field entertained fans, but it was his speed and incredible control that made him a star. Gibson was less verbal and let his bat do his talking. He excelled behind the plate and became one of the greatest home run hitters of all time while playing for Pittsburgh and Homestead.

World War II and Integration

The Negro National League did well during World War II, when it was one of the most successful businesses in the black community. Good players could make $300 a month. The Negro League World Series was reinstituted in 1942, teams were profitable, and the leagues became important cultural institutions for the African American community, providing recreation, racial pride, and opportunities for socializing.

At the same time, there also was a growing movement for equal rights and racial integration. Many African Americans were fighting alongside whites in the war, and at home, African American laborers were finding new opportunities in wartime industries. Sportswriters such as Wendell Smith, Lester Rodney, and Sam Lacy promoted integration of organized base-

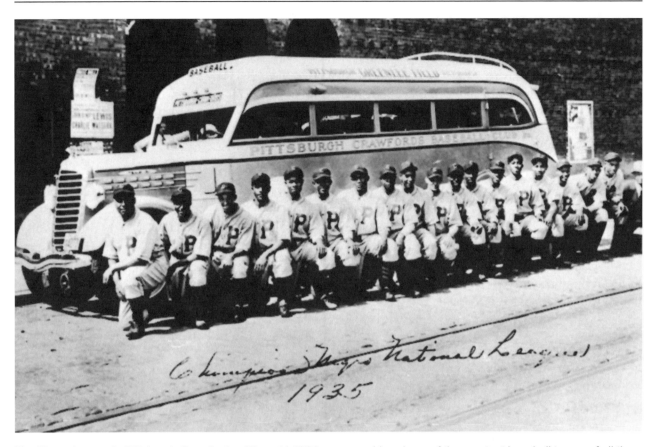

The Negro League's Pittsburgh Crawfords of the mid-1930s are considered one of the greatest baseball teams of all time. The 1935 club, posing here, included Hall of Famers Josh Gibson, Satchel Paige, "Cool Papa" Bell, Judy Johnson, and Oscar Charleston. *(Associated Press)*

ball. A few major league teams publicized tryouts for black players, but they failed to offer contracts to any. Most major league owners opposed integration, because they believed that white fans and players would incite racial violence, threatening attendance at games.

In 1945, Branch Rickey, an executive with the Brooklyn Dodgers, with the support of Gus Greenlee, owner of the Pittsburgh Crawfords, and others, began to scout for African American players. Rickey wanted to find just the right player to break the color barrier in baseball. He found the man he wanted in Kansas City Monarchs infielder Jackie Robinson, who had been a star on integrated teams at the University of California, Los Angeles before the war, but had not earned a college degree, and had served with distinction in the military. Rickey signed Robinson to a contract with the Montreal Royals, the top Dodgers farm team, in 1946. Canada did not suffer the same racial tensions as the United States, and Rickey believed it might be easier to begin the transition there. Robinson used the

year to hone his skills, giving Rickey time to prepare for his arrival in Brooklyn, New York.

Robinson joined the Brooklyn Dodgers in 1947, becoming the first black player in the majors since 1884, opening the door for others to follow him into the major leagues. Other young players from the Negro Leagues were recruited for the majors (sometimes without compensation to their Negro League teams), among them Monte Irvin, Larry Doby, Willie Mays, Joe Black, and Hank Aaron. Satchel Paige even got a chance when he joined the Cleveland Indians in 1948 as the oldest rookie in major league history. Josh Gibson and a number of other Negro League stars were past their prime playing days and never played in the big leagues.

It was clear from the beginning that the integration of organized baseball meant the end of the Negro Leagues. Each year, more black players made their way into organized baseball, and the appeal of the Negro Leagues declined. The Negro National League folded in 1948, leaving just the Negro American League, which ended operations in 1958.

In 1970, the National Baseball Hall of Fame appointed a Committee on Negro Baseball Leagues to review the performance of its stars and to recommend players deserving induction. The committee named nine players for induction before being disbanded in 1977, and thereafter nine more were added by the Veterans Committee.

Then, in 2006, the Special Committee on Negro Leagues selected five pre-Negro Leaguers, seven Negro Leaguers, and five Negro team owners. The latter included Effa Manley, the only woman in the Hall of Fame. Manley co-owned the Newark Dodgers with her husband Abe and served with great success as the team's general manager in the late 1930s and 1940s. The Newark Dodgers won the Negro League World Series in 1946, the year before Jackie Robinson appeared with the Brooklyn Dodgers.

Leslie Heaphy

See also: African American Baseball, Before 1920; African Americans; Crawfords, Pittsburgh; Grays, Homestead; Monarchs, Kansas City; Race and Race Relations.

Further Reading

Bruce, Janet. *The Kansas City Monarchs: Champions of Black Baseball.* Lawrence: University Press of Kansas, 1985.

Heaphy, Leslie A. *The Negro Leagues, 1869–1960.* Jefferson, NC: McFarland, 2003.

Lanctot, Neil. *Fair Dealing and Clean Playing: The Hilldale Club and the Development of Black Professional Baseball, 1910–1932.* Syracuse, NY: Syracuse University Press, 2007.

———. *Negro League Baseball: The Rise and Ruin of a Black Institution.* Philadelphia: University of Pennsylvania Press, 2004.

Lester, Larry. *Baseball's First Colored World Series: The 1924 Meeting of the Hilldale Giants and Kansas City Monarchs.* Jefferson, NC: McFarland, 2006.

Peterson, Robert W. *Only the Ball Was White.* Englewood Cliffs, NJ: Prentice Hall, 1970.

Rogosin, Donn. *Invisible Men: Life in Baseball's Negro Leagues.* New York: Atheneum, 1983.

Snyder, Brad. *Beyond the Shadow of the Senators: The Untold Story of the Homestead Grays and the Integration of Baseball.* Chicago: Contemporary Books, 2003.

Tygiel, Jules. *Baseball's Great Experiment: Jackie Robinson and His Legacy.* New York: Oxford University Press, 1983.

African Americans

Despite a history burdened by slavery, segregation, and racial prejudice, African Americans have played a major role in the development of American sports at all levels, from the jockeys and fighters of the slave South in the 1800s to the superstar professional athletes of the late twentieth and early twenty-first centuries. But these achievements did not come easily. Blacks were barred from most college and professional sports leagues, forcing them to establish institutions of their own. And when top black athletes threatened white supremacist ideas about the inferiority of African Americans' skills and competitive spirit, they were met with prejudice, prosecution, and even violence.

The advances of the civil rights movement after World War II, however, made it possible for African American athletes to compete in previously white-only professional sports leagues and on teams at colleges that once rejected or severely limited their participation. With these barriers torn down, African American athletes have excelled, dominating such popular sports as football and basketball and representing a major presence in baseball, tennis, and track and field.

Slavery Era

During the colonial and antebellum eras, masters used slaves for their amusement. Slaves were involved in spotlighting deer during hunting expeditions and carrying the carcasses, in fighting slaves from other plantations, and in exhibition dancing. Slaves and free African Americans also engaged in the training of gamecocks, hunting dogs, and horses, and they served as jockeys in horse races.

On their own time, slaves enjoyed singing, dancing, and conversing, but they also participated in tests of strength, such as boxing and wrestling; played ball games, such as shinny (an early informal version of hockey); and engaged in foot races and swimming competitions. Some enslaved blacks on Southern plantations played an early version of baseball during their time off. Free blacks played billiards and quoits (similar to horseshoes) and attended horse races and cockfights.

The first prominent African American athlete was prizefighter Bill Richmond, born a slave in New York City. He fought in England, then the center of boxing, losing a title fight to Tom Cribb in 1805. Richmond later became a boxing teacher. Next came Tom Molyneaux, who fought bouts arranged by his master against slaves from other plantations, and thereby gained his freedom. He migrated to England, where he trained with Richmond. Molyneaux earned a reputation as a fearsome opponent, and in 1810, he fought Cribb, the new English champion, losing in 34 rounds.

Post–Civil War Era

Approximately 90 percent of African Americans in the late nineteenth century lived in the rural South, many working as impoverished sharecroppers in a segregated society that prohibited them from using most public and private recreational facilities, including athletic fields, public parks, beaches, and, later, swimming pools. Meanwhile, urban African Americans had access to few athletic facilities as well.

In 1853, a colored branch of the Young Men's Christian Association (YMCA) opened in Washington, D.C.; it was soon followed by others in Charleston and Boston. Blacks in Chicago initially had access to the YMCA, but they encountered growing discrimination by 1900. The association barred them in 1910, which led to the opening three years later of the all-black Wabash Avenue YMCA, financed largely by white philanthropists.

While few African Americans attended college before the Civil War, by the 1880s, blacks played baseball at such colleges as Oberlin and the University of Michigan. Others participated in sports at the new black colleges formed during Reconstruction, such as Howard University in Washington, D.C., but most administrators preferred to spend their funds on academic activities. The first athletic contests were intramural class competitions.

Booker T. Washington's Tuskegee Institute in Alabama was at the forefront of black college sports. The school hired a sports director in 1890 and held its first track meet in 1892. That year, a number of black colleges began intercollegiate competition in baseball and football. The first black college baseball game pitted Biddle (now Johnson C. Smith) College against Livingstone College in 1892, with the former winning 5–0.

Black colleges tried to provide athletic leadership in the community, but at schools such as Howard, Shaw, Lincoln, Virginia Union, and Hampton, most students had limited time for sports. There also was little opportunity to engage in sports at the high school level. Few blacks then attended high school, although there were some black athletes at Northern schools. In Washington, D.C., there were significant opportunities available through the Interscholastic Athletic Association, founded by educator Edwin B. Henderson in 1905.

Another early option for young black men was the military, which encouraged sports among enlisted men to promote physical fitness and morale. The Twenty-Fifth Infantry, which comprised mainly residents of New Orleans, then the capital of antebellum black sports, had several athletes. They played baseball during the Civil War and enjoyed other sports, including billiards, bowling, gymnastics, wrestling, and trick riding. Black cavalrymen, known as "Buffalo Soldiers," played baseball throughout the West.

Baseball

The main African American sport of the late nineteenth century was baseball, which was played in the Northeast before the Civil War. The first prominent black club was the Philadelphia Pythians, founded in 1867 by civil rights activist Octavius Valentine Catto and businessman and educator Jacob C. White, Jr. The team played white clubs, even though the National Association of Base Ball Players shunned them. Southern baseball was largely segregated, except in New Orleans, where there were interracial games until 1890.

Despite such prejudice, some 70 African Americans played in organized baseball in the nineteenth century, starting with John "Bud" Fowler, who pitched for a team in Lynn, Massachusetts, in the International Association in 1878. In 1883, Moses Fleetwood "Fleet" Walker, who had caught for Oberlin College and the University of Michigan, played with the Toledo Blue Stockings of the Northwestern League. One year later, Toledo joined the American Association, a rival to the National League, and Walker became the first black major leaguer. His brother, Welday "Weldy" Walker, briefly played with the club as well.

Black players in organized baseball encountered prejudice from fans who jeered at them, as well as from their teammates and club owners. Opposing players threw balls at them, runners spiked them, and teammates would not sit for photographs with them. In 1887, manager Cap Anson of the Chicago White Stockings refused to play the Newark Giants of the International League unless the team's black players—Moses Walker and star pitcher George Stovey—sat out the game, which they were forced to do.

After the 1887 season, the owners of the International League, the highest-level minor league, made a "gentleman's agreement" to limit each team to no more than two black players and to sign no new black players in the future. Two years later, there were no blacks in the International League, and by 1900, there were no African Americans in any of the majors.

Instead, many talented black players found spots on all-black squads, such as the Cuban Giants, founded in 1885. The team played other black teams, college squads, and even major league clubs. In 1889, the Cuban Giants and the black New York Gorhams played in the otherwise all-white Middle States League.

Top black teams in the early 1900s had more than 100 games a year, usually playing at home on Sundays, "barnstorming" the rest of the week, and playing in winter leagues in California. Top clubs included the Cuban Giants, Philadelphia's Cuban X-Giants, and the Leland Giants, who went 110–10 in 1907. Among the outstanding players were John Henry Lloyd, shortstop for the Indianapolis ABCs, dubbed the "Black Honus Wagner," and Andrew "Rube" Foster, who went 54–1 pitching one year for the Cuban X-Giants.

Horse Racing

African American slaves were prominent jockeys and trainers, and after the Civil War, people of color continued to play important roles in racing. Owners and racing fans at the time considered jockeys to be minor contributors to the outcome of races, expecting the best-bred horses to win—a belief that allowed white thoroughbred owners to use black jockeys in major events. In the first Kentucky Derby in 1875, for instance, 14 of the 15 jockeys were African American, including Oliver Lewis, the winning rider. African American jockeys won 13 of the first 27 Derbies, while Edward "Brown Dick" Brown trained the 1877 Derby winner.

The best-known African American jockey was Isaac Murphy, who won the Derby three times, a record unequaled until 1930. Murphy earned a total of $250,000 during his career, but he eventually gained too much weight and had to quit. There were several other top jockeys in this era, including Willie Simms, who earned about $300,000.

The color line was drawn in the early 1900s, when white jockeys united to cut out the competition. The last black jockey in the Derby rode in 1911, by which time most African Americans had left the sport or had gone to Europe, such as Jimmy Winkfield, winner of the Kentucky Derby in 1901 and 1902. Thereafter, African Americans were relegated to work as exercise boys or stable hands.

Prizefighting

Athletes at the bottom of the social ladder who had few avenues for social mobility traditionally dominated boxing, and boxers of African descent achieved considerable renown in the lower weight divisions during the late nineteenth and early twentieth centuries.

George Dixon, the first Canadian and the first black world boxing champion, captured the bantamweight championship in 1890; a year later, he won the featherweight title, which he held for ten years.

The first African American champion was Joe Gans, considered by experts one of the finest lightweight fighters of all time. However, the "Old Master" had a tough time getting fights, and he was forced to throw a match in 1900 to featherweight champion "Terrible" Terry McGovern. Gans won the lightweight title in Fort Erie, Ontario, in 1902, defeating Frank Erne by a first-round knockout. He held the crown for six years.

In the heavyweight division, where white boxers ruled and their prowess was seen as proof of racial superiority, black participation was far more controversial. When powerful black boxers entered the scene, the sport's color line was drawn strong and tight. Champion John L. Sullivan (1882–1892), for example, refused to fight Canadian George Godfrey, who was considered the best black boxer of the 1880s. Sullivan's successor, James J. Corbett, refused to fight Peter Jackson, a black Australian, with whom he previously had fought a 60-round draw. Another great black fighter, Canadian Sam Langford, who had 130 knockouts (200–46–51) in a career that spanned 1902 to 1926, never got a title bout. He repeatedly fought other black boxers, including 18 bouts against Harry Wills, the number one contender in the 1920s.

The color barrier finally was broken by John Arthur "Jack" Johnson, who was born in Galveston, Texas. A top contender for several years, he could not get a title shot because of his race. In 1908, Johnson chased champion Tommy Burns around the world to Australia, where the titleholder agreed to fight him for a $30,000 guaranteed purse. Promoters advertised the contest as a chance to prove that blacks were inferior people who lacked the toughness and heart for such a manly activity as boxing. However, Johnson's skills and behavior during the fight dispelled those notions, and he emerged victorious.

Johnson attracted a huge following among African Americans, and he appealed to a smaller group of white boxing fans, who admired his patient fighting style. However, white America was not ready for a black champion, especially one who punched holes in prevailing racial theories that identified whites as superior in intelligence and physicality. Many considered Johnson obnoxious, presumptuous, and even threatening, complaining about his lavish lifestyle, his relationships with white women (three of his wives were white), and his flaunting of social and racial conventions.

Johnson defeated several "White Hopes," including former undefeated champion Jim Jeffries in 1910, sparking riots and the killing of African Americans across the country. In the aftermath of the violence, screenings of the film of the fight were banned in many states. Federal authorities soon acted to cut short Johnson's career. In 1913, he was indicted for violating the Mann Act, which criminalized the transportation of women across state lines for immoral activity. Johnson fled the country, and fought and traveled overseas for two years. On April 5, 1915, in Havana, Cuba, he lost his title to Jess Willard in 26 rounds. Thereafter, no black fighter would get a shot at the heavyweight title until 1937.

The National Association for the Advancement of Colored People (NAACP), founded in 1909, used sports and sports personalities to further the goals of black advancement and to attain integration. In the 1920s, W.E.B. Du Bois and other NAACP leaders asked how boxing could be any more reputable with the white Jack Dempsey, who had been a homeless vagabond, as champion than it had been with Jack Johnson. The association's spokesmen wondered why black athletes, who had proven their ability to compete with and against whites, were not allowed to compete in society as well.

Bicycling, Track, and Football

The color line also was drawn in bicycling, then a popular spectator sport, by the League of American Wheelmen in 1894, which led to the rise of black cycling clubs and races. Nonetheless, Marshall "Major" Taylor became one of the best bicyclists in the world, even though he could not compete in the South because of his race. He raced in the North, where he encountered prejudice from other professional riders, and in Europe and Australia. He set several world records and, in 1899, won the world championship in Montreal in the 1-mile (1.6-kilometer) sprint.

African Americans also set up track clubs in the early 1900s, including the Smart Set Club in Brooklyn, New York. At the 1904 Olympic Games in St. Louis, Missouri, George Poage won a bronze medal in the 400-meter (437-yard) hurdles, and four years later, John "Doc" Taylor ran a leg on the winning 4×400-meter relay.

A few African American football players also gained recognition at predominantly white colleges. The first black All-American was center William Henry Lewis (1892–1893), who attended Harvard Law School. Another two-time All-American was end Paul Robeson (1917–1918), an all-around athlete who scored the highest-ever marks on the New Jersey High School Examination and received an academic

scholarship to attended Rutgers University, where he excelled at football, basketball, and track and field. Robeson played professional football from 1920 to 1922 in Akron and Milwaukee while attending law school, and later became a widely acclaimed professional concert singer and actor. His teammate, African American Fritz Pollard, a star football player at Brown University, coached the Akron Pros in 1921, making him the first black coach in the National Football League (NFL).

Interwar Years

The black population of the North grew dramatically as a result of the "Great Migration" from the South during the first half of the twentieth century, as African Americans sought to leave behind Jim Crow laws and poverty for better jobs and living conditions in the cities of the North. This led to the emergence of black ghettoes, but it also opened up new opportunities for black businesses, which sponsored black professional sports teams and associations.

Basketball

African Americans in the interwar years amply demonstrated their athletic prowess, despite the burden of racism. They gained recognition in traditional inner-city sports, as well as in other athletic endeavors. Basketball became popular in urban ghettoes, as it was inexpensive and could be played on outdoor playgrounds or indoor gymnasiums.

The first well-known professional black team was the New York Renaissance, known as the Rens, founded in 1923 by businessman Bob Douglas, known as the "Father of Black Basketball." The Rens played and defeated the finest white teams, but they were barred from participating in white leagues. Their record was nothing short of phenomenal: The 1933 team won 88 straight games and, six years later, the Rens captured the first World Professional Tournament.

The other great black team of this period was the Harlem Globetrotters, founded in 1927 in Chicago by white entrepreneur Abe Saperstein. A barnstorming team, they played 150 games each year, winning more than 90 percent of them. In 1940, the Globetrotters won the second World Professional Tournament. Over the next few years, they added clowning to their repertoire to increase fan interest, although critics charged that this played into white stereotypes. Still, any doubts about their skills were put to rest in 1949, when the Globetrotters defeated the Minneapolis Lakers, then two-time champions of the Basketball Association of America (predecessor of the National Basketball Association).

Negro League Baseball

In 1920, black businessman Rube Foster organized the Negro National League as a "race" business that would employ black ballplayers, as well as black executives and black secretaries, and would cater primarily to an inner-city black audience. Seven of the original eight Midwestern teams were owned by African Americans, including the Chicago American Giants, the Indianapolis ABCs, and the Detroit Stars. The only white owner was J.L. Wilkinson of the Kansas City Monarchs. Foster provided strong leadership of the league, and he tried to make the teams competitive with each other.

The Negro National League participated in the Negro League World Series (1924–1927) against its rival, the Eastern Colored League. However, the future of the league was hurt by Foster's retirement in 1926 because of mental illness, and by the Great Depression. The league went out of business in 1931.

A new Negro National League was established two years later—largely by men in the numbers racket—and lasted until 1948. The top team was the Homestead (Pennsylvania) Grays, champions from 1937 to 1945, which featured such stars as Satchel Paige, Josh Gibson, Buck Leonard, and James "Cool Papa" Bell.

College Football

Opportunities increased in the interwar era for black college athletes at such athletic powerhouses as the University of Michigan, Ohio State University, the University of California, Los Angeles, and Syracuse University. However, opposing coaches, mainly from the South, requested, demanded, or forced teams to refrain from playing their black athletes.

In 1937, the highly rated Syracuse football team did not play star quarterback Wilmeth Sidat-Singh against the University of Maryland. However, four years later, Cornell University refused to prevent Samuel Pierce from taking the field against Navy. This was the first time an African American player competed against a white team in the South.

Jesse Owens and Joe Louis

In 1936, Jesse Owens led a predominantly African American track team to glory at the Summer Olympics in Berlin, then the capital of Nazi Germany under Adolf Hitler. The Nazis sought to use the games to demonstrate the superiority of the Aryan (white) race and of fascist society, but Owens helped put that myth to rest, winning four gold medals, including the 100-meter (109-yard), 200-meter (218-yard), 4×100-meter (437-yard) relay, and long jump, an achievement unequaled until Carl Lewis's performance at the 1984 Olympics.

One year later, Joe Louis became the first African American to fight for the heavyweight boxing title since Jack Johnson. He was a great talent and a hero to all African Americans. In 1937, Louis won the title from champion Jimmy Braddock, and a year later, he fought former world champion German Max Schmeling, who had defeated Louis in 1936. The rematch had enormous international significance, as it was seen as a battle between the fascist Nazi system (although Schmeling was not a Nazi) and democracy. Louis won with a first-round knockout at New York's Yankee Stadium, becoming an American hero. He won all 25 title defenses before retiring in 1949.

Jackie Robinson and the Integration of Baseball

Many historians regard Jackie Robinson's integration of Major League Baseball as the single most important event in the history of modern African American sports. Civil rights activists and journalists in the 1930s and 1940s worked to integrate the game; however, in spite of the proven ability of African American athletes such as Paige, Owens, and Louis, there was considerable opposition from players, fans, and owners. Baseball was the national pastime, and its integration would have enormous symbolic importance.

Robinson was signed on October 23, 1945, by Brooklyn Dodgers president Branch Rickey, who referred to the integration of baseball as the "Great Experiment." Convinced that it was the right thing to do, Rickey also believed that Robinson could help the Dodgers win the National League pennant and bring black fans to the game. Robinson had played one year for the Kansas City Monarchs, but he was not their best player. Nonetheless, Rickey felt that stars such as Satchel Paige and Josh Gibson were too old and did not have the background to adjust to the difficulties they would encounter in the major leagues. On the other hand, Robinson was a gifted all-around athlete who had grown up outside the South, gaining a reputation as an able scholar and a star athlete at the University of California, Los Angeles and serving as an army officer during World War II. Rickey felt that Robinson had the fortitude to stand up to any challenge he might encounter. After a year at the team's minor league franchise in Montreal, Robinson joined the Dodgers in 1947.

Rickey was right. Not only did Robinson overcome opposition from teammates, rival players, and the public, he also was named Rookie of the Year and helped lead the Dodgers to the pennant. Robinson's achievement was a major victory for civil rights, and demonstrated the potential for additional future advances. His success opened the door for other stars such as Larry Doby, Willie Mays, and Hank Aaron, but the pace of integration was slow, and black players had to be significantly more talented than whites in order to make the majors. Only in 1959 did the last major league team, the Boston Red Sox, integrate. This integration process led to the demise of the one remaining Negro League, which folded in 1958.

Integrating the South

In the 1950s and early 1960s, when the civil rights movement focused on the South, efforts were under way to desegregate major college sports. One of the first steps forward occurred in 1948, when the Cotton Bowl in Dallas was integrated, followed by El Paso's Sun Bowl (1952), Miami's Orange Bowl (1955), and the Sugar Bowl in New Orleans (1956). Yet until 1963, Mississippi State University repeatedly declined bids to the National Collegiate Athletic Association (NCAA) basketball championship, rather than play an integrated team.

The segregation of Southern teams pushed many outstanding black athletes to enroll at historically black colleges or to migrate to the North. The first Southern schools to recruit blacks for football were second-tier institutions, notably North Texas State College in 1957. Nine years later, Texas Western University (now the University of Texas at El Paso) defeated basketball power University of Kentucky 72–65 to take the NCAA basketball championship with an all-black starting five. One year later, the Southeastern Conference recruited its first black football and basketball players. By 1972, the last holdouts, the universities of Georgia and Mississippi, had black football players.

The quintessential Southern sport was NASCAR racing, which promoted itself as the sport of "good old boys," especially bootleggers who drove Southern back roads to evade revenuers. The first black driver in a NASCAR race was Elias Bowie in San Mateo, Califor-

nia, in 1955, and one year later, Charlie Scott came in nineteenth in a Daytona event.

In 1963, Wendell Scott became the only African American to win the Grand National/Winston Cup Series at Speedway Park in Jacksonville, Florida. However, racing officials did not announce his victory for fear of upsetting the white crowd in attendance. Scott competed in 495 Cup races from 1961 to 1973, and he finished in the top 10 in 1966, 1968, and 1969.

Black Athletic Revolt and After

The fight against subtler forms of discrimination in the North began in the mid-1960s. These were turbulent years that saw riots in the streets and the assassinations of Malcolm X and the Reverend Martin Luther King, Jr.

In 1964, Olympic heavyweight boxing champion Cassius Clay stunned the boxing world by defeating Sonny Liston, and then shocked the public by declaring that he was a Black Muslim and changing his name to Muhammad Ali. He further alienated mainstream Americans by opposing the war in Vietnam and refusing to enter the U.S. Army in 1967 on religious grounds. He was stripped of his title and convicted of draft dodging. Ali's actions made him a hero to African Americans, opponents of the war, and others around the world. He later was vindicated in court and regained his crown.

Ali was a role model for the "black athletic revolt," which was led by sociologist Harry Edwards of San Jose State College. The movement tried to raise public consciousness about racism in sports in the United States and around the world, an effort that resulted in protests at 37 campuses between 1967 and 1971 and an unsuccessful effort to boycott the 1968 Olympic Games in Mexico City. That year, track and field medalists Tommie Smith and John Carlos held up their clenched black fists in protest when the U.S. flag was raised, a demonstration against American racism. They promptly were expelled from the Games.

Another athlete who stood up for his rights was centerfielder Curt Flood of the St. Louis Cardinals. After Flood was traded to the Phillies, he refused to go to Philadelphia, a city that was considered inhospitable to African American athletes. Flood sued Major League Baseball through Commissioner Bowie Kuhn to gain free agent status; however, the U.S. Supreme Court ruled in 1972 in *Flood v. Kuhn* that it could not interfere because of baseball's antitrust exemption.

By the first decade of the twenty-first century, African Americans dominated two of the nation's three premier professional sports, representing 70 percent of all NFL players and 80 percent of athletes in the National Basketball Association (NBA). Baseball was the lone exception, as the percentage of African American players fell from 27 percent in 1974 to 9.5 percent in 2010; their places often were taken by a new generation of Latino athletes. Numbers alone do not tell the story, however. In basketball, in particular, African American players—such as Bill Russell, Kareem Abdul-Jabbar, Earl Monroe, and Michael Jordan—dramatically altered the game, making it more dynamic.

At the management and coaching levels, progress was substantially slower. In 1975, nearly three decades after Jackie Robinson integrated the field, Frank Robinson (no relation) became the first Major League Baseball manager, taking the helm of the Atlanta Braves. By 2008, there were five black major league managers, compared to seven NFL and 12 NBA coaches. The NBA had the most integrated front office of any major sports league, with seven African American team presidents.

In 2003, media magnate Robert L. Johnson became the first black owner of an NBA team when he took the newly formed Charlotte Bobcats into the league (though businessmen Peter Bynoe and Bertram Lee had bought a partial interest in the Denver Nuggets 14 years before). In 2010, Michael Jordan bought the Bobcats for $275 million.

African American Women

African American women played an important role in sports during the 1930s and 1940s. At a time when middle-class white women were discouraged from competitive sports, black physical educators saw athletic competition for women as a positive force. The Tuskegee Institute, for one, sent excellent teams to compete at the National Women's Amateur Athletic Association track and field meets, winning 14 titles from 1937 to 1951.

African American women were important members of U.S. track and field teams after World War II, culminating in the success of Wilma Rudolph, who won three gold medals at the 1960 Olympic Games in Rome. The best-known African American female athlete of the era, however, was Althea Gibson, who won the singles tennis championships at both Wimbledon and Forest Hills in 1957 and 1958. Recent years have seen athletic superstars such as three-time Olympic gold medalists Florence Griffith Joyner and Jackie Joyner-Kersee, and sisters Venus and Serena Williams, who have 20 singles tennis Grand Slam titles between them.

African Americans in the Twenty-First Century

By the early twenty-first century, African American athletes had become integral to virtually every major American sport, college and professional, with the possible exception of ice hockey. By the early 2000s, blacks represented roughly four-fifths of players in the NBA and two-thirds in the NFL, though less than 10 percent of major league baseball players. Moreover, blacks had broken barriers within team sports that once relegated them to nonleading positions, such as quarterback or starting pitcher. Increasing numbers of black managers and coaches, many of them former athletes, could be seen on the sidelines and in the dugouts at major sporting events. Even such bastions of white sporting privilege as tennis and golf featured successful black competitors.

It would seem that the long and sorry story of racial exclusion from American sports had ended. Still, the business of sports remains largely a white profession. It was not until 2005 that an NFL franchise, the Minnesota Vikings, had a black limited partner, Randy Fowler. As of 2011, not a single Major League Baseball team has ever been owned by an African American.

James R. Coates, Jr.

See also: African American Baseball, Before 1920; African American Baseball, Negro League Era; Harlem Globetrotters; Historically Black Colleges; Race and Race Relations.

Further Reading

Ashe, Arthur, and Arnold Rampersad. *Days of Grace: A Memoir.* New York: Alfred A. Knopf, 1993.

Baker, William J. *Jesse Owens: An American Life.* New York: Free Press, 1986.

Bass, Amy. *Not the Triumph but the Struggle: The 1968 Olympics and the Making of the Black Athlete.* Minneapolis: University of Minnesota Press, 2002.

Carroll, John M. *Fritz Pollard: Pioneer in Racial Advancement.* Urbana: University of Illinois Press, 1992.

Djata, Sundiata. *Blacks at the Net: Black Achievement in the History of Tennis.* Syracuse, NY: Syracuse University Press, 2006.

Edwards, Harry. *The Revolt of the Black Athlete.* New York: Free Press, 1969.

Hoberman, John M. *Darwin's Athletes: How Sport Has Damaged Black America and Preserved the Myth of Race.* Boston: Houghton Mifflin, 1997.

Hotaling, Edward. *The Great Black Jockeys: The Lives and Times of the Men Who Dominated America's First National Sport.* Rocklin, CA: Forum, 1999.

Lanctot, Neil. *Negro League Baseball: The Rise and Ruin of a Black Institution.* Philadelphia: University of Pennsylvania Press, 2004.

Lomax, Michael E. *Black Baseball Entrepreneurs, 1860–1901: Operating by Any Means Necessary.* Syracuse, NY: Syracuse University Press, 2003.

Martin, Charles H. *Benching Jim Crow: The Rise and Fall of the Color Line in Southern Colleges, 1890–1980.* Urbana: University of Illinois Press, 2010.

Olsen, Jack. *The Black Athlete: A Shameful Story.* New York: Time-Life, 1968.

Rampersad, Arnold. *Jackie Robinson: A Biography.* New York: Alfred A. Knopf, 1997.

Ritchie, Andrew. *Major Taylor: The Extraordinary Career of a Champion Bicycle Rider.* Baltimore: Johns Hopkins University Press, 1996.

Roberts, Randy. *Papa Jack: Jack Johnson and the Era of White Hopes.* New York: Free Press, 1983.

Ruck, Rob. *Sandlot Seasons: Sport in Black Pittsburgh.* Urbana: University of Illinois Press, 1987.

Sammons, Jeffrey T. *Beyond the Ring: The Role of Boxing in American Society.* Urbana: University of Illinois Press, 1988.

Shropshire, Kenneth L. *In Black and White: Race and Sports in America.* New York: New York University Press, 1996.

Tygiel, Jules. *Baseball's Great Experiment: Jackie Robinson and His Legacy.* New York: Oxford University Press, 1983.

Weiss, Stuart L. *The Curt Flood Story: The Man Behind the Myth.* Columbia: University of Missouri Press, 2007.

Whitaker, Matthew C., ed. *African-American Icons of Sport: Triumph, Courage, and Excellence.* Westport, CT: Greenwood, 2008.

White, Sol. *History of Colored Base Ball, with Other Documents on the Early Black Game, 1886–1936.* Lincoln: University of Nebraska Press, 1995.

Wiggins, David K. *Glory Bound: Black Athletes in a White America.* Syracuse, NY: Syracuse University Press, 1997.

Zang, David W. *Fleet Walker's Divided Heart: The Life of Baseball's First Black Major Leaguer.* Lincoln: University of Nebraska Press, 1995.

Agents

Professional athletes employ agents primarily to negotiate their contracts. Agents have been an integral part of the sports industry for decades, mainly in individual sports—horse-racing jockeys long made use of them—but agents for team players did not become common until the 1960s and 1970s. This was because team owners generally resisted dealing with agents, preferring instead to negotiate directly with players.

Gradually, agents became an accepted and important part of the industry. While players' associations determine the basic parameters of players' contracts through the collective bargaining process, they do not negotiate individual salaries. Agents fill that void and also offer financial advice and seek endorsement opportunities for clients. Depending on the player's needs and the agent's expertise and relationship with the player, agents might deal with matters such as athletic training, public relations, legal counseling, immigration, foreign tax law, and dispute resolution.

Origins of Sports Agents

The first widely known sports agent was promoter C.C. "Cash and Carry" Pyle, who represented a number of prominent athletes during the 1920s and 1930s, most notably football star Harold "Red" Grange, the "Galloping Ghost," for whom he negotiated a contract with the Chicago Bears after Grange completed his college eligibility at the University of Illinois in 1925. Grange made $325,000 in salary and endorsements in one year, an extraordinary sum at a time when star athletes were fortunate to earn even five-figure salaries. Pyle's client list also included tennis stars Mark K. Brown and Suzanne Lenglen, for whom he signed contracts for $50,000 in 1926.

Still, the use of agents in sports was rare until the 1970s, because owners insisted on complete control over negotiations. In 1963, for instance, the management of the Green Bay Packers made a decision, reportedly on the advice of Coach Vince Lombardi, to trade star center Jim Ringo, after they learned that Ringo had brought in an agent to help him with his contract negotiations.

In 1965, William Hayes, a Hollywood agent, helped Los Angeles Dodgers pitching aces Don Drysdale and Sandy Koufax plan a two-man holdout even though Dodgers owner Walter O'Malley refused to deal directly with the agent, fearing the precedent it would set. The players demanded combined salaries amounting to $1 million over three years (or $333,000 per season). In the end, they accepted a collective salary offer of $235,000 per season, an amount that represented a considerable increase for both players.

Several important changes in sports during the 1970s led to the widespread use of agents. Television was key, as it raised the value of players, both in terms of their salaries and, through national exposure, their potential as product endorsers. As players began to realize their money-making potential, they started to challenge the reserve and option clauses, which bound them to specific teams. The latter development was aided by the growing power of players' unions. The unions demanded, for example, that salaries be disclosed publicly, so that players would know what their competitors were being paid. All of these factors increased the players' value and negotiating power, making it both possible and financially worthwhile for agents to interject themselves into the negotiating process.

Another important development in the field was the creation of sports marketing conglomerates. Attorney Mark McCormack started out with Arnold Palmer in 1960, and he soon represented other golfers, helping to make the sport a business. McCormack then branched out, founding the International Management Group (IMG), which he made into a sport and entertainment conglomerate.

The modern fathers of the sports agent industry in team sports were Bob Woolf, an attorney who entered the business in 1964, and Martin Blackman, who is best known for obtaining lucrative endorsement deals, such as the innovative Miller Lite beer commercials. Woolf's clients included baseball star Carl Yastrzemski, basketball standout Julius "Dr. J" Erving, and hockey pro Derek Sanderson. But the top agent in the 1970s was Mike Trope, who got his start as a college student at the University of Southern California, where he negotiated contracts for six Heisman Trophy winners.

Trope was eclipsed by Leigh Steinberg, a student at the University of California, Berkeley. In 1975, Steinberg negotiated a record $650,000 contract for University of California quarterback Steve Bartkowski, who lived in the dormitory where Steinberg served as a student advisor. Steinberg, an excellent self-promoter who emphasized public relations, was the model for the eponymous agent in the Hollywood movie *Jerry Maguire* (1996).

Agents in Team Sports

By the early twenty-first century, agents had become ubiquitous in American professional sports: the National Football League Players Association (NFLPA) certified 1,700 agents for its 1,800 active players; the National Basketball Players Association (NBPA) featured 313 agents and 414 players; the Major League Baseball Players Association (MLBPA) had around 300 certified agents; and there were roughly 150 agents certified with the National Hockey League Players' Association (NHLPA). The MLBPA and NHLPA have no caps on agent fees, but the NFLPA has a cap of 3 percent, and the NBPA 4 percent.

Agents receive a much greater share for obtaining endorsement and sponsorship opportunities for their clients, usually 20 percent. Instead of commissions, agents may charge a flat rate, an hourly rate, or some combination of the two. Players who rely on an agent for simple contract negotiations sometimes prefer a flat or hourly rate when there is no need for an extensive time commitment by the agent.

Each sport features high-profile agents who represent a number of established star players. Scott Boras arguably is the single most powerful agent in any professional sport, representing 75 Major League Baseball players. He is best known for negotiating Alex Rodriguez's ten-year, $252 million contract with the Texas Rangers in 2001, then the richest in baseball; Boras topped this achievement in 2007 when he inked a ten-year, $275 million deal with the New York Yankees for the third baseman. In 2005 alone, Boras negotiated $500 million in free agent contracts.

Conflicts of Interest and Monitoring

The sports agent industry also has its problems. Opportunities to make money and the lure of working with professional athletes have led to unscrupulous behavior by agents trying to break into a competitive and lucrative business. Agents, say critics, have been known to do or say anything to land a client.

The signing bonus alone for a first-round National Football League (NFL) draft pick can result in a $300,000 commission for an agent. As a result, agents have used financial inducements to convince promising college players to sign with them for years. A newer means of attracting clients is to offer "marketing guarantees," which are cash advances that agents pay to players in anticipation of future endorsement contracts.

Agents regularly try to woo players away from their existing agents. For example, some 30 percent of the 233 National Basketball Association (NBA) players active in both 2001 and 2005 had switched agents at least once over the intervening years. The incentive for an agent to try to induce a player to switch increases as the financial payoff escalates.

This has led to a number of cases in which agents have been sued for unprofessional conduct. In 1984, Billy Sims and the Detroit Lions successfully voided a contract in *Detroit Lions v. Argovitz* because Sims's agent, Jerry Argovitz, also was the co-owner of the Houston Gamblers of the United States Football League.

Perhaps the most prominent recent case involved NFL agent Tank Black, who was convicted of stealing more than $12 million from his clients in 2002. He also had violated National Collegiate Athletic Association (NCAA) regulations to sign up clients, providing them with financial inducements while still in college.

In another major case, a judge in 2004 awarded basketball star Scottie Pippen $11.8 million from his former financial advisor for reportedly losing $17 million of Pippen's money. A recent study by the NFLPA found that between 1999 and 2002, 78 NFL players were defrauded of more than $42 million by their agents and financial advisors.

Inappropriate conduct includes soliciting student athletes with remaining collegiate eligibility or underage athletes (such as junior hockey and high school basketball players). Agents also are prohibited from violating the rules of their professional associations, including the American Bar Association. Other problems include conflicts of interest, such as representing players on the same team, players at the same position in the same sport, players seeking similar endorsement opportunities, or players in the same free agent or draft pool.

Industry stakeholders have developed monitoring and certification programs to address these concerns. They deal with professional standards for agents, agent conduct, and parameters for solicitation. The four major professional players' associations have developed agent certification programs, such as the NFLPA's Registered Financial Advisor Program, and several states have implemented programs that focus on protecting college athletes from inappropriate solicitation. The NCAA has developed its own regulations regarding agents.

Trends

Since the turn of the century, the agent industry has undergone a substantial upheaval. Industry giant IMG divested its interests in representing individual athletes in 2006, while entertainment firms Wasserman Media Group and Creative Artists Agency (CAA) have attempted to dominate the industry by luring established agents to their companies. CAA has built up a sports division that represents more than 300 professional athletes, including Peyton Manning and LaDainian Tomlinson of the NFL and the New York Yankees' Derek Jeter. The involvement of Wasserman and CAA signals the continued merging of the sports and entertainment industries.

Each sports league is dominated by a handful of agents and firms who represent a bulk of its players. The five biggest firms handling the NBA represent 147 players, or 35.5 percent of the league. In baseball, SFX represented players who earned $229 million in 2004, an amount second only to that of Scott Boras's clients, who made $234 million in the same year. In hockey, Newport Sports Management ($166 million) and IMG ($142 million) have dominated the market.

It is not clear what effect new and powerful agencies with ties to other segments of the entertainment industry will have on the profession. As larger agencies with multiple connections and interests in the industry increase in prominence, so, too, will the opportunity for conflicts of interest. When it comes to player representation, say experts, the onus will be on players' associations to diligently monitor agent behavior in order to protect players' interests and the interests of agents who act fairly toward their clients.

Daniel S. Mason

See also: Business of Sports; Endorsements, Athlete; Major League Baseball Players Association; National Football League Players Association; National Hockey League Players' Association; Reserve Clause.

Further Reading

Gallner, Sheldon. *Pro Sports: The Contract Game.* New York: Charles Scribner's Sons, 1974.

Mason, Daniel S. "Player Agents." In *Handbook on the Economics of Sport,* ed. Wladimir Andreff and Stefan Szymanski. Cheltenham, UK: Edward Elgar, 2006.

Powers, Alex. "The Need to Regulate Sports Agents." *Seton Hall Journal of Sport Law* 4 (1994): 253–276.

Ruxin, Robert H. *An Athlete's Guide to Agents.* Lexington, MA: Stephen Greene, 1989.

Shropshire, Kenneth L., and Timothy Davis. *The Business of Sports Agents.* Philadelphia: University of Pennsylvania Press, 2003.

Air Racing

Air racing, like automobile racing, is both a contest between machines and a competition between their human operators. From 1909 to the late 1940s, piston-engine racing airplanes represented the cutting edge of aviation technology, and air races were used as showcases and testing grounds for new designs. The advent of high-performance jets and scientific flight testing after World War II put an end to this era. After 1950, air racing became a pure sporting event in which increasingly stringent class rules constrained designs and ensured close competition.

Air racing was born in a series of contests held in the French city of Reims in 1909. American Glenn Curtiss, a motorcycle racer turned aviator, won two of the signature events at Reims. The next year, when the first air meets were held in the United States, however,

Curtiss failed to repeat his triumphs. American pilots remained minor players in international air racing for a decade, in part because the Wright brothers were unwilling to send their technically advanced planes to competitions.

The golden age of air racing in the United States began with the establishment of a trophy for the sport by newspaper magnate Joseph Pulitzer in 1919. The first races, held on Long Island, New York, in 1920, drew a crowd of 25,000. That year, the trophy went to Curtis Moseley, a captain in the U.S. Army Air Corps.

Military pilots and military aircraft dominated American air races throughout the 1920s, as both the army and navy used the events as proving grounds for their latest fighter planes. Twelve of the 15 planes in the 1922 race were military types, as were all seven planes in the 1923 race and three of the four in the 1923 race.

Races for the John L. Mitchell Trophy, established by U.S. Army Air Corps officer William "Billy" Mitchell in honor of a younger brother killed in World War I, were military affairs. Pilots from the First Pursuit (Fighter) Squadron competed annually from 1922 to 1930 and from 1934 to 1936 in a five-lap race around a 4-mile (6.4-kilometer) course marked by tall pylons. The Pulitzer Trophy race merged with the new National Air Races in 1924, and the Mitchell Trophy races were held in conjunction with the national event throughout the 1920s.

Clifford W. Henderson, a car dealer and aviation promoter who staged the 1928 National Air Races in Los Angeles, took air racing to a new level at the 1929 contest in Cleveland. Henderson produced a ten-day program of races, aerobatics, and demonstration flights that drew an estimated 300,000 spectators and turned a profit of $90,000.

That year, the race for the newly established Thompson Cup became air racing's premier closed-course event: five laps around a 10-mile (16-kilometer) triangular course at speeds approaching 200 miles (322 kilometers) per hour. The trophy was named for Charles Thompson, president of Thompson Products, who sponsored the event. The initial race was won by Doug Davis, an airline pilot flying a custom-built racing plane; Lieutenant R.G. Breen of the U.S. Army Air Corps took second in a U.S. Army P-3A, marking the end of military dominance in American air racing; and Gilmore Oil Company pilot Roscoe Turner finished third in a modified Lockheed Vega. The race was renamed the Thompson Trophy in 1930. Until 1939, it remained the culmination of the National Air Races, which were dominated by civilian pilots flying specialized racing machines.

Interest in long-distance air racing increased markedly after Charles Lindbergh's 1927 solo flight across the Atlantic Ocean. Art Goebel won the "Pineapple Derby" race from Oakland to Honolulu later that year, and the 1929 National Air Races included a women-only race from Santa Monica to Cleveland (dubbed the "Powderpuff Derby" by humorist Will Rogers), among many other distance events.

The transcontinental Bendix Trophy race, first flown in 1931, became distance racing's equivalent of the Thompson Trophy, and it drew many of the same pilots, including Doug Davis, Jimmy Doolittle, and Roscoe Turner. Women, who raced separately from men in closed-course events, were allowed to compete head to head with male pilots in the Bendix Trophy race, beginning in 1934. Two years later, Louise Thaden became the first woman to win it, with Laura Ingalls finishing second and Amelia Earhart fifth.

The growing threat of war, the diminishing novelty of aviation, and the retirement or death of leading pilots, such as Davis, Doolittle, and Turner, sent air racing into decline by the late 1930s. Suspended during World War II, the National Air Races—including the Thompson and Bendix trophy races—were revived for a time after the war, dominated by modified war-surplus fighters and trainers flown by civilian pilots such as Paul Mantz, Jacqueline Cochran, and Alvin "Tex" Johnston.

A division for "midget" racers, powered by engines with a displacement of 190 cubic centimeters (12 cubic inches) or less, was added in 1947 in an effort to bring back the spirit of the 1930s races. The National Air Races were run for the last time in 1949, but the midget racers continued to fly in local and regional competitions through the 1950s.

Air racing on the national level resumed in 1964, when Nevada rancher Bill Stead revived the National Air Races at Reno to celebrate the centennial of Nevada statehood. The 1964 races featured an Unlimited Class for World War II fighters as well as separate divisions for midget racers, biplanes, and woman pilots. Stead died after the 1965 running, but the National Air Races continued and were held each September at a decommissioned air force base owned by the city of Reno. The Unlimited, Midget (renamed Formula One in 1968), and Biplane classes remain on the program, along with a T-6 Class for the mass-produced World War II advanced trainer (added in 1967), a Sport Class for powerful home-built aircraft (1998), and an invitation-only Jet Class (2002).

The Red Bull Air Race World Series and the Aero GP Series, both launched in Europe in 2000, have drawn some interest from American pilots and have produced one American champion, Kyle Chambliss, winner of the Red Bull series in 2006. Both competitions add tests of skill—precision aerobatics in the Red Bull races, mock dogfights and "bombing" with bags of flour in the Aero GP contests—to American air racing's traditional emphasis on speed. The addition of such skill elements and the staging of races near major international cities represent the first serious attempts to adapt air racing to the demands of television coverage.

A. Bowdoin Van Riper

See also: Technology.

Further Reading

Gandt, Robert. *Fly Low, Fly Fast: Inside the Reno Air Races.* New York: Viking, 1999.

Matthews, Birch. *Race with the Wind: How Air Racing Advanced Aviation.* Osceola, WI: MBI, 2001.

Vorderman, Don. *The Great Air Races.* Garden City, NY: Doubleday, 1969.

Ali, Muhammad (1942–)

Considered one of the best boxers ever, Muhammad Ali was a three-time world heavyweight champion in the 1960s and 1970s. First appearing on the international sporting scene as a seemingly shy young Olympic contender in 1960, he became a contentious figure in 1964, when he won the heavyweight title, announced his membership in the divisive Nation of Islam, and changed his name. During the Vietnam War, he refused induction into the armed forces as a conscientious objector, even when this meant he was banned from boxing, an action that made him one of the most controversial sports stars of the century. Once reinstated, he took his boxing career to new heights. At the pinnacle of his fame, Muhammad Ali, known as "The Greatest," was among the most recognized personalities in the world, having fought before adoring crowds in Europe, Africa, and Asia, as well as at home.

Cassius Clay: The Early Years

He was born Cassius Marcellus Clay, Jr., on January 17, 1942, in Louisville, Kentucky, to Cassius Marcellus Clay, Sr., a sign painter, and Odessa Clay, a maid. Clay first became interested in boxing at the age of 12, after his bicycle was stolen. Angry about the incident, Clay complained to police officer Joe Martin that he wanted

to beat up the perpetrator. Martin, who trained amateur boxers, invited Clay to join his boxing program.

Clay's rise to prominence was rapid, and he enjoyed an excellent amateur career, compiling a 100–5 record. In 1959 and 1960, he won the U.S. National Amateur Light Heavyweight championships; in 1960, he also won an Olympic gold medal in the light-heavyweight division of under 178.6 pounds (under 81 kilograms).

The Making of a Champion

A few months after his Olympic championship, Clay turned professional. He signed a six-year contract with the Louisville Sponsoring Group, a syndicate of 11 white men from his hometown, nearly all of whom were millionaires. His backers' wealth ensured that Clay could devote himself full time to boxing without having to take another job. He had the best sparring partners, facilities, and medical care, and his sponsors made certain that he would not be hustled prematurely into dangerous matches. The Louisville group hired Angelo Dundee, one of the sport's most respected trainers, to guide the young boxer.

In the early years, Clay remained modest, but soon he began inventing rhymes and quips about himself and his fights. In the ring, he showed intelligence, quickness, and enough power to finish off an opponent. He became a box office draw whose fights helped revive an ailing sport. The boxing world had been living under the cloud of reports of fixed fights and control by mobsters. By contrast, Clay seemed to be a clean-living, honestly managed, and promising prospect. Major magazines including *Sports Illustrated* ran feature stories about him in his first year. By his eighth match, he was fighting on national television.

Clay's first ten fights from October 1960 to November 1961 showed him to be a polished fighter with superb hand and foot speed, a strong jab, and good power. Yet his style was unorthodox: He rarely threw body punches, pulled straight back instead of side to side when avoiding punches, and held his hands low. Ali described his technique as "float like a butterfly, sting like a bee." His natural abilities were enough to defeat his early marginal opponents, but many observers questioned whether he would be able to manage tougher bouts.

By 1962, Clay's handlers were ready to move him into larger markets such as New York and Los Angeles. After reeling off four straight wins to start the year, two of them nationally televised, Clay knocked out the ranked Alejandro Lavorante, paving the way for a match against the once-brilliant Archie Moore—at age 49, long past his prime—in Los Angeles. As Clay predicted, "Moore fell in four." The bout was a blockbuster, setting a state indoor box office record for a sporting event.

It was clear by 1963 that Clay was the biggest attraction in the sport. His January bout against Charlie Powell set an indoor attendance record in Pittsburgh, even though it was held on one of the coldest days in the city's history. In March, despite a newspaper strike that limited coverage, his fight with contender Doug Jones was the first boxing event in Madison Square Garden's 38-year history to sell out in advance. The gross receipts were the arena's largest in ten years. The fighter was becoming an international phenomenon and was featured on the cover of *Time.* A June bout with England's Henry Cooper drew 55,000 fans, Great Britain's largest fight crowd in 25 years. Clay took the rest of the year off to prepare for his biggest match against the seemingly invincible heavyweight champion of the world, Sonny Liston.

During this period, it was suspected that Clay had become a member of the Nation of Islam, a black separatist group that had earned the enmity of many Americans because of its antiwhite rhetoric. Although Clay had been hiding his interest in the group for years, he was less inclined to do so as a title fight became imminent. He refused to deny a newspaper report that placed him at a Nation of Islam meeting in Philadelphia. In Miami, where he was training for his February 25, 1964, bout with Liston, he was joined at his training camp by Malcolm X, the Nation of Islam's national spokesperson.

Although opposition to Clay began to materialize in light of these revelations, it did not become an issue, since the public expected that he would lose the bout to Liston, who was heavily favored (7–1) to beat Clay. In a surprise result, the challenger dominated the bout, and Clay won the title when Liston refused to answer the bell for the seventh round. With the championship in hand, Clay revealed that he was, indeed, a member of the Nation of Islam. Shortly thereafter, he was renamed Muhammad Ali by Nation of Islam leader Elijah Muhammad. The press and the public turned against him.

After winning a controversial rematch against Liston on May 25, 1965, that lasted only one round—a fight that many believed was fixed—Ali set his sights on popular contender Floyd Patterson, the man whom Liston had beaten for the title. Press coverage of the November 22 bout contrasted the two boxers, with Patterson presented as the hero and Ali as the villain. Ali defeated Patterson by a technical knockout in the twelfth round, but some boxing writers accused him of toying with Patterson, punishing him for many rounds instead of knocking him out earlier.

After the Patterson fight, Ali continued to fight and defeat one opponent after another. He fought twice in Great Britain and once in West Germany, then returned to the United States, where he had three more victories, over Cleveland "Big Cat" Williams, Ernie Terrell, and Zora Folley.

Political Controversies

Several of Ali's professional and personal decisions aroused controversy. First, he replaced the Louisville Sponsoring Group with a Nation of Islam–led promotional outfit called Main Bout. Ali's professional affiliation with the Nation of Islam upset established boxing promoters in the United States (some reputedly supported by mobsters), who were used to making big money on the sport's major bouts. Their reluctance to schedule contests with Main Bout encouraged Ali to fight in Britain and Europe in 1966.

Second, when Ali received a compulsory draft notice during the escalating war in Vietnam, he refused to be inducted into the U.S. Army, claiming exemption as a conscientious objector. Conservative politicians, including many in the South, earned political capital by challenging Ali's draft refusal, accusing him of being cowardly and unpatriotic.

The government denied Ali's claim as a conscientious objector and summoned him to appear for induction. He appeared in April 1967 but declined to step forward when his name was called for induction. He was arrested and charged with draft evasion. In June, a judge found him guilty. Ali announced that he would appeal the decision. Within days, he was stripped of his heavyweight crown by U.S. boxing authorities, who took away his license.

Ali's boxing career came to a halt. State athletic commissions around the country refused to license him. Worse, as a convicted felon, he was unable to travel abroad. For the next three and a half years, Ali remained exiled from the sport.

Ali Returns to the Ring and Boxing Glory

State court decisions in his favor in Georgia and New York allowed Ali return to the ring in 1970. He defeated two ranked contenders and agreed to face Joe Frazier, the new heavyweight champion, on March 8, 1971. In one of the greatest events in boxing history—a heavyweight title bout between two undefeated champions—Frazier won a unanimous decision over Ali.

Despite Ali's loss to Frazier, 1971 was a great year for the former champion. The U.S. Supreme Court overturned his draft evasion conviction because of a technical error made by the Justice Department, which had never indicated exactly why Ali's conscientious objector claim had been rejected. He was free.

For the next three years, Ali pursued the world heavyweight championship, fighting all over the world. Although he suffered setbacks, including a loss to unknown Ken Norton, Ali eventually earned a rematch against Frazier and then was signed to an October 30, 1974, meeting in Kinshasa, Zaire, against George Foreman, who had won the championship from Frazier with a brutal and decisive knockout. Foreman also had destroyed Norton, and Ali's chances for victory

Outspoken, controversial, and supremely talented in the ring, heavyweight boxer Muhammad Ali (born Cassius Clay) won the second of his three world championships by knocking out the powerful George Foreman in Kinshasa, Zaire, in 1974. *(Sports Illustrated/Getty Images)*

looked slim. But in the "Rumble in the Jungle," Ali, as he had done in his bout against Liston, shocked fans by handling a seemingly invincible champion, regaining the title against the heavily favored Foreman with an eighth-round knockout. Many people felt that the bout had symbolic importance, because it was the first world heavyweight championship match held in Africa, and Ali was a black nationalist.

The fight not only reinforced Ali's popularity around the world, it also marked his return to the good graces of many Americans who had been appalled by his draft resistance. By 1974, public opinion had turned against the Vietnam War, and Americans began to view Ali from a new perspective. Furthermore, his gallant ring performances and determination to triumph against adversity won over many fans. President Gerald Ford, perhaps sensing the nation's about-face, invited the new champion to the White House to officially congratulate him and try to heal the wounds of Vietnam, Watergate, and racism.

Ali remained champion until 1978, but by then his skills had eroded, and he absorbed punishment that would contribute to serious health problems later in life. The most telling example was his epic third fight with Joe Frazier in 1975, billed as the "Thrilla in Manila." Ali won when Frazier could not come out after the fourteenth round, which ensured Ali's status as a boxing legend, but he suffered severe physical punishment. He lost the title in 1978 to upstart Leon Spinks, regained it later that year, and then retired. However, the lure of the ring brought Ali back for a 1980 match against Larry Holmes, who had succeeded him as champion. Holmes demolished Ali, who refused to answer the bell for round 11. Ali fought once more the following year and then retired.

The years immediately following his retirement were difficult, as he faced health, personal, and financial problems. However, Ali made a remarkable return to public life during the late 1990s. At the 1996 Olympic Games, he lit the Olympic flame.

In spite of his controversial stance on the Vietnam War, his legendary boxing career earned him widespread support. He eventually rejected the Nation of Islam's antiwhite rhetoric and adopted a more orthodox form of Islam, and in later years, he battled against Parkinson's disease. Ali was reborn as a cherished American icon because of his athletic prowess, his courage in speaking up for what he believes, and the moderation of his religious ideas. He remains one of the world's most beloved sports figures.

Michael Ezra

See also: African Americans; Boxing; Race and Race Relations.

Further Reading

Cottrell, John. *Muhammad Ali, Who Once Was Cassius Clay.* New York: Funk & Wagnalls, 1968.

Early, Gerald, ed. *The Muhammad Ali Reader.* Hopewell, NJ: Ecco, 1998.

Ezra, Michael. *Muhammad Ali: The Making of an Icon.* Philadelphia: Temple University Press, 2009.

Gorn, Elliott J., ed. *Muhammad Ali, the People's Champ.* Urbana: University of Illinois Press, 1995.

Hauser, Thomas. *Muhammad Ali: His Life and Times.* New York: Simon & Schuster, 1991.

Marqusee, Mike. *Redemption Song: Muhammad Ali and the Spirit of the Sixties.* London: Verso, 1999.

Remnick, David. *King of the World: Muhammad Ali and the Rise of an American Hero.* New York: Random House, 1998.

Sheed, Wilfrid. *Muhammad Ali: A Portrait in Words and Photographs.* New York: Crowell, 1975.

All-America Football Conference

The All-America Football Conference (AAFC) was a major professional football league that operated for four seasons (1946–1949) immediately after World War II, in competition with the National Football League (NFL). During its short life, the innovative AAFC was led by the Cleveland Browns, one of the top teams in professional football, and 15 of its players eventually were elected to the Pro Football Hall of Fame. War between the leagues ended with three AAFC teams merging into the NFL.

Arch Ward, sports editor of the *Chicago Tribune,* who had masterminded both the College All-Star Game in football and the Major League Baseball All-Star Game in the 1930s, believed that there was a sufficient market for two professional football leagues to exist and cooperate. By late 1944, however, when the AAFC publicized its plans, overt hostility from the NFL made it clear that coexistence was an unrealistic goal. Jim Crowley, a former member of Notre Dame University's renowned "Four Horsemen" backfield, became commissioner of the rival league.

The AAFC comprised eight teams: the Brooklyn Dodgers, Buffalo Bisons, Chicago Rockets, Cleveland Browns, Los Angeles Dons, Miami Seahawks, New York Yankees (whose owner, Dan Topping, had defected from the NFL), and San Francisco 49ers. Their proprietors were significantly wealthier than their peers in the NFL, whose football teams were their main source of income. AAFC owners included Arthur "Mickey" McBride of the Browns, a real estate and taxi magnate; John L. Keeshin, a Chicago trucking executive; and Benjamin Lindheimer of the Dons, a Chicago realtor and racetrack owner. The teams played at such spacious fields as New York's Yankee Stadium and Chicago's Soldier Field. The league, organized into two divisions, set up a double round-robin schedule of 14 games, and signed an unprecedented contract with United Airlines to fly its teams to away games.

The AAFC intended to begin play in 1945, but World War II pushed back their plans. Once the war was over, the AAFC's owners got into a bidding war with the NFL for talent, signing 44 of the 60 players from the 1946 College All-Stars, along with many veteran NFL players. Eventually, approximately 100 NFL veterans joined the AAFC, resulting in lawsuits over contracts—most notably, after former Heisman Trophy winner Angelo Bertelli signed contracts with both the Los Angeles Dons and the Boston Yanks of the NFL, and Chet Adams signed with both the Los Angeles Rams of the NFL and the Browns. Particularly significant was the breaking of pro football's color barrier when the Browns signed African Americans Marion Motley and Bill Willis before the 1946 season.

The first regular-season AAFC game took place on September 6, 1946, at Cleveland's Municipal Stadium, where a crowd of 60,135 watched the Browns defeat Miami, 44–0. Although the league lost money, attendance was surprisingly high, except in Miami, which was plagued by two hurricane-induced postponements. Cleveland drew more than 70,000 fans twice at home and became a popular road team, attracting 51,962 when they visited the Chicago Rockets.

The quality of play was high right from the start, although there was a talent gap between teams, and some cities had coaching turmoil. Miami replaced its coach in mid-season, Brooklyn went through three head coaches, and Chicago's Dick Hanley was fired after just three games, replaced by three players until Pat Boland took over. Cleveland finished 12–2–0 to win the Western Division, while New York took the East with a 10–3–1 mark. The Browns won the championship game, 14–9.

Before the 1947 season, the league dumped Miami, which had lost $80,000, and awarded the franchise to Baltimore, which played in Municipal Stadium. Admiral Jonas H. Ingram became the new commissioner, as Crowley resigned to become part owner and head coach of the tumultuous Chicago Rockets.

The AAFC's second year was its high point. Attendance was good—the Yankees and Dons drew more than 82,000 fans at the Los Angeles Memorial Coliseum—except in Brooklyn and Chicago (both cities had three pro teams), and the overall quality of play improved. A November match in New York between the Browns and Yankees, ending in a 28–28 tie, is regarded as the league's greatest game. The Yankees again won the East with an 11–2–1 record, while the Browns went 12–1–1 to capture the West. In the championship game, Cleveland won its second title, 14–3, before 61,879 fans. In a serious setback off the field, Arch Ward tried but failed to replace the NFL champion as the pro team in the College All-Star game with the AAFC champion Browns.

When play got under way in 1948, the Browns and 49ers dominated, while the rest of the teams took turns beating each other. Attendance declined. Cleveland piled up a perfect record of 14–0–0, handing San Francisco (12–2–0) its only losses by scores of 14–7 and 31–28. In the weaker East, Buffalo and Baltimore tied for first (7–7), with Buffalo prevailing in a playoff, 28–17. The Bisons subsequently were trounced 49–7 by Cleveland in the championship game.

By the end of the season, nearly every pro team had lost money, as attendance declined and player salaries continued to rise. In December, the two leagues began tentative efforts at peace talks. The AAFC wanted to merge four teams, but the NFL only wanted Cleveland and San Francisco, and negotiations broke down.

Going into the 1949 season, the AAFC had its third commissioner, Oliver O. Kessing, and Brooklyn merged with the Yankees, forming the Brooklyn-New York Yankees. Down to seven teams, the AAFC dropped its divisional alignment and cut back to a 12-game schedule. However, little changed on the gridiron, as Brooklyn-New York, Cleveland, and San Francisco remained the dominant teams in the league, although Cleveland's 18-game winning streak ended in the season opener with a 28–28 tie against Buffalo. Five weeks later, the 49ers snapped the Browns's 29-game unbeaten streak. In the postseason playoffs, Cleveland defeated Buffalo, while San Francisco beat Brooklyn-New York. In the championship game, the Browns won their fourth consecutive AAFC title, 21–7 over the 49ers.

The season was another financial disaster for both leagues, and within days of its close, they agreed on a merger that moved Baltimore, Cleveland, and San Francisco into the NFL. Players on the other teams were dispersed among NFL teams, mostly through a special draft. Escalating player salaries, falling attendance,

higher travel costs, and, ultimately, the dominance of the Cleveland Browns all contributed to the failure of the AAFC, which every year of its existence outdrew the NFL, helped integrate the sport, and promoted a higher quality of play.

Raymond Schmidt

See also: 49ers, San Francisco; Brown, Paul; Browns, Cleveland; Football, Professional.

Further Reading

Brown, Paul, with Jack Clary. *PB, the Paul Brown Story.* New York: Atheneum, 1979.

Coenen, Craig R. *From Sandlots to the Super Bowl: The National Football League, 1920–1967.* Knoxville: University of Tennessee Press, 2005.

Littlewood, Thomas B. *Arch: A Promoter, Not a Poet.* Ames: Iowa State University Press, 1990.

Piascik, Andy. *The Best Show in Football: The 1946–1955 Cleveland Browns, Pro Football's Greatest Dynasty.* Lanham, MD: Taylor Trade, 2007.

All-American Girls Baseball League

In the fall of 1942, less than a year after the United States entered World War II, the U.S. government announced that because of wartime manpower needs, professional sports would have to be curtailed or cancelled for 1943. The announcement prompted talk among Major League Baseball owners of devising alternative attractions to fill their stadiums.

Philip K. Wrigley, whose family controlled the Wrigley chewing gum company and owned the Chicago Cubs, came up with a viable option. Before the winter was over, Wrigley had formed the All-American Girls Softball League. He reasoned that women were working in wartime trades once thought to be suited only to men. Why not employ them on the baseball field?

Wrigley proposed to his fellow big league owners that they create women's teams for their big city ballparks, but few were interested. Undeterred, Wrigley proceeded anyway. He found a ready pool of talented players in the hundreds of women's recreational softball teams that blossomed in the 1930s, and he discovered a real enthusiasm for women's baseball in the smaller industrial cities of the upper Midwest.

Wrigley based the league on a nonprofit trustee organization, with himself, Brooklyn Dodgers president Branch Rickey, and Chicago Cubs attorney Paul V. Harper as trustees. He invested over $100,000 to establish the league and recruited leading businessmen in league cities as team underwriters. Each group of guarantors invested $22,500 toward their team's establishment and operation. Their responsibilities included promoting teams in their communities, recruiting local residents to house players, securing equipment, and administering facilities. Wrigley mandated that the league own all of the players and used an allocation procedure to equalize competition among teams.

Wrigley placed his four-team women's league in the war production cities of Kenosha and Racine, Wisconsin; Rockford, Illinois; and South Bend, Indiana. He recruited the best players from all over the United States and Canada through the Cubs' scouting system, hiring former professional male ballplayers as team managers. Wrigley employed chaperones to supervise the players, whom he required to adhere to strict rules governing their behavior on and off the field. In the first game, played on May 30, 1943, the South Bend Blue Sox defeated the Rockford Peaches 4–3 in 13 innings at South Bend's Bendix Field.

Wrigley believed in persistent advertising to ensure business success, and he applied this principle to the women's league. He also wanted the league to appeal to a broad spectrum of fans. Through prolific publicity, Wrigley and his advertising agent, Arthur E. Meyerhoff, emphasized the players' femininity, their strict rules of conduct, and their stylish uniforms. The league adopted skirted uniforms resembling the outfits then worn by women in tennis, golf, figure skating, and field hockey. In their advertising, Wrigley and Meyerhoff emphasized themes such as "Recreation for War Workers," "Family Entertainment," and "Community Welfare." The slogans remained fundamental promotional themes throughout the league's existence.

By the end of the 1944 season, it was clear that men's professional baseball would continue once World War II came to an end. Wrigley turned his attention back to the major leagues and sold the women's league to Meyerhoff, who continued many of Wrigley's policies, but changed the league's organization. Meyerhoff established franchises in each interested city, to be sold

A member of the Rockford Peaches slides safely into third during an All-American Girls Professional Baseball League game in 1946. The Peaches, featured in the 1992 film *A League of Their Own,* won four AAGPBL titles between 1945 and 1950. *(Transcendental Graphics/Getty Images)*

to local backers and supported by a percentage of gate receipts. He also changed the name of the organization to the All-American Girls Baseball League.

Meyerhoff made several innovations over the next six seasons. Most noteworthy, in 1948, the pitching style changed from underhand to overhand, the base paths were lengthened to 72 feet (22 meters), the pitching distance was extended to 50 feet (15 meters), and the ball's circumference was reduced from 12 inches (30.5 centimeters) to 10.375 inches (26.3 centimeters). A 10-inch (25.4-centimeter) ball with red seams was introduced in 1949. It remained in use until it was replaced by the regulation 9-inch (22.8-centimeter) baseball on July 1, 1954. Teams played more than 100 games a season from mid-May through mid-September. Player salaries ranged from $45 to $125 per week. Top players, such as Dorothy Kamenshek and Dorothy "Snookie" Doyle, commanded the highest salaries.

Meyerhoff also initiated recognition of All-Star players, the creation of a minor league in Chicago, the operation of rookie touring teams, and league-wide Southern spring training camps in Pascagoula, Mississippi (1946); Havana, Cuba (1947); and Opa-Locka, Florida (1948). Through the training camp in Cuba, several Cuban players became members of All-American teams, and league players found opportunities for postseason exhibition tours in Central America, Cuba, Puerto Rico, and Venezuela.

By 1949, the teams were having more and more trouble staying afloat. The postwar economy was booming, and people had more money and more recreational choices. Believing that Meyerhoff's administration was spending too much, the team owners established their own league administration after the 1950 season and cut costs. Nonetheless, deficits continued to grow. Between 1951 and 1954, the league dwindled from eight teams to five, and the club presidents halted operations on February 1, 1955.

The All-American Girls Baseball League was fondly remembered in the popular 1992 film *A League of Their Own,* featuring Geena Davis, Tom Hanks, and Madonna.

Merrie A. Fidler

See also: Baseball, Semiprofessional; Women.

Further Reading

Berlage, Gai Ingham. *Women in Baseball: The Forgotten History.* Westport, CT: Praeger, 1994.

Browne, Lois. *Girls of Summer: In Their Own League.* Toronto, Canada: HarperCollins, 1992.

Fidler, Merrie A. *The Origins and History of the All-American Girls Professional Baseball League.* Jefferson, NC: McFarland, 2006.

Gregorich, Barbara. *Women at Play: The Story of Women in Baseball.* San Diego: Harcourt Brace, 1993.

Heaphy, Leslie A., and Mel Anthony May, eds. *Encyclopedia of Women and Baseball.* Jefferson, NC: McFarland, 2006.

Johnson, Susan E. *When Women Played Hardball.* Seattle, WA: Seal, 1994.

Macy, Sue. *A Whole New Ball Game: The Story of the All-American Girls Professional Baseball League.* New York: Henry Holt, 1993.

Madden, W.C. *The Women of the All-American Girls Professional Baseball League: A Biographical Dictionary.* Jefferson, NC: McFarland, 1997.

Amateur Athletic Union

For nearly a century, from its founding in 1888 until 1979, the Amateur Athletic Union (AAU) governed amateur sports in the United States, with a particular emphasis on track and field. It was established by elite athletic clubs to maintain strict standards of amateurism through the sanctioning of competitions and the disciplining of athletes. The AAU represented the conservative social and cultural values of upper- and upper-middle-class whites in the United States. In the late 1960s, however, many athletes began to question the authoritarian policies of the organization, leading to its decline.

The AAU was created in 1888 by the New York Athletic Club and similar sports groups to maintain strict standards of amateurism. Modeled on England's Amateur Athletic Association, the AAU replaced the National Association of Amateur Athletes of America (1879–1888), which had been accused of mismanagement and failure to stimulate interest in sports beyond metropolitan New York. The AAU's fundamental principle was that sports should serve as its own reward; athletes were forbidden to receive remuneration for playing and coaching or to "capitalize" on their fame. It was implicit that upper-class amateur athletes should not compete with lower-class professional athletes.

The AAU's first secretary was James E. Sullivan, a 26-year-old track athlete, the self-educated son of an Irish immigrant railroad worker, and the publicist for the Spalding sporting goods company. Until his death in 1914, Sullivan was known as the "czar" of amateur sport. From its start, the AAU moved aggressively to establish formal agreements with the governing bodies of individual amateur sports and collegiate sports in the United States, as well as with athletic associations in Canada and Great Britain. It encompassed virtually all of the Olympic sports and the American Olympic Committee. The AAU disdained women's athletics.

The AAU's Board of Governors was composed of wealthy and socially prominent white men who sought to protect the established social order by preaching the values of mass recreational sport. They dealt harshly with perceived violations, often hypocritically and with prejudice. Lifetime bans were meted out for the receipt of excessive expense money to champion sprinter and Irish American Arthur Duffey of Georgetown University (1905) and to Abel R. Kiviat, the Jewish 1,500-meter (1,640-yard) world record holder (1915) and captain of the Irish American Athletic Club. The most notable scapegoat was Jim Thorpe, pentathlon and decathlon winner at the 1912 Olympic Games in Stockholm, Sweden. The AAU pushed the International Olympic Committee to strip Thorpe of his medals and records and to permanently suspend him from amateur sports, because he had played semiprofessional baseball while in college. These three men represented minority ethnic or religious institutions, whereas other athletes charged with similar violations went unpunished.

Fred Rubien succeeded Sullivan as secretary-treasurer in 1914 and consolidated his predecessor's gains. His tenure was marked by an escalating power struggle with the National Collegiate Athletic Association (NCAA) over the right to register athletes for amateur competitions and control of the American Olympic Committee. In 1927, Avery Brundage, an Olympic competitor in the decathlon in 1912 and a wealthy Chicago builder, became the AAU's president. He reached an accord with the NCAA in 1929–1930, granting it greater control of its own athletes and a prominent role in the Olympics. This freed the AAU to focus on more constructive development. In track and field, swimming, and boxing, the 1930s marked the heyday of amateur sports in America.

Dan Ferris took over as secretary-treasurer in 1927. A former sprinter for the Irish American Athletic Club and a newspaper reporter, he had worked for the AAU since 1907. Ferris had a well-earned reputation as a "tiger" in adhering to the amateur code. Yet the soft-spoken Ferris also gained renown in world capitals as a diplomat. He was tested by controversies at home, such as the debate over U.S. participation in the 1936 Olympic Games in Berlin. AAU President Jeremiah T. Mahoney, a former New York Supreme Court judge, joined with prominent Catholic, liberal Protestant, and Jewish spokesmen to promote a boycott of the games

that was only narrowly defeated. Mahoney did not stand for reelection, and Brundage returned to the presidency of the AAU.

Brundage was ambivalent about the role of women in sport, but as AAU president, he supported female participation in the AAU track championships in 1924, one of the few competitions then open to women. In 1952, Ferris called for "more co-ed sports," and within a few years, a series of dual track meets between the United States and the Soviet Union under AAU auspices opened new avenues for talented women.

The AAU under Ferris was an expansive and dominating force, but in the post–World War II era, elite athletes and coaches questioned the effectiveness and relevance of the AAU's policies and programs, spurring drastic changes. They pushed the AAU to become a leader in basketball for college graduates in small Western towns and cities. Its centerpiece was the annual AAU tournament (first played in 1898) held in Kansas City, Missouri, from 1921 through 1934 and then in Denver, Colorado, from 1935 to 1968. The basketball champions typically were large corporations such as Phillips Petroleum and Peoria Caterpillar, which recruited players with the promise of job training and career advancement. Although the AAU defined these leagues as amateur, many observers considered them semiprofessional, as the companies gave players jobs in return for their play. The AAU tournament was discontinued in 1968 due to the growth of the National Basketball Association and professional basketball.

By the close of Ferris's long tenure in 1957, the AAU's control over amateur athletics was being widely questioned, especially by the NCAA, for promoting its self-interest rather than that of athletes—charges that had far-reaching implications in the Cold War era, when the United States was trying to defeat the Soviet Union in international competitions. Many even began to consider the distinction between amateur and professional athletes to be obsolete.

In 1962, gymnastics, track, and basketball formed their own federations, which the AAU refused to recognize. AAU control of Olympic sports continued. Following the 1972 Olympics, the NCAA withdrew from the United States Olympic Committee (USOC), prompting President Gerald Ford to appoint a blue-ribbon Presidential Commission on Olympic Sports. Its recommendations eventually led to passage of the Amateur Sports Act of 1978, which reorganized the USOC into a coordinating agency for the nation's amateur sports and required the AAU to divest itself of its Olympic sports divisions.

Thereafter, the AAU shifted its focus from elite athletes to broad-based participatory programs. Its headquarters in Orlando, Florida, currently administers a youth program in 32 sports, gives annual physical fitness tests to millions of students, and runs adult programs in sports and fitness. The organization continues to honor the nation's outstanding amateur athlete each year with the James E. Sullivan Memorial Award.

Alan S. Katchen

See also: Amateurism; Intercollegiate Athletic Associations and Conferences; Olympics, Summer.

Further Reading

Cahn, Susan K. *Coming on Strong: Gender and Sexuality in Twentieth-Century Women's Sport.* New York: Free Press, 1994.

Flath, Arnold William. *A History of Relations Between the National Collegiate Athletic Association and the Amateur Athletic Union of the United States (1905–1963).* Champaign, IL: Stipes, 1964.

Grundman, Adolph H. *The Golden Age of Amateur Basketball: The AAU Tournament, 1921–1968.* Lincoln: University of Nebraska Press, 2004.

Hunt, Thomas M. "Countering the Soviet Threat in the Olympic Medals Race: The Amateur Sports Act of 1978 and the American Athletics Policy Reform." *International Journal of the History of Sport* 24:6 (June 2007): 796–818.

Lucas, John. "The Hegemonic Rule of the American Amateur Athletic Union 1888–1914: James Edward Sullivan as Prime Mover." *International Journal of the History of Sport* 11:3 (December 1994): 355–371.

Turrini, Joseph M. *The End of Amateurism in American Track and Field.* Urbana: University of Illinois Press, 2010.

Amateurism

In the context of sports, an amateur athlete is unpaid, a participant who ostensibly "plays fair" and engages in sports for the love of the game. The amateur's counterpart is the professional athlete, whose primary motive is presumed to be financial gain. The distinction between the two—along with an ideology that celebrated the amateur as purer and more noble than the professional—emerged at the same time that modern organized sports began to develop in the mid-nineteenth century. Consequently, the ideology of amateurism had a dramatic impact on the founders of many important athletic movements and organizations, most notably the Olympics and the National Collegiate Athletic Association (NCAA). Over time, however, the amateur ideal has come under attack and has been substantially watered down.

Birth of Amateurism

The late Victorian era witnessed a blossoming of organized sports, particularly among the laboring classes. Wealthy Britons and Americans feared for the sanctity of the sports they enjoyed and looked to protect them from the pernicious influence—as they saw it—of working-class athletes, particularly those skillful enough to make a living as sportsmen.

Thus the first known definition of amateurism, penned by British rower Edwin S. Brickwood in 1866, was highly elitist, including only military offices, government officials, attorneys, clergymen, physicians, college men, graduates of English public (private boarding) schools, and members of clubs; it excluded tradesmen or working mechanics. In fact, a significant point in the development of amateurship came in 1873 when the entrance rules for Great Britain's Henley regatta stipulated that manual laborers, artisans, tradesmen, and mechanics were considered professionals and could not participate. In practice, the British model revolved around strict class bias against athletes not of upper-class birth, because they were not considered gentlemen. Ultimately, the British defined an athlete as a professional if he played for pay or taught sports, or if his principal job provided him with undue exercise and gave him an advantage in muscular development over sedentary workers or members of the leisure class.

The need to create a clear distinction between amateur and professional arose out of three specific concerns on the part of British and American elites. The first was the corrupting influence of money. Elites feared that teams might be torn apart if players were loyal to an employer rather than to their teammates, or that games and matches would be subject to bribery and other chicanery. Second was ensuring a level playing field. They were concerned that if amateur athletes were compelled to compete against stronger, faster, and more experienced professionals, they would lose enthusiasm and stop participating in sports. The final concern was preserving the spirit and etiquette of fair play. Elites believed that they could be counted on to understand and maintain standards of chivalry and gentlemanly behavior, while the lower classes could not.

It should be clear, then, that from the beginning, the ideology of amateurism blended noble impulses—upholding chivalry, ensuring a level playing field, and maintaining the integrity of sporting contests—with more than a tinge of elitism. Further, the men who promoted this ideology naturally were most concerned about the sports in which they themselves competed. Therefore, amateurism always has been most important in the sports favored by the well-to-do, such as collegiate athletics, golf, rowing, tennis, and track and field.

In the United States, the foremost early advocate of amateurism was William B. Curtis, who is remembered as the "Father of American Amateur Athletics." An outstanding all-around athlete and a former seminarian, Curtis was a firm believer in the philosophy of "muscular Christianity," which valued sports as a means of ennobling the soul. In 1867, he opened a gymnasium in New York City, and the next year, he founded, together with Henry Buermeyer and John Babcock, the New York Athletic Club.

Curtis served as president of the club for several years, and then left in 1879 to become editor of *The Spirit of the Times*. In his 20 years at the helm of the journal, he transformed it into the preeminent sporting publication of the era. During that time, Curtis also helped found the Amateur Athletic Union (AAU) and served as the organization's treasurer and president.

Curtis utilized the platform afforded by *The Spirit of the Times* to advocate the ideals of amateurism, promoting honesty, honor, and gentlemanly behavior. At the same time, he railed against what he called the "Barnumization" of sport—after the famed circus promoter P.T. Barnum, who was known for being phony and dishonest. The editor had a special bias against blood sports, particularly professional boxing, believing that they diminished the moral fiber of participants and spectators. He also labored to eliminate gambling, which often led to fixed contests, or "hippodroming" in the parlance of the day.

Curtis's New York Athletic Club began emulating the British amateur codes in the 1870s. It allowed only men who had never competed for pay with professionals for a prize or taught athletics as a living to compete. These requirements were adopted three years later by the National Association of Amateur Athletes of America. Theses rules made sports more class based and also eliminated as potential athletic competitors anyone who worked at play, trained more diligently, and practiced against other full-time athletes.

Unlike the English, however, American "gentlemen" athletes had little compunction about winning at all costs, and not all clubs held strictly to the guidelines. Consequently, in 1888, the New York Athletic Club organized the AAU to tighten up enforcement. James E. Sullivan, who served as the AAU's secretary or president from 1889 to 1914, diligently enforced its strict amateur codes, barring any athlete who competed for prizes or money.

Curtis was not wholly opposed to professional sports, however. He believed that professional athletes could have honor and dignity, as long as they were of good character and eschewed the unwholesome aspects of sports, particularly gambling and contest fixing. Moreover, he lambasted some of the amateur athletic associations for their elitism. He even criticized the AAU on occasion, arguing that the organization had a responsibility not merely to monitor codes of amateurism for the benefit of a few gifted athletes but to encourage athletics for everyone.

Olympic Games

The modern Olympics resulted from the efforts of Baron Pierre de Coubertin, who founded the International Olympic Committee (IOC) in 1890. An aristocratic Frenchman, Coubertin was an enthusiastic believer in the ideology of amateurism. At its first meeting, the IOC decided that the first Olympic Games would be held in Athens, Greece, in 1896. Following Coubertin's lead, the organization decreed that only amateur athletes would be allowed to participate. This remained the official IOC policy for nearly a century.

In the early years of the Olympic movement, the rules regarding amateurism were enforced strictly. In 1912, for example, American Jim Thorpe won the pentathlon and the decathlon. Then, it was discovered that he once had been paid to play amateur baseball. This was not unusual, as most elite athletes at the time earned pocket money in this way. Thorpe's mistake, however, was using his real name instead of an alias, which made it easy to verify his participation. As a result, he was stripped of his Olympic medals.

Thorpe's experience illustrates flaws in the ideology of amateurism that had become apparent even in the early years of the Olympic movement. It takes a great deal of time and energy to become an elite athlete. As early as the 1910s or 1920s, it was impossible to earn a living and still have the time needed to train for world-class competition in most disciplines. In this circumstance, amateurism did not level the playing field. In fact, it threatened to do the exact opposite—to make certain that only wealthy people who did not need to work could compete in the Olympic Games.

By the 1970s, the pressure on the IOC to dispense with its restrictions on professional athletes had grown intense. However, IOC Chairman Avery Brundage, who prided himself on being "the last pillar of the Olympic idea," remained resolute, insisting that there would be no change in the rules on his watch.

Shortly before the 1972 Winter Olympics at Sapporo, Japan, Brundage unsuccessfully tried to keep out skiers who had earned money as coaches. The IOC ultimately decided to ban only the most egregious offender, legendary Austrian skier Karl Schranz. Brundage retired several months later. He was succeeded by Lord Killanin and then Juan Antonio Samaranch, both of whom were far more open to change.

In 1981, a number of different types of income for athletes were legalized: They could sell sponsorships, accept subsidies, teach classes, or coach individuals and still remain "amateurs." In 1983, the IOC took a major symbolic step when it posthumously restored Thorpe's medals. Finally, in 1991, the IOC dispensed with nearly all of its remaining restrictions on professional athletes, clearing the way for the 1992 "Dream Team" of American NBA superstars. Today, the only Olympic sport that still is restricted to amateurs is boxing. This distinction is not made for ideological reasons, but because of safety concerns.

College Sports

American colleges, particularly those whose sports were highly commercialized, long skirted the issue of amateurism. In the late nineteenth century, college baseball teams often had professionals on the rosters, and, at the turn of the century, players often earned money by playing for pay during the summer. College football teams lured top players, some of whom jumped from school to school, with room and board, tuition, easy classes, junkets, and paid vacations. These practices were criticized by muckraking journalists and a few sports writers, notably Caspar Whitney, who was less concerned about the class elements of amateurism than he was about having middle- and upper-class athletes adhere to the amateur code and follow the precepts of good sportsmanship.

Founded in 1905, the NCAA, like the IOC, was established when the ideology of amateurism was in full bloom. The NCAA's first formal definition of amateurism, adopted in 1916, stated, "An amateur is one who participates in competitive physical sports only for the pleasure, and the physical, moral, and social benefits derived there from."

The NCAA strongly opposed all benefits for college athletes, including athletic scholarships. However, athletic contests were an important source of revenue for universities, and they attracted much positive media attention. Victories served to make alumni happy, keeping donations flowing, and also gave voters a connection to the state schools that their tax dollars funded.

Under these circumstances, administrators spent much money on coaches, equipment, training facilities, and recruitment. Sports stars were given jobs they did not have to actually work at, loans they did not have to repay, or outright cash payments from secret university slush funds. A 1929 study found that 81 of the NCAA's 112 member schools were compensating athletes in one way or another. That same year, the term "shamateurism"—describing a situation in which athletes pretend to be amateurs but are not—first appeared in the sports pages.

The NCAA of the 1920s was not powerful enough to punish schools for violating the tenets of amateurism. Finally, in the 1950s, the organization settled on a "carrot and stick" approach to the problem. The "stick," which came first, was that the NCAA began to sanction schools that violated the organization's guidelines. The penalties range in severity, from warning letters and small fines up to the most draconian punishment of all—the NCAA "death penalty." The death penalty is reserved for schools that commit gross violations of NCAA rules on multiple occasions. When it is levied, a school is required to completely suspend the offending sport for a period of one or more years, granting no scholarships and playing no games. This punishment has been imposed only five times, beginning with the University of Kentucky basketball program, which was forced to forgo its 1952–1953 season.

The "carrot" was implemented in 1957, when the NCAA declared that athletic scholarships were acceptable after all. Critics argued that this represented a form of payment, as college athletes were earning something in exchange for their play. NCAA officials took the position that athletic scholarships were similar to academic scholarships.

Then in 1973, the NCAA decided that athletic scholarships would not be conferred for four years. Instead athletes would be granted a series of one-year scholarships, with each subsequent year being renewable at the discretion of the university. With these changes, it is difficult to argue that modern athletic scholarships do not function as a form of salary, as athletes are "paid" when performing well and are vulnerable to being "fired" if they are no longer needed.

A Surviving Ideology

The cases of the NCAA and the Olympics are the two most prominent examples of how the ideology of amateurism has been challenged and forced to evolve over time. They certainly are not the only examples, however. In particular, competitive tennis and golf existed primarily as amateur sports through the 1930s and 1940s, then became hybrid amateur-professional sports in the 1950s and 1960s, and finally emerged as predominantly professional by the 1970s.

In all of these cases, the ideology of amateurism is not nearly as strong as it once was, but it is not dead, either. It still echoes in the philosophy and the spirit of the Olympics. Many college athletes—Ivy Leaguers and those at Division III schools—still adhere to the notion of amateurism as it was understood in 1916, playing sports without benefit of athletic scholarships. The United States Tennis Association still stages important annual tournaments for amateurs, as does the United States Golf Association. The amateur ideology thus seems poised to survive, albeit in a scaled-down form, well into the twenty-first century.

Christopher G. Bates and Paul J. DeLoca

See also: Amateur Athletic Union; Athletic Clubs; Business of Sports; Class, Economic and Social; Endorsements, Athlete; Little League Baseball; Military, Sports and the; Olympics, Summer; Olympics, Winter; Physical Education; Public Schools Athletic League; Sokol Movement; Turnvereins; Young Men's Christian Association and Young Women's Christian Association; Young Men's/Women's Hebrew Association.

Further Reading

Allison, Lincoln. *Amateurism in Sport: An Analysis and a Defence.* London: Frank Cass, 2001.

Guttmann, Allen. *The Games Must Go On: Avery Brundage and the Olympic Movement.* New York: Columbia University Press, 1984.

Pope, Stephen W. *Patriotic Games: Sporting Traditions in the American Imagination, 1876–1926.* New York: Oxford University Press, 1997.

Smith, Ronald A. *Sports and Freedom: The Rise of Big-Time College Athletics.* New York: Oxford University Press, 1988.

American Basketball Association

The American Basketball Association (ABA) was a professional basketball league founded in 1967 that challenged the monopoly of the National Basketball Association (NBA). It survived until 1976, when four of the remaining franchises joined the NBA and three disbanded. The ABA introduced many innovations to the game and employed some of the most spectacular players of its era, helping to popularize a high-flying style of basketball. The ABA was one of the most successful challengers to an established sports league in modern times.

A number of basketball entrepreneurs were dissatisfied with the NBA because of its slow pace of expansion. From 1952 to 1961, the NBA had just eight teams. In the next five years, under great pressure to expand, it added only two more teams. The time seemed right for a new league.

From the beginning, the ABA aimed to attract fans by encouraging a different style of play. The league adopted the 3-point shot from the short-lived American Basketball League, which had challenged the NBA for two seasons (1961–1963). A less radical rule change was to extend the NBA's 24-second clock to 30 seconds to allow more time for pattern offenses. In addition, the league used eye-catching equipment and uniforms. The official ball was colored red, white, and blue.

The new league began play in the 1967–1968 season with 11 teams. Initially, it hoped to induce established NBA players to sign with the ABA for more money, but few did. Players were drawn from the minor Eastern League, Amateur Athletic Union teams, and colleges through the ABA's draft. In addition, the league signed players who had been blacklisted by the NBA for scandals involving gambling and bribery (though they never were convicted), including Roger Brown, Connie Hawkins, Tony Jackson, Doug Moe, and Charlie Williams.

The league lost about $2.5 million in its first year, but all 11 teams finished the season. There were 11 teams the next year as well, though some had moved to different cities. The Pittsburgh Pipers, led by Connie Hawkins, defeated the New Orleans Buccaneers with Doug Moe and Larry Brown to win the first ABA championship. The Pipers moved to Minnesota the next season, replacing the Muskies, who moved to Miami. This franchise hopping continued throughout the life of the league, with no fewer than 16 franchise changes in nine years.

In 1968, superstar Rick Barry, the 1966–1967 NBA scoring champion for the San Francisco Warriors, joined the ABA's Oakland Oaks. He had signed a contract the previous year, but a superior court ruling enjoined him from playing for any team but the Warriors. He sat out the season before joining the Oaks in 1968–1969. Barry's impressive scoring, together with the addition of Larry Brown, Doug Moe, and top rookies such as Warren Armstrong, led Oakland to the championship. The Oaks' Alex Hannum was named Coach of the Year, an honor he previously had won in the NBA with the Warriors (1963–1964).

In 1969, the Denver Nuggets signed Spencer Haywood, the star of the 1968 U.S. Olympic basketball team. Haywood had completed only one year at Trinidad State Junior College and one at the University of Detroit and had not finished his college eligibility. The NBA, whose teams were not allowed to sign undergraduates, protested, but the league soon altered its stance, fearing that it would continue to lose young players to the ABA. Haywood gained wide attention, leading the ABA in scoring and rebounding in his first season, but the league's gains were offset when stars Rick Barry and Connie Hawkins defected to the NBA. Barry was forced to complete his ABA contract, playing for one year in Washington, D.C., where the Oakland franchise had relocated, and for two years in New York with the Nets. Negotiations between the two leagues were suspended, as both were signing the other's players.

The ABA struggled against poor attendance and the lack of a television contract, but in 1971, the league signed collegiate stars Artis Gilmore and Julius "Dr. J" Erving. The networks began reconsidering the ABA, and in 1973, the league signed a limited contract with HBO.

The two leagues continued battling each other, but they did agree to exhibition games. The upstart ABA held its own, winning 79 of 155 of interleague games between 1971 and 1975. The ABA also played two closely contested All-Star games against the NBA, losing 125–120 in 1971 and 106–104 a year later.

The ABA lost a franchise during the 1972–1973 season and continued to struggle. The following year, Wilt Chamberlain was signed as a player-coach in San Diego, a move that was expected to bolster fan interest; however, the Los Angeles Lakers obtained an injunction to prevent Chamberlain from playing, because he still owed them the option year on his contract. The next year, he resigned as coach, and he never played in the ABA.

In 1974–1975, the Carolina franchise moved to St. Louis as the Spirits and hired young Bob Costas as their radio announcer. By then, rumors of the ABA's imminent collapse were rampant. In 1975, the Utah Stars signed Moses Malone directly out of high school, and his phenomenal success opened the door for more high school signings over the next 30 years. The Kentucky Colonels, led by Artis Gilmore, won the ABA title and challenged the NBA champions, the Golden State Warriors, to a series, but to no avail.

After that season, the ABA named Dave DeBusschere, the former New York Knicks Hall of Famer and New York Nets general manager, as league commissioner. The ABA started the 1975–1976 season with nine teams, but only seven finished, and it became clear that the ABA could not survive.

DeBusschere negotiated a deal with the NBA that allowed the New York Nets, the Indiana Pacers, the Denver Nuggets, and the San Antonio Spurs to join the NBA. The other three ABA franchises—Kentucky, St. Louis, and Virginia—folded. The merger brought new stars to the NBA, increased television interest, and eliminated the battle for young talent coming out of high school and college.

Murry R. Nelson

See also: Basketball, Professional, NBA Era.

Further Reading

Bradley, Robert. *Compendium of Professional Basketball.* Tempe, AZ: Xaler, 1999.

Neft, David. *The Sports Encyclopedia: Pro Basketball.* New York: St. Martin's, 1975.

Pluto, Terry. *Loose Balls: The Short, Wild Life of the American Basketball Association.* New York: Simon & Schuster, 1990.

Shouler, Ken, Bob Ryan, Sam Smith, Leonard Koppett, and Bob Belotti, eds. *Total Basketball: The Ultimate Basketball Encyclopedia.* Wilmington, DE: Sports Classics, 2003.

America's Cup

A prestigious international yacht racing award, the America's Cup is the oldest active trophy in world sports competition. In 1851, the Royal Yacht Squadron of Great Britain invited five members of the fledgling New York Yacht Club to enter the running of its annual race around the Isle of Wight. The New York club built a sleek racing schooner named *America,* designed by George Steers. Unexpectedly, *America* defeated its British competitors handily.

The owners of *America* kept the trophy awarded for their victory and brought it back to the United States. In 1857, they presented it to the New York Yacht Club, with the stipulation that any foreign yacht club should have the right to challenge for it. Beginning in 1870, American yachts successfully defended the America's Cup 25 straight times in more than 100 years—a record sometimes considered the longest winning streak in sports.

The first six America's Cup series (1870–1886) consisted of competitions between two very different types of yachts. The American defenders tended to have low, broad hulls with shallow keels or retractable centerboards for stability, and carried their mast well forward of the midpoint. The British and Canadian challengers tended to have high, narrow hulls with deep keels; they carried their mast at or just ahead of the midpoint. British yachtsmen noted that their boats were more habitable and seaworthy, but the Americans won the races. The 1887 British challenger, *Thistle,* was built broad and shallow in the American style, but it was soundly beaten by the Americans' even broader and shallower *Volunteer.*

America's Cup competitors, like all yachts of the era, were assigned a rating—a rough measure of their performance that enabled dissimilar vessels to compete on equal terms. The formula used to determine the ratings was changed in 1888, and designers quickly took advantage of this change.

Nathanael Greene Herreshoff, whose yachts defended the America's Cup five times between 1893 and 1903, pushed the formula the most, designing the *Vigilant* (1893), *Defender* (1895), *Columbia* (1899, 1901), and *Reliance* (1903), ships that were very large but extremely light. Shallow "skimming dish" hulls with towering masts and huge expanses of sail, they were pure racing machines, totally impractical for any other purpose. They could reach 15 knots in a moderate breeze but risked catastrophic equipment failures in anything stronger. Alarmed, New York Yacht Club officials sought to establish a new rating rule that would penalize such extremism.

The new rule, drafted by Herreshoff himself, took effect in 1904, and it was applied formally to future America's Cup series in 1910. The first challenge under the new rule, in 1920, featured boats that were somewhat smaller but significantly more seaworthy than their immediate predecessors. That year's race also broke with tradition by moving the course from the approaches to New York Harbor to the less constricted and less crowded waters off Newport, Rhode Island. The defending yacht was skippered by an amateur, not a paid captain—also unusual for the time—though the physically demanding work of sail handling continued to be done by a paid crew.

A further break with tradition took place ten years later, when J-class yachts were designated the official boat of America's Cup competition, and handicaps were eliminated because all such boats were, for scoring purposes, considered to be equally competitive. They had a waterline length of 79 feet (24.1 meters) to 87 feet (26.5 meters), an overall length of 120 feet (36.5 meters), and a displacement of up to 160 tons (145 metric tons). Conceived during the booming 1920s, these yachts competed for the America's Cup only in 1930, 1934, and 1937. The 1930 race marked the fifth and final challenge by Sir Thomas Lipton, the self-made British tea magnate. After the 1937 race, the

Great Depression and World War II temporarily put off any plans for further challenges.

The next challenge took place in 1958, and it was governed by completely new specifications for the yachts. The J-class yachts were too large and too expensive. Instead, the new standard was the 12-Meter class, which was relatively smaller and cheaper. The 12-Meter era (1958–1992) marked the first time the America's Cup was contested on a regular schedule: once every three to four years. It was also the only time in the history of the America's Cup that amateurs dominated the competition.

The amateur skippers of the 1920s and 1930s had been independently wealthy men who were comfortable handling giant yachts and paid crewmen. By contrast, the 12-Meter skippers tended to have white-collar jobs and hold championship records in small as well as large vessels. The 12-Meter crews of the 1960s and 1970s were mostly amateurs who could afford to leave their jobs for the duration of a "Cup summer." The brief all-amateur era ended in the early 1980s, when hard-driving skippers such as Dennis Conner began to insist that their crews train year-round and be paid by the syndicate that funded their boat.

Early in the 12-Meter era, Australia emerged as a serious threat to American dominance. The first Australian challenger, *Gretel* (1962), was fast and aggressively sailed and might have won the series were it not for a spectacular performance by American skipper Emil "Bus" Mosbacher. Finally, in 1983, an Australian challenger succeeded. *Australia II,* designed by Ben Lexcen, was smaller than most 12-Meter yachts and employed a smaller than normal keel with horizontal "wings" at its tip. The innovative design gave the yacht less wetted surface, less drag, and thus better speed than the American defender *Liberty,* which *Australia II* defeated 4–3 in a seven-race series. Following the America's Cup tradition, the next challenge was held in Australian waters in 1987. The U.S. craft *Stars and Stripes* defeated Australia's *Kookaburra III* off Fremantle, Australia. This marked the end of the 12-Meter era.

In a controversial 1988 series, New Zealand and the United States entered ships of wildly divergent designs, sparking a controversy that ultimately was decided in the U.S. courts in favor of the American defender. Following the disputed result, a new International America's Cup Class boat design was designated the vessel of choice for future America's Cup competition.

In the first two International America's Cup Class challenges, the United States won in 1995 and lost to New Zealand in the finals in 1998. In 2000, 2003, and

In 1987, the U.S. 12-Meter yacht *Stars and Stripes (right)*, captained by Dennis Conner, won back the America's Cup by defeating Australia's *Kookaburra III (left)*. In 1983, Conner had suffered the first Cup defeat for the New York Yacht Club in 132 years. *(Tony Feder/Stringer/Getty Images)*

2007, the United States failed to make the finals. New Zealand successfully defended the America's Cup in 2000 but lost in 2003 to *Alinghi,* representing Switzerland. *Alinghi* successfully defended the Cup in 2007. The competition took place off the Atlantic coast of Spain, as Switzerland, the Cup-holding nation, had no sea frontage of its own.

The United States returned to the front ranks of the competition in 2010, when the Golden Gate Yacht Club's *BMW Oracle Racing* defeated Switzerland's *Alinghi* 2–0 to take the Cup and the right to host the 2011 match in the waters off San Francisco, where the club is headquartered.

A. Bowdoin Van Riper

See also: Bennett, James G., Jr.; Class, Economic and Social; Yacht Racing.

Further Reading

Conner, Dennis, and Michael Levitt. *The America's Cup: The History of Sailing's Greatest Competition in the Twentieth Century.* New York: St. Martin's, 1998.

Shaw, David W. *America's Victory: The Heroic Story of a Team of Ordinary Americans, and How They Won the Greatest Yacht Race Ever.* New York: Free Press, 2002.

Whipple, Addison B.C. *The Racing Yachts.* Alexandria, VA: Time-Life, 1980.

Archery

Use of the bow and arrow, a weapon that dates to prehistoric times, became a recreational sport in England during the fifteenth and sixteenth centuries, after the weapon no longer was employed in military combat. The sport of bow and arrow, known as archery, developed slowly in North America during the late nineteenth century, but it enjoyed huge growth by the 1930s for hunting game and competitive target shooting. In competition, the United States dominated the sport for decades, winning 12 of 16 men's world championships from 1957 to 1985, and 14 team titles in 1957 and 1959–1983. Currently, there are more than 10 million archers in the United States.

North American archery was based on the example of Native Americans and the English bowmen who fought the French in the Hundred Years' War (1337–1453). Painter Titian Ramsay Peale was fascinated with these traditions, and his interest prompted the formation of the United Bowmen of Philadelphia in 1828, the first archery club in North America. It usually had 16 to 20 members at any time. They used longbows at practice matches and tournaments for 30 years, until the club stopped holding contests in 1859. Interest switched to baseball, boat racing, and horse racing.

U.S. archery receded during the Civil War years, resuming in the late 1870s as a popular pastime, still dominated by the middle and upper classes. The revival is credited to lawyer and writer Maurice Thompson, who as a child made bows and arrows to hunt game. He regarded archery as a healthful pastime that demanded physical and mental discipline. Thompson increased interest in the sport with his books *Hunting with the Long Bow* (1877) and *The Witchery of Archery* (1878), preferring shooting as a roving bowman, although he recognized that most people preferred stationary target shooting.

Thompson encouraged women to participate because, he said, the sport developed left- and right-hand balance and promoted muscle tone and a beautiful physique. He believed that if women approached men in physical power, they also would earn greater respect for their minds. In 1877, the Ladies Club for Outdoor Sports (primarily a tennis club) on Staten Island was organized; by 1880, there were more than 25 women's clubs. Archery became a popular activity among female college students.

On August 12, 1879, the eight-club National Archery Association held its first tournament at Chicago's White Stocking Park. The event was favorably reviewed by *Harper's Weekly* (the cover art depicted a women's archery club on Staten Island), which noted the presence of ladies and gentlemen of high status. In the tournament, women used smaller and lighter bows, but otherwise competed on an equal footing with men in target shooting. William H. Thompson won the gentlemen's medal, using the distances established by the English National Association. In the team event, four archers shot "American" rounds of 30 arrows per man at distances of 40, 50, and 60 yards (37, 46, and 55 meters).

Interest in archery declined at the turn of the century, although the sport was included in the 1900 Olympic Games in Paris. Four years later, at the Games in St. Louis, Missouri, only Americans competed. They won all 17 medals, including three gold medals won by 45-year-old Mathilda Howell. After 1920, archery was dropped from Olympic competition because of a disparity in rules among nations. In response, the Fédération Internationale de Tir à l'Arc (FITA) was founded in Paris in 1931 to standardize rules for international competition; that year, the federation held the first world championship tournament. It was won two years later by American D. Mackenzie.

Hunting with bow and arrow increased in popularity after World War I. Wisconsin became the first state to establish a bow hunting season in 1934, and other states followed. Fred Bear, considered the father of modern bow hunting, popularized the sport in books, films, and television appearances from the 1940s through the 1970s.

In 1939, the National Field Archery Association of the United States was established to promote hunting, roving, and field archery. In roving, archers set up many marks on the field and shoot at them in sequence—they proceed to each target striked, then shoot at the next—winning by taking the fewest shots. In field archery, archers shoot at stationary targets from a position in a field or the woods; the targets often are at unmarked distances and may be life-size animal targets.

Technological innovations soon followed. Physicist and rocket scientist Clarence N. Hickman, known as the "Father of Scientific Archery," redesigned the English bow to make it flat and more efficient, basing his designs on studies of the ballistics of bows and arrows. In 1937, he used a high-speed camera to study what was known as the "archer's paradox." He found that when an arrow shaft is fired, it flexes away from the target, indicating that the archer must aim slightly to the side in order to strike a bull's-eye.

The longbow dominated the sport, but it was difficult to use and easily affected by changing temperatures and humidity. By mid-century, it was replaced with the recurved or compound bow, a composite made of laminated wood, plastic, and fiberglass. Unaffected by climate, it has a rigid midsection that provides a good grip, has very strong limbs, is 30 percent to 40 percent more accurate, and can send an arrow more than 850 yards (777 meters), compared to 300 yards (274 meters) for the longbow. Another technological innovation was the replacement of wooden arrows with aluminum-alloy or fiberglass tubing arrows with plastic fins and a steel point.

In 1972, target archery returned to the Olympics. International competitors shoot at targets that are 48.8 inches (123.9 centimeters) in diameter, with a bull's-eye of 4.8 inches (12.2 centimeters). A bull's-eye is worth 10 points, with each outer ring valued at 1 point less. Competitive archers normally shoot Olympic rounds of 72 arrows at 70 meters (77 yards), or FITA rounds of 36 arrows shot from 30, 50, 70, and 90 meters (33, 55, 77, and 98 yards) for men and 30, 50, 60, and 70 meters (33, 55, 66, and 77 yards) for women. In Olympic competition, archers are eliminated in successive rounds until the two undefeated competitors meet in the final round to compete for the gold and silver medals, with the two semifinal losers competing for the bronze.

Archery in the Olympics is divided into four events: men's and women's individual, and men's and women's team competitions. The United States has been a world power in Olympic competition, second only to Korea. The top U.S. bowmen were Rick McKinney, world champion in 1977, and Darrell Pace, world champion in 1975 and 1979, and Olympic champion in 1976 and 1984. The leading women archers were Olympic gold medalists Doreen Wilber in 1972 and Luann Ryon in 1976. Overall, U.S. archers won 13 Olympic medals, including eight gold, through 2008.

The sport became institutionalized in the post–World War II era with the opening of the Archery Hall of Fame and Museum in Springfield, Missouri in

1971 and the Bowhunters Hall of Fame in Squaw Valley, California, in 1990.

Steven A. Riess

See also: Olympics, Summer.

Further Reading

Davidson, Robert B. *History of the United Bowmen of Philadelphia.* Philadelphia: Allen, Lane & Scott, 1888.

Fadala, Sam. *Traditional Archery.* 2nd ed. Mechanicsburg, PA: Stackpole, 2011.

Grayson, Charles E., Mary French, and Michael J. O'Brien. *Traditional Archery from Six Continents: The Charles E. Grayson Collection.* Columbia: University of Missouri Press, 2007.

Kinney, Christian D. *Archery: An Olympic History, 1900–2004.* Los Angeles: World Sport Research & Publications, 2005.

Koppedrayer, Kay. "Native American Prisoners and a Victorian Women's Archery Club: Patterns of Changing Social Relations in Late Nineteenth Century North America." *International Journal of the History of Sport* 21:1 (January 2004): 67–96.

Schumm, Maryanne M. *Clarence N. Hickman: The Father of Scientific Archery.* Minisink Hills, NJ: Maples, 1983.

Arledge, Roone (1931–2002)

Roone Arledge, a pioneering ABC sports producer and executive, revolutionized the coverage of sports on television in the 1960s. He was responsible for creating *ABC's Wide World of Sports,* one of the longest-running shows on television, and *Monday Night Football,* which made the sport a staple of prime-time entertainment. In addition, he altered the way in which sports were broadcast, giving the home audience a better view than those who paid to see an event in person. His advancements included handheld cameras, slow motion replay, instant replay, and background segments on the athletes.

Roone Pinckney Arledge, Jr., was born on July 8, 1931, in Forest Hills, New York, to Roone Arledge, Sr., a lawyer, and Gertrude Arledge, a homemaker. He grew up in the town of Merrick on Long Island, New York. He attended Columbia University with the intention of becoming a sports journalist, and there he learned the importance of narrative and the role of the hero. Years later, Arledge would teach ABC Sports announcers to emphasize the story line of the game they were covering and to focus on a star whose personal story transcended the outcome of the game. He aimed to get the audience emotionally involved so that they would enjoy the program even if they did not care about the outcome of the contest.

Arledge graduated from Columbia in 1952 and briefly worked for the Dumont network as an assistant program director. He later worked as a stage director and producer for legendary puppeteer Shari Lewis's children's show in New York, for which he won a local Emmy.

In April 1960, Arledge joined ABC Sports as an assistant producer. His first job was to produce National Collegiate Athletic Association (NCAA) football broadcasts, which he thought needed enlivening. At the time, the philosophy of television sports was that the fan's view at home should not be any better than that of the fan in the worst seat in the ballpark. A typical broadcast featured a couple of cameras behind home plate or on the 50-yard line, resulting in bland coverage. During the 1960s, Arledge introduced innovations that have become standard, including shots of the town and stadium from a nearby tall building (later from a blimp), cuts to cheerleaders or the band, close-ups of coaches' faces, dramatic close-ups of the action, and microphones placed on the field to bring the sound of the sport into viewers' living rooms. He used videotape recorders to replay key action during halftime. After seeing a samurai movie in Japan that used slow motion, Arledge got the idea of creating slow-motion instant replays. He also insisted that the television network select the announcers (until then, individual sports leagues chose the announcers).

In 1961, Arledge produced a new show, *ABC's Wide World of Sports,* as a way to fill Saturday afternoon wintertime programming. The show frequently used videotaped rather than live coverage. It started off with track and field, and soon introduced Americans to such international sports as Australian rules football, curling, hurling, jai alai, and the 24-hour Le Mans auto race. It lasted through 1997, one of the longest runs in television history. In Canada, CTV broadcast a Canadian version during the 1970s and 1980s. Arledge also obtained the rights to televise events that did not get national television exposure, from the Indianapolis 500 to the Professional Bowlers Association championship tour. Bowling became a mainstay of Saturday afternoon television.

Arledge became president of ABC Sports in 1968. Between 1964 and 1988, he supervised coverage of ten Summer and Winter Olympic Games. ABC's coverage of the 1972 Games in Munich became an international news event when terrorists attacked the Israeli athletes and held them hostage. ABC provided round-the-clock coverage of the crisis. Arledge's work with the Olympics turned the event from a minor attraction into must-see television.

Arledge led sports programming out of its weekend ghetto into prime time, beginning with the 1968 Mexico City Olympics, which ran during prime time on weekday evenings. This success led to the creation of *Monday Night Football,* which Arledge designed to provide entertainment as well as game coverage. He brought in a three-man crew that included Howard Cosell, an abrasive New York announcer who would become the most famous American sportscaster of the 1970s, and former NFL players Frank Gifford and Don Meredith.

Prime-time advertising budgets for sporting events prompted an explosion of sports. New leagues sprang up to challenge established leagues, and old leagues moved to new cities. Arledge's success in increasing sports broadcasting was a major factor in the expansion of the sports business.

After revolutionizing sports on television, Arledge was chosen in 1977 to head ABC's struggling news department. The choice sparked controversy, as Arledge's professional background was in entertainment, not journalism. He created successful news magazines for ABC, including *20/20* and *Prime Time Live,* as well as the nighttime show *Nightline.*

Arledge was not easy to work with, however, as he had a large ego and a prickly personality. He also came under fire for his extravagant spending. As networks began to focus on cutting costs and boosting shareholder value, Arledge no longer felt comfortable at ABC. He retired from broadcasting in 1998.

In 1990, *Life* magazine named Arledge one of the most influential Americans of the century; four years later, *Sports Illustrated* ranked him as the third most influential person in sports since 1950. Arledge won 37 Emmys, including the first Lifetime Achievement Award in 2002.

A workaholic, Arledge's success took a toll on his private life. He died of cancer in New York City on December 5, 2002.

Caryn E. Neumann

See also: Cosell, Howard; *Monday Night Football;* Television; *Wide World of Sports, ABC's.*

Further Reading

Arledge, Roone. *Roone: A Memoir.* New York: HarperCollins, 2003.

Gunther, Marc. *The House That Roone Built: The Inside Story of ABC News.* New York: Little, Brown, 1994.

Roberts, Randy, and James Olson. *Winning Is the Only Thing: Sports in America Since 1945.* Baltimore: Johns Hopkins University Press, 1989.

Armstrong, Lance (1971–)

Lance Armstrong is a professional road race cyclist who won the Tour de France a record seven consecutive times after surviving testicular cancer. The Tour, which covers some 2,200 miles (3,540 kilometers) over three weeks, is the flagship event of world cycling and one of the most grueling competitions in sport. Armstrong was only the second American after Greg LeMond to win the Tour, riding for the U.S. Postal Service team from 1999 to 2004 and for the Discovery Channel in 2005. Armstrong is widely considered one of the greatest athletes in North American history, and likely the fittest ever. His victories helped spur American interest in the Tour de France.

He was born Lance Edward Gunderson in Plano, Texas, on September 18, 1971, the son of Linda Walling and Eddie Charles Gunderson. After his father left the family in 1973, his mother married Terry Keith Armstrong, who adopted Lance the following year. Armstrong began competing as a triathlete at age 12. Four years later, he was the top-ranked triathlete in the country in the 19-and-under age group. Armstrong turned professional at age 16 and won the United States National Triathlon Sprint competition in 1989 and 1990.

Armstrong began to focus on cycling, his best event, and in 1991, he won the United States National Amateur Road Race competition. In 1992, he finished fourteenth in the road race at the Summer Olympic Games in Barcelona. The following year, he was both the U.S. cycling champion and the world cycling champion. In 1993 and 1994, Armstrong, riding for Team Motorola, finished second in America's Tour du Pont. In the same two years, he started strong in the Tour de France, winning a few stages, but he failed to finish both times.

Shortly after his twenty-fifth birthday, Armstrong was diagnosed with testicular cancer. The cancerous testicle was removed, but the cancer had spread to his abdomen, lungs, and brain. Despite brain surgery and an aggressive course of chemotherapy, doctors believed that he had little chance for survival. The chemotherapy caused Armstrong permanent kidney damage; at the same time, it destroyed his musculature. Armstrong returned to training soon after leaving the hospital, but exhaustion and depression forced him to quit. His coach, Chris Carmichael, and agent, Bill Stapleton, convinced him to keep going. Returning to racing in Spain's five-day Ruta del Sol in 1998, Armstrong finished fourteenth.

Armstrong's success as a cyclist has been attributed to his incredible physical fitness—he ranks near the top in both aerobic and anaerobic capacity—and to his total dedication to training. Between 1999 and 2005, he devoted nearly every waking minute to training for the Tour de France. According to physicians, Armstrong's heart is one-third larger than that of an average man of his size; his resting heart rate is extremely low at 30 beats per minute, with a maximum in excess of 200. His body contains an exceptionally low level of lactic acid. These factors contributed to Armstrong's ability to spin (pedal) as fast as 120 revolutions per minute, a cadence faster than most, if not all, of his competitors, resulting in less fatigue.

The Tour de France is a decidedly team sport, despite the glory accorded the winning rider. The Tour combines time trials, long flat races, and mountain stages; it was in the mountains that Armstrong proved unbeatable. Teams consist of support personnel as well as *domestiques*—a role that Armstrong played in earlier Tours—whose function is to protect and "pull" the team's best rider. The best rider in the pack (*peloton*) drafts, or is pulled along by his teammates, saving as much as 40 percent of his energy. The team consists of riders who are strong climbers or speedsters who perform exceptionally well in time trials. Though Armstrong always had done well in time trials, following his bout with cancer, he became the best climber in the world.

Armstrong rode six times with the U.S. Postal Service team. Although he rode with a highly skilled and carefully trained team whose function was to protect their star, he often raced far ahead of his team. The support team functioned as a cohesive unit, with a number of elite manufacturers working to supply cutting-edge bicycle frames, tires, and other components.

Reports of drug use have tarnished Armstrong's reputation, although none has been substantiated. Allegations charge that he began using performance-enhancing substances as early as 1995, when he raced for the Motorola team. Teammates reported that they had witnessed Armstrong violating the drug rules, and support personnel claimed that he had attempted to enlist them in cover-ups. In a 1999 urine test, a trace amount (too small to be in the positive range) of corticosteroids was detected. Armstrong produced a medical certificate showing that he had used an approved cream for saddle sores that contained corticosteroids. As of 2011, rumors continued to circulate regarding his use of drugs for performance enhancement.

Prior to Armstrong, only four men had won the Tour de France five times, and just Spanish cyclist Miguel Indurain had won in consecutive years. Armstrong's 2001 victory posted the third-fastest time in the 100-year history of the Tour. *ABC's Wide World of Sports* named Armstrong Sportsman of the Year in 1999, and the Associated Press chose him as Male Athlete of the Year from 2002 to 2005. Armstrong retired from professional cycling after the 2005 Tour as the first American to win with an American team. He returned to competition in 2009, finishing third in the Tour de France for the Astana team. He also competed in 2010, coming in twenty-third, although he helped Team RadioShack win the team title. His final international race was the Tour Down Under in Adelaide, South Australia, in 2011, but he continued to compete in the United States with the RadioShack domestic team.

In 1997, Armstrong established the Lance Armstrong Foundation to inspire and empower those fighting cancer. The foundation provides cancer patients with the practical information and tools necessary to live full lives. Its signature yellow "Livestrong" wristbands have raised tens of millions of dollars for the foundation.

Duncan R. Jamieson

See also: Cycling; Endorsements, Athlete.

Further Reading

Armstrong, Lance, with Sally Jenkins. *Every Second Counts.* New York: Broadway, 2003.

Coyle, Daniel. *Lance Armstrong's War: One Man's Battle Against Fate, Fame, Love, Death, Scandal, and a Few Other Rivals on the Road to the Tour de France.* New York: HarperCollins, 2005.

Gutman, Bill. *Lance Armstrong: A Biography.* New York: Simon & Schuster, 2004.

Wilcockson, John, and Andrew Hood. *The 2005 Tour de France: Armstrong's Farewell.* Boulder, CO: VeloPress, 2005.

Arts, Visual

American sports art has a long and distinguished history dating to the Revolutionary War and continuing to the present. Nearly every important American artist, from Benjamin West and John Singleton Copley to Andy Warhol and LeRoy Nieman, has dabbled in the subject at one point or another.

This art can be organized, loosely speaking, into two categories. Fine artists primarily are interested in exploring broad themes—the beauty of the landscape or of the body, the importance of community, the sublime pleasures of everyday life, and so forth. Often, these themes can be handled most easily in small, intimate scenes. Therefore, most sports-themed fine art portrays individual sports or focuses on an individual participating in a team sport, relegating the teammates to the background. Further, for fine artists, sports are simply a means to an end, one possible subject among many. Thus, sports-themed works by fine artists tend to be part of larger portfolios that are dominated by non-sports-related works.

Popular artists and photographers, by contrast, tend to be interested in the essence of the sports. They are documentarians who strive to capture specific moments in time for a popular audience and for posterity. While popular artists and photographers certainly have given much attention to individuals, they have inherited almost sole responsibility for portraying team sports. In addition, it is much more common for these artists to spend much or all of their careers working on sports-related compositions.

Early American Sports Art

The first sports art in America was created during the nation's late colonial and early republic periods. At that time, American artists had not yet developed their own traditions, so they took their cues from Great Britain. In that era, British painters—and thus American painters—favored dramatic scenes of the wealthy and powerful.

Benjamin West, regarded as the first great American painter, arguably also was the first American sports artist. In 1763, he executed the oil painting *The Cricketers,* depicting five aristocratic Southerners posing with their bats, making clear to the world that they are Englishmen of high status. West's student John Singleton Copley—who lived in England for most of his career—followed his mentor's lead. In 1782, he painted *Richard Heber,* which also depicts a cricketer. The youngster stands leaning on his cricket bat with ball in hand, a self-assured son of wealth.

Another popular subject in early American sports art—again, borrowed from the British—was the thoroughbred horses owned by the wealthy. This tradition began around 1822, when breeder Charles H. Hall hired Alvan Fisher to paint *Eclipse with Race Track.*

American artists of the nineteenth century also—like their British counterparts—painted a great many hunting scenes. William Rainey, a member of the New York Cricket Club, is particularly associated with this tradition. He produced several portrayals of bird hunting in the New Jersey marshes, emphasizing the sport's social aspects.

Hudson River School, Luminism, and Western Art

In the middle decades of the nineteenth century, American artists began to move in different directions than their European counterparts, developing uniquely American traditions of art. The nation's first distinct art movement, which emerged in the 1830s, is known as the Hudson River school. The painters of this school produced landscapes with the intention of showing the majesty and the raw power of nature. People generally did not appear in these paintings, and when they did, they were relegated to the background or otherwise given secondary importance. Consequently, this first American art movement did not include images of sports or of athletes.

There were, however, several offshoots from the Hudson River school. Among them was luminism, which reached its peak between the 1850s and 1870s. Like the impressionists who were working in Europe at this time, luminists experimented with light, color, and technique. Though they tended to produce many landscapes, like the painters of the Hudson River school, the luminists were less interested in celebrating nature and more focused on capturing the sublime in American life. Given this, they often found room for human subjects in their paintings, including athletes. The most notable example is George Caleb Bingham's *Shooting for the Beef* (1850). It depicts a rural marksmanship contest watched by about a dozen interested spectators in front of a post office and grocery store and speaks to notions of community and sociability on the frontier.

Another important American genre that emerged in the middle of the nineteenth century was Western art. Western artists were excited by the foreignness, drama, and danger of the frontier. They often depicted Native Americans (and later cowboys) as their subjects, and their work included many scenes of athletes and athletic contests. The most important of the first generation of Western artists was George Catlin. He spent considerable time in the early 1830s with the native peoples in the West, painting about 500 canvasses of an idealized primitive society. His paintings became very popular, offering Americans an appealing depiction of "exotic" Native Americans. Catlin was deeply interested in mythic aspects of ball play, and he saw Native American sports as a link to an earlier time in human development. He executed several paintings of Native American sporting contests, most notably *Ball Play of the Choctaws: Ball Up* and *Ball Play of the Choctaws: Ball Down* (both 1835). The canvases portray a huge number of participants involved in an apparently chaotic lacrosse-like game with few rules. They suggest that the removal of the Choctaw from their native lands had not hurt their way of life, a message that surely must have pleased Catlin's white audience.

Among the generation of Western artists who succeeded Catlin, the most significant was Frederic Remington. Remington began his career in the employ of *Harper's Weekly,* sent by his editors to do pictures of the Indian Chief Geronimo and of the "real" West. Remington's early portraits earned him national fame, allowing him to work independently and to do watercolors, oil paintings, and sculptures. Stylistically, Remington's work was much less realistic than Catlin's—he felt free to experiment with color and to paint idealized images of people and things that had never actually existed as he depicted them. In that way, Remington (like the luminist George Caleb Bingham) echoed the impressionists of his time. Thematically, however, Remington and Catlin were very similar, with an interest in the exotic, untamed, and uncivilized elements of the West.

Remington executed several paintings of Native American sports, particularly hunts; however, he was most interested in cowboys, both at work and at play. His famous cowboy sculptures, most notably *The Broncho Buster* (1909), capture (or at least anticipate) the sport of rodeo. Sporting subjects sometimes found their way into Remington's other Western works as well. *The Right of the Road* (1900) shows a bicyclist in twentieth-century garb sharing a dusty road with a stagecoach. It speaks to the difficulty that the "old" West and "new" West had in trying to coexist. Finally, Remington—himself a former football player—also found much of the spirit of the West in the athletic contests of the East. As such, his non-Western works often took sports as their subject. Most notable is *Yale-Princeton Football Game, Thanksgiving Day, 1890* (1891), which captures the violence, savagery, and romance of a football game.

Popular Prints and Illustrations

The first technique for making high-quality reproductions of images—lithography—was invented in 1796.

The technique improved dramatically over the course of the next several decades, becoming both more efficient and more affordable. This made possible the printmaking firm founded by Nathaniel Currier and James Merritt Ives in 1834.

Currier & Ives prints were geared toward a popular audience. Indeed, at a cost of as little as 5 cents for black-and-white images and as little as $1 for hand-colored images, they were the only artwork within the budget of many Americans. The firm's business model required that they focus on subjects with mass appeal. Further, given that they published more than 7,500 works in their seven decades of existence, it was necessary to find a great many subjects. Given that sports—particularly professional sports—were growing in popularity and prominence during the heyday of the firm, they were an obvious choice.

Over time, Currier & Ives produced roughly 1,000 different images of athletes and sporting events, including pictures of horse races, boxing matches, fishing, yachting, and—especially—hunting. Though many artists combined to produce this output, the firm's specialist in sports-related images was the English-born artist Arthur Fitzwilliam Tait. He earned particular renown for his hunting scenes, among them *The Check: Keep Your Distance* (1852), *Life on the Prairie, The Buffalo Hunt* (1862), and *Good Hunting Ground: The Home of the Deer* (1882).

Hunting's rival for the distinction of most-portrayed sport in nineteenth-century popular art was baseball. The first drawing of adults playing a baseball game appeared in *The Spirit of the Times* on September 12, 1857. It depicted a contest at the Elysian Fields in Hoboken, New Jersey, between the Eagles and the Gothams of New York. Two years later, *Harper's Weekly* published an illustration of a match between the Brooklyn Atlantics and the New York Mutuals. In 1865, Currier & Ives produced *The American National Game of Baseball.* The lithograph became one of their signature images, and it sold so well that the firm produced a steady stream of baseball-related pictures thereafter.

In the twentieth century, the most prominent creator of sports-themed illustrations for a mass audience was Norman Rockwell. Working both independently and in the employ of the *Saturday Evening Post,* the artist spent his 65-year career creating quaint, nostalgia-evoking scenes that celebrated everyday American life and the American spirit. Not surprisingly, he was enamored of sports, particularly baseball. In fact, his first cover for the *Post* (May 20, 1916) depicted an unhappy boy pushing a baby carriage past his taunting buddies as they head off to play baseball. Other baseball-themed covers included *Gramps at the Plate* (August 5, 1916), *The Dugout* (September 4, 1948), *Game Called Because of Rain* (April 23, 1949), and *The Locker Room* (March 2, 1957). The artist also portrayed many other sports, including basketball, cycling, football, hockey, skiing, running, sledding, and weight lifting.

Realism

For most of the nineteenth century, fine and popular artists tended to create idealized images of American sporting life. The late nineteenth and early twentieth centuries, by contrast, saw many painters embrace a European fine art movement known as realism. Realists stood in direct opposition to the impressionists. Broadly speaking, they tried to capture unadorned scenes of ordinary people engaged in everyday activities. Quite often, these images focused on the unpleasant or sordid elements of daily life.

The preeminent realist painter of American sports was Thomas Eakins. A sportsman himself, he executed paintings that reflected his fondness for athletics and vigorous activity. His work celebrates male achievement, but at the same time reflects the artist's deeply held apprehensions in an era of rapid and often bewildering change. Eakins's most famous sports-themed paintings were his series of 11 images of oarsmen, particularly *Max Schmitt in a Single Scull* (1871). Presented as a landscape of the Schuylkill River, with the city of Philadelphia in the background and Eakins himself rowing off in the distance, the painting depicts Schmitt as a tired, aging athlete in the autumn of his career, resting after his victory.

Eakins also depicted other sports. He did a series of hunting pictures from 1873 to 1876, notably *Whistling for Plover* (1874), and did several baseball paintings, beginning with an 1875 watercolor entitled *Baseball Players Practicing* that was exhibited at the Philadelphia Centennial Exposition. Eakins also produced three major paintings and roughly ten sketches about boxing, a subject then considered beneath the talents of a serious artist. He respected prizefighters who carefully disciplined their bodies and minds and earned a livelihood by their prowess.

The boxing paintings feature protagonists who display confidence and dignity, but at the same time emphasize the struggles that test human character. *Between Rounds* (1898) depicts a boxer resting in his corner between rounds, while *Taking the Count* (1899) depicts the conclusion of a fight, with the winner standing over his foe as the referee counts him out. *Salutat* (1899) portrays a scene in which a victorious fighter acknowledges the crowd's plaudits.

Eakins was not the only painter of the realist school to embrace sports as a subject. Winslow Homer was among the preeminent artists of the movement, and he did a number of canvases that depict people swimming, fishing, and hunting. Most notable, perhaps, is *Right and Left* (1909), which shows a duck at the moment that it is being struck by a hunter's bullet.

Earlier in his career (1866), Homer painted a series of five croquet paintings among the few sporting paintings to highlight women. Croquet was a popular fad among middle class men and women in the mid-1860s, providing Victorians with an excellent social outlet. In *Croquet Scene,* he depicts three fashionable young women and a gentleman who is positioning a ball for a lady in red for whom any movement in her huge hoop skirt would be very difficult, if not unladylike; or maybe he wants to catch a glimpse of her ankle.

Edward Hopper also was an important realist and a sportsman. Among his most prominent works is *French Six-Day Bicycle Ride* (1937). It portrays a cyclist resting in his cubicle, alone in his thoughts, while his partner has taken over the riding.

Ashcan School and Regionalism

Realism spawned a number of important offshoots. Among them was the Ashcan school, which emerged in New York City during the first decade of the twentieth century. The artists of the Ashcan school took the general tenets of realism—accuracy, brutal honesty, and a willingness to show the seamy side of daily life—magnified them, and applied them to art featuring the city in which they lived.

Among the Ashcan artists, the one who most frequently turned his attention to sports was former athlete George Bellows. Among his first paintings was *Forty-Two Kids* (1907), in which he observed the behavior of unsupervised lads swimming nude in a New York City river, while others roughhoused, gambled, smoked, or urinated.

Bellows was drawn to New York's subterranean boxing world. The state officially banned prizefighting in 1900, but a loophole allowed boxing clubs to continue operating as long as they did not promote their contests as prizefights. Bellows executed three boxing scenes between 1907 and 1909, most notably *Both Members of This Club* (1909). Bellows's paintings, unlike those of Eakins, depicted frenzied action inside the ring and the attendees as ghoulish fans out for blood. Nonetheless, he admired the fighters, defining their muscular bodies with long, sweeping strokes of color, reinforcing an ideology of masculinity.

Masculinity was not the only theme of Bellows's sports-related work. Indeed, his *Business-Men's Class, YMCA* (1916) and *The Shower Bath* (1917) actually mock and critique American notions of masculinity. Both depict a paunchy crowd of middle-class sportsmen. In 1920, the artist painted *Tennis Tournament,* which shows a small and disinterested audience of elites on a beautiful summer afternoon, looking on as a player is posed to hit a ball. The work argues that upper-class life is ultimately empty and without passion.

In 1924, Bellows returned to boxing in one of his last and best-known works, *Dempsey and Firpo,* which recapitulates one of the most violent fights in American sports history, between heavyweight champion Jack Dempsey and Luis Firpo of Argentina. Like his earlier works on boxing, the painting celebrates the masculine qualities of the fighters while also recording the brutality of the sport. As the same time, the artist appears to have mellowed in his final years—the crowd in *Dempsey and Firpo* is far less bloodthirsty than the one in *Both Members of This Club.*

Another offshoot of realism was regionalism, which reached its apogee in the 1930s. Regionalist painters, such as the realists, rejected impressionism and tried to honestly and accurately capture the essence of daily life. They are distinguished, however, by their focus on small towns and rural living. As the regionalists were at work during the tail end of the Industrial Revolution and throughout the Great Depression, their emphasis on rural themes implied a clear critique of industrialization and other aspects of modern life.

For some regionalist artists, pastoral scenes of sporting contests meshed very well with these themes. The most prominent example is Thomas Hart Benton, a self-proclaimed "enemy of modernism." His *People of Chilmark* (1920) takes sports as a central theme, incorporating elements of basketball, wrestling, swimming, and rowing. Sports figure even more prominently in Benton's masterwork, *The Arts of Life in America* (1932), a collection of murals that document American culture. Among the murals are scenes of baseball, harness racing, hunting, and rodeo.

Early Sports Photography

Photography, of course, is another route to achieving realistic depictions of events. The technology dates to the 1830s, although sports photography did not begin to emerge as a genre until the 1890s, for two reasons. First, early cameras required long exposure times, which meant that subjects had to remain stationary for long periods of time. It was not until the turn of the century that cameras advanced to the point that they could capture shots of athletes in action. Second, both photography and most sports were regarded as lowbrow in the nineteenth century, and therefore not the province of wealthy elites. There was little demand for sports photographs until they could be reproduced for a mass popular audience in magazines and newspapers. The first viable technique for doing so was developed by Frederic Ives (no relation to James Merritt Ives) in 1881.

The first important sports photographer in the United States was Charles Conlon. He began his career as a copyeditor for the *Troy* (New York) *Press* and then New York City's *Evening Telegram,* with photography as a hobby on the side. In 1904, *Evening Telegram's* sports editor John Foster (also assistant editor of *Spalding's Base Ball Guide*) encouraged Conlon to take some photographs at the Polo Grounds. Conlon lugged his glass negatives and heavy equipment around, taking portraits. Two years later, he was taking action shots, stationing himself on the field during games near first or third base. Though he handled all of the era's sports, Conlon became a specialist in baseball, taking thousands of shots of minor and major league players. His best-known photo—one of the iconic images American baseball—shows Ty Cobb sliding hard into third base during a 1909 game between the Detroit Tigers and the New York Highlanders (later the New York Yankees).

Following the path blazed by Conlon—and legendary in his own right—was Nat Fein, who began a three-decade career in the employ of the *New York Herald Tribune* in 1933. Fein's résumé is a virtual duplicate of Conlon's: He began as a copyeditor, then was recruited as a photographer, and eventually became a generalist who shot all sports but specialized in baseball. His most important image was captured at the June 13, 1948, game between the Yankees and the Cleveland Indians. On that day, Yankee great George Herman "Babe" Ruth—13 years after retiring and two months before he died—returned to the "House That Ruth Built" for the last time, donning his old uniform and participating in a tribute in his honor. Fein's photograph captures the "Sultan of Swat" from behind, with his familiar number 3 at the center of the image. Clearly wasting away, Ruth leans on a bat as he takes one last, long look at the outfield he once patrolled. Entitled *The Babe Bows*

Out, the image earned Fein the only unshared Pulitzer Prize ever to be won by a sports photographer.

Abstract Art and Pop Art

In the twentieth century, particularly after 1920, the dominant trend in American fine art was toward abstraction. This movement grew out of impressionism, which argued that artists did not have a responsibility to interpret their subjects literally, and that they should feel free to take artistic license in order to capture the essence of their subjects. Abstract painters took this notion a step (or sometimes many steps) farther, sometimes grotesquely distorting their subjects, other times representing them with indistinct collages of shapes or colors. The many different schools of thought included under the general umbrella of "abstract art" each have their own notion of exactly what the term means.

Abstract artists often focus on weighty subjects— war, suffering, the decay of civilization, and so forth. Even more commonly, they have no specific subject at all, preferring instead to let the viewer reach his or her own interpretation. Therefore, there are relatively few abstract art pieces that can be described as specifically sports themed.

The most notable exception to this rule is the work of LeRoy Nieman, who generally is categorized as an abstract impressionist. That is to say, his works are too representational to be considered wholly abstract, but they are too abstract to be regarded as classically impressionist. Nieman began his career with *Playboy* magazine in the 1950s, producing depictions of athletes and sports events. When he began to work independently, he retained his popular orientation and continued to focus on sporting subjects in a variety of mediums, including lithographs, oils, pencil drawings, and watercolors.

The other important trend in mid- to late-twentieth century American art was pop art, which emerged in the 1950s. Pop artists reject abstraction and instead are interested in understanding the deeper meaning of popular culture. To explore this meaning, they extract images, icons, and personalities from their context, displaying them with minimal background or ornamentation. Pop art thus invites viewers to examine and evaluate the artist's subject on its own merits.

The preeminent pop artist was Andy Warhol, famous for his works featuring Campbell's soup cans. Warhol regularly turned to the world of sports for inspiration. In 1977, for example, he executed a series entitled *Athletes* that included a dozen paintings of the most prominent sports stars of that time. The image of boxer Muhammad Ali is the best-known work from the group; also represented were Kareem Abdul-Jabbar, Ron Duguay, Chris Evert, Vitas Gerulaitis, Rod Gilbert, Dorothy Hamill, Jack Nicklaus, Pelé, Tom Seaver, Willie Shoemaker, and O.J. Simpson. In the early 1980s, Warhol did a series of Polaroid images of athletes. Ali and Simpson again were included, as were Wayne Gretzky and John McEnroe, among others. In 1985, shortly before his death, Warhol completed *Pete Rose,* a screen print based on a baseball card of the famous hitter.

Sculpture

Sculptors have made significant contributions to sports art. One of the most significant such artists was R. Tait McKenzie (1867–1938), a Canadian surgeon and physical educator at the University of Pennsylvania, whose sculptures stemmed from his role as physical eductor. In his beautiful, lifelike figures, such as *The Sprinter* (1902), McKenzie strove to portray ideals of physical development and to capture the precise moment of sports action that summarized the totality of the psychological challenge and movement involved in that event. He also produced some intriguing works that captured the struggles of a sprinter (runner); he entitled this group *Exhaustion, Fatigue, Violent Effort,* and *Breathlessness* (1900–1901). His most notable sports sculptures include *The Athlete* (1903), *The Competitor* (1907), *The Relay* (1909), and *The Onslaught* (1911), which depicts a halfback carrying a football, led by his blockers, busting through the line.

Another outstanding sculptor was Joseph Brown (1909–1985), a collegian and professional boxer who studied with McKenzie. He was instructor of boxing at Princeton for 25 years and taught sculpture there from 1938 to 1977. He produced over 35 boxing sculptures, typically depicting tired, fallen, and frustrated boxers, such as *Pieta* (1944) and *Not a Word* (1958), emphasizing action and technique. He also produced baseball, football and basketball works, including *Bill Bradley from Life* (1965).

Recent Sports Photography

Since the 1950s, the field of sports photography has blossomed, so much so that photographers now dominate sports art. The preeminent photographer of the era was Robert Riger, who recorded more than 90,000 images between 1950 and 1994. He delighted in suspending in time the intensity of the great athletes.

Riger covered all sports, but, by contrast with his predecessors who tended to be generalists, he specialized in football. His 40,000 photos of the sport include iconic shots of Frank Gifford, Vince Lombardi, Bart Starr, and Johnny Unitas. Riger also worked in television, winning nine Emmy Awards for his work on football and the Olympics.

Many other photographers specialized in sports in the postwar years. Walter Iooss's career spanned more than 40 years, during which he covered baseball, basketball, football, tennis, and the Olympics; his images made the cover of *Sports Illustrated* more than 300 times. Neil Leifer has 150 *Sports Illustrated* covers of his own, though he is best known for his famous 1965 shot of Muhammad Ali standing over a knocked-out Sonny Liston. Toni Frissell earned rave reviews for the grace and artistry of her photographs, and she is remembered as America's first successful female sports photographer.

Through the 1980s, the best sports photographers were those who could handle any assignment and any sport. Since then, however, the trend has been toward specialization. Each sport presents unique challenges in terms of the photographer's location, timing, and framing. Consequently, the best sports photographers of the current generation largely have built their careers around a single sport. They include Andrew D. Bernstein (basketball), Aaron Chang (surfing), and Darren Heath (auto racing).

Sports Documentaries

Finally, some attention must be given to those photographers who work with moving images—that is, filmmakers. The tradition of sports documentaries dates to 1930s Germany and the films made at the 1936 Berlin Olympics by Leni Reifenstahl.

American filmmakers began to follow Reifenstahl's lead in the 1950s, particularly Bud Greenspan, whose first project was a 1952 film on weightlifting, followed by *Jesse Owens Returns to Berlin* (1964). In 1976, he directed a collection of 22-hour-long films called *The Olympiad*, a series that won rave reviews and numerous honors and awards. Greenspan thereafter was regarded as America's preeminent chronicler of Olympic sports; he earned a lifetime achievement award from the Directors Guild of America and was inducted into the U.S. Olympic Hall of Fame.

A number of important documentarians followed in Greenspan's footsteps. Ed Sabol, for example, started by filming his son's high school football games, then moved on to professional games, eventually founding NFL Films in 1965. Ken Burns, known for his films on

American history, directed an 18-hour study of baseball in 1994 (expanding it to 20 hours in 2010). Ira Opper has earned recognition for his films chronicling surfing culture.

A Vital Tradition

Sports does not represent a major genre in the fine art world, but great artists have used it to capture the anxiety of competition, the joy of winning, and the agony of defeat. They also have used sporting themes to depict honor, sportsmanship, and the toll of pain and fatigue. On the other hand, there is a long tradition of depicting sports among popular artists and, more recently, photographers and filmmakers, for whom the spirit of sports is their primary interest, and who enjoy a growing popular market.

Since the 1959 founding of the National Art Museum of Sport (housed since 1990 in Indianapolis, Indiana); the American Sports Art Museum and Archives at the United States Sports Academy in Daphne, Alabama (founded in 1984); the National Sporting Art Museum in Middleburg, Virginia (established in 2011); and, of course, the rise of the Internet, the opportunities for Americans to enjoy popular sports art has greatly expanded.

Christopher G. Bates and Steven A. Riess

See also: Film; Newspapers and Magazines.

Further Reading

Clark, Carol, and Allen Guttmann. "Artists and Athletes." *Journal of Sport History* 22:2 (Summer 1995): 85–110.

Crawford, Alta. "Frederic Remington: Artist of the People." *Kansas Quarterly* 9:4 (1977): 89–118.

Doezema, Marianne. *George Bellows and Urban America.* New Haven, CT: Yale University Press, 1992.

Drumm, Russell. Still Magic. *Walter Iooss: A Lifetime Shooting Sports & Beauty.* New York: Graphis Press, 1999.

Goodyear, Frank, III. "'Nature's Most Beautiful Models': George Catlin's Choctaw Ball-Playing Paintings and the Politics of Indian Removal." *International Journal of the History of Sport* 23:2 (March 2006): 138–153.

Junker, Patricia, ed. *Winslow Homer, Artist and Angler.* New York: Thames & Hudson, 2002.

Kozar, Andrew J. R. *Tait McKenzie: The Sculptor of Athletes.* Knoxville: University of Tennessee Press, 1975.

Neiman, Leroy. *Winners: My Thirty Years in Sport.* New York: Harry N. Abrams, 1983.

Oates, Joyce Carol. "Bellows' Bouts: A Celebrated Novelist and Boxing Specialist Looks at America's Most Popular Prizefighting Paintings." *Arts & Antiques* 4:9 (Summer 1987): 66–73.

Peters, Harry T. *Currier & Ives: Printmakers to the American People.* Garden City, NY: Doubleday, 1942.

Smith, Carl S. "The Boxing Paintings of Thomas Eakins." In *Prospects: An Annual of American Cultural Studies,* vol. 4, ed. Jack Salzman. New York: Burt Franklin, 1979.

Ashe, Arthur (1943–1993)

Arthur Ashe was the first great African American male tennis player, achieving success in the 1960s and 1970s in a sport that long had been identified with upper-middle-class white society. He was a National Collegiate Athletic Association (NCAA) champion and the winner of 11 Grand Slam tournament titles and seven Davis Cup championships. A versatile, graceful player who conducted himself as a gentleman on and off the court, Ashe also was a social activist. He fought racism in tennis and in other areas, promoted higher standards for students seeking athletic scholarships, and wrote movingly about the African American experience in sport.

Early Life

Arthur Robert Ashe, Jr., was born on July 10, 1943, in Richmond, Virginia. His mother, Mattie Cunningham, died when he was six years old. His father Arthur Ashe, Sr., was a park caretaker. As a resident of the Old South, Ashe lived in a racially segregated society. He attended segregated schools and played tennis on segregated courts, where he could not play a white opponent in public.

Ronald Charity, a part-time playground instructor, noticed Ashe's talent on the court and began working with him. Later, Ashe was coached by Dr. Robert Walter Johnson, an African American who trained young black players at his home in Lynchburg, Virginia. Johnson had established the American Tennis Association, which organized tournaments for African American players.

As a teenager, Ashe won several titles in the boys' division, starting in 1955. In 1959, he traveled to New York City to compete in the Eastern Junior and Boys Championships of the U.S. Lawn Tennis Association—a predominantly white organization—at Forest Hills, New York. He was seeded number one, but lost to Hugh Lynch III of Maryland. Lynch, who was white, and Ashe would not have been able to play one another in a Southern tournament, but the association had opened its national tournament to African Americans.

Tennis Achievements

During his career in tennis, Ashe often was the first or the only African American man in tournaments and other competitions. (In women's tennis, Althea Gibson was the first African American to win the U.S. and British women's championships in 1957.) In 1963, Ashe became the first black player to be named to a U.S. Davis Cup team. He considered it an honor to compete for his country and became a fixture on the Davis Cup teams, participating on ten squads between 1963 and 1978, with a brilliant record of 28-6.

Also in 1963, Ashe entered the University of California, Los Angeles (UCLA). He became the NCAA men's singles champion in 1965 and led the school to the NCAA championship. By this time, he was ranked in the top ten in the world. He graduated from UCLA in 1966 with a degree in business. During the next two years, he fulfilled his military obligation by serving in the U.S. Army.

In 1968, Ashe won the U.S. Amateur Championship and then entered the U.S. Open, which included both amateurs and professionals. Seeded fifth, he reached the finals, where he defeated Tom Okker in five sets. As an amateur, he received $280 for his expenses, while Okker, a professional, received $14,000. After his victory, Ashe was ranked number one in the world.

During the late 1960s, the tennis world began to change as more world-class players gave up their amateur status to turn professional. Ashe turned professional in 1969, and he soon began to take an interest in the plight of professional tennis players. While the sport was attracting large crowds and television audiences, the players' share of the revenues was very small. In 1969, he was a founding member of the organization that would become the Association of Tennis Professionals, which worked to protect the interests of professional players.

Ashe captured the Australian Open singles title in 1970, but in the next few years, he failed to win any of the four Grand Slam tournaments—the Australian, French, British, and U.S. Opens. In 1975, however, he played through the British Open field at Wimbledon all the way to the finals, where he met the young sensation Jimmy Connors. Although Ashe had lost to Connors in three previous matches, in a surprise upset, Ashe defeated Connors convincingly: 6–1, 6–1, 5–7, 6–4. By year's end, Ashe had earned $338,337 in prize money and again was ranked number one in the world.

Like other top players of the 1970s, Ashe earned additional income by endorsing tennis equipment and clothing. He worked with AMF Head, which created the Arthur Ashe Competition Racquet and later the Arthur Ashe Competition 2 model, an aluminum and fiberglass racket that Ashe helped design and develop. He also signed contracts with Le Coq Sportif, a subsidiary of Adidas that manufactured a shoe model named for him, and endorsed Catalina Martin of Los Angeles, a company that introduced a new line of tennis wear. By 1973, Ashe was conducting tennis clinics for American Express and Coca-Cola, working in minority recruitment for Aetna Insurance, and providing tennis commentary for ABC Sports.

Health problems began to hinder Ashe's career in 1977, when he had calcium deposits removed from his left heel. That year, he married photographer Jeanne Moutoussamy; they had two daughters. Two years later, at age 35, he reached the semifinals of the Australian

Arthur Ashe was the first African American player to win a Grand Slam tennis event, claiming victory in the U.S. Open (1968), as well as the Australian Open (1970) and Wimbledon (1975, seen here). He also fought racism and advocated for AIDS awareness. *(Focus on Sport/Getty Images)*

Open and advanced to the final of the Grand Prix Masters.

Following a heart attack that led to quadruple bypass surgery in 1979, Ashe retired in 1980. He later became the national campaign chairperson for the American Heart Association.

Ashe served as a nonplaying Davis Cup captain from 1980 to 1985; during that time, the team won the title in 1981 and 1982. He was inducted into the International Tennis Hall of Fame in 1985, in his first year of eligibility, having won 33 tournaments, 800 matches, and three Grand Slams. In 1992, he was the first athlete to be named by *Sports Illustrated* as Sportsman of the Year after retirement.

Off the Court

Off the court, Ashe was outspoken on social issues and the concerns facing professional tennis. He played a benefit match to raise money for the Black Economic Union and Food First relief program in Holly Springs, Mississippi. He served as president of the Association of Tennis Professionals in 1974–1975.

Ashe also became involved in the fight against apartheid in South Africa. In 1970, he requested a visa from South Africa to play in that country's open tournament. When the request was denied because of his race, he called for the expulsion of South Africa from the Davis Cup.

In 1973, Ashe decided to challenge apartheid by playing in South Africa, believing that it was crucial for black South Africans to see a black tennis professional. He demanded total integration at the match site, Ellis Park in Johannesburg, and insisted that he be recognized as a black man rather than be given "honorary white" status, a common practice at the time for foreign blacks visiting the country.

Despite his opposition to apartheid, Ashe rejected the blackballing of white South African tennis players. In 1985, when he was arrested outside the South African embassy in Washington, D.C., while protesting apartheid, Ashe admitted that he had erred in traveling to South Africa earlier in his career. He was arrested a second time outside the White House, during a protest against the George H.W. Bush administration's policy toward Haitian refugees in 1992.

In addition to writing a number of articles for tennis magazines and business newsletters, Ashe penned a biweekly column for the *Washington Post,* and he also wrote several books, including *Arthur Ashe: Portrait in Motion* (1975); an introspective memoir, *Days of Grace*

(1993); and *A Hard Road to Glory* (1988), a three-volume encyclopedic history of blacks in sports. In the early 1980s, he taught an honors course, "Education and the Black Athlete," at Florida Memorial College (now Florida Memorial University) in Miami.

Ashe waged his final battle against AIDS, which he contracted from a blood transfusion performed when he underwent heart surgery in 1983. Ashe made a public announcement that he had AIDS, but maintained his right to privacy. Once again, he became a catalyst for public debate.

He worked as an activist for public awareness of HIV/AIDS, and addressed the United Nations on World AIDS Day, requesting increased funding for AIDS research. In 1992, he founded the Arthur Ashe Foundation to fund AIDS research, became a spokesperson for improved health care, and continued to work as a broadcaster for HBO at Wimbledon.

Ashe died of AIDS complications on February 6, 1993. At the time of his death, he was helping former United States Tennis Association president David Markin carry out the expansion of the National Tennis Center, which had replaced Forest Hills as the home of world-class tennis. The new stadium was named in his honor.

After his death, Ashe was widely honored for his contributions to the sport. In 1996, a 12-foot (3.6-meter) statue of Ashe, sculpted by Paul De Pasquale, was unveiled in Richmond, Virginia, where he had once been excluded from interracial competition. ESPN established the Arthur Ashe Courage Award, and the U.S. Postal Service honored Ashe with a commemorative stamp in 2005.

Sundiata A. Djata

See also: African Americans; Race and Race Relations; Tennis.

Further Reading

Ashe, Arthur, and Arnold Rampersad. *Days of Grace: A Memoir.* New York: Alfred A. Knopf, 1993.

Ashe, Arthur, with Frank Deford. *Arthur Ashe: Portrait in Motion.* Boston: Houghton Mifflin, 1975.

Djata, Sundiata A. *Blacks at the Net: Black Achievement in the History of Tennis.* Syracuse, NY: Syracuse University Press, 2006.

Martin, Marvin. *Arthur Ashe: Of Tennis and the Human Spirit.* New York: Franklin Watts, 1999.

Steins, Richard. *Arthur Ashe: A Biography.* Westport, CT: Greenwood, 2005.

Towle, Mike, comp. *I Remember Arthur Ashe: Memories of a True Tennis Pioneer and Champion of Social Causes by the People Who Knew Him.* Nashville, TN: Cumberland House, 2001.

Astrodome

When the city of Houston, Texas, gained a new franchise in baseball's National League in 1962, team owners promised to find a solution to the city's summer heat and humidity. The most prominent of the new owners, Roy Hofheinz (1912–1982), already had been dreaming of a domed stadium that would shut out heat, humidity, and rain, and provide its own controlled environment. The result was the Astrodome, which opened in the spring of 1965. The stadium succeeded in attracting Houston sports fans, lured by the prospect of watching baseball while getting out of the heat. It also allowed the team to avoid rain delays and postponements. The Astrodome's success made it a model for a series of new covered stadiums in the 1970s and 1980s.

Hofheinz borrowed the idea of a vast indoor stadium from visionary architect Buckminster Fuller, the designer of the geodesic dome. As Hofheinz noted in *Inside the Astrodome* (1965), "Fuller convinced me that it was possible to cover any size space if you didn't run out of money." Indeed, Hofheinz needed plenty of money for the facility he had in mind. The Astrodome cost more than $45 million to build, of which the owners put up $6 million, while the municipality paid the rest.

The new edifice introduced several Texas-sized innovations. The covered area measured 642 feet (196 meters), making the Astrodome the longest clear-span building in the world. It addition, it was the only fully air-conditioned sports stadium in the United States, and its huge illuminated scoreboard, nearly 500 feet (152 meters) tall, was the largest of its kind in the world. In the spirit of the times, the stadium was designed for multiple uses. In addition to the Houston Astros baseball team, it also was home to the Houston Oilers football franchise, the University of Houston football team, and the Houston Livestock and Rodeo Show.

Initial reactions to the Astrodome were overwhelmingly positive, but there were some unexpected problems. The stadium originally was built with a real grass playing field; translucent skylights admitted enough sunshine for the grass to prosper. Major league fielders soon learned, however, that the glare from the skylights made it almost impossible to see and catch fly balls. To solve the problem, many of the skylights were painted over, but the lack of sunlight killed the grass. The solution was another Astrodome first—AstroTurf. Hofheinz worked with the Monsanto Corporation to develop the first successful artificial playing surface in major

The world's first domed stadium, Houston's "space age" Astrodome opened in 1965. The semitransparent panes on the roof caused glare on the field and were replaced by white ones, which killed the grass. The solution? A synthetic surface called AstroTurf. *(Transcendental Graphics/Getty Images)*

league sports. During the 1970s, AstroTurf and other competing surfaces were installed on playing fields across the country. Although the artificial surfaces were expensive to install, compared to grass, they were much easier and cheaper to care for, requiring no sun, water, fertilizer, or maintenance.

The major league franchises that occupied the Astrodome never achieved their sports' highest honors. In 35 years, the Astros won four division titles but never advanced to a World Series. In 2000, the team moved into a new stadium, Minute Maid Park, which was scaled especially for baseball and had a retractable dome, allowing for play in the open air in good weather. In 33 years, the Oilers played only five playoff games at the Astrodome and never went to a Super Bowl. In 1998, the team moved to Nashville and became the Tennessee Titans. Houston was awarded a new National Football League (NFL) franchise, the Texans, but the team began play in 2002 in a brand new stadium with a retractable

roof. The venerable Astrodome was left without any major league franchises.

The Astrodome had its share of great moments. On January 20, 1968, the University of Houston basketball team played the top-ranked University of California, Los Angeles, and won 71–69, ending UCLA's 47-game winning streak. The crowd of 52,693 was the largest up to that time to see a basketball game in North America. Five years later, the stadium hosted one of the most anticipated tennis matches of all time. Former men's tennis star Bobby Riggs claimed that he could defeat the current women's champion, Billie Jean King. King accepted his challenge, and the match took place on September 20, 1973, before more than 30,000 fans and a national television audience. King beat Riggs in three straight sets.

The success of the Astrodome led to the construction of several other multipurpose, synthetic turf stadiums, notably Cincinnati's Riverfront Stadium and Pittsburgh's Three Rivers Stadium (both opened in 1970) and Philadelphia's Veterans Stadium (1971). These stadiums followed the basic design of the Astrodome, although none had a dome.

By the end of the 1970s, however, sports teams, fans, and players began to find fault with multipurpose stadiums. Baseball teams wanted cozier parks with seats closer to the diamond. Football teams wanted more seats, as they played only eight regular-season home games each year. Many NFL teams gained their own stadiums by 1990. In 1992, the Baltimore Orioles opened Camden Yards—an open air, grass stadium in the heart of the city. Other cities, including Houston, soon began building new parks as a means of downtown revitalization. Both the Astros and the Texans moved to new, dedicated stadiums. The new Houston stadiums were not designed as multiuse venues, but both adopted the Astrodome's main feature: a roof to keep out unwanted weather.

The Astrodome continues in use, still run by the Houston Sports Association, and it is now known as the Reliant Astrodome. The Dome hosts trade shows, pop concerts, and, on occasion, sporting events. In 2004, the Astrodome was the site of the championship game in the movie about Texas high school football, *Friday Night Lights*.

Brad Schultz

See also: Stadiums and Arenas; Technology.

Further Reading

Inside the Astrodome. Houston, TX: Houston Sports Association, 1965.
Lipsitz, George. "Sports Stadia and Urban Development: A Tale of Three Cities." *Journal of Sport and Social Issues* 8:2 (Summer/Fall 1984): 1–18.
Ray, Edgar W. *The Grand Huckster: Houston's Judge Roy Hofheinz, Genius of the Astrodome.* Memphis, TN: Memphis State University, 1980.

Athletic Clubs

Athletic clubs emerged in North America during the second half of the nineteenth century and flourished in the 1870s and 1880s. Originally, they were voluntary associations formed by wealthy white men who wanted to participate in sports and socialize with like-minded peers. The clubs functioned as a home away from home for men, who exercised, dined, and drank at these members-only establishments. Athletic clubs in the United States focused mainly on track and field, while Canadian clubs emphasized winter sports.

These athletic clubs resembled earlier hunting and fishing lodges, but they operated in cities rather than in the countryside. Such clubs helped establish organized amateur sports competition and played a vital role popularizing physical conditioning as a recreational activity.

New York Athletic Club

The first American track and field club was San Francisco's Olympic Club, founded in 1860. But the one that set the standard for all others was the New York Athletic Club, which was established in 1866 by three wealthy athletes who were interested in competing in track and field with men of similar interests and social status; two years later, the club incorporated. The New York Athletic Club was inspired by the London Athletic Club, founded in 1863, and the initial English amateur championship track meet in 1866.

The New York club built the first cinder track in North America and sponsored the first national championships in track and field (1876), swimming (1877), and boxing and wrestling (1878). It became a model for other clubs, including the Manhattan Athletic Club (1877), Los Angeles Athletic Club (1880), Boston Athletic Association (1887), and Detroit Athletic Club (1887). By 1883, there were about 150 metropolitan athletic clubs in the country; by 1900, most large and midsize U.S. cities boasted at least one club.

In Canada, the Montreal Amateur Athletic Association began in 1881, combining the city's snowshoe, bicycle, and lacrosse clubs. A decade later, the Toronto Athletic Club was organized; its building, completed in 1894, had the first indoor pool in the city.

By 1882, the New York Athletic Club no longer focused exclusively on sports, but became a status institution. In 1885, when it opened its $150,000, five-floor structure, it had 1,500 members of high social standing. Seven years later, the club built an even more impressive structure, but it was surpassed in 1893 by the Chicago Athletic Club's $1 million, nine-story edifice.

Club applicants had to be recommended by two current members, underwent a rigorous application process and background check, and had their membership put to a vote. Members could blackball candidates without explanation. The top athletic clubs, regardless of ethnicity, typically set high fees—$100 for initiation and $50 for annual dues—to discourage less affluent applicants. Elite club members were predominantly white Anglo-Saxon Protestants; this led New York's elite German Jews to form their own City Athletic Club.

Club Structure

Athletic clubs were run by a cabinet of elected officers and specialized committees that managed the clubhouse, handled membership and finances, organized athletics programs, and scheduled entertainment and social activities. Members enjoyed a wide range of amenities in a facility that provided escape from domestic matters in the company of other men and the opportunity to make business connections. Clubs typically were open from 8 A.M. to midnight or later, and they provided dining rooms, parlors, a library, a smoking room, a card room, billiards, bowling, and exercise and training facilities. Most clubs even offered apartments for long-term rentals.

Club life encompassed a full spectrum of entertainment and social events that included musical and dramatic groups and sponsored guest lectures, concerts, and plays. More affluent clubs, such as the Manhattan Athletic Club, even constructed concert halls and stages. Many clubs published newsletters that reported on club events, social news, and local happenings. The Detroit Athletic Club's *DAC News* and the Los Angeles Athletic Club's *Mercury* both circulated outside the club and functioned as their respective city's society magazine.

Athletic Programs, 1880–1939

The competitive impulse among clubs varied. Clubs that took competitive sports seriously often had "athletic memberships" that provided gifted athletes with temporary member status so that they could compete for the club. These clubs sponsored athletes who competed on the regional, national, and even Olympic level.

The Manhattan Athletic Club, for example, was a fierce competitor, staging athletic meets and sending representatives to distant competitions. Lon Myers, the American record holder in distances from 50 yards (48 meters) to 1 mile (1.6 kilometers), was employed by the club in the mid-1880s as its secretary and was provided with benefits that netted him $4,000. This kind of financing reeked of professionalism. The New York Athletic Club was aghast at such violations of the amateur code, and in 1888, it led the creation of the Amateur Athletic Union to control U.S. amateur sports (and perhaps to further its own competition with the Manhattan Athletic Club).

By the 1890s, some clubs were running into financial difficulties, partly as a result of the 1893 economic depression, and they struggled to survive. Some were consolidated, such as New York's Berkeley Athletic Club, which was absorbed by the University Athletic Club. The Los Angeles Athletic Club met financial ruin in 1901, but was resurrected four years later. The Detroit Athletic Club also faced financial difficulties and was saved by a benefactor who personally financed the club's activities. At the same time, the New York Athletic Club spent liberally in support of sport, and in 1905, it reportedly spent more than $25,000 on athletic competitions and training in sports such as cycling, fencing, ice-skating, water polo, and track and field events.

Some clubs, especially those formed in the twentieth century, recognized that focusing on all members' fitness, rather than a few select athletes, was a better financial strategy. The Minneapolis Athletic Club was organized specifically to serve members' physical, recreational, and social needs rather than to provide sporting entertainment. Its athletic director encouraged individual physical development through the use of ropes, ladders, Indian clubs, pommel horses, rings, and dumbbells. Handball, racquetball, and squash also were popular pursuits.

Swimming, under the "bath department," was a vital aspect of club programs. The Illinois Athletic Club and the New York Athletic Club dominated national swimming and water polo championships; the latter won 20 men's titles by 1939. The swimming pool, or "plunge," united the athletic aspects of the club with the social. Pool rooms often were decorated ornately. Minneapolis's pool boasted a waterfall, balcony, and palm trees, and at the Los Angeles club, alcoves with Moorish decor and sculpture overlooked the pool, where members could lunch poolside. Bath departments typically provided Russian, Turkish, and needle baths, massages, and barbering services.

Working-Class and Women's Athletic Clubs

Working-class athletic clubs proliferated in New York during the early 1900s, though they seldom had any athletic facilities or social pretensions. There were more than 700 small clubs in the city with as few as ten members. Working-class athletic clubs were sponsored by neighborhood organizations, occupations (such as firemen and postal workers), unions (such as the Building Trades Athletic Association), ethnic groups (such as the Irish American Athletic Club), and employers (such as the Millrose Athletic Association, organized by John Wanamaker). Athletes from the Irish American Athletic Club won nine gold medals at the 1908 Olympic Games in London.

Meanwhile, certain late-nineteenth-century athletic clubs included "lady members" who had family ties to male members. Women were spectators, social guests, and competitors, which helped raise club revenues, enhance social activities, and increased male loyalty to the club. The Brooklyn Athletic Club, for instance, opened its billiard and bowling facilities to women on Mondays and Fridays, and hired a female fencing instructor. In 1889, the Berkeley Athletic Club constructed a $200,000 midtown clubhouse for women members, set aside tennis courts and a running track at the Berkeley Oval in the Bronx, and allotted time for female scullers at its boathouse.

Several clubs created special areas for women—for example, the Minneapolis Athletic Club had a ladies' dining room to encourage women who were shopping downtown to lunch at the club—and developed programs, especially swimming lessons, for members' children. However, most athletic clubs did not admit women as full-fledged members until the 1970s.

Upper-class women organized their own athletic clubs and, in 1901, established the Federation of Women's Athletic Clubs. In 1898, the Chicago Woman's Athletic Club opened its $100,000 building, which included a gymnasium, pool, bowling alley, and billiard room. The 275 members included the leading women in the city. They paid $100 for initiation and $40 for dues.

Athletic Clubs After 1920

Few of the clubs founded in the late nineteenth century still exist today. Their decline began during World War I, when many members were deployed for military service. In the 1920s, Prohibition ended lucrative alcohol sales at club bars. Then, during the Great Depression, members' financial difficulties further hurt membership. World War II proved a large drain on membership, and after the war, suburbanization encouraged the establishment and growth of suburban country clubs at the expense of downtown clubs.

Survivors, such as San Francisco's Olympic Club, the Los Angeles Athletic Club, and the Detroit Athletic Club, became more financially savvy, increased their membership rolls, and developed modern athletic programs that emphasized new trends in fitness and health. Only a few, such as the New York and Los Angeles

athletic clubs, remained prominent in amateur competition by the 1950s, as a result of formalized rules governing amateur participation, the growing influence of organizations such as the Amateur Athletic Union, and the high cost of club programs. Open competition in the 1970s led to the professionalization of elite athletes.

The New York Athletic Club alone remains at the forefront of athletic clubs, with 7,000 members. Its current home on fashionable Central Park South is 24 stories tall. The New York Athletic Club was targeted on its one-hundredth anniversary in 1968 by an athletic boycott led by activist Harry Edwards to protest anti-Semitic and racist membership policies; the first women joined in 1987. The club's athletes have produced 215 Olympic medals, including 11 in 2004.

Shelly McKenzie

See also: Amateurism; Class, Economic and Social; Settlement Houses; Sokol Movement; Turnvereins; Young Men's Christian Association and Young Women's Christian Association; Young Men's/Women's Hebrew Association.

Further Reading

Fair, John D. "Strongmen of the Crescent City: Weightlifting at the New Orleans Athletic Club, 1872–1972." *Louisiana History* 45:4 (Fall 2004): 407–444.

Hilliard, Celia. *The Woman's Athletic Club of Chicago, 1898–1998: A History.* Chicago: Woman's Athletic Club, 1999.

Rader, Benjamin G. *American Sports: From the Age of Folk Games to the Age of Televised Sports.* 6th ed. Upper Saddle River, NJ: Prentice Hall, 2009.

Voyles, Kenneth H., and John A. Bluth. *The Detroit Athletic Club, 1887–2001.* Chicago: Arcadia, 2001.

Willis, Joe, and Richard Wettan. "Social Stratification in New York City Athletic Clubs, 1865–1915." *Journal of Sport History* 3:1 (Spring 1976): 45–63.

Young, Betty Lou. *Our First Century: The Los Angeles Athletic Club, 1880–1980.* Los Angeles: LAAC Press, 1979.

Athletics, Oakland/ Kansas City/ Philadelphia

Few baseball teams have had as wide a gap between their highs and lows as have the Athletics, who finished last in their league or conference 23 times, yet trail only the New York Yankees among American League (AL) teams in pennants (14) and World Series victories (9). The Athletics, who have played in three cities, enjoyed three different dynasties—two under legendary owner-manager Cornelius "Connie" Mack in Philadelphia and, after a 13-year hiatus in Kansas City, one under mercurial owner Charlie Finley in Oakland. Beginning in the 1990s, the Athletics became a model for small-market major league teams when they discarded traditional baseball metrics to ascertain a baseball player's worth in determining salaries in favor of an approach nicknamed "moneyball."

When Byron Bancroft "Ban" Johnson declared the year-old American League a major league in 1901, he sought to establish a team in Philadelphia. He chose Mack, a manager in the Western League (forerunner of the AL) and a former National League (NL) catcher, to lead the team. Mack named the team the Athletics to reflect the city's baseball legacy, which dated back to the original Athletics of the 1860s. Mack received a 25 percent interest in the club, while Cleveland coal baron Charles W. Somers put up the remainder of the seed money.

Philadelphia Origins

Arriving in Philadelphia, Mack enlisted two local sportswriters, Samuel "Butch" Jones and Frank Hough, to locate a ballpark site, which became Columbia Park, the Athletic's, or A's, home for the team's first eight years. Jones and Hough also introduced Mack to Ben Shibe, a partner of Al Reach, a former professional baseball player who had founded a prominent sporting goods company. Shibe acquired a half interest in the team, and Jones and Hough bought out the rest of Charles Somers's interest. As an inducement for Shibe, Mack persuaded league president Johnson to let the Reach company supply baseballs to the new league.

Jones and Hough became ardent promoters of the team, a role common among local sportswriters in those days. Hough was helpful to Mack in recruiting five players, most notably Napoleon Lajoie from the local NL Phillies. Lajoie won the first AL Triple Crown in 1901, hitting .426, still the highest season average in AL history. Mack acquired three more Phillies players before the 1902 season, in which the A's won their first championship and more than doubled their rival's attendance. The A's remained the city's favorite baseball team until after World War II.

The raids on the Phillies' roster, later curtailed by a court action, and Mack's strategy of recruiting collegians, such as future Hall of Famers Eddie Plank and Eddie Collins, enabled the A's to win six pennants and three World Series in 13 years, from 1902 to 1914, establishing the first AL dynasty. During that period, Mack developed a personal rivalry with New York Gi-

ants Manager John McGraw, who had called the A's "white elephants" because of their costly recruiting. Mack responded by adopting the elephant as the team mascot; he put a likeness on the uniform, and even gave McGraw a replica before their meeting in the 1905 World Series, which the Giants won.

Mack gained more than revenge as the A's defeated the Giants in two subsequent Series meetings, in 1911 and 1913. The elephant stayed on the uniform until 1928, returned when the team shifted to Kansas City in 1955, disappeared again when Charlie Finley bought the team in 1960, and then came back in 1988 to inspire the Oakland team to three successive pennants. The team's current mascot is an elephant, depicted on the A's uniform, named "Stomper."

Facilitating the first A's dynasty was Shibe Park. It opened in 1909 as the first steel-reinforced concrete baseball stadium and a harbinger of a major league building boom that saw older wooden parks replaced, culminating in the opening of Yankee Stadium in 1923. Shibe's namesake park featured a French Renaissance style and a domed tower, which included Mack's "oval office." The park's appeal helped set a record attendance of 675,000 in the first year and continued to provide added income to fund the dynasty.

After the A's 1913 World Series victory, Shibe countered the Yankees' pursuit of Mack with a financial restructuring that enabled Mack to become half owner of the team. In 1914, however, attendance dropped to 346,541, reducing the revenue needed to offset escalating salaries and causing Mack to speculate that fans preferred a contender to a repeat winner.

Immediately after the A's upset sweep by Boston's "Miracle Braves" in the 1914 World Series, Mack decided to dismantle the team in order to bring down its deficit. As a result, the 1915 A's were the first team in major league history to drop from first place to last in one year. Attendance plummeted to 146,223, while the rival Phillies captured their first NL pennant. The A's would finish in last place for six consecutive years before rebuilding during the more prosperous 1920s.

In 1922, Ben Shibe died, and he was succeeded in the front office by his sons Tom and Jack. On the field, the A's emerged from the cellar, then advanced to second place in 1925, drawing a record 869,703 fans. After finishing second or third for the next three years, the Shibes and Mack established a second dynasty with three consecutive pennants, winning more than 100 games each year.

Growing attendance had allowed Mack to purchase promising minor leaguers, including future Hall of Famers Robert Moses "Lefty" Grove, Al Simmons,

Jimmie Foxx, and Mickey Cochrane (whom he secured by buying the entire Portland Pacific Coast League team), creating one of the greatest teams of all time. The 1929 club went 104–46, taking the pennant by 18 games and the World Series in five over the Chicago Cubs. They went 102–52 in 1930 and took the Series in six over the St. Louis Cardinals.

In 1931, the A's won a franchise record 107 games, but they were upset by the St. Louis Cardinals' "Gashouse Gang" in the World Series. Following a second-place finish in 1932, Mack once again began to sell off players in order to offset the Depression-related attendance decline. He completed the purge by trading Foxx to the Boston Red Sox for $150,000 and two journeymen after the A's finished 1935 back in the cellar.

Tom and Jack Shibe died in 1936 and 1937, respectively, and Mack became president of the club. Beginning in 1935, the A's would finish in last place in 10 of Mack's final 16 years as manager.

Kansas City Hiatus

After the 1950 season, Mack's sons, supported by the Shibes, removed the 87-year-old "grand old man" from managing on the field. He remained titular president until the club was sold to Chicago businessman Arnold Johnson after the 1954 season and was moved to Kansas City. Mack died two years later, and the Phillies, who had played in Shibe Park since 1937, renamed it Connie Mack Stadium.

The A's spent an unlucky 13 years—six in last place—in Kansas City, six under Johnson and seven under another Chicago businessman, Charlie Finley, who moved the team to Oakland, California, in 1968. The A's lowly finishes were partly the result of team owner Johnson's close business relationship with New York Yankees owners Dan Topping and Del Webb. Before the A's arrived in Kansas City, its minor league team, the Kansas City Blues, had been a top farm club for the Yankees. Now, even though the A's played in the majors, they made 16 trades with the Yankees involving 59 players during Johnson's ownership, primarily sending top prospects to New York in exchange for over-the-hill veterans. The most notable transaction sent Roger Maris to the Yankees two years before he broke Babe Ruth's fabled 60-homer record.

Upon buying the A's, Finley vowed never to trade with the Yankees again. When General Manager Frank "Trader" Lane violated that promise four months later, Finley fired him. Finley operated as his own general manager for most of his 20-year tenure, personally signing top prospects, executing numerous trades, and

making 18 field managerial changes. Despite his volatile personality, which tended to alienate fans, media, managers, players, and fellow owners, he was responsible for several on-field innovations, including night All-Star and World Series games, the designated hitter, minor league rehabilitation for injured players, and interleague play.

Oakland Years

Finley's Oakland years saw another A's dynasty and its demise. Buoyed by key acquisitions and the development of homegrown talent, including Hall of Famers Roland "Rollie" Fingers, Jim "Catfish" Hunter, and Reggie Jackson, the A's moved from the cellar in a ten-team league in 1967, the last year in Kansas City, to 101 wins and a divisional championship four years later. A colorful, long-haired, mustached squad, the A's won the World Series in three straight years (1972–1974) for the first time in team history.

The A's earned another division championship the following year, but the team drew only slightly more than a million fans under Finley in 1973 and 1975. Finley then imitated Mack by beginning a wholesale player selloff that dropped them to the bottom of the division by 1977.

Despite a decline in salaries, continuing low attendance, which had dropped to 306,763 by 1979, prompted Finley to sell the club to avoid further financial losses. The team nearly moved to Denver, but the stadium lease blocked the sale. Then Walter Haas, Jr., chief executive officer of Levi Strauss and a local philanthropist, bought the team and recommitted to Oakland. The team, with strong community promotion, drew 1.3 million fans in 1981, 200,000 more than Finley's best, in a strike-shortened season of 109 games.

A return to glory occurred later in the decade. A rebuilt farm system, which had gone fallow during the late Finley era, produced three consecutive Rookie of the Year titles (1986–1988) and three straight pennants (1988–1990). The A's took the World Series in four straight games over the Bay Area rival San Francisco Giants in 1989, in the only postseason series ever postponed by an earthquake. The A's set an attendance record of 2,900,217 in 1990; however, the team also produced the highest payroll in the majors. Haas died in 1995, and the team was sold one year later to a syndicate of local real estate developers, Steve Schott, Dave Eethride, and Ken Hoffman.

The new owners promptly cut costs, but also reemphasized scouting and development, with a Mack-like focus on college players, such as Jason Giambi, as well as Latino recruits, such as Miguel Tejada, the AL's Most Valuable Player in 2002. However, the team's low-budget "moneyball" approach precluded them from keeping top players once they achieved free agent status. (The "moneyball" approach used nontraditional measures—such as slugging and on-base percentages—to help identify undervalued players.)

Despite the financial constraints of a small market, the A's have remained a perennial contender, finishing first or second in their division for eight straight years and making the playoffs five times through 2006, when they lost the AL championship to the Detroit Tigers. The current owner Lewis Wolff, who bought the team in 2005, continued his predecessors' quest for a new baseball-only stadium in the Bay Area. In November 2006, Wolff announced a plan to construct a new stadium in Fremont, 20 miles (32 kilometers) south of the current stadium, but the project was never carried forward.

Robert F. Lewis II

See also: Baseball, Major League; Mack, Connie.

Further Reading

Dickey, Glenn. *Champions: The Story of the First Two Oakland A's Dynasties and the Building of the Third.* Chicago: Triumph, 2002.

Jordan, David M. *The Athletics of Philadelphia: Connie Mack's White Elephants, 1901–1954.* Jefferson, NC: McFarland, 1999.

Kashatus, William C. *Connie Mack's '29 Triumph: The Rise and Fall of the Philadelphia Athletics Dynasty.* Jefferson, NC: McFarland, 1999.

Lewis, Michael. *Moneyball: The Art of Winning an Unfair Game.* New York: W.W. Norton, 2003.

Markusen, Bruce. *A Baseball Dynasty: Charlie Finley's Swingin' A's.* Haworth, NJ: St. Johann, 2002.

Peterson, John E. *The Kansas City Athletics: A Baseball History, 1954–1967.* Jefferson, NC: McFarland, 2003.

Atlas, Charles (1892–1972)

Charles Atlas was a twentieth-century pioneer in the fields of physical fitness and mail-order marketing. After becoming one of the first champion body builders, Atlas published his 12-week bodybuilding course, Dynamic-Tension, in 1923. Over the years, the course was bought by millions of consumers around the world, and it continues to be sold by the company that Atlas co-founded in 1929. The Dynamic-Tension program instructs students in how to perform exercises based on the principles of isometric contractions and offers basic nutritional advice.

Charles Atlas was born Angelo Siciliano on October 30, 1892, outside the town of Acri in the southern Italian region of Calabria, where he was apprenticed to a shoemaker at the age of six. Siciliano emigrated from the port of Naples with his mother, Francesca Fiorelli, arriving at Ellis Island, New York, on February 12, 1904. They settled in Brooklyn.

Like many immigrants of the time, Siciliano attended public school through the eighth grade, then sought paid labor to contribute to the family income. He took a series of jobs, including sweeping the floors of a candy factory and managing other immigrant laborers at a leather factory, utilizing the skills he had gained as an apprentice in Italy.

Siciliano was inspired to pursue physical fitness and bodybuilding after visiting the Brooklyn Museum of Art's Greek and Roman statuary rooms with a group from the Italian Settlement School. The physically fit Siciliano recognized a similarity between his own body and that depicted in a public sculpture of Atlas, the figure from Greek mythology. He adopted the name Charles Atlas.

From 1914 to 1921, Atlas used both names interchangeably as he began to seek employments for his muscular physique. In November 1914, he posed for the cover of the British edition of the popular magazine *Physical Culture*, and he performed as a strongman at Brooklyn's Coney Island amusement park (where he also worked as a janitor). In 1918, Atlas married Margaret Cassano in New York, and the couple had two children.

In the early 1920s, he modeled for several artists in New York's Greenwich Village, and from 1920 to 1926, he began producing testimonials for products sold by physical fitness entrepreneurs and companies, such as Earle Liederman and the Battle Creek Sanitarium. During this time, he began to gain a foothold in the competitive world of "physical culture"—a contemporary term encompassing activities as diverse as calisthenics and weightlifting.

Atlas first achieved national recognition in 1921 when he won the "Most Handsome Man" contest sponsored by *Physical Culture*, the magazine owned by fitness entrepreneur and editor Bernarr Macfadden. The following year, Atlas won another of Macfadden's contests, "The World's Most Perfectly Developed Man," at Madison Square Garden. Both victories awarded Atlas with prominent coverage in *Physical Culture* and a $1,000 prize. He used the money to found his first mail-order fitness company in 1923. He subsequently opened a gymnasium for men in Midtown Manhattan and a summer camp for children in the Catskill Mountains.

In the late 1920s, Atlas overextended himself financially and was forced to declare bankruptcy. Soon afterward, however, he entered into an important business partnership that would bring his name and message to millions around the world. On February 28, 1929, Atlas and Charles Roman, a young graduate of New York University with some marketing experience, formed Charles Atlas, Ltd. Roman overhauled the advertising for Atlas courses, focusing prominently on photographs and drawings of Atlas's body.

Atlas's best-known advertisement, "The Insult That Made a Man Out of 'Mac,'" first appeared in 1931 in *Physical Culture*. It still is a mainstay on the back covers of comic books worldwide. Considered the longest-running advertisement in American history, it employed a comic-strip format to describe the tale of its protagonist, a "97-pound weakling" whom Atlas likened to himself before he began working out. The scrawny boy first appears on the beach with a date, and a muscular bully humiliates them, kicking sand in their faces. Mac vows revenge, and sends away for Atlas's bodybuilding course. After completing the course, a physically transformed Mac returns to the beach, punches the bully, and regains the favor of his female companion. The ubiquity of "The Insult" in comic books from the 1940s on, as well as the advertisement's simple but powerful theme of personal metamorphosis, inspired scores of imitations. Nevertheless, it remains linked in the popular imagination with Atlas, whose photograph usually appeared beneath the comic strip in the ads.

By 1935, many of Atlas's former mentors and competitors, such as Liederman, had gone out of business, damaged by the Great Depression and the company's bold new advertisements. Atlas still faced competition from weightlifter Bob Hoffman, who alleged in 1935 in his magazine *Strength and Health* that Atlas had used weights to shape his physique rather than the isometrics that Dynamic-Tension promoted. Atlas sought the intervention of the Federal Trade Commission, claiming that Hoffman's allegations were untrue and that they had caused his business to suffer. Despite the opinion of several contemporary and present-day experts in anatomy and kinesiology that Atlas must have lifted weights in order to achieve his muscular bulk and definition—as well as Atlas's own statement in 1921 that he had begun his career in physical culture by using a homemade barbell—the commission sided with Atlas.

Thereafter, Atlas appeared frequently in the press as an expert in the fields of fitness and bodybuilding,

and as a groundbreaking entrepreneur. He died of heart failure on December 24, 1972.

Atlas had an enormous influence on North American popular culture and sports history. Generations of young people encountered his advertisements, which exhorted young men to tone their bodies and build muscle by purchasing and following the Dynamic-Tension program. Atlas's closing to each week's lesson—"Yours in perfect manhood"—symbolized his cultural import. Standing as a visual incarnation of ideal masculinity, Atlas helped ensure that broad shoulders, a trim waist, bulging biceps, and tanned skin would become synonymous with Americans' notions of a "real man." His legacy is apparent in the literature and songs inspired by his career (such as David Mamet's *Brown Paper Wrapper*, Sergio Ramirez's *Even Charles Atlas Dies*, and *The Rocky Horror Picture Show*'s "Charles Atlas Song"), as well as in the contemporary awareness of the importance of physical fitness to overall health and well-being.

Dominique Padurano

See also: Bodybuilding.

Further Reading

Bushyeager, Peter. "The World of Atlas." *Men's Health* 6:5 (October 1991): 56–61.

Danna, Sam. "The 97-Pound Weakling Who Became 'The World's Most Perfectly Developed Man.'" *Iron Game History* 4:4 (September 1996): 3–4.

Automobile Racing

The sport of automobile racing dates back more than 100 years. It began, as did bicycling racing, as a venue for testing the quality of different models, promoting products, and publicizing the need for good roads. Even manufacturers such as Henry Ford participated in early races.

The first races were open-road contests over hundreds or thousands of miles at a time when most roads were unpaved. These races tested the mettle of drivers, mechanics, and automobiles alike. By 1910, off-road racing was introduced, primarily as a test of speed and, second, of equipment. Off-road racing, most notably of open-wheel cars at the Indianapolis Motor Speedway, known as the Brickyard, soon became one of the most popular spectator events in North America.

Car racing's popularity skyrocketed after World War II with the rise of stock car racing under the auspices of the National Association of Stock Car Automobile Racing (NASCAR). It began as a Southern sport, but by 2000, it had become national in scope, watched by as many as 75 million fans on television, making it the second most popular televised sport after professional football.

Origins of Car Racing in North America

The first true automobile race took place in 1895, a grueling 732-mile (1,178-kilometer) epic in France from Paris to Bordeaux and back again. The top finisher completed the grind in 48 hours, but he was disqualified from victory because he drove a two-seater. The 31,000-franc prize went to M. Koechlin, who completed the course in a four-seater Peugeot in 59 hours.

The first car race in North America took place on November 28, 1895. It was a 54-mile (87-kilometer) round-trip race from Chicago to Evanston, Illinois, won by auto manufacturer Charles Duryea in 10 hours, 23 minutes. Chicago hosted the race because of the publicity given to transportation innovations at the recent World's Fair, the city's access to transportation routes, its relatively smooth streets, and the sponsorship of the *Chicago Times-Herald.* Despite all of these advantages, only two of the six cars finished the race.

In 1900, renowned sportsman and publisher James G. Bennett, Jr., publisher of the *New York Herald,* established the Gordon Bennett Cup, the first international race, with the goal of encouraging the production of superior automobiles. Each country was allowed three representatives. The races were staged annually in Europe through 1905.

In North America, the emphasis was on open-road racing, beginning in 1904 with the Vanderbilt Cup, which was run on open roads in Nassau County, New York. Railroad magnate and sportsman William K. Vanderbilt, who worried that American automobiles were inferior to their European counterparts, initiated the contest.

The same year, the American Automobile Association (AAA) sponsored its first major tour from Boston to New York and then on to St. Louis, site of the World's Fair, to promote car travel and sales and to campaign for safer roads. The annual race, known as the Glidden Tours, in honor of Charles J. Glidden, a financier and automobile fan who donated a trophy for the 1905 race, lasted through 1914. The tour gave manufacturers a chance to test their cars and promote their products, as the route followed difficult terrain, while publicizing the need for good roads. Drivers and their ride-along mechanics demonstrated their prowess by driving fast and showed off their mechanical and technical proficiency and ingenuity by making repairs on the fly.

Racing on public roads was hazardous to participants, spectators, and innocent bystanders. During the first stage of a 1903 race from Paris to Madrid, a crash on the road to Bordeaux resulted in the deaths of two drivers, a mechanic, and five spectators. Three years later, crowd control was so poor for the 1906 Vanderbilt race, which drew some 250,000 people, that the promoters cancelled the event in 1907.

That year, the French newspaper *Le Matin* and *The New York Times* jointly sponsored an automobile race from New York to Paris. Teams representing six nations set out on a westward course from New York on February 12, 1908. The American entry in the race was a Thomas Flyer, valued at $4,000, an enormous sum at the time. Before that time, only nine men had driven cross-country. The teams drove to Chicago and then on to San Francisco. From there, the racers traveled by ship to Japan and on to Vladivostok, Russia. Finally, they drove west to Paris, covering a total distance of 22,000 miles (35,406 kilometers). Mechanic George Schuster, who had taken over the driving from his teammate Montague Roberts in San Francisco, won the race, finishing with two other cars. Schuster completed the journey in 169 days—26 days ahead of the Germans and 49 days ahead of the Italians.

Off-Road Racing

Once automobile races left the public roads and moved to dedicated tracks, speed rather than endurance became the primary objective. The first racetrack designed specifically for automobiles was Brooklands, built by Hugh Locke-King on his estate near Weybridge, England, in 1907. It was primarily a site for testing and developing engines and other high-performance automobile parts. American enthusiasts seeking to encourage tourism in their regions soon organized races on enclosed tracks in Atlanta, Georgia; Daytona Beach, Florida; and Indianapolis, Indiana. Car manufacturers contributed to the Indianapolis track, which opened in 1909 and was constructed of 3.1 million paving bricks. It served not only as a racing site, but also as a testing facility for new technology and late-model cars.

The first important venue for all-out speed testing was Daytona Beach. The flat, wide, hard sand beaches of the town offered a surface that was superior to the roads and tracks of the 1920s and 1930s. Sir Malcolm Campbell of Great Britain became the first man to reach 150 miles (241 kilometers) per hour on the Daytona sands, but his goal of 300 miles (483 kilometers) per hour was unattainable on the beach. As a result, speed testing moved west in 1935 to the alkaline Bonneville Salt Flats of Utah.

By the 1980s, however, the salt flats at Bonneville had outlasted their usefulness for setting speed records. Serious testing moved to a longer course at Black Rock, Nevada, where Richard Noble set a land speed record of 403.10 miles (648.7 kilometers) per hour. In 1997, Andy Green exceeded the speed of sound in Noble's Thrust SSC.

Automobile racing was not merely the pastime of European and American playboys who built and drove their own machines. Local entrepreneurs in the early twentieth century constructed dirt tracks or converted horseracing ovals for the use of local men testing their cars and their mettle.

Grand Prix Racing

Grand Prix racing, in which cars race over an irregular road course featuring a variety of curves and hills, was inaugurated in 1906, with a six-lap race on a circuit at Le Mans, France. However, the sport did not debut in the United States until 1948, when a race was run in the hamlet of Watkins Glen, New York. It was the brainchild of law student Cameron Argetstinger, who had fallen in love with Grand Prix races during his summer vacations in Europe. The original course stretched 6.6 miles (10.6 kilometers) over asphalt, cement, dirt roads, and railroad crossings in and around Watkins Glen. The date became known as "The Day They Stopped the Trains."

A permanent 2.3-mile (3.7-kilometer) road course at Watkins Glen, built in 1956, has hosted NASCAR Grand National, Formula 1, Can-Am, Trans-Am, Six-Hour, Formula 5000, and CART/Indy races since then. Despite the Glen's relative success, Grand Prix racing has struggled to remain popular in North America. Changes in car design rendered the Glen course obsolete in 1980 and sent the Formula 1 Grand Prix on a two-decade-long search for a new, more viable venue.

Races in Sebring, Florida (1959); Riverside (1960) and Long Beach, California (1975, 1976, 1983); Las Vegas, Nevada (1981, 1982); Detroit, Michigan (1982); Dallas, Texas (1984); and Phoenix, Arizona (1989–1991) were sometimes competitive successes, though they rarely were financially rewarding for promoters.

The third Phoenix race drew only 18,000 fans to the city streets. The scorching heat also hindered the drivers, and only nine finished the course.

Thereafter, there was no Formula 1 racing in the United States until 2000, when it took place at the Indianapolis Motor Speedway for the first time. The race was a resounding success, drawing 225,000 attendees and a vast television audience. Unfortunately, tire issues turned the 2005 race into a farce, when seven of the ten teams withdrew from the race after the parade lap, unnerved by problems with their Michelin tires. The last Grand Prix was in 2008. The Canadian Grand Prix, held annually since 1967 (except for 1987), also was halted after the 2008 race.

Open-Wheel Racing

Open-wheel race cars usually are manufactured for racing only. Their wheels are situated outside the car's main body, and there is usually just one seat. The most famous venue for these cars is the Indianapolis 500, which was first run in 1911 and was attended by 80,000 fans. The winner was Ray Harroun, who achieved an average speed of 74.6 miles (120 kilometers) per hour. A national championship was sponsored by the AAA in 1905, but it soon was halted after several serious injuries. Following a four-year gap, the AAA resumed its backing of the Indianapolis 500; this backing continued until the 1955 race, in which driver Bill Vukovich was killed in an accident. That same year, a sports car in the Le Mans 24-hour endurance race in France crashed into a crowd of spectators, killing 80 people.

Thereafter, Indianapolis Motor Speedway owner Tony Hulman organized the United States Auto Club (USAC) to regulate championship automobile racing, which encompassed racing at the highest levels. The USAC also sanctioned other types of events, including sports car, sprint car, and stock car racing until 1984. The organization was jeopardized in 1978 when eight of its executives were killed in a plane crash, shortly after Hulman's death. Indy car owners and drivers demanded major innovations in racing, as events were poorly attended and television rights were sold for low rates. They also opposed the organization's efforts to keep the dated Offenhauser engine competitive with the more advanced Cosworth DFV engine.

Consequently, in 1979, team owners and drivers formed CART (Championship Auto Racing Teams) and left the USAC because of disputes over race promotion and prize money. The new organization took over negotiating television contracts and cultivating sponsorships for the races it promoted. The USAC fought back, but the top teams joined CART, which subsequently sponsored 13 of 20 open-wheel races in the United States.

The other top open-wheel racing series in the United States is the Indy Racing League (IRL), formed in 1994 by Tony George, owner of the Indianapolis Speedway, who wanted to create a more cost-efficient open-wheel series that would feature American drivers on American tracks. Not coincidentally, the creation of the IRL also gave George complete control over the teams and drivers in the Indianapolis 500. In 1996, the IRL's first year of competition, the IndyCar Series competed with CART, employing less expensive equipment and American drivers. A few low-profile teams and second-tier drivers competed at the Indianapolis 500, while the superior teams and drivers with CART sat on the sidelines.

Since then, the IRL has risen to dominate American open-wheel racing, attracting top teams and drivers, such as Roger Penske and Mario Andretti, Dan Whel-

don and Dario Franchitti, and, in the process, forcing CART into bankruptcy. CART emerged as the Champ Car World Series, and the competition between the two series continued. In 2008, the IndyCar Series merged with the Champ Car World Series, ending three decades of division in open-wheel racing.

Stock Car

Stock cars are production-based cars used for racing. Legend has it that stock car racing began in the southern Appalachian Mountains, where unruly young men drove untaxed moonshine liquor to market over twisting mountain roads in souped-up cars that could outrun the federal revenue men. The myth of stock car racing's origins can be attributed to a few colorful drivers, such as Robert Glen "Junior" Johnson of North Wilkesboro, North Carolina, who did in fact transport moonshine from the family still to cities in the Carolina Piedmont, was caught and convicted, and spent ten

In 1959, Lee Petty (42), one of the early superstars on the stock car racing circuit, leads the inaugural Daytona 500, which he won in a photo finish. He was also the father of Richard Petty, the most successful driver in the sport's history. *(ISC Archives/ Getty Images)*

months in a federal penitentiary. Johnson's exploits were vividly portrayed in a 1965 essay by Tom Wolfe, "Junior Johnson Is the Last American Hero. *Yes!*" in *Esquire*. Wolfe painted a heroic picture of Johnson outrunning and outwitting the law using his own native intelligence and frontier spirit. The essay is rightly a classic, even if it misrepresents the reality of stock car racing. Stock car racing grew up as a local sport on scores of tracks beginning in the mid-1930s.

In 1948, Bill France, Sr., owner of the Daytona Beach Roach course since 1938, led a syndicate of businessmen to form NASCAR. The organization rapidly became the governing body of stock car racing. NASCAR gradually moved the sport from its original dirt tracks to paved super-speedways in just over a decade.

NASCAR immediately attracted top drivers from across the country who were eager for better tracks and bigger purses. Jim Roper of Kansas won the first NASCAR race on June 19, 1949, at Charlotte, North Carolina, after the judges disqualified Glenn Dunnaway, the apparent winner, for modifying his shocks.

By 2000, NASCAR racing was the fastest-growing spectator sport in the United States, attracting huge audiences, in person and on television, lucrative sponsorships, and the envy of all other motor sports. NASCAR currently operates three circuits. At the top is the Nextel Cup, featuring the top drivers on top teams. The second-tier Busch Series mixes competition between veteran Nextel Cup drivers and younger, emerging drivers, often on tracks that do not host a Nextel Cup race. The Craftsman Truck Series is the third-tier circuit, offering opportunities to young and journeymen drivers and catering to the American taste for pickup trucks.

The most prestigious stock car race is the Daytona 500. From 1949 to 1958, the race was run on Daytona's road course, which incorporated parts of Highway A1A and the flat, hard-packed sand beach. In 1959, Lee Petty, patriarch of the legendary Petty racing clan, won the first 500 at the new Daytona International Speedway. Since then, the Daytona 500 has lived up to its moniker, "The Great American Race," just as NASCAR has grown into the most successful auto racing organization in the nation.

Drag Racing

Drag racing began on the dry lakebeds of the Southern California desert in the 1930s. It differed in several ways from the speed testing at venues such as Bonneville. The races pitted drivers against one another in one-on-one competition, in which the point was to accelerate

quickly. The cars were simply souped-up street cars. The term "drag racing" most likely referred to the popular practice of racing street cars down the "main drag"—or main street—of small towns, illegally in the wee hours of the morning.

In the early 1950s, promoters began building legal racing strips for quarter-mile (0.4-kilometer) racing, a move that authorities supported. The National Hot Rod Association (NHRA) began in 1953 to govern the emerging sport. The founder and first president of the organization was Wally Parks, a native of Goltry, Oklahoma, who had moved to California as a child. The NHRA moved drag racing off the streets and out of the desert into the fairgrounds, from which the sport eventually moved into specialized drag strips built for speed and safety.

The NHRA has grown into the largest sanctioning body in motor sports, with 80,000 members, 35,000 of them licensed competitors. Drag racing also is one of the more welcoming sports for women drivers. Legendary driver Shirley "Cha Cha" Muldowney began her career racing a Corvette. She fought the NHRA for the right to drive top-fuel dragsters and funny cars (supermodified stock cars that burn nitromethane fuel) and went on to win three NHRA Winston Top Fuel championships and 18 NHRA national events. In the mid-1980s, she surpassed 250 miles (402 kilometers) per hour, and she reached 312 miles (502 kilometers) per hour in 1998 at age 58.

Top-fuel dragsters and funny cars have vied for popularity throughout the years, but both have endured. Today, both have national cable television contracts and attract huge crowds to highly sophisticated drag strips across the country.

Sprint Cars and Midget Cars

Many top drivers on auto racing's professional circuits got their start in sprint car or midget car racing. Sprint cars are high-powered vehicles raced on short tracks, both paved and dirt. Sprint cars come in two types—those with wings and those without. The USAC took over the Sprint Car Racing Association in 1956, and thereafter sanctioned racing for nonwinged sprint cars, including the prestigious Silver Crown series beginning in 1971. The main promotional organization of winged sprint cars was Ted Johnson's World of Outlaws, the leading dirt sprint car racing series since 1978. Despite the danger implied by that name, the winged cars are easier to handle and less likely to go airborne than nonwinged cars.

Midget car racing features miniature, front-engine cars running on short (0.25- to 0.5-mile/0.4- to 0.8-kilometer) tracks, paved and dirt, that generally cover 2.5 to 25 miles (4 to 40 kilometers). The sport began at Gilmore Stadium in Los Angeles in 1934, and it thrived there until the facility closed in 1950. Midget racing is not child's play. Midget cars may weigh only 1,000 pounds (454 kilograms), but they carry engines of 200 to 300 horsepower and can accommodate adult drivers. Top races include the Chili Bowl, held in early January in Tulsa, Oklahoma. Young racers, ages 5 to 16, may begin their careers driving quarter midget cars, which are one-quarter the size of midgets. They are relatively low in cost and horsepower, and are raced on banked ovals only a twentieth of a mile (less than 300 feet/91 meters) in length.

The popularity of automobile racing was established early, within years of the technological innovations that led to the first motorcars. Over the years, various forms of racing—involving different venues and types of cars—have proliferated in the United States, Europe, and other parts of the world. In the past century, the sport in all of its manifestations has survived global war and depression, and supporters say, it certainly will outlast current concerns about the environmental impact of the automobile and the transition from the internal combustion engine to other forms of cleaner propulsion.

Darcy Plymire

See also: Endorsements, Athlete; Hot Rodding; Indianapolis 500; Industrialization; Motorcycle Sports; NASCAR; Technology.

Further Reading

Chapin, Kim. *Fast as White Lightning: The Story of Stock Car Racing.* New York: Three Rivers, 1998.

Charters, David Anderson. *The Chequered Past: Sports Car Racing and Rallying in Canada, 1951–1991.* Toronto, Canada: University of Toronto Press, 2007.

———. "It's a Guy Thing: The Experience of Women in Canadian Sports Car Competition." *Sport History Review* 37:2 (November 2006): 83–99.

Cole, Terrence M. "Ocean to Ocean by Model T: Henry Ford and the 1909 Transcontinental Auto Contest." *Journal of Sport History* 18:2 (Summer 1991): 224–240.

Hall, Randal L. "Before NASCAR: The Corporate and Civic Promotion of Automobile Racing in the American South, 1903–1927." *Journal of Southern History* 68:3 (August 2002): 629–668.

———. "Carnival of Speed: The Auto Racing Business in the Emerging South, 1930–1950." *North Carolina Historical Review* 84:3 (July 2007): 245–275.

National Hot Rod Association. "NHRA History: Drag Racing's Fast Start." http://sportsman.nhra.com/content/about.asp?articleid=3263&zoneid=101.

Nye, Doug. *The United States Grand Prix and Grand Prize Races, 1908–1977.* Garden City, NY: Doubleday, 1978.

Shackleford, Ben. "From Dirt Tracks to Superspeedways: The Modernization of Southern Auto Racing." *Atlanta History: A Journal of Georgia and the South* 46:2 (2004): 60–80.

Thompson, Neal. *Driving with the Devil: Southern Moonshine, Detroit Wheels, and the Birth of NASCAR.* New York: Crown, 2006.

Avalanche, Colorado/Quebec Nordiques

A National Hockey League (NHL) franchise with a roller-coaster history, both on and off the ice, the Colorado Avalanche began its existence as the Quebec Nordiques, competing with the archrival Montreal Canadiens for the affections of French Canadian fans. The team began in the upstart World Hockey Association (WHA) in 1972 before joining the NHL in 1979, when the two leagues merged. However, Quebec City's population of about 170,000 was too small to sustain the franchise even in hockey-mad Canada, and it moved to Colorado in 1995. There, the team was enormously successful, winning the Stanley Cup in its first year.

The birth of the Nordiques was unexpected. In 1972, a group of Quebec City businessmen led by Paul Racine and Marius Fortier sought a franchise in the new WHA, which they were able to secure only because funding for a San Francisco team fell through. The club was named "Les Nordiques," in reference to its northern geographic location (although four WHA cities actually were farther north). Few observers believed the WHA would succeed, especially the Quebec franchise.

The WHA's franchises tried to establish its credibility by stealing away big NHL stars. The Nordiques hired the Montreal Canadiens' Jean-Claude Tremblay and Marc Tardif. Then they convinced French Canadian icon Maurice "Rocket" Richard to become their head coach, but he resigned after only four games. The team made the WHA playoffs in five straight years (1974–1979) and won the championship trophy, the Avco Cup, in 1977.

In 1979–1980, the WHA shut down, and, after intense discussions, the Quebec, Edmonton, Winnipeg, and New England (Hartford, Connecticut) teams joined the NHL for a $6 million fee each. The expansion Nordiques did not make the playoffs. Team president Marcel

Aubut, a lawyer, decided to speed up the building process by "stealing" elite European players Peter, Anton, and Marián Šťastný from communist Czechoslovakia in 1980 and 1981.

The impact of the Šťastnýs, combined with that of such rising young stars as Michel Goulet and Dale Hunter, was to give the Nordiques more credibility. They made the playoffs in 1980–1981 and again the following year. In the 1981–1982 playoffs, they beat the legendary Montreal Canadiens in overtime in a decisive fifth game in Montreal. Until then, hockey cognoscenti had considered the Nordiques the Canadiens' weaker little brother. Their shocking victory made them an enemy of the Canadiens and split the province's fans in two.

The rivalry between the Canadiens and the Nordiques became one of the most intense in the NHL. The competition reached epic proportions and generated intense passions, even dividing families. French Canadian journalists lost their impartiality and became fans, cheering for their teams and coming close to fighting their own colleagues. The enmity was most intense during the Christmas holidays and during the playoffs. The worst moment came during the 1984 playoffs, when, on Good Friday, two bench-clearing brawls occurred. Suddenly, everyone realized that the contention had gone too far.

After the intensity of the early 1980s, when the Nordiques reached the conference finals twice, in 1982 and 1985, the club failed to make the playoffs for five straight years (1988–1992). In response, the team made high draft choices, including Eric Lindros in 1991; however, the projected superstar refused to play for Quebec, mainly because of language and marketing concerns, and sat out the season. The "Lindros Saga" ended when the Nordiques concluded a blockbuster trade with the Philadelphia Flyers for five established players, two first-round picks (including goaltender Jocelyn Thibault), the rights to Swedish teen star Peter Forsberg, and $15 million. Observers called the deal one of the most lopsided trades in NHL history.

After a very promising 1992–1993 campaign in which the team doubled its point total from 52 to 104,

the Nordiques returned to the playoffs but lost in the first round to the rival Canadiens, who went on to win the Stanley Cup. During the 1994–1995 season, the league played only 48 games because of an owners' lockout over a labor dispute. The Nordiques earned the best record in the Eastern Conference, but they lost in the first round of the playoffs. Unfortunately, President Aubut had major financial problems, paying players in U.S. dollars but selling tickets in Canadian dollars. Furthermore, they played in the smallest market in the NHL (and second smallest in North American team sports after the Green Bay Packers), which was virtually monolingual in French. Aubut sought aid from the provincial government, which refused to grant a bailout or build a new arena.

The team was sold to the COMSAT Entertainment Group of Denver. Renamed the Colorado Avalanche, the club played in McNichols Sports Arena and went on to have 487 consecutive sellouts over nearly 11 seasons. In their first year, the Avalanche, led by Joe Sakic, Forsberg, and newly acquired goaltender Patrick Roy, captured the Pacific Division and won the Stanley Cup in four straight games over the Florida Panthers.

Quebec hockey fans who had been left empty handed finally saw their championship dreams come true, albeit in another city. The Avalanche became a dominant NHL team with eight divisional titles and a second Stanley Cup in 2001–2002. They returned to postseason play in 2005–2006, 2007–2008, and 2009–2010, but did not advance beyond the semifinals in those seasons.

Jocelyn East

See also: Ice Hockey; World Hockey Association.

Further Reading

Diamond, Dan, ed. *The Official National Hockey League 75th Anniversary Commemorative Book.* Toronto, Canada: McClelland & Stewart, 1991.

Quebec Nordiques. *The Quebec Nordiques: 1995 Official Yearbook.* Quebec: Quebec Nordiques Communications Department, 1995.

Baker, Hobey
(1892–1918)

Hobey Baker, the only athlete to be inducted into both the College Football Hall of Fame and the International Hockey Hall of Fame, was one of the great amateur athletes of the early twentieth century. For many Americans, he was a symbol of all that was good about American intercollegiate sports, and he has remained a lasting icon of intercollegiate sophistication, sportsmanship, and gallantry. He was a sort of "Frank Merriwell"—the fictional, all-around Yale University sports hero of the turn of the century—in flesh and blood, as well as a tragic figure who died young defending his country.

Hobart Amory Hare "Hobey" Baker was born in Wissahickon, Pennsylvania, near Philadelphia, on January 15, 1892, one of two children of A. Thornton Baker, a wealthy manufacturer, and his wife Mary Augusta. At the age of 10, Hobey was sent off to St. Paul's School in Concord, New Hampshire, where he played all of the sports the school offered and developed into an outstanding all-around athlete.

From the age of 14, Baker was recognized as a budding hockey superstar. Possessed of blazing natural skating speed and maneuverability, and equally fast going forward or backward, he developed into a superb puck handler through long practices in the dark on the outdoor pond at St. Paul's. Baker led his team to stunning victories over highly regarded teams from Princeton and Harvard universities.

He entered Princeton in fall 1910, a very muscular 5 feet, 9 inches (1.8 meters) and 160 pounds (73 kilograms), and immediately immersed himself in the school's athletic life. Faculty rules restricted him to two varsity sports; he chose to play football and hockey, even though he also was an outstanding baseball outfielder and a strong swimmer.

A halfback, he broke into the football team's lineup by mid-season 1911 and led the way to a 30–0 win over Colgate University with two touchdown runs. From his first game, Baker—who never wore a helmet—was the team's punt returner, catching the ball on the dead run to build up momentum. In a 1911 game against Yale, he returned 13 punts, a school record, as Princeton completed an 8–0–2 season and was considered by the press the unofficial or mythical national champion.

One year later, Princeton compiled a 7–1–1 record, while Baker added field goal kicking as a drop-kicker to his repertoire. He broke off a 75-yard run against Dartmouth, and in a 6–6 tie with Yale, he kicked two field goals and piled up 180 yards of punt-return yardage. Baker scored a total of 92 points for the season (a school record that stood for more than 50 years), was named a first-team All-American by Parke Davis and Hamilton Fish, and was on Walter Camp's third-team list. In the 1913 season, Baker captained the 5–2–1 Tigers, highlighted by an 85-yard punt return for a touchdown against Dartmouth College and a 43-yard field goal to produce a 3–3 tie with Yale. Again he was named a third-team All-American by Camp.

As outstanding as he was at football, Baker was even better at ice hockey. Stepping in as a sophomore at the "rover" position, he was at once a dominating player. His speed and puck-handling skill often sent him roaring up the ice in an end-to-end rush as he led the Princeton attacks on goal. Teams frequently used extremely rough play to try to slow him down, yet he never retaliated and soon was recognized as a sterling example of gentlemanly sportsmanship. Because Princeton had no on-campus ice rink, the team played all of its home games at St. Nicholas Arena in New York City. Baker soon was acclaimed as the premier player in college hockey, and an appearance by Princeton attracted boisterous sellout crowds.

Early in his sophomore hockey season of 1911–1912, Baker poured in six goals against Williams College. Princeton lost just twice and generally was considered the intercollegiate champion. In his junior hockey season of 1912–1913, Baker was team captain, and Princeton again lost only two games. In 1913–1914, he led the Tigers to another national championship.

Baker was a hardworking student majoring in the Department of History, Economics, and Politics, and he graduated in 1914. After the excitement and glamour of his college days, he faced an uncertain future. He toured Europe on a motorcycle after graduation and then became a trainee at the J.P. Morgan Bank for $80 per month.

Working in a variety of minor clerical jobs, Baker chaffed under his new lifestyle and was frustrated by the relative inactivity. Seeking a return to athletic excitement, he joined the amateur St. Nicholas Arena hockey team, starring for one of the top teams in the East. In his first game in 1914–1915, Baker scored five goals in a narrow win over Toronto's top team, and he followed that with three goals against the defending Canadian champions. At the end of the season, St. Nicholas won the American championship. The high point of Baker's amateur days came in late 1915, when he tallied two goals and three assists in a 6–2 win over the Montreal Stars in the Ross Cup series.

Baker joined the U.S. Army in 1917, when the United States entered World War I. Having taken flying lessons, he became a pilot. He was among the first American airmen sent to France as a first lieutenant in the Lafayette Escadrille. The chance to engage in aerial combat brought a return of the thrills that Baker had experienced as an athletic superstar. He was credited with three official "kills" of enemy planes and was awarded the Croix de Guerre (Cross of War).

In August 1918, Baker was promoted to the rank of captain and placed in charge of the newly formed 141st Squadron. Ordered to return home after the war, he insisted on one last test flight in a squadron airplane that had just undergone repairs. To the horror of onlookers, the plane lost power shortly after takeoff. Baker attempted to land the plane, but it crashed short of the airfield. He died on December 21, 1918, in an ambulance on the way to the hospital.

From his athletic career through his wartime days as a pilot, Baker was regarded as one of the foremost symbols of his generation. F. Scott Fitzgerald patterned a character in his novel *This Side of Paradise* after him. He is commemorated in Toul, France, where his fatal accident occurred, with a gymnasium and football field named for him, and Princeton's ice rink is named in his honor. Baker was elected to the International Hockey Hall of Fame in 1945 and the College Football Hall of Fame in 1977.

Raymond Schmidt

See also: Football, College; Ice Hockey.

Further Reading

Davies, John. *The Legend of Hobey Baker.* Boston: Little, Brown, 1966.

Fimrite, Ron. "A Flame That Burned Too Brightly." *Sports Illustrated* 74:10 (March 18, 1991): 78–90.

Royce, Bob. "He Lived For Excitement." *College Football Historical Society* 7:3 (May 1994): 16–18.

Salvini, Emil R. *Hobey Baker: American Legend.* St. Paul, MN: Hobey Baker Memorial Foundation, 2005.

Baseball, to 1870

Contrary to popular mythology, Civil War General Abner Doubleday did not invent baseball in 1839 when he was a West Point cadet living in Cooperstown, New York. In reality, baseball evolved over many years from several different versions of ball games. During the early days of the sport, players standardized rules taken from different sports and from variations on the game.

Baseball's modern rules were set down in 1845 by the Knickerbocker Base Ball Club. By the 1850s, enthusiasts had organized a number of clubs and leagues. The game spread beyond the Northeast, and soon it was considered the national pastime. By the late 1860s, baseball was becoming professionalized and commercialized.

Origins in the British Isles

Baseball evolved from a variety of English and Gaelic stick and ball games, such as old cat, cricket, and rounders. Rounders resembled cricket more than baseball, with a player bowling a ball to a "striker" or batter, but unlike cricket, it had a circuit of safe areas, like baseball. Although baseball's connection to such ball games is not exactly clear, it competed with all of them for popularity during the first half of the nineteenth century.

Games of "base" were played before the American Revolution and at Valley Forge, Pennsylvania, in 1778. "Baste ball" was banned at Princeton College in 1787 because it was considered dangerous and inappropriate for gentlemen. Four years later, the town of Pittsfield, Massachusetts, forbade the playing of baseball and several other ball sports near the town hall. Baseball historian David Block uncovered a German text published in 1796 that contains elementary rules for such a game and even mentions the word "baseball."

During the early nineteenth century, Americans played versions of a game called town ball. This game

Union prisoners play a game of baseball at the Confederate prison in Salisbury, North Carolina, during the Civil War. The conflict helped make baseball a national phenomenon, as Northern soldiers carried the game south and west. *(Library of Congress)*

differed significantly from modern baseball: It lacked foul territories and employed "soaking" (putting a player out by hitting him with the ball); the field was shaped in a square, with the batter standing between third and fourth (home) base. Innings lasted different lengths, depending on the region. In some versions, every player batted during an inning, while in others, there was only a single out per inning.

The "Massachusetts game" was similar to town ball, and it competed with the "New York game." The Massachusetts game allowed overhand pitching and required that players catch a batted ball on the fly to make an out. The New York game allowed outs to be called when a fielder caught a batted ball on one bounce.

The first known game of "baseball" was played in New York City by two clubs in Manhattan in 1832, one of which later became the New York Club. Ten years later, a group of young office workers who considered themselves "gentlemen" began to gather at Manhattan's Madison Square for informal ball games. They played under an evolving set of rules, and these rules formed the basis of modern baseball.

The main figure in this group was Alexander Cartwright, a New York bookseller, who in 1845 formalized the group as the Knickerbocker Baseball Club and helped draw up 14 rules for playing baseball. The field was diamond shaped, with foul lines. Batters could be put out by catching a batted ball on the fly, tagging the runner with the ball, or gaining a force-out. "Soaking," or throwing the ball at a runner to put him out, was not allowed. The distance across the diamond, from home to second base and from first to third base, was set at 105 feet (32 meters), making each base 74.25 (22.6 meters) feet apart. Pitching was underhand, and innings lasted until three outs were made. All teams had an equal number of turns at bat, and a winner was decided when 21 aces (runs) were scored. On pitches, no balls or strikes were called.

An intrasquad game was played on October 6, 1845, using the new rules. On October 21, the New York Base Ball Club (not to be confused with the Knickerbocker Club) defeated the Brooklyn Base Ball Club 24–4 at the Elysian Fields in Hoboken, New Jersey, just across the Hudson River from New York City. There was a rematch four days later in Brooklyn, won by New York 37–19. It is not clear which version of the rules these two games used.

The Elysian Fields became the primary field for the Knickerbockers, as there was no adequate place to play in Lower Manhattan. They played the New York

Club there on June 19, 1846, losing 23–1 in what is considered the first intersquad game using modern baseball rules. By the 1850s, there were dozens of clubs in metropolitan New York, particularly in Brooklyn, including the Eagles, Eckfords, Gothams, and Mutuals. Several of the finest teams were organized as social clubs of small merchants and clerks. Other teams were organized by neighborhood, political affiliation, or occupation (such as butchers, shipwrights, and firemen). More clubs soon appeared elsewhere in the Mid-Atlantic area.

At this time, players played without gloves (leading to many injuries), frequently made their own bats and balls, and played on irregularly sized fields. They practiced and played intrasquad games, which led to exhibitions against other clubs.

In 1857, a convention of New York baseball players revised the length of games to nine innings and standardized the size of teams to nine players. They formed the National Association of Base Ball Players, an amateur organization, to oversee the rules and create a championship. The Brooklyn Atlantics won the first league championship in 1859 and defended it for the next two years.

The growing seriousness of play led to professionalization. The first paid player was New Yorker James Creighton, who was recruited to play for the Excelsiors of Brooklyn in 1860. Creighton was the dominant pitcher of his day; he created the fastball and changeup pitches and pitched the first shutout game. He also was one of the era's best hitters.

Other groups also had begun to play baseball. On July 1, 1859, Amherst College defeated Williams College 73–32 under the Massachusetts rules in the first recorded intercollegiate baseball game. African Americans usually played in segregated clubs and were excluded from white clubs and leagues.

Origins of the Modern Game

Eventually, the New York game became the predominant version. It rapidly surpassed the popularity of the other main bat-and-ball game, cricket, which had dominated in the 1840s. Baseball had simpler rules, did not require a perfectly laid out field, did not take days to complete, and was considered an "American" game.

The success of the New York game also relied on factors outside the game. The growth of New York City was a key factor in baseball's dramatic expansion. Urbanization and an increasingly sedentary lifestyle in cramped apartments and factories drove the baseball craze. New York was the economic, commercial, and information center of the country, and its businessmen and periodicals exported the game to other regions of the country. Such local publications as *The Spirit of the Times,* the *New York Clipper,* and the *National Police Gazette* promoted the city's sporting culture and carried regular baseball coverage. English immigrant Henry Chadwick, a passionate supporter of baseball, who invented the box score and was the game's first statistician, wrote for the *New York Clipper.* He also helped make the game more demanding, mainly by campaigning successfully for the fly-out rule (1864), which disallowed outs on balls caught on one bounce.

By the eve of the Civil War, cartoons and newspapers had declared baseball the "national pastime," but it did not become a true national phenomenon until the war. The conflict took young men away from their hometown teams, which struggled during the war years, but it also helped spread the game to the West and the South. Northeastern soldiers taught the game to soldiers from other regions, and it provided a means of escaping intense boredom in camps or prisons. Union soldiers routinely played baseball in the camps and fortresses that surrounded Washington, D.C., with attendance in the tens of thousands, as soldiers and civilians watched and gambled on games. The game also was taught to Confederate prisoners, including officers who played while incarcerated in a prison camp on Johnson's Island in Lake Erie.

After the war, baseball exploded in popularity, and it quickly displaced other sports for the nation's attention. The game began a transition from a recreational activity to a business. Clubs built fences around their fields and charged admission for spectators or "kranks" to watch their best players or "first nine" play against another team's first nines. The first to do this was William H. Cammeyer, who remodeled his skating rink in Brooklyn into an enclosed baseball field in 1862 and charged spectators 10 cents to sit on his benches.

Teams also employed professional players, at first surreptitiously, to ensure victories. At the end of 1868, the National Association of Base Ball Players established a professional category, and in 1869, 12 teams declared themselves professional. The Cincinnati Red Stockings, the first openly salaried professional baseball team, toured the country, with a record of 57–0–1 over other National Association teams. The Red Stockings followed up in 1870 with 26 victories until the team finally was defeated by the Brooklyn Atlantics.

The Red Stockings were led by player-manager Harry Wright and his brother George, the team's best player. The Wrights' father had been a professional

English cricket player. As manager, Harry Wright was an excellent evaluator of talent, recruiter, motivator, and tactician, who developed some of baseball's first strategies. The Red Stockings, however, struggled at the box office, earning just $1.39 in 1869, their record-breaking season. The team disbanded after the 1870 season. Nonetheless, their success on the field encouraged other teams to become completely professional.

In 1871, amateurs and professionals separated. The pros set up the National Association of Professional Base Ball Players, the first professional baseball league, and 18 amateur clubs organized the National Association of Amateur Base Ball Players. Baseball had changed from a regional pastime into a modern national game with standardized rules across the country.

Aaron W. Miller

See also: African American Baseball, Before 1920; Baseball, Major League; Reds, Cincinnati.

Further Reading

Adelman, Melvin L. *A Sporting Time: New York City and the Rise of Modern Athletics, 1820–70.* Urbana: University of Illinois Press, 1986.

Block, David. *Baseball Before We Knew It: A Search for the Roots of the Game.* Lincoln: University of Nebraska Press, 2005.

Goldstein, Warren. *Playing for Keeps: A History of Early Baseball.* Ithaca, NY: Cornell University Press, 1989.

Kirsch, George B. *Baseball in Blue and Gray: The National Pastime During the Civil War.* Princeton, NJ: Princeton University Press, 2003.

Martin, Jay. *Live All You Can: Alexander Joy Cartwright and the Invention of Modern Baseball.* New York: Columbia University Press, 2009.

Rader, Benjamin G. *Baseball: A History of America's Game.* 3rd ed. Urbana: University of Illinois Press, 2008.

Ryczek, William J. *When Johnny Came Sliding Home: The Post–Civil War Baseball Boom, 1865–1870.* Jefferson, NC: McFarland, 2006.

Seymour, Harold. *Baseball.* 3 vols. New York: Oxford University Press, 1960–1989.

Tygiel, Jules. *Past Time: Baseball as History.* New York: Oxford University Press, 2000.

Wright, Marshall D. *The National Association of Base Ball Players, 1857–1870.* Jefferson, NC: McFarland, 2000.

Baseball, Major League

Major League Baseball (MLB) is the highest level of competition in America's national pastime. It is the oldest professional sports league in the world and the most stable professional sports circuit, dating to 1876.

Star players became local and national icons, and heroes to North American youth. It comprises the National League (currently 16 teams) and the American League (14 teams). No franchise has gone out of business since 1902, none moved between 1903 and 1952, and no new clubs were initiated from to 1903 through 1959.

The MLB's purpose was to make money for its owners, who operated as a monopsony (a market structure in which the product or service of several sellers is sought by only one buyer), and it successfully has blocked the rise of rival leagues since 1903, when the American and National Leagues merged. MLB tried many schemes to increase attendance and to limit costs, particularly player salaries through the use of the reserve clause. Management dominated relations with employees until the mid-1970s, when players were empowered to become free agents and vigorously negotiate contracts.

The National Association

The first overtly professional team was Harry Wright's Cincinnati Red Stockings in 1869, and their success on the diamond encouraged businessmen in other cities to back professional clubs, hoping to boost their cities' reputations. In 1871, entrepreneurs organized the National Association of Base Ball Players (NA), the first professional league. The NA maintained amateur traditions of player leadership, with little central control. Membership cost just $10 per team.

There were franchises in very small cities, schedules were haphazardly arranged, players switched teams on their own in mid-season, and several squads abruptly quit during the campaign. There was little competition, as the NA was dominated by Wright's Boston team (composed mostly of former Red Stockings), which won four championships, dampening fan interest. Player salaries averaged about $1,400, and even Boston totaled only $38,000 in gross receipts, almost entirely from ticket sales.

The National League: Becoming a Business

In 1876, William Hulbert of the Chicago White Stockings (which later became the Cubs) spearheaded a drive to form a new owner-dominated league that was aimed at making a profit. Called the National League (NL), it had stricter rules, charged prospective owners $100 for membership, required a minimum population of 75,000 for any host city, and delegated schedule making to the league. To attract respectable middle-class patrons, the NL banned gambling (charges of gambler influence had tarnished earlier organizations), the sale of beer or liquor at parks, and Sunday games.

Six of the initial eight franchises in the NL came from the NA. However, some strong pro teams did not seek membership in the new league and threatened to mount strong competition to the NL. Furthermore, the NL teams in Philadelphia and New York did not finish the 1876 season and were expelled from the league. A year later, four players of the Louisville Grays were banned for fixing games.

In 1879, Boston Red Stockings co-owner Arthur Soden introduced the reserve clause. By making players the exclusive "property" of a team, the new clause restricted players' ability to quit one team to play for another and weakened their bargaining position in negotiating for higher pay. The system allowed owners to maintain team continuity and, more important, to reduce pressure to pay higher player salaries, which was their largest expense. Pay declined about 20 percent over the next few seasons, and teams became profitable.

During the 1880s and early 1890s, NL owners also worked to perfect the game. They allowed pitchers to throw the ball overhand and called for a mound (a slight elevation in the middle of the infield) for the pitcher to throw from. These innovations tipped the game too far in favor of the pitcher, however, so the league lengthened the distance from the pitcher's rubber to home plate from 45 feet (13.7 meters) to 60 feet, 6 inches (18.4 meters). These new regulations remain in force today.

The top team of the early 1880s was the Chicago White Stockings, who captured five pennants between 1880 and 1886, led by the versatile Hall of Famer Mike "King" Kelly, the most popular player prior to Babe Ruth. Attendance averaged about 3,000 per game, and most teams were making money. The NL's success encouraged town boosters and baseball fans outside the league to form rival organizations.

The American Association began play in 1882, and a third league, the Union Association, opened in 1884, producing a record 33 major league teams that season. The Union Association survived only a single season. The American Association had more success, appealing to working-class fans. Admission was only 25 cents, alcohol was sold at the park, and games were played on Sunday, the only day most workingmen could attend, as they were required to work a six-day week.

In 1883, the American Association and the National League, together with some minor leagues, signed a National Agreement in which they agreed to honor each other's player contracts, including the reserve clause. A year later, teams in the two leagues played the first World Series, which was won by the Providence Grays (National League) over the New York Metropolitans (American Association) in three games.

Less positive was the racial stance of "organized baseball" during this period. In 1884, two African American brothers, Moses Fleetwood "Fleet" Walker and Welday "Weldy" Walker, played for the Toledo Blue Stockings of the American Association, but despite efforts by John Ward and a few others, the leagues' owners banned blacks from the majors. Minor league owners soon curtailed the hiring of African Americans by establishing unwritten "gentlemen's agreements," and by 1900, prejudice had forced them out of organized baseball altogether. African Americans would not be permitted to participate again until 1947, when Jackie Robinson joined the Brooklyn Dodgers.

Players' League

The National League's New York Giants reportedly ended the 1883 season with more than $100,000 in profit, gained largely by paying their players minimal salaries. The players responded by forming sport's first union, the Brotherhood of Professional Baseball Players, in 1885 under the leadership of Giants star shortstop and pitcher John Montgomery Ward. The Brotherhood began pressuring owners in the major league to increase player salaries. Soon, the players and owners went to war.

After the 1888 season, former pitching star Albert Spalding, owner of the Chicago White Stockings and a major entrepreneur in sporting goods, organized an around-the-world tour, in which Chicago would play Ward's All-Star team, to demonstrate baseball to the rest of the world. While the members of the tour, including Ward and other Brotherhood leaders, were far from home, major league owners passed a Classification Plan that would slash player salaries to a $2,500 maximum.

When Ward and his lieutenants learned of the plan, they began organizing a cooperative, revenue-sharing Players' League, which began play in spring 1890. Because the new league guaranteed free agency, many leading NL players jumped to the Players' League, investing their savings to organize teams and build new parks. Additional capital was contributed by the owners of interurban trolley companies, who understood that baseball crowds could increase their business.

All three leagues lost heavily in 1890, with salaries at an all-time high, but the National League was the only one rich enough to survive the tough times. Spalding played an important role in the National League's victory. He invited Players' League owners to consider membership in the established National League. Some jumped at the chance, leaving the Players' League with too few teams and too little appeal to continue. The innovative and popular league soon folded.

Monopoly Baseball

In 1892, the American Association also folded, and the National League added its four strongest teams, becoming the only major league. The 12-team circuit established and strictly enforced a $2,400 pay limit for players, cutting the salaries of many veterans. However, business declined, partly because of the economic depression of 1893 and its aftermath, and also because the owners' monopoly tactics and reports that bitter players were paid by gamblers to throw crucial games drove fans and sportswriters away. Many wooden ballparks burned down in the 1890s, but owners refused to build more expensive fire-resistant parks.

The dominant style of play in these years emphasized speed and inside strategy. This style was pioneered by Baltimore Orioles manager and president Ned Hanlon, whose club won three straight pennants (1894–1896).

American League Creates a Formula for Success

In 1900, the faltering 12-club NL dropped four franchises: Baltimore, Louisville, Washington, and Cleveland. The Cleveland team had won only 20 games and lost 134 after its owners traded all of the club's best players to St. Louis, which was under the same ownership.

The NL's downsizing provided an opportunity for a new circuit to move in. Former sportswriter Ban Johnson, who had become president of the Western League, recruited Charles Somers of Cleveland as the league's primary investor, and former players Charles Comiskey and Cornelius "Connie" Mack, both of whom had played in the Players' League and the National League, as key organizers. The minor Western League became the American League (AL) in 1900, and it went to the majors a year later with eight teams, including Comiskey's Chicago White Sox and owner-manager Mack's Philadelphia Athletics. The new league vigorously raided the older circuit, landing at least 74 National Leaguers.

Johnson's American League delivered open competition and cleaner play, and it recruited fan-friendly owners. The junior circuit also beat the National League at the box office. In 1903, the National League sued for peace. A modified National Agreement was drawn up, in which each league recognized the contracts of the other. In addition, the National Commission was created—the two league presidents plus Cincinnati Reds owner Garry Herrmann, an associate of Johnson—to resolve disputes in professional baseball and to establish an annual World Series. Pro leagues that did not sign the National Agreement were considered "outlaws."

Baseball became a profitable business, with attendance doubling by the end of the first decade. It was not uncommon for teams to make $100,000 in just one season and for the value of teams to rise rapidly. One of the most profitable teams, the NL Chicago Cubs, was bought in 1905 for $105,000, and sold for $500,000 in 1916, having made its owners $1.26 million in the interim. Such profits encouraged baseball magnates to build large, new concrete-and-steel ballparks, and the owners' powerful political connections enabled them to obtain excellent locations near mass transit. This started with Forbes Field in Pittsburgh and Shibe Park in Philadelphia in 1909, and by 1915, nearly all of the teams had new fire-resistant ballparks seating 25,000 to 40,000 people.

At the same time, the sport received widespread press and magazine coverage. Its popularity led William Howard Taft in 1910 to initiate the tradition of the president throwing out the first ball on opening day in Washington, D.C., to project an image as a man of the people.

The years between 1893 and 1920 are known as the "dead-ball era" because the baseballs then in use were too soft and irregular to be hit great distances. Teams tried to score by using scratch hits and daring base running. On defense, the era was dominated by pitching, particularly Christy Mathewson of the New York Giants, who had an NL record of 373 wins and the best control in baseball history, and Walter Johnson of the Washington Senators (AL), who won 417 games with a 2.17 earned run average. These players were considered Christian gentlemen and outstanding role models. The finest offensive player was the malevolent outfielder Ty Cobb of the Detroit Tigers, who hit for an all-time average .366 and stole 892 bases, a record that stood until 2001. The top clubs were Mathewson's New York Giants in the NL, managed by John McGraw, and the Philadelphia Athletics and Boston Red

Sox of the AL. Each of these teams won six pennants between 1900 and 1920.

In 1914, the Federal League, formerly a minor league, announced that it would become a major league. The men who were prominent in promoting the Federal League included John Montgomery Ward, who had been a founder of the Players' League in the 1880s, and Ned Hanlon, who owned the Baltimore franchise. The league had strong financial backing, with owners such as oilman Harry Sinclair and ice magnate Phil Ball. They broke the monopoly of the other major leagues, offering star players large sums of money to jump to the new league, which spurred a big increase in major league salaries. In addition, the league brought an antitrust suit against MLB and its claims of exclusive territorial rights for team owners.

The Federal League faced major difficulties. The established leagues worked hard to keep their stars from jumping, and several of the Federal League franchises were financially shaky. By the end of the 1915, it was clear that the league could not continue. The established leagues bought out the teams in Brooklyn, Buffalo, Newark, and Pittsburgh. The owner of the Federal League St. Louis Terriers was allowed to buy the St. Louis Browns of the AL, and Charlie Weeghman, owner of the Chicago Whales, bought the Chicago Cubs of the NL. Two other Federal League cities—Kansas City and Baltimore—were left with no major league teams. However, the Baltimore club carried through on the Federal League's antitrust suit. Seven years later, in 1922, the U.S. Supreme Court rejected the suit and conferred special antitrust immunity to the surviving major leagues.

Stability in War and Depression

In the 1919 World Series, the Cincinnati Reds stunned the baseball world by defeating the highly favored Chicago White Sox. Then, at the end of the 1920 season, the nation was shocked by revelations that the 1919 series had been fixed. Eight White Sox players were suspected of receiving money from gamblers to lose the series to Cincinnati. When the major leagues' ruling National Commission failed to hush the scandal, frantic owners dissolved the commission and appointed baseball's first commissioner, retired federal judge Kenesaw Mountain Landis, and gave him absolute power.

Seven of the suspected "Black Sox" were tried for committing a confidence game. They were acquitted by a jury who carried them out of the courtroom on their shoulders. However, Commissioner Landis quickly banned all eight players from organized baseball for life, imposing the game's own justice. Landis continued to administer stern, sometimes arbitrary justice until his death in 1944, restoring public confidence and owner control in the national game.

Coincidentally, Landis's appointment came months after baseball's next big transformation. Star pitcher turned outfielder Babe Ruth became the first player to take full advantage of recent changes in the game. Owners had banned the spitball, a pitch that gave many hurlers an extra edge, and they introduced a livelier ball to encourage powerful hitters. In 1920, Ruth hit an unprecedented 54 home runs, playing for the New York Yankees, nearly doubling his 1919 record of 29. Only one other *team* in the majors hit 54 homers that season.

The dead-ball era was over, and fans flocked to stadiums to see the great power hitters of the new era. Ruth and first baseman Lou Gehrig led the "Murderer's Row" batting order in Yankee Stadium, which opened in 1923. Ruth's enthusiastic, bigger than life personality fit the Roaring Twenties, and the Yankees won six pennants and four world championships in the decade. In 1930, major league teams reported record profits of $2,318,847, with 10.2 million in attendance. The average player salary was a robust $4,500, and stars such as Ruth and Gehrig were paid many times that amount.

The Great Depression brought smaller crowds to baseball in the early 1930s, but popular innovations helped teams weather the storm. In 1933, sports editor Arch Ward of the *Chicago Tribune* organized the first major league All-Star Game in conjunction with the World's Fair then being held in Chicago, and the contest became an annual ritual. In 1935, major league teams played their first night game in Cincinnati, an innovation that allowed working-class fans to attend. (Night games had been pioneered earlier by teams in the minors and in the Negro Leagues.)

In 1936, the newly established Baseball Hall of Fame elected its first five members: Ty Cobb, Walter Johnson, Christy Mathewson, Babe Ruth, and Honus Wagner. The Hall of Fame opened in Cooperstown, New York, in 1939, honoring a legend that Civil War General Abner Doubleday had "invented" the game there a century earlier.

During the 1930s, many minor league clubs that had been independently owned were bought out by major league teams, which were establishing a system of "farm teams" to develop young baseball talent. The farm system was pioneered by team executive Branch Rickey, first for the St. Louis Cardinals and later for the Brooklyn Dodgers. The Cards had five farm clubs in

1929 and 28 by 1936. The farm system produced talent for the associated big league club, and other promising players could be sold to other teams for cash.

In 1942, in the months after the bombing of Pearl Harbor, the U.S. government determined that baseball should continue uninterrupted during World War II to keep up morale on the home front. However, wartime service interrupted the careers of hundreds of players. In wartime, even the major leagues had to make do with very young and old players and with men who were deemed physically unfit for the military. Pitcher Warren Spahn, who won 362 games, missed three seasons. The great hitter Ted Williams served as a fighter pilot during World War II and again during the Korean conflict, missing four and a half seasons in all.

Prosperity and Integration, 1946–1949

Baseball boomed after the war. Profits skyrocketed as attendance achieved all-time records, doubling to 16,000 per average game. The Cleveland Indians drew a record 2.6 million fans in their world championship 1948 season.

A key development after the war was the integration of organized baseball. African American journalists had been calling for integration since the 1930s. During World War II, many thousands of African Americans served in the armed forces, and their exclusion from baseball seemed an injustice. Branch Rickey, president of the Brooklyn Dodgers, saw a chance to right a social wrong and build his team's roster, and he took the decisive step. He recruited Jackie Robinson, who was playing at the time for the Kansas City Monarchs in the Negro Leagues, and signed him to a major league contract. Robinson had been a star athlete at the University of California, Los Angeles, and he had served as a U.S. Army officer during the war. Rickey assigned Robinson to play for Montreal, Brooklyn's top farm team, in 1946, and called him up to the Dodgers in 1947. Many of Rickey's fellow owners opposed integration, as did many players. The civil rights era of the

A 1927 series between the New York Yankees and Philadelphia Athletics brought four of the greatest baseball stars of the early twentieth century to Yankee Stadium: (*left to right*) Lou Gehrig, Tris Speaker, Ty Cobb, and Babe Ruth. (*Transcendental Graphics/Getty Images*)

1950s and 1960s was still in the future, and much of the country remained segregated by law.

Rickey's persistence and Robinson's great play and coolness under the pressure of taunting fans and hostile players helped win many over to the integration project. Robinson and other African Americans helped build a Dodger dynasty in Brooklyn through the mid-1950s. Other owners soon recognized that African American players offered a huge reservoir of baseball talent. Soon after Robinson's debut with the Dodgers, Cleveland owner Bill Veeck signed Larry Doby for his Indians, integrating the AL.

The integration of baseball was a milestone in postwar history, because it demonstrated the potential for the broader integration of American society. But the process took place slowly, and it was not until 1959 that the last team to integrate, the Boston Red Sox, brought in its first black player. Furthermore, teams seldom had more than a few black players on their roster, and they had to be far superior to white players in order to make it onto a team. During the 1950s, the Yankees were the dominant team, with eights pennants and six World Series titles, but the overall quality of play was better in the NL, perhaps because the NL teams were quicker to welcome great African American talents, such as Hank Aaron, Ernie Banks, and Willie Mays.

Franchise Shifts and Expansion

Beginning in 1950, major league game attendance fell. Millions of consumers were buying their first television sets, and more fans were staying at home. At the same time, the U.S. population was shifting from cities (where major league parks were located) to the suburbs, and from the Northeast and Midwest (where all major league franchises were located) to the West and South.

As late as 1952, no new major league team had been created and no existing team had moved for half a century, but changing demographics put pressure on baseball owners to move teams or create new ones for cities without major league sports. Such cities were eager to help pay for new ballparks and offered television markets without competition (baseball's revenue from televising games increased about 500 percent during the 1950s).

Finally, in 1953, the changes began. The struggling Boston Braves (which lost out to the more successful Red Sox) moved to Milwaukee. The next year, the St. Louis Browns (second fiddle to the Cardinals) became

the Baltimore Orioles. In 1955, the Philadelphia Athletics moved to Kansas City, and in 1958, two of the three teams in New York City moved to California— Brooklyn's prosperous and beloved Dodgers moved to Los Angeles, and the New York Giants moved to San Francisco.

The loss of two teams in New York set off a chain reaction. In 1959, a group of influential political and business leaders announced the formation of the Continental League, a third major league. The league planned for teams to begin competition in eight new cities in 1961, and it sought to negotiate with the existing leagues for approval rather than operate as an "outlaw" competitor. Once again, however, the major league owners managed to defeat the challenge of an interloping league.

In 1960, the struggling Washington Senators moved to Minneapolis, one of the Continental League cities. Soon afterward, the owners voted to expand the number of franchises for the first time. In 1961, the AL added the Los Angeles Angels and a new franchise in Washington, D.C. (where prominent politicians were angry about the loss of the old franchise). In 1962, the NL added the Houston Colt .45s (later the Astros) and the New York Mets. With its most promising cities taken by the established leagues, the Continental League collapsed without playing a single game.

To accommodate the new teams, baseball switched from a 154-game schedule to 162 games in 1961. That season, Yankee slugger Roger Maris threatened Babe Ruth's venerable record of 60 home runs in a season (set in 1927). Maris broke the record, but not within the old 154-game span, so he was forced to settle for a controversial asterisk next to his name in baseball record books.

Other changes in field specifications favored pitchers, however. Baseball raised the pitcher's mound a few inches and increased the size of the strike zone. During the 1960s, baseball was dominated by great pitching from Bob Gibson, Sandy Koufax, Juan Marichal, and others.

The long dominance of the New York Yankees ended after 1964. Other teams were able to catch up because of the rise of the amateur draft of high school and college players in 1965. Four small-market organizations took over: owner Jerry Hoffberger's family-like Baltimore Orioles; flamboyant owner Charlie Finley's combative Oakland Athletics, world champions from 1972 to 1974; Cincinnati's "Big Red Machine," which won four pennants and two World Series in the 1970s; and brewer Gussie Busch's St. Louis Cardinals.

The era saw a number of franchise moves, as teams went to the South and West, areas with large television markets and publicly financed stadiums. The Milwaukee Braves moved to Atlanta in 1966, followed by the Kansas City Athletics, which went to Oakland in 1968, and the second Washington Senators team, which became the Texas Rangers in 1972. Other teams threatened to move and secured multipurpose stadiums that cost some $50 million to $60 million from their hometowns to keep them there. Many such cookie-cutter parks were located near the center of cities as part of urban renewal programs. The new fields, located near major traffic interchanges, had little positive impact on urban renewal, though their huge parking lots attracted suburban fans who arrived by freeway.

During this time, some new teams were created as well. In 1969, four new expansion teams joined the major leagues: the Kansas City Royals (a replacement for the Athletics) and Seattle Pilots (who became the Milwaukee Brewers a year later) in the American League, and the San Diego Padres and Montreal Expos, the first Canadian team, in the National League. That year, the leagues each divided into two divisions and instituted a playoff system leading up to the World Series.

The powerful reserve rule helped maintain a $6,000 minimum salary in the majors as late as 1968. That year, the average salary increased beyond a modest $20,000, and superstar Willie Mays was paid only $125,000. The players' share of team revenues was only 15 percent, and most players were paid so little that they needed off-season jobs. The players' union, the Major League Baseball Players Association, had been formed in 1954, but only gained significant influence after labor economist Marvin Miller became its director in 1966. In 1968, he negotiated the first collective bargaining agreement, which raised the minimum wage to $10,000 and provided for arbitration of grievances beginning two years later. The owners did not realize that arbitration soon would upset organized baseball's power balance.

Players Empowered

In 1969, 31-year-old Curt Flood, the Cardinals' outstanding veteran center fielder, was traded to the Phillies. Unwilling to go to Philadelpia, he filed an antitrust suit to block the trade, with the support of the Players' Association. Three years later, the U.S. Supreme Court upheld the reserve clause in *Flood v. Kuhn,* based on the 1922 precedent exempting organized baseball from antitrust jurisdiction, but recommended that Congress reconsider the matter. (Flood played in 1971 for the Washington Senators but never again played in the major leagues.)

In April 1972, there was a 13-day strike over the collective bargaining agreement; owners eventually granted more money for the players' pension fund. There was nearly another strike a year later, but an agreement gained the required salary arbitration and enabled a player with ten years of service, including five with his current team, to refuse any trade. Two years later, arbitrators declared Jim "Catfish" Hunter a free agent after Oakland A's owner Charlie Finley failed to pay an annuity clause in his contract. Then, just before the 1976 season, arbitrators ruled in favor of free agency for veteran pitchers Dave McNally of the Montreal Expos and Andy Messersmith of the Los Angeles Dodgers, who had played in 1975 without signing contracts.

One of the most prominent owners of this era was Finley, who had moved the Kansas City A's to Oakland in 1968 and helped build the team into a dynasty. He was well known for his promotions, encouraging his players to grow moustaches, hiring ball girls, and campaigning for the designated hitter rule and a bright yellow baseball. At the same time, there was enormous animosity between Finley and his players, whom he regularly embarrassed in public and under paid. Broadcasting executive Ted Turner bought the Atlanta Braves in 1976 and made them the centerpiece of WTBS, television's first superstation. Then there was George Steinbrenner, whose syndicate bought the New York Yankees in 1973 for $10 million. He was renowned for his pursuit of free agents and for going through 20 managers in 23 years. These men were the first among a new breed of owners who muscled their way into the spotlight, unlike the old "gentleman owners," such as Boston's Tom Yawkey and Baltimore's Jerry Hoffberger, who remained behind the scenes.

The sport suffered a decline in the early 1970s and was surpassed by professional football as the most popular American spectator sport. Because fans, especially younger ones, were bored by baseball's low scoring, the AL adopted the designated hitter rule, in which a tenth player bats in place of the team's pitcher but does not play the field. The new rule made a dramatic difference in the AL's style of play. The owners also lowered the pitcher's mound to 10 inches (25.4 centimeters) and squeezed the strike zone to further build up offense. Another innovation was the playoff system, which made more teams eligible for the postseason.

By the mid-1970s, higher ratings increased the value of television contracts in big markets, doubling some owners' net revenue. The New York Mets, for example, increased revenue by about 1,000 percent from 1962 to 1980. The American League added two more franchises in 1977, the Seattle Mariners and the Toronto Blue Jays.

The greatest player achievement of the 1970s came when Atlanta Braves hitter Hank Aaron's passed Babe Ruth's long-venerated record for career home runs. Traditionalist fans and race baiters made Aaron's life miserable as he approached the record of 714. He received hundreds of death threats for daring to challenge a "white man's record." He finally hit homer number 715 on April 8, 1974, in Atlanta. Several national fan polls voted the achievement the greatest moment in baseball history.

In January 1981, five years after free agency was granted, team owners blocked any compromise on a compensation plan to force a strike. The players walked out in June and did not return until August. The owners split the season into two halves, with the four division leaders from the first half automatically qualifying to play the winners of the second half in the postseason. In 1987 and 1989, MLB was found guilty of colluding to restrict free agency; in 1989, the owners locked the players out of spring training. Nonetheless, average attendance per game increased about 18 percent from 1980 to 1990.

The owners became dissatisfied with their high-profile commissioners in the 1980s. They forced Commissioner Fay Vincent, who had served only three years, to resign in 1993 with a no-confidence vote of 18–9. In place of Vincent, they appointed one of their own, Bud Selig, the longtime owner of the small-market Milwaukee Brewers, first as acting commissioner, and then as permanent commissioner. In addition, the owners themselves were changing, as local, family owner-operators sold teams to deep-pocket, out-of-town corporate owners, for whom MLB presented an investment opportunity that could be linked with their other businesses.

In the 1990s, owners once again demanded new ballparks from taxpayers to replace their old multipurpose stadiums, with sport-specific parks equipped with lucrative skyboxes and added activities for families. The first such park designed to fit its surroundings was Baltimore's $235 million Oriole Park at Camden Yards (1992), whose homer-happy, fan-friendly formula to revitalize downtown areas was imitated widely.

By 2009, only seven major league ballparks built before 1990 still were in use. The new ones include two billion-dollar parks in New York City, Yankee Stadium and Citi Field. A new revenue source for owners is the leasing of naming rights for stadiums to locally based corporations. The Mets received $20 million a year from CitiBank for the right to name their new park Citi Field.

The next major league expansion came in 1993, when the National League added the Florida Marlins and the Colorado Rockies. Both leagues reorganized to add a third division. The price to buy a franchise was $95 million, a pricetag that further expanded MLB's coffers, but immediately burdened new owners and hosting cities with heavy debt.

Tradition Versus Innovation

New parks and more home runs accelerated profits. With billions pouring into MLB from television contracts and aggressive merchandising, relations between the owners and players deteriorated further. In 1994, negotiations came to an impasse. In August, the players went on strike, and the remainder of the season was cancelled. For the first time in 90 years, there was no World Series.

In March 1995, a U.S. district court forbade the owners from unilaterally enforcing new financial conditions and ordered that circumstances revert to those of 1994. The first 18 games were cut from the new schedule to allow time for a postseason, as wild card teams had been added to the playoffs. No longer could fans and the media ignore the business aspect of baseball—it was now central to all sports.

Strike-weary fans did not rush back to the ballparks, although they were energized by Orioles shortstop Cal Ripken's run on Lou Gehrig's record of 2,103 consecutive games, which long had been considered unbreakable. Ripken broke the mark on September 6, 1995, in Baltimore and went on to surpass it by 502 games. Ripken's work ethic, family values, and free availability to fans were principles that many appreciated.

Besides Ted Turner, other media giants also secured baseball teams. The Tribune Company previously had bought the Chicago Cubs in 1981, while Disney took over the California Angels in 1996 (the team was renamed the Anaheim Angels), and Australian media baron Rupert Murdoch acquired the Los Angeles Dodgers (1997). The expansion of television markets via cable and the emergence of free agency exacerbated the revenue gap between large-market franchises and small-market clubs such as Kansas City, Milwaukee, and Pittsburgh, especially because MLB, unlike the National Football League, has little revenue sharing. Big-budget teams such as the Atlanta Braves under General Manager John Schuerholz and Manager Bobby Cox and the New York Yankees under Manager Joe Torre became dynasties in the 1990s. It was difficult for low-budget teams to compete. These years saw the AL dominate the World Series and the All-Star games.

Major league baseball players—including some of the game's biggest stars—testify on steroid use before a U.S. House committee in 2005. The use of performance-enhancing drugs tainted more than 100 players and over a decade of statistics. *(Win McNamee/Getty Images)*

Low-budget franchises had a hard time acquiring North American talent, because amateurs and their agents could leverage a ballplayer's ability to go to or stay in college, and then reenter the draft to drive up offers and pick the team with whom they would sign. This, along with the declining presence of African Americans (9 percent in 2007) in the baseball pipelines, led to heavy recruitment of Latino ballplayers who were outside the amateur draft. In the late 1990s, the majors extended their talent hunt to the Far East. The disciplined, already well-paid Japanese stars from the two Nippon Leagues proved successful and brought millions of enthusiastic, open-pocketed East Asian viewers with them. In 2007, 20 percent of major leaguers were from Latin America, 4 percent were Hispanics from the United States and Puerto Rico, and 2 percent were Asian.

In 1996, small-market franchises welcomed two reforms that long had been rejected by owners in the new poststrike Major League Agreement: a payroll tax on big-budget franchises redistributed to small-revenue clubs, and interleague play. Even so, the 1999 Yankees's payroll was $88 million, compared to the Florida Marlins's $15 million. Two years earlier, the Marlins took advantage of revenue sharing to temporarily overspend and win the World Series. The introduction of limited interleague play in 1997 helped MLB, concerned about its aging fan base, stay in the running for young fans, who preferred the inventive, faster-paced National Football League and the National Basketball Association.

Another big attraction was the dramatic 1998 home run race between Mark McGwire of the St. Louis Cardinals and Sammy Sosa of the Chicago Cubs. Both shattered Maris's season mark with 70 and 66 homers, respectively, helping to set attendance and television ratings records.

That year also marked further expansion to the Sun Belt with franchises for Tampa Bay (the Devil Rays, later renamed the Rays) and Phoenix (the Arizona Diamondbacks). Also in that year, the Milwaukee Brewers (run by Selig's daughter while he served as commissioner) moved from the AL to the NL, the first such switch since 1891. Selig and the corporate owners worked to reduce the separation of the two leagues. The AL and NL were disbanded as official corporations, divested of league offices, and relieved of managing their own umpiring staffs.

Organized baseball continued to struggle to maintain its traditional appeal compared to new professional sports that make frequent modifications to satisfy changing tastes without infuriating fans. By the 1980s and 1990s, the All-Star Game had become more of an exhibition than a serious competition, and it also had become a lucrative festival staged at new parks. In the 2002 game in Milwaukee, both managers ran out of pitchers in the eleventh inning, leading Selig to end the game and call it a draw. The fiasco in his family's new park prompted him to confer home-field advantage in the World Series to the winning league, hoping to force managers and All-Stars to take the game more seriously.

Beginning in the mid-1990s, muscle-bound hitters suddenly were launching monster home runs and new gargantuan pitchers were throwing at speeds of up to 100 miles (161 kilometers) per hour. These crowd-pleasing feats, it was suspected, were the result of the use of performance-enhancing drugs. After revelations of steroid use in the major leagues, especially by slugger José Canseco in his best-selling book *Juiced: Wild Times, Rampant 'Roids, Smash Hits & How Baseball Got Big* (2005), off-the-record finger pointing and media speculation spiraled. The Players Association had the power to prevent greater drug testing, and Commissioner Selig was accused of being asleep at the wheel as revenue soared. Suspected users include former home run kings McGwire and Sosa.

After the Bay Area Laboratory Co-operative (BALCO) steroid scandal, MLB increased drug testing and penalties. BALCO had long promoted new season home-run record holder Barry Bonds of the San Francisco Giants as its model client. The multitalented left fielder, often accused of surliness toward fans and the media, broke Hank Aaron's career home run record of 755 on August 7, 2007, in San Francisco, but his achievements remained under a cloud, as the hitter was suspected of using performance-enhancing drugs.

Baseball's finances are currently as skewed as they have ever been. The most likely challenger to Bonds' record, Alex Rodriguez of the New York Yankees, made about $25 million yearly in 2005, just $4 million less than Tampa Bay's entire 25-man roster. This was at a time when the Yankees' payroll was about $208 million and the team posted a loss of $37 million. The average 2005 franchise was worth $332 million, and the wealthiest franchises were worth over five times as much as the poorest. Regular-season ticket price averages increased about 225 percent from 1991 to 2001 ($19.70). By 2010, they reached an average of $26.74.

The inequality is most striking in local television revenue. In 2005, Montreal's television package was just $600,000, compared with the Yankees' $56 million. The disparity led the Montreal Expos to move to Washington, D.C., where it became the third Washington franchise (the Nationals) hoping to succeed in the nation's capital.

Baseball was truly big business at the end of the first decade of the twenty-first century. In 2009, MLB reported record revenues of $6.6 billion. The average MLB player in 2010 made $3,340,133. In 2010, the 27-time world champion Yankees were worth $1.6 billion, a value 54 percent higher than the team's value in 2002, with revenues of $441 million. The next most valuable team was the Boston Red Sox, at $730 million, and the average MLB team was worth $491 million. But big payrolls were not necessarily a prerequisite for profitability, as the Florida Marlins demonstrated. In 2009, with a value of $317 million, fourth lowest in baseball, the franchise had the highest operating income of $46.1 million, despite the lowest revenue in MLB ($144 million), a situation that reflected the team's low payroll.

David Stevens

See also: African American Baseball, Before 1920; African American Baseball, Negro League Era; Baseball, Minor League; Baseball, Semiprofessional; Brotherhood of Professional Baseball Players; Federal League; Major League Baseball Players Association; National Association of Professional Base Ball Players; Pacific Coast League; Reserve Clause; Stadiums and Arenas.

Further Reading

Burgos, Adrian, Jr. *Playing America's Game: Baseball, Latinos, and the Color Line.* Berkeley: University of California Press, 2007.

Burk, Robert F. *Much More Than a Game: Players, Owners, and American Baseball Since 1921.* Chapel Hill: University of North Carolina Press, 2001.

———. *Never Just a Game: Players, Owners, and American Baseball to 1920.* Chapel Hill: University of North Carolina Press, 1994.

Canseco, Jose. *Juiced: Wild Times, Rampant 'Roids, Smash Hits and How Baseball Got Big.* New York: Regan, 2005.

Goldstein, Richard. *Spartan Seasons: How Baseball Survived the Second World War.* New York: Macmillan, 1980.

Koppett, Leonard. *Koppett's Concise History of Major League Baseball.* Philadelphia: Temple University Press, 1998.

Kyle, Donald G., and Robert B. Fairbanks, eds. *Baseball in America and America in Baseball.* College Station: Texas A&M University Press, 2008.

Levine, Peter. *A.G. Spalding and the Rise of Baseball: The Promise of American Sport.* New York: Oxford University Press, 1985.

Pietrusza, David. *Major Leagues.* Jefferson, NC: McFarland, 1991.

Rader, Benjamin G. *Baseball: A History of America's Game.* 3rd ed. Urbana: University of Illinois Press, 2008.

Riess, Steven A. *Touching Base: Professional Baseball and American Culture in the Progressive Era.* Rev. ed. Urbana: University of Illinois Press, 1999.

———, ed. *Encyclopedia of Major League Baseball Clubs.* 2 vols. Westport, CT: Greenwood, 2006.

Seymour, Harold. *Baseball.* 3 vols. New York: Oxford University Press, 1960–1989.

Stevens, David. *Baseball's Radical for All Seasons: A Biography of John Montgomery Ward.* Lanham, MD: Scarecrow, 1998.

Vincent, Ted. *Mudville's Revenge: The Rise and Fall of American Sport.* New York: Seaview, 1981.

Voigt, David Quentin. *American Baseball.* 3 vols. University Park: Pennsylvania State University Press, 1966–1983.

Baseball, Minor League

The minor leagues of baseball began more than 130 years ago to entertain fans in smaller communities and to train young talent. Leagues were ranked by the population of their cities and by the quality of competition. Teams originally were independent until the rise of the "farm system" in the 1920s and 1930s, when major league clubs began to buy existing minor league teams and establish new ones.

The minor leagues peaked in popularity during the late 1940s, when there was pent-up interest in baseball following World War II, but they declined sharply thereafter. Beginning in the 1990s, there was a resurgence of interest in minor league play. Attendance increased, and some teams became profitable in their own right.

Early Years: 1877–1920

In 1876, the National League was established, becoming the second major league in baseball, followed a year later by the International Association, a loose-knit organization of high-quality professional teams, and the New England League. The New England League was effectively a "minor" league. But the first league to be so designated "officially" was the Northwest League (1883–1884), which signed the National Agreement of 1883 with the National League and the year-old American Association. In this document, the Northwest League agreed to honor the terms under which the two major leagues claimed control of their teams and their players. The most important minor league in the nineteenth century was the International League, which was established in 1886 and actually was one level below the majors.

A second National Agreement was ratified in 1892 to protect teams from having their rosters raided. The pact established a system for transferring players during the postseason, allowing higher-level leagues to "draft" players from lower-level leagues. In return, the higher-level teams agreed to pay a fee to the lower-level team. For example, the National League agreed to pay $1,000 to draft a player on a Class A minor league team and $500 for a player from a Class B team. In addition, Class A teams could draft players from Class B franchises.

By 1900, there were 13 minor leagues. That year, the Western League was renamed the American League, restructuring itself as a more national organization. One year later, it proclaimed itself a major league.

After the 1900 season, President Patrick T. Powers of the Eastern League organized the 14-league National Association of Professional Baseball Leagues to protect the independence of the minor leagues. It set up an extensive classification system that ranked leagues from Class A (highest level) to Class D (lowest level). Team owners typically were local small businessmen, who often were involved in retail business or local politics.

In 1903, a new National Agreement was signed when the American and National leagues merged. It regulated compensation for players sold to higher leagues. Major league clubs could take up to two players from any Class A team for $750 apiece. The prices for drafting players from lower-level teams were less; for example, Class D teams received only $200 when a major league club drafted a player. In addition, when major league teams sent players down to the minor leagues, they often chose a team with which they had negotiated an understanding that allowed them to keep their rights to the player and to call him back up to the majors for a specified fee.

In 1909, the Eastern League (formerly the International League), American Association (1903–1963), and Pacific Coast League (1903–) were elevated to Class AA status. By 1912, there were 45 minor leagues, with rosters ranging from 20 in the top leagues to 13 for Class D. Top minor leaguers could earn more than $1,600 a season, while Class D players earned $50 to

$100 a month. However, the number of minor leagues dropped to 31 in 1915, and then to 24 in 1916, after the Federal League, a new self-proclaimed major league, increased the pool of major league players in 1914 and 1915. The Federal League ended operation after 1915, but in 1917, the United States entered World War I. Thousands of young men were drafted or enlisted for service. By 1918, there were only eight minor leagues left, and only one finished the season.

Golden Age of the Minor Leagues: 1921–1950

The National Association of Professional Baseball Leagues withdrew from the National Agreement with Major League Baseball (MLB) in 1919, temporarily ending the draft system. A new agreement was reached in 1921, which raised the draft price for Class AA players to $5,000 and raised the price for Class D players to $1,000. However, it also allowed a minor league to exempt itself from the draft by forgoing its own right to draft lower-level players, an option that was selected by five leagues, including the three with AA ratings.

The leagues that opted out of the draft agreement could prosper by selling promising prospects to major league teams for much more than the draft prices. Jack Dunn's Baltimore Orioles were particularly successful. They captured the International League championship seven straight years (1919–1925), with a winning percentage of .688. The 1921 team won 119 games against 47 losses and batted .313. It was rated the second-best minor league team ever. Dunn reportedly made more than $400,000 by selling his talent, including $100,500 for hurler Robert Moses "Lefty" Grove in 1925. Soon afterward, however, the major leagues amended the National Agreement to keep any league from opting out of the draft.

The 1921 agreement also allowed minor league teams to be owned by major league teams. Branch Rickey, business manager of the St. Louis Cardinals, saw this as a great opportunity to develop a "farm system" to recruit and nurture talent. Other owners thought that leaving recruitment to independent minor league teams was more cost-effective. By 1928, the Cards owned seven teams; in 1940, they had 32, in addition to having "working agreements" with eight other teams, attaching some 600 minor league players to the Cardinals and prohibiting those players from accepting larger monetary offers to other major league teams. The system produced three times as many players as the Cardinals needed, enabling them to sell off their surplus to other teams in the majors and minors, a business that produced $2 million in 1942.

The Cardinals' success convinced other major league teams to set up farm systems. MLB Commissioner Kenesaw Mountain Landis opposed this recruitment model, arguing that it was detrimental to players because it limited their ability to get promoted to the majors and also hurt contending minor league teams, which would lose key players late in the season. In 1938, Landis granted free agency to 74 Cardinals farmhands because of various improprieties, and he did the same for 91 Tigers minor leaguers two years later. Landis never succeeded, however, in ending the farm system.

Operating under tight budgets, the minors were generally more innovative than the majors. The first permanent lighting installation for night baseball was employed on May 2, 1930, in Des Moines, Iowa, a franchise of the Western League. Three years later, General Manager Frank Shaughnessy of the Montreal Royals established a postseason playoff between the four top teams in the International League to maintain fan interest. Owner Bill Veeck of the minor league Milwaukee Brewers built a movable outfield fence in the early 1940s; when a team of sluggers came to town, Veeck moved the fence back to reduce home runs.

The minors struggled during the Great Depression, and there were just 14 leagues and 102 clubs in 1932. Nonetheless, they continued to play good baseball. The Pacific Coast League ran with more independence than many others. Because the climate was mild, the league scheduled up to 200 games per season. The long schedule allowed them to pay players more, and some players stayed in the league for their whole careers. The 1934 Los Angeles Angels played 187 games, winning 137 of them, and later was judged the best minor league team ever. However, attendance was down in the Pacific Coast League, partly because of the Great Depression and partly because of the domination of the Angels. Minor league attendance increased in the late 1930s, but with the entry of the United States into World War II, minor league play was drastically curtailed. Because so many players joined the military and travel in the United States was restricted, only 10 leagues operated, attracting just 6 million paying fans.

After the war, the minors bounced back and reached their peak in 1949, with 59 leagues, 448 clubs, and paid attendance of more than 39 million, a record until 2004. In 1946, the American Association, International League, and Pacific Coast League were reclassified as

Class AAA leagues (the highest in the minors). The Pacific Coast League did so well that it even tried to gain recognition as a third major league.

Modern Era: 1950–Present

The glory years of the minor leagues ended in the early 1950s. A period of increasing prosperity gave Americans many more recreational choices as millions of people moved out of cities and into suburbs. Television brought another revolution in the 1950s. When people could find commercial entertainment at home, they went out less often. Attendance at movies plunged along with attendance at minor league games.

The major leagues also contributed to the decline of the minors. They brought MLB to new cities: Milwaukee (1953), Baltimore (1954), Kansas City (1955), Los Angeles and San Francisco (1958), and Minneapolis-St. Paul (1961). All of these cities had prosperous minor league teams, which quickly moved to less promising territories or went out of business. MLB also changed the rules governing teams' farm systems, restricting powerful farm organizations such as those of the Cardinals and Yankees from controlling hundreds of players. Teams focused more attention on drafting promising young players out of high school or college.

In 1951, major league teams owned 207 minor league franchises; by 1957, they owned only 38. In 1963, after the loss of its teams in Kansas City, Milwaukee, and Minneapolis, the venerable American Association ended operation, and its remaining teams moved to other leagues. The following year, there were only 20 minor leagues and 132 clubs, with attendance down to 10 million.

From this low point, it was a long climb for minor league baseball to its current popularity. A new Class AAA American Association began play in 1969 and continued until 1997. On July 4, 1982, 65,666 fans attended an American Association game in Denver's Mile High Stadium, the largest audience in minor league history. Five years later, minor league attendance surpassed 20 million, a level unattained since 1953, and attendance steadily rose to 38.8 million in 2001.

Minor league owners had become excellent promoters who advertised their product as inexpensive, clean family fun in new ballparks that provided a friendly small-town atmosphere with plenty of music and other entertainment. Franchise values escalated, and new teams were established in suburbs where land was cheap and accessible by nearby highways.

In 2009, minor league attendance was 41.6 million, just below the all-time record of 43,263,740 set in 2008. As of early 2011, there were 19 leagues in seven classes, with rosters composed of 45 percent foreign-born players.

Steven A. Riess

See also: Baseball, Major League; Baseball, Semiprofessional; Pacific Coast League.

Further Reading

Johnson, Lloyd, and Miles Wolff, eds. *The Encyclopedia of Minor League Baseball: The Official Record of Minor League Baseball.* Durham, NC: Baseball America, 1993.

Obojski, Robert. *Bush League: A History of Minor League Baseball.* New York: Macmillan, 1975.

Rader, Benjamin G. *Baseball: A History of America's Game.* 3rd ed. Urbana: University of Illinois Press, 2008.

Sullivan, Neil J. *The Minors: The Struggles and the Triumph of Baseball's Poor Relation from 1876 to the Present.* New York: St. Martin's, 1990.

Zingg, Paul J., and Mark D. Medeiros. *Runs, Hits and an Era: The Pacific Coast League, 1903–58.* Urbana: University of Illinois Press, 1994.

Baseball, Semiprofessional

Semiprofessional baseball represents a level of play between the strictly amateur, played for the love of the game, and the professional, paid to play. Semiprofessional baseball flourished from baseball's beginnings to the mid-1970s, providing an opportunity for athletes to be compensated for playing on a part-time basis. The growth of the professional game largely killed off semipro baseball, although there are still tournaments at which baseball players can compete for the love of the game and minimal compensation.

Baseball started out as a fully amateur game, but by the 1860s, some teams began paying their pitchers and catchers and some other players with money that came from passing a hat, admission fees, and side bets. Semiprofessional teams flourished by the late nineteenth century, when there were hundreds of company and neighborhood teams that paid players to play on weekends.

Early hotbeds of semipro baseball were Chicago, Cleveland, metropolitan New York, and Philadelphia. In Chicago, the eight-team City League was formed in 1887; players shared in the gate receipts (admission was 25 cents for adults), usually drawing more than

1,000 people per game on Sundays. The league broke up in 1895, and the teams began to play independent schedules. Rosters included youngsters who wanted to become major leaguers and former big leaguers who were in the twilight of their careers.

Semipro ball in Chicago experienced a golden age from 1906, when the Logan Squares played and beat both the Cubs and the White Sox in a postseason series, to 1910. In 1907, New York Giants star Mike Donlin, one of the best hitters in the National League, sat out a season in the majors to play semipro ball in Chicago. In 1909, there were 26 semipro teams that received coverage in the major daily papers, and the top six formed a new City League, including the black Leland Giants, who won the championship that year. That team, like several other top black teams of the day, was composed of full-time professionals who played baseball for a living. Semipro ball remained an important Chicago institution until the 1930s.

Independent teams and leagues worked together to increase interest at the state, regional, and national levels. The National Baseball Federation (NBF) started in Cleveland after the 1914 city tournament between Telling's Strollers and Gus Hanna's Street Cleaners drew 83,000 fans. In 1915, the organization sponsored the first national semiprofessional championship tournament, which succeeded because most teams had industrial support. After World War I, the NBF expanded, dividing teams into classes: A (Amateur) for those who had never played professionally; AA (Industrial) for those who had never played in the major leagues; and AAA (Semipro) for those who played for money, but not full time.

The increased interest in baseball after the war encouraged the development of other leagues and tournaments, usually limited to nonprofessionals. Boston sponsored a successful twilight league, and in Denver, the *Post* sponsored a seven-state invitational tournament. Some outstanding athletes started in semipro baseball and then moved to the majors, including Joe DiMaggio, who played for a San Francisco olive oil dealer's team. Others, such as John Pickett of the Cheyenne Indians, winner of the 1923 *Denver Post* tournament, remained semiprofessional, playing baseball while pursuing his career as a lawyer.

Leagues grew during the 1930s to provide a diversion from the woes of the Great Depression. The NBF continued to hold tournaments in Ohio, but some players became disenchanted with the federation and created the amateur American Baseball Congress in Dayton in 1935; in two years, it was larger than the

NBF. Another newcomer that year was the primarily semipro National Baseball Congress. Its origins date to a 1931 Wichita, Kansas, league started by sporting goods salesman Hap Dumont in order to to provide Sunday entertainment. The inaugural 1935 tournament was won by Satchel Paige's Bismarck, North Dakota, club, which received a guaranteed payment of $1,000 to participate.

The semipro season was highlighted by the annual *Denver Post* tournament (1915–1947). Some of the top Western teams competed for purses, including such renowned traveling teams as the House of David and the black Kansas City Monarchs—both won championships. The 1937 crown was captured by an African American team headed by Paige and Josh Gibson that had won the Caribbean championship for Dominican Republic dictator Rafael Trujillo.

During World War II, some industrial leagues stopped play, because so many men were drafted into the military. However, the Utah Industrial League continued to field teams and even improved its standard of play. Professional ballplayers stationed at the defense installations in Utah wanted to play, and the league allowed local teams to recruit them.

Many believe that the immediate postwar period was the golden era of semiprofessional baseball. Nebraskan Hobe Hays, like other returning veterans who had played baseball during the war, wanted to continue playing, and he joined the McCook team while working for the local newspaper. The players were all locals at first, but in 1948, several former professional ballplayers who drifted from town to town and worked at odd jobs began joining local teams. These "baseball bums," along with "college hotdogs" (collegians off for the summer), changed the status of the semiprofessional leagues, as their combined wages from their daytime jobs and baseball salaries earned them more money and gave them more freedom than many minor league players.

Throughout the 1950s, semiprofessional baseball continued to be a starting point for several major league players. Hank Aaron, for example, played shortstop for the Mobile Black Bears, a semipro team; then after high school, he played for the traveling Indianapolis Clowns, a team that belonged to the Negro American League.

Semipro ball faded quickly in the 1950s, however, as baseball began to be televised and the major and minor leagues expanded. For example, the semipro baseball team in Canton, Ohio, disbanded in 1953, even though it had had for years the support of members of the community, who switched their loyalty to the Cincinnati Reds. Similarly, the minor leagues pulled fans and funds from semiprofessional teams. In 1956, when the Nebraska Independent League folded, the six towns that had semipro teams plus two more became homes for the eight-team Class D Rookie League. Other semiprofessional leagues also become minor leagues.

Semiprofessional baseball nearly disappeared after the mid-1970s, particularly with the resurgence of interest in the minor leagues and the absence of factory-sponsored teams. Still, the American Baseball Congress, National Baseball Congress, and National Baseball Federation continue to hold yearly tournaments.

Jessie L. Embry

See also: African American Baseball, Before 1920; African American Baseball, Negro League Era; All-American Girls Baseball League; Baseball, Major League; Baseball, Minor League; Baseball, to 1870.

Further Reading

Broeg, Bob. *Baseball's Barnum: Ray "Hap" Dumont, Founder of the National Baseball Congress.* Wichita, KS: Center for Entrepreneurship, W. Frank Barton School of Business Administration, Wichita State University, 1989.

Embry, Jessie L. "'The Biggest Advertisement for a Town': Provo Baseball and Provo Timps, 1913–1958." *Utah Historical Quarterly* 71:3 (Summer 2003): 196–214.

Hays, Hobe. *Take Two and Hit to Right: Golden Days on the Semi-Pro Diamond.* Lincoln: University of Nebraska Press, 1999.

Parr, Royse. "Semipro Baseball's Golden Era (1935–1941): A Tale of Two Cities." *NINE: A Journal of Baseball History and Culture* 15:1 (Fall 2006): 54–67.

Sanford, Jay. *The Denver Post Tournament.* Cleveland, OH: Society for American Baseball Research, 2003.

Schmidt, Raymond. "The Golden Age of Chicago Baseball." *Chicago History* 28:2 (2000): 38–59.

Seymour, Harold. *Baseball.* 3 vols. New York: Oxford University Press, 1960–1989.

Thornley, Stew. *Baseball in Minnesota: The Definitive History.* St. Paul: Minnesota Historical Society Press, 2006.

Basketball, College

There are currently 31 conferences and 325 institutions playing basketball in Division I of the National Collegiate Athletic Association (NCAA). The sport has been played at colleges for more than 100 years, providing entertainment to spectators, promoting school spirit, and leading to lucrative professional contracts for top athletes.

College basketball has evolved from a simple, rough game into a world-class sport played by outstanding athletes, many of them from poor inner-city neighborhoods, drawn by scholarships and the hope of a professional career. College basketball usually was the first or second most popular game on campuses in the early twentieth century, after football, and it became a profitable spectator sport by the 1930s. Today, the season culminates in the NCAA Tournament, a staple of television viewing and sports betting since the 1970s.

Origins

Educator James Naismith first devised a game of "basket ball" for a class that he taught at the International Young Men's Christian Association (YMCA) Training School (now Springfield College) in December 1891. He drew up 13 rules for a game, the object of which was to toss a large ball into a peach basket; Naismith's goal was to create a game that emphasized agility, fitness, and skill rather than strength. The first formal intercollegiate rules, drawn up in 1905, required a center jump, in which play resumed at center court after every basket, when the referee threw the ball up between each team's best leaper.

Educator Senda Berenson quickly adapted the game for women at Smith College, and in 1892, the first women's interinstitutional game was played between the University of California, Berkeley, and Miss Head's School, a local establishment. On April 8, 1893, the men of Geneva College defeated the New Brighton YMCA at Beaver Falls, Pennsylvania. The first intercollegiate game took place on February 9, 1895, when the Minnesota State School of Agriculture (now part of the University of Minnesota) defeated Hamline College, 9–3.

Teams at first used seven to nine players, but in 1897, Yale University beat the University of Pennsylvania, 32–10, playing five on five. In 1904, the Hiram College team, out of Ohio, won the first college basketball tournament.

At that time, basketball was a rough game. Any out-of-bounds ball went to the team that retrieved it. To lower the level of physical contact, a player committing five fouls was ejected beginning in 1908.

Interwar Years

At first, basketball was played conservatively and deliberately. Offenses passed to set up a two-handed set shot against a zone defense, and scores usually were in the low 20s. Colleges recruited top players from the poor sections of major cities, where they learned the game at settlement houses, YMCAs, and school gyms, or from small towns in states such as Illinois, Indiana, and Kentucky, where basketball was popular in small towns.

New York was the center of the collegiate game during the interwar years, and its teams relied heavily on local Jewish ballplayers (just as colleges since the 1960s have relied on African Americans, also primarily of inner-city origins). The St. John's University "Wonder Five," for instance, which went 68–4 in 1929–1931, consisted primarily of local Jewish athletes. Urban commuter colleges found basketball a less expensive and less land-intensive option than football. The teams played in armories and dance halls before building their own gyms.

In the 1930s, New York's Madison Square Garden became the center of intercollegiate basketball. On January 21, 1931, Mayor Jimmy Walker staged a tripleheader, organized by sportswriter Ned Irish, to raise money for Depression-era relief. The event was a success, and it gave Irish the idea of staging weekly doubleheaders between local teams and nationally renowned quintets. His first promotion, on December 29, 1934, featured New York University and the University of Notre Dame and drew 16,138 spectators, resulting in a $20,000 gate.

Irish successfully fought to make the game more spectator friendly. He convinced the collegiate Rules Committee to end stalling by adding a centerline in 1935 that had to be crossed within ten seconds and to open up play by limiting offensive players to three seconds inside the foul lane. Two years later, the center jump was eliminated. In the 1930s, New York's top teams—New York University, Long Island University, St. John's University, and the City College of New York—were nationally renowned and produced several All-Americans. The Long Island University Blackbirds, coached by Clair Bee, won 43 straight games in 1935–1936 by an average margin of 23 points. They were favored to represent the United States at the 1936 Olympic Games in Berlin, but the team boycotted the Olympic trials because the Games were to be held in Nazi-ruled Germany.

Top programs in the heartland included the University of Kansas, the University of Kentucky, and Oklahoma A&M (now Oklahoma State). Naismith, Kansas's first coach, was replaced by Forrest "Phog" Allen (1907–1909, 1920–1956), who compiled a 591–219 record. His main competitor was Hank Iba of Oklahoma A&M (1934–1970), who went 767–338, including NCAA titles

in 1945 and 1946. Iba coached a slow-paced game that fell out of favor in the 1950s. Kansas alumnus Adolph Rupp coached the University of Kentucky (1930–1972) to 875 wins and four NCAA titles. He dominated the Southeastern Conference with 27 conference titles, employing an energetic, fast-breaking offense.

Tournaments

The first national collegiate basketball tournament was an eight-team event for smaller institutions held at Kansas City's Municipal Auditorium in 1937, the brainstorm of Naismith, a few coaches, and local boosters. Central Missouri State University won the first two national championships. The tournament was taken over in 1940 by the new National Association of Intercollegiate Basketball, renamed the National Association of Intercollegiate Athletics (NAIA) in 1952. The NAIA began admitting historically black colleges to the tournament in 1953.

Games at Madison Square Garden continued to receive national coverage. In December 1936, Long Island University, with a 43-game winning streak, faced Stanford University, whose star, Hank Luisetti, was an early practitioner of the one-handed jump shot. To the dismay of Long Island fans, Luisetti and his team won 46–31, ending the streak.

In 1938, Ned Irish, determined to take advantage of the venue at Madison Square Garden, created the National Invitation Tournament (NIT), to be played by six teams selected by the Metropolitan Basketball Writers Association. In the first NIT, Temple University defeated the University of Colorado, 60–36. It was the most prestigious postseason series through the 1940s, but it declined in popularity after the basketball scandals of 1950–1951.

In 1939, the National Association of Basketball Coaches started an eight-team tournament (taken over by the NCAA in 1940), which was won by the University of Oregon over Ohio State University, 46–33. The tournament grew to 16 teams in 1951 (with automatic bids to conference champions), 32 in 1975, and currently 68. The University of California, Los Angeles (UCLA) has won the most championships (11), followed by the University of Kentucky (7) and Indiana University (5).

The basketball ranks were hard hit by World War II, but teams did not need a big roster, and anyone over 6 feet, 6 inches (about 2 meters) was exempt from the military draft. The outstanding quintet in 1941–1942 was the University of Illinois "Whiz Kids," a sophomore-laden team led by two-time All-American Andy Philip. They won the NCAA Tournament final but went 17–1 the next year. The team was forced to decline an NCAA Tournament bid in 1943 because three of its players had joined the military. Doubleheaders at Madison Square Garden remained popular, playing to 98 percent capacity in 1945–1946.

As the war came to an end, two 6-foot, 10-inch (2.1-meter) centers made a big impact. George Mikan was a three-time All-American at DePaul University, and Bob Kurland of Oklahoma A&M led the Cowboys to two straight NCAA championships (1945–1946). Mikan was awkward, nearsighted, and brittle, with little high school experience, but he was a hard worker who had been molded by Coach Ray Meyer. Mikan led DePaul University to the NIT title in 1945, twice led the nation in scoring, and was named Helms Player of the Year in 1944 and 1945. Mikan and Kurland were so adept at blocking shots on their downward trajectory that in 1945, the NCAA banned goaltending.

Basketball Scandals

Gambling proved to be the bane of college basketball. People originally bet on who would win, but there was not much interest in uneven match-ups regardless of the odds. In the late 1930s, bookmakers introduced the point spread—that is, a bet on the margin of victory. This innovation dramatically increased betting, but also encouraged the fixing of games, as players only had to hold down the point differential and did not actually have to lose the game.

A national betting scandal was revealed in February 1951, when three players at City College of New York, the defending NIT and NCAA champion, and Long Island University's Sherman White, the *Sporting News* Player of the Year, were arrested for shaving points. New York City District Attorney Frank Hogan reported that 86 games had been fixed, involving 32 colleges across the country, including Kentucky, NCAA champion in 1948, 1949, and 1951. Most of the players who were indicted took plea bargains and received suspended sentences, but the principal gambler, 45-year-old jeweler and fixer Salvatore Sollazzo, got 12 years in jail. The scandal undermined the stature of the NIT. City College of New York downgraded its sports program to small-college status, and Kentucky canceled its 1952–1953 season.

Then, in 1961, another basketball scandal rocked the sports world, this one involving 49 players and 67 games between 1957 and 1961. The man behind it was

Jack Molinas, a 6-foot, 5-inch (1.9-meter) All-American at Columbia University in 1953, and the fourth player selected in the National Basketball Association (NBA) draft. The Fort Wayne Pistons suspended Molinas two months into the 1953–1954 season for gambling, and the NBA subsequently banned him from basketball. Molinas had carefully cultivated many inner-city high school stars in the late 1950s, and he bribed some of them to fix games. Some of the accused, such as freshman Connie Hawkins of the University of Iowa, were innocent (freshmen were ineligible to play then), but the taint ruined their college and pro careers. Molinas served five years of a 10- to 15-year sentence.

Rise of African American Players

After the scandals, the focus of college basketball shifted away from New York. Fans' attention was diverted by two prodigious scorers. In 1953, 6-foot, 9-inch (2.1-meter) Clarence "Bevo" Francis of Rio Grande College in Ohio averaged 50.1 points, albeit against modest competition, followed by 48.0 points a year later against stronger teams. The NCAA's top scorer in 1954, Furman University guard Frank Selvy, averaged 41.7 points per game, scoring 100 against Newberry College. An important rule change awarded a bonus foul shot if the penalized team had an excessive number of fouls.

Before the 1950s, there were few African American basketball players at white institutions anywhere in the country, including the Big Ten Conference, which was not integrated until 1947. In 1955 and 1956, center Bill Russell led the University of San Francisco to 55 straight wins and two NCAA titles. His defensive dominance led to the widening of the foul lane from 6 feet (1.8 meters) to 12 feet (3.7 meters). In 1957, sophomore Wilt Chamberlain led the University of Kansas to the NCAA championship game, which they lost in triple overtime to North Carolina, 54–53. He averaged 30.1 points the following season but, discouraged by triple teaming, left to play for the Harlem Globetrotters. The All-America first team in 1958 had four African Americans: Chamberlain, Elgin Baylor of Seattle, Guy Rodgers of Temple University, and Oscar Robertson of the University of Cincinnati. Robertson was a three-time Player of the Year and was rated the second-best college player of all time.

Even as individual African Americans found more opportunities at predominantly white universities, college basketball was slow to admit teams from historically black colleges. When a steering committee of African American coaches applied for consideration, the NCAA dragged its feet. The NAIA, made up primarily of small colleges, was more welcoming, inviting historically black colleges to its postseason tournament in 1953. From 1957 to 1959, Tennessee State University, a historically black college led by coach John McLendon, won the NAIA championship three times in a row. McLendon, who had studied with James Naismith at the University of Kansas (but had not been allowed to play on the basketball team there), went on to coach in pro and international play, and was elected to the Naismith Memorial Basketball Hall of Fame in 1979.

The success of African American players spurred increased recruitment by universities in the early 1960s, except in the Deep South. The University of Kentucky did play against integrated teams, mainly away games, but Mississippi State University refused to play against any team with black players, even in the NCAA Tournament. The coaches of integrated teams typically played no more than three black players on the road and two at home. In 1963, however, Loyola University of Chicago won the NCAA championship over Cincinnati, starting four African Americans, and sometimes playing five, while the rival Bearcats started three.

Then, in 1966, Texas Western University (now the University of Texas at El Paso, or UTEP), coached by Don Haskins, started an all–African American lineup (backed by two black reserves) and went 23–1 during the regular season, third in the nation. They were a stark contrast in the NCAA finals to the all-white Kentucky Wildcats. Coach Rupp felt that black athletes had talent but lacked self-control and intelligence. He was proven wrong by UTEP's ball-control offense and tough defense, and Kentucky lost, 72–65.

Shortly thereafter, all Southeastern Conference schools recruited African Americans, with Mississippi State the laggard until 1972. By the 1980s, two-thirds of Southeastern Conference basketball players were African American.

The first African American coach at a major university was Will Robertson at Illinois State University in 1970, followed by George Raveling at Washington State in 1972 (Coach of the Year in 1992), along with John Thompson at Georgetown University (1972–1989), whose Hoyas played in three Final Fours in three years (1982, 1984–85), winning in 1984. In 1985, the University of Arkansas hired Nolan Richardson, who promised opponents "forty minutes of hell." By the 1990s, African Americans were coaching top Southern programs, including Tubby Smith at the University of Kentucky, who won the NCAA championship in 1997.

The Wooden Era

Midwestern colleges dominated basketball in the early 1960s. Ohio State University went 78–6 from 1960 to 1962, led by Jerry Lucas and John Havlicek. They captured the NCAA tourney in 1960 and came in second the next two years to Cincinnati.

One of the top collegiate players was 6-foot, 5-inch (1.9-meter) Rhodes Scholar Bill Bradley of Princeton

Coach John Wooden of UCLA, known as the "Wizard of Westwood," built a dynasty in college basketball. His Bruin teams won a total of ten NCAA championships in 12 years, from 1964 to 1975. He won Coach of the Year honors four times. *(Sports Illustrated/Getty Images)*

University, who averaged 30.2 points per game over his career and went on to become the Sullivan Amateur Athlete of the Year in 1965 when he led the Tigers to third place in the NCAA Tournament. He scored a tournament-record 177 points, including 58 in his final game, then the NCAA record. Then there was 6-foot, 5-inch "Pistol" Pete Maravich of Louisiana State University, Player of the Year in 1970 and the leading NCAA Division I scorer in history with 3,667 points (44.2 per game). An expert ball handler, he was probably the single biggest draw of any college player ever.

But the team of the decade was UCLA, coached by John Wooden (1948–1975), a traditionalist who ran extremely organized practices and coached a disciplined game with a controlled fast break, yet was adaptable and pragmatic. Wooden won back-to-back titles in 1964 and 1965 with guard-oriented teams and then won seven straight titles (1967–1973) with towering players such as Lew Alcindor (now known as Kareem Abdul-Jabbar) and Bill Walton. Alcindor was the dominant player in college basketball, leading UCLA to three straight national championships (1967–1969), with a record of 88–2. His style of play prompted the implementation of the "no dunk" rule.

UCLA's 47-game winning streak was broken by Elvin Hayes and the University of Houston Cougars, 71–69, on January 20, 1968, at the Houston Astrodome. The game drew a record crowd of 53,693 fans to the first nationally televised regular-season college game. Center Bill Walton, the Sullivan Award winner in 1973, led UCLA to 88 straight victories. He scored 44 points in the 1973 NCAA finals against Memphis, making 21 of 22 shots.

Television and NCAA Basketball

The first televised college basketball game took place at Madison Square Garden on New York's W2XBS on February 28, 1940. Pittsburgh defeated Fordham, 50–37. The Final Four first was broadcast on local television in 1954 and went national in 1969 after NBC paid $2 million for the telecast rights.

Ten years later, the 1979 NCAA finals, which matched up Larry Bird and undefeated Indiana State University against Earvin "Magic" Johnson and Michigan State University, was seen by 25 million viewers, with a rating of 24.1, the highest ever for a college game. Michigan State won 76–64.

Revenue from the NCAA Tournament, which outdraws the World Series, skyrocketed from less than $20 million in 1985 to more than $150 million in 1994. In 2002, CBS signed an 11-year, $6.2 billion deal to cover the tournament.

NCAA Basketball Since 1980

College basketball has seen some rule changes since the 1980s, including the 3-point shot, first allowed in 1980, and the addition of the shot clock in 1985 (45 seconds), which was reduced to 35 seconds in 1993. Division I basketball programs earn an NCAA Tournament berth by winning their conference season, or conference tournament, or by getting an at-large bid. This certifies their success and that of their coaches, who must justify their high salaries. Coaches also are under pressure to generate revenue, which means producing winning teams that fill large arenas. The average salary of the 65 coaches in the NCAA Tournament in 2006 was nearly $800,000, plus bonuses and outside money from athletic apparel companies. Four years later, there were ten coaches making more than $2 million, led by John Calipari of the University of Kentucky at $4 million.

As for athletes, the pressure, critics say, results in large numbers of unprepared or uninterested students being recruited to play basketball. Many recruits see college basketball as training for a pro contract, and the most talented high school stars often stay in college for only one year. Not surprisingly, only 21 percent of NBA players active in 2009 had college degrees. Still, graduation rates have improved, and among student players enrolling in 2001, 62 percent graduated. However, 44 percent of the tournament teams had a 20 percent or greater gap in graduation between white and black students. Among the coaches who managed to win and to graduate students were Bobby Knight (902 wins) and Mike Krzyzewski (900), the two winningest coaches in men's Division I basketball.

Today, college basketball is more popular than ever. In 2010, the total attendance for Division I was a record 27.5 million, an average of 5,245 a game. Three schools—Kentucky, North Carolina, and Syracuse—average more than 20,000 per game. The NCAA Tournament, dominated since 1980 by the Big East (five titles) and the Atlantic Coast Conference (eight titles), draws enormous television coverage over three weeks, dubbed "March Madness" by CBS. At the same time, the tournament is a magnet for betting in Las Vegas and unofficial betting in workplaces and online across the country.

Steven A. Riess

See also: Basketball, Professional, NBA Era; Basketball, Women's; College Basketball Scandal of 1951; Football, College;

Historically Black Colleges; Intercollegiate Athletic Associations and Conferences; Interscholastic Sports.

Further Reading

Bjarkman, Peter C. *Hoopla: A Century of College Basketball.* Indianapolis, IN: Masters, 1996.

Cohen, Stanley. *The Game They Played.* New York: Farrar, Straus and Giroux, 1977.

Einhorn, Eddie, with Ron Rapoport. *How March Became Madness: How the NCAA Tournament Became the Greatest Sporting Event in America.* Chicago: Triumph, 2006.

Fabian, Ann. "Gamblers in the Garden: The Political Consequences of the Fix." *South Atlantic Quarterly* 95:2 (Spring 1996): 501–521.

Fox, Larry. *Illustrated History of Basketball.* New York: Grosset & Dunlap, 1974.

Grundy, Pamela. *Learning to Win: Sports, Education, and Social Change in Twentieth-Century North Carolina.* Chapel Hill: University of North Carolina Press, 2001.

Henderson, Russell J. "The 1963 Mississippi State University Basketball Controversy and the Repeal of the Unwritten Law: 'Something More than the Game Will Be Lost.'" *Journal of Southern History* 63:4 (November 1997): 827–854.

Horger, Marc. "A Victim of Reform: Why Basketball Failed at Harvard, 1900–1909." *New England Quarterly* 18:1 (March 2005): 49–76.

Isaacs, Neil D. *All the Moves: A History of College Basketball.* Rev. ed. New York: Harper & Row, 1984.

Martin, Charles H. "Jim Crow in the Gymnasium: The Integration of College Basketball in the Deep South." In *Sport and the Color Line: Black Athletes and Race Relations in Twentieth-Century America,* ed. Patrick B. Miller and David K. Wiggins. New York: Routledge, 2004.

Rosen, Charles. *Scandals of '51: How the Gamblers Almost Killed College Basketball.* New York: Holt, Rinehart and Winston, 1978.

———. *The Wizard of Odds: How Jack Molinas Almost Destroyed the Game of Basketball.* New York: Seven Stories, 2001.

Roy, George, and Steven Hilliard Stern, dirs. *City Dump: The Story of the 1951 CCNY Basketball Scandal.* New York: HBO Sports, 1998.

Smith, Dean E., with John Kilgo and Sally Jenkins. *A Coach's Life: My Forty Years in College Basketball.* New York: Random House, 1999.

Basketball, Professional, Pre-NBA

Basketball was invented in 1891 at the International Young Men's Christian Association (YMCA) Training School (now Springfield College) in Springfield, Massachusetts. By 1898, a professional league had been formed with six teams that played in the Philadelphia and Trenton, New Jersey, area. The early professional players were local and working-class ethnics, who learned the game at YMCA and settlement houses. Pro basketball was a minor sport for the first half of the twentieth century, with struggling regional leagues in the East and Midwest, as well as independent teams that barnstormed the country.

Rise of the Professional Game

In 1891, James Naismith, a physical education teacher at the International YMCA Training School, laid down 13 basic rules for a game of "basket ball." Initially, a peach basket with its bottom cut out was used for a hoop. The court size was not standardized, and the basket might or might not have a backboard.

Naismith's guidelines banned running with the ball, established fouls for holding, striking, pushing, or tripping opponents, and set 15-minute halves, with new rules added as the game developed. The game was very rough, emphasizing low scoring and ball possession. Jump balls were held after every basket or free throw, and a good "tipper" could help his team control the action by retaining possession of the ball. Professional basketball originally had no foul limit, so players could be disqualified from the game only for extremely rough play, as judged by a single referee.

Originally, the player with the ball could not move with it—the ball could be advanced only by passing. A rule change allowing players to move with the ball while bouncing it (dribbling) was adopted during the game's earliest years. In some early versions of the game, players had to bounce the ball with both hands, but by 1908, only the one-handed dribble was allowed in the amateur game. Some professional leagues required the two-handed dribble until 1925.

Some professional leagues in the 1890s used a steel cage to surround the court in order to protect spectators in small, cramped gymnasiums. As it turned out, the cage served as much to protect the players from unruly fans as it did to protect the fans from the ball. It also allowed for a faster game, as the ball was always in play, even when it bounced off the cage. Players could climb on and could push off the cage to gain leverage against their opponents. The cage was used in various forms by some leagues until 1930. Decades later, news reports still called basketball players "cagers."

In its first decade, the sport used balls that were larger and heavier than basketballs today, and the laces protruded prominently, making dribbling a challenge and ball handling more difficult. At the time, basketball shoes were a new invention, and they were not universally worn.

Almost all of the first "professionals" were paid by the game, usually about $5 per contest, and they held other jobs. Players played with any number of teams, depending on their schedules and the payment offered. There generally were no formal contracts binding players to particular teams.

The first professional league, the National League of Professional Basketball, was formed in 1898. It included six teams from metropolitan Philadelphia: Philadelphia, Germantown, and Kensington in Pennsylvania, and Camden, Trenton, and Millville in New Jersey. The league lasted six years, with a varying roster of teams. Some teams had ties to particular trades or businesses, as indicated by team nicknames such as the Drivers, Glass Blowers, Electrics, Ironworkers, Potters, Shoe Pegs, and Wheelmen. Early in the twentieth century, there were at least six other professional leagues in Allegheny County, Pennsylvania; New Hampshire; and central, western, and eastern Massachusetts.

Teams often scored no more than two or three baskets during a game. Players lobbed two-handed set shots, and few ever left the floor to shoot or rebound, mainly because it was risky to be in midair amid a tough scrum. The game resembled hockey in its constant pace and movement, rough-and-tumble action, and minimal scoring. When foul shots were awarded, the team's best shooter usually took them. Spectators were mostly working-class fans who cheered lustily, especially for the roughhouse play.

The first great team was the Buffalo Germans, which was formed in Buffalo, New York, at a local YMCA in 1895 as a 14-and-under team. In 1901, the team won the Pan-American Exposition tournament in Buffalo and the amateur championship at the 1904 Olympic Games in St. Louis, where basketball was a demonstration sport. The Germans turned professional in 1904 and toured for the next 22 seasons. They won consistently, going on a 111-game winning streak during the 1907–1909 seasons. The team played under various banners and sponsors, ending as the Buffalo Bisons of the American Basketball League in 1925–1926, when they won only 10 of their 30 games and then disbanded.

Professional Basketball in the 1920s

During World War I, most professional leagues shut down due to a lack of players and travel restrictions on the railroads. Two of the top players of the era were Barney Sedran and Marty Friedman, the so-called Heavenly Twins. Jewish players from New York City who got their start in the settlement houses, they played as teammates on championship teams in the Interstate, Pennsylvania State, and Eastern leagues between 1914 and 1921. One season, Sedran made $12,000, playing in three leagues at one time.

After the war, the Original New York Celtics emerged as the top team in basketball. Led by future Hall of Famers Johnny Beckman, Henry "Dutch" Dehnert, Nat Holman, and Joe Lapchick, the Celtics won several league championships in the early 1920s, and barnstormed much of the country in the mid-1920s. They went 193–11–1 in 1922–1923.

In 1925, the first truly national professional league, the American Basketball League (ABL), was established by Joe Carr, president of the National Football League, from primarily independent eastern teams. These teams included the Boston Whirlwinds, Brooklyn Arcadians, Buffalo Bisons, Chicago Bruins, Cleveland Rosenblums, Detroit Pulaskis, Fort Wayne (Indiana) Caseys, Rochester (New York) Centrals, and Washington, D.C., Palace Five. Three owners had NFL connections: George Halas of the Chicago Bears owned the Bruins; Max Rosenblum of the Cleveland Bulldogs owned the Rosenblums; and George Preston Marshall of the Palace Five was the future owner of the Redskins. The Rosenblums won the first championship.

The Brooklyn Celtics joined the ABL for the 1926–1927 season, won the championship, and then moved to New York and repeated as champions in 1927–1928 with a record of 40–9. The ABL broke up the Celtics because of their dominance. The Cleveland Rosenblums (with four former Celtics in the lineup) won the title the next two years. The ABL was very unstable, with 19 teams in five seasons, and the league lasted only until 1931, when it disbanded amid the Great Depression.

In the late 1920s, the Celtics' toughest adversaries were the independent New York Renaissance, or the "Rens," the first dominant African American team (soon to be rivaled by the Chicago-based Harlem Globetrotters), and the South Philadelphia Hebrew Association team or "SPHAs." The Rens, established by Robert Douglas, were named after their home court, Harlem's Renaissance Ballroom. The team went everywhere on their own bus, as travel for African Americans on public bus lines in those days was difficult or impossible. In 1948–1949, their last year, the Rens competed as an all-black team in the National Basketball League, then the top professional league, but the players were past their prime and did not perform well. The SPHAs were organized by Basketball Hall of Famer Eddie Gottlieb, who served as their first coach.

A second, exclusively eastern ABL was organized for the 1934–1935 season, and it remained in operation through the 1952–1953 season. The league was dominated by Jewish players, who made up more than 40 percent of the rosters, and the preeminent team was the SPHAs, who captured seven championships through 1945. The new ABL struggled, going through 40 franchises in just 20 years. The league suspended operations in 1953–1954 and went out of business the following year.

In 1935, as the hardships of Depression began to ease, Indianapolis grocer Frank Kautsky and Paul Sheeks, the recreation director for the Firestone Tire and Rubber Company of Akron, decided to form a new professional league, the Midwest Basketball Conference. The league consisted of nine teams, playing independently scheduled games. John Wooden, a former Purdue University All-American and future legendary college coach, was the leading scorer. The league was successful enough to inspire Sheeks and Kautsky to restructure and expand it in 1937 as the National Basketball League (NBL).

The NBL was very different from previous professional leagues, mainly because of the players' backgrounds. Most prior professional basketballers had not graduated from or even attended college, but the NBL was composed largely of college graduates, most of whom held jobs and worked regular hours in the off-season. Some squads were sponsored by corporations, such as Akron's Firestone and Goodyear teams. The companies often employed the players in some capacity during the rest of the year. Other teams, such as the Indianapolis Kautskys and the Columbus Athletic Supply, were sponsored by smaller businesses, and the players held outside jobs. There also were community-supported teams, such as the Sheboygan Red Skins and the Oshkosh All-Stars, which sold shares to local boosters and fans. The number of NBL franchises fluctuated from 13 in 1937–1938 to 4 during World War II and then rose back to 13 in 1946–1947.

The league had the best young players in the game, particularly Leroy Edwards and Bob McDermott. Edwards was a 6-foot, 4.5-inch (1.9-meter) center and forward who played one year of varsity basketball at the University of Kentucky before turning pro in 1935 with the Indianapolis U.S. Tires team. Edwards played for the entire life of the NBL (1937–1949). He was a great rebounder, was ranked as the league's all-time leading scorer, and led Oshkosh to two NBL ti-

tles. McDermott played with a number of NBL teams and often acted as a player-coach. He led the league in scoring once and took his team to three titles.

The league's dominant player was 6-foot, 10-inch (2.1-meter) George Mikan, who led the Chicago American Gears to the championship in 1947. However, the Gears dropped out of the NBL when owner Maurice White organized the 16-team Professional Basketball League of America. Unfortunately, the new league lasted only three weeks. The Gears players were distributed throughout the NBL; Mikan ended up with the Minneapolis Lakers and led them to an NBL title.

Outside of league play, the pro game was highlighted by the World Professional Tournament, sponsored by the *Chicago Herald-American* from 1939 to 1948. Top independent fives competed with league teams in a single-elimination format that packed venues in Chicago. In 1939, the New York Rens defeated the Oshkosh All Stars (34–25) in the inaugural tournament, solidifying their claim as the best professional team in basketball. The Harlem Globetrotters finished third, having been bracketed with the Rens so that they could not meet in the finals. There were cries of racism, but it was more likely an economic decision, as games played between black and white teams were controversial and drew larger crowds than all-black games. The next year, the Harlem Globetrotters captured the title, and in 1943, a team of former Rens, playing as the Washington Bears, won the championship. Thereafter, the World Tournament was won five straight years by an NBL team.

In 1946, a group of hockey club owners, most of whom owned their arenas, sought additional attractions for their facilities. They formed the Basketball Association of America (BAA), a strong competitor to the NBL. The league began with 11 teams, mostly in large Eastern cities and including a team in Chicago to compete with the local NBL franchise. The BAA had few stars other than the Philadelphia Warriors' Joe Fulks, who led the team in scoring in its first two years.

The potential of basketball in big-city arenas clearly challenged the NBL, many of whose franchises were located in small to middle-sized cities. NBL owners understood this, and before the 1948–1949 season, the Fort Wayne Zollner Pistons, Indianapolis Jets, Minneapolis Lakers, and Rochester Royals joined the rival BAA, with the Lakers taking the championship. The following year, both leagues were in financial distress, and they agreed to merge, forming the 17-team National Basketball Association.

Murry R. Nelson

See also: Basketball, Professional, NBA Era; Harlem Globetrotters; Renaissance, New York.

Further Reading

Basloe, Frank J., with D. Gordon Rahman. *I Grew Up with Basketball: Twenty Years of Barnstorming with Cage Greats of Yesterday.* New York: Greenberg, 1952.

Bole, Robert D., and Alfred C. Lawrence. *From Peachbaskets to Slamdunks: A History of Professional Basketball, 1891–1987.* Canaan, NH: B&L, 1987.

Gould, Todd. *Pioneers of the Hardwood: Indiana and the Birth of Professional Basketball.* Bloomington: Indiana University Press, 1998.

Holman, Nat. *Winning Basketball.* New York: Charles Scribner's Sons, 1932.

Lapchick, Joe. *50 Years of Basketball.* Englewood Cliffs, NJ: Prentice Hall, 1968.

Nelson, Murry R. *The National Basketball League: A History, 1935–1949.* Jefferson, NC: McFarland, 2009.

———. *The Originals: The New York Celtics Invent Modern Basketball.* Bowling Green, OH: Bowling Green State University Popular Press, 1999.

Peterson, Robert W. *Cages to Jump Shots: Pro Basketball's Early Years.* Lincoln: University of Nebraska Press, 2002.

Shouler, Ken, Bob Ryan, Sam Smith, Leonard Koppett, and Bob Belotti. *Total Basketball: The Ultimate Basketball Encyclopedia.* Wilmington, DE: Sports Classics, 2003.

Westcott, Rich. *The Mogul: Eddie Gottlieb, Philadelphia Sports Legend and Pro Basketball Pioneer.* Philadelphia: Temple University Press, 2008.

Basketball, Professional, NBA Era

The National Basketball Association (NBA) originated in 1949, when professional basketball was still a regional, small-time operation. The NBA was formed by the merger of two existing leagues: the Basketball Association of America, founded by owners of big-city arenas, and the National Basketball League, which was tied to small industrial cities in the Midwest and Northeast.

During the league's first several years, weaker franchises were moved to larger cities or were eliminated, and the league made refinements to the rules to speed up the game. In the 1960s, an influx of stars, including many African American players, brought the NBA new popularity and encouraged expansion. Basketball became the third major team sport in America, following baseball and football. In 1967, the league's dominance was challenged by the American Basketball Association; this led to a period of instability that finally resulted in expansion and further success. Shrewd leadership, tele-vision revenue, and marketable stars spurred an NBA boom in the 1980s.

Beginning in that decade, basketball was established as a popular spectator sport in other parts of the world as well. Soon, U.S. teams (made up of NBA players) faced challenges in the Olympics and other international competitions. Beginning in the 1990s and continuing to the present, outstanding players from Eastern and Western Europe, Africa, and South America made increasing contributions to NBA teams and offered a new pool of talent for the future. In 2010, there were 29 NBA teams in the United States, and there was one in Canada. This commercial and cultural blossoming established basketball's place in the pantheon of American professional sports.

Origins

On June 6, 1946, 11 men, mainly from major East Coast and Midwest cities, met at the Hotel Commodore in New York City to organize the Basketball Association of America (BAA). Five-foot- (1.5-meter-) tall, Russian-born, Yale-educated Maurice Podoloff served as commissioner. Five of the founders owned franchises in the American Hockey League, of which Podoloff was president, and another five had connections to National Hockey League franchises. Ten of the owners were members of the Arena Managers Association of America. Though they were not experts in basketball, they had experience in promoting and publicizing sporting events, and they represented big-city arenas with open dates for pro basketball.

The BAA attracted many players from the American Basketball League (ABL), which had been in operation since 1925, with franchises in the New York and Philadelphia areas and in smaller industrial cities of the Northeast. In its early years, the ABL featured the most talented players of the day. But by the 1940s, the ABL had lost its top position to the National Basketball League (NBL), which had operated since 1937, with franchises in smaller industrial cities of the Midwest, and had attracted most of the leading stars of college play. The NBL viewed the new BAA as a rival, and few of its players jumped to the new league.

The BAA's first season was difficult. For the 1947–1948 season, it shrunk to eight teams. It also cut back its schedule and instituted a territorial draft, which allowed franchises preemptive rights to graduating stars of local universities. With its big-city arenas, the BAA had the potential for growth that the NBL lacked; however, the NBL had greater basketball talent.

During the 1947–1948 season, it became clear that neither league was likely to succeed on its own. Merger talks began, and before the 1948–1949 season, four NBL franchises joined the BAA, including the Minneapolis Lakers, whose 6-foot, 10-inch (2.1-meter) center George Mikan was the most promising player in the game. In summer 1949, the NBL ceased operation. The BAA absorbed seven other teams from the NBL, and it adopted a new name, the National Basketball Association. The NBA began the 1949–1950 season with 17 teams organized into three divisions.

The league was an ungainly mess, marred by the financial demands of team owners. Some teams played 68 games, while others played 64 or 62. Small-city franchises in Sheboygan (Wisconsin), Waterloo (Iowa), and Anderson (Indiana) soon folded, and the Denver team withdrew because of the hardships of cross-country travel in the era before jet airliners. More troubling, franchises in Chicago and St. Louis also folded. In the ensuing years, franchises in Baltimore, Indianapolis, and Washington, D.C., dropped out, leaving the NBA with only eight teams by the start of the 1954–1955 season. It had franchises in the major East Coast cities of Boston, New York, and Philadelphia, as well as in Milwaukee and Minneapolis. Other clubs were located in smaller cities: Fort Wayne, Indiana, and Rochester and Syracuse, New York.

The NBA suffered from a reputation as a "bush league." Fans regularly taunted the visiting team, players often brawled, and owners did little to discourage rough play. Referees were overwhelmed by screaming fans, intimidating coaches, and physical play. Home teams won an inordinate share of the games. Some teams used slowdown tactics, leading to plodding and unappealing games. The regular season existed only to keep the league afloat until the playoffs— six of the eight teams qualified—which provided the season highlights.

College basketball remained much more popular than pro ball, and the barnstorming, all-black Harlem Globetrotters attracted larger gates than NBA teams. The Globetrotters regularly played exhibitions before NBA games to attract more paying customers. By the mid-1950s, the NBA had established itself, but it had not yet achieved a significant claim on the loyalties of American sports fans.

The NBA Emerges

By the early 1950s, several factors pointed to the NBA's future growth. One was the league's first dynasty, the Minneapolis Lakers, which boasted the game's greatest player in Mikan, a behemoth with a repertoire of low-post power moves. Stocked with talent, the Lakers won five championships in the six seasons between 1949 and 1954. The engaging, charismatic Mikan also served as the league's most visible representative. Before a game against New York, for instance, the marquee at Madison Square Garden read "Mikan vs. Knicks." Mikan and the Lakers established a standard of team excellence, a measuring stick for competing franchises.

The NBA also benefited from the college basketball scandals of the early 1950s. In 1951, the New York City district attorney had begun investigating rumors of point shaving in college games held at Madison Square Garden; by April 1953, a grand jury investigation resulted in accusations against 32 players of fixing 86 games in 17 states. Though college basketball gradually recovered, fans began paying more attention to the professional game.

NBA Commissioner Podoloff encouraged further growth through increased television coverage. First the Dumont Television Network and then NBC broadcast NBA games to national audiences.

The All-Star Game, begun in 1951, showcased the game's greatest stars. Besides the Minneapolis contingent of Mikan, Vern Mikkelsen, and Jim Pollard, the NBA boasted such appealing sharpshooters as Paul Arizin of the Philadelphia Warriors, Dolph Schayes of the Syracuse Nationals, and Bob Pettit of the St. Louis Hawks. Perhaps no player was as beloved as Boston Celtics guard Bob Cousy, a local college hero from Holy Cross. The diminutive Cousy possessed long arms and amazing court vision. He flung creative passes and dazzled crowds, while spurring the Celtics' trademark fast break.

Two key rule changes in 1954 made the game more appealing. The owners adopted a rule (known as the shot clock) requiring the team with the ball to shoot within 24 seconds. Syracuse owner Danny Biasone proposed this change to prevent teams from stalling after establishing a lead. The owners further agreed to count team fouls in order to discourage excessive fouling. On the first six nonshooting fouls in a quarter, the ball was turned over to the team fouled against. On any further nonshooting fouls in the quarter, the fouled team was awarded a free throw. If the foul came in the act of shooting, the opposing player received three chances to make two foul shots. These changes discouraged slowdown tactics and encouraged fast breaks rather than deliberate set plays. Scoring increased, and professional basketball now guaranteed 48 minutes of action.

The 1956–1957 season began the NBA's journey into national sports prominence thanks to the revolutionary play of Bill Russell. Russell had led the University of San Francisco to two National Collegiate Athletic Association titles and a 55-game winning streak, and he remained an amateur long enough to become a leader on the 1956 U.S. Olympic basketball squad. Soon after the U.S. victory, he joined the Boston Celtics. Boston Coach Red Auerbach also had drafted Russell's college teammate, K.C. Jones, and Holy Cross star Tommy Heinsohn. Veteran Celtics included playmaker Cousy and scoring whiz Bill Sharman. The Celtics compiled the best record in the league during the regular season and won their first league title in the playoffs, defeating the St. Louis Hawks in the finals.

Russell revolutionized the sport. His physical and intellectual skills concentrated on defense. He leaped to block shots under the basket, disrupting pattern offenses designed to end with a layup. By taking away layups, Russell forced opponents to shoot more midrange jumpers and compelled a more dynamic style of play. He also offered the perfect complement to his offensively oriented teammates. The Celtics lost to the St. Louis Hawks in the 1958 NBA finals, but then won ten titles in 11 years (1957–1969). During that period, the Celtics evolved from a team of offensive superstars, including Tommy Heinsohn and Sam Jones, into one rooted in aggressive defense. When Auerbach was named the Celtics' general manager in 1966, Russell became player-coach, and Boston won two titles in his three final seasons. The Celtics had become a dynasty on par with the New York Yankees of baseball and the Montreal Canadiens of hockey.

Russell was destined to be a superstar. There had been black players in the NBA since 1950, starting with Earl Lloyd of the Syracuse Nationals, Chuck Cooper of the Celtics, and Nat "Sweetwater" Clifton of the Knicks. But beginning with Russell, a host of dynamic African American stars appeared. In 1958, Elgin Baylor joined the Minneapolis Lakers. His sweeping, bullish drives to the basket made him an instant star, and he returned the Lakers to prominence. Wilt Chamberlain joined the Philadelphia Warriors the next year. The most powerful offensive force in the history of the sport, Chamberlain possessed remarkable strength and grace in a 7-foot (2.1-meter) frame, and he immediately shattered scoring and rebounding records. In 1960, Oscar Robertson joined the Cincinnati Royals. Perhaps the most complete player ever, Robertson could shoot, pass, rebound, defend, and run the floor with equal aplomb.

Along with Russell and Jerry West, these players constituted the pantheon of NBA superstars in the 1960s.

Another sign of the NBA's growing national profile was the migration of franchises from small cities to large ones. The Fort Wayne Pistons moved to Detroit and the Rochester Royals moved to Cincinnati in 1958, and then the Lakers left Minneapolis for Los Angeles in 1960. In 1961, the Chicago Packers joined the league, changed their name to the Zephyrs in 1962, and then moved to Baltimore as the Bullets in 1963. That same year, a new Chicago franchise, the Bulls, replaced the Packers. Also in 1963, the Philadelphia Warriors moved to San Francisco, becoming the second West Coast team, and the Syracuse Nationals became the Philadelphia 76ers. With these moves, the NBA had a foothold in nearly all major U.S. markets.

The NBA's strategy for strengthening its franchises was partly a response to a new challenge. Abe Saperstein, the impresario behind the Harlem Globetrotters, launched the competing American Basketball League (ABL) in 1961. Saperstein's Globetrotters had been a phenomenon since the 1930s, entertaining audiences with their basketball artistry and comic antics. Until the mid-1950s, they also may have been the best team in basketball, as they were able to defeat leading NBA teams in exhibition play. Later African American stars, beginning with Bill Russell, turned down offers from the Globetrotters and instead chose to play in the NBA. In addition, league salaries were increasing, and many black players disapproved of the Globetrotters' "clowning," which they felt reinforced racial stereotypes. In the 1960s the Globetrotters remained popular, but more as entertainment than as a legitimate team.

Saperstein's ABL had eight teams across the nation, including franchises in Los Angeles, San Francisco, and Hawaii, but the league lacked financial resources and never really threatened the NBA's supremacy. It folded at the end of December 1962, in the middle of its second season. The ABL did leave a legacy, however, as the NBA soon adopted its wider foul lane. The ABL also used a scoring system that gave 3 points for field goals shot from behind a line marked on the court; the NBA initially resisted the 3-point rule, but finally adopted it in 1979.

By the mid-1960s, the NBA had taken steps toward stable economic growth. In 1963, Walter Kennedy replaced Maurice Podoloff as league commissioner. While Podoloff had successfully negotiated the competing demands of rival owners throughout his tenure, critics maligned him unfairly as a symbol of the bush league era, because he had little power. Kennedy, who

The televised showdowns between rival big men Bill Russell (*left*) and Wilt Chamberlain (*right*) in the 1960s helped bring professional basketball to prominence and reflected its changing racial mix. By mid-decade, nearly half of NBA players were black. *(National Basketball Association/Getty Images)*

had a professional background in publicity, offered the league an air of polished respectability. In 1964, he negotiated a three-year contract with ABC. The Sunday afternoon "Game of the Week" became a regular fixture on television in the 1960s, and it earned the league new levels of television revenue. In 1965, Jack Kent Cooke bought the Los Angeles Lakers for $5 million, more than five times the price of the Warriors franchise when it moved west three years earlier.

Economic growth also was accompanied by the difficulties of modern labor relations. Most of the original owners ran their teams paternalistically, treating even established stars as hired hands. The National Basketball Players Association, led by Bob Cousy, was founded in 1954, but there was no collective bargaining until 1957, and salaries remained paltry. Players begged for such tiny concessions as a 20-game limit on the exhibition season. They consistently agitated for a pension fund, but with little success.

A turning point came in January 1964. Players at the nationally televised All-Star Game in Boston refused to participate without concessions from the own-ers. As ABC threatened to cancel its contract, the players persisted, until Kennedy promised a good-faith negotiation for a pension plan. The owners were outraged, but the pension plan went into effect the next year. The league's paternalistic system of labor relations started to erode. In 1965, Robertson became the Players Association president. He and attorney Larry Fleisher acted with the assumption that players and owners had an adversarial relationship.

Television fostered basketball's growing national appeal, but the on-court product drove the sport's emergence. By the mid-1960s, players' skills had reached unprecedented levels. An NBA fan could expect to see pressing defense, fast breaks, dunks, off-balance jump shots, 30-foot (9-meter) shots, and deft passing. The college game also was booming, and college teams developed a deep pool of talent for the league. The NBA provided an exciting mix of polished skills and breath-taking athleticism.

Throughout most of the 1960s, the sport's preeminent narrative was the rivalry between Russell and Chamberlain. While Russell led the Boston Celtics to title after title, Chamberlain dominated the sport on an individual level. Fans and reporters constantly debated their respective merits. Russell was a team-oriented winner, the leader of the finely tuned Celtics machine who concentrated on defense and rebounding. Chamberlain was the sport's Colossus, the perennial scoring and rebounding champion whose teams always fell short in the playoffs. In fact, Chamberlain lost to Russell in the playoffs seven times; Chamberlain's team prevailed only in 1967, when the Philadelphia 76ers beat the Celtics in the Eastern Conference finals and then captured the NBA championship. Russell conveyed an image as a shrewd, cagey competitor, who further enhanced his stature by becoming the NBA's first black coach. He won 11 championships in 13 seasons. Chamberlain, by contrast, often hurt his cause with egotistical self-justifications. Their professional rivalry was fascinating theater, a central thread running through the NBA's emergence in the 1960s.

Russell's and Chamberlain's rivalry further signified the game's changing racial texture. In 1958, African Americans composed 13 percent of NBA players, and just seven years later, they made up 49 percent. Furthermore, they represented two-thirds of starters and three-fourths of All-Stars. That proportion kept growing in subsequent years. Some executives and reporters questioned whether the sport would suffer, but the influx of black players occurred simultaneously with the game's explosion on a national level.

A Challenge to the NBA

In 1967, another rival league challenged the NBA. The American Basketball Association (ABA) was organized by advertising executives seeking a lucrative marketing venture. The league hired George Mikan as its first commissioner and established 11 teams nationwide in major markets. Basketball had surged in popularity, but the NBA still had only ten teams, and other cities had large arenas and enthusiastic fan bases. The ABA thus began on a firmer footing than the ABL had in 1961. In time, the ABA lured such young stars as Julius "Dr. J" Erving, Dan Issel, Moses Malone, George McGinnis, David Thompson, and Connie Hawkins, a breathtaking talent who had been banned from the NBA for alleged ties to gambling during his one college year. The ABA hired some of the NBA's best referees and promoted such novelties as the 3-point shot and a red, white, and blue ball.

The ABA threat accelerated change within the NBA. The senior league had been planning expansion,

but now Kennedy announced an aggressive addition of franchises. By 1970, the NBA had 17 teams. This growth lined the pockets of existing NBA owners, as new teams had to pay multimillion-dollar fees to join the league.

The players also profited, because the ABA competition gave them leverage in salary negotiations. They knew that team owners were prosperous thanks to expansion fees. In addition, they could threaten to jump to the other league. The ABA was attracting some established NBA stars, including Rick Barry, the San Francisco Warriors star who joined the Oakland Oaks. Rumors followed that such luminaries as Chamberlain, Robertson, and John Havlicek would jump leagues.

The NBA Players Association took advantage of the competition to bargain aggressively, even threatening to strike during the 1967 playoffs. By the end of the decade, owners were required to pay a minimum salary to all players, and players qualified for medical insurance, generous severance pay, and pension benefits. They flew first class and stayed in luxury hotels. Many players earned more than $50,000, and some stars earned more than $100,000. No one could call the NBA a bush league any more.

Following Russell's retirement in 1969, the Boston Celtics crumbled, and new rivalries emerged. The New York Knicks produced fluid and exciting teams in the early 1970s that meshed the backcourt grace of Walt Frazier, the cerebral efficiency of Bill Bradley, and the heroic work ethic of Willis Reed. Long an ill-managed team, the Knicks captured the heart of the nation's media capital as it won championship titles in 1970 and 1973.

The elegant center Lew Alcindor, Jr. (soon to be known as Kareem Abdul-Jabbar), chose the NBA over the ABA. Teaming with veteran superstar Robertson, he led the Milwaukee Bucks to the 1971 championship. Chamberlain and West led a dynamic, fast-breaking Los Angeles Lakers team to a 33-game winning streak and the 1972 title, lending the league more glamour.

The ABA continued to operate, however, despite frequent franchise moves and its own bush league reputation. Backed by significant investors, the league sought to survive long enough to win a national television contract and force a merger with the NBA. In 1970, the NBA agreed to a proposed merger, but the Players Association challenged the process in court. The players had profited from the competition between the leagues—the average salary jumped from $18,000 in 1965 to $110,000 in 1975. The players argued that the merger would create a monopoly, and the courts issued an injunction against the merger. The NBA and ABA continued to exist independently, competing for players and visibility.

In 1975, the NBA owners lost a motion to dismiss the protracted suit by the Players Association. The case finally was settled in February 1976, with stipulations that allowed player movement and included a financial settlement for players. The end of the suit freed the way for four ABA teams—Indiana, New York (Nets), San Antonio, and Denver—to join the NBA by paying hefty entry fees and giving up television revenue for three years. The remaining ABA teams were dissolved, and their players were drafted by NBA teams. The NBA now had 22 teams.

An Era of Prosperity

By the late 1970s, the NBA had traveled far from its roots, with television revenues creating a surge of money and teams. In 1978, the league signed a four-year, $74 million contract with CBS. Multimillionaires and corporations that profited from television, advertising, and tax write-offs replaced the old generation of owners, whose bottom line had been dependent on gate revenue.

Larry O'Brien, an influential political strategist and former postmaster general, took over as league commissioner in 1975. He oversaw the league merger, the CBS contract, and increases in game attendance, but he had weak public relations skills, and his league suffered from malaise. The league now cast a wider net, but fewer fans felt close ties to their teams, due to frequent player movement and the NBA/ABA shakeout. Players were in so many games that they sometimes seemed lethargic, a spirit far removed from the rivalries of the 1960s. Those with no-cut contracts could not even be fired for lazy play.

NBA rosters had become over three-quarters black. The league's marketers capitalized on the grace and speed of new African American players, but they still worried about alienating their predominantly white fan base. The NBA's television ratings were down, even for playoff finals. In 1980 and 1981, CBS refused to show some of the finals games live, broadcasting them instead on tape delay to avoid preempting popular weekend prime-time programming.

The NBA exploded into the popular consciousness in the mid-1980s, driven by a sustained rivalry between the Celtics and the Lakers. These two teams won eight of the nine NBA championships between 1980 and 1988. Heightening the rivalry was the perfect, poetic contrast between the game's two greatest stars. Earvin "Magic" Johnson, the ebullient African American point guard, keyed the Lakers' "Showtime" attack with flair. Larry Bird, the stoic white forward with the great jump shot, exemplified the gritty image of the Celtics.

Commissioner David Stern oversaw the NBA's rise to prosperity. When he took over the league in 1984, 17 of the 23 teams were losing money. Stern exploited the burst of sports interest and television programming, exemplified by the popular all-sports cable network ESPN. The former lawyer convinced the Players Association to accept a salary cap and convinced the owners to accept a revenue-sharing system to maintain relative parity among teams. Stern further instituted marketing and advertising campaigns that emphasized individual stars such as Johnson and Bird.

Michael Jordan, acknowledged as the greatest player—and most prolific product spokesman—in the history the sport, brought a new level of excitement, media attention, and international interest to pro basketball in the 1980s and 1990s. *(AFP/Getty Images)*

The game's popularity accelerated in the 1990, thanks in part to the emergence of the game's greatest superstar, Michael Jordan of the Chicago Bulls. Arriving in the NBA in 1984, the same year as Stern, Jordan's graceful, gravity-defying style captivated the public, and he led the Chicago Bulls to six NBA titles between 1991 and 1998. Jordan also became a familiar presence in advertising, particularly for Nike, the sports apparel company.

Commissioner Stern, cashing in on the wide popularity of Jordan and other stars, negotiated lucrative television contracts with NBC in 1990 and with ABC in 2002. He expanded the league to 30 teams. Average player salaries skyrocketed from $325,000 in 1985 to $4.2 million in 2000. In 1997, Stern introduced the Women's National Basketball Association, and the NBA since has instituted a developmental league, a popular Web site, and a 24-hour television network. During his tenure, the league's revenue has increased 500 percent.

From the 1990s on, the NBA has benefited from the robust growth of international basketball. The trend began with the appearance of the U.S. basketball team at the 1992 Olympics in Barcelona, Spain. Because of a rule change, the "Dream Team," as the squad was known, was composed of leading NBA stars, not college players, as in the past. Its stars included all-time basketball greats Larry Bird, Magic Johnson, and Michael Jordan, and the team demonstrated its mastery of the game, easily defeating all challengers to win the gold medal. Their performance inspired players and spectators in many parts of the world. In succeeding years, substantial professional leagues grew up in Eastern and Western Europe, providing training and livelihoods for hundreds of basketball professionals.

By the late 1990s, the NBA was looking at veteran European stars and promising rookies as a new source of basketball talent. By the end of the first decade of the new century, there were scores of players in the NBA born outside the United States, not only from Europe, but also from Africa, South America, and Asia. Some became championship players. The San Antonio Spurs won four NBA titles in 1999, 2003, 2005, and 2007, relying heavily on Tim Duncan, born and raised in the U.S. Virgin Islands and the NBA's Most Valuable Player (MVP) in 2002 and 2003; Tony Parker, born in Belgium and raised in France by an African American father and a Dutch mother; and Manu Ginòbili from Argentina. German Dirk Nowitzki, the first European-born MVP (2007), led the Dallas Mavericks to win the NBA title in 2011.

Of course, the immigrant players faced strong challenges from stars born in the United States, including Kobe Bryant, LeBron James, Shaquille O'Neal, and others. The NBA continues to thrive. League revenues reached a record $3.8 billion in the 2007–2008 season, and the average team pretax profit was $10.6 million.

Aram Goudsouzian

See also: American Basketball Association; Basketball, College; Basketball, Professional, Pre-NBA; Basketball, Women's; Celtics, Boston; Lakers, Los Angeles/Minneapolis.

Further Reading

Axthelm, Pete. *The City Game: Basketball from the Garden to the Playgrounds.* New York: Viking, 1991.

Cole, Lewis. *A Loose Game: The Sport and Business of Basketball.* Indianapolis, IN: Bobbs-Merrill, 1978.

George, Nelson. *Elevating the Game: Black Men and Basketball.* New York: HarperCollins, 1992.

Halberstam, David. *The Breaks of the Game.* New York: Ballantine, 1981.

———. *Playing for Keeps: Michael Jordan and the World He Made.* New York: Random House, 1999.

Koppett, Leonard. *The Essence of the Game Is Deception: Thinking About Basketball.* Boston: Little, Brown, 1973.

———. *24 Seconds to Shoot: The Birth and Improbable Rise of the National Basketball Association.* Kingston, NY: Total/Sports Illustrated Classics, 1999.

Pluto, Terry. *Loose Balls: The Short, Wild Life of the American Basketball Association.* New York: Simon & Schuster, 1990.

———. *Tall Tales: The Glory Years of the NBA* Lincoln: University of Nebraska Press, 1992; 2000.

Salzberg, Charles. *From Set Shot to Slam Dunk: The Glory Days of Basketball in the Words of Those Who Played It.* Lincoln: University of Nebraska Press, 1987.

Taylor, John. *The Rivalry: Bill Russell, Wilt Chamberlain, and the Golden Age of Basketball.* New York: Random House, 2005.

Thomas, Ron. *They Cleared the Lane: The NBA's Black Pioneers.* Lincoln: University of Nebraska Press, 2002.

Basketball, Women's

Women's basketball began in 1892 at Smith College in Northampton, Massachusetts, when physical educator Senda Berenson introduced the game—invented only a year earlier in nearby Springfield—to her students, adapting it to meet prevailing stereotypes about women's athletic abilities and needs.

Women's play flourished during the sport's early years but diminished in the early 1900s. Interest awoke in the 1930s, when women played in industrial leagues, but virtually disappeared again after World War II. Interest in women's basketball revived on high school and college campuses in the 1970s following the passage of Title IX of the Education Amendments of 1972. American women became the best female players in the world, and in the late 1990s, a professional women's basketball league was established.

Origins and Initial Rules

Berenson, who observed "basket ball" played indoors at the International Young Men's Christian Association (YMCA) Training School in Springfield, Massachusetts, shortly after James Naismith invented the game there in 1891, was impressed with the sport as a means of providing exercise and fostering moral development. Berenson explained in "The Significance of Basket Ball for Women" (1899) that basketball "develops physical and moral courage, self-reliance and self-control." However, she modified Naismith's original rules to make the game more appropriate for girls, as she felt that his version was too aggressive.

Berenson's rules emphasized cooperation and downplayed competition. As a result, women's basketball differed from men's basketball in several key aspects. She diminished physical exertion by creating "line basketball." The court was divided into three equal zones: backcourt, midcourt, and frontcourt. Depending on the size of the gymnasium, teams had between six and nine players. Ideally, three would play in each zone, and players could not enter the other zones, as this would "concentrate energy, encourage combination plays [and] equalize team work."

To further discourage "star playing" and to promote teamwork, players could hold the ball for only three seconds and could dribble only three times before passing. Berenson's rules also prohibited aggressive behavior such as snatching or batting the ball from another player. Berenson's version of the game, with six players on a side, was played by high school girls in Iowa until 1993.

Early Collegiate Games

Smith students embraced basketball enthusiastically, and games began to attract audiences. Their first known competitive game took place between sophomores and freshmen on March 22, 1893, with Berenson serving as referee. The sophomores won 5–4. Spectators overflowed the gym, but all of them were women. In keeping with the Victorian ideal of gender propriety, no men were permitted to watch.

Some months earlier, the University of California, Berkeley, had played Miss Head's School in the first interinstitutional game. In the next several years, women played basketball at Mount Holyoke, Sophie Newcomb College, Wellesley, Vassar, and Bryn Mawr, all women's colleges. The first intercollegiate game was held in California on April 4, 1896, when Stanford University beat Berkeley 2–1, with nine players on each side. Although cultural mores still banned men from the audience, the gymnasium was full.

Intercollegiate games initially proved difficult, because institutions followed different rules. Clara Gregory Baer of Sophie Newcomb College published the first book of rules for women's basketball (then called *basquette*) in 1895. In 1899, the Basketball Committee for Women was established to codify the rules of the game. Berenson chaired the committee and disseminated her rules as editor of the A.G. Spalding Sporting Goods Company's first *Basket Ball for Women* (1901).

Spread of Basketball from Women's Colleges to Communities

Women's basketball began to wane in popularity at colleges, losing ground to individual pursuits such as tennis and swimming, but it survived and prospered in high schools and local communities. The game had the advantage of being inexpensive, as it could be played in existing gymnasiums or outdoors, where makeshift hoops could be connected to trees. High schools in rural or impoverished areas improvised courts, and in many cities, churches, YMCAs, settlement houses, and other civic groups sponsored basketball teams for teens. Many African American communities also embraced women's basketball.

The game differed greatly from Berenson's vision. At community games, both men and women came to cheer on the teams and often paid for admission. Even at the high school level, some individual girls earned acclaim for their talents. Many girls learned to play the game by playing against boys; in the 1920s and 1930s, many African American colleges allowed women to play the game according to men's rules.

Amateur Players and the Fight for Equality

In 1926, the Amateur Athletic Union sponsored the first national women's basketball championship in Pasadena, California, attracting the most skilled women players from across the country. The best teams were sponsored by businesses and factories as a form of publicity. Some women players, such as Mildred "Babe" Didrikson; Alline Banks of the Nashville Business College, an 11-year All-American; and Ora Washington, who starred for the African American Philadelphia Tribunes (1932–1942), earned celebrity status in the 1930s and 1940s. These stars attracted paying crowds to home games and engendered a fierce sense of competition between towns. Players typically worked for the company whose team they played for, and companies began recruiting women from across the country for their squads.

During World War II, when a large proportion of able-bodied men were serving in the military, the popularity of women's basketball spiked. After the war, however, men returned to the factories, displacing women, and many women's teams were disbanded. Interest persisted only in companies with a large share of women employees, such as Hanes Hosiery and Dr. Pepper. Even there, women team members were expected to dress and behave in traditionally feminine ways. They were required to wear lipstick and were warned not to wear their basketball uniforms off the court.

Although African American women had been playing the sport for years, and it was an important sport at historically black colleges in the 1930s, no African American colleges were invited to the annual Amateur Athletic Union tournament until 1955. In that year, Missouri Arledge, star of the Philander Smith College team, became the first African American woman to be chosen to an All-America team.

Despite this breakthrough, the popularity of women's basketball declined sharply from 1955 through the early 1960s. Corporate sponsors became reluctant to support women's teams, and women's teams in schools and colleges received scant funding compared to men's teams.

Title IX and Its Impact

The first women's intercollegiate basketball championships were held in 1969. One, sponsored by the Conference on Intercollegiate Athletics for Women, was won by West Chester State College (which came in second the next three years). The second, the National Women's Invitational Tournament, was won by Wayland Baptist College, which repeated its victory for each of the next eight years.

A landmark in the history of women's athletics occurred in 1972, when the U.S. Congress passed the Education Amendments. Title IX of that act mandated that educational institutions could not discriminate against any student on the basis of sex. One area targeted was athletic participation, where most schools and colleges spent the vast majority of funds on men, while apportioning a tiny fraction to women. In the following years, women's basketball programs were able to claim dramatically increased support from educational institutions.

The Association for Intercollegiate Athletics for Women (a successor to the Conference on Intercollegiate Athletics for Women) sponsored a women's national championship beginning in 1972. In 1975, the first women's basketball game was televised nationally. The following year, Madison Square Garden hosted its first women's basketball game between New York's Queen's College and Philadelphia's Immaculata College, attracting more than 12,000 fans.

Despite pockets of enthusiasm, women's collegiate basketball failed to attract the widespread national following of men's. Still, by 1982, the National Collegiate Athletic Association (NCAA) supplanted the Association for Intercollegiate Athletics for Women and organized its first national women's championship, won by Louisiana Tech.

By the 1990s, women's basketball had gained much greater visibility. Regular season games and final tournaments were televised. Leading colleges began to recruit promising players, offering athletic scholarships. Certain schools and coaches gained national recognition for their programs. At the University of Tennessee, Coach Pat Head Summit won 1,071 games and eight NCAA titles. At the University of Connecticut, Geno Auriemma's Lady Huskies won seven championships and set a record for the most consecutive wins in college basketball—men's or women's—with a streak of 90 victories, ending in December 2010. Outstanding players included Jennifer Azzi (Stanford), Lisa Leslie (Southern California), Nancy Lieberman (Old Dominion), Cheryl Miller (Southern California), Maya Moore (Connecticut), Candace Parker (Tennessee), Dawn Staley (Virginia), and Sheryl Swoopes (Texas Tech).

In 1976, women's basketball was added to the Olympic Games. The U.S. team, made up of amateurs until 1992 and thereafter by pros and amateurs, has won a medal in every Olympics it has competed in, including a silver in 1976, a bronze in 1992, and six gold medals, four of them since 1996.

Rise of Professional Women's Basketball

Women played professional basketball as early as the 1930s. During World War II, teams such as the All-American Redheads and the Arkansas Travelers barnstormed across the country, playing against men's teams according to men's rules. Although they were fiercely competitive athletes, the women players were expected, once off the court, to exhibit "lady-like" behavior.

The Women's Professional Basketball League was launched in 1978. Funded by corporate sponsorship, the league highlighted players' sex appeal to attract audiences. The league gained wide attention, but few devoted fans, and it disbanded after three seasons.

By the 1990s, however, the outlook for a women's pro game had changed dramatically. In 1996, the American Basketball League began play and appeared to have a promising future. But the next year, the powerful National Basketball Association announced that it would establish the Women's National Basketball Association (WNBA). The two leagues competed for attention in 1997–1998. In fall 1999, the American Basketball League folded after playing only a dozen games. Four of its teams gained franchises in the WNBA, which attracted increasing attention in the early 2000s.

Marilyn Morgan

See also: Basketball, College; Basketball, Professional, NBA Era; Title IX; Women.

Further Reading

Berenson, Senda. *Line Basket Ball.* New York: American Sports, 1901.

———, ed. *Spalding Basket Ball Guide for Women.* New York: American Sports, 1903.

Grundy, Pamela, and Susan Shackelford. *Shattering the Glass: The Remarkable History of Women's Basketball.* Chapel Hill: University of North Carolina Press, 2007.

Hult, Joan S., and Marianna Trekell, eds. *A Century of Women's Basketball: From Frailty to Final Four.* Reston, VA: National Association for Girls and Women in Sport, 1991.

Ikard, Robert W. *Just For Fun: The Story of AAU Women's Basketball.* Fayetteville: University of Arkansas Press, 2005.

McElwain, Max. *The Only Dance in Iowa: A History of Six-Player Girls' Basketball.* Lincoln: University of Nebraska Press, 2004.

Baugh, Sammy (1914–2008)

Samuel Adrian "Slingin' Sammy" Baugh was an all-time great college and professional football player. He was a single-wing tailback and T-formation quarterback, as well as a star defensive back and punter who helped revolutionize play in the National Football League (NFL) during his 16-year career from 1937 to 1952. Named to the All-Star team seven times, Baugh played a pivotal role in transforming the focus of football from running and kicking to passing. The only NFL player to lead the league in an offensive, defensive, and special teams category, Baugh has been rated as high as the third greatest player in the history of both college and professional football.

Baugh was born in Temple, Texas, to farmers James and Katherine Baugh. The elder Baugh gave up farming during the early years of the Great Depression and moved the family to Sweetwater, where he worked as a checker for the Atchison, Topeka, and Santa Fe Railroad. Sam entered Sweetwater High School as a sophomore.

Because of his height (6 feet, 2 inches, or 1.9 meters), he won a starting position on the football team as an end, later moving to the backfield because of his athletic versatility. Baugh improved his passing ability by throwing a football through a swinging automobile tire in his backyard. He led Sweetwater to the quarterfinals of the Texas State high school football playoffs in 1930 and the semifinals in 1932. He also was an outstanding professional baseball prospect who played semiprofessional baseball in Abilene while in high school.

After graduating from high school in 1933, Baugh enrolled at Texas Christian University, where he received a scholarship and a loan to cover additional expenses, which was repaid from his pro football earnings. As a sophomore, he compiled nearly 1,000 all-purpose yards (914 meters) and proved to be a skilled defensive back.

Then, in 1935 and 1936, Baugh achieved All-American honors as an outstanding passer and punter. He led Texas Christian to a 3–2 victory over Louisiana State University in the 1936 Sugar Bowl and a 16–6 win over Marquette University in the 1937 Cotton Bowl, which cemented Baugh's college football reputation. During his college years, the Horned Frogs star threw 587 passes and completed 270 for 3,384 yards (3,094 meters) and 39 touchdowns. He earned letters in football, baseball, and basketball.

After graduating from college, Baugh worked in Pampa in the Texas Panhandle. He played semiprofessional baseball and signed a contract with the St. Louis Cardinals. But after assessing his prospects as a third baseman, he chose to play pro football. He was named to the 1937 College All-Star team that defeated the Green Bay Packers, 6–0.

Baugh was the sixth player selected in the 1937 NFL player draft, going to the Redskins, who were moving from Boston to Washington, D.C. Baugh thought that

Washington was too big a city for him, but he agreed to play for the Redskins for $8,000 a season. Owner George Preston Marshall decided to promote his new field general from Texas by having him appear at a press conference wearing a ten-gallon hat and cowboy boots. When Baugh protested that he did not own either a cowboy hat or boots, Marshall told him to buy them and send him the bill.

Quarterbacks at this time were being mauled by rushing defensive linemen. Marshall pressured the NFL to change the rules to protect passers from unnecessary roughness. Baugh took advantage of the new rule, which sheltered him from constantly getting knocked down, and he transformed the game of football with his great passing. He used his large hands to grip the football with his thumb on the laces, which enabled him to throw spiral passes. He played both offense and defense, as did all of the Redskins starters.

In 1937, Baugh led the Redskins to the NFL title, defeating the Chicago Bears 28–21 in the championship game, throwing for 335 yards (306 meters) and three touchdowns. In 1940, the Redskins faced the Bears in another championship. Using their new T-formation, the Bears slaughtered the Redskins, 73–0. Two years later, the Redskins had their revenge, beating the undefeated Chicagoans 14–6 to win the NFL championship. But the Bears bounced back in 1943 to take the title, 41–21.

The Redskins finally switched to the T-formation in 1945. Baugh responded by setting a 70.3 percent completion record that lasted until 1982. The Redskins again made it to the NFL championship game, only to lose 15–14. Baugh played his best game two years later, when he threw for six touchdowns against the Chicago Cardinals.

Baugh married Edmonia Gary Smith, his college sweetheart, on April 12, 1938. They had two sons, Todd and Davey. While an active player, Baugh lived in a hotel during the season and spent most nights going to the movies. He returned to the Texas Panhandle in the off-season, where in 1941 he bought a ranch near Sweetwater, which he ultimately expanded to 21,000 acres (8,498 hectares) with 700 head of cattle.

Baugh retired after the 1952 season, having played longer in the NFL than any other player up to that time. Slingin' Sammy was the league's leading passer in six seasons, and he ended his career with 1,695 completions on 2,995 attempts and 187 touchdowns. Baugh also had a lifetime punting average of 45.1 yards (41.2 meters), and his average of 51.4 yards (47 meters) in 1940 is still the single-season record. On defense, he even led the league in pass interceptions one season. Baugh was elected to the College Football Hall of Fame, and he was one of 17 charter members of the Pro Football Hall of Fame.

After retirement, Baugh starred in a Republic Studio movie, *King of the Texas Rangers* (1941). He later coached football at Hardin-Simmons University (1955–1957) and worked briefly with the New York Titans of the American Football League and the Houston Oilers, but his heart was never fully in his coaching. He also announced Redskin games. He died in Rotan, Texas, on December 17, 2008.

Keith McClellan

See also: Football, College; Football, Professional; Redskins, Washington.

Further Reading

Coenen, Craig R. *From Sandlots to the Super Bowl: The National Football League, 1920–1967.* Knoxville: University of Tennessee Press, 2005.

Whittingham, Richard. *What a Game They Played: An Inside Look at the Golden Age of Pro Football.* Lincoln: University of Nebraska Press, 2004.

Bears, Chicago

The Chicago Bears, together with the Arizona (originally Chicago) Cardinals, are the two remaining charter franchises of the National Football League (NFL). In the early years of the league, the Bears succeeded both on the field and at the box office, led by George Halas, who recruited such all-time greats as Harold "Red" Grange in 1925 and Bronko Nagurski in 1931. The team won eight NFL titles between 1920 and 1969.

In the Super Bowl era, the Bears have continued to produce All-Star players and often have made the playoffs, but they have reached the Super Bowl only twice and have won once, in Super Bowl XX, after the 1985 season. They reached the big game again after the 2006 season but lost in Super Bowl XLI to the Indianapolis Colts. Nicknamed the "Monsters of the Midway," the Bears have seen 26 of their players elected to the Pro Football Hall of Fame, the most of any team.

Origins

The team began as the Decatur Staleys in 1919, an independent semiprofessional club representing the A.E. Staley Starch Works of Decatur, in downstate Illinois. Augustus Staley hired former University of Illinois star athlete George Halas in 1919 as the company's athletic director and coach to improve labor relations. One year later, the Staleys became a professional team and a member of the newly organized American Professional Football Association (renamed the National Football League in 1922). The Staleys won their first pro game 20–0 over the Moline Indians and went 10–1–2 for the 1920 season, coming in second to the undefeated Akron Pros (8–0–3).

Staley gave Halas control of the team, and Halas took on teammate Ed "Dutch" Sternaman as a partner and moved the franchise to Chicago for the 1921 season. The Chicago Staleys played at Cubs Park (later renamed Wrigley Field) on the North Side and won the league title with a 10–1–1 record. Before the 1922 season, the team changed its nickname to the Bears.

The Bears notched consecutive second-place finishes in the NFL from 1922 to 1924, then created a stir near the end of the 1925 season by signing the sensational college halfback Red Grange immediately following his last game for the University of Illinois. Grange and his agent, C.C. Pyle, signed a lucrative contract to play a series of postseason exhibition games with the Bears. Bob Zuppke, Grange's coach at Illinois, and his fellow college coaches criticized Grange's decision. They believed that pro football demeaned the sport and its players. The outcry from major college coaches and fans soon forced the NFL to adopt a rule against professional teams signing players before their college graduation.

Grange made his debut with the Bears on Thanksgiving Day in Chicago before 36,000 fans, an astonishing crowd for pro football. The team then embarked on a hastily arranged Eastern tour, playing eight games in just 12 days. After resting briefly, the Bears and Grange began on Christmas Day another nine-game tour that lasted one month, traveling from Florida to the West Coast. A high point was a game at the Los Angeles Memorial Coliseum that drew 75,000 fans, a new attendance record for pro football.

Grange jumped to the new American Football League 1926, playing for the New York Giants, then returned to the Bears in 1929. That year, the Bears suffered their first losing record, prompting Halas to resign as head coach.

Under new coach Ralph Jones, and with the powerful 235-pound (107-kilogram) running back Bronko Nagurski on the squad, the team bounced back in 1930 and 1931, and won the NFL championship in 1932 with an unusual record of 7–1–6. The title was decided at the end of the season, when the Bears handed the Portsmouth (Ohio) Spartans a 9–0 defeat in a game played indoors at the Chicago Stadium because of extremely bad weather. After the 1932 season, Halas became sole owner of the Bears after buying out Sternaman's share of the team.

Halas again took over as head coach in 1933, when the NFL split into two divisions. The Bears captured the Western Division and then defeated the New York Giants 23–21 in the first NFL title game. Before the 1934 season, the Bears appeared in the *Chicago Tribune's* inaugural College All-Star Game at Soldier Field against a team of newly graduated college players. The game ended in a 0–0 tie. One year later, the Bears returned, this time winning 5–0. The Bears appeared a record seven times in the event, going 5–1–1. The preseason annual summer spectacle played a major role in building widespread popularity for professional football and ensuring its long-term success.

The Bears won the division title in 1934 and were undefeated going into the championship game against the New York Giants. They played at New York's Polo Grounds on a frozen field. The Bears led 10–3 at halftime, when the Giants switched from cleats to sneakers, which helped them get better traction. The Giants went on to win 30–13. That year, Bears halfback Beattie Feathers rushed for 1,004 yards (918 meters), a new NFL record, averaging 8.4 yards (7.7 meters) a carry. The Bears took their division in 1937 (9–1–1), but they lost the title match to the Washington Redskins, 28–21.

The T-Formation

Before the 1939 season, Halas drafted Sid Luckman from Columbia University to play quarterback in the new T-formation that he had installed with the help of Clark Shaughnessy. These moves quickly paid off with a division title in 1940. In the championship game, the Bears (8–3) played the Redskins, who had defeated them earlier in the season. The Bears rolled to an amazing 73–0 victory at Griffith Stadium, with ten different players scoring touchdowns.

After adding star players such as George McAfee and Clyde "Bulldog" Turner, the "Monsters of the Midway" won an NFL championship in 1941. After six games of the 1942 season, Halas left for service with the U.S. Navy. Luke Johnson and Heartley "Hunk" Anderson took over as co-coaches, but the Bears lost the title match. The team bounced back to win the NFL crown in 1943. Luckman led the way by passing for 2,194 yards (2,006 meters) and 28 touchdowns, a team record that stood until 1995. Halas returned as coach for the 1946 season, and the Bears responded with another NFL title, defeating the Giants 24–14.

Thereafter, other teams dominated the NFL as many key Bears neared the end of their careers and were not replaced with comparable talent. The Bears finished in a tie for the division title with Los Angeles in 1950, but they lost a special playoff game. Halas again retired as coach after the 1955 season. He was succeeded by Paddy Driscoll, who led the Bears to a division title and the NFL championship game in 1956. The New York Giants drubbed the Bears 47–7. That season, fullback Rick Casares of the Bears led the NFL in rushing with 1,126 yards (1,030 meters), while quarterback Ed Brown led in passing with 1,307 yards (1,195 meters).

Halas returned as head coach yet again for the 1958 season, and the team compiled winning records in four of the next five seasons, finally breaking through behind a great defense to another division title in 1963, and then a 14–10 victory over the Giants for the NFL crown on an icy day in Chicago. The 1965 season saw the debut of two outstanding rookies, halfback Gale Sayers, who led the NFL with 22 touchdowns that season, and linebacker Dick Butkus. Halas retired for the last time after the 1967 season, having compiled a career record of 326–151–32.

In 1971, the Bears moved their home games to Soldier Field, and in 1977, the team returned to the playoffs for the first time since 1963. They were led by halfback Walter Payton (1975–1986), who rushed for 1,852 yards (1,693 meters), including an NFL record 275-yard (251-meter) game against the Minnesota Vikings. In his career, Payton ran for 16,716 yards (15,285 meters), scored 125 touchdowns, and played in 186 straight games.

In 1982, Halas named former Bears tight end Mike Ditka as head coach. The next year, Halas, who had owned the Bears, either in part or fully, for 63 years, died at the age of 88. His daughter, Virginia McCaskey, succeeded him as team owner, controlling 80 percent of the franchise.

Ditka Era

The club under Ditka entered another outstanding era, beginning with a trip to the NFL playoffs in 1984. The next year, the Bears compiled an impressive 15–1 record, rolled through the playoffs, and won Super Bowl XX in a 46–10 romp over the New England Patriots. Behind Ditka's fiery and controversial leadership, the Bears advanced to five playoffs between 1986 and 1992. Ditka finally was dismissed after a losing record and

many disputes with team president Michael McCaskey, Halas's grandson.

Between 1993 and 2010, the Bears advanced to the playoffs on five more occasions, winning division titles in 2001, 2005, 2006, and 2010. After the 2006 season, they advanced to Super Bowl XLI, losing to the Indianapolis Colts, 29–17. During the 2010 season, the Bears captured their seven-hundredth regular-season victory—the first NFL team to do so—on November 18 over the Miami Dolphins by a score of 16–0. They went to the National Football Conference championship but lost to the Green Bay Packers. The Bears finished the 2010 season with an all-time regular season record of 704–512–42 (an NFL leading .579 winning percentage) and a playoff record of 17–18.

Raymond Schmidt

See also: Football, Professional; Grange, Red; Halas, George; Luckman, Sid.

Further Reading

Halas, George S., with Gwen Morgan and Arthur Vesey. *Halas by Halas: The Autobiography of George Halas.* New York: McGraw-Hill, 1979.

Keteyian, Armen. *Ditka: Monster of the Midway.* New York: Pocket Books, 1992.

Lamb, Kevin. *Portrait of Victory: Chicago Bears 1985.* Provo, UT: Final Four Productions, 1986.

MacCambridge, Michael. *America's Game: The Epic Story of How Pro Football Captured a Nation.* New York: Random House, 2004.

Roberts, Howard. *The Chicago Bears.* New York: G.P. Putnam's Sons, 1947.

Vass, George. *George Halas and the Chicago Bears.* Chicago: Regnery, 1971.

Bennett, James G., Jr. (1841–1918)

James Gordon Bennett, Jr., was one of the leading American newspaper publishers of the late nineteenth century. He also was a sportsman and a sports promoter and used sports to sell newspapers and achieve social prominence and fame. He was especially associated with all kinds of racing, ranging from the ocean, to the track, and even the sky. While Bennett's main goals may have been financial success and personal notoriety, his support for elite sporting events helped raise public awareness of those pursuits.

Bennett was born on May 10, 1841, in New York City. His father was James Gordon Bennett, Sr., publisher of the *New York Herald.* The elder Bennett made his fortune and fame as a sensationalist publisher. He recognized that the American public craved lurid details and descriptions of scandals and crimes, which most established newspapers refused to print. Bennett's style of journalism scandalized New York high society. Although he possessed wealth and fame, the elder Bennett never was considered a member of fashionable society.

Bennett's mother raised him in Europe to spare him the scandals that dogged his father. The younger Bennett was educated by tutors until he entered the École Polytechnique in Paris. He returned to the United States in early 1861. His father had become a supporter of President Abraham Lincoln and had allowed his yacht to be taken into naval service during the Civil War.

Bennett, Jr., received a lieutenant's commission and served aboard the family yacht until the U.S. Navy no longer needed it, after which he resigned. He then began working at the *Herald,* under his father's direct supervision. In 1866, after only two years of intense internship, Bennett was named managing editor of the *Herald.* The next year, the elder Bennett retired, and Bennett the younger assumed proprietary control.

Unlike his outcast father, Bennett wanted to be a member of New York's high society, which was known as the "Four Hundred." With his good looks, European education, virtually unlimited funds, and extravagant personality, he was popular among the "fast" set. Bennett, a sportsman from an early age, recognized that participation in elite sports could help him assume a leading role in society. While still a teenager, he became the owner of a 77-ton (70-metric-ton) yacht and, at age 16, joined the New York Yacht Club. The club was the oldest major voluntary sports organization in New York City and the exclusive preserve of wealthy society families. Acceptance into the club equaled acceptance into the highest ranks of society.

Bennett cemented his reputation in yachting by winning the first transatlantic yacht race in 1866 aboard the *Henrietta* (which he named after his mother) in 13 days and 22 hours. Weather conditions were dreadful during the race, and six crewmen from the competing *Fleetwing* were lost overboard. Bennett's reputation for daring was enhanced by his side bets, which earned him $60,000 in cash. The race was highly promoted and stirred more excitement than any other yachting event since the first America's Cup race in 1851. In recognition of Bennett's contributions, he was elected commodore of the New York Yacht Club in 1871, the youngest member ever to receive the honor.

Bennett found that his successes not only brought him personal fame but also helped him to sell newspapers. The *Herald* covered the events in detail and included exclusive interviews with the participants. In 1873, Bennett began promoting foot-racing events. The most important intercollegiate competition at the time was the annual rowing regatta held at Saratoga, New York. Bennett donated a prize plate worth $500 to the winner of a 2-mile (3.2-kilometer) race held the day after the rowing championship in the first intercollegiate track meet. By the following year, the event had expanded to include a 100-yard (91-meter) dash, 120-yard (110-meter) high hurdles, a 1-mile (1.6-kilometer) run, a 3-mile (4.8-kilometer) run, and a 7-mile (11.3-kilometer) walk.

Bennett also helped promote professional long-distance walking races, which were the rage during the 1870s and 1880s. He financed some of the competitors, including Daniel O'Leary, and often walked the last few laps with them. In 1874, Bennett and attorney John Whipple held a highly publicized walking race from Bennett's home on 38th Street in Manhattan to Jerome Park in the Bronx, a distance of more than 10 miles (16 kilometers), for a $3,000 bet, while others bet a total of $50,000 on the contest. Bennett won with a time of 1 hour, 46 minutes, and 55 seconds.

Bennett was responsible for introducing the sport of polo to the United States. On an 1875 trip to England, he witnessed a polo game, and he was immediately fascinated. He hired an English player to teach his friends the game, and he imported mallets and balls. Bennett had a herd of Texas cow ponies brought to New York, and he staged the first American polo match at Dickel's Riding Academy in what is now Midtown Manhattan. He founded the Westchester Polo Club in 1876, the first such organization in America. The sport quickly spread to Newport, Rhode Island, the summer retreat of many wealthy New Yorkers.

Bennett also played a significant role in the rise of lawn tennis, which came to North America in 1874. He built the Newport (Rhode Island) Casino, an exclusive sports club for the very rich. It was the site of the U.S. national tennis championships from 1881 to 1914.

Bennett also encouraged the development of motor sports. He created the Gordon Bennett Cup in 1900 for international motorcar racing, which became Grand Prix racing. Six years later, he established the Coupe Aéronautique to recognize hot-air balloon competitions, which continues today. Finally, the Gordon Bennett Trophy was created in 1909 for airplane racing.

Aviator Glenn Curtiss won the first year, and the contest continued through 1920.

Bennett proved to be an erratic but overall successful newspaper publisher. He spent money to make news that helped sell newspapers. In 1869, he commissioned Henry Stanley to travel to Africa to find medical missionary Dr. David Livingstone at any price. He also sponsored an expedition led by George Washington DeLong to find the North Pole in 1879, in which the entire party of 20 died.

In 1877, Bennett went into self-exile in France, after causing a public scandal when he got drunk and urinated into a fireplace in front of his fiancé and a mixed company of guests. Even while overseas, he continued to run the *Herald* autocratically and to promote sports. By the time of his death on May 14, 1918, it was estimated that he had spent $30 million promoting sports—and himself—in the United States.

Tim J. Watts

See also: Newspapers and Magazines; Polo; Yacht Racing.

Further Reading

Crockett, Albert Stevens. *When James Gordon Bennett Was Caliph of Bagdad.* New York: Funk & Wagnalls, 1926.

Crouthamel, James L. *Bennett's* New York Herald *and the Rise of the Popular Press.* Syracuse, NY: Syracuse University Press, 1989.

O'Connor, Richard. *The Scandalous Mr. Bennett.* Garden City, NY: Doubleday, 1962.

Seitz, Don C. *The James Gordon Bennetts, Father and Son, Proprietors of the* New York Herald. Indianapolis, IN: Bobbs-Merrill, 1928.

Berenson, Senda (1868–1954)

A pioneering physical educator at Smith College in Northampton, Massachusetts, Senda Berenson Abbott is known as the "Mother of Basketball" for her promotion of the sport among women students. In 1892, she modified the rules of the men's game, which she felt was too aggressive, to make it appropriate for females. She organized the first collegiate women's basketball game the next year, and edited several guide books that codified the rules of women's basketball. Berenson's rules remained in effect until the 1960s.

Born on March 19, 1868, in Vilnius, Lithuania, she was one of five children of Albert and Judith Valvrojen-ski (later changed to Berenson). In 1874, her father immigrated to Boston. One year later, his wife, sons Bernard and Abraham, and Senda joined him. Berenson's sisters were born in America.

As a child, Berenson attended the Boston Latin School as well as the Boston Conservatory of Music. Back problems prevented her from finishing those programs, so she began classes at the Boston Normal School of Gymnastics. As her health and stamina improved, she became convinced of the benefits of physical activity for women and, in 1892, took a job as a physical education teacher at the all-female Smith College.

Shortly after starting at Smith, Berenson learned about a new sport called "basket ball," which had been invented a year earlier at the International Young Men's Christian Association Training School in nearby Springfield by James Naismith. She praised the coordination, confidence, values, and team-building skills that basketball instilled and decided to introduce the game to her students at Smith.

Although Berenson applauded the physical and social benefits of basketball, she adhered to Victorian standards of gender propriety and considered the game too rough for women. At the time, sports such as football, prizefighting, and basketball, which required physical strength, skill, and aggression, were considered masculine activities. The prevailing middle-class ideology insisted that intense physical activity could harm women's bodies, especially their reproductive capabilities. Some conservative members of society cautioned that if women engaged in physical competition, they would become aggressive, unnatural, and "unsexed," and therefore unravel the established social structure.

To protect women from overexertion and competitiveness and to make the game more inclusive, Berenson modified Naismith's rules. She decreased the physical exertion of players by dividing the court into three equal zones: backcourt, midcourt, and frontcourt. Berenson's teams were composed of six to nine players, with two to three players assigned to each zone; players could not enter the other zones. Stationed in this manner, they would be protected from overexerting themselves. Furthermore, the game would not be dominated by the most skilled players, thereby giving all women a chance to play.

Berenson endeavored to equalize play among all and to promote team cooperation. Her rules decreased the chances for aggressive, unladylike behavior and rough physical contact by forbidding players from snatching or batting the ball out of their foes' hands. When shooting a basket, women could use only one hand, as many feared that using two hands would flatten the chest and restrict breathing. Berenson also prevented highly skilled players from dominating the game by limiting participants to three dribbles and allowing them to the hold the ball for no more than three seconds. Thus, women's basketball, as conceived by Berenson, emphasized cooperation and socialization over competition.

The new game became so popular in physical education classes that Smith students clamored for a schoolwide game. The first known collegiate women's basketball game took place on March 22, 1893, before an all-female audience. Men appeared at the gymnasium, interested in attending, but they were banned from watching. Berenson served as referee as the sophomore team beat the freshmen team 5–4.

Students embraced the game enthusiastically, and its popularity spread to other women's colleges. At first, several sets of rules existed, making it difficult for schools to compete against one another. The American Association for the Advancement of Physical Education met in Springfield in 1899 to regulate the rules for all colleges. The association organized the Women's Basketball Rules Committee, with Berenson as chair, to create and codify official rules for women's basketball, based on Berenson's game.

In 1901, the A.G. Spalding Sporting Goods Company published Berenson's *Line Basket Ball, or Basket Ball for Women,* which explained her theories about basketball's psychological and physiological benefits for women. Two years later, she edited *Spalding's Official Basket Ball Guide for Women.* Berenson continued to edit and revise the rules for women's basketball until 1917.

Berenson initiated an effective physical education program during her 19-year tenure as Smith's first physical education director. She promoted not only basketball, but also Swedish gymnastics, volleyball, field hockey, fencing, and folk dancing as character-building activities for female students. In 1893, she helped organize Smith's Gymnastic and Field Association, and in 1897, she studied fencing in Stockholm, Sweden, becoming the second American woman to attend the Royal Central Institute of Gymnastics.

Berenson married Herbert Vaughan Abbott, a professor of English at Smith College, in 1911. Soon afterward, she resigned from Smith to become the director of physical education at the Mary A. Burnham School for girls in Northampton. After retiring from that position in 1921, she traveled to Europe to visit her brother, well-known art historian Bernard Berenson.

Upon her husband's death in 1929, she moved to California, where she lived with a sister until her death on February 16, 1954. She was the first woman honored by the Basketball Hall of Fame (1985), a member of the International Jewish Sports Hall of Fame (1987), and one of two charter inductees into the Women's Basketball Hall of Fame (1999).

Marilyn Morgan

See also: Basketball, Women's; Women.

Further Reading

Melnick, Ralph. *Senda Berenson: The Unlikely Founder of Women's Basketball.* Amherst: University of Massachusetts Press, 2007.

Reynolds, Moira Davison. *Immigrant American Women Role Models: Fifteen Inspiring Biographies, 1850–1950.* Jefferson, NC: McFarland, 1997.

Spears, Betty. "Senda Berenson Abbott: New Woman: New Sport." In *A Century of Women's Basketball: From Frailty to Final Four,* ed. Joan S. Hult and Marianna Trekell. Reston, VA: National Association for Girls and Women in Sport, 1991.

Billiards

Billiards is a generic term for games played on a rectangular cloth-covered table with raised, cushioned edges in which a cue ball strikes an object ball. In the past, the term "billiards" was used to refer to carom games, and the term "pool" referred to games played on pocketed tables. Traditionally, the sport was both an elite recreation played at home or exclusive social clubs, as well as a popular sport among the working class, who played in pool halls and saloons with sometimes less than savory reputations. The sport was played professionally by the mid-nineteenth century, and formal championships were held, but many of the finest players worked as hustlers, earning money through private betting arrangements. Today, billiards is the sixth most popular participatory sport in the United States, with 32 million players, many of whom play eight-ball in bars on coin-operated tables that measure 4.5 feet (1.4 meters) wide by 9 feet (2.7 meters) long.

Billiards was played in America as early as 1709, by plantation owner William Byrd II of Westover, Virginia, who had his own table. Many prominent colonials enjoyed the sport, including George Washington. But the game was so controversial that President John Quincy Adams's installation of a table in the White House became a minor campaign issue in his 1828 bid for reelection. (He lost to Andrew Jackson.)

By 1830, there were public rooms devoted to billiards, and by 1850, New York had 50 to 60 billiard rooms to fill the growing demand for a competitive sport that was inexpensive and individualistic, and fit in with the bachelor subculture. At the same time, the general public had a negative impression of the sport because of the gambling, drinking, and crime that was associated with pool halls, and many municipalities enacted laws to license and regulate the sport.

The most popular game in the early 1800s was four-ball carom, played on a 6-foot (1.8-meter) by 12-foot (3.7-meter) table with six pockets, using two red and two white balls. Points were scored by making the cue ball pocket an object ball, by hitting two object balls with the cue ball in one stroke, or by scratching. The balls were made of ivory until 1869, when John Wesley Hyatt invented a process to make balls out of a synthetic plastic called celluloid.

The first star player was William Phelan, who advanced the sport through his publications, manufacturing of tables, and challenge matches. In 1850, he wrote *Billiards Without Masters,* the first book on the sport in the United States. Phelan also invented an India rubber (latex) cushion that returned a rebounding ball at a predictable angle, and he owned a successful billiards parlor in New York. In 1854, he formed the Phelan & Collender Company to manufacture tables.

The leading firm in the industry was the J.M. Brunswick Manufacturing Company, which began in 1845 in Cincinnati, Ohio, making carriages. The owner, John Moses Brunswick, decided that he could earn more money making billiard tables by manufacturing a less expensive product than the best tables imported from England. In 1873, the firm merged with that of Julius Balke. In 1884, Phelan's firm merged with J.M. Brunswick & Balke, forming the Brunswick-Balke-Collender Company.

In 1859, Phelan defeated John Seereiter for the first national four-carom championship in Detroit for a $15,000 purse. Six years later, he organized the American Billiard Players Association.

By the mid-nineteenth century, four-carom was seen as too easy, and it went through several alterations, beginning in the early 1870s with straight rail, a game with three balls (red, white, and white with a spot) and no pockets. A balkline was introduced in 1879 to divide the table into rectangular sections. By 1903, this had evolved into the 18.1 and 18.2 balkline, in which a line was drawn 18 inches (46 centimeters) from one end of the table to the other end, creating eight rectangular zones, called balks. The balls could only remain in one rectangle for one shot (18.1 balkline) or for two shots (18.2 balkline). Players could only score once or twice if both object balls were in the same rectangle (balk area) before directing a ball out of one balk area into another.

Three-cushion billiards was a more difficult and very defensive game that was invented in the 1870s. The object was to hit the cue ball off an object ball, contacting at least three rails before striking the second object ball.

Pocket billiards was derived from 15-ball pool, which was played with 15 balls and a six-pocket table. It also was known as 61-pool, in which the player received points equivalent to the number of the ball that he sunk. In 1878, the first American pool championship was contested, employing the 61-pool game, and it was won by Canadian Cyrille Dion. In 1888, the game became 14.1 continuous pool, in which only the number of balls was counted, and the fifteenth ball was used to break a new rack of 14 balls. By 1900, pocket billiards was the most popular game. Other popular variants were eight-ball, which was invented shortly after 1900, and nine-ball (or rotation), which was introduced in the early 1920s.

There were about 30,000 pool halls in the early 1900s; many were small businesses with just a few tables in working-class ethnic neighborhoods. A good new table cost $500, but a used table could be bought for half that amount. The sport also was a common amusement at saloons. For instance, half of Chicago's 7,600 saloons had a table.

Pool halls were stereotyped as gathering places for young inner-city loafers who gambled and plotted crimes. But downtown pool halls often were much larger and fancier. Detroit's Recreation Hall had 142 tables. Graney's in San Francisco, which had a 400-seat gallery known as the Billiard Academy, was considered the finest, grossing up to $15,000 a week.

By 1920, there were 42,000 pool halls in the United States, including 4,000 in New York City and 2,244 in Chicago, up from 1,169 ten years earlier. In 1922, New York City established a Billiards Commission to regulate the business. The beginning of Prohibition in 1920 caused the number of pool halls to drop by two-thirds, but the number rebounded after the repeal in 1933.

The Brunswick Company ardently tried to bolster the status of the game by publishing instructional materials, changing the sport's name to "pocket billiards," and renaming the pool halls "billiard parlors." An intercollegiate tournament held in 1933, conducted by telegraph, was won by the University of Michigan. By the late 1930s, there were 10 million players, mainly at reopened taverns and at pool halls, which were known as billiard parlors.

The game had its stars, beginning with Willie Hoppe, who won his first 18.2 title in 1906 against Maurice Vignaux. He won 36 world balkline titles, but when the game lost its popularity during the 1930s, Hoppe switched to three-cushions and won 12 world titles. The next superstar was Ralph Greenleaf, who won 14 world pool titles between 1919 and 1937. He toured the vaudeville circuit for $2,000 a week, making trick shots. He was succeeded by onetime child prodigy Willie Mosconi, the greatest pocket billiardist of all time, who earned 15 world titles from 1941 to 1957. In an exhibition in 1954, he pocketed 526 straight balls in 140 minutes.

The sport declined during World War II, and it struggled so much afterward that the world championship was discontinued in 1958. By 1961, there were only 257 pool halls in New York. This changed as a result of the popular film *The Hustler* (1961), starring Paul Newman, and the sport became a popular fad. Nearly 3,000 family billiard centers opened in 1966. However, the sport again faded, until it was reinvigorated in 1986 by the film *The Color of Money,* the sequel to *The Hustler.* The new billiard parlors provided quality equipment, expert instruction, and sociability, especially for young singles.

Billiards in North America is supervised by the Billiard Congress of America (BCA), a 45,000-member organization established in 1948, which sanctions leagues and tournaments, hosts the annual BCA International Billiards and Home Recreation Expo, and operates the BCA Hall of Fame in Colorado Springs, Colorado. When the BCA reduced purses for tournament wins in the late 1970s, professional players left the organization to form their own organizations.

The American Poolplayers Association (APA), founded in 1979, has more than 250,000 members in North America. The APA conducts the U.S. Amateur Championship, the pool world's most prestigious amateur tournament, and its feature event is the $500,000 APA 8-Ball National Team Championship.

The APA is affiliated with the Women's Professional Billiard Association (WPBA), which was organized in 1976. The WPBA's finest players include Jean Balukas, winner of seven U.S. Opens, and Allison Fisher, winner of more than 50 major titles since 1995. Women's billiards in the twenty-first century received considerable television coverage, and women currently are at the forefront of the sport, including Jeanette Lee, known as the "Black Widow," winner of more than 30 national and international titles.

Steven A. Riess

See also: Gambling; Saloons, Taverns, and Sports Bars.

Further Reading

Adelman, Melvin L. *A Sporting Time: New York City and the Rise of Modern Athletics, 1820–70.* Urbana: University of Illinois Press, 1986.

Grissim, John. *Billiards: Hustlers and Heroes, Legends and Lies, and the Search for Higher Truth on the Green Felt.* New York: St. Martin's, 1979.

Polsky, Ned. *Hustlers, Beats, and Others.* Chicago: Aldine, 1967.

Riess, Steven A. *City Games: The Evolution of American Urban Society and the Rise of Sports.* Urbana: University of Illinois Press, 1989.

Black Colleges

See Historically Black Colleges

Black Sox Scandal

A year after the Chicago White Sox lost the 1919 World Series to the Cincinnati Reds, four White Sox ballplayers confessed that they had conspired with gamblers to intentionally lose the best-of-nine series. The incident, dubbed the "Black Sox scandal," became front-page news nationwide. An act of betrayal by players and a source of disillusionment for fans, it remains the most infamous sports scandal in American history.

At the time, the scandal was clouded by uncertainty, which most likely contributed to its appeal as a public spectacle. There was confusion about who had played their best, who had accepted money from gamblers, and who had known what and when. What is certain is that in early October 1919, the highly touted White Sox, led by outfielder "Shoeless" Joe Jackson and pitcher Eddie Cicotte, were strongly favored to beat the Reds in the World Series, but they lost five games to three.

Many Chicagoans, especially team owner Charles Comiskey and Manager Kid Gleason, were disappointed by the team's poor play. Often exceptional during the regular season, hurlers Cicotte and Claude "Lefty" Williams were unusually erratic on the pitching mound, and first baseman Arnold "Chick" Gandil, who had organized much of the plot, shortstop Charles August "Swede" Risberg, and center fielder Oscar

In the Black Sox scandal of 1919, eight members of the Chicago White Sox were accused of accepting bribes from gamblers and intentionally losing the World Series to the Cincinnati Reds. The seven players whose cases went to trial were acquitted, but all eight were expelled from baseball for life. This game was played at Chicago's Comiskey Park. *(APA/Getty Images)*

"Hap" Felsch generally played poorly. Utility man Fred McMullin had just two at bats.

On the other hand, Jackson and third baseman George "Buck" Weaver were impressive. Jackson had a World Series record 12 hits, including the only home run in the Series and a .375 batting average, and Weaver hit and fielded well.

In late September 1920, after the publication of several investigative reports and as rumors of wrongdoing persisted, Cicotte, Jackson, and Williams testified before a Cook County grand jury about the previous year's World Series. Cicotte and Williams confessed that they had conspired with gamblers to lose the Series. Jackson explained that he had known of the scheme and unwillingly had accepted $5,000 in bribe money, but that he had played to win. In addition, Felsch admitted to a sports writer that the Series had been fixed.

According to legend, after Jackson's testimony, a disillusioned street urchin confronted him on the steps of the courthouse. "It ain't true is it, Joe?" the youngster asked, to which Jackson replied, "Yes, kid, I'm afraid it is." Jackson always denied that such an exchange had occurred. Nevertheless, the story encapsulates how many people felt after learning that White Sox players had lost the Series for money. As Chicago writer Nelson Algren

later put it, they were "Benedict Arnolds! Betrayers of American Boyhood, not to mention American Girlhood and American Womanhood and American Hoodhood."

All told, eight ballplayers—including Weaver, who consistently denied being involved in the conspiracy—were implicated. Eventually, the so-called Black Sox and a handful of gamblers were tried in court. The novelty of major leaguers on trial stirred great public excitement and media interest. To add to the drama, the prosecution announced that the ballplayers' original confessions and immunity waivers mysteriously had disappeared from the state attorney's office. As a result, Cicotte, Jackson, and Williams recanted their confessions, which nonetheless were read into the record by court reporters.

From a legal standpoint, though, it did not matter. The complexity of the indictments, which outlined five different conspiracies, made it difficult for the prosecution to convict the defendants. Further, the judge's instructions to the jury that the state must prove that the defendants had intended to defraud the alleged victims identified in the indictments and the public—not merely to lose the World Series—made a guilty verdict unlikely.

On August 2, 1921, the indicted ballplayers and gamblers were acquitted of all charges. The defendants, their attorneys, and many baseball fans were elated. The next day, however, Kenesaw Mountain Landis, a federal judge who recently had been appointed the first commissioner of baseball by team owners anxious to lend an aura of integrity to the game, declared that all of the ballplayers charged would be banned from baseball. Landis's decision was well received nationally. Despite attempts by some of the ballplayers and their supporters to change his mind, Landis never reversed his ruling.

In retrospect, the causes of the Black Sox scandal are clear. By 1919, there already was a long history of baseball players and gamblers associating with one another; fixed games were nothing new. With few exceptions, though, the baseball establishment chose to ignore such malfeasance or to punish players inadequately. Moral laxity and a lack of leadership fostered conditions under which game fixing occurred.

In addition, exceedingly poor labor–management relations had plagued professional baseball for decades. Many major leaguers felt that they were exploited by their employers, partly because of the reserve clause, instituted in 1879, which bound players to their teams indefinitely. This engendered a sense of powerlessness and bitterness on the part of some ballplayers.

Finally, the 1919 White Sox were beset by acute internal dissension and fractiousness. One faction, comprised almost entirely of poorly educated working-class men from rural communities, barely spoke to their teammates and harbored deep enmity toward owner Comiskey, whom they considered parsimonious. Yet the extent of Comiskey's tightfistedness and his culpability for game fixing are debatable.

For many reasons, the Black Sox scandal has long interested baseball fans. Some believe that it represents betrayal, avarice, and the loss of innocence. Others see the event differently. Historian David Q. Voigt argues that the scandal's mythological function, the "single sin myth," explains its endurance. He contends that the baseball establishment had a vested interest in publicizing the affair as an aberration, as a singular transgression—which it was not.

Writer Harvey Frommer suggests that "it is all of the unanswered questions as well as a powerful sense that justice miscarried, that the ignorant were duped by the clever, that the powerless suffered and the strong prevailed, that makes the story of Shoeless Joe and his teammates live on." Certainly, the Black Sox scandal remains an oft-told, intriguing, and contested story. Indeed, numerous journalists, poets, playwrights, novelists, historians, and filmmakers have put the event to multifarious uses.

Daniel A. Nathan

See also: Baseball, Major League; Comiskey, Charles; Crime, Organized; Gambling; Landis, Kenesaw Mountain.

Further Reading

Asinof, Eliot. *Eight Men Out: The Black Sox and the 1919 World Series.* 1963. New York: Henry Holt, 1987.

Carney, Gene. *Burying the Black Sox: How Baseball's Cover-Up of the 1919 World Series Fix Almost Succeeded.* Washington, DC: Potomac, 2006.

Frommer, Harvey. *Shoeless Joe and Ragtime Baseball.* Lincoln: University of Nebraska Press, 2008.

Nathan, Daniel A. *Saying It's So: A Cultural History of the Black Sox Scandal.* Urbana: University of Illinois Press, 2003.

Seymour, Harold. *Baseball.* 3 vols. New York: Oxford University Press, 1960–1989.

Voigt, David Q. "The Chicago Black Sox and the Myth of Baseball's Single Sin." In *America Through Baseball,* ed. David Q. Voigt. Chicago: Nelson-Hall, 1976.

Blackhawks, Chicago

The Chicago Blackhawks, founded in 1926, were among the "Original Six" franchises of the National Hockey League in operation from 1942 through 1967, when the league underwent its first expansion. Although they were a top club through the 1960s, with superstars such as Bobby Hull and Stan Mikita, they won only three Stanley Cups in their first four decades (1933–1934, 1937–1938, 1960–1961). In the late 1960s, the Blackhawks entered a long period of decline, and it seemed that fans in Chicago would abandon them. The team's rebirth began in 2006 with the arrival of promising new stars such as Patrick Kane and Jonathan Toews, and in June 2010, the Blackhawks won their first Stanley Cup in nearly a half century. Through their many ups and downs, the Blackhawks attracted some of the most ardent and raucous sports fans in North America.

The founders of the team were Major Frederic McLaughlin, a millionaire who had made his wealth in coffee, and Huntington R. "Tack" Hardwick, a former All-American football player at Harvard and an investment banker, who secured the franchise for $14,000. They bought the Portland Rosebuds of the Western Hockey League (which was going out of business) for $100,000 from hockey legend Lester Patrick; the Rosebuds provided the core for their first season. McLaughlin named the new team after his unit in World War I, the 86th (Blackhawk) Division.

The Blackhawks debuted at the 6,000-seat Chicago Coliseum on November 17, 1926, defeating the Toronto Maple Leafs 4–1. They finished the season

19–22–3 and lost in the first round of the Stanley Cup playoffs. Thereafter, the team won just seven games in each of the next two seasons; they went through 12 coaches in 13 seasons.

On December 16, 1929, the team moved into the new 19,500-seat, $7 million Chicago Stadium, then the world's largest indoor sporting arena. The Blackhawks won their initial clash there before 14,212 fans, 3–1 over the Pittsburgh Pirates. The Blackhawks' raucous fans gave them a big home advantage, and they were egged on by the roaring of the stadium's $120,000 organ.

In 1930–1931, the club made the Stanley Cup finals but lost to the Montreal Canadiens. Then, in 1933–1934, they beat the Detroit Red Wings in a best-of-five series to capture the Cup. The Blackhawks returned to the Stanley Cup finals four years later, despite a dismal 14–25–9 record, and defeated Toronto in the biggest upset in Cup history. They again made the Cup finals in 1943–1944, but were swept by the Canadians.

McLaughlin died in 1944 and the team was sold to a syndicate led by team president Bill Tobin. However, the man in charge was Canadian wheat merchant James E. Norris, owner of the Detroit Red Wings and a partner with stadium owner Arthur Wirtz. Norris used the Blackhawks as a farm team for the Red Wings, and they did not have a winning season from 1945–1946 through 1958–1959.

Norris died in 1952, and shortly thereafter, his son, James D. Norris, Jr., together with Wirtz, took over the franchise. They rebuilt the club, hiring Tommy Ivan, formerly of the Red Wings, as general manager, and then Rudy Pilous as coach (1958–1963). Ivan developed an outstanding farm system that helped develop future greats Bobby Hull, Stan Mikita, and Pierre Pilote.

In 1957–1958, the Blackhawks received goalie Glen Hall and veteran forward Ted Lindsay from Detroit in a trade. They improved sufficiently to make the playoffs in 1958–1959 and 1959–1960. In 1960–1961, they came in second during the regular season, and went on to defeat the Red Wings for their first Stanley Cup since 1944. The team also reached the finals in 1961–1962 and 1964–1965.

Hull was a superstar with great skating speed and a 120 mile (193 kilometer) per hour slapshot. He had four 50-goal seasons and 604 goals as a Hawk. Mikita played 22 years for the Blackhawks and won two consecutive scoring titles, while Pilote won three straight Norris Trophies as the best defenseman. Goalie Hall made eight All-Star teams and played 502 games in a row. The team finished first overall in 1967 but was ousted in a disappointing playoff series.

In 1967–1968, the NHL expanded and placed all of the Original Six in the Eastern Conference. That same season, the Blackhawks made a disastrous trade, sending three promising young players—Phil Esposito, Ken Hodge, and Fred Stanfield—to the Boston Bruins. The newcomers helped the Bruins win two Stanley Cups. The next year, Hull scored 58 goals, yet the team fell into the cellar. In 1970–1971, they moved to the much weaker Western Division and went 46–17–5 but lost Game 7 of the Stanley Cup finals to the Canadiens.

The Blackhawks dominated the West, with seven division titles in the decade. But in 1972, underpaid superstar Bobby Hull jumped to the new World Hockey Association, accepting a $1 million contract to play for the Winnipeg Jets. The Blackhawks still were strong enough in 1972–1973 to make it back to the Cup finals, but they again lost to Montreal.

The Blackhawks made the playoffs throughout the 1980s but could not get back to the Stanley Cup finals. In 1990–1991, the Blackhawks took the Presidents' Trophy for best regular-season record, but they were immediately bounced from the playoffs. One year later, led by Jeremy Roenick's 53 goals, Chris Chelios on defense, and Eddie Belfour in goal, the Blackhawks returned to the Cup final for the first time in 19 years but were swept by the Pittsburgh Penguins.

In 1995, the Blackhawks moved into the $175 million, 20,500-seat United Center, owned by Blackhawks owner Bill Wirtz (son of Arthur Wirtz) and Jerry Reinsdorf of the Chicago Bulls; however, the team was in a tailspin. In 1998, they failed to make the playoffs for the first time in 29 years and continued to struggle for the next half-dozen years. In 2004, ESPN named the Blackhawks the worst franchise in professional sports.

A Blackhawks game had long been one of the hottest tickets in Chicago, but interest faded because of the team's poor play and anger at owner "Dollar Bill" Wirtz, who sharply increased ticket prices to an average of $50 and barred the televising of home games. In 2004–2005, the team finished 26–43–13, twenty-seventh in a 30-team league, and twenty-sixth overall the next year. They also fired popular television and radio announcer Pat Foley, a 25-year veteran.

The team began a major turnaround with the draft in 2006 and 2007, when they selected future stars Patrick Kane and Jonathan Toews, and made some astute trades. Wirtz died in 2007 and was replaced by his son, William "Rocky" Wirtz, who turned the team's management upside down. In 2008, the team televised all of its games for the first time since 1979–1980 and rehired

Foley as broadcaster. Former stars Hull and Mikita were brought back as "ambassadors" for the team.

The franchise preceded the 2009–2010 season with an outdoor game at Wrigley Field in August that drew more than 40,000 spectators. The game was a prelude to a magical season. The Blackhawks went 52–22–8 in the regular season and entered the Stanley Cup play-offs with high hopes. After dispatching the Nashville Predators and Vancouver Canucks, each in six games, they beat the San Jose Sharks for the Western Conference title and faced the Philadelphia Flyers in the finals. In the sixth game, with the Blackhawks leading three games to two, regulation play ended in a 3–3 tie. After four minutes of overtime, Patrick Kane scored the winning goal, bringing the Blackhawks their first Stanley Cup in 49 years. Captain Jonathan Toews was awarded the Conn Smythe Trophy as Most Valuable Player in the playoffs.

Steven A. Riess

See also: Ice Hockey.

Further Reading

Greenland, Paul. *Hockey Chicago Style: The History of the Chicago Blackhawks.* Champaign, IL: Sagamore, 1995.

Pfeiffer, Gerald L. *The Chicago Blackhawks: A Sixty Year History, 1926–1986.* Chicago: Windy City, 1987.

Verdi, Bob. *Chicago Blackhawks: Seventy-Five Years.* San Diego, CA: Tehabi, 2000.

Weinberg, Mark. *Career Misconduct: The Story of Bill Wirtz's Greed, Corruption, and the Betrayal of Blackhawks' Fans.* Chicago: Blueline, 2001.

Wong, John Chi-Kit. "Entrepreneurship and the Chicago Blackhawks." In *The Chicago Sports Reader: 100 Years of Sports in the Windy City,* ed. Steven A. Riess and Gerald R. Gems. Urbana: University of Illinois Press, 2009.

———. *Lords of the Rinks: The Emergence of the National Hockey League, 1875–1936.* Toronto, Canada: University of Toronto Press, 2005.

Blue Jays, Toronto

The Toronto Blue Jays are a Major League Baseball team in the Eastern Division of the American League (AL). An expansion team, the franchise entered the league in 1977 along with the Seattle Mariners. The Blue Jays were the second major league team based in Canada (after the Montreal Expos). In 1992, the Blue Jays became the first and only team outside the United States to win a World Series, an achievement they repeated in 1993. From 1985 through 1994, the Blue

Jays drew more fans than any other team in the American League. After 1998, however, they fell to the bottom half of the league standings, and attendance declined.

Professional baseball has a long history in Toronto. The Toronto Maple Leafs were a flagship team in the International League, a minor league one level below the majors, from 1896 to 1967, when the franchise moved to Louisville, Kentucky. In 1977, a new major league franchise was awarded to an ownership group that included Labatt Breweries, maker of the popular Canadian beer Labatt Blue, Imperial Trust, and the Canadian Imperial Bank of Commerce. The team's nickname, the Blue Jays, chosen from fan suggestions, was an ideal fit, as both the Argonauts in the Canadian Football League and the Maple Leafs in the National Hockey League sported blue uniforms.

The Blue Jays played their first game at home on April 7, 1977 against the Chicago White Sox, winning 9–5 at a snow-covered Exhibition Stadium (capacity 43,737), home of the Argonauts. The team went on to set new attendance records for an expansion team even though they finished the season with more than 100 losses, a performance that was repeated in each of the next two years under manager Roy Hartsfield.

In 1983, the team finally achieved a winning record under manager Bobby Cox. In 1985, Toronto won their first AL East division title with a record of 99–62, but they lost the American League Championship Series (ALCS) to the Kansas City Royals after taking a three-game lead. In 1987, the team led the AL in attendance for the first time.

In 1989, the Blue Jays' new retractable-roof home, the SkyDome, opened on June 5 with a capacity of 50,598; it came complete with luxury hotel suites facing the outfield, providing a unique way to watch a game. The novelty of the new park and the high quality of the team would propel the Blue Jays to record attendance for six straight years.

Also in 1989, manager Jimy Williams was fired after going 12–24. He was replaced with hitting instructor Cito Gaston. The team went 77–49 for the rest of the season and captured the AL East but lost the ALCS to Oakland in five games.

In 1990, Dave Stieb pitched the team's only no-hitter, beating the Indians 3–0 at Cleveland's Municipal Stadium. After the season, the Blue Jays traded short-stop Tony Fernández and first baseman Fred McGriff to the San Diego Padres for outfielder Joe Carter and second baseman Roberto Alomar. These new recruits led the team to its third division title in 1991. The Jays lost the ALCS to the Minnesota Twins in five games. The exciting season helped propel attendance to a major league record of 4 million spectators.

The Blue Jays built up their team for the 1992 season, acquiring pitcher Jack Morris and designated hitter Dave Winfield. They captured their second straight AL East title with a record of 96–66, led by Morris (21–6), the club's first 20-game winner. After finally winning the ALCS 4–2 over the Oakland Athletics, the Blue Jays went to the World Series, defeating the Atlanta Braves (managed by Bobby Cox) in six games. Catcher Pat Borders batted .450 and was named World Series Most Valuable Player.

The 1993 squad had an outstanding season, with seven men selected to the All-Star team. First baseman John Olerud, designated hitter Paul Molitor, and Alomar had the top three batting averages in the AL. The team won its third straight AL East crown (95–67), besting the Chicago White Sox 4–2 in the ALCS. The Blue Jays repeated these successes in the World Series, topping the Philadelphia Phillies. In Game 4 of the Series, the team came back from a 14–9 deficit to win 15–14 in the highest-scoring game in World Series history. In Game 6, Carter hit a three-run homer in the bottom of the ninth to win the game and the championship, the only time that the Series was decided by a walk-off home run by a team trailing in the bottom of the ninth.

The Blue Jays struggled in the strike-shortened 1994 season, going 55–60, mainly because of poor pitching. This was the first of many losing seasons, as the team fell into mediocrity, unable to compete with the New York Yankees and Boston Red Sox in the AL East. Team ownership changed when Labatt was bought by Interbrew, a Belgian company, only the second time a major league team was owned by non–North Americans. General Manager Pat Gillick, who had brought the Blue Jays to success, resigned and was replaced by Torontonian Gord Ash, who would stay with the team through 2001.

The 1995 season was a disaster. The team came in last in the AL East (56–88), and attendance declined sharply. The team added pitcher Roger Clemens in 1997 for a $24.75 million contract, and he led the AL with a record of 21–7, a 2.05 earned run average, and 292 strikeouts. Yet the team still went 76–86.

In 1998, Manager Gaston was fired and was replaced by Tim Johnson. Clemens achieved a second straight pitching Triple Crown (20–6, 2.65 earned run average, 271 strikeouts), and the Blue Jays finished

with their first winning record since 1993 (88–74). But Johnson, who had lost the confidence of both players and owners, was fired; he was replaced by veteran skipper Jim Fregosi, who led the team to two straight winning seasons. In 2000, seven players hit 20 or more home runs, led by Carlos Delgado, who hit .344 with 41 home runs and 137 runs batted in.

At the end of the 2000 season, Rogers Communications, Inc., purchased 80 percent of the club, with Interbrew (now called InBev) keeping a 20 percent share. This marked a new descent in the standings, as the majority owners ordered management to cut player payroll. Broadcaster Buck Martinez became manager, but he was fired in mid-2002 and was replaced by third base coach Carlos Tosca, who, in turn, was replaced two years later by first base coach John Gibbons.

In November 2004, Rogers Communications purchased the SkyDome from Sportsco International for $21.24 million, renaming the facility the Rogers Centre. The next year, the company increased the salary budget, and Toronto signed pitchers B.J. Ryan and A.J. Burnett for $47 million and $55 million, respectively, but the losses continued. Ryan's effectiveness was cut short by an injury; Burnett played out his option and signed with the Yankees in 2008 for $82.5 million; and star pitcher Roy Halladay was traded before the 2010 season as his contract was expiring. The Blue Jays could not compete financially with the Yankees and Red Sox, making Manager Gaston's tenure in his return from 2008 to 2010 a daunting task, with three straight fourth-place finishes.

Ron Reynolds

See also: Baseball, Major League; Stadiums and Arenas.

Further Reading

Bradford, Rob. *Chasing Steinbrenner: Pursuing the Pennant in Boston and Toronto.* Washington, DC: Brassey's, 2004.

Goodman, Michael E. *History of the Toronto Blue Jays.* Mankato, MN: Creative Education, 2003.

Morgan, Joe, Buck Martinez, and Jon Rochmis. *A Series to Remember: The Official Book of the 1993 World Series.* San Francisco: Woodford, 1993.

Blue Laws

Blue laws are legislative acts that regulate moral standards, especially activities on Sunday, the Christian Sabbath. They are based on the Fourth Commandment: "Six days shalt thou labor and do thy work, but the seventh day is the Sabbath of the Lord thy God."

This English tradition was enforced in seventeenth-century Anglican Virginia, Puritan New England, Dutch Reformed New York, and Quaker Pennsylvania to limit amusements on Sunday.

Blue laws restricted many activities, including the sale of alcoholic beverages, and a variety of recreations, including sporting events. Professional sports were forbidden on Sundays in parts of the United States and in English-speaking Canada into the 1920s. Today, most laws restricting Sunday sports have been repealed.

Colonial Era

Most early English and Dutch colonists were adherents of Calvinist churches that advocated strict observance of the Sabbath. They believed that the Sabbath should be reserved for worship, prayer, and contemplation, and disapproved of both work and idle amusements on Sunday. When newer immigrants from different traditions arrived, however, disagreements arose.

In New England, Puritan town leaders established laws to restrict public sports and amusements on Sunday. Blue laws were adopted in most English-speaking colonies, as well as in many of the new territories as settlers moved west. By contrast, Catholic immigrants to Maryland and French-speaking citizens of Quebec had a more tolerant view, adopting the custom that was prevalent in many parts of Europe of holding festivals and sporting events on Sundays.

Blue Laws in the Nineteenth Century

Acceptance of blue laws in the United States began to wane in the early nineteenth century. In most parts of the country, newspapers were printed, mail was delivered, and public conveyances transported travelers on Sundays. However, strict Sabbatarians continued to advocate public laws restricting activities on Sunday. They had considerable success in closing stores, taverns, and theaters on Sundays, and in banning sporting activities, especially those involving professional players or gambling.

By the late nineteenth century, blue laws had become more liberal, especially in large cities such as Chicago, Cincinnati, and St. Louis, where substantial communities came from Catholic and politically liberal countries in Europe. These cities and others in the Far West never developed the strong Sabbatarian traditions of those in the East and South. Supporters of abolishing the blue laws often pointed out that workingmen of the

time put in long hours six days a week, and only had leisure to enjoy amusements on Sundays. As the laws were liberalized, more people participated in Sunday sporting activities and attended professional events.

Reforms of blue laws in the East did not take place until after 1900. Protestants in Eastern cities fought for strict Sabbath laws, in part to maintain social control over lower-class immigrant populations. They favored amateur sporting events that could be scheduled on weeknights and Saturdays and attended by middle-class office workers, who generally had shorter workweeks than manual laborers.

Baseball and Circumventing Sunday Blue Laws

The main sport limited by Sunday blue laws was professional baseball. While religious groups led the campaign, support also came from those who championed more gentlemanly sports practiced by wealthy and middle-class amateurs. They feared that allowing such professional sports would reduce support for their own events; there was a greater tolerance for amateur and even semiprofessional sports.

When it began operation in 1876, baseball's National League scheduled no Sunday games, hoping to present itself as a respectable pastime to middle-class fans. The American Association, which was established in 1882, had more working-class fans; it permitted Sunday ball from the outset. When the two leagues merged for the 1892 season, the National League permitted Sunday baseball in cities where it legally could be conducted. The issue remained contentious for years, and until the 1910s, most teams in the new American League could not play Sunday games in their home parks.

Within blue law states, professional baseball games typically were better tolerated in workingmen's towns than in major cities. In Ohio, for instance, industrial Canton was more liberal on the issue of Sunday games than was the city of Cleveland. Baseball clubs located in blue law states actively searched for ways around the law, as a Sunday crowd was often twice or four times as large as a weekday crowd. In some cases, when the law prohibited events charging admission, team owners advertised their Sunday games as free, but then required customers to buy scorecards or refreshments and merchandise at inflated prices. Another dodge was to represent the Sunday event as a religious one by presenting a brief concert of sacred music before the game.

Some teams were forced to play Sunday games in a different municipality than their weekday games to avoid the no-Sunday law altogether. In the 1880s, the Brooklyn club in the American Association played Sunday games in Ridgewood, just across the county line. Similarly, the Philadelphia club played Sundays in Gloucester, New Jersey. Later, in 1898, the New York Giants of the National League played some Sunday games in Weehawken, New Jersey, just across the Hudson River from New York City. In the American League, Cleveland staged Sunday games in 1902 at various sites in Ohio and Indiana, including Canton, Columbus, Dayton, and Fort Wayne. Most of these Sunday-only grounds fell into disfavor because the ballparks were small and could not hold large paying crowds. In some cases, nonpaying fans filed into the park in later innings, sometimes overflowing onto the field and disrupting the game.

The courts often were not kind to club owners' evasions. In Brooklyn, where the free-admission ruse was used in 1904—owners charged inflated prices for scorecards instead—the city sued, and the court ruled that this approach violated the state's blue law. In 1906, the Brooklyn club asked for voluntary contributions at Sunday games, to be deposited in a box by spectators. The court ruled that this, too, violated the law.

Modifying the Sunday Blue Laws

Proponents of Sunday sports first attempted to overturn blue laws through the courts. When court challenges were unsuccessful, proponents worked to change the laws through legislative action or, when that failed, through voter referenda. Legislative action permitted professional Sunday baseball in Ohio in 1911, in the District of Columbia in 1918, and in New York in 1919. New York voters believed that men who had fought overseas for freedom should be free to watch baseball on their day off. Both Ohio and New York instituted "local option" laws that enabled each city to decide the issue of Sunday ball for itself.

However, legislative efforts to modify blue laws in Massachusetts and Pennsylvania failed. It took referenda to overturn the bans in those states, first in Massachusetts in 1928, abetted by the large Democratic turnout for presidential candidate Al Smith. Boston got Sunday ball the next season. In 1933, Pennsylvania voters also approved a referendum to permit Sunday ball that would raise badly needed revenue for the state government. The major league teams in Philadelphia and Pittsburgh finally were able to play on Sundays in 1934. In both states, games were restricted by time (2 P.M. to 6 P.M.), and by location in Massachusetts (not within 1,000 feet or 305 meters of a church).

Certain minor league Southern cities did have Sunday baseball in the early 1900s, mainly ports with large foreign-born populations, such as Memphis, Mobile, and New Orleans, and cities in West Texas. Cities in the Bible Belt, such as Atlanta, did not stage Sunday games until the mid-1930s and some not until the 1950s.

Football

Sunday blue laws restricted indoor sports, such as boxing, basketball, and ice hockey, but were less of a hindrance because these sports could be effectively conducted under artificial lighting and attended by working people on weeknights and Saturdays. Six-day bicycling events would begin at midnight on Sundays and then end at midnight the next Saturday.

Blue laws had a significant impact on early professional football, which could not compete with the popularity of college football on Saturdays. Before World War I, pro football was centered in the industrial cities of the Midwest, where Sunday laws were relatively liberal. The National Football League (NFL), launched in 1920, expanded to Eastern cities in the mid-1920s, locating franchises in New York City and Providence, Rhode Island, as well as in Frankford and Pottstown, Pennsylvania. Frankford, a community near Philadelphia, played home games on Saturdays, while Pottstown, 50 miles (80 kilometers) northwest of Philadelphia, played on Sundays because authorities there looked the other way.

It was not until 1929 that an NFL franchise was located in Boston, and not until 1933 until that Philadelphia and Pittsburgh entered the league, anticipating the overturning of the Pennsylvania blue laws in the fall elections.

Charlie Bevis

See also: Class, Economic and Social; Religion; Urbanization.

Further Reading
Bevis, Charlie. *Sunday Baseball: The Major Leagues' Struggle to Play Baseball on the Lord's Day, 1876–1934.* Jefferson, NC: McFarland, 2003.

Daniels, Bruce C. *Puritans at Play: Leisure and Recreation in Colonial New England.* New York: St. Martin's, 1995.

Gilkeson, John S., Jr. "The Rise and Decline of the 'Puritan Sunday' in Providence, Rhode Island, 1810–1926." *New England Quarterly* 59:1 (March 1986): 75–91.

Homel, Gene Howard. "Sliders and Backsliders: Toronto's Sunday Tobogganing Controversy of 1912." *Urban History Review* 10:2 (October 1981): 25–34.

Jable, J. Thomas. "Pennsylvania's Early Blue Laws: A Quaker Experiment in the Suppression of Sports and Amusements, 1682–1740." *Journal of Sport History* 1:2 (November 1974): 107–122.

McCrossen, Alexis. *Holy Day, Holiday: The American Sunday.* Ithaca, NY: Cornell University Press, 2000.

Peterson, Robert W. *Pigskin: The Early Years of Pro Football.* New York: Oxford University Press, 1997.

Riess, Steven A. *Touching Base: Professional Baseball and American Culture in the Progressive Era.* Rev. ed. Urbana: University of Illinois Press, 1999.

Bobsled, Luge, and Skeleton

The bobsled (or bobsleigh), luge, and skeleton all are vehicles used for traveling down ice-covered or snow-covered tracks at high speeds. The sledding sports are popular with Olympic audiences, although participation largely is limited to a handful of countries with the wealth and facilities needed to support professional teams.

A means to carry goods across snow and ice was first employed by the Innu and Cree of Northern Canada, who fabricated a wooden sleigh structure to hold various items and ease transport. The luge, skeleton, and bobsleigh are believed to be modern adaptations of the original practice of sledding.

In the 1870s, Swiss entrepreneur Caspar Badrutt began to market the town of St. Moritz as a winter resort for wealthy American and European tourists. Badrutt envisioned his visitors eating, drinking, skiing, and participating in indoor activities in the comfort of his hotels. It was not long, however, before his most adventurous guests began borrowing the sleds employed by delivery boys, using them to zip around on the hilly roads of the town.

Desiring faster travel and greater thrills, these tourists soon looked to develop speedier vehicles. In 1875, a group of Britons developed the skeleton, a low-lying sled with a sliding seat. Riders on the skeleton travel headfirst, shifting their weight on the seat in order to steer. Eleven years later, Englishman William Smith took a wooden platform (toboggan) and attached a crude hand brake, a pivoting sled in front, and a stationary sled in back. Thus was born the first bobsled. The luge, by contrast, did not need to be invented by the patrons of St. Moritz. A small sled ridden feet first, the luge had been in existence since the sixteenth century.

On the streets of St. Moritz, it was dangerous enough to have sleds traveling at high speeds among regular foot and vehicle traffic, and the new, speedier vehicles made matters worse. Consequently, Badrutt built the first half-pipe (U-shaped ramp) sledding track in the world in 1870. This was followed by a dedicated skeleton and luge track in 1884 and a dedicated bobsled track in 1903. Thus began the sports of bobsledding, luge, and skeleton.

The three sports quickly gained popularity. The first skeleton club was organized sometime in the 1880s, while the first bobsled club followed in 1896, and the first luge club in 1898. By 1900, organized competitions were being held in all three sledding sports. In 1923, the Fédération Internationale de Bobsleigh et de Tobogganing (FIBT) was founded in Paris; it has staged annual world championships since 1930, and it remains the governing body for all three disciplines. The FIBT began with only seven members—Austria, Belgium, Canada, France, Great Britain, Switzerland, and the United States. By 1945, the list had grown by only 12 more nations, with all of the new additions, except for Argentina and Japan, located in Europe.

Bobsledding was the first of the three sledding sports to find a permanent place on the international stage, with world championships starting in 1931. The four-man bobsled was added to Olympic competition in 1924, while two-man bobsledding became an Olympic sport in 1932. North America's first artificial bobsled run was built in 1911 at Montebello, Quebec; the first run in the United States was built at Mount Van Hoevenberg, near Lake Placid, for the 1932 Winter Olympics, when the two-man bobsled competition was added to the program.

In accordance with modern rules, bobsled participants begin their race by pushing their sled for 50 meters (55 yards). After climbing into the vehicle, the front man steers, while the rest of the crew simply tries to reduce their profile (and thus wind resistance). They travel down a track that is 1,200 to 1,600 meters (1,300 to 1,750 yards) in length with grades from 8 percent to 15 percent. As greater weight makes for faster runs, four-person teams are limited to a maximum weight of 630 kilograms (1,400 pounds), and two-person teams are limited to 375 kilograms (825 pounds). The winners are those with the shortest aggregate time over four runs; a winning time is somewhere in the range of 3 minutes, 40 seconds.

International bobsledding has been dominated by a handful of nations since its inception. Using Olympic medals as a measure, the leader of the sport is Germany

(40 Olympic medals since 1924), followed by Switzerland (30), the United States (20), Italy (12), and Canada (6). All of the other nations of the world combined have a total of 16 Olympic medals. Women's bobsledding was added to the Olympics in 2002.

The United States dominated early bobsledding, winning at least one gold medal in bobsledding in 1928, 1932, 1936, and 1948, at least in part due to technological innovations. In the late 1930s, brothers Bob and Bill Linney built a two-man sled with a steel plank linkage that permitted more speed through the turns, followed by the first sled with side-mounted handles to facilitate a flying start. In 1946, they fabricated the first all-steel sled with shock absorbers.

In the latter part of the twentieth century, U.S. bobsledders did not fare as well at the Olympics. It was not until 2010 that Steve Holcomb drove the four-man U.S. team to its first gold medal since 1948.

In the 1920s, the skeleton appeared to be headed down the same path as bobsledding. It was chosen as an Olympic sport in 1926, with the first medals awarded at the 1928 St. Moritz Games. Then it was eliminated until 1948, when the Winter Olympics returned to St. Moritz. Thereafter, interest in the skeleton waned for several decades, leading to a 54-year gap before skeleton became a permanent Olympic sport in 2002.

The skeleton has much in common with the luge; it is run on the same tracks and has similar weight limits—92 kilograms (202 pounds) for women and 115 kilograms (250 pounds) for men. As with lugers, the winners of the skeleton are those recording the single fastest run. There are a few differences as well—beyond the fact that skeleton riders use a different type of sled and travel headfirst. Doubles skeleton rarely is staged, and it is not an Olympic event.

Given the skeleton's relatively brief international and Olympic history, it is difficult to speak of any nation as a power in the sport. However, the United States has claimed the most Olympic medals (6), followed by Great Britain (5), Canada (4), and Switzerland (3).

Modern luges, which feature flexible runners that the rider can manipulate by moving his or her legs, were developed in the 1930s. The luge was the last of the three sledding sports to emerge on the world stage; three events—men's singles, women's singles, and doubles—were added to the Olympic program in 1964. While it theoretically is possible for women to compete in doubles events, in practice, the teams always are made up of two men.

According to FIBT rules, luge tracks range from 800 to 1,300 meters (875 to 1,420 yards) in length, with a grade of 8 percent to 11 percent, and riders are judged based on their single fastest run. As with bobsledding, there are maximum allowable weights—75 kilograms (165 pounds) for women, and 90 kilograms (200 pounds) for men. Riders who fall short of these weights are allowed to wear special weighted vests.

The leaders in the luge are Germany (70 Olympic medals), Austria (18), and Italy (16). Only three other nations have claimed even a single Olympic medal in the luge, among them the United States with two silver medals (1998 and 2002 doubles) and two bronze medals (also in the 1998 and 2002 doubles).

The sledding sports thus are firmly ensconced in Olympic competition and attract wide attention in Olympic years. Otherwise, however, they reach only a niche audience. With a few minor exceptions—most notably the emerging discipline of street luge—amateurs cannot try these sports for themselves; they are too dangerous and proper equipment and courses are not available. Further, there are only 19 FIBT-approved tracks in the world, with just two in Canada (Calgary and Whistler) and two in the United States (Lake Placid and Park City). This makes it impossible for most North Americans to attend a sledding event in person, and such events rarely are broadcast on television outside Europe.

The lack of courses and the prohibitive cost of equipment (a used bobsled costs a minimum of $25,000) also make it difficult for aspiring professionals. The heartwarming story of the four-man Jamaican bobsled team—who never had seen snow before arriving to compete in the 1988 Winter Olympics—notwithstanding, it seems fair to say that the sledding sports will remain the preserve of a handful of individuals in a small number of wealthy, snowy countries, much as they always have been.

Christopher G. Bates and Steven A. Riess

See also: Olympics, Winter.

Further Reading

Lori, Chris, with Ken Lori. *Fiercely Driven.* Toronto, Canada: University of Toronto Press, 2000.

O'Brien, Andy. *Bobsled and Luge.* Toronto, Canada: Colban, 1976.

Wallechinsky, David. *The Complete Book of the Winter Olympics.* Vancouver, Canada: Aurum, 2009.

Bodybuilding

Although the practice of bodybuilding as an exercise regimen to enhance muscular development and athletic proficiency has roots as far back as ancient Greece, it did not become a competitive sport until the twentieth century. Like its sister sports—weightlifting, powerlifting, and strongman events—bodybuilding involves the lifting of heavy objects, chiefly barbells and dumbbells, but not in actual competitions. Rather, lifters employ weights to develop muscle tone and an exaggerated and defined muscle mass to produce an overall aesthetic effect. Muscularity, symmetry, definition, and posing ability are major components in the judging of physique. With so much emphasis on bodily appearance and little direct interaction among competitors, most authorities regard bodybuilding as much an artistic endeavor as a sport.

Early Contests

Eugen Sandow, often dubbed the "Father of Bodybuilding," staged the world's first physique contest in 1901 at London's Royal Albert Hall, with the title going to William Murray of Nottingham. Two years later, physical culturist Bernarr Macfadden organized the first American competition for the "Most Perfectly Developed Man" and the "Most Perfectly Developed Woman" in New York City; the competition was won by Al Treloar of Michigan and Emma Newkirk of California, respectively.

Charles Atlas, the winner of contests staged by Macfadden for the "Most Handsome Man" (1921) and "World's Most Perfectly Developed Man" (1922), became a bodybuilding icon and inspired generations of young men worldwide to develop their bodies through his highly successful mail-order program. Otherwise, there were few physique contests between the wars.

In 1939, John Hordines in Amsterdam, New York, initiated a revival of bodybuilding competitions with the first Mr. America Contest, which was won by Bert Goodrich of California. It soon gained official recognition as an adjunct to the national weightlifting championships under the Amateur Athletic Union (AAU), which, under the leadership of Bob Hoffman of York, Pennsylvania, sponsored the event for the next 60 years. Hoffman's *Strength & Health* magazine provided extensive coverage of bodybuilding.

John Grimek of York, Mr. America in 1940 and 1941, was the greatest bodybuilder of his era. Over the next three decades, the amateur event was the preeminent bodybuilding contest in the world. Its standing was boosted in 1947 by Mr. America Steve Reeves, who attained fame starring in "sword-and-sandal" movie epics, most notably *Hercules* (1959). During the 1950s, however,

with less emphasis on muscularity and greater stress on such holistic criteria as character, education, personality, and athletic ability, the event seemed to some to be a male counterpart to the annual Miss America Contest in Atlantic City.

Meanwhile, other bodybuilding organizations, less wedded to these ideals and more attuned to form (appearance) over function (athleticism), began to emerge in the late 1940s. The Mr. Universe Contest, conceived at the 1947 world weightlifting championships in Philadelphia and first won by American Steve Stanko, began in 1950 under the aegis of the National Amateur Bodybuilders Association (NABBA). The contest was headed for several decades by Oscar Heidenstam, editor of *Health & Strength,* and it featured such titlists as Grimek (1948); Reeves (1950); Great Britain's top bodybuilder Reg Park (1951, 1958); and Mickey Hargitay (1955), who was best known as a member of Mae West's troupe of musclemen and the husband of actress Jayne Mansfield. In 1967, Austrian-born Arnold

Bodybuilding icon Charles Atlas (Angelo Siciliano) inspired generations of young men to develop their physiques with magazine advertisements depicting the transformation of "97-pound weaklings" into bully-defying, girl-winning beach heroes. *(The Granger Collection, New York)*

Schwarzenegger, at 6 feet, 2 inches (1.9 meters) and 248 pounds (112 kilograms), with 21-inch (53-centimeter) arms and a 57-inch (144-centimeter) chest, won the title; he went on to claim the NABBA professional championship for the next three years.

By the 1960s, Southern California had become a haven for bodybuilders, in part because of the enthusiasm sparked by a collection acrobats, gymnasts, and weightlifters who started performing at Muscle Beach in Santa Monica as early as 1938. The proximity of Muscle Beach to Hollywood helped popularize and glamorize bodybuilding. Contributors to the movement included fitness guru Jack LaLanne; Abbye Stockton, the first woman bodybuilder; Vic Tanny, founder of the first national chain of gyms; and Harold Zinkin, inventor of the Universal Gym.

No less critical to raising bodybuilding to a higher level of public consciousness and its development as a sport were the promotional activities of Joe and Ben Weider of Montreal, who in 1947 founded the International Federation of Bodybuilders (IFBB) to conduct physique contests worldwide. While Ben remained in Canada, Joe moved his business operations, including numerous magazines (most notably *Muscle and Fitness*) and fitness products (especially dietary supplements), to New Jersey and eventually to Woodland Hills, California, in 1972. The Weiders created their own Mr. America and Mr. Universe titles and offered greater opportunities for professionalism. Their professional Mr. Olympia Contest, launched in 1965, soon eclipsed the AAU's Mr. America Contest in prestige, chiefly because of the popularity of Arnold Schwarzenegger, whom Joe Weider brought to America and effectively showcased.

Bodybuilding also benefited from the promotional efforts of Dan Lurie of Brooklyn, New York, and Peary Rader of Alliance, Nebraska. Lurie, after winning Most Muscular Man awards in early Mr. America contests, gained public recognition as "Sealtest Dan the Muscle Man" on the CBS show *Sealtest Big Top,* which was televised from Philadelphia in the 1950s. Eventually Lurie created his own organization, the World Bodybuilding Guild, copycat titles of Mr. America and Mr. Olympus, a line of fitness products, and a promotional journal, *Muscle Training Illustrated.* He also sponsored a series of banquets in New York City, which formed the basis for the Association of Oldtime Barbell & Strongmen created by naturopath Vic Boff in the 1980s.

Rader, after founding *Iron Man* magazine in 1936, became the iron game's most independent voice. Less commercially motivated than other promoters, Rader provided the most balanced coverage of events and inspired the greatest confidence among bodybuilders for decades. John Balik of Santa Monica bought *Iron Man* in 1986, bringing further notoriety to Southern California's muscle culture.

Performance-Enhancing Drugs

Another important aspect of bodybuilding's development was the introduction of performance-enhancing substances. Following the lead of California physical culturist Paul Bragg, who had stressed the importance of diet for decades, Chicago nutritionist Irvin Johnson introduced dietary supplements in the early 1950s to promote the ingestion of protein and to stimulate muscle growth. Production and sale of such supplements by Hoffman, Weider, and other entrepreneurs in the 1960s became very profitable and, by internalizing training protocol, paved the way for ergogenic (performance-enhancing) drugs.

Testosterone and its derivative, anabolic steroids (isolated in 1935 by Charles Kochakian), were not used in sports until Russian weightlifters began using the former in the 1950s and Maryland physician John Ziegler started administering the latter to American lifters in the early 1960s. Their widespread use by bodybuilders in subsequent decades to enhance muscle mass and recovery virtually revolutionized the sport.

Undoubtedly, Schwarzenegger has had the greatest influence in popularizing bodybuilding. In his 15-year career, the "Austrian Oak" won 14 world titles, including seven Mr. Olympia competitions. What made him an international icon, however, was his movie career, first in bodybuilding roles in *Stay Hungry* (1976) and *Pumping Iron* (1977) and then in such blockbuster thrillers as *Conan the Barbarian* (1982) and *The Terminator* (1984). Schwarzenegger's star status set the stage for his 2003 election as governor of California; however, he did not abandon his bodybuilding roots.

In 1989, Schwarzenegger established the Arnold Classic, a major physique contest held annually in Columbus, Ohio, which became, in 1993, the Arnold Fitness Weekend, the largest multisport competition outside the Olympics. In 2006, the event attracted an estimated 17,000 athletes from 39 sports (including 14 Olympic sports), with bodybuilding still as its centerpiece.

By this time, women held a prominent place in bodybuilding. In 1977, Henry McGhee of Canton, Ohio, held the first women's physique contest, which was won by Gina LaSpina. In 1978, McGhee established the United States Women's Physique Association and held the first National Women's Physique Championships.

By 1984, many IFBB-affiliated nations were adding a women's component to traditional male physique contests. The American affiliate boasted more than 2,000 competing members, and the Ms. Olympia Contest was well in place as the counterpart to the Mr. Olympia Contest, bodybuilding's leading professional event. The most notable female bodybuilders were Texan Rachel McLish, the first Ms. Olympia (1980), and Californian Cory Everson, the winner from 1984 to 1989. Throughout these years, there was controversy among promoters and judges over evaluating competitors for their feminine charm as well as their physique.

The emergence of women bodybuilders also helped transform training environments from dingy, dark, sweaty gyms to modern fitness centers with chrome, mirrors, hardwood floors, and computerized machines. Setting the pace was Gold's Gym, the most famous fitness franchise in the world, founded in 1965 by Joe Gold in Venice, California. It attracted Schwarzenegger and other Weider stars and eventually spread to more than 600 facilities in 42 states and 30 countries with 3 million members. The Gold's Gym in Venice remains at the center of the bodybuilding world.

Arguably the greatest effect of bodybuilding has been to spark a worldwide fitness revolution and a preoccupation with sports beginning in the 1970s. Indeed, the iconography of bodybuilding, from buff movie stars to children's hypertrophied toy action figures, reflects a larger societal emphasis on health, fitness, and muscular appearance. Ironically, many elite bodybuilders, because of drugs and extreme dietary and training regimens, are neither healthy nor fit, and they may appear grotesque to the general public.

John D. Fair

See also: Atlas, Charles; Schwarzenegger, Arnold; Weightlifting.

Further Reading

Chapman, David L. *Sandow the Magnificent: Eugen Sandow and the Beginnings of Bodybuilding.* Urbana: University of Illinois Press, 1994.

Ernst, Joseph. *Weakness Is a Crime: The Life of Bernarr Macfadden.* Syracuse, NY: Syracuse University Press, 1991.

Fair, John D. *Muscletown USA: Bob Hoffman and the Manly Culture of York Barbell.* University Park: Pennsylvania State University Press, 1999.

Hotten, Jon. *Muscle: A Writer's Trip Through a Sport with No Boundaries.* London: Yellow Jersey, 2005.

Lowe, Maria R. *Women of Steel: Female Bodybuilders and the Struggle for Self-Definition.* New York: New York University Press, 1998.

Roach, Randy. *Muscle, Smoke and Mirrors.* Bloomington, IN: AuthorHouse, 2008.

Schwarzenegger, Arnold, with Douglas Kent Hall. *Arnold: The Education of a Bodybuilder.* New York: Simon & Schuster, 1977.

Wayne, Rick. *Muscle Wars: The Behind-the-Scenes Story of Competitive Bodybuilding.* New York: St. Martin's, 1985.

Webster, David. *Barbells and Beefcake: An Illustrated History of Bodybuilding.* New York: Arco, 1979.

Bonds, Barry (1964–)

Barry Lamar Bonds was one of the greatest, and most controversial, hitters in the history of professional baseball. He was a five-tool player—one who excels in hitting (both for power and for consistency), throwing, fielding, and base running—who late in his career became the greatest power hitter of all time, setting a new record for the most home runs ever hit. However, his achievements were clouded by his apparent use of performance-enhancing drugs. Bonds's 22-year career ended after the 2007 season. At the end of that year, he became a free agent, but no team in the majors would sign him for 2008 because of the drug controversy.

Bonds was born in Riverside, California, on July 24, 1964, the son of former major league right fielder Bobby Bonds and the godson of Hall of Famer Willie Mays. He excelled in baseball, basketball, and football at Junipero Serra High School in San Mateo, California, and went on to become an All-American baseball player at Arizona State University, graduating in 1986. The Pittsburgh Pirates selected Bonds as the sixth pick in the 1985 Major League Baseball draft and assigned him to the Prince William Pirates of the Carolina League. The next year, he began the season with the Hawaii Islanders of the Pacific Coast League and was called up to Pittsburgh at the end of May.

During his seven years with the Pirates, Bonds was a slender speedster with power, initially a lead-off hitter who stole bases, hit home runs, and drove in runs. He averaged 35 stolen bases a year in Pittsburgh (with a high of 52 in 1990), 25 home runs, and 79 runs batted in. From the beginning of his career, he demonstrated great hitting discipline by refusing to swing at bad pitches, which led to many walks. He led the league in several categories and was an excellent fielder, winning three Gold Glove awards (1990–1992).

During Bonds's last three years with the Pirates, his consistently high level of performance earned him Most Valuable Player (MVP) awards in 1990 and 1992. The Pirates took three straight division championships starting in 1990, but they never advanced to the World Series. A free agent following the 1992 season, Bonds signed a six-year contract for more than $43 million with the San Francisco Giants, the team for which his father and godfather had played.

Bonds continued to dominate with the Giants. In 1993, he led the National League in home runs (46), runs batted in (123), slugging (.677), total bases (365), and intentional walks (43), and was named the National League MVP. During his first 12 years, he was at least the equal of any player in baseball during a similar time span. During the last four years of this stretch, he won the National League MVP award each year, bringing his total to seven, and in 2001, he was named Male Athlete of the Year by the Associated Press.

His tenure with the Giants was marked by many milestones. In 1996, he was the first National Leaguer to hit 40 homers and steal 40 bases in a season. Two years later, he became the first major leaguer to hit 400 home runs and steal 400 bases in a career. Opposing teams—especially pitchers—both respected and feared him, and he often was walked intentionally. In 2004, Bonds reached an all-time high walk total of 232.

Bonds helped the Giants win 103 games in 1993; take the National League West division title in 1997, 2000, and 2003 (when the team won 100 games); and win the National League pennant as a wild-card team in 2002. However, the club lost the World Series to the Anaheim Angels (4–3) in the highest-scoring World Series ever.

Baseball's landscape changed dramatically during the 1998 and 1999 seasons, when Mark McGwire of the St. Louis Cardinals and Sammy Sosa of the Chicago Cubs hit home runs at an unprecedented rate. Before this time, only Roger Maris (61 home runs in 1961) of the New York Yankees had surpassed Babe Ruth's record of 60 in 1927. McGuire and Sosa exceeded Maris's total in both seasons, with McGwire hitting 70 in 1998. In those two years, Bonds hit a combined 71 home runs.

While Bonds had been the best player in baseball in the 1990s, he now had greater aspirations. He began to build up his physique and focused more than ever on increasing his power. He hit 49 homers in 2000, his all-time high. In 2001, he hit 73 homers to surpass McGwire for the single-season record and also set the single-season record for slugging (.863). Then he led the league in batting average in 2002 (.370) and 2004

San Francisco Giants slugger Barry Bonds, facing controversy and later federal charges pertaining to his alleged steroids use, broke one of Major League Baseball's most cherished records with his 756th career home run on August 7, 2007. *(Bloomberg/Getty Images)*

(.362). He led the majors in OBP (on base average plus slugging) five years out of six beginning in 2001. In 2004, his OBP (1.422) set an all-time record, and he reached base more frequently than the number of official plate appearances (his 232 walks did not count as at bats).

Bonds's sudden home run explosion positioned him to break the lifetime home run record (755) set by Henry Aaron of the Atlanta Braves. After missing all but 15 games of the 2005 season because of a knee injury that required surgery and a long rehabilitation, he returned to form in 2006. The next season, he surpassed Aaron's lifetime home run total, finishing the season with 762. Bonds concluded his 22-year career with seven MVP awards and seven slugging crowns. He was the all-time major league leader in bases on balls (2,558) and intentional walks (688). He earned a total of $188,245,322 from baseball, peaking in annual salary at $22 million in 2005.

By 2007, however, Bonds's career was overshadowed by controversy. His amazing display of hitting power in the 2000s and his bulked-up physique raised eyebrows. Fans wanted to know whether Bonds and other home run heroes such as McGwire and Sosa had used performance-enhancing drugs. In 2002, a federal investigation targeted the Bay Area Laboratory Co-operative (BALCO), a company that conducted urine and blood analyses. In 2003, several athlete customers of BALCO, including Bonds, were summoned to testify before a grand jury. Bonds denied that he had used steroids, but other testimony raised further questions. Later, reporters Mark Fainaru-Wada and Lance Williams discovered that in 2003, BALCO had given an undetectable steroid to athletes.

In November 2007, Bonds was indicted on four counts of perjury in his grand jury testimony and one count of obstruction of justice in the BALCO case. In April 2011, a federal jury found him guilty of obstruction of justice but could not reach a decision on the perjury accusations, forcing the district court judge to declare a mistrial on those charges. The verdict seemed to give no clear determination of Bonds's guilt or innocence, leaving fans and critics to judge his conduct for themselves.

Benjamin Franklin V

See also: Baseball, Major League; Drugs, Performance-Enhancing; Giants, San Francisco/New York (Baseball).

Further Reading

Fainaru-Wada, Mark, and Lance Williams. *Game of Shadows: Barry Bonds, BALCO, and the Steroids Scandal That Rocked Professional Sports.* New York: Gotham, 2006.

Pearlman, Jeff. *Love Me, Hate Me: Barry Bonds and the Making of an Antihero.* New York: HarperCollins, 2006.

Bowl Games, College Football

Postseason bowl games between major college football teams originated as exhibition contests during the Christmas and New Year holidays, with no competitive bearing for the teams. The bowls were planned by boosters in warm weather regions to publicize their region and leading industries. However, the games gradually achieved great popularity. The National Collegiate Athletic Association (NCAA), which oversees college football, stepped in to provide some regulation in 1949, but it was later forced to cede oversight to the individual athletic conferences in 1984. Meanwhile, bowl competition took on added significance as television made bowl appearances more and more lucrative for universities and conferences.

At the same time, the games took on greater importance as sports journalists struggled to determine a national college champion each year. By 1971, the wire service polls of coaches and sportswriters ranking major teams included bowl results in their end-of-season standings.

Finally, bowl organizations took matters into their own hands, seeking to maintain control of their events and to identify a national champion. The result was the Bowl Championship Series (BCS), established in 1998. The results of the BCS remained controversial, however, and critics of bowl games proposed substituting a postseason tournament to determine a national champion.

The Rose Bowl

In 1890, members of the exclusive Valley Hunt Club in Pasadena, California, organized a floral festival known as the Tournament of Roses to advertise the temperate climate and available real estate of the Southern California/Los Angeles basin. The venture quickly became a huge civic undertaking, and participants created the Tournament of Roses Association. Supporters and members of the association included some of the wealthiest, most prominent landowners in the region. The tournament and the region were publicized in the Midwinter Edition of the *Los Angeles Times,* which was distributed free in Eastern and Midwestern markets.

At the turn of the century, college football was gaining popularity as major universities developed rivalries and drew national attention on the sports pages. In 1902, the Tournament of Roses organizers added a football game to the New Year's Day program. In this first game, Stanford University, a leading team in the West, played the University of Michigan, a powerhouse in the Midwest. Michigan drubbed Stanford 49–0. (The student manager of the Stanford team was Herbert Hoover, who would be elected U.S. president in 1928.)

Football did not return to the Tournament of Roses program until 1916. Games were played in Pasadena's Tournament Park until 1923, when the Rose Bowl Stadium, modeled on the Yale Bowl, opened on January 1, accommodating 57,000 spectators. The stadium was enlarged several times and accommodated more than 100,000 people beginning in 1978, making it the largest football stadium in the country. Seating later was reduced to about 94,000. Like the 1903 game, other early matches featured a team from the Pacific Coast Conference (predecessor of the Pac-10) against a Midwestern or Eastern team.

Beginning in 1947, the Rose Bowl usually brought together the champions of the Pacific Coast Conference and the Big Nine (now the Big Ten) of the Midwest. Until 1975, teams in both conferences were not allowed to accept any other invitation; thereafter, the league champions continued to accept Rose Bowl invitations, while teams with poorer records could accept other bowl bids. This system ended in 1998, when the Rose Bowl became a part of the BCS.

New Bowls Arise

The Tournament of Roses inspired other prominent bowl games. In Florida, the city of Miami witnessed a meteoric rise in the early 1920s as a result of a land boom. That growth, however, was halted by a hurricane in 1926, the stock market crash of 1929, and the beginning of the Great Depression.

Hoping to restore Miami's image, civic booster and local utility executive George Hussey founded the Palm Festival in 1933, with the financial assistance of the city's hospitality and real estate interests. One of the festival's events was a football game, in which the University of Miami upset the highly ranked Manhattan College on January 1, 1933, at Moore Park.

The following year, the Palm Festival organizers, in conjunction with the Miami Chamber of Commerce, created the Orange Bowl as a means to advertise the Florida citrus industry and other benefits of the region in order to draw tourists, new residents, and investors to Miami. The first official Orange Bowl saw Bucknell University defeat Miami 26–0 on a rainy New Year's Day in 1935.

At nearly the same time, civic and political leaders in New Orleans, together with the *New Orleans Item,* created the New Orleans Mid-Winter Sports Association to host football and basketball events over the New Year's holiday in an attempt to draw visitors to the Crescent City. Sports editor Fred Digby suggested

The Rose Bowl, known as the "Granddaddy of Them All," is the oldest college football bowl game. Held on New Year's Day in Pasadena, California, the annual match-up dates to 1902. The 1969 Rose Bowl pitted perennial powers Ohio State and USC. *(Focus on Sport/Getty Images)*

calling the event the Sugar Bowl to tout the region's sugarcane industry. The games were played at Tulane University's stadium, site of a former sugar plantation. Like the Orange Bowl organizers, the Mid-Winter Association maximized gate revenue by inviting the local Tulane University team, which beat Temple University 20–14 in the inaugural game on January 1, 1935.

In El Paso, Texas, the local Kiwanis Club, soon joined by other service organizations, initiated a Sun Carnival in 1934 to advertise the temperate climate of the West Texas border town. For the 1935–1936 carnival, organizers added a New Year's Day football game between nearby New Mexico A&M (now New Mexico State University) and Hardin-Simmons University. The game ended in a tie.

The last significant Depression-era bowl emerged in Dallas a year later. Oilman J. Curtis Sanford had attended the 1936 Rose Bowl, and he decided to establish a similar program to advertise the Dallas region. Sanford personally financed the first four games and, like his predecessors in Miami and New Orleans, identified the game with the city's most prominent economic institution—in this case, the famed Cotton Exchange.

The inaugural Cotton Bowl in 1937 matched Texas Christian University against Marquette University, with the former winning 16–6. Having established the game as a fixture on New Year's Day, Sanford turned the game over to the Cotton Bowl Athletic Association in 1939. Boosters in other cities organized scores of other bowl games during the 1930s, but most lasted just a year or two.

Regulating the Bowls

Bowl games operated outside the existing organizational framework of college football, lacking any national coordination or planning. Most bowl games came and went, with unstable financing and limited local appeal. In the worst instances, bowls failed to draw enough live gate revenue to meet their financial guarantees to the teams.

As a result, in 1949, the NCAA's Extra Events Committee began regulating bowl games. Technically, the NCAA had no control over the games, but it threatened that schools participating in uncertified bowl games would be expelled from the association. In response, bowl games opened their books to NCAA officials, providing evidence of sound financing and guaranteeing the participating universities a prearranged number of tickets and 80 percent of all revenue (this was changed to 75 percent the following year).

Within three years, the number of recognized bowl games dropped from 14 to 7, while the number of fly-by-night games dropped from near 50 to zero. By the mid-1970s, the number of bowl games stood at only 11.

Though regulation by the Extra Events Committee established some stability in the bowl system, it did nothing to change the status of the games as exhibitions. Many schools and conferences opposed or banned participation in bowl games. Ivy League schools, once the dominant powers in college football, largely shunned bowl games, and the University of Notre Dame refused invitations until 1971. In 1921, the Big Ten prohibited all members from appearing in bowl games, as did the Southern Conference soon afterward. The Big Eight Conference in the Midwest followed suit in 1950. However, the prohibition meant that conferences and their member schools also gave up the extra revenue and public exposure that bowl games brought.

To address this problem, the major conferences agreed with bowl officials to establish permanent bowl rivalries. Thus, in 1946, the Big Ten negotiated an exclusive contract with the Pacific Coast Conference to play annually in the Rose Bowl. Other conferences arranged similar contractual tie-ins. The Cotton Bowl already had contracted with the Southwest Conference to invite one of its teams in 1941. In 1953, the Atlantic Coast Conference and the Big Eight agreed to send teams to the Orange Bowl. The Sugar Bowl did not have a formal arrangement with the Southeast Conference (SEC) until 1977, but in 36 of the 40 years prior to the arrangement, an SEC team had been invited.

Still wary that bowls could be a commercially corrupting influence, and desiring to protect the exclusivity of the Rose Bowl, the Big Ten and Pac-10 mandated that the Rose Bowl was the only bowl game in which their conference members could participate. This provision, together with the continued refusal of independents such as Notre Dame, left the field wide open for conferences with no such restrictions. SEC and Big Eight schools received and accepted numerous bowl invitations each year. In 1971, SEC and Big Eight schools accounted for 10 of the 22 teams invited to the 11 bowl games.

This imbalance allowed the conferences disproportionate television exposure, which increased their income and helped them recruit top players and build fan support. Because several teams in these conferences might play in bowl games in a given year, the conferences had that much more money from television to share. Faced with this competitive disadvantage, the Big

Ten and Pac-10 lifted most restrictions on teams accepting bowl bids in 1974. In most years, the conference champions continued to play in the Rose Bowl, but at the same time, strong conference teams were playing in other postseason games.

Bowls and the National Championship

Early on, many bowl games were understood to be simple exhibitions, not an extension of regular-season play. The games gave players and team boosters a chance to enjoy a short vacation in a warm climate and a friendly contest with a nonconference opponent. By the 1970s, however, major bowl games had become an important element in determining a team's overall success for the year.

In 1936, the Associated Press (AP) began polling its sportswriters to rank college football teams on a weekly basis. The winner of the final AP poll, taken at the end of the regular season, generally was regarded as the national champion. However, the AP system (along with a rival poll of leading college coaches conducted by United Press International), increasingly came under fire. In 1940, for example, 23 teams took unbeaten records into bowl games and then lost. How could a team ranked as the national champion in early December lose its bowl game and still be considered a champ? Between 1936 and 1969, seven AP national champions lost their bowl games: Southern Methodist (1936), Oklahoma (1951), Tennessee (1952), Maryland (1954), Minnesota (1961), Alabama (1965), and Michigan State (1966). Finally, bowing to pressure from fans, the AP changed its system—the last ranking of the year was conducted *after* the bowl games, and the bowl results counted.

The 1980s brought further challenges to the bowl system. In 1984, the U.S. Supreme Court ruled that the NCAA's regulation of contracts for televised college football violated the Sherman Antitrust Act and decreed that conferences and schools should be able to negotiate their own television coverage. This ruling came just as the volume of sports coverage on television was increasing at a record rate. Cable television offered hundreds of new channels; national stations such as WTBS (Atlanta) and WGN (Chicago) offered expanded sports coverage; and the all-sports channel ESPN was just beginning operation. As a result, the number of college football games on television exploded. Organizers in many cities saw an opportunity to create more bowl games,

and the number of annual events grew from 16 in 1984 to 32 by 2006.

The increased television coverage provided exposure for corporate sponsors that used the games as an advertising vehicle. In September 1985, the Fiesta Bowl signed a multimillion-dollar sponsorship package with the Sunkist Growers Corporation to change the official name to the Sunkist Fiesta Bowl. (The game later was sponsored by IBM and then by Frito Lay, and recently became the Tostitos Fiesta Bowl.) Other bowls rapidly followed suit, creating the USF&G Sugar Bowl and the John Hancock Sun Bowl in 1987, and the Federal Express Orange Bowl and the Mobil One Cotton Bowl in 1988. The overt commercialization of the bowl system made many college football enthusiasts squirm, as games were renamed the Poulan Weed Eater Independence Bowl (1990–1996) and the IBM OS/2 Warp Fiesta Bowl (1993–1995), or dropped the historical name altogether for that of a corporate sponsor, such as the John Hancock Bowl (1986–1993).

As the number of bowl games increased, invitations to lesser events went to more and more teams with mediocre records in their regular-season schedules. The major bowls continued to prosper, but the tangle of agreements with conferences confused any hope of scheduling a game between the two leading teams in the nation in order to determine a national champion. Fans and sports journalists increased pressure on the NCAA and the major conferences to develop a championship game, or even a postseason playoff. The organizers of the major bowl games stepped in to create a championship system that would satisfy fans but preserve their traditional midwinter events.

In 1992, the Sugar, Fiesta, Orange, and Cotton Bowls agreed to create the Bowl Coalition (later reorganized as the Bowl Championship Series). Under the coalition, each year one of the four bowls would give up its usual conference match-ups and instead would select the two highest-ranked teams, in the hope of staging a national championship game. Because the Rose Bowl organizers and the Big Ten and Pac-10 conferences declined to participate in the Bowl Coalition, this system soon became problematic. For the 1995 game, top-ranked Penn State, a recent addition to the Big Ten, was obligated to play in the Rose Bowl, making a match-up between the two top teams impossible. Two years later, unbeaten number two Arizona State of the Pac-10 was required to play in the Rose Bowl, and thus could not face top-ranked Florida State.

Finally, in 1998, the bowls created the Bowl Championship Series, which included the Rose Bowl and Big

Ten and Pac-10 conferences. However, the new organization developed a bewildering system for identifying the top two teams. It included media polls and a sophisticated computer model that considered additional factors, such as strength of schedule and "quality wins." The system raised so many questions that the BCS was forced to make major adjustments to the complex formula in 2001, 2002, 2004, and 2006.

Even so, the BCS succeeded in drawing more and more attention to the major bowls and conferences. As a result, attendance at the smaller bowls steadily dwindled. With such a vexed history and a controversial present, the future of the college bowl system appears uncertain.

Kurt Edward Kemper

See also: Football, College; Notre Dame, University of; Stadiums and Arenas; Television.

Further Reading

Dunnavant, Keith. *The Fifty-Year Seduction: How Television Manipulated College Football, from the Birth of the Modern NCAA to the Creation of the BCS.* New York: Thomas Dunne, 2004.

Hibner, John Charles. *The Rose Bowl, 1902–1929: A Game-by-Game History of Collegiate Football's Foremost Event, from Its Advent Through Its Golden Era.* Jefferson, NC: McFarland, 1993.

Mulé, Marty. *Sugar Bowl: The First Fifty Years.* Birmingham, AL: Oxmoor House, 1983.

Ours, Robert M. *Bowl Games: College Football's Greatest Tradition.* Yardley, PA: Westholme, 2004.

Smith, Loran. *Fifty Years on the Fifty: The Orange Bowl Story.* Charlotte, NC: East Woods, 1983.

Stowers, Carlton. *Cotton Bowl Classic: The First Fifty Years.* Lexington, KY: Host Communications, 1986.

Watterson, John Sayle. *College Football: History, Spectacle, Controversy.* Baltimore: Johns Hopkins University Press, 2000.

Bowling

With a history stretching back to the colonial era, bowling always has been one of the most popular participatory sports in America, as it is inexpensive, generally requires little skill for beginning play, and promotes sociability among competitors. From the nineteenth century, bowling remained primarily an urban ethnic working-class sport through World War II. After the war, upscale bowling alleys using automatic pin spotters became a staple of burgeoning suburban shopping centers, and bowling emerged as a popular middle-class family recreation. Television helped popularize bowling in the late 1950s, and for several decades, it was a mainstay of weekend programming. By the late 2000s, about 7 million people competed in sanctioned league play each year, while about 60 million Americans bowled at least once a year.

Origins

American colonists played different versions of the game, beginning at Jamestown, Virginia, where settlers bowled in the streets from the earliest days. In 1631, the Dutch burghers of New Amsterdam ventured outside the village walls to play skittles, a traditional bowling game that used nine pins set in a triangle.

While Massachusetts Puritans bowled at taverns, which provided facilities to attract thirsty customers, they also restricted the sport to discourage gambling. Alleys consisted of planks of wood 90 feet (27 meters) long and 18 inches (46 centimeters) wide, or of lawns such as New York's Bowling Green, which was laid out in 1733.

Before the Civil War, bowling was popular with the sporting fraternity, but the sport was identified mainly with German immigrants. The first indoor bowling alley was the Knickerbocker Alleys, built in New York City, using clay for the bowling surfaces. In 1850, there were more than 400 alleys in New York City, which was considered the bowling capital of North America. However, the early versions of the sport were difficult to master, and there were complaints about gambling and hustlers, so the sport gradually faltered. In addition, several American cities regulated bowling because of gambling.

Bowling was revived in the late nineteenth century, primarily by German Americans in cities such as Chicago, Cincinnati, Detroit, Milwaukee, New York, and St. Louis. Aficionados formed the United Bowling Clubs of New York in 1885. German bowlers laid out lanes in their clubhouse basements, churches, beer gardens, and saloons; they also bowled outdoors at picnic grounds. The game enjoyed some popularity among elite men and women, who had slate bowling lanes installed in their mansions and private clubs.

An alternative form of bowling was duckpins, which uses smaller balls and pins and allows three balls to be tossed in each frame. The origin of duckpins is unclear; it was mentioned in the press as early as 1893, seven years before its reported "invention" at a Baltimore bowling alley owned by two renowned Orioles baseball players, Wilbert Robinson and John McGraw. The National Duck Pin Bowling Congress was established in 1927, and by 1938, there were 200,000 league bowlers and 600,000 duckpin players in the United States. Currently, there are about 60 duckpin alleys in the United States, half of which are in Maryland.

Rise of Organized Bowling

Bowling's first organization was the short-lived 27-club National Bowling Association, which was founded in 1875. The association tried to modernize the sport by regulating the ball size and the rules. It was supplanted in 1890 by the American Bowling League, which eliminated the third ball in a frame. The highest possible score at the time was 200 with 10 strikes.

In 1895, Joe Thum established the American Bowling Congress (ABC), which has governed the sport ever since. The ABC standardized ball weights, pin dimensions, and pin spacing; organized national competitions for men; adopted the 300-point scoring system; and drew up a constitution that barred women in 1906 and nonwhites in 1916.

In 1901, 41 teams from 17 cities competed in the first National Bowling Championship in Chicago, using balls made out of lignum vitae, a very hard wood. Four years later, the "Evertrue," the first rubber ball, was introduced. In 1941, the ABC Hall of Fame was created, the third-oldest such hall in sports.

Meanwhile, the sport gained in popularity. By 1900, New York had about 100 bowling alleys, typically located in saloon basements. They were crude operations in shabby neighborhoods that provided a place for working-class ethnic men to meet. The bowling alleys were affordable and accessible, and they served as centers of the bachelor subculture, which meant a lot of drinking and gambling. At the time, Chicago was another big center of bowling, with 10 bowling leagues and 20,000 players.

In 1907, the ABC held national tournaments for men and women, though the sport had not yet gained respectability among the middle classes. Ten years later in St. Louis, bowling proprietor Dennis Sweeney established the Women's National Bowling Association. The organization was renamed the Women's International Bowling Congress (WBIC) in 1971.

The first great American bowler was Jimmy Smith (born Jimmy Mellilo) of Brooklyn, the unofficial champion from 1905 until 1922, when the first official match play championship was held. In 1927, Smith made a national tour, and while in Denver, Colorado, he played Floretta McCutcheon in two blocks of three games. He won the first set by eight pins, and McCutcheon cap-

tured the second by seven pins (704–697). McCutcheon subsequently went on a 51-city exhibition tour and later established the Mrs. McCutcheon School of Bowling Instruction, which was attended by some 500,000 women.

Bowling flourished during Prohibition when saloons were closed. The disassociation from saloons helped create a family image for the game. It was seen as a clean and inexpensive pastime (a game cost about 25 cents) that tested skill and promoted sociability. There were fewer bowling alleys than before, but the average number of lanes (which cost about $1,500 apiece to construct) rose from 6.5 in 1919 to 10.6 in 1933. Manufacturers such as Brunswick encouraged proprietors to build well-lit facilities in multistory recreation centers to foster the growing female interest, an achievement reflected by the 10,000 members of the Women's National Bowling Association in 1927. The fanciest alleys were downtown, but most were in ethnic working-class neighborhoods.

Bowling remained popular during the Great Depression, experiencing less of a drop in participation than other sports. During the 1930s, the alley was an important part of street corner life, giving young men a hangout where they could socialize, a game to test their skills, and a good place to meet young women. Chicago had 500,000 bowlers and more than 900 leagues by this time, sponsored by church, ethnic, company, and other organizations. The annual *Chicago Evening American* tournament drew 10,000 female competitors.

Nationally, there were 4,600 bowling alleys in 1939, which generated nearly $49 million in revenues, more than major league baseball. The ABC championships offered $170,000 in prize money. Top players in cities such as Detroit and St. Louis joined company teams, especially those sponsored by brewers, which played virtually full time. Men such as Italian American Hank Marino, "Bowler of the Half Century," became ethnic heroes.

African Americans bowled during the saloon era, but they were barred from the ABC and the WIBC. Thereafter, they were unwelcome in bowling alleys and lacked the capital to build facilities in black neighborhoods. In 1939, the National Negro Bowling Association was organized in Detroit to encourage bowling by getting proprietors to keep their lanes open late at night for blacks. Five years later, the organization was renamed the National Bowling Association, to reflect its large nonblack membership.

The NBA used the courts to force the ABC and WIBC to remove their restrictive clause in 1950, though individual alley proprietors continued to discriminate. In

1962, the Congress of Racial Equality and the Student Non-Violent Coordinating Committee, two leading civil rights organizations, staged sit-ins in St. Louis to successfully desegregate local alleys. Then they took their fight to the South, where, in 1968, three young men were killed in the so-called Orangeburg (South Carolina) Massacre over access to the local bowling alley.

Bowling After World War II

In 1947, there were more than 16 million bowlers in the United States, spending over $200 million annually, although the sport still had a seedy image. Within a few years, however, bowling would enjoy its greatest boom, making it a family entertainment, and remaking the bowling alley into the "peoples' country club."

The sport followed many of its players to the suburbs with large new recreational centers that cost hundreds of thousands of dollars to construct and boasted dozens of lanes and new technology. The biggest development was the introduction in 1952 of automatic pin spotters to replace pin boys, making the game move faster. (Pin boys had a reputation for rude and boisterous behavior, so their removal from bowling establishments also contributed to the new image of bowling as a sport that was appropriate for families.)

Other innovations included arrow markers to increase accuracy and underground ball returns to promote safety. Facilities were open 24 hours, and proprietors catered to housewives and children who played in the mornings and afternoons. The new facilities included nurseries for children, snack bars, cocktail lounges, and restaurants. By 1964, there were 39 million bowlers.

While the number has increased since then, the sport experienced a 40 percent drop in league bowling by the 1980s. To help reverse this trend, the United States Bowling Congress was created in 2005, merging the ABC, WIBC, Young American Bowling Alliance, and USA Bowling, serving more than 2.6 million Americans.

Bowling and Television

In the 1950s, bowling received considerable television exposure. The first network coverage was NBC's *Championship Bowling,* and a host of local shows, such as *Make That Spare* (1960–1964) and *Bowling for Dollars* (1968), gave participants a chance to win prizes.

In 1958, Eddie Elias, a successful promoter, agent, and entrepreneur, founded the Professional Bowlers Association (PBA) with 33 members, mainly from Detroit and Chicago brewery-sponsored leagues. Three years later, the association was on network television. ABC telecast the Pro Bowlers Tour hosted by Chris Schenkel (1961–1997), which originally outdrew college football and basketball. Bowling was so popular that in 1964, Don Carter, considered the greatest bowler of all time, became the first athlete to sign a $1 million endorsement deal, with bowling manufacturer Ebonite. The Ladies Pro Bowlers Tour, established in 1981 (now the Professional Women's Bowling Association) was one of the first women's pro sports to appear on television.

The PBA was bought in 2000 by three former Microsoft executives—Rob Glaswer, Chris Peters, and Mike Slade—who hoped to save the organization by assuming its debts and providing imaginative leadership for the future. PBA events are covered by ESPN on Sunday afternoons. Prize money doubled to $5.6 million in 2009. The current star is Walter Ray Williams, Jr., a six-time Player of the Year who holds the records for all-time PBA career titles (44) and earnings (more than $4 million).

In 2010, the PBA gave Kelly Kulick, the winner of the Women's World Championship, a spot in its Tournament of Champions. Kulick averaged 226 for 90 games and won the title, 265–195 over Chris Barnes. She is the first woman to win a PBA crown.

Steven A. Riess

See also: Urbanization.

Further Reading

Browne, Christopher, prod. *A League of Ordinary Gentlemen.* New York: Magnolia Home Entertainment, 2006.

Rigali, James H., and John C. Walter. "The Integration of the American Bowling Congress: The Buffalo Experience." *Afro-Americans in New York Life and History* 29:2 (July 2005): 7–43.

Hemmer, John G., and W.J. Kenna. *The Western Bowlers' Journal Bowling Encyclopedia: A History of Bowling.* Chicago: Western Bowlers' Journal, 1904.

Hurley, Andrew. *Diners, Bowling Alleys and Trailer Parks: Chasing the American Dream in the Postwar Consumer Culture.* New York: Basic Books, 2001.

Riess, Steven A. *City Games: The Evolution of American Urban Society and the Rise of Sports.* Urbana: University of Illinois Press, 1989.

Weiskopf, Herman. *The Perfect Game: The World of Bowling.* Englewood Cliffs, NJ: Prentice Hall, 1978.

Boxing

First becoming popular in America during the early nineteenth century, boxing is a sport in which two participants use their fists—originally bare and, later, in padded gloves—to score points or knockouts by landing blows against opponents. Bouts usually are conducted in rings—actually, enclosed squares surrounded by ropes—and divided into a number of timed rounds. A referee patrols the ring to prevent illegal blows and holds. Judges score points and name the winner, unless a fighter is incapacitated by a punch, leading to a knockout or a technical knockout.

Given the sport's violent nature, the American public exhibited a mixed attitude toward boxing, condemning it as brutal, but also celebrating it as a symbol of manliness and courage. This ambivalent attitude led to restrictive legislation against boxing, often putting it on the margins of legitimate recreational activity. Another issue that divided the public was boxing's traditional association with high-stakes gambling and suspicions that the outcomes of big fights may be determined beforehand by unscrupulous officials, some with connections to the criminal underworld.

As for the boxers themselves, most have been working-class men (and, very recently, women), often from the most impoverished and lowest-status ethnic and racial groups, who have tried to use the sport to gain upward social and economic mobility. Prizefighting was permitted in only a few states until after World War I, when it became one of the most popular spectator sports in North America, while amateur boxing remained a widely practiced participatory sport.

Politicians, organized crime networks, business tycoons, state athletic commissions, and world sanctioning organizations—many of which have not served the athletes or the sport well—all have had a hand in shaping the prizefighting, or professional boxing, industry. Not surprisingly, boxing long has been beset by controversy over the integrity of the sport and its impact on the health of its practitioners.

Origins of Boxing

The sport of boxing dates to ancient times and was part of the Greek Olympic games in 688 B.C.E. It largely disappeared from the historical record from approximately 500 C.E. through the early 1700s, when it reemerged in the form of bare-knuckle fighting in England.

The first codified boxing rules, drafted by Jack Broughton in 1743, specified that each match would go on for an unlimited number of rounds, until one of the boxers was knocked down and could not continue within a half-minute time limit. While permitting wrestling holds and mauling, the "Broughton rules" prohibited eye gouging, hitting below the belt, and striking a fallen opponent. Broughton also invented boxing gloves—or "mufflers"—which, at the time, were used only in sparring contests. Early bare-knuckle bouts were fought in a circle formed by spectators around the fighters; the purse was divided publicly after the bout, with two-thirds given to the winner.

In 1838, the Broughton rules were modified to introduce a 24-foot (7.3-meter) square ring made of turf and formed by eight stakes and ropes. Colored handkerchiefs tied onto the stakes of the opposite corners were claimed by the winner as trophies. The new "London Prize Ring rules" banned holding stones in your hands, low blows, head-butting, kicking, hitting below the waist, and biting as foul tactics; they also established guidelines for umpires, referees, seconds, and "bottle-holders." Rounds lasted until a knockdown, and then fighters had 30 seconds to rest, and then eight more seconds to return to the scratch line.

Rise of Boxing in North America

Before the sport became widely popular in the United States, slave owners often sponsored matches between slaves and wagered money on the outcome, sometimes granting slaves their freedom as a prize for a victorious fight. Bill "The Black Terror" Richmond of Staten Island, New York, for example, was a former slave who traveled to England in 1809 and fought as a protégé of the Duke of Northumberland. In 1810 and 1811, Tom Molyneaux, a former slave from Virginia who was trained by Richmond, twice challenged and lost to English champion Tom Cribb; despite the losses, Molyneaux was hailed as a celebrity in England.

The first recognized U.S. bare-knuckle bout took place between Jacob Hyer and Tom Beasley in New York in 1816. The victorious Hyer generally is referred to as the "Father of the American Ring." These early bouts were chronicled in the periodical *American Fistiana* and later were compiled into a history of U.S. pugilism, or boxing, of the same title, first published in 1849.

U.S. pugilism developed in tandem with urbanization and the commercialization of leisure culture, especially in immigrant hubs such as Baltimore, Boston, New Orleans, New York, and Philadelphia. Urban neighborhoods, rife with interethnic conflicts and labor tensions, served as breeding grounds for aspiring boxers, who otherwise had few prospects for upward mobility or chances at fame. The ethnic working class spent much of their leisure time in drinking establishments—saloons, brothels, and taverns—where boxing matches generally were staged, complete with vigorous betting wagered on the side.

The bare-knuckle contests took on strong nationalistic undertones, epitomized by Hyer's son Tom, who became the U.S. heavyweight champion when he defeated Yankee Sullivan (James Ambrose) on February 7, 1849, at Still Pond Creek, Maryland. Sullivan, who enjoyed a maverick reputation, ran a saloon in New York, where he fought many of the best boxers of the day, although he only claimed the heavyweight title after Hyer's retirement in 1851.

Notwithstanding the actual practice, boxing was prohibited by law in many states because of the violence (and occasional deaths), the riotous crowds, and the gambling. New Jersey was the first state to implement legislation against prizefighting in 1835; Massachusetts followed suit in 1849, and New York in 1858. By the 1880s, all 38 existing states had made boxing illegal.

On October 12, 1853, Sullivan met John Morrissey for the heavyweight championship in Boston Corners, New York. After the thirty-sixth round, a riot broke out when Sullivan hit Morrissey while he was down, and spectators spilled into the ring. After the chaos was quelled, the referee awarded the fight to Morrissey based on low blows and Sullivan's failure to come to scratch, the line in the middle of the ring. On October 20, 1858, Morrissey defeated John C. Heenan at Long Point, Canada, to become the heavyweight champion of America (the United States and Canada).

After the bout, Morrissey retired from boxing, while Heenan went on to meet British champion Tom Sayers in Farnborough, England, on April 17, 1860, for a world championship contest that was invested with ideas of American versus British manliness. Heenan seemed to be making his way toward victory, but after the forty-second round, the crowd broke into the ring and the bout was declared a draw, with each boxer awarded a championship belt.

Irish Americans

Amid the great wave of Irish immigration in the mid-nineteenth century, an increasing number of first- and second-generation Irish immigrants became involved in boxing, and by the late nineteenth century, most champions were of Irish descent. While these immigrant youth were used to settling scores in brawls in the streets, boxing matches offered them a payday, social mobility, and respect among their peers. Neighborhood gangs often had close links to political organizations that had a stake in the ongoing religious (Protestant versus Catholic), political (Whig versus Democrat), and citizenship (nativist versus immigrant) debates. New York's notoriously corrupt Tammany Hall, for example, hired physically

strong Irish men to intimidate wavering voters from their own ranks as well as members of their rival organizations, such as the anti-Catholic Know-Nothing or American Party. The best known of these so-called shoulder-hitters was Morrissey, who, after retiring from boxing, was elected to the U.S. House of Representatives in 1866 and—after a falling-out with Tammany Hall—became a New York state senator in 1875.

A curious symbiosis between sports and politics was forged: politicians sponsored fighters, served as managers and matchmakers, and used their leverage with the police to gain approval and protection for semipublic boxing matches. Newspapers had an important role in promoting boxing matches, and boxers used the papers to issue challenges to one another through printed advertisements, known as "cards." Richard Kyle Fox, an Irish immigrant and the publisher of the *National Police Gazette,* was one of the most prominent promoters. He declared the winners of fights and gave out championship belts to boxers whom he considered the best in each weight class. Popular boxing reporting appeared in a number of newspapers and periodicals, including the *Boston Post,* the *Daily Picayune* (New Orleans), *Leslie's Weekly Illustrated* (New York), the *New York Clipper,* the *New York Herald,* and *The Spirit of the Times* (New York).

A late-nineteenth-century culture of physicality that celebrated masculine prowess—in particular, the white male body—brought wider attention to sports, but boxing provided the era's most famous hero and raised the sport's financial stakes to new levels. Irish American John L. Sullivan became known for his crowd-pleasing bravado, offering a handsome sum of money to any man of any size who would challenge him in the ring. The ability of the "Boston Strong Boy" to knock his opponents out turned the charismatic Sullivan into a publicity magnet, particularly embraced by working-class men.

On February 2, 1882, when Sullivan fought the reigning champion, Patrick "Paddy" Ryan, for the heavyweight crown in Mississippi City, Mississippi, both boxers brought $25,000 to the ring under the agreement "winner takes all." The fight, which Sullivan won, originally had been scheduled to take place in New Orleans, but, as often was the case with the illegal matches, it had to be moved across state lines to evade the law.

On July 8, 1889, Sullivan engaged in a bout in Richburg, Mississippi, with Jake Kilrain, who previously had been declared heavyweight champion by

Fox. After 75 rounds, Kilrain was unable to continue in what turned out to be the last heavyweight bare-knuckle championship fight.

Legalized Prizefighting

Boxing's status improved near the end of the century, as it became known as the "manly art of self-defense." In 1888, the Amateur Athletic Union began organizing local, state, and national amateur boxing championships in the United States. This encouraged the legalization of boxing, first in Texas in 1889, and then New Orleans in 1890.

On September 7, 1892, John L. Sullivan met James J. "Gentleman Jim" Corbett in the three-day "Carnival of Champions" tournament, which also included a featherweight fight between George Dixon and Jack Skelly, and a lightweight match between Jack Mc-Auliffe and Billy Myer. It was a legal event organized by the Pelican Athletic Club in New Orleans, and the boxers followed the Marquis of Queensberry rules.

Drafted by John Graham Chambers, a member of England's Amateur Athletic Club, under the sponsorship of John Sholto Douglas, the ninth Marquis of Queensberry, in 1867, the Queensberry rules introduced boxing gloves, three-minute rounds—with a minute between rounds and ten seconds to get up after a knockdown—while banning wrestling and hugging holds. Sullivan and Corbett both wore 5-ounce (142-gram) gloves to the contest. The younger and more technically skillful Corbett knocked out the aging Sullivan in the twenty-first round, marking the demise of a decade-old hero who had turned boxing into a major sporting attraction.

Boxing soon was legalized in New York under the Horton Law (1896–1900), which allowed athletic clubs licensed by local municipalities to organize sparring sessions. In practice, these "exhibition contests" often were fronts for prizefights, at times prevented and at other times ignored by the police. Prizefighting was legalized in Nevada (1897) and Colorado (1899), although the latter state soon repealed its decision.

African American and Women Boxers in the Late Nineteenth Century

Although boxing initially was not segregated along racial lines, by the end of the nineteenth century, interracial matches, especially among heavyweights, were rare. John L. Sullivan adamantly refused to meet any nonwhite challengers during his career, while Corbett fought an interracial match to a 61-round draw against the popular Peter "Black Prince" Jackson in San Francisco on May 21, 1891. But Corbett also drew the color line as champion. The so-called Negro circuit produced many boxers of renown, including Canadian George "Little Chocolate" Dixon, the first black fighter to win a world boxing championship in 1890 as a bantamweight, and Joe Gans, lightweight champion of the world from 1902 to 1908.

In addition, some women in late-nineteenth-century North America sporadically stepped into the ring. The first known women's boxing match was Nell Saunders's 1876 victory over Rose Harland in New York City; in 1884, Nellie Stewart of Norfolk, Virginia, was crowned the first "Female Champion of the World."

Boxing, 1900–1920

The early twentieth century saw a lull in the mainstream popularity of boxing, which operated with little legal protection. Prizefighting was banned in New York in 1900 (although boxing clubs survived there under the guise of "membership" clubs) and in Chicago in 1905. San Francisco became the main scene for championship fights under the protection of city boss Abe Reuf, who also was the city's leading boxing promoter.

The volatile racial relations of the Progressive Era aided antiboxing crusades across the nation. The rise of African American Jack Johnson as the first publicly acknowledged black fighter to challenge for the heavyweight championship raised violent opposition. On December 26, 1908, the "Galveston Giant," as Johnson was known, defeated Canadian Tommy Burns in Sydney, Australia, upsetting the century-long reign of white boxers for the most prestigious boxing crown. This shocked Americans who believed in the supremacy of the white race and led to an ongoing quest for the "Great White Hope."

Former champion Jim Jeffries agreed to come out of retirement to challenge Johnson in Reno, Nevada, the only state that would allow the fight, on July 4, 1910. In the promotions, Johnson was billed as the "Negroes' Deliverer" and Jeffries as the "Hope of the White Race." Jeffries's loss to Johnson provoked riots and mob violence throughout the United States, galvanizing a movement to ban prizefighting outright. At a time when motion pictures were becoming a popular form of entertainment, many states banned the showing of the Johnson–Jeffries fight film. This prompted Congress in 1912 to bar the interstate commerce of all fight films for public viewing, a ban that lasted until 1940.

Johnson finally was dethroned in Havana, Cuba, on April 15, 1915, by Jess Willard, who restored the racial status quo in and out of the ring. After Johnson, no African American boxer would get a shot at the heavyweight title until 1937.

Some restrictions on boxing broke down in the 1910s, with New York's Frawley Law, which allowed for "no decision" contests from 1911 to 1917, and in California, four-round bouts were allowed between 1914 and 1924. As the United States' entry into World War I became imminent, boxing received widespread positive publicity as part of soldiers' training for combat, prompting many states to allow prizefights again, including New Jersey, whose Hurley Law in 1918 permitted eight-round bouts.

Interwar Years

The 1920s often are referred to in the United States as the "golden age of sports," when large numbers of people enjoyed prosperity and had more leisure time than ever before. Spectator sports boomed, and each sport seemed to have its own great hero. In New York in 1920, the Walker Act, sponsored by James J. Walker, minority leader of the state senate, legalized prizefights, allowed them to be concluded by a decision, and established the first state athletic commission to regulate the industry. Other states soon followed.

In 1921, the National Boxing Association, comprising the state commissions and their international equivalents, was formed to sanction world championship title bouts. Promoter George "Tex" Rickard made a ten-year arrangement to stage boxing shows at New York's Madison Square Garden, a lucrative deal that turned Rickard into the preeminent boxing promoter and established New York as the sport's national center. Radio broadcasting of fights, publication of Nat Fleischer's magazine *The Ring* (launched in February 1922), and newspaper coverage of heavyweight champion Jack Dempsey turned the preeminent prizefighter of the era into an international superstar.

Under the tutelage of manager Jack "Doc" Kearns, Dempsey, known as the "Manassa Mauler," became a national celebrity, hailed as the incarnation of white masculine "Americanness." Dempsey, together with the emerging mass entertainment industry, contributed to boxing's rising popularity and turned the sport into

big business. It is estimated that some 12 million Americans followed prizefighting in the 1920s. Men and women of all socioeconomic backgrounds—including members of high society—wanted to be seen at fights, especially championship bouts at arenas such as Madison Square Garden.

Dempsey's most popular fights were billed as patriotic contests against foreign challengers, including Georges Carpentier of France and Luis "Wild Bull of the Pampas" Firpo of Argentina. On July 2, 1921, Dempsey defeated Carpentier in New Jersey in a fight dubbed the "Battle of the Century," the first bout sanctioned by the National Boxing Association. It was also the first world title fight broadcast over radio and the first million-dollar gate, with gross receipts of $1,789,238.

Notwithstanding his popularity, Dempsey frequently was taken to task for his military record. Unlike his nemesis, Gene Tunney, who had served in the U.S. Marine Corps during World War I and was celebrated as a war hero, Dempsey's public image was shadowed by insinuations of draft dodging. On September 23, 1926, Tunney dethroned Dempsey in Philadelphia before more than 120,000 spectators who paid a total of $1.8 million to attend. Their rematch at Soldier Field in Chicago on September 22, 1927, produced a gate of $2.65 million, a record that stood for more than 50 years.

The 1927 fight was one of the most controversial pugilistic encounters of all times. In the seventh round, Dempsey knocked down Tunney, but the referee did not start the count until Dempsey had retreated to the farthest neutral corner, giving Tunney extra time to recover. He went on to win the bout, which became known in fistic annals as the "long-count" fight.

Like other heavyweight champions, Dempsey refused to meet any African American challengers, particularly the number-one contender, Harry Wills. However, the 1920s saw the emergence of the first black middleweight champion when Theodore "Tiger" Flowers defeated Harry Greb in New York on February 26, 1926. The ring was dominated by Americans, although there were significant changes in their ethnicity.

After the overwhelming dominance of Irish boxers until 1916, the early decades of the twentieth century experienced a brief Jewish boxing boom. Alongside increasing Eastern European immigration, there were no fewer than 26 Jewish world champions between the years 1910 and 1940; Jews also had a strong presence in boxing as trainers, managers, and promoters. The most famous Jewish boxer, lightweight Benny Leonard (Benjamin Leiner), held his championship title for eight years, from 1917 to 1925. Barney Ross (Beryl

Jack Dempsey knocked down Gene Tunney in the seventh round of their heavyweight championship rematch in 1927—dubbed the "long-count fight"—but Tunney retained the title. The gate of $2.65 million at Chicago's Soldier Field was a record. *(New York Daily News/Getty Images)*

David Rosofsky) won the world championship in three weight categories: lightweight, junior welterweight, and welterweight.

When Max "Slapsie Maxie" Rosenbloom, the world light heavyweight champion from 1930 to 1934, was defeated by Bob Olin in New York on November 16, 1934, it marked the last time two Jews fought for a championship. After 1936, Italian Americans reigned in the boxing ring for more than a decade, while Jews mainly were active in the business side of boxing, as promoters (Mike Jacobs, the leading promoter in the late 1930s and 1940s), writers (Nat Fleischer, founder of *The Ring* magazine), or entrepreneurs (Jacob Colomb, founder of Everlast boxing gear).

The prominence of Italian Americans in the ring reflected that group's widespread poverty. Most Italian immigrants who came to America near the turn of the century were unskilled and uneducated, and they were slated for the lowest occupational positions. They also became the object of discrimination by mainstream society, who stereotyped them as dangerous criminals and even questioned whether they were white. Many first- and second-generation Italian boxers fought under Anglicized aliases. For example, Giuseppe Carrora became lightweight champion in 1921 as Johnny Dundee.

The greatest fighter of the era was not an Italian, but an African American—Joe Louis (Joseph Louis Barrow), who, on June 22, 1937, defeated James Braddock in Chicago to become the second African American world heavyweight champion. Promoted by Jacobs and African American managers John Roxborough and Julian Black, Louis's career—unlike that of Jack Johnson before him—was celebrated in the United States. Louis was billed in the media as a symbol of American democratic ideals, as opposed to the oppressive regime of Nazi Germany, homeland of Louis's nemesis Max Schmeling, who had knocked out the American boxer in 1936. Their rematch in New York on June 22, 1938, with the stakes much higher, was Louis's most famous bout. With his first-round knockout victory, Louis was hailed as a victor for American democracy and racial egalitarianism, while Schmeling was depicted as a token for Nazi nationalism and racism—though, in fact, Schmeling had assisted Jews in Germany. A month after the Japanese attack on Pearl Harbor on December 7, 1941, pushed the United States into World War II, Louis enlisted in the U.S. Army; he mainly performed in exhibition tours overseas, while his image was used by the Office of War Information to publicize the war effort.

Even as African Americans were rising in the male boxing world, female boxing remained very much on the fringes. In 1910, Crystal Bennett of Kansas City, Missouri, was crowned "Female Lightweight Champion of the World." In the 1920s, boxing was part of ladies' health education in Boston. Then, in the 1930s, former middleweight champion Mickey Walker toured the United States with a troupe of fighting women.

In the interwar era, control of boxing shifted away from politicians to organized crime networks. In ethnic neighborhoods where boxing gyms were located, fighters and criminals—both scraping for a living—grew up together or met later on, giving underworld figures ready access to boxers and their handlers. The structural deficiencies in boxing, including dysfunctional state athletic commissions and the lack of a federal governing body, facilitated corruption in the sport. During the Great Depression, when boxing was second in popularity only to baseball, notable mobsters—among them, Paul John "Frankie" Carbo, Max "Boo Boo" Hoff, and Owen "Owney" Madden—moved in on the business side of the sport.

The gangsters took a cut from boxers' purses—if not stealing them outright—and there also was money to be made from selling tickets and fixing fights. Abetted by a nexus of "fronts" across the nation, they served as de facto managers and matchmakers, and few boxers could become contenders, let alone champions, without their blessing. Carbo, for example, made his living from boxing and claimed a virtual monopoly on the middleweight division, while Madden managed many heavyweights, including the Italian heavyweight champion Primo Carnera. Notorious for his lack of boxing skill, Carnera won many fights in the 1930s amid cries of foul play, and his 1967 obituary in *The New York Times* referred to his career as a "hoax."

As a result of fight fixing, bribery, and extortion, the criminal influence penetrated all aspects of prizefighting. Boxers, trainers, managers, matchmakers, promoters, fight officials, athletic commissions, and even sportswriters all were influenced by the underworld.

Postwar Era Through the 1980s

The postwar era witnessed enormous public interest in prizefighting, especially among the urban ethnic working class. Boxing was a sport that perfectly fit the needs of the new medium of television, with its constant action and all the activity focused in a small space. By 1950, televised boxing shows—including ABC's *Wednesday Night Fights* from Chicago and NBC's *Gillette Friday Night Fights* (1948–1960) from New York on prime time—gave exposure to popular boxers, including Carmen Basilio, Rocky Graziano (Rocco Barbella), Jake LaMotta, Cuban Kid Gavilán (Gerardo Gonzalez), and African American "Sugar Ray" Robinson (Walker Smith, Jr.), as well as to many previously unknown fighters, especially in the welterweight and middleweight divisions. In 1955, *Gillette Friday Night Fights,* broadcast from the Madison Square Garden, won an Emmy Award for best sports program of the year. The popularity of boxing on television and the revenues it generated only intensified the sport's already rampant corruption and ties to organized crime, which were depicted in a slew of popular films of the day, including *Body and Soul* (1947), *Champion* (1949), *The Set-Up* (1949), *On the Waterfront* (1954), *The Harder They Fall* (1956), and *Somebody Up There Likes Me* (1956).

The pattern of ethnic succession continued after World War II, when African Americans began to dominate the sport, followed by Italians and Mexicans. Louis, the preeminent figure in the ring, retired in 1949, after 25 successful title defenses. However, financial problems forced him back into the ring for a few more bouts, including his final fight on October 26, 1951, when Italian American Rocky Marciano defeated him. One year later, Marciano dethroned African American "Jersey Joe" Walcott to become the new superstar heavyweight champion.

The 1950s also saw the emergence of a famed female boxer, "Battling" Barbara Buttrick, of Great Britain, who won the first "Undisputed Women's World Boxing Title" against Phyllis Kugler in San Antonio, Texas, on October 6, 1957. Buttrick was the first woman boxer to appear in *The Ring* (1957 and 1959), and she fought Gloria Adams in the first women's boxing bout ever broadcast by a radio station, WCKR Miami, on October 1, 1959.

The International Boxing Club

During the 1950s, the International Boxing Club (IBC) controlled the promotional side of boxing, while the underworld continued to exercise covert control of the matchmaking process. In January 1949, Chicago businessmen James D. Norris and Arthur M. Wirtz incorporated the International Boxing Club of Illinois and New York to promote championship boxing in major cities in the United States. Within months, they had gained control of most boxing promotions. Between 1949 and 1953 alone, they staged 36 of 44 championship bouts.

The sweeping takeover was accomplished through several tactics, beginning with their ownership of the main fight arenas, including Chicago Stadium, Detroit's Olympia Stadium, Madison Square Garden, and the St. Louis Arena. Second, to eliminate competition, they bought or made special agreements with all their major promotional rivals. Third, they imposed exclusive three- to five-year contracts on all boxers, complete with film and broadcasting rights, making it next to impossible for unaffiliated contenders to get championship bouts. Finally, their close connections with the underworld helped them secure a monopoly on the heavyweight, middleweight, and welterweight divisions.

These questionable business practices led the Federal Bureau of Investigation and the U.S. Department of Justice to launch investigations into the prizefighting business, resulting in antitrust action against the IBC, which controlled the rights to televise, broadcast, and film boxing matches. In *United States v. International Boxing Club of New York* (1955), a federal district court found the IBC guilty of monopolizing the promotion of professional championship matches as interstate commerce. The court ordered the IBC to be dissolved and denied its exclusive rights to Madison Square Garden and Chicago Stadium, ordering Norris and Wirtz to sell all of their stock in Madison Square Garden. The IBC appealed, but in 1959, the U.S. Supreme Court upheld the ruling.

Carbo and several other mobsters who had control of the industry were arrested soon after. Carbo, Frank "Blinky" Palermo, Joe Sica, Louis Dragna, and Truman Gibson were found guilty of extortion, bribery, and racketeering and sentenced to fines and imprisonment.

Muhammad Ali Era

During the 1960s, several sanctioning organizations were established to award championship belts and to rank contenders worldwide, which only served to increase chaos in the industry. The National Boxing Association was renamed the World Boxing Association in 1962, the World Boxing Council was created in 1963, and the North American Boxing Federation came into being in 1969. From then on, championships were fought under the rules and regulations of each individual organization. Many title bouts were organized outside of North America and broadcast on closed-circuit television in the United States.

African American champions dominated the heavyweight division—most notably Muhammad Ali (Cassius Clay), Joe Frazier, and George Foreman—and raised the popularity of the sport worldwide, as many fans appreciated the boxers' skills and identified with their underdog status. Ali had a unique career, starting off as a popular amateur Olympic champion before upsetting the fearsome Sonny Liston in 1964. However, by joining the Nation of Islam, an early advocate of Black Power, and by refusing to serve in the U.S. armed forces in Vietnam, the witty and articulate Ali represented a new type of champion, one who brought attention to the politics of racial relations at home while garnering attention abroad for his pacifist stance—all the while jeopardizing his career.

Among Ali's most popular fights were a trilogy of bouts with "Smokin'" Joe Frazier and his second heavyweight title against Foreman in Kinshasa, Zaire (now Congo), on October 30, 1974, known as the "Rumble in the Jungle." During his heyday and even after his retirement in 1981, Ali often was named as the most famous athlete in the world.

Post-Ali Era

In the 1980s, the welterweight and middleweight divisions produced a number of outstanding boxers, including African Americans "Sugar" Ray Leonard, "Marvelous" Marvin Hagler, and Thomas "Hit Man" Hearns and Latinos Julio César Chávez, Hector "Macho" Camacho, and Roberto Duran. Two legendary duels between Leonard and Duran, in particular, epitomized the African American and Latino dominance of the lower weight categories.

The most prominent figure in the ring during the late twentieth century was an African American, "Iron" Mike Tyson, who on November 22, 1986, knocked out Trevor Berbick of Jamaica in the second round of his first title bout to become, at age 20, the youngest heavyweight champion in prizefighting history. Tyson's ferocious early-round knockouts produced the biggest live gates and television sales ever seen in boxing, turning him into an instant celebrity across the globe. However, his frequent problems with the law, complete with several convictions and prison sentences, brought negative publicity to the sport. No charismatic heavyweight emerged to fill the gap, and network television dropped the broadcasting of boxing for a decade.

Turn of the Twenty-First Century

Late-twentieth-century boxing was dominated by African Americans in the middleweight divisions and up, and by Latinos in the lighter weight categories. Mexicans, in particular, already had strong traditions of boxing in their homeland. Boxing gyms in the American barrios provided a cheap athletic option, while providing skills to defend oneself amid interethnic feuds. Superstar Latino boxers such as Oscar De La Hoya and Felix Trinidad brought a mainstream following to the sport, and Spanish-language television stations attracted an increasing number of Latino viewers, especially in the Southwest.

At the same time, a growing cohort of women became involved in the sport, and some, most notably Christy Martin, Laila Ali (daughter of Muhammad Ali), and Lucia Rijker, even claimed celebrity status. This surge in women's boxing was reflected in several films, including *Shadow Boxers* (2000), *Against the Ropes* (2004), *Girl Fight* (2000), *New Waterford Girl* (2000), and *Million Dollar Baby* (2005), which won the Academy Award for best motion picture.

Prizefighting in the United States has offered successive groups of impoverished athletes the means to demonstrate their physical prowess, make a living, and bolster their sense of community. The sport is a lucrative business for some, mainly the promoters, but only 5 percent of professional boxers make it to the world championship level. The world sanctioning bodies today grant championships in 17 different weight divisions (as opposed to the original eight), all with different champions, disparate ratings, and inconsistent regulations.

In the 1990s, Senators John McCain of Arizona and Richard Bryan of Nevada initiated government intervention in the industry to establish minimum health and safety standards, uniform business policies, and a national umbrella organization for the sport. This led to the Professional Boxing Safety Act of 1996 and the Muhammad Ali Boxing Reform Act of 2000, both of which were enacted into federal law.

Although these laws brought about some generally accepted business principles and rules regarding the deductions made from boxers' purses, many of their provisions regulating the prizefighting industry remain to be implemented. The initiative for a national umbrella organization stalled, and boxers have no collective forum protecting their interests and no minimum social benefits, health and life insurance, or basic pension plans. The sport continues to grapple with unscrupulous promoters, incongruous regulations, and rigged results worldwide.

Even more threatening to boxers than corrupt promoters or the lack of bargaining rights is the potential for brain injury, particularly a form of neurodegenerative disease or dementia known as *dementia pugilistica*. It long has been known—indeed, it is a cliché of the sport—that experienced boxers often suffer a number of symptoms, particularly as they age, including loss of memory, declining mental acuity, speech problems, and physical unsteadiness. And it long has been suspected that these symptoms were the result of repeated blows to the head, even though symptoms of dementia pugilistica may not arise for up to 20 years after the boxer has left the ring.

In recent years, advances in brain research and new diagnostic tools have allowed scientists a better understanding of the mechanics of this form of dementia, including the loss of neurons, buildup of water on the brain (hydrocephalus), the accumulation of different forms of plaque on the brain, and the scarring of brain tissue. In some notable cases, such as that of Ali, another degenerative brain and nervous system disorder—Parkinson's disease—may be linked to the repeated blows to the head received by boxers and other contact-sport athletes, such as football players.

The growing scientific evidence linking boxing to degenerative brain disorders has led to renewed calls for banning professional boxing in recent years. If that cannot be achieved, reformers seek to require that professional boxers wear the kind of protective headgear already required in most amateur and all Olympic bouts. However, some experts question the extent to which such protective headgear prevents brain injury.

Benita Heiskanen

See also: Crime, Organized; Gambling; Injuries, Protection Against and Remediation of; Violence in Sports.

Further Reading

Erenberg, Lewis A. *The Greatest Fight of Our Generation: Louis vs. Schmeling.* New York: Oxford University Press, 2006.

Gorn, Elliott J. *The Manly Art: Bare-Knuckle Prize Fighting in America.* Ithaca, NY: Cornell University Press, 1986.

Heiskanen, Benita. "The *Latinization* of Boxing: A Texas Case-Study." *Journal of Sport History* 32:1 (Spring 2005): 45–66.

Hietala, Thomas R. *The Fight of the Century: Jack Johnson, Joe Louis, and the Struggle for Racial Equality.* Armonk, NY: M.E. Sharpe, 2002.

Isenberg, Michael T. *John L. Sullivan and His America*. Urbana: University of Illinois Press, 1988.

Roberts, Randy. *Jack Dempsey: The Manassa Mauler*. Baton Rouge: Louisiana State University Press, 1979.

————. *Papa Jack: Jack Johnson and the Era of White Hopes*. New York: Free Press, 1983.

Sammons, Jeffrey, T. *Beyond the Ring: The Role of Boxing in American Society*. Urbana: University of Illinois Press, 1988.

Braves, Atlanta/Milwaukee/Boston

The Atlanta Braves, winners of three World Series and 11 National League pennants, is the oldest continuously operating U.S. sports franchise. The team dates back to the Boston Red Stockings, which in 1876 formed the core of the Boston Red Caps, an original National League squad, later renamed the Beaneaters, Doves, Rustlers, and Bees. The name that eventually stuck was the Boston Braves.

The team was one of Major League Baseball's weakest-performing and least profitable franchises until 1953, when the team moved to Milwaukee, seeking greater returns and success on the playing field. This was the first franchise move in Major League Baseball in 50 years. Then, just 13 years later, the club moved to Atlanta, again in search of more revenue. There, team owner Ted Turner was an innovator in cable broadcasting, and his club became a dominant National League squad, with 11 division championships between 1995 and 2005. The Braves returned to the National League Division Series in 2010, losing in four games to the San Francisco Giants.

Rise and Fall of the Triumvirs: Boston, 1871–1952

In 1871, Harry Wright, manager of the Cincinnati Red Stockings, the first professional team, moved to Boston with shortstop and brother George Wright and other Cincinnati players to play for Ivers Whitney Adams, a twine manufacturer and aspiring baseball owner. Adams's team, called the Boston Red Stockings, played in the National Association of Professional Base Ball Players, the first professional baseball league. They won four straight pennants (1872–1875) while playing at the South End Grounds. In 1876, when the more business-oriented National League supplanted the National Association, the Red Stockings franchise, owned by Nicholas T. Apollonio, became the Red Caps.

Under new owner Arthur Soden, the Red Caps took consecutive National League championships in 1877 and 1878. Then, in 1879, after shortstop George Wright and two other stars left the Red Caps, Soden and his two partners, known together as the Triumvirs, drew up baseball's reserve clause, a rule intended to keep players from jumping from team to team and to drive down salaries. In 1883, the Boston club, renamed the Beaneaters, won the pennant. The Triumvirs attracted Irish fans by signing Irish players, such as colorful catcher and right fielder Mike "King" Kelly, a national favorite who was acquired from the Chicago White Stockings for $10,000.

In 1890, Boston hired manager Frank Selee, who brought with him rookie fireballer Charles "Kid" Nichols. Nichols won 297 games for Boston over the next decade, the most wins by a pitcher in a ten-year span. Selee piloted the club superbly, winning five National League pennants (1891–1893, 1897–1898). Three straight championships (1891–1893) garnered Boston permanent possession of the Dauvray Cup, named after the wife of New York Giants player John Montgomery Ward, actress Helen Dauvray. In 1894, the club's insufficiently insured wooden ballpark burned down, and a smaller field replaced it.

The emergence of a rival major league in 1901 brought unwanted competition to the National League. Several Beaneaters stars jumped to the new American League franchise in Boston, then known as the Americans. The Beaneaters finished no better than sixth from 1903 to 1912. The team changed its name to the Doves in 1907 and to the Rustlers in 1911.

In 1911, John Montgomery Ward formed a syndicate to buy the team and became its president. Ward tried to revive the team by naming them the Braves, to give the club an identity that was infused with spirit and pride. The name also honored majority owner James Gaffney, a leader of New York City's Tammany Hall political machine, whose members were nicknamed "Braves." The ball club was the first major professional team to carry a Native American name. Ward also redesigned the club's plain uniforms to feature a colorful Native American profile.

In 1914, the Braves were in last place in early July, 15 games out of first place, but went on to capture the top spot in a remarkable turnaround, going 66–18 for rest of the season. The "Miracle Braves" under manager George Stallings pulled off a sweep of the Philadelphia Athletics in a shocking World Series upset. One year later, the team built Braves Field, a fireproof stadium seating 40,000.

The Braves contended in 1915 and 1916, and then began a lengthy stretch of weak teams and meager attendance, primarily under owner Emil Fuchs, who bought the team in 1923. From 1917 through 1932, the Braves finished only once in the first division and returned to the second division from 1935 to 1945. Fuchs sold the team in 1935 to Red Sox president Bob Quinn, and the team briefly was renamed the Bees until 1941.

In 1944, three construction company owners—Lou Perini, Guido Rugo, and Joe Marey, known as the "Three Little Steam Shovels"—bought the team. The team finally became a contender in 1946, led by star hurlers Warren Spahn and Johnny Sain. The two pitchers were so much better than the rest of the squad that sportswriters described the rotation as "Spahn, Sain, then pray for rain." The chant became famous in 1948, when the Braves returned to the World Series for the first time since 1914, losing to the Cleveland Indians in six games. Spahn continued to pitch for the Braves through 1964, winning all but 7 of his 363 career wins for them.

Seduced and Abandoned? Milwaukee, 1953–1965

The Braves' attendance soon returned to its normal low level, and the team lost $500,000 in 1952. The next season, the Steam Shovels moved the Braves to Milwaukee, where they owned the Milwaukee Brewers, the Braves' top minor league club. Milwaukee badly wanted a major league franchise to demonstrate its progressive environment and to promote business, and the city provided the team with the County Stadium.

Featuring exciting young sluggers Hank Aaron and Eddie Mathews and a sterling pitching staff still led by Spahn, the team's attendance exploded to a record 1.8 million in 1953. The Braves enjoyed some of the largest profits of any major league team, which inspired other money-losing franchises in Philadelphia and St. Louis to relocate. Manager Fred Haney's Braves won the pennant in 1957 and 1958. They defeated the New York Yankees in the World Series in 1957 and lost in 1958, with both series going to seven games.

The team lost its monopoly in the Upper Midwest in 1961, when the American League put a team in Minnesota. The next year, a consortium headed by Chicago insurance executive Bill Bartholomay bought the Braves for $6.5 million. In 1966, the new owners moved the club to Atlanta, which was becoming a major center in the Deep South. Atlanta offered the team a new publicly financed venue, 52,000-seat Fulton County Stadium.

America's Team? Atlanta 1966–Present

Television revenue and attendance rose, but the team's performance dipped. The Braves made the playoffs only once during their first 16 seasons in Atlanta. Nonetheless, Aaron provided one of the greatest moments in all of baseball history, belting home run number 715 to break the legendary record of Babe Ruth on April 8, 1974. Aaron courageously overcame hundreds of death threats for menacing a "white man's record." Another important player for the Braves was knuckleballer Phil Niekro, who won 318 games (298 for the Braves) and starred on the 1969 and 1982 playoff teams.

In 1976, television mogul Ted Turner acquired the team, which became a cornerstone in the growth of his local cable station, renamed WTBS in 1979. Turner placed the station on cable systems across the South and later nationwide, broadcasting every Braves game. Despite losing teams, Turner's wild promotions and innovations attracted fans across the country but riled baseball's establishment. The Braves were one of the first teams to hire African Americans as executives. (General Manager Bill Lucas, from 1976 until his untimely death in 1979, was at the time the highest-ranking black executive in the majors.) After he retired as a player, Aaron worked in the Braves organization for many years and pioneered the recruitment of talent from the Caribbean.

The team struggled in the late 1980s, when Turner ceased his controversial hands-on, anything-for-publicity approach and gave the reins to President Stan Kasten. In 1990, Kasten brought back former manager Billy Cox (1978–1981) and hired John Schuerholz as general manager. Mobilizing the massive revenues generated by Turner's burgeoning empire, the team vaulted from last place in 1990 to consecutive National League pennants in 1991 and 1992. Constant TBS close-ups of Turner and his wife, actress Jane Fonda, grinning while leading Atlanta crowds in the "Tomahawk chop" spurred vigorous protests by Native American activists.

In 1995, the Braves won the World Series, defeating the Cleveland Indians in six games behind their "Young Guns"—pitchers Tom Glavine, Greg Maddux, and John Smoltz—who were tutored by pitching coach Leo Mazzone, a member of the Braves organization from 1979 to 2005. The team won two more pennants in 1996 and 1999. In 1997, the team moved into Turner Field, site of the 1996 Olympic Games. Turner lost control of the Braves in 2001, when his broadcasting empire merged with AOL Time Warner.

Solid pitching and the batting strength of Chipper Jones and Andruw Jones powered the team for several more seasons. In 2005, the Braves captured their fourteenth straight National League division championship, and Braves broadcaster Skip Caray's son, Chip, joined his father in Atlanta, continuing a family tradition. After the 2010 season, manager Bobby Cox retired after 25 years with the Braves, having won one World Series and five pennants.

David Stevens

See also: Aaron, Hank; Baseball, Major League; Television.

Further Reading

Aaron, Hank, with Lonnie Wheeler. *I Had a Hammer: The Hank Aaron Story.* New York: HarperCollins 1991.

Caruso, Gary. *The Braves Encyclopedia.* Philadelphia: Temple University Press, 1995.

Kaese, Harold. *The Boston Braves, 1871–1953.* Boston: Northeastern University Press, 2004.

Stevens, David. "Atlanta Braves." In *Encyclopedia of Major League Baseball Clubs,* vol. 1, *The National League,* ed. Steven A. Riess. Westport, CT: Greenwood, 2006.

Schuerholz, John, with Larry Guest. *Built to Win: Inside Stories and Leadership Strategies from Baseball's Winningest General Manager.* New York: Warner, 2006.

Stevens, David. *Baseball's Radical for All Seasons: A Biography of John Montgomery Ward.* Lanham, MD: Scarecrow, 1998.

Brotherhood of Professional Baseball Players

The Brotherhood of Professional Baseball Players (or simply the Brotherhood), the first organization of players, began in 1885 in secret because players were afraid of reprisals from autocratic team owners. By the end of that decade, however, the organization found itself in such a bitter battle with owners that its remedy was to found its own association, the Players' League. This demonstrated the players' determination to have a say in their welfare and fate as professional athletes. However, the Players' League lasted just one season (1890), and with its failure, the power of the Brotherhood was destroyed.

The Brotherhood operated during a period of rapid evolution in baseball, both on the field and as a business. When the 1880s began, pitchers could throw only underhand, it took eight balls for a walk, and substitutions were allowed only in the event of an injury. Rosters were small, franchises were unstable, and it was common for teams to fold in mid-season if their stars defected to other teams offering them more money.

The reserve system, inaugurated in 1879, allowed teams to "reserve" five players for the following season, protecting teams from raids on their stars. By the mid-1880s, however, the owners figured out that if they reserved all of the players on their roster, they could transfer the contracts themselves from one team to another through trades and sales. Thus, they could control all player movement and avoid the higher salaries that resulted from multiple teams competing for a player's services.

John Montgomery Ward, star shortstop and pitcher of the New York Giants and a recent law school graduate, wrote an article early in 1885 challenging the legality of the "reserve clause." Later that year, he and eight New York teammates secretly formed the first local chapter of the Brotherhood. Within a year, more than 100 players had joined the organization, and there were chapters in every major league city. Ward went public with the Brotherhood's protests against the newly instituted salary cap ($2,000 maximum per player) and other abuses by owners, and there followed a period of limited cooperation between players and owners. Roster sizes were increased, creating more jobs, some contract language was changed, and the players pledged to curb dissipation. *Sporting News* hailed Ward as "the St. George of baseball, for he has slain the dragon of oppression."

Ward knew better. He wrote a lengthy manifesto titled "Is the Base-Ball Player a Chattel?" that was published in *Lippincott's Magazine* in August 1887. Because the team that initially signed a player owned the rights to him forever, Ward declared that the reserve clause "has been used as a handle for the manipulation of traffic in players, a sort of speculation in live stock, by which they are bought, sold, and transferred like so many sheep." (That language was echoed more than 80 years later by Curt Flood, who wrote in his 1971 book *The Way It Is* that players subject to the same clause "ranked with poultry.")

Ward protested that the owners could release a player with ten days' notice, while the players had no reciprocal power to seek positions on other teams. He likened the system to serfdom, compared the reserve clause to the Fugitive Slave Law, and declared that the "claim by one set of men of a right of property in another is as unnatural to-day as it was a quarter century ago." The only issue to be resolved in Ward's mind was whether the remedy for these wrongs would "come from the clubs, or from the players, or from both conjointly."

There would be no remedy from the clubs. Competition between the National League and the American Association had driven up salaries, with many stars signing lucrative multiyear contracts. After the 1889 season, while Ward and other Brotherhood leaders were occupied with a winter-long world tour, the National League passed the Brush Classification Plan, authored by Indianapolis owner John T. Brush. This was another form of salary cap that preserved the salaries of stars already under contract, but it effectively prevented new players and emerging stars from signing similar deals. Ward hurried home early from the tour, but the damage was done. The new plan effectively alienated stars from the rank-and-file, which had less influence than ever. Ward and the Brotherhood resolved to find a remedy.

During the 1889 season, as confrontations between players and owners escalated, Ward and others worked behind the scenes to court investors who were willing to create a league that would be operated by and for the players. By September, the plan had become public knowledge, and when the season ended, players planning to participate in the new league refused to sign contracts with National League teams. The new Players' League would operate in eight cities, seven of them already sporting National League franchises. Players were encouraged to invest in their teams, the reserve clause was abolished, and a system of pooled profits was established. The majority of National League players joined the Players' League, and attempts by the National League to get injunctions against jumping players were defeated in the courts.

Although the Players' League had better players and higher attendance figures than the other two major leagues in 1890, all three leagues suffered financially and were in danger of ruin if the conflict continued into 1891. The idealistic system advocated by Ward and other Brotherhood leaders was at odds with the capitalistic principles of the league's financial backers. The owners of Federal League franchises approached National League officials after the 1890 season and revealed that their greatest desire was not to continue funding a rival league, but to use their current leverage to join the ownership ranks of the established league.

The National League seized this opportunity. Before Ward could mobilize his forces, most of his investors had traded their Players' League interests for shares in National League teams. Thus ended the Players' League, and with it, the Brotherhood's well-intentioned but doomed experiment.

Gabriel Schechter

See also: Baseball, Major League; Major League Baseball Players Association; Reserve Clause.

Further Reading

Burk, Robert F. *Never Just a Game: Players, Owners, and American Baseball to 1920.* Chapel Hill: University of North Carolina Press, 1994.

Seymour, Harold. *Baseball.* 3 vols. New York: Oxford University Press, 1960–1989.

Sullivan, Dean A., ed. *Early Innings: A Documentary History of Baseball, 1825–1908.* Lincoln: University of Nebraska Press, 1995.

Brown, Jim (1936–)

Jim Brown was an outstanding all-around athlete at Syracuse University who went on to become the best running back in the history of the National Football League (NFL). He was named by *Sporting News* in 2002 as the greatest player ever in professional football. He retired in his prime, unusual among athletes, and became a successful movie actor who refused to be stereotyped into "black" roles. Brown also was an ardent civil rights and social activist, and he worked vigorously to promote black capitalism.

James Nathaniel Brown was born on February 17, 1936, on St. Simon Island, Georgia, the only child of Swinton Brown, a professional boxer and itinerant worker, and his wife Theresa. His parents separated soon after his birth, and he was raised mainly by his great-grandmother, Nora Peterson, until he was eight years old. He then joined his mother in Manhasset on Long Island, New York.

At Manhasset High School, Brown demonstrated exceptional athletic ability. Mentored by football coach Ed Walsh and attorney Kenneth Molloy, Brown became the most outstanding athlete in Manhasset and Long Island history, earning 13 varsity letters in track, basketball, lacrosse, and football. Brown had more than 40 college scholarship offers to play football, but Molloy convinced the young player to attend his own alma mater, Syracuse University. Brown did not know at the time that he had no scholarship to the New York school and that Molloy was raising funds for his first-year expenses with the hope that Brown later would earn a football scholarship.

From the start, Brown ran into difficulties at Syracuse. The freshmen coaches questioned his ability and shook his confidence. As a result, he decided to drop out of school. Raymond Collins, the Manhasset superintendent of schools, drove to Syracuse and convinced Brown to remain in school and on the team.

After injuries thinned the Syracuse backfield in 1954, Brown got an opportunity to play. In his second year, he became a starting halfback, and in the next two seasons, he amassed 2,091 total yards (1,912 meters), 25 touchdowns, and 187 points. In his senior year (1956), he set a major college record by scoring 45 points in a single game, against Colgate University.

Syracuse was invited to play in the Cotton Bowl in Dallas, and Brown became one of the first African Americans to play there. He led Syracuse against Texas Christian University, scoring three touchdowns, but Syracuse lost 28–27. He later recalled, "everyone looks back on my problems because I am well-known, but the situation in America at the time hurt all blacks."

Brown was selected a unanimous All-American in football and lacrosse in 1956–1957, and he earned letters in basketball and track. Considered one of the greatest lacrosse players of all time, who scored 43 goals in his senior year, he is a member of the National Lacrosse Hall of Fame (1984), as well as the National Collegiate Football Hall of Fame (1995). Brown also was an excellent basketball player, but he did not play in his senior year because of a policy imposed by the Syracuse coaching staff that called for only one black player in a game at a time. Brown was so good that he was drafted by the Syracuse Nationals of the National Basketball Association, but he never played.

The Cleveland Browns selected Jim Brown in the first round of the NFL draft, and he became the team's outstanding fullback. At 6 feet, 2 inches (1.9 meters) and 228 pounds (103 kilograms), Brown showed the power, quickness, and speed that would make him the most dominating running back in NFL history. He was the Rookie of the Year in 1957 and led the Browns to the league championship game, which Cleveland lost to the Detroit Lions.

Opposing teams targeted Brown during his nine-year NFL career, but he never missed a game because of injury, often playing hurt. Chuck Bednarik, one of league's best linebackers, maintained that Brown was the most difficult back to bring down. "You can forget about your [Bronko] Nagurskis and Jim Thorpes," concluded Bednarik. "I'll take Jimmy Brown."

Brown continued his remarkable offensive performances during the late 1950s and early 1960s. He broke Steve Van Buren's NFL record for yards rushing in 1958 with 1,527 (1,396 meters). Despite Brown's impressive performances, Cleveland failed to win an NFL championship under longtime coach Paul Brown. When Blanton Collier replaced Paul Brown in 1963, Jim Brown had more confidence in his new coach, who employed a more open style of offense, and he recorded his best season in terms of rushing with 1,863 yards (1,703 meters).

In 1964, Brown led Cleveland to a conference title in a 57–20 romp over their archrivals, the New York Giants. In the NFL championship game against the Baltimore Colts, Brown's effective running game contributed to a 27–0 victory for the Browns. In 1965, Brown scored 21 touchdowns, leading Cleveland to another conference title, but the Browns lost the championship to the Green Bay Packers. During summer 1966, Brown stunned the NFL and his fans by announcing his retirement in order to pursue a film career. In nine seasons, Brown had gained 12,312 yards (11,258 meters) rushing, averaging 5.2 yards (4.7 meters) per carry, and scoring 126 touchdowns.

In 1966, Brown founded the Black Economic Union in an attempt to create more businesses and jobs in black communities. He was convinced that economic progress was more important for African Americans than social protest. Brown mobilized financial and moral support among prominent black athletes, such as Muhammad Ali and Kareem Abdul-Jabbar, and he leveraged the skills of successful black businessmen. In the late 1980s, Brown founded the Amer-I-Can Program to combat inner-city gangs and to divert youthful offenders from lives of crime and violence. He established such antigang programs in more than a dozen states.

After his retirement from football, Brown also became a successful movie actor. He received wide recognition for his role in the 1967 film *The Dirty Dozen*. By the late 1960s, he became a pioneer in breaking down racial stereotyping in Hollywood films. He played a role scripted for a white man in *Ice Station Zebra* (1968) and played white actress Jacqueline Bisset's lover in *The Grasshopper* (1970).

In 1968, feminist Gloria Steinem described Brown as the "Black John Wayne." Jim Brown agreed: "I could ride a horse, shoot guns, rip the blouse off the girl, and mastermind the heist." Interestingly, John Wayne became a film star after dropping out of the University of Southern California, where he played tackle on the football team. Brown has appeared in more than 30 films.

John M. Carroll

See also: Browns, Cleveland; Football, College; Football, Professional.

Further Reading

Brown, Jim, with Myron Cope. *Off My Chest.* Garden City, NY: Doubleday, 1964.

Brown, Jim, with Steve Delsohn. *Out of Bounds.* New York: Kensington, 1989.

Freeman, Mike. *Jim Brown: The Fierce Life of an American Hero.* New York: HarperCollins, 2006.

Lee, Spike, dir. *Jim Brown: All-American.* 40 Acres & A Mule Filmworks, 2002.

Terzian, James P., and Jim Benagh. *The Jimmy Brown Story.* New York: Julian Messner, 1964.

Brown, Paul (1908–1991)

Paul Eugene Brown had perhaps the most profound effect on the game of football of any coach in the twentieth century. He was not only one of the most successful coaches in football history, winning national championships at every level, but he also was one of the game's great innovators. Many of his contributions to football's equipment, plays, and coaching techniques became standard in the sport, and a few, such as detailed film study, have been adopted by other sports as well. By redefining the modern football coaching profession and introducing offensive and defensive techniques that still are used today, Paul Brown changed the way football is coached and played.

Born September 7, 1908, in Norwalk, Ohio, to railroad dispatcher Lester Brown and his wife Ida, Paul moved with his family to football-mad Massillon, Ohio, at the age of nine. By age 15, he was the starting quarterback for Washington High, leading his team to a 15–3 record over two years. Graduating at 16, he first tried to play for Ohio State University, but he was too small for big-college football. He transferred to Miami University of Ohio, where he led the Redskins to a 13–4 record in two years as quarterback and punter.

After graduating in 1929, Brown considered taking a Rhodes Scholarship or starting law school. However, with the Great Depression worsening, and having just married his high school sweetheart, Katy Kester, he decided to take a job coaching football and teaching at Severn School in Maryland, a preparatory school for the U.S. Naval Academy. His teams went 16–1–1 over two years. In 1932, he left to become head coach of his old high school team.

Brown's Massillon teams were among the best high school teams ever assembled. In his first three seasons, his record was 20–7–1, but he was only warming up. Between 1935 and 1940, his teams went 58–1–1, winning six state titles and four Associated Press wire service national championships. These six teams outscored their opponents 2,393–168, and their only loss came on a night when half of the team was out with the flu.

Brown thought that his last Massillon team might have been better than his first one at Ohio State. It outscored opponents 477–6, won state and national honors, and scored more than 50 points in a shortened scrimmage against Kent State University, the collegiate champion of the Ohio Conference.

Brown's tremendous success at Massillon prompted Ohio State to hire him as head football coach in 1940, despite his relatively young age and lack of college-level experience. His three-year tenure at Ohio State resulted in an overall 18–8–1 record, including the Buckeyes' first national championship in 1942. Frustrated by Reserve Officers' Training Corp (ROTC) restrictions during World War II that forced him to play almost exclusively freshmen in his 3–6 campaign in 1943, Brown accepted a naval commission in 1944 and became head coach of the Great Lakes Naval Station team in Illinois. His Bluejackets went 15–5–2 in two years (including a major 39–7 upset of the University of Notre Dame in 1945).

Rather than return to Ohio State after the war, Brown accepted an offer from Cleveland businessman Arthur "Mickey" McBride to create a new team in the fledgling All-America Football Conference (AAFC), which was seeking recognition as a major league alongside the NFL. Brown built a team mostly from players he had either coached or coached against in the past. His first team included six future Hall of Famers: Frank Gatski, Otto Graham, Lou Groza, Dante Lavelli, Marion Motley, and Bill Willis.

Brown's hiring of Motley and Willis—along with the Los Angeles Rams' hiring of Kenny Washington and Woody Strode the same year—marked the reintegration of professional football after a 13-year "gentlemen's agreement" to exclude black players. Although Brown often was lauded for his role in football's reintegration, he shied away from such praise. As journalist Lonnie Wheeler recounted in "Father Football" (1998), Brown once said, "I honestly believe I should not get a lot of credit for bringing blacks into professional football . . . Motley and Willis were both my former players, I thought they were exceptional, and I was just building a football team without trying to do any social thing."

Named for their coach, the new Cleveland Browns launched one of the most impressive dynasties in professional sports history. Starting in 1946, the Browns won the championship in each of the four years of the AAFC's existence. After the AAFC merged with the NFL, the Browns continued their streak, making the NFL championship game six years in a row. Brown compiled a 52–4–3 record in the AAFC and a league-high 62–16–1 in his first six NFL seasons.

Overall, the Browns achieved a record of 167–53–8 during Paul Brown's tenure and suffered only one losing season in his 17 years. However, Coach Brown clashed with new owner Art Modell, who bought the team in 1961 and wanted to play a direct role in its operations. In addition, several players, including star Jim Brown, were uncomfortable with Brown's dictatorial style, leading Modell to fire his coach early in 1963.

In 1967, Paul Brown returned to football when he created the Cincinnati Bengals for the American Football League, which would merge with the NFL three years later. As coach and general manager during the Bengals' first eight years, he led the team to three playoff appearances and a 55–59–1 record before becoming full-time general manager, a post he held until his death on August 5, 1991. His 222 professional wins and .660 winning percentage over 25 years are among the best ever.

Brown's influence on football extended far beyond his victories and championships "Precision Paul" was not only a strict disciplinarian but also a meticulous organizer whose systematic approach to the game eventually became the norm. He introduced elaborate organized playbooks, intensive use of classroom techniques, a year-round coaching schedule for himself and his assistants, detailed film study to grade players and evaluate the opposition, and systematic scouting of college players. He developed a series of tests, including the 40-yard (36.5-meter) dash and intelligence tests, to evaluate players, and he earned a patent for the modern facemask. In addition, he employed hand signals and "messenger guards" to send in plays, modern "pocket" pass protection, extensive use of timing routes, and a number of plays that are common today, including the "down-and-out" pass play.

Some innovations were far ahead of his time. For example, in 1956, Brown became the first coach to send in plays through a helmet radio, an innovation that was not widely adopted until decades later. Similarly, former Browns assistant Bill Walsh admitted that his famous "West Coast Offense" as coach of the San Francisco 49ers was essentially Brown's offense

from the 1950s and 1960s. Walsh is one of more than 40 NFL coaches who played or worked under Brown, including Hall of Famers Weeb Eubank, Chuck Noll, and Don Shula. In 1967, Brown became the first modern-era coach inducted into the Pro Football Hall of Fame.

Kevin F. Kern

See also: All-America Football Conference; Browns, Cleveland; Football, College; Football, Professional.

Further Reading

Brown, Paul, with Jack Clary. *PB, the Paul Brown Story.* New York: Atheneum, 1979.

Clary, Jack. *Cleveland Browns.* New York: Macmillan, 1973.

Piascik, Andy. *The Best Show in Football: The 1946–1955 Cleveland Browns, Pro Football's Greatest Dynasty.* Lanham, MD: Taylor Trade, 2007.

Browns, Cleveland

The Cleveland Browns began as a charter member of the upstart All-America Football Conference (AAFC) in 1946 before joining the National Football League (NFL) four years later when the two leagues merged. The Browns dominated the AAFC under Coach Paul Brown and continued their competitive performance in the NFL. One of the best teams in football during the first decade of their existence, the Browns won eight league championships and sent 16 players to the Pro Football Hall of Fame. In subsequent decades, the Browns were a moderately successful team on the field while, at the same time, boasting some of the most loyal fans in the NFL. When owner Art Modell moved the team to Baltimore in the 1990s, the city and fans successfully sued to have the Browns name stripped from the team. In 1999, the NFL granted the city a new Cleveland Browns franchise.

Arthur "Mickey" McBride, a real estate and taxicab company executive and a principal in the Continental Press Service, popularly known as the "racing wire," originally tried to buy the Cleveland Rams of the NFL. When the league rejected his offer, he established a team in the rival AAFC. He hired Paul Brown, a former Ohio State University coach, as his head coach and general manager, paying him the princely salary of $20,000 and 15 percent of the profits.

The team chose its nickname through a contest, selecting "Browns" in honor of their coach, who already was a legend in Ohio football circles. The club hired several outstanding players, notably quarterback

Otto Graham and talented ends Dante Lavelli and Mac Speedie. The AAFC had no color barrier, and Brown quickly recruited two powerhouse African Americans, fullback Marion Motley and guard Bill Willis, who both played eight seasons in Cleveland en route to the Pro Football Hall of Fame.

The Cleveland Browns played their first regular-season game on September 6, 1946, at Municipal Stadium, where 60,135 fans enjoyed their 44–0 romp over the Miami Seahawks. The Browns won their first seven games before losing to the San Francisco 49ers, 34–20. Graham passed for 1,834 yards (1,677 meters), leading the Browns to a 12–2 record, He capped the season with a victory over the New York Yankees (an AAFC team from 1946 to 1949) in the AAFC title game, connecting with Lavelli for a late touchdown and a 14–9 victory.

In 1947, the Browns rolled to a 12–1–1 season, as Graham led the league's passers with 2,753 yards (2,501 meters) and 25 touchdowns; Motley rushed for 889 yards (813 meters); and Speedie had 67 pass receptions. Cleveland again knocked off New York in the championship by a score of 14–3.

In 1948, the Browns were even more impressive, winning all 14 games, as Motley led the AAFC in rushing with 964 yards (881 meters), while Graham passed for 2,713 yards (2,481 meters) and 25 touchdowns. The Browns crushed the Buffalo Bills in the championship game, 49–7.

In the following season, the AAFC dropped to seven teams. The Browns posted a 9–1–2 record, defeating Buffalo 31–21 in the playoffs and then knocking off San Francisco 21–7 to capture their fourth consecutive championship.

Both the AAFC and the NFL were feeling the pressure of competition for football talent and of keeping marginal franchises from bankruptcy. In December 1949, the leagues agreed on a merger. Three AAFC teams would be merged into the NFL—the Cleveland Browns, Baltimore Colts, and San Francisco 49ers. The remaining AAFC teams were dissolved, and their players were apportioned to other NFL teams, most through a special draft.

In 1950, the Browns played their first game in the NFL against the defending champion Philadelphia Eagles, who were expected to put the Browns in their place. Instead, the Browns hammered the Eagles in Philadelphia, 35–10. Over the season, the Browns sported a 10–2–0 record, tied the New York Giants for the American Conference title, and then outlasted the Giants in a playoff game, 8–3. The Browns went on to defeat the Los Angeles Rams, 30–28, for the NFL championship when Lou "The Toe" Groza kicked a field goal in the game's waning seconds.

Over the next three seasons, the Browns rolled to three more division titles—including 11–1 records in both 1951 and 1953—yet they were defeated in all three championship games. After the 1953 season, McBride sold the team for $600,000 to a syndicate headed by David R. Jones.

In 1954, the Browns went 9–3 and defeated the Detroit Lions, 56–10, for the NFL title. Graham passed for three touchdowns and ran for three more. One year later, the Browns again took the East, and then defeated Los Angeles 38–14 in the championship game. Graham retired after the 1955 season, ending the greatest era in franchise history.

In 1957, the arrival of the sensational Jim Brown, a powerhouse running back from Syracuse University, inaugurated a new era. The slashing ball carrier played nine seasons (1957–1965), leading the NFL in rushing eight times—including 1,863 yards (1,704 meters) in 1963—and ending with 12,312 rushing yards (11,258 meters). In his Rookie of the Year campaign, the Browns went to the championship, but the Detroit Lions clobbered them, 59–14.

In 1961, Art Modell, a New Yorker who worked in advertising, public relations, and television production, purchased the franchise for $4 million, of which only $250,000 was his own money (he borrowed $2.7 million, and the rest came from his partners). Almost from the start, Modell believed that Paul Brown exercised too much authority in the organization. After the 1962 season and a string of slightly above-average campaigns, Modell fired Coach Paul Brown.

The new coach was Blanton Collier. The Browns compiled a good record in his eight seasons (1963–1970), which included the 1964 NFL championship, a 27–0 win over the Baltimore Colts in which quarterback Frank Ryan threw three touchdown passes to Gary Collins. The Browns returned to the title game one year later, but they came up short against the Green Bay Packers, 23–12. Cleveland returned to the NFL championship in 1968 and 1969, but lost both outings. When Collier left after the 1970 season, the Browns began a long parade of head coaches, and the team struggled to regain its old glory.

In 1980, the Browns posted an 11–5 record to win their division but then lost in the first playoff game to the eventual champion, the Oakland Raiders. That season quarterback Brian Sipes led the NFL in passing, with 4,132 yards (3,778 meters), and he earned the Associated Press NFL Most Valuable Player award. The team did not return to the playoffs until 1985, when it finished 8–8. The Browns put together strong seasons in 1986 (12–4), 1987 (10–5), and 1989 (9–6-1), yet fell short each year, losing the American Football Conference title game to the Denver Broncos.

On November 6, 1995, in the midst of a losing season, Modell announced a deal to move the team to Baltimore. (The Baltimore Colts had moved to Indianapolis after the 1983 season, taking both the team and its nickname with them, and the city had been without an NFL team for 12 years.) Almost immediately, the city of Cleveland and Browns fans filed nearly 100 lawsuits against Modell.

Lawyers for the NFL believed that some of the suits could pose a real problem to the league, and they advised quick action. In response, the league announced in February 1996 that the Browns merely were being "deactivated" for three years (1996–1998), and that an existing or expansion team known as the Browns would take up residence in Cleveland for the 1999 season. Modell's Baltimore team became known as the Ravens, and he surrendered the Browns's name, colors, records, and history.

In 1998, the NFL announced that realtor and banker Al Lerner had bought the Browns franchise for a record $530 million. Pro football returned to Cleveland in 1999, with the latest Browns playing at the new 73,200-seat, $283 million Cleveland Browns Stadium, constructed on the site of Municipal Stadium. The new Browns struggled on the field, although they went 9–7 in 2002 and 10–6 in 2007 before falling to 4–12 in 2008 and 5–11 in 2009 and 2010.

Raymond Schmidt

See also: All-America Football Conference; Brown, Jim; Brown, Paul; Football, Professional; Motley, Marion.

Further Reading

Clary, Jack. *Cleveland Browns.* New York: Macmillan, 1973.
Levy, Bill. *Return to Glory: The Story of the Cleveland Browns.* Cleveland, OH: World, 1965.
————. *Sam, Sipes, & Company: The Story of the Cleveland Browns.* Cleveland, OH: J.T. Zubal & P.D. Dole, 1981.
Morgan, Jon. *Glory for Sale: Fans, Dollars, and the New NFL.* Baltimore: Bancroft, 1997.

Bruins, Boston

The Bruins, a professional hockey team based in Boston, Massachusetts, entered the National Hockey League (NHL) in 1924 as its first U.S.-based franchise. The third-oldest club in the NHL, the Bruins were one of the "Original Six" teams in the league. Since their inaugural 1924–1925 campaign, the Bruins have celebrated five Stanley Cup championships (1928–1929, 1938–1939, 1940–1941, 1969–1970, and 1971–1972). Bruins alumni include some of the most skilled and colorful players in NHL history, 46 of whom have been named to the Hockey Hall of Fame.

The Bruins trace their roots to grocery store magnate Charles Adams, who spent $15,000 in November 1924 for the rights to a Boston NHL franchise. Adams, who believed that Bostonians would welcome professional hockey with the same enthusiasm they had shown for the amateur game, adorned his team in the brown and yellow of his First National Stores and accepted a team secretary's suggestion to name the team the Bruins.

Adams selected Art Ross, a widely respected figure in Canadian hockey, as general manager, coach, and scout. Within three years, the duo had assembled a formidable lineup that included Aubrey "Dit" Clapper, Lionel Hitchman, George Owen, Eddie Shore, and goaltender Cecil "Tiny" Thompson. Ross's Bruins, known for their physical, aggressive style, dominated the 1928–1929 regular season en route to the Stanley Cup.

Shrewd marketing bolstered the team's rising esteem among Bostonians. A cooperative press emphasized the merits of professional hockey to an audience accustomed to watching amateurs, and when Boston and Springfield radio stations began broadcasting games in 1926, announcers tailored their commentary to make the game appealing to female fans. Rising attendance prompted the expansion of the Boston Arena's balcony in 1926, by which time the Bruins had implemented a season ticket program. By November 1927, the team's popularity inspired boxing promoter Tex Rickard to spearhead an effort to build a new arena featuring the Bruins as the anchor tenant. The Boston Garden, designed to seat approximately 14,000 hockey fans, was completed in time for the 1928–1929 season.

Adams remained team president until 1936, when he was succeeded by his son, Weston W. Adams. The Bruins remained competitive throughout the 1930s, but on the eve of the 1938–1939 season, the Bruins, now clad in black, gold, and white, failed to match their 1929 championship. The season began ominously when Eddie Shore held out over a contract dispute. Although Shore later returned, the season appeared to take another discouraging turn in mid-November, when Ross sold fan favorite Tiny Thompson to Detroit.

Thompson's replacement, rookie goalie Frank Brimsek, soon vindicated the unpopular move by notching 33 wins and 10 shutouts over the remaining 43 regular season games. Earning the moniker "Mr. Zero," Brimsek led a Bruins team into the playoffs that featured several veterans from the 1929 championship, as well as Bobby Bauer, Woody Dumart, and Milt Schmidt, a trio of emerging star forwards from Kitchener, Ontario, who became known as the "Kraut" line. After edging out the New York Rangers in a seven-game semifinal series, the Bruins defeated the Toronto Maple Leafs in five games to win their second Stanley Cup.

The Rangers eliminated the Bruins in the following year to spoil Boston's bid to repeat as champions. The Bruins rebounded with a strong 1940–1941 season and reclaimed the Stanley Cup after sweeping Detroit in the 1941 finals.

Although many predicted that the powerful Bruins would win several more championships, the onset of World War II prompted the premature dismantling of the squad. Sixteen Bruins players would serve in Allied military forces, including Bauer, Dumart, and Schmidt, who enlisted in the Royal Canadian Air Force. The Bruins honored the trio after a February 11, 1942, game against Montreal in a ceremony that ended with both teams carrying the Krauts—now dubbed the "Kitchener boys"—off the ice. Although Bauer, Brimsek, Dumart, Schmidt, and others rejoined the team after the war, the reassembled Bruins could not match their prewar accomplishments.

From 1942 to 1959, the team compiled an uneven record of achievements. Although the Bruins reached the Stanley Cup finals five times (1942–1943, 1945–1946, 1952–1953, 1956–1957, 1957–1958), they also missed the playoffs entirely on three occasions. In 1948–1949, the team commemorated its twenty-fifth season by unveiling jerseys with a new spoked "B" logo that remains in use six decades later. When Willie O'Ree donned the jersey in a January 18, 1958, game against Montreal, he became the first black player in NHL history. Off the ice, Boston Garden General Manager Walter Brown replaced Adams as president in 1951 and purchased 60 percent of the team.

The Bruins' exit from the 1959 playoffs began an eight-year postseason absence during which Boston finished in last place six times. Boston's revival began in 1966–1967, when 18-year-old superstar defenseman Bobby Orr made his widely anticipated debut in a Bruins uniform. General Manager Milt Schmidt continued to rebuild the team over the next few years, most notably by acquiring center Phil Esposito from the Chi-cago Blackhawks in a June 1967 trade. Thus began the "Big Bad Bruins" era, during which Boston earned notoriety for prolific scoring, individual flamboyance, and physical and intimidating play. This era, highlighted by Stanley Cup championships in 1970 and 1972, ended when Orr and Esposito departed Boston in 1976.

Following their final Stanley Cup victory in 1972, the Bruins remained one of the NHL's elite teams until the end of the decade, reaching the Stanley Cup finals in 1973–1974, 1976–1977, and 1977–1978. Boston reemerged as a powerhouse in the late 1980s, appearing in both the 1987–1988 and 1989–1990 finals. From the mid-1970s to the end of the Cold War, the Bruins hosted six games against Soviet clubs as part of the nine NHL-Soviet "Super Series" exhibitions that took place from 1976 to 1991.

In 1975, arena concessionaire Jeremy M. Jacobs purchased the Bruins and the Boston Garden for $10 million from Storer Broadcasting, which owned the team from 1973 to 1975. Jacobs presided over the construction of a new, privately financed, 17,565-seat arena that replaced the Boston Garden in 1995. Known originally as the Fleet Center, the facility was renamed the TD Banknorth Garden after the Maine-based banking company purchased the naming rights to the facility in 2005. In 2010–2011, the Boston Bruins defeated the Vancouver Canucks in seven games to win the Stanley Cup, led by Cup MVP goalie Tim Thomas. It was the Bruins's first championship since 1971–1972.

H. Matthew Loayza

See also: Ice Hockey.

Further Reading

Booth, Clark. *Boston Bruins: Celebrating 75 Years.* Del Mar, CA: Tehabi, 1998.

Hardy, Stephen. "Long Before Orr: Placing Hockey in Boston, 1897–1929." In *The Rock, the Curse, and the Hub: A Random History of Boston Sports,* ed. Randy Roberts. Cambridge, MA: Harvard University Press, 2005.

Roberts, Randy. "Number 4 Is the One: The Emergence of Bobby Orr." In *The Rock, the Curse, and the Hub: A Random History of Boston Sports,* ed. Randy Roberts. Cambridge, MA: Harvard University Press, 2005.

Brundage, Avery (1887–1975)

Avery Brundage was a preeminent American Olympic leader. He participated in the Games as an athlete in

1912 and, more importantly, directed the United States Olympic Committee (USOC) from 1929 to 1953 and served as president of the International Olympic Committee (IOC) for two decades (1953–1972). Brundage helped preserve the Olympic Games after the devastation of World War II, extended the Olympic ideals of international understanding to the global community, and championed Olympic principles during an era when the games were becoming commercialized. Brundage also had many critics, particularly later in his career, who saw his decisions as anachronistic and authoritarian.

Brundage was born on September 28, 1887, in Detroit, Michigan. Five years later, the Brundages moved to Chicago, and soon after that, his father abandoned the family. Avery went to work as a newsboy in 1899, and like many newsboys, read the papers and did well in school. He enjoyed summer vacations in Michigan with his Uncle Edward, an attorney and a rising figure in Chicago politics.

He attended Crane Technical High School, where he competed in track and field, making his own hammer for the hammer throw. In 1905, he entered the University of Illinois. Brundage completed the civil engineering curriculum, worked on the student newspaper, participated in campus dances, and excelled on the intercollegiate track and field and basketball teams. He worked summers on Chicago construction projects.

After graduating in 1909, Brundage joined the architectural firm of Holabird and Roche as a construction superintendent. He continued his athletic career as a member of the Chicago Athletic Association's Cherry Circle teams, competing in amateur athletic meets. He entered national competitions in the all-around (forerunner of the decathlon) from 1910 to 1918, winning the championship in 1914, 1916, and 1918. In 1912, he qualified for the U.S. team selected for the Olympic Games in Stockholm, where he came in sixth in the pentathlon and sixteenth in the decathlon. He was profoundly impressed by the Olympic ideology and the spectacle of international athletic competition.

Returning to Chicago, he founded the Avery Brundage Company in 1915. An innovative construction engineer, he prospered during the postwar building boom, building lakeshore apartment houses, a Ford automobile assembly plant, lakefront bridges, and the Baha'i Temple. He was an active handball player and chaired the Handball Committee of the Amateur Athletic Union (AAU) in 1925–1927.

Brundage attended the 1924 Olympic Games in Paris; he also went to the Amsterdam Games four years later. In 1928, he was elected president of the AAU, and the next year, he was made president of the United States Olympic Committee, succeeding General Douglas MacArthur. He remained AAU president through 1934 and USOC president until 1953. In 1932, he was the national Olympic committee host for the Summer Games in Los Angeles. The huge Coliseum, modern sports venues, and Olympic village impressed foreign participants and the American public. During a period when sports became a popular form of public entertainment and urban athletic clubs lost influence in sporting organizations, Brundage negotiated agreements on control and eligibility with the National Collegiate Athletic Association.

The economic depression of the 1930s wiped out much of Brundage's fortune and halted most private building. His construction experience and determination enabled him to take a leading role in reorganizing bankrupt firms and to launch a second career as a clever property manager and investor in Chicago and Southern California. The income from his investments after World War II allowed him to devote more time and money to the support of the Olympic Games.

Between 1933 and 1935, a movement arose in the United States to boycott the 1936 Olympic Games in Berlin to protest the policies of Adolf Hitler and the Nazi Party in Germany. The Nazis were openly hostile to Jews and considered the Aryan race of Northern Europe superior to other races. Brundage led the opposition to the boycott, believing that the Olympics should transcend local politics.

Brundage's later words and actions suggest that he admired the German Olympic organizers and government officials and was impressed by their emphasis on physical training and athletics. To reassure those who pressed for a boycott, Brundage met with German officials and gained assurances that no athlete would suffer discrimination during the Games. Finally, in December 1935, the AAU voted in favor of participation, prompting the organization's new president, Judge Jeremiah T. Murphy, to resign in protest.

Brundage played a leading role in raising public contributions to send a U.S. team to the Games. The Berlin Olympics attracted worldwide attention for the spectacular staging of the competition and for the efficiency of the German organizers. At the same time, it provided a stage for the victories of African American Jesse Owens in track and field, which challenged the racist dogma of the German government.

In July 1936, the International Olympic Committee chose Brundage for membership. As major sporting events were becoming commercialized, he joined the IOC's Executive Committee and participated in its efforts to redefine amateurism amid changing world conditions. He believed that the Olympic movement should be neutral in international affairs (though he also was a dedicated anticommunist). In 1939, following Germany's invasion of Poland and the beginning of World War II, Brundage opposed U.S. involvement in the war, joining the "America First" movement, but he resigned when the organization objected to his pro-German views. After the United States entered the war in December 1941, Brundage built military facilities and promoted physical training programs and the creation of the first Pan-American Games.

The scheduled Olympic Games in 1940 and 1944 were canceled because of the war. When the war ended in 1945, Brundage worked with IOC Vice President Sigfrid Edstrom and surviving members of the committee to reestablish and promote the Olympic Games. With little time to plan, Brundage and Edstrom worked with Great Britain's Lord Burghley to organize the 1948 Games in London. At the Helsinki Games in 1952, Brundage replaced Edstrom as IOC president. In the next 20 years, he faced major challenges arising from the growth of professional sports, the creation of new nations from former colonies, political divisions in Germany and China, animosities created by racial segregation and discrimination, and the emergence of television revenue as a major source of support for IOC programs.

Olympic idealism and internationalism also were tested by the Cold War between the Soviet Union and the United States. It became clear that countries in the Soviet bloc were developing institutes to train leading athletes full time to compete in prominent sports. This put athletes from other countries, including the United States, at a significant disadvantage, pitting part-time athletes against Russian teams that were, in fact, made up of professional athletes. Brundage resisted nearly all initiatives to ease standards of amateurism in Western countries, as he regarded this as an important Olympic ideal. His critics replied that his policies excluded gifted athletes who were not rich enough to finance their own intensive training. At the same time, Brundage refused to take any steps against the doubtful amateurism in Soviet-bloc countries.

Brundage opposed any efforts to boycott Olympic events. In 1968, he spoke out against the African boycott of the Mexico City Games, a protest against the oppressive system of apartheid in South Africa. During the Games, African American gold medalists Tommie Smith and John Carlos raised their black-gloved hands on the winners' stand during the playing of the U.S. national anthem, a show of support for the Black Power movement. Brundage had them evicted immediately from the Olympic Village and expelled from the U.S. team. He believed that their protest had broken a cardinal rule of the Olympic movement—the introduction of politics.

In 1972, Brundage made another controversial decision. During the Games, Arab terrorists invaded the Olympic site in Munich, kidnapping members of the Israeli team. In the ensuing violence, the kidnappers killed 11 Israeli athletes and coaches. The events were covered around the clock by television networks, and there was widespread sentiment for canceling the remaining events. Brundage stood firm. After a pause and a memorial service for the victims, he decreed that "the Games must go on." Soon after the Munich Games, Brundage resigned as IOC president, but he remained in the public eye. He died on May 8, 1975, at Garmisch-Partenkirchen, Germany, and was buried in Chicago.

Brundage's work and his views remain controversial. In the years since his death, the IOC has allowed professional athletes in many sports to compete equally in the Games, bringing wide visibility and huge revenues from television rights. On one hand, his views on amateurism in sports still have many defenders; on the other hand, the opening of the Games to professionals has democratized participation in international sports, allowing talented athletes, rich or poor, to compete.

Maynard Brichford

See also: Amateur Athletic Union; Amateurism; Olympics, Summer; Olympics, Winter.

Further Reading

Brichford, Maynard. "Avery Brundage: Chicago Businessman." *Journal of the Illinois State Historical Society* 91:4 (Winter 1998): 218–232.
———, ed. *Avery Brundage Collection, 1908–1975.* Koln, Germany: Verlag Karl Hofmann Schorndorf, 1977.
Espy, Richard. *The Politics of the Olympic Games.* Berkeley: University of California Press, 1979.
Guttmann, Allen. *The Games Must Go On: Avery Brundage and the Olympic Movement.* New York: Columbia University Press, 1984.

Bryant, Bear (1913–1983)

Paul William "Bear" Bryant was a renowned American college football coach who served as head coach at the University of Maryland, the University of Kentucky, and Texas A&M University from 1946 to 1957. Bryant achieved his greatest fame at the University of Alabama, where, from 1958 to 1982, he led six teams that won or shared the national championship (1961, 1964–1965, 1973, 1978–1979). Bryant's record for National Collegiate Athletic Association (NCAA) Division I career victories (323) stood for 20 years, until Joe Paterno at Penn State surpassed that mark in 2001. Bryant was among the top coaches in collegiate athletic history and became a prominent cultural figure in the American South.

Bryant was born on September 11, 1913, in Moro Bottom, Arkansas, the eleventh of 12 children of William Monroe and Ida Kilgore Bryant. Plagued with both mental and physical illness, Bryant's father struggled to support the family through sharecropping. His mother, a strong-willed and deeply religious woman, served as head of the Bryant household. When he was 14, the young Bryant earned the nickname "Bear" after wrestling with a muzzled bear to promote a local theater. Although the name became famous, Bryant disliked it, and close friends rarely used the nickname when referring to him.

Bryant played football at Fordyce (Arkansas) High School, which won the state title in 1930, and earned a scholarship to attend the University of Alabama. He struggled academically yet maintained his eligibility for sports and played blocking end on dominant Crimson Tide football teams that went 23–3–2 during his career. His team went 10–0 in 1934 and won the national championship, defeating Stanford University in the 1935 Rose Bowl.

After graduating in 1936, Bryant turned down offers to play professionally and instead turned to coaching. He took a job briefly with Union College in Tennessee but soon returned to Alabama after the Crimson Tide offered him an assistant coaching position. Alabama football remained successful in the late 1930s, racking up a 29–5–3 record while Bryant was an assistant coach.

In 1940, Bryant left Alabama to serve as an assistant at Vanderbilt University. The University of Arkansas offered him a head coaching position in 1941, but following the Japanese attack on Pearl Harbor on December 7, he enlisted in the U.S. Navy. He rose to lieutenant commander, with service in North Africa, and then coached the football team at North Carolina Pre-Flight.

In 1945, Bryant took his first head coaching job at the University of Maryland. It was a tumultuous tenure, as Bryant clashed with administrators over control of the program. Although he was wildly popular with the student body, he left reluctantly after one season with the Terrapins, finishing 6–2–1.

He then took the head coaching job at the University of Kentucky, where he served for eight seasons (1946–1953). He led the Wildcats to four postseason games, including the Great Lakes, Orange, and Cotton Bowls, and to their only Southeastern Conference title in 1950. Kentucky ended the season with a victory in the Sugar Bowl over the Oklahoma Sooners, the number one team in the country. Despite his success, the coach was convinced that Kentucky administrators favored the distinguished basketball program of Adolph Rupp over football. As evidence, Bryant pointed out that after one season, the university gave Rupp a new car and gave Bryant a cigarette lighter. He quit after the 1953 season and moved on to become head coach and athletic director at Texas A&M University.

At Texas A&M, Bryant inherited a little-known, inexperienced team that had not won the conference championship since 1941. Before the 1954 season, he took his players to Junction, Texas, and subjected them to an infamous training camp in grueling heat. More than 100 players made the trip, but just 29 survived the camp and made the team. The so-called Junction Boys became a legendary example of Bryant's coaching style and the growing dedication of student athletes in postwar America. After suffering through a 1–9 season in 1954, the Aggies made a dramatic comeback, and in 1956, they went 9–0–1, were ranked ninth in the country, and went to the Gator Bowl, which they lost to Tennessee, 3–0. The team contended for the national championship the following year, led by running back John David Crow, recipient of the Heisman Trophy. Meanwhile, long-standing rumors circulated that Alabama was interested in wooing Bryant, and in 1958, the Crimson Tide offered him the job of head coach. He accepted.

After turning around Texas A&M and compiling a 25–14–2 record, Bryant engineered an immediate improvement at Alabama. After going 5–4–1 in his first season, he coached the Crimson Tide for 25 years, compiling a 232–46–9 record. Bryant won six national championships at Alabama and took the team to 24 consecutive bowl games. Known for his exceptional motivational skills, he won 15 bowl games, including eight Sugar Bowls. In 1981, he coached his 315th victory over Auburn University, breaking Amos Alonzo Stagg's record for career wins. Bryant retired in 1982 with 323 total victories.

By the late 1960s, Bryant's popularity in Alabama was unmatched by any politician or public figure in the state. At the 1968 Democratic National Convention, two Alabama delegates even cast ballot votes for Bryant to succeed Lyndon B. Johnson as president of the United States. Bryant's tenure at Alabama coincided with extensive changes in NCAA policies and an expansion of college football's role in shaping American culture and society.

He also presided over the team during a period of racial unrest, when African Americans faced discrimination throughout the South and could not attend the university. Bryant's desire to pursue black athletes—inspired by Alabama's loss to the University of Southern California and its black running back, Sam Cunningham, in 1970—reportedly prompted a change, albeit minimal, in the state's education policy. By 1971, the Crimson Tide was recruiting black players, and soon after, African Americans became prominent fixtures on Alabama football teams. Defensive end John Mitchell was the first black player on the team, earning All-American honors in 1972.

Bryant died of a heart attack on January 26, 1983. He passed away only weeks after coaching the Crimson Tide to a victory over Auburn in the Liberty Bowl at the end of his final season. One month after his death, Bryant was posthumously awarded the Presidential Medal of Freedom, the nation's highest civilian award, by President Ronald Reagan.

Lane Demas

See also: Bowl Games, College Football; Football, College; Race and Race Relations.

Further Reading

Barra, Allen. *The Last Coach: A Life of Paul "Bear" Bryant.* New York: W.W. Norton, 2005.

Dent, Jim. *The Junction Boys: How Ten Days in Hell with Bear Bryant Forged a Championship Team.* New York: St. Martin's, 1999.

Dunnavant, Keith. *Coach: The Life of Paul "Bear" Bryant.* New York: Simon & Schuster, 1996.

Robe, Mike, dir. *The Junction Boys.* Stamford, CT: ESPN Original Entertainment. 2002.

Bulls, Chicago

The Chicago Bulls were the dominant team in the National Basketball Association (NBA) during the 1990s, winning six championships with Michael Jordan, the league's most influential superstar. The Bulls became a marquee NBA franchise, reflected in its 2009 value of more than $300 million and the team's 21,711-seat United Center arena, shared with hockey's Chicago Blackhawks since 1994. After Jordan's retirement in 1998, however, the team struggled to regain the championship.

In 1966, a group of investors led by businessman and former professional basketball player Dick Klein paid $1.6 million for an NBA franchise, the third attempt to establish a successful NBA organization in Chicago. The Chicago Stags (1946–1950) had failed, and the Chicago Packers (1961, renamed the Zephyrs in 1962) had moved to Baltimore in 1963.

The Bulls were no overnight success. They began with four straight seasons below .500, although they did register the best first-year record for an NBA expansion team (33–48) in their initial campaign under Coach Johnny "Red" Kerr. They made the playoffs that year, suffering an early exit. The Bulls played at the 9,000-seat International Amphitheatre, drawing fewer than 1,000 fans to some games before moving to the Chicago Stadium in 1967. The club finished a dismal 29–53 in 1967–1968, but again made the playoffs.

Dick Motta replaced Kerr as head coach in 1968, and a trade for scoring machine Bob Love helped change the franchise's fortunes. During the 1969–1970 season, the team improved to 39–43, scoring 114.9 points per game. In each of the next four seasons, they were more than 20 games over .500. Assisting Love were high-scoring forward Chet Walker, prolific rebounder Tom Boerwinkle, scrappy defender Jerry Sloan (the first player to be signed by the Bulls franchise), and tough-nosed point guard Norm Van Lier. Motta won Coach of the Year honors in 1971 as the Bulls nearly upended the Los Angeles Lakers in the division semifinals. That year and again the following season, Love averaged more than 25 points a game. In 1974, the Bulls went to the Western Conference finals, only to lose to Milwaukee Bucks, led by Kareem Abdul-Jabbar and Oscar Robertson.

Motta left the team in 1976 following a 24–58 season, his worst record up to that point. In the spring, the Bulls hired Jerry Krause as director of player personnel, and then a few months later, they hired Ed Badger as head coach. The Bulls also added 7-foot, 2-inch (2.2-meter) center Artis Gilmore from the American Basketball Association player dispersal draft. However, a near decade of futility followed, in which the Bulls finished above .500 only twice.

The team's fortunes changed in 1984 when management chose Jordan, a junior from the University of North Carolina, as the third pick overall in the NBA draft, though General Manager Rod Thorn admitted that he had hoped for a 7-foot (2.1-meter) rookie. Jordan exceeded all expectations in his first season by averaging 28.2 points per game and leading the Bulls to the playoffs. The average attendance at Bulls home games nearly doubled.

Midway through Jordan's rookie campaign, Jerry Reinsdorf bought a controlling stake in the Bulls for $16 million from a syndicate that included Lamar Hunt, George Steinbrenner, and William "Dollar Bill" Wirtz, which had owned the team since 1972. Jordan's presence undoubtedly encouraged Reinsdorf's bid. The Bulls made the playoffs in 14 straight years, from 1985 through 1998, Jordan's last season with the team.

In 1985, Reinsdorf hired Jerry Krause as general manager to replace Thorn, and Krause brought in Doug Collins as coach a year later. Krause gained renown for his 1987 drafting of Horace Grant and for trading his draft pick, Olden Polynice, for unheralded rookie Scottie Pippen. The team made progress under Collins, but after the 1988–1989 season, when they lost a six-game series in the Eastern Conference finals to the Detroit Pistons, the eventual NBA champion, Krause unexpectedly fired Collins and hired the relatively unknown and unconventional Phil Jackson. Within a few years, the decision looked masterful, as Jackson won over many players with his team-oriented philosophy, which he claimed melded Zen Buddhism, Christianity, and Lakota spirituality, along with his implementation of the triangle offense.

In 1990–1991, the Bulls won the championship over the Los Angeles Lakers in five games; they repeated their success the next two years, with victories over the Portland Trail Blazers and the Phoenix Suns. However, Jordan retired in 1993 to play minor league baseball. The club did well without him in 1993–1994, propelled by the play of Pippen, but the Knicks eliminated the Bulls in the second round of the playoffs.

Jordan returned to the team late the next season, but he was rusty, and the team quickly was eliminated in the playoffs. This only seemed to stoke Jordan's competitive fire, however, as he led the Bulls to a record 72 victories in 1995–1996 with the help of Pippen, European import Toni Kukoc, and flamboyant rebounder Dennis Rodman. The Bulls captured the NBA crown over the Seattle Supersonics and went on to another triple-title "three-peat," with championships the next two seasons over the Utah Jazz.

Following the 1997–1998 season, Coach Jackson left amid rumors that he could not get along with Krause.

Jordan refused to play without Jackson as coach, and the Bulls dynasty came to an end.

In the post-Jordan era, the Bulls suffered a string of losing seasons, going 119–341 over the next six years under coaches Tim Floyd, Bill Cartwright, and Scott Skiles. In 2003, Krauss retired, and Reinsdorf hired former Jordan-era marksman John Paxson as vice president of basketball relations. He replaced Cartwright with the discipline-minded Skiles and made some effective personnel moves by drafting Kirk Hinrich in 2003 and then Ben Gordon, Chris Duhon, and Luol Deng. The Bulls began to turn around, with three straight seasons over .500 from 2004 to 2007. However, a return to the NBA finals never materialized.

In 2007–2008, the Bulls struggled early on, leading to Skiles being fired 25 games into the season. The team finished under .500. The rebuilding process continued when top draft pick Derrick Rose was named Rookie of the Year in 2009. The Bulls went 41–41 in 2008–2009 and again 41–41 in 2009–2010. The team's value in 2009 was $511 million, third highest in the NBA. Longtime Boston Celtics assistant coach Tom Thibodeau took the helm in 2010.

Carson J. Cunningham

See also: Basketball, Professional, NBA Era; Jordan, Michael.

Further Reading

Halberstam, David. *Playing for Keeps: Michael Jordan and the World He Made.* New York: Broadway, 2000.

LaFeber, Walter. *Michael Jordan and the New Global Capitalism.* Expanded ed. New York: W.W. Norton, 2002.

Smith, Sam. *The Jordan Rules.* New York: Simon & Schuster, 1992.

Business of Sports

Sports are big business today. Large multinational corporations manufacture lucrative sporting goods, while spectator sports are a popular and profitable form of entertainment. From payrolls to ticket sales, spectator sports account for billions of dollars a year. They entertain millions of fans, most of whom never make it to the stadium but instead follow their favorite teams on television and radio, in newspapers, and on the Internet.

The development of sports as a business began more than 150 years ago, when entrepreneurs started charging admission to horse races, baseball games, and other sporting events, and as artisans began making and selling equipment such as billiard tables. The rapid rise of spectator sports and the retailing of sporting goods began primarily in the late nineteenth century and was fueled by a booming interest in sports and the growth of urban populations. Industrialization spurred advances in transportation, eventually improved living standards and incomes, and led to shorter work weeks, giving Americans more opportunities to engage in leisure activities.

Compared to other forms of entertainment, spectator sports did not rely directly on changing technology for its basic structure. Radio and television, for example, did not change the essential concept of spectator sports, but they did transform the way in which most spectators consumed sports. In addition, the vast amount of money produced by television altered the structure of organized sports leagues.

In 1920, the U.S. Census Bureau first began tracking spending on spectator sports, estimating it at $257 million ($2.9 billion in current dollars). The consulting firm of W.R. Hambrecht reported that in 2010 that figure had increased to $22.4 billion, more than Americans spent on movies or theater. As large as that amount seems, it was just 3 percent of the total amount spent on all forms of leisure and recreation. Americans spent nearly twice as much on their flower gardens, three times as much on books, and seven times as much on other entertainment.

The Early Sports Enterprise

The first promoters of sports in North America were inn and tavern keepers who sponsored races, feats of skill (billiards, bowling, shuffleboard, darts), foot races, or blood sports (dog fighting, cockfighting, wrestling, boxing), offering prizes to the winners. During colonial times, taverns exploited the concentrated populations in and around the cities to sponsor sporting events, such as bowling, cockfights, horseshoes, and quoits (similar to horseshoes), to draw crowds who were hungry, thirsty, and in need of lodging.

Foot races became popular in the early nineteenth century. In 1835, John C. Stevens first commercialized the sport when he offered a $1,000 prize ($23,000 in 2005 dollars) to anyone who could run 10 miles (16 kilometers) in less than one hour. The publicity that his offer generated attracted a crowd of 30,000 curious onlookers at the Union Course on Long Island. Over the next quarter century, crowds numbering as high as 50,000 attended races that awarded prizes of up to several thousand dollars. The most successful contestants, such as John Gildersleeve and William Howett, could earn a living traveling around the country running races and promoting themselves for public challenges.

In 1859, the All-England cricket club toured North America, an event that foreshadowed the vast potential of team sports as a vehicle for mass entertainment. The English team played to sellout crowds across the continent. The tour also revealed an emerging connection between organized team sports and civic pride. The best example was the team's hastily arranged final match at Rochester, New York. In a surprisingly modern scenario, local officials appropriated public funds to upgrade the city's cricket grounds to entice the English team to come. The mayor claimed that the money was well spent and that the event demonstrated Rochester was no less a metropolis than New York or Philadelphia.

Pugilism

Prizefighting was outlawed nearly everywhere in the nineteenth century because of its brutality, its association with gambling, and the general character of its participants, sponsors, and fans. Newspapers opined against the sport but covered it nonetheless to satisfy readers' demands. Early matches, and even championships, were organized by backers of particular fighters for side bets and usually were staged in the back of a barroom or at a secret location. Promoters typically were saloon keepers or machine politicians.

The business of boxing took a step forward under Richard Kyle Fox, who promoted the sport in the late nineteenth century in order to sell copies of the *National Police Gazette,* one of the original practitioners of "yellow" or sensational journalism. Sports provided the backbone of his approach to news coverage, which appealed to the masses through a publication that also featured sensational crime reports and sex scandals. Still, Fox cleaned up boxing, introduced weight classes to even out the competition, offered championship belts at each weight class, and arranged contests. In the 1880s, his innovations made him the most important fight promoter in the industry.

In the early 1890s, the sport briefly was legalized in New Orleans and New York. Promoters staged prize fights under the Marquis of Queensberry rules (established to create fairer matches and to protect fighters from life-threatening injuries) and offered purses to the competitors, making money by charging spectators for admission. By the end of the decade, additional revenue was earned from motion pictures made of championship fights.

Boxing still was prohibited in most states. It came and went in New York until it was legalized permanently in 1920 under the supervision of the state boxing commission. Madison Square Garden became the national center of the sport, which was guided to profit and prominence by its top promoter, Tex Rickard. Boxing's success was epitomized by the 1927 bout between Jack Dempsey and Gene Tunney in Chicago, which was attended by 104,943 and earned a record $2.7 million gate ($32.4 million in 2010).

The Emergence of the Sporting Goods Industry

Sporting goods appeared on the shelves of retailers before the Revolutionary War, when merchants offered products such as cricket balls, tennis rackets, and fishing rods, mostly imported from England. American sports publications and the sporting goods industry began in the early nineteenth century to supply information and tools for outdoor recreational sports, such as hunting and fishing. The public interest in sports provided the reason for the creation of the first sports publications, such as the *American Farmer* (1819) and *The Spirit of the Times* (1831), and provided a market for sporting goods.

Artisans such as John W. Brunswick, a carpenter who started a flourishing business in 1845 manufacturing billiard tables, established the first sporting goods companies. In the post–Civil War era, when participation in sports boomed, sporting goods became a natural industry for retired athletes to enter. They could bank on their name to attract business, often beginning in retail, which was easier to enter than manufacturing, because of the capital commitment necessary to start a firm.

Spalding capitalized on his fame as a baseball player to open a sporting goods store and a publishing company that focused on sports publications when he joined the Chicago White Stockings in 1876. His sporting goods line became so profitable that he left playing baseball to develop the business. Spalding's company was the dominant sporting goods firm by the end of the nineteenth century, and he nurtured that position through vertical integration of the industry. He owned, for example, a lumber mill to control the source of wood for his baseball bats. Spalding also expanded horizontally by buying out some of his main sporting goods competitors, including, in the 1980's, Albert Reach and George Wright, both former baseball pioneers.

Spalding's publishing business flourished as well. He sold history books, rule books, and guidebooks and established his company as preeminent in the field. He advertised heavily in his own publications and other sports publications, which helped him capture a large market share.

By the late 1880s, guidebooks were the fastest-growing and most widely distributed sporting goods item. They listed rules and season statistics, and they featured advertising for the publisher's sporting good products. Many were published for baseball, but they were published for many other sports as well. Spalding published his first *Official Baseball Guide* for the National League in 1876. (Spalding himself, not the league, declared the book "official," a marketing ploy.) Others followed suit. Reach began publishing the official *American Association Guide* in 1883, and George Wright, brother of Harry Wright, published an official guide for the Union Association in 1884. Manufacturers saw the baseball leagues as good guarantors of quality. They sought to have a league use their equipment and then advertised the equipment as "official," capitalizing on the publicity. Indeed, this official connection became so valuable that leagues soon were paid to use a particular company's baseballs. In the late 1870s, Spalding's baseball became the official ball of the National League, after his company paid the league $1 a dozen for the privilege of supplying teams with baseballs.

Sporting goods manufacturers actively worked to promote sports to increase their potential markets. The more people golfed, fished, played ball, and bowled, the more customers would buy golf clubs, fishing rods, baseball equipment, and bowling balls. Rule books and instructional pamphlets fueled interest in these sports, and publishers added legitimacy to their publications by seeking endorsements from coaches, players, sports journalists, and league administrations. The manufacturers also helped lower the prices of their products through mass production in factories and mass sales in outlets that ranged from sporting goods stores to department stores and mail-order catalogs.

The Growth of Sports Leagues

Big-time sports leagues all evolved in a monopoly framework, seeking to control the competition, consumer base, and labor pool, with varying degrees of success. In team sports, owners formed cartels. Organizers of individual sports such as tennis and golf attempted to control the tournaments, while boxing was monopolized in the 1940s and 1950s by the mob, which controlled matchmaking, venues, and the television rights to heavyweight championship fights in the 1950s.

Without fail, the most financially successful sports leagues were cartels that grew and thrived by exploiting their athletes and granting individual owners exclusive access to discrete geographic markets. Competing leagues arose to challenge the monopoly leagues and their profits in football, hockey, basketball, and baseball. When these challengers failed, they went bankrupt. The only success they could hope to gain was a merger—of the entire league or some of its franchises—with the established league. No challenger league continued to operate independently, and each of the major sports leagues still enjoys monopoly status.

The market structure of team sports is exemplified by professional baseball. Major League Baseball (MLB) is a highly successful oligopoly (a market structure with few producers) of professional baseball teams. The teams successfully have protected themselves against competition from rival leagues for more than 130 years. The closest call came from the challenger American League, which became a part of the National League's monopoly in 1903 to form the structure—known as "organized baseball"—that exists to this day.

The MLB monopoly lost some of its power in 1976, when the arbitrators granted free agency to players, diminishing the league's exclusive control over the player labor market. Now, franchise owners must share a greater percentage of their revenue with the players, whereas until 1976, they strictly controlled how much of the revenue was diverted to the players.

In fact, the owners of professional baseball teams have acted in unison since the beginning of the major leagues. They conspired to hold down the salaries of players with a secret "reserve clause" agreement in 1879. This created a monopsony in which players could offer their services to only one buyer, organized baseball, and were bound by a contract to a single team within that organization. Virtually every new professional sports league in the future would adopt the reserve clause to keep down salaries. And this stranglehold on the labor market lasted for a century.

The legitimacy of MLB's organizational structure was tested legally when the shunned owner of the Baltimore club in the Federal League, a failed competitor to the big leagues in 1914 and 1915, sued MLB for violation of antitrust law. The U.S. Supreme Court's 1922 decision in *Federal Baseball Club v. National League*, written by Justice Oliver Wendell Holmes, Jr., ruled that baseball was not a form of interstate commerce, and therefore it was exempt from antitrust laws. In the 1950s, the courts ruled that baseball alone enjoys this exemption, but the basic league structure remains the same for all team sports.

Teams have cooperated off the field for many years to control the market for their sport and to maximize

profits. These efforts have taken place primarily through monopolization of the franchises and monopsonization of the labor markets. The franchises established local monopolies to minimize competition.

At the same time, all professional sports leagues used a labor contract that restricted players' ability to move to other teams, thus holding down their wages. This combination of restrictions has allowed teams to maximize their profits by increasing ticket revenue and lowering player salaries (historically the largest expenses for professional sports teams) beyond the levels that would be possible in competitive markets.

Monopoly control of franchises is the backbone of any sports league. Sports leagues control schedules, maintain the quality of play, and try to maximize profits. This is done in a number of ways—first of all, by cornering the market on playing talent, desirable markets, and media income. Leagues do so by signing the best available players and then tying up the next tier of young talent at the minor league level. This prepares developing players for the major leagues and keeps them away from potential competitor leagues.

Leagues also attempt to control the best markets by locating teams in large cities where there are the largest potential audiences, making it more difficult for competitors to enter the market. At the same time, leagues limit the number of franchises to fewer than the market will bear. This ensures that they can exploit monopoly profits by limiting the output of their product. Since the 1950s, this has been most evident in franchises threatening to leave town unless more fans buy season tickets and cities build them new stadiums.

These efforts have not always stifled competition. The lure of high proceeds in all major league team sports has resulted in the formation of competing leagues. In every case, however, the new leagues either failed or merged with existing leagues. Baseball has done the best job of maintaining its monopoly, such as holding off the competing Federal League in 1914–1915. An effort to organize the Continental League in 1959 nudged the majors to expand, and the competing league never got off the ground.

Basketball has a longer history of mergers, mainly encompassing regional leagues. There were several early attempts to formally organize basketball, beginning in 1898. The most successful were the Eastern League (1909–1936) and the Metropolitan League (1921–1933). The East Coast–based American Basketball League was founded in 1925, but it fell to minor league status in the 1930s. The National Basketball League was founded in 1926 as a Midwestern league. In 1946, it was challenged by the Basketball Association of America, which was established by the owners of sports arenas in major cities who hoped to find new activities for their facilities to supplement hockey. The two leagues competed for three seasons then merged to create the National Basketball Association (NBA) in 1949. The NBA weathered a long-lasting challenge from the American Basketball Association, which began in 1967. Finally, after nine seasons of competition, the leagues merged in 1976 to form the current NBA. Four of the seven surviving American Basketball Association teams were allowed to join the NBA.

Facing eight antitrust lawsuits in 1950, MLB requested that the U.S. Congress pass a bill granting antitrust immunity to all professional sports leagues. During congressional hearings, league officials and even active players testified in favor of the bill, convinced that the reserve clause was necessary to maintain a competitive balance. No legislative action was taken, however. In 1957, the House Antitrust Subcommittee revisited the issue, once again recommending no change in the status quo.

Beginning in the mid-1970s, major league players mounted a concerted attack on the teams' power over them. The Major League Baseball Players Association won the right to salary and trade arbitration, which effectively ended baseball's reserve clause in 1976. However, organized baseball maintained its rights to restrict the location of teams and to preserve each team's local monopoly. The leagues also restrict television broadcasts of games by one team within another team's television market.

Other major team sports do not have this unusual antitrust immunity, with obvious results. Other leagues have seen many more franchise relocations, as owners of teams seek the best markets in which to sell their product. From 1970 through 2006, only two MLB teams moved (the Washington Senators became the Texas Rangers in 1972, and the Montreal Expos became the Washington Nationals in 2005). During the same period, 25 teams in the other three professional sports leagues moved. There also is a substantial difference in the rate of expansion: MLB added six teams, while the other leagues added a total of 38 franchises.

Young baseball fans urge major league players not to go on strike in August 1994. The union walked out the following day, leading to the cancellation of the rest of the season. Labor disputes come as a harsh reminder to fans that pro sports are big business. *(Otto Greule Jr/Stringer/Getty Images)*

To date, none of the established team sports leagues has failed. The popularity of sports, the quality of competition at the highest level, the vast sums of television and sponsorship dollars, and the monopoly status of leagues have generated revenues sufficient to guarantee large paychecks for athletes and profits for owners. Yet even in a period of prosperity, players' conflicts with the leagues and team owners continued. Baseball in particular was damaged by two long work stoppages—called "strikes" by the owners, "lockouts" by the players—one in 1981 and the other in 1994.

Franchise Values

Sports have been about profits since the first admission fee was charged. The first professional league, the National Association of Professional Base Ball Players, founded in 1871, charged a $10 franchise fee. The latest teams to join MLB paid $130 million apiece for the privilege in 1998. The most recent expansion franchise in major North American team sports was the Charlotte Bobcats of the NBA, which paid $300 million to join the league in 2004.

The value of franchises has ballooned over time. In the early twentieth century, owning a sports franchise was a career decision. Most owners operated their team as their full-time occupation. Teams occasionally were partnerships, usually with political connections, but were not owned by corporations. In some instances, it was a natural choice for an entrepreneur with financial interests in a related business, such as a brewery, that provided complementary goods.

In 1915, the New York Yankees were sold for $460,000 (comparable to an investment of $10.3 million in 2011 dollars). In 2011, the team's value was $1.7 billion, a value attributable to its location in New York, new ballpark, lengthy history of championships and high-quality players, and lucrative media outlets. The Yankees was the highest-valued team in MLB by a large margin, followed by the Boston Red Sox ($912 million) and the Los Angeles Dodgers ($800 million), with the league average at $523 million. The least valuable franchise was the Pittsburgh Pirates ($304 million).

The most valuable teams are in the National Football League (NFL), where the average team in 2010 was worth $1.02 billion. At $1.8 billion, the Dallas Cowboys were the most valuable team in the league and the second most valuable sports franchise in the world, surpassed only by soccer's Manchester United ($1.87 billion). The Jacksonville Jaguars were the least valuable franchise ($725 million).

The average NBA team value in 2010–2011 was $369 million, ranging from the New York Knicks ($655 million) to the Milwaukee Bucks ($258 million). That same season, the average National Hockey League (NHL) franchise was worth $228 million, up from $125 million in 1997–1998. In 2010, NHL teams ranged in value from the Toronto Maple Leafs ($505 million) down to the Phoenix Coyotes ($134 million).

The higher price of a professional sports franchise is symptomatic of changes in teams' ownership structure. The typical owner of a professional sports team is now either a conglomerate, such as Disney, AOL Time Warner, or the Tribune Company, or a wealthy individual who may own a related business and operate the team on the side, perhaps as a hobby or as a complementary business. Corporate ownership allows the cross marketing of products. For example, Madison Square Garden owns not only the historic arena, but also the city's franchises in the NBA (the Knicks) and the NHL (the Rangers), and a cable television outlet to broadcast basketball, hockey, and other sporting events.

The most significant change in franchise values between 1990 and 2010 occurred as a result of new stadium construction. The construction of a new stadium or arena creates additional sources of revenue for a team owner, which influences the value of the franchise. The increase in franchise value is potentially the most profitable part of ownership. Nearly 100 new stadiums and arenas have been constructed since 1990 for the 122 teams in MLB, the NBA, the NFL, and the NHL. The value of those franchises increased an average of 20 percent the year the new stadium opened.

Sports Facilities

The construction of arenas enclosed for the purposes of convenience and controlling admission fees dates to the early nineteenth century. For example, early arenas included race courses and indoor structures for cockfighting and other baiting sports. The latter housed up to 2,000 to 3,000 spectators, each of whom paid up to a dollar for admission.

The first enclosed baseball field opened in 1862. For nearly 50 years, parks had small capacities, were wooden firetraps, and offered little sense of permanence. In the early twentieth century, fireproof structures began to be built, starting with Harvard Stadium, the first fully concrete field, in 1903. Between 1909 and 1915, most MLB teams also built fire-resistant structures with seating capacities up to 40,000.

Beginning in 1960, municipally funded sports stadiums became an important component of the commercialization of sports and reflected the perceived economic benefits to a city of hosting big-league sports. Most professional sports stadiums in North America were constructed in the center city, primarily with public monies, as teams argued that they could not afford the expense and threatened to move to a more accommodating city.

Local governments became sports promoters in the name of urban renewal and economic development, using their authority over eminent domain, bond issuance, and taxation to secure land for stadiums and parking. Cities could claim "big league" status. The teams could avoid tying up hundreds of millions of dollars in a stadium, while, at the same time, making money by selling high-priced tickets, luxury boxes, and stadium naming rights.

Commercial Aspects of College Sports and the NCAA

Intercollegiate American sports also had a commercial element from the beginning. The first intercollegiate athletic contest was the Yale–Harvard crew match in 1852. It was sponsored by the Boston, Concord, and Montreal Railroad, which paid all of the expenses for the two crews as part of a business promotion aimed at transporting spectators to the event. When college sports began to blossom by the 1870s, they were the exclusive province of student-run athletic associations that financed, recruited and coached players for, and scheduled matches for their teams.

Football became the big game at elite Eastern colleges, and coaches such as Walter Camp revised the rules to make the game more appealing as a spectator sport. As college sports became increasingly violent and popular, faculty and administration sought to take control, both to reduce the brutality and to capture the growing profits. In 1903, the Yale Athletic Association made about $100,000, more than 10 percent of the entire college budget. For large schools in the early twentieth century, football became the second-largest source of revenue after tuition, helping to make coaches and alumni fund-raisers influential on campus. Permanent stadiums were built, beginning with Harvard in 1903, followed by Princeton (capacity of 45,750) and Yale (70,869) in the 1910s, and the University of Michigan (72,000) in the 1920s.

College sports, particularly men's basketball and football, can be lucrative sources of revenue. In 2006–2007, the top college in both revenue and profits was the University of Texas, with a revenue of $63.8 million and profits of $43.2 million.

Such huge profits are not the rule, however. A study of the 330 Division I schools found that just 17 earned a net profit between 2004 and 2006, with ticket sales and private donations accounting for more than half of all revenue. All but one were from the Football Bowl Subdivision (formerly known Division 1-A).

The Media

A symbiotic relationship also has evolved between sports and the media. Sports coverage in the press sells newspapers. Broadcasts help convince fans to buy the gear, then subject them to highly profitable ads between innings and during time-outs.

Information on ball games in progress was telegraphed to saloons as early as the 1890s. In 1897, "broadcast" rights were sold for the first time to Western Union, whose telegraph wires sent a running account to local offices. Each National League team received $300 worth of free telegrams as part of a league-wide contract to transmit play-by-play coverage over the telegraph wire. The movie industry purchased the rights to film and showed highlights of the 1910 World Series for $500; a year later, the fee was $3,500. In 1913, Western Union began paying each MLB team $17,000 per year for five years for the rights to transmit inning-by-inning results of games.

The first commercial radio broadcast of a sporting event was a boxing match in early 1921 by Pittsburgh's KDKA. It was soon followed by the broadcast of the heavyweight championship match between Jack Dempsey and Georges Carpentier by New York's WJY in July of that year. In October, Newark's WJZ re-created the New York Giants and Yankees World Series. KDKA also broadcast the first college football game, between Pittsburgh and West Virginia. Such broadcasts encouraged people to buy radios and prompted stations to sell advertising to be broadcast during the games.

Team owners originally saw radio, and later television, as a threat to the value of their franchises. They resisted broadcasting their games for fear that customers would stay home and listen or watch the games for free rather than come to the stadium. They soon discovered that these media represented a source of free advertising and helped to attract even more fans. At first, teams charged little or nothing for the rights to broadcast their games, but before long, they came to see how valuable those rights could be.

The Chicago Cubs were the first team to regularly broadcast their home games, giving them away to local radio in 1925. By 1939, every team had begun regular radio broadcasts of their games. The New York teams held out the longest until 1938, when they received $100,000 in contracts for their rights. In 1946, the New York Yankees became the first team with a local television contract, when they sold the rights to their games for $75,000. By the end of the century, the team was selling those rights for $52 million per season.

The financial success of sports since 1960 is attributable largely to television exposure. The NFL and MLB, the most successful sports leagues, generate more money from television rights than they do from ticket sales. In 2005, the NFL earned nearly $4 billion per year in national television rights (more than $100 million per team), about 66 percent of total league earnings. The NFL pioneered the national television contract in 1962, sharing the revenues equally among teams regardless of market size or the number of games broadcast for each team.

MLB and the NBA in 2010 earned more than $700 million from national television rights (more than $20 million per team). The NHL's national television revenues, however, are just about $2 million per team, merely 3 percent of its total gross.

An important innovation in the business of sports was the use of sponsorship fees to promote golf and tennis by increasing the size of purses in order to attract top players and boost fan interest. Private sponsors also attached their names to postseason college football bowls. In college football, for example, the season-ending bowl games were almost all sold to sponsors, and many major bowl games were renamed to include the name of the sponsor. The money paid by the sponsors, when combined with television rights, fees, and ticket sales, made the major bowl games multimillion-dollar paydays for the participating universities.

Finally, virtually all sports stadiums and arenas were named or have been renamed for corporate backers. The average annual value of 12 major stadium deals completed in 2006 was $5.25 million, 61 percent higher than the average deal in 1999. Though most sponsors were local companies, in 2007 Barclays PLC, an international bank with no retail presence in New York, agreed to a 20-year, $400 million fee for the naming rights to a new basketball arena in Brooklyn.

The Sports Labor Revolution

In all team sports, the labor pool was exploited because the league, as a monopoly, was the only employer. The standard player contract had a form of reserve clause, instituted under the rationale that it was required to keep teams balanced, games competitive, and the league viable. The team had the right to renew a player's contract each year, restricting the player's ability to bargain, thus depressing wages. Rarely did players have any leverage, except when an insurgent rival league existed.

There were several attempts by players to organize unions to level the playing field, beginning with the Brotherhood of Professional Baseball Players in 1885, which formed its own league five years later. The Players' League consisted of cooperative teams that were owned in part by the players. Their contracts were free of the reserve clause. However, it folded after one season.

The first successful independent organization of professional athletes was the Major League Baseball Players Association, formed in 1954; however, the association became influential only after 1966, when it hired Marvin Miller, a former negotiator for the United Steelworkers union. Miller began by winning the players' confidence with a series of small gains, including increases in the minimum salary, pension contributions by owners, and limits on the maximum salary reduction that owners could impose. The union soon used its power to strike in order to gain collective bargaining, the use of agents to negotiate players' contracts, and arbitration of grievances, and it became one of the strongest labor unions in the world. Football, basketball, and hockey players followed suit, forming their own unions that staged multiple work stoppages to gain concessions.

Free Agency and Big Money

In 1970, star center fielder Curt Flood of the St. Louis Cardinals was traded to the Philadelphia. When he refused the trade, MLB Commissioner Bowie Kuhn ruled that Flood had no right to veto the trade and ordered him to play for Philadelphia or not at all. Flood chose the latter and sued MLB for violation of antitrust laws. In the 1972 ruling in the case of *Flood v. Kuhn,* the U.S. Supreme Court refused to overturn the 1922 precedent of *Federal Baseball Club v. National League,* while acknowledging that MLB's antitrust exemption was an anomaly that Congress could rectify.

The Major League Baseball Players Association challenged this system in 1974 when Oakland Athletics owner Charlie Finley failed to fulfill his contract with star hurler Jim "Catfish" Hunter, whom arbitrators declared a free agent. He signed with the New York Yankees for $3.75 million over five years. Then, just before the 1976 season, arbitrators also ruled in favor of free agency for veteran pitchers Dave McNally and Andy Messersmith, who had played in 1975 without signing a contract.

Flood lost his legal battle (and never played in the majors again), but the players ultimately won the war. In a series of labor market victories buoyed by strikes, players won the right to free agency, individual contract negotiations with agent representation, and hearing committees for disciplinary actions, among other gains. The biggest victory was free agency. These rights spread from baseball to other professional team sports. Players are no longer restrained by the reserve clause in any sport. As a result, current professional athletes are among the highest-paid workers in the world.

No longer shackled to one team forever, players earned the right to bargain with other teams for their services, changing the landscape of team sports dramatically. The average salary for a professional athlete skyrocketed from $45,000 in 1975 ($163,000 in 2005 dollars) to more than $2 million by 2005. Ballplayers now earned 100 times the average American's income, compared to five times in 1900. Of course, other factors played a role, particularly much higher revenues, thanks to television, creating a bigger pie for all to share. In 2010, the average player in the NBA made $5.85 million, in MLB, $3.3 million. In the NFL, players averaged $2.4 million, and in the NHL, they averaged $1.9 (a median of $770,000).

In addition, star athletes, going back to Babe Ruth and Honus Wagner, supplemented their income by endorsing products. Such opportunities have become so lucrative that some athletes can earn more from endorsements than from playing a sport. Furthermore, some athletes became wealthy even before accomplishing anything. In 1990, for instance, 14-year-old tennis player Jennifer Capriati received $5 million in endorsement contracts before her first pro match.

Basketball superstar Michael Jordan took endorsements to a completely new level when he signed deals with Nike and many other products, earning $30 million a year. Golfer Tiger Woods surpassed even Jordan, earning more than $100 million per year before his earning power was damaged by personal scandal.

Conclusion

The business of sports started modestly in colonial taverns. It remained relatively small in scale during the nineteenth century, when sports became increasingly commercialized, professionalized, and spectator oriented, driven by entrepreneurs who organized boxing matches, horse races, and baseball leagues. Monopsony developed in big-time sports, increasing owners' power over individual athletes. At the same time, the growing popularity of sports spurred the creation of the sporting goods industry, which, in turn, made it possible for more people to participate. In addition, as sports became big-time entertainment, publishers of books and newspapers helped stoke enthusiasm, increasing their own profits along the way.

The business took a step forward in the 1910s and 1920s with the construction of large arenas and ballparks that held larger crowds. Sportswriters helped invent and promote a golden age of sports during the 1920s, making star athletes national celebrities. The business of sports slackened during the Great Depression. Yet during this time, MLB did better than nearly every other business in America except for the motion picture industry.

After World War II, the main sports advanced with the advent of television and the building of new stadiums in the 1960s and again after 1990. Management dominated labor relations and kept down expenses by limiting wages. Owners of sports franchises were more and more often corporations that intended to create a synergy between their sports investments and their primary businesses. By the 1970s, certain sports, especially pro football, were generating enormous revenues, and the profit potential accelerated. By the mid-1970s, there was a revolution in labor–management relations that led to a dramatic increase in player salaries, resulting in many becoming multimillionaires.

Michael J. Haupert

See also: Agents; Class, Economic and Social; Crime, Organized; Drugs, Performance-Enhancing; Endorsements, Athlete; Globalization; Government, Local; Government, U.S.; Industrial Sports; Industrialization; Reserve Clause; Sporting Goods Industry; Stadiums and Arenas; Television; Urbanization.

Further Reading

Adelman, Melvin L. *A Sporting Time: New York City and the Rise of Modern Athletics, 1820–1870.* Urbana: University of Illinois Press, 1986.

Burk, Robert F. *Much More Than a Game: Players, Owners, and American Baseball Since 1921.* Chapel Hill: University of North Carolina Press, 2001.

———. *Never Just a Game: Players, Owners, and American Baseball to 1920.* Chapel Hill: University of North Carolina Press, 1994.

Gorn, Elliott J. *The Manly Art: Bare-Knuckle Prize Fighting.* Ithaca, NY: Cornell University Press, 1986.

Gorn, Elliott J., and Warren Goldstein. *A Brief History of American Sports.* New York: Hill and Wang, 1993.

Hardy, Stephen. "Adopted by All the Leading Clubs: Sporting Goods and the Shaping of Leisure, 1800–1900." In *For Fun and Profit: The Transformation of Leisure into Consumption,* ed. Richard Butsch. Philadelphia: Temple University Press, 1990.

———. "Entrepreneurs, Organization, and the Sports Marketplace." In *The New American Sport History: Recent Approaches and Perspectives,* ed. S.W. Pope. Urbana: University of Illinois Press, 1997.

Holliman, Jennie. *American Sports (1785–1835).* Philadelphia: Porcupine, 1975.

Lowenfish, Lee. *The Imperfect Diamond: A History of Baseball's Labor Wars.* New York: Da Capo, 1980.

McClellan, Keith. *The Sunday Game: At the Dawn of Professional Football.* Akron, OH: University of Akron Press, 1998.

Rader, Benjamin G. *American Sports: From the Age of Folk Games to the Age of Spectators.* Englewood Cliffs, NJ: Prentice Hall, 1983.

Riess, Steven A. "The Profits of Major League Baseball, 1900–1956." In *Baseball in America and America in Baseball,* ed. Donald G. Kyle and Robert B. Fairbanks. College Station: Texas A&M University Press, 2008.

———. *Sport in Industrial America, 1850–1920.* Wheeling, IL: Harlan Davidson, 1995.

Rottenberg, Simon. "The Baseball Players' Labor Market." *Journal of Political Economy* 64:3 (1956): 242–258.

Sammons, Jeffrey T. *Beyond the Ring: The Role of Boxing in American Society.* Urbana: University of Illinois Press, 1988.

White, G. Edward. *Creating the National Pastime: Baseball Transforms Itself, 1903–1953.* Princeton, NJ: Princeton University Press, 1996.

Camp, Walter (1859–1925)

Walter Camp, known as the "Father of American Football," was one of the most influential figures in American college football and college athletics, initiating crucial gridiron rule changes as well as pioneering the role of the football coach and athletic director. From 1878 to 1910, he was an unpaid advisor to Yale University's football team, and later he acted as Yale's athletic director while working as a businessman in New Haven, Connecticut. He also served on a variety of intercollegiate football rules committees from 1876 to 1925.

He was born in New Britain, Connecticut, on April 7, 1859, the son of Leverett L. Camp, a schoolmaster and publisher, and Ellen Cornwell. He graduated from Hopkins Grammar School in 1876. Entering Yale University, he participated in football, baseball, track, tennis, and rowing. He played on the football team for six years—four years as an undergraduate and two years as a medical student—serving as captain for three years. Because of his extensive knowledge of football, he acted as coach to the team while he was captain and continued to coach or "advise" the team after he left medical school in 1882.

Camp was most influential as a delegate to the annual intercollegiate football rules conventions. In 1880, the convention adopted his proposal that the team having possession of the ball would continue to hold it. This change substituted the more systematic football scrimmage for the far less orderly and predictable rugby scrum. The new rule took American football along a different path than British rugby. Because teams insisted on retaining possession of the ball for an entire half, Camp next proposed the yards and downs rule, which required a team to gain 5 yards (4.6 meters) in three downs in order to keep the ball. Camp also was responsible for the rule mandat-

ing 11 men on a team and numerical scoring. Later in the 1880s, committees on which he served introduced rules that allowed tackling below the waist and interference or blocking in front of the ball carrier. These changes led to a more systematic, compact, line-oriented, and rougher game. The rules also expanded football's strategic possibilities and made the game far more spectator friendly, as well as uniquely American.

After leaving Yale, Camp went to work for the Manhattan Watch Company, and then in 1883, he transferred to the New Haven Clock Company, where he spent the rest of his business career, eventually advancing to president and chairman. In 1888, he married Alice Graham Sumner, the younger half-sister of famed sociologist William Graham Sumner. Alice Camp attended football practices when her husband was unavailable and met with team leaders who gathered at their home in the evening to discuss the practices and devise strategy.

During the 1888 season, when Camp was unable to devote enough time to football and Alice functioned as co-coach, the Yale team outscored its 13 opponents 698–0. Overall, Camp's teams from 1878 to 1910, when he or his wife served as coach-advisor, recorded 285 wins, 14 losses, and 12 ties, including 29 victories over the archrival Harvard University team. Camp also traveled to California in 1892 and 1894 to assist Stanford University in preparing for their "Big Game" with the University of California, Berkeley.

Camp wrote extensively, mainly on sports and games. In 1888, he and sportswriter Caspar Whitney devised the All-America team, which initially consisted only of players from Harvard, Yale, and Princeton. As college football programs spread in the 1890s, Camp either traveled to watch key games or relied on a network of friends and correspondents to supply information about All-American candidates until his death in 1925. He also wrote more than 200 articles and wrote or edited nearly 30 books, including juvenile fiction. The

A player and coach at Yale and Stanford universities, Walter Camp—the "Father of American Football"—proposed rule changes that defined the modern game. His innovations include the 11-man team, down system, and hike from scrimmage. *(Hulton Archive/Getty Images)*

best-known of his books for boys were *The Substitute* (1908) and *Jack Hall at Yale* (1909). He collaborated with Harvard's Lorin F. Deland, inventor of the flying wedge, on *Football* (1896), and for 31 years edited *Spalding's Official Intercollegiate Football Guide*.

Beginning in the 1890s, the sport of football came under attack as brutal and unsportsmanlike. Because of his expertise, Camp was asked to head a Harvard-appointed committee that sent questionnaires to players, former players, faculty, and athletic authorities. His edited responses were included in *Football Facts and Figures* (1894), a work heavily weighted in favor of the existing style of play. In 1894, the intercollegiate rules committee made additional changes to the game, eliminating the flying wedge and certain formations from scrimmage. Nevertheless, criticism of football persisted, growing especially heated after the serious injury or death of a player.

In 1905, Camp attended a White House meeting called by President Theodore Roosevelt, who hoped to convince the six coaches and advisors to alter the game to make it less violent and more sportsmanlike. In spite of the president's intervention, a spate of serious injuries and deaths, mainly in high school or sandlot games, put Camp and his rules committee on the defensive. On December 28 of that year, at a conference of faculty representatives, a reform committee was appointed. The changes triggered by the crisis of 1905–1906 reduced Camp's power over rulemaking and led to a series of reforms, one of which was the forward pass. Camp was opposed to the forward pass, but he devised plays that employed it. In 1910, Camp resigned as coach-advisor to the Yale team, though he returned briefly in 1916.

When the United States entered World War I in 1917, Camp became director of the U.S. Navy Training Camps' Physical Development Program. Camp commuted to Washington, D.C., where he worked with President Woodrow Wilson's cabinet to keep them in shape, earning them the nickname "Walter Scamps." He also founded the Senior Service Corps in New Haven for men past the age for military service. Members spent an hour a day, three days a week in physical training, such as sit-ups and military drills.

From his attempts to promote fitness, Camp distilled 12 exercises that he dubbed the "Daily Dozen." Appalled by the poor physical condition of American military personnel, Camp published his exercises in a magazine article and in a pamphlet entitled "Daily Dozen." Although his profits from the pamphlet were modest, he toyed with commercial fitness ventures in the postwar period.

On March 14, 1925, while attending an intercollegiate football rules committee meeting in New York, Camp failed to show up for a morning session. He had died of a heart attack during the night. Three years later, before the Yale–Dartmouth game on November 3, 1928, the massive $300,000 Walter Camp Memorial Gateway was dedicated near the entrance of the Yale Bowl. It was paid for with contributions in Camp's memory from more than 220 universities and 270 prep schools.

John Watterson

See also: Football, College; Roosevelt, Theodore.

Further Reading

Camp, Walter. *American Football*. New York: Harper & Brothers, 1892.

Martin, John S. "Walter Camp and His Gridiron Game." *American Heritage* 12 (October 1961): 50–55, 77–81.

Powel, Harford, Jr. *Walter Camp, the Father of American Football.* Boston: Little, Brown, 1926.

Smith, Ronald A. *Sports and Freedom: The Rise of Big-Time College Athletics.* New York: Oxford University Press, 1988.

Canadiens, Montreal

The oldest and most storied franchise in professional hockey, the Montreal Canadiens have won the Stanley Cup 24 times, all but once as a member of the National Hockey League (NHL). The team has come to represent the nationalistic hopes, aspirations, and struggles of the French-speaking Quebecois. It is said that every francophone boy has dreamed of playing for his beloved Canadiens. The affection of the team's fans is reflected in the sheer number of nicknames: the "Habs" (from *les habitants,* loosely meaning "the locals"), the "Flying Frenchmen," and the "Tricolor," or *Bleu, Blanc, et Rouge* (blue, white, and red), referring to its jersey colors.

Origins

The "Flying Frenchmen" were born in 1909 when John Ambrose O'Brien took the lead in establishing Canada's National Hockey Association (NHA). In the league's first season, a Montreal franchise appeared as "Les Canadiens," which O'Brien hoped to sell to a francophone sportsman as soon as possible.

After the first brief season in winter and spring 1910, Montreal sports promoter George Kennedy (born George Washington Kendall) brought a suit against the NHA and O'Brien for copyright infringement. Kennedy claimed that his sports club, the Club Athletique Canadien, owned title to the name "Canadiens." O'Brien, who still had control of the Canadiens franchise, and others in the league, offered to settle with Kennedy by giving him uncontested rights to the name and the players from one of his other NHA teams, the Haileybury Comets. Kennedy agreed, and the new Canadiens began the 1910–1911 season under Kennedy's ownership.

From the beginning, the NHA's plan was for the Canadiens to sign only French-speaking players. Soon, however, the rule was changed to allow the Candiens two Anglophone players, and to allow the other teams two Francophone players each.

In 1914, Kennedy introduced the now-iconic red jerseys with a horizontal blue stripe framed by white stripes across the middle. The Canadiens won their first Stanley Cup in 1916, defeating the Portland Rosebuds of the Pacific Coast Hockey Association. The next year, they lost to the Seattle Metropolitans, the first U.S.-based team to win the Stanley Cup.

In 1917, a series of disputes with combative Toronto Blueshirts owner Eddie Livingstone led Kennedy and four other owners of NHA franchises to withdraw from the association and form the National Hockey League. Except for the exclusion of Livingstone, the new league continued with the same rules and procedures as the NHA.

The Canadiens soon proved themselves the dominant force in the new league. They lost the first NHL championship in 1918 to the Toronto Arenas, the eventual Stanley Cup winner and the forerunner of Montreal's bitter rival, the Maple Leafs. But in 1918–1919, the Canadiens dominated the NHL and again faced Seattle for the Cup. With the series tied at 2–2–1, the deadly Spanish flu reached Seattle, forcing the cancellation of the rest of the games. Nearly every Canadiens player fell ill, and one, Joe Hall, died.

Team owner Kennedy never recovered from the flu's effects; he died on October 19, 1921, at age 39. Two weeks later, on November 3, 1921, his widow sold the Canadiens for just $11,000 to businessmen Joseph Cattarinich, Leo Dandurand, and Louis A. Letourneau. Cattarinich and Dandurand later bought out Letourneau.

Dandurand was an excellent promoter, and he built the Canadiens and the NHL around the swift-skating Howie Morenz, the "Babe Ruth of Hockey." Despite stars such as Morenz, Aurial Joliat, and Billy Boucher, the Habs's overall playoff performance often was mediocre, although the team won its second Stanley Cup in 1924. The next year, star goalie Georges Vezina died of tuberculosis. In his honor, the Canadiens gave the NHL the Vezina Trophy to recognize the best goaltender in the league.

Montreal won the Stanley Cup in both 1930 and 1931, but with Joliat and Morenz now aging, the team soon fell into the NHL's lower ranks. When it finished with the league's worst record in the 1935–1936 season, the Canadiens received from the worried NHL exclusive rights to all French Canadian players for two years.

Montreal's fortunes improved in 1936–1937, and it finished with the league's the second-best record, but that campaign was dampened by the death of 34-year-old Morenz on March 8, 1937. In a January 28 game, Morenz suffered multiple leg fractures when his skate got caught in the boards after a hard check by Chicago's Earl Seibert. Morenz developed several blood clots in his injured leg, which led to a fatal embolism. More than 10,000 mourners filed by his coffin, which lay in state at center ice in the Forum.

In 1935, Cattarinich and Dandurand sold the Canadiens to the Canadian Arena Company, which owned the rival Montreal Maroons, for $165,000. The Maroons folded amid the Great Depression, and the Canadiens struggled on and off the ice as well.

After winning just ten games in 1939–1940, Montreal hired Toronto's former coach, Dick Irvin, who soon turned the team into a powerhouse. Led by its fabled "Punch Line" of Elmer Lach, Hector "Toe" Blake, and Maurice "Rocket" Richard, Montreal lost only five games in the 50-game 1943–1944 season and raised the Cup for the fifth time. They won the Cup a sixth time in 1946 but spent the last years of the 1940s in the shadow of the Maple Leafs and much of the early 1950s chasing the Detroit Red Wings.

Molson Takes Over

Besides Irwin, the owners of the team also hired Toronto General Manager Frank Selke in 1946 after he resigned following a series of disputes with Leafs owner Conn Smythe. Selke built a strong farm system for the cash-strapped Canadiens, obtaining young players such as goalie Jacques Plante and rugged defenseman Doug Harvey. The Canadiens even bought the entire Quebec Senior League just to acquire center Jean Béliveau. The moves paid off with a Stanley Cup victory in 1953 and sowed the seeds for the future. The team's money woes ended when Molson Breweries purchased the Canadiens in 1957.

Montreal's obsession with its team during this era was epitomized by the public reaction to the suspension of Richard on March 13, 1955, for the balance of the season and the playoffs by NHL president Clarence Campbell for hitting a linesman during a fight in Boston. Campbell foolishly attended the Habs's next home game on March 17 with Detroit. Montreal fans verbally and physically abused the league president, and when a tear gas bomb exploded, Campbell ordered the game forfeited. Angry Habs fans rioted in the streets, causing several million dollars in damage. Playing without Richard, the Canadiens lost the Cup finals to the Red Wings.

Irvin left the club after the 1954–1955 season to coach the Chicago Blackhawks. He was replaced by Toe Blake, who molded a dynasty that won five straight Cups from 1956 to 1960. The Canadiens, without the newly retired Richard, appeared set to win a sixth

straight Cup in 1961, but the Blackhawks stunned Montreal in the semifinals and went on to win the Cup.

Montreal did not hoist the Cup again until 1965; the team repeated this success the following year. However, in 1967, Canada's centennial year, an over-the-hill Toronto team upset the heavily favored Canadiens in the last Cup final before the league expanded.

In the first and second years of expansion, the Canadiens twice won the Cup, defeating the expansion St. Louis Blues. They missed the playoffs in 1970, but with rookie Ken Dryden in goal, the Canadiens roared back in 1971 and defeated Chicago to claim the Cup. The Habs's beloved captain, Béliveau, retired after the victory.

Under Coach Scotty Bowman, Montreal won the Cup in 1973, and in 1976 the team began a streak of four straight Cup wins. That team featured Guy Lafleur, who scored 50 goals in six straight seasons, and three All-Star defensemen in Serge Savard, Guy Lapointe, and Larry Robinson. In 1976–1977, Montreal lost just eight games in an 80-game schedule.

By the 1980s, many of the Habs's best players had either retired or had been traded. They won the Cup in 1986, defeating the Calgary Flames behind rookie Patrick Roy's phenomenal goaltending, and only one Cup in the 1990s, the twenty-fourth, and last, against the Los Angeles Kings in 1993.

Montreal struggled from 1995 into the new century, missing the playoffs five times from 1995 to 2007, and going through seven coaches. Disputes between players and management also colored those years, leading to acrimonious trades of players such as Patrick Roy, Guy Carbonneau, and Brian Savage. In 1996, the Canadiens abandoned the historic Forum for the new Molson (now Bell) Centre, which proved less hospitable. Then, in 2000, longtime owners Molson sold the team to American investor George N. Gillett, Jr., after he promised to keep the franchise in Montreal.

The team has enjoyed few highlights in recent years. On November 22, 2003, the Canadiens participated in the Heritage Classic, the first outdoor game in NHL history, defeating the Edmonton Oilers 4–3 at Commonwealth Stadium in Edmonton. The game was seen by a record crowd of more than 55,000 spectators.

Problems continued to plague the team, with General Manager Bob Gainey firing Coach Claude Julien in January 2006 and taking over behind the bench himself. Gainey also traded controversial goalie Jose Theodore, a former league Most Valuable Player, to Colorado. The team barely qualified for the playoffs and lost in the opening round to the Carolina Hurricanes, the eventual

Cup winner. Under new coach Guy Carbonneau, the team's fortunes did not improve in 2006–2007, and Montreal missed the playoffs by 1 point on the last day of the season. This was not the performance the Canadians expected of its once-great franchise. The team did somewhat better in subsequent years, advancing as far as the conference finals in 2009–2010, before losing to the Philadelphia Flyers.

Nigel Anthony Sellars

See also: Ice Hockey.

Further Reading

Béliveau, Jean, with Chrys Goyens and Allan Turowetz. *My Life in Hockey.* Toronto, Canada: McClelland & Stewart, 1994.

Cohen, Richard. "Montreal Canadiens." In *Professional Sports Team Histories: Hockey,* ed. Michael L. LaBlanc. Detroit, MI: Gale Research, 1994.

Goyens, Chrys, and Allan Turowetz. *Lions in Winter.* Toronto, Canada: Penguin, 1987.

"Montreal Canadiens." In *Total Hockey,* 2nd ed., ed. Dan Diamond. Kingston, NY: Total Sports, 2000.

Richard, Maurice, and Stan Fischler. *The Flying Frenchmen: Hockey's Great Dynasty.* New York: Hawthorn, 1971.

Canine Sports

Dogs have played several important roles in North American sport. They were, and remain, an integral part of the hunting experience as locators and retrievers of game, and in some cases as hunters. Dogs also were employed in the nineteenth century to bait and kill animals ranging from rats to bulls to other dogs for the viewing pleasure of spectators. This pastime has long been banned in North America, yet it continues illegally to this day. Finally, in the twentieth century, dogs raced in the Great North pulling sleds, and greyhounds raced at dog tracks for the purpose of wagering.

Hunting

North American hunters always have employed dogs to find and retrieve game. Huntsmen used Newfoundland retrievers along the Atlantic shore to hunt in bays and salt marshes, while setters were used in the rough country of the Northeast to hunt woodcock and grouse, and pointers were popular in the South for hunting bobwhite quail. Hounds often did the actual killing of game.

Some hunters used sight hounds, such as whippets, which have excellent vision and speed and stalk their prey. More commonly, hunters utilized scent hounds, such as coonhounds and basset hounds, which have extremely sensitive noses and hunt by scent. Most breeds of scent hounds have deep, booming voices and use them actively when running and especially when following a scent trail.

These dogs were used to trail game, such as foxes, often in packs. The first fox hunting club was the Gloucester Fox Hunting Club, founded in Philadelphia in 1766. Hunters typically were led on long chases that ended with the dogs either treeing the quarry or killing it.

Baiting Sports

English colonists brought a tradition of baiting animals to the New World. Tavern keepers, for example, sponsored matches between bulldogs and bulls. Bulldogs were extremely strong and determined, and they inherited a propensity to grab the bull by the nose, rather than by other body parts. Terriers usually were used to bait rats. Spectators wagered on the time and number of rats killed—15 in a minute was considered an excellent score.

These sports were banned in Great Britain in 1835 but were very popular among the North American sporting fraternity. Tournaments held in the 1850s almost daily at Kit Burns's Sportsman Hall in New York City drew as many as 400 people, taxing the 250-seat arena. Reformers in the state banned blood sports in 1856, but enforcement was lax. One year later, the *New York Clipper,* a popular sporting weekly, devoted an entire section to rat baiting and dog fighting. Dog baiting survived in New York until the 1880s.

Dog Fighting

Dog fighting was a popular underground sport in the United States into the late nineteenth century. Promoters mainly used the English Staffordshire bull terrier, which first was imported around 1817 and became commonplace at mid-century when it was brought over by Irish and English immigrants. Over time, these dogs were bred to be larger and stockier, creating the American pit bull terrier. They were used to fight dogs in matches all over the country, including those at Burns's Sportsman Hall.

Most states banned dog fighting in the 1860s, forcing the sport underground. *The New York Times* in the 1870s reported a number of illegal fights in the metropolitan area. Despite its illegality, the United Kennel

Club, founded in 1898 (and still in existence) to promote working dogs, briefly sanctioned dog fighting.

The sport of dog fighting currently is a felony in every U.S. state, as well as in the District of Columbia, Puerto Rico, and the Virgin Islands. However, enforcement was lax until the early 2000s, by which time it had become popular in inner-city neighborhoods and closely connected to the activities of street gangs. The Animal Fighting Prohibition Enforcement Act of 2007 made interstate or foreign transport of animals for fighting purposes a federal crime, with a penalty of up to three years in jail and a $250,000 fine for each offense.

Psychologists say that many owners of fighting dogs see them as a positive reflection of their manhood. The practice has been glorified in urban music and gained popularity among professional athletes, most notably Atlanta Falcons quarterback Michael Vick, who was sentenced to 23 months in federal prison for his involvement in promoting dog fighting.

Sled Racing

Sled racing, or mushing, probably started as an impromptu challenge between two trappers. It became a popular sport in winter when Alaskan mining towns were being shut down.

The first official race was the All Alaska Sweepstakes in 1908. John Hegness won the 408-mile (657-kilometer) round-trip from Nome to Candle in 119 hours, 15 minutes, and 12 seconds. Two years later, John "Iron Man" Johnson completed the race in 74 hours, 14 minutes, and 37 seconds. His record lasted until 2008, when Mitch Seavey won with a time of 61 hours, 29 minutes, and 45 seconds, earning a $100,000 prize.

The 1910 race introduced the first Siberian huskies to Alaska. They soon replaced the Alaskan malamute and various mongrels as the favored sledding dog; however, other types of dogs still are used in the sport.

The most famous event in Alaskan mushing was the 1925 "Great Race of Mercy." At the time, Nome was suffering a diphtheria epidemic, which was especially deadly for the local population because Inuit children had no natural immunity to the disease. The nearest location with serum was Anchorage, but it was impossible to get the antitoxin by plane. No one had ever flown the route in winter, and furthermore, the planes had been dismantled for the season. Governor Scott Bone had a 20-pound (9-kilogram) cylinder of serum sent by train to Nenana, where a relay began using 22 mushers and more than 100 sled dogs, who carried the package 674 miles (1,085 kilometers) to Nome in less than six days.

The most renowned race, and the most popular sporting event in Alaska, is the Iditarod Trail Sled Dog Race, which follows a 1,049-mile (1,688-kilometer) route from Willow to Nome. It began in 1973, when the sport was enjoying a resurgence. The record for the race was set in 2002 by Swiss musher Martin Buser at 8 days, 22 hours, 46 minutes, and 2 seconds. The first woman champion was Libby Riddles in 1985, who was named Professional Sportswoman of the Year by the Women's Sports Foundation; she was followed by Susan Butcher, who won in 1986–1988 and in 1990. The Iditarod typically draws more than 50 mushers from around the globe and 1,000 dogs. The best teams cost between $80,000 and $100,000 a year to train and support. The top prize is about $69,000, but additional money comes from sponsorships, lectures, endorsements, and book deals.

Outside Alaska, the best-known race was the American Dog Derby, held in 1917 in Ashton, Idaho, until 1961, when it was supplanted by snowmobiling. The race was reinstituted in 1993.

Dog Racing

While some greyhounds were brought to America by early Europeans explorers and later settlers, the breed was first imported in large numbers from England and Ireland in the mid-1800s to help protect crops from jackrabbits. These dogs can reach speeds of 40 miles (64 kilometers) per hour, and speed competitions developed, sometimes at county fairs, in which two competing dogs would chase a live rabbit (coursing).

U.S. cavalry officers often kept greyhounds to catch game and help scouts. In 1878, Major James H. "Hound Dog" Kelly's four greyhounds set what was considered a record by running down 6 out of 12 antelope, marking the start of American coursing.

In 1905, Owen Patrick Smith, director of the chamber of commerce in Hot Springs, South Dakota, set up a coursing meet to promote tourism. Feeling that it was a cruel sport, he experimented with the idea of greyhounds chasing a mechanical hare around an oval track. In 1910, he patented an "inanimate hare conveyor," which he tried out nine years later at Emeryville, California, using a motorized four-wheel cart to carry the hare around the track. The meet was a failure, but a second at Tulsa, Oklahoma, at which bookmakers took bets on the races, was a success.

Smith took his invention to Florida in 1922 and built a track at Humbuggus (later renamed Hialeah), adding night racing three years later, which helped the business take off. Smith formed a partnership in 1926 with Edward "Eddie" J. O'Hare, his lawyer and a St. Louis politician, establishing the International Greyhound Racing Association. The pair opened a track outside Kansas City with the support of local bootleggers and politicians, and another in Miami Beach.

Smith died in 1927, and O'Hare moved to Chicago, where he became Al Capone's lawyer. He opened the Hawthorne Kennel Club in Stickney for Capone and soon opened a track in Massachusetts and two more in Florida. Although dog racing was illegal in Illinois, with bribes and gangster support, it went on without interference. Hawthorne faced competition from the Fairview Kennel Club track, owned by rival mobster George "Bugs" Moran, but Capone had it burned down in retaliation for Moran's hijacking a liquor shipment.

Capone took over the International Greyhound Racing Association, which controlled racing in Miami, Tampa, and Jacksonville, where pari-mutuel racing was legalized in 1932, and in New Orleans, where it was not. Dog racing ended in Illinois in 1933 after a prolonged legal fight when the state would not permit pari-mutuel betting at dog tracks. By 1935, there were eight dog tracks in Florida, and dog racing continued in other states.

The sport reached the peak of its popularity in 1992, when attendance approached 3.5 million. Nearly $3.5 billion was wagered at pari-mutuel windows on 16,827 races at more than 50 tracks in 15 states, making it the sixth most popular spectator sport.

Since then, the sport has declined in the face of pressure from animal rights groups protesting the abuse of the animals, especially dogs that no longer race. It also has been affected by competition due to the legalization of casinos and other gambling venues. By 1998, betting had dropped to $983.7 million, revenues had fallen by nearly 50 percent, and 13 tracks had closed. The most successful dog racing tracks are located in Iowa, Rhode Island, and West Virginia, where attendees also can gamble at slot machines or video lottery terminals.

In 2010, there were 40 tracks in 12 states, including 16 in Florida, and the sport drew about 15 million spectators, who bet over $2 billion. States and county governments receive over $100 million annually in revenue from greyhound racing.

Steven A. Riess

See also: Cockfighting; Gambling; Violence in Sports.

Further Reading

American Dog Derby, Ashton, Idaho. http://www.americandog derby.org.

Cantwell, Robert. "Run, Rabbit, Run: No Harebrained Scheme, Owen Smith's Mechanical Bunny Put Dog Racing on the Track and Helped Nab Al Capone." *Sports Illustrated* 39:9 (August 27, 1973): 64–67, 70–72, 74.

Eidinger, Joan. "Nowhere to Run: Dog Racing in Decline." *Animals' Agenda* (September/October 2000).

Fleig, Deiter. *The History of Fighting Dogs.* Neptune City, NJ: 124 T.F.H. Publications, 1996.

Gibson, Hanna. "Dog Fighting Detailed Discussion." Michigan State University College of Law, Animal Legal and Historical Center, 2005. http://www.animallaw.info.

"The Greyhound Racing Association of America, Inc." http://www.gra-america.org.

Homan, Michael. *A Complete History of Fighting Dogs.* New York: Howell Book House, 1999.

Jones, Caroline. "Fox Hunting in America." *American Heritage* 24:6 (October 1973): 62–68, 101.

Krout, John Allen. *Annals of American Sport.* Vol. 15, *The Pageant of America.* New Haven, CT: Yale University Press, 1929.

Mozee, Yvonne. "Dog Racing Capital of the World." *Alaska Journal* 14:2 (1984): 40–47.

Raitz, K.B. "Fox Hunting." In *The Theater of Sport,* ed. K.B. Raitz. Baltimore: Johns Hopkins University Press, 1995.

Canoeing

Canoeing is a recreational sport in which a light boat, either a canoe or a kayak, is propelled through the water with a paddle. Canoeing originated in North America among Native Americans, who constructed boats from tree bark that were used on streams, rivers, and lakes. In the Far North, the Inuit used animal skins to fashion kayaks, which they paddled on the inland and ocean waters.

By the nineteenth century, canoeing had become a competitive sport among European settlers, who engaged in flatwater sprint races. Whitewater canoeing became an international sport in the 1940s. North Americans dominated canoeing for a generation, but then endured years of mediocrity in the sport. Canadians and Americans regained championship status in canoeing in the 1980s.

Canoes come in two types: the open vessel, known internationally as the Canadian or C-boat, in which the paddler kneels and propels the boat with a single-blade paddle, and the closed-deck kayak or K-boat, in which the paddler sits and uses a double-blade paddle. Formal competition involves one, two, or four paddlers (C-1, C-2, and C-4; K-1, K-2, and K-4). Only men compete in canoes, but both men and women vie in kayaks. Racing events include flatwater sprint races of 200, 500, and 1,000 meters (219, 547, and 1,094 yards); slalom, in which contestants pass through a set of "gates" on a whitewater course; and marathons, usually 35–40 kilometers (22–25 miles).

The Emergence of Canoe Racing

In 1535, French explorer Jacques Cartier was the first European to adopt the canoe in place of heavy rowboats for speedier inland waterway travel. Other European explorers, settlers, and fur traders soon adopted the lighter boats as well. Canoe races initially were held by Native Americans and later by settlers.

By the early 1800s, rowing regattas incorporated canoe races into their meets, and before long there were a number of North American boating clubs devoted to canoeing. In the 1870s, canoe races became a part of aquatic carnivals, which introduced the sport to a broader audience.

The formation of the American Canoe Association (ACA) in 1880 and the running of its first regatta helped generate interest, though the first national championships in canoeing and kayaking were not established until 1930. Canadian clubs formed the ACA's northern division until 1900, when they organized the Canadian Canoe Association and staged the first national Canadian championships.

Twentieth Century

Canoeing became an international sport with the founding of the International Representation for the Canoeing Sport in 1924. It was renamed the International Canoe Federation (ICF) in 1946.

Canoeing entered Olympic competition in 1924 as a demonstration sport, employing American and Canadian paddlers. It became a permanent Olympic sport at the Berlin Games in 1936. That year, Canada's Frank Amyot won a gold medal (C-1, 1,000 meters/1,093 yards), and the Canadian team went on to take a silver (C-2, 10,000 meters/10,936 yards) and a bronze (C-2, 1,000 meters). For the United States, Ernest Riedel, winner of 11 national titles, earned a bronze medal (K-1, 10,000 meters). Women only gradually came into canoeing, making their first Olympic appearance in kayaking in 1948.

Whitewater canoeing grew in popularity after World War II, employing a descending 300-meter (328-yard) course through turbulent rapids, currents, and eddies while navigating through gates. The ICF introduced World Cup competition in whitewater in 1949;

it became an Olympic sport in 1972; and it achieved permanent status 20 years later.

The United States performed well in the World Cup championships during the 1980s, taking seven consecutive world titles in C-1 team competition beginning in 1979. That year, a team led by five-time C-1 world titlist Jon Lugbill and two-time C-1 world titlist David Hearn won the World Cup. American women took K-1 team titles in 1973 and 1979, the latter led by K-1 titlist Cathy Hearn. In 2002, Rebecca Giddens won a world title in K-1. In the discontinued mixed C-2 competition, the United States won four consecutive world titles (1973–1981). David Ford earned Canada's first world championship in slalom when he took the K-1 title in 1999.

A newer variation of canoeing is wildwater racing. The first international competition took place in 1959. Paddlers originally competed as individuals and as part of a team, racing their craft down a whitewater course of 4–7 kilometers (2–4 miles) in the fastest time possible. More recent events are wildwater sprints of 400 and 800 meters (437 and 875 yards). North Americans rarely have medaled in wildwater, but the U.S. men took the bronze in C-1 team competition in 1971 and in the C-2 team competition in 1977. In women's K-1 team competition, the United States took the silver medal in 1973 and the gold in 1979.

In the late 1950s, long-distance flatwater canoeing was eliminated from competition. After 1956, the 10,000-meter event was dropped from the Olympic Games; after 1993, the World Cup eliminated 10,000-meter events for men and 5,000-meter (5,468-yard) events for women and added 200-meter (219-yard) events. However, marathon canoeing gradually rose in popularity. The United States Canoe Association, founded in 1968, promoted the event.

Twelve years later, the Canadian Marathon Canoe Racing Association was established, and its first national championships were held the following year. The ICF introduced World Cup competition in the marathon in 1988. North Americans lagged behind their European competition, with only a Canadian pair taking a C-2 second place in the 2,000-meter (2,187-yard) World Cup. There are also extreme distance events, notably the Missouri River 340 (340 miles/547 kilometers, the longest nonstop event) and the Yukon River Quest (461 miles/742 kilometers).

After World War II, North American paddlers failed to maintain competitiveness in international flatwater competition, but they returned to prominence in the 1980s. At the 1984 Olympic Games in Los Angeles, a Canadian pair took the 1,000-meter K-2, and Larry Cain won the 500-meter (547-yard) C-1. At the 1988 Games in Seoul, Korea, American Gregory Barton took the gold medal in the 1,000-meter K-1 and the 1,000-meter K-2 (with Norman Bellingham). Barton also won three world titles in the 10,000-meter K-1 from 1985 to 1991.

Modern Competition

Canadian Caroline Brunet is recognized as the greatest North American kayaker in history. She won two silver medals and one bronze in the 500-meter in three Olympics (1996–2004), and ten world titles in the 200-, 500-, and 1,000-meter races (1997–2003).

Founded in 1989, the U.S. Canoe and Kayak Team, which was renamed USA Canoe/Kayak in 2005, currently selects and trains U.S. Olympic teams. Hoping to improve American competitiveness against the Eastern European powers, the organization opened a huge flatwater training facility in Oklahoma City and a large training facility for slalom in Charlotte, North Carolina, in 2006.

The Canadian Canoe Association, which was renamed CanoeKayak Canada in 2005, also has worked to upgrade its canoeing program. The Canadian men captured the silver medal at the 2008 Olympic Games in Beijing, China, in the 500-meter K-1 and the bronze in the 1,000-meter C-1.

The International Canoe Federation sponsors marathons of at least 20 kilometers (12.4 miles) for men and 15 kilometers (9 miles) for women, although world championship races usually are twice these lengths. The longest canoe race in the world is the Yukon 1000 (1,600 kilometers/1,000 miles), which runs from Whitehorse, Yukon, Canada, downriver to the Pipeline Bridge on the Dalton Highway, the Yukon River's final road access point in Alaska.

Robert Pruter

See also: Fishing; Rowing.

Further Reading

Franks, C.E.S. "White Water Canoeing: An Aspect of Canadian Socio-Economic History." *Queen's Quarterly* 82:2 (1975): 175–188.

Poling, Jim, Sr. *The Canoe: An Illustrated History.* Woodstock, VT: Countryman, 2000.

Ruffan, James, and Bert Horwood, eds. *Canexus: The Canoe in Canadian Culture.* Toronto, Canada: Betelgeuse, 1988.

Canucks, Vancouver

Vancouver, Canada, has a long and rich hockey heritage. Its professional team, the Vancouver Canucks, was established in 1911 and played in the Pacific Coast League and, until 1970, in the Western Hockey League. In that year, Vancouver received a franchise in the National Hockey League (NHL) and adopted the name "Canucks," a common nickname for Canadians. The team, which plays at Rogers Arena, has made seven appearances in post-season play but has never won the Stanley Cup.

The new squad joined the NHL, together with the Buffalo Sabres, during the league's second phase of expansion in 1970. The Canucks have never won the Stanley Cup, but they enjoyed sustained playoff runs to reach the Stanley Cup finals in 1982 (losing to the New York Islanders) and 1994 (losing to the New York Rangers). The second defeat sparked rioting among disappointed fans in downtown Vancouver on June 14, 1994, causing $1.1 million in property damage. Despite sustained periods when on-ice success was scarce, the franchise's ownership situation, its early interest in European players, and its involvement in at least three legal controversies all highlight important themes in North American sports history.

The arrival of the NHL franchise in Vancouver, and its continued operation, depended on both local and external ownership. When local attempts to secure an NHL expansion franchise proved unsuccessful in the 1960s, the Minnesota-based Medical Investment Corporation (Medicor) was approached to assume majority control of the franchise and to assist with the $6 million franchise fee.

In 1974, the Vancouver-based Western Broadcast Sales Corporation, headed by Frank Griffiths, purchased the team. Ownership of the team later passed to Griffiths's son Arthur, who maintained control of the franchise and its parent company, Northwest Entertainment Group, until 1995. To support plans to develop a franchise in the National Basketball Association (the Vancouver Grizzlies) and build the new General Motors Place arena (seating 18,630 for hockey), Griffiths sold a controlling interest in Northwest Entertainment Group to Seattle billionaire John E. McCaw, Jr.

The Canucks returned to local ownership in March 2005, when the Aquilini Investment Group secured 50 percent of McCaw's shares, then became sole owner in November 2006, when it bought out McCaw's remaining interest. A lawsuit launched by two of Francesco Aquilini's former business partners contesting his ownership of the club was dismissed by the British Columbia Supreme Court in January 2008.

The team generally has lacked marquee players, with the exceptions of Pavel Bure (1991–1999) and Roberto Luongo (2006–). The team's two most celebrated players, Stan Smyl (1978–1991) and Trevor Linden (1988–1998, 2001–2008), provided solid offensive contributions, while developing strong reputations for leadership, an unceasing work ethic, and community involvement with local charities.

In an attempt to improve the team's on-ice performance, the Canucks were among the first NHL teams to embark on a sustained effort to secure European talent. In the late 1970s and early 1980s, the team focused its recruitment efforts on Sweden, obtaining players such as Thomas Gradin (1978–1986), Lars Lindgren (1978–1983), Lars Molin (1981–1984), and Patrick Sundstrom (1982–1987). In 1981, the Canucks turned their attention to Czechoslovakia to secure the services of veteran international stars Ivan Hlinka (1981–1983) and Jiri Bubla (1981–1986).

By the mid-1980s, their focus shifted to the Soviet Union, as they obtained the rights to two members of the Central Red Army team's top line: Igor Larionov (1989–1992) and Vladamir Krutov (1989–1990). The decision to draft Bure in 1989 resulted in the Canucks's most productive Soviet signing. More recently, the team has returned to its focus on Swedish talent, signing players such as Markus Naslund (1995–2008), Mattias Ohlund (1997–), Daniel Sedin (2000–), and Henrik Sedin (2000–).

The Canucks's first major legal dispute involved accusations of tampering and conflict of interest. In 1987, the franchise was embroiled in a dispute with the NHL as it reached an agreement with Coach Pat Quinn of the Los Angeles Kings to become the Canucks's general manager and president. Concerned about public perceptions of impropriety, as Quinn still was under contract with the Kings, NHL President John Ziegler levied a $310,000 fine against the Canucks and banned Quinn from coaching in the league until 1990. The team contested the ruling in court, and the fine was reduced to $10,000. The parties reached a compromise that allowed Quinn to take up his managerial duties at the end of the 1987 season.

Two other legal controversies focused on the extent to which on-ice violence in the NHL should be subject to legal prosecution. During a February 21, 2000, game, the Boston Bruins's Marty McSorley violently struck Vancouver Canuck Donald Brashear on the head with his stick, knocking him unconscious. McSorley received a one-year suspension from the NHL. The case went to court, and McSorley was convicted of assault with a weapon, but he received a suspended sentence.

A 2004 case revisited the issue of violence in sports—but this time, a Canuck was the aggressor. On March 8, 2004, Todd Bertuzzi violently attacked the Colorado Avalanche's Steve Moore from behind, leaving Moore with injuries that ended his playing career. Bertuzzi was suspended by the NHL until August 2005. He pleaded guilty to a charge of assault causing bodily harm but received a conditional sentence of probation and community service.

The Canucks made the playoffs in 2003–2004, 2006–2007, and 2008–2009 through 2010–2011, when they won the Presidents' Trophy, coming in first in the NHL with 117 points, led by Daniel Sedin, whose 104 points led the league, following his twin Henrik, who had led the year before. The Canucks captured the Western Conference championship but lost the Stanley Cup in seven games to the Boston Bruins.

Michael Dawson

See also: Ice Hockey.

Further Reading

Boyd, Denny. *History of Hockey in B.C.: From the Denman Arena to the Pacific Coliseum.* Vancouver, Canada: Canucks, 1970.
———. *The Vancouver Canucks Story.* Toronto, Canada: McGraw-Hill Ryerson, 1973.
Jewison, Norm. *Vancouver Canucks: The First Twenty Years.* Winlaw, Canada: Polestar, 1990.

Cardinals, St. Louis (Baseball)

The St. Louis Cardinals have one of the richest traditions in baseball, having won the most pennants (17) in National League history and standing second only to the New York Yankees in the number of World Series titles (10). The Cardinals were Major League Baseball's westernmost and southernmost representative until 1958, when the Brooklyn Dodgers relocated to Los Angeles. The franchise benefited from the astute leadership of field manager and vice president Branch Rickey, who established a minor league farm system that funneled talent to the majors. The Cardinals play in a small venue, yet they were the eighth most valuable major league franchise in 2010, valued at $488 million.

St. Louis in the Late Nineteenth Century

The Cardinals originated as the St. Louis Brown Stockings (later shortened to the Browns) in 1882 as part of the major league American Association. Under flamboyant owner Chris von der Ahe, a local brewer, the Browns enjoyed an impressive four-year run (1885–1888) in which they twice met Albert Spalding's Chicago White Stockings (later renamed the Cubs) of the National League in a championship series. A fierce rivalry was born in those meetings that persists to the present day.

In 1892, the American Association dissolved, and four franchises, including the Browns, joined the National League. Von der Ahe sold the franchise in 1898 to Frank and Stanley Robison, who renamed the team the Perfectos. The team first was called the Cardinals in 1899, when it switched its uniform colors from brown to red; it officially adopted the nickname the following season.

In 1899, the Cardinals benefited from a controversial trade that caused an uproar in baseball. The Robisons also owned the Cleveland Spiders, a new National League team. Early in the season, they transferred their best players from Cleveland to St. Louis. The Cardinals, previously stuck in the lower half of the league standings, finished the season 84–67, fifth in the 12-team league. The Spiders went 20–134, the worst record in major league history, and disbanded at the end of the season. In 1902, the Cardinals faced local competition when the new American League established a St. Louis franchise, using the Cardinals's old nickname, the Browns. The Browns and Cardinals coexisted for 51 years.

Branch Rickey and the Cardinals Juggernaut

In 1911, when Frank Robison died, his daughter, Helene Hathaway Britton, became the first female owner in the major leagues. She sold the team after the 1916 season to a syndicate led by local car dealer Sam Breadon. In 1919, the new owners brought in Branch Rickey of the Browns as their business manager and field manager. A year later, he was named the team's vice president.

Rickey was an excellent evaluator of talent and an innovative leader who established a minor league farm system that supplied a steady stream of talent for the Cardinals. He helped the team escape decades of mediocrity to become one of the National League's premier

franchises. Breadon fired Rickey as field manager during the 1925 season, but he stayed on in his other positions, helping the team to eight pennants and five World Series titles over the next 15 years.

In 1926, led by player-manager Rogers Hornsby, the National League's hard-hitting answer to Babe Ruth, the Cardinals won their first pennant and went on to upset Ruth's powerful New York Yankees in a seven-game World Series. In the legendary Game 7 of that Series, Grover Cleveland Alexander, who had pitched the Cardinals to victory the previous day, came on in relief to strike out slugger Tony Lazzeri with the bases loaded, saving the game.

The Cardinals returned to the Series in 1928, only to be swept by the Yankees. They won another pennant in 1930 but lost the World Series in six games to the Philadelphia Athletics. They had their revenge a year later, though, when they won the Series over the Athletics in seven games.

In 1934, the imagination of the Depression-scarred nation was captivated by the antics of the "Gashouse Gang," led by pitchers Dizzy and Paul Dean, along with infielders Frankie Frisch, Rip Collins, and Pepper Martin and outfielder Joe Medwick. Known for their scruffy appearance, hard hitting, and equally hard fighting—even with each other—the Gashouse Gang defeated the Detroit Tigers in the World Series, winning Game 7 in an 11–0 shutout. The team's fortunes dipped, however, when arm troubles in 1937 derailed the outrageous Dizzy Dean.

The exuberant Cardinals of the 1930s gave way to another successful team in the 1940s. Manager Billy Southworth and emerging star Stan Musial led the team, hailed as the "St. Louis Swifties" for their base-running exploits, to three consecutive pennants between 1942 and 1944, winning more than 100 games each season. The 1944 team met their cross-town rivals, the Browns, in a "Streetcar Series" in which the Cardinals triumphed four games to two. Two years later, they defeated the potent Boston Red Sox in the World Series, taking Game 7 after Enos Slaughter made his famous "mad dash" from first to home on a single to score the decisive run in the eighth inning.

Gussie Busch and St. Louis Baseball

The Cardinals's star dimmed after their 1946 triumph. A year later, a New York reporter famously, if not accurately, linked the team with a planned boycott (which never took place) against the Brooklyn Dodgers and their black rookie, Jackie Robinson. In 1952, Cardinals owner Fred Saigh was convicted of income tax evasion and was forced to sell the team.

It seemed—as Browns owner Bill Veeck wished—that the franchise might be moved out of town. However, the Cardinals remained in St. Louis when August A. "Gussie" Busch, Jr., owner of the Anheuser-Busch brewery, bought the team. After the 1953 season, the Browns left St. Louis, becoming the Baltimore Orioles. The Cardinals now were the only team in town.

Life with Busch was not always easy. Demanding a winner, he routinely juggled managers and general managers throughout the 1950s. Gussie renovated the team's home at Sportsman's Park, renaming it Busch Stadium. In 1966, he replaced that park with a new downtown stadium. He demanded that the team invest in black talent, and by the mid-1960s, the Cardinals featured one of the most diverse rosters in baseball.

Musial retired after the 1963 campaign, and in 1964, the Cardinals, thanks in part to the acquisition of speedy outfielder Lou Brock from the Chicago Cubs, outlasted the exhausted Philadelphia Phillies in one of baseball's great pennant races. In the World Series, the Cardinals, featuring black stars Brock, first baseman Bill White, and pitcher Bob Gibson, ousted the aging—and still predominantly white—New York Yankees in seven games.

The 1967 "El Birdos" team, which won 101 games, featured a remarkably diverse mix of black, white, and Latino players. Propelled by first baseman Orlando Cepeda, the Cardinals topped the Boston Red Sox in the World Series, led by Gibson's three victories. They returned to the Series a year later, thanks in large part to Gibson's Cy Young–caliber pitching performance (he had a 1.12 earned run average, the lowest in the National League in 54 years), only to lose to the Detroit Tigers in seven games.

The Cardinals's fortunes dipped following the 1969 expansion and the realignment of Major League Baseball into four divisions. The 1970s were a decade of change, when the team generally was mediocre, coming in third or fourth. Longtime announcer Harry Caray, whose bombastic personality had carried Cardinals baseball across the Midwest over the airwaves of KMOX, was dismissed amid controversy in 1969. Partner Jack Buck became the team's voice; he forged his own legacy before passing away during the 2002 season.

The Cardinals were one of baseball's highest-paid teams during the 1960s, but Busch began to tighten his pocketbook as labor turmoil engulfed baseball in the early 1970s. When the Cards traded All-Star outfielder Curt Flood to Philadelphia in 1970, Flood refused to accept his reassignment, and the ensuing court case paved the way for free agency in 1975. An increasingly disgruntled Busch packed talented hurler Steve Carlton off to Philadelphia in 1972 rather than renegotiate his contract, and Busch's confrontational style may have sparked a players' labor strike that occurred that year.

During the 1980s, manager Whitey Herzog presided over a new era of success with notoriously light-hitting teams that used speed and defense to take advantage of the hard turf at Busch Stadium. "Whiteyball" earned the Cardinals three pennants in the 1980s, and in 1982, they captured the franchise's ninth World Series championship over the Milwaukee Brewers.

In the 1985 World Series, against the Kansas City Royals, the Cardinals had victory in their grasp in Game 6 with a 1–0 lead in the ninth. Aided by a controversial call by umpire Don Denkinger, however, the Royals scored two runs to win, and buried the Cards 11–0 in Game 7.

Bye, Bye Busch, Welcome Tony LaRussa

Busch died in 1989, signaling the end of an era in more ways than one. Herzog resigned midway through the 1990 campaign, and the team regressed badly. Then, in 1995, Anheuser-Busch sold the team and the stadium to businessman William DeWitt, Jr., the son of a longtime baseball executive, and his syndicate.

New manager Tony LaRussa led the team to a division title in 1996, but slugger Mark McGwire, who arrived by trade in 1997, defined the rest of a mediocre decade. In 1998, McGwire hit 70 home runs, defeating Cubs outfielder Sammy Sosa in a race to break the single-season home run mark. The competition helped breathe new life into a sport that still was reeling from the 1994 player's strike. However, controversy regarding the use of performance-enhancing drugs tainted the accomplishments of McGwire and others who followed.

After a string of playoff defeats, LaRussa's Cardinals finally captured the National League pennant in 2004, but they were swept in the World Series by the Boston Red Sox. Despite the bat of emerging superstar Albert Pujols, the team fell just short of a return to the Series in 2005, its last season at Busch Stadium II.

In 2006, the team inaugurated a new downtown ballpark, also named Busch Stadium. They limped into the playoffs with a modest 83–78 mark and then shocked baseball fans by defeating the young Detroit Tigers in the World Series, capturing the franchise's tenth World Series title, the most in National League history.

Nathan M. Corzine

See also: Baseball, Major League; Rickey, Branch.

Further Reading

Cash, Jon David. *Before They Were Cardinals: Major League Baseball in Nineteenth-Century St. Louis.* Columbia: University of Missouri Press, 2002.

———. "St. Louis Cardinals." In *Encyclopedia of Major League Baseball Clubs,* vol. 1, *The National League,* ed. Steven A. Riess. Westport, CT: Greenwood, 2006.

Golenbock, Peter. *The Spirit of St. Louis: A History of the St. Louis Cardinals and Browns.* New York: Spike, 2000.

Halberstam, David. *October 1964.* New York: Villard, 1994.

Hood, Robert E. *The Gashouse Gang.* New York: William Morrow, 1976.

Lieb, Frederick G. *The St. Louis Cardinals: The Story of a Great Baseball Club.* 1944. Carbondale: Southern Illinois University Press, 2001.

Catholic Youth Organization

The Catholic Youth Organization (CYO) originated in Chicago during the depths of the Great Depression. Inspired by his experiences as an athlete and prison chaplain, Bernard J. Sheil, auxiliary bishop of the archdiocese of Chicago, founded the CYO in 1930 as an athletic association to compete for the attention of working-class, Roman Catholic adolescent males who might be tempted by the glamour of vice and crime during the era of Al Capone.

Embracing a Catholic version of "muscular Christianity," Sheil's CYO was modeled on the Protestants' progressive Young Men's Christian Association (YMCA), established in the previous century. The CYO, however, distinguished itself ideologically from the YMCA and other church-sponsored athletic programs by framing its mission within the context of Catholic social teachings and New Deal ideology.

Significantly, Sheil's CYO, under the patronage of archbishop George Cardinal Mundelein, did not discriminate against members on the basis of race, religion, or gender. A generation before the modern civil rights movement and the church reforms of the Second Vatican Council, the CYO accepted African Americans, Latinos, Asian Americans, Protestants, and Jews, who competed alongside European American Catholics under the banner of fair play and patriotism. The rise of the CYO signified the Americanization of the nation's immigrant Catholics and provided an opportunity for significant interracial and ecumenical cooperation among the nation's urban youth during the 1930s and 1940s.

Capitalizing on the popularity of boxing during the Depression years, the CYO sponsored citywide tournaments that drew 15,000 to 20,000 spectators annually to the old Chicago Stadium, and thousands more followed the action through live radio broadcasts. Chicago's CYO champions went on to fight against challengers from the archdioceses of New York and San Francisco, as well as international pugilists, in front of summertime crowds of 30,000 to 40,000 at Soldier and Wrigley fields. In addition, Sheil arranged for Chicago's CYO boxing champions to go on publicity tours, sending working-class boys across the country and overseas traveling in first-class accommodations. The commitment of resources paid dividends. Three of the 14 members of the 1936 U.S. Olympic boxing team came from the Chicago CYO.

Although boxing dominated, other CYO sports such as basketball, track and field, and softball drew even larger numbers of participants, both boys and girls. In 1932, Sheil opened the CYO Center in Chicago's downtown Loop, complete with training facilities and a regulation boxing ring. Organization, however, began at the parish level, where seminarians, nuns, and lay volunteers coached teams ranging in age from kindergarten through young adulthood. Interparish competition culminated in massive citywide tournaments, which in 1934, for example, included 360 basketball teams, 110 of them girls' teams. By 1940, the Chicago CYO counted more than 200,000 participants competing in activities that included tennis, golf, bowling, checkers, marbles, and water polo.

Remarkably, the CYO sponsored interracial swim meets as early as the 1930s. While all CYO sports except boxing included girls from its inception, boys received most of the public's attention until the late 1940s, when the Chicago CYO women's track and field team earned national recognition. Coach Joe Robichaux recruited talented African American sprinters from the city's South Side Bronzeville neighborhood. Standouts Barbara Jones and Mabel Landry went on to compete in the 1952 Olympic Games.

The CYO was more than an athletic association, however. It was an expansive array of civic-religious social and educational programs. Catholic social teachings regarding the rights of workers and communal responsibilities, known as Catholic Action, provided its conceptual framework. This emphasis on social justice, complemented by the New Deal ethos of the 1930s, shaped the organization's ideology. Franklin D. Roosevelt, who counted Cardinal Mundelein as an important political ally, demonstrated his support by choosing CYO official and future federal judge William J. Campbell to oversee the Illinois office of the National Youth Administration.

Chicago's Democratic political machine also assisted Sheil by hosting CYO summer vacation schools in public parks throughout the city, which were staffed in part by municipal and Works Progress Administration workers. In addition to providing free milk, these vacation schools emphasized the ideals of patriotism, pluralism, and tolerance.

Moreover, the CYO operated a social service department, neighborhood community centers, youth homes, overnight camps, an employment agency, an aeronautics school, a commercial college, and an FM radio station. In 1943, the CYO opened the Sheil School of Social Studies, a downtown "labor school" that offered night classes for working men and women.

The Chicago CYO soon became a model for Catholic dioceses across the United States. By the mid-1930s, a number of cities, including New York, Los Angeles, and San Francisco, had begun their own CYOs. Most Catholics embraced the CYO emphasis on athletics, but some church leaders distanced themselves from Sheil's social progressivism.

Between the late 1930s and the mid-1950s, the national media covered Bishop Sheil's often controversial support of organized labor and civil rights for African Americans, as well as his sharp denunciations of anti-Semitism and McCarthyism. In 1954, Sheil abruptly announced his resignation as CYO director, citing failing health, financial mismanagement, and increasing alienation from church hierarchy.

Without its singular leader, Chicago's CYO empire soon was dismantled by Mundelein's successor, archbishop Samuel Cardinal Stritch. Sheil's vision of working-class urban pluralism sustained by an ecumenical commitment to justice faded away as the postwar American Catholic Church turned its focus to fighting communism and building new parishes to serve the booming population of white middle-class Catholics settling in the suburbs.

The CYO reached its zenith during the Great Depression and World War II, but the name and concept continued during the postwar period, with millions of young participants in cities and towns throughout the nation. American Catholic bishops maintained a small CYO office in Washington, D.C., which provided leadership training and program suggestions, but funding, operations, and control remained at the local level.

In 1983, the Washington office changed its name to the National Federation of Catholic Youth Ministry, ending national recognition of the CYO. Some parishes and dioceses continued to use the CYO name to describe their athletic leagues, but they did not necessarily address the issues of social justice championed by Bishop Sheil during the middle of the twentieth century.

Timothy B. Neary

See also: Athletic Clubs; Boxing; Class, Social and Economic; Muscular Christianity; Young Men's Christian Association and Young Women's Christian Association.

Further Reading

Avella, Steven M. *This Confident Church: Catholic Leadership and Life in Chicago, 1940–1965.* Notre Dame, IN: University of Notre Dame Press, 1992.

Gems, Gerald R. "Sport, Religion, and Americanization: Bishop Sheil and the Catholic Youth Organization." *International Journal of the History of Sport* 10:2 (August 1993): 233–241.

Neary, Timothy B. "Crossing Parochial Boundaries: African Americans and Interracial Catholic Social Action in Chicago, 1914–1954." PhD diss., Loyola University Chicago, 2004.

Treat, Roger L. *Bishop Sheil and the CYO: The Story of the Catholic Youth Organization and the Man Who Influenced a Generation of Americans.* New York: Messner, 1951.

Celtics, Boston

Founded in 1946, the Boston Celtics are the most historically significant franchise in professional basketball. During the 1950s and 1960s, the Celtics created a dynasty, winning eight consecutive National Basketball Association (NBA) titles, a record that probably will never be bested, and the most championships in NBA history. Like Vince Lombardi's Green Bay Packers in professional football or Mickey Mantle's New York Yankees baseball clubs, the Boston Celtics were more than just a successful sports franchise. They established and maintained a level of excellence that passed into legend and that others still seek to emulate. In the

A founding franchise of the NBA and one of the most successful teams in all of American sports, the Boston Celtics have won a record 17 league titles. A banner for each championship has hung from the rafters of the old Boston Garden and its successor arena. *(National Basketball Association/Getty Images)*

process, the franchise also broke new ground by being the first team to draft an African American player (1950), the first to field an all-black starting five (1963), and the first in all of professional sports to hire an African American head coach (1966) since Fritz Pollard coached the Akron Pros in 1921.

Origins of the Celtics

On June 6, 1946, 11 men met at the Commodore Hotel in New York to form a new professional basketball league, the Basketball Association of America (BAA). Among them was Walter Brown, who had succeeded his father as manager of the Boston Garden, a 14,890-seat arena built in 1928. Brown named his franchise the Celtics in the hope of appealing to the local Irish American population. He recruited and hired John "Honey" Russell as the organization's first head coach.

The Celtics played their first home game on November 5, 1946, a 57–55 loss to the Chicago Stags, before a crowd of just over 4,300 fans at the Boston Arena.

Prior to the 1949–1950 season, the BAA merged with the rival National Basketball League to form the National Basketball Association, with the Celtics as one of the new league's original 17 franchises.

Auerbach, Russell, and a Dynasty

The Celtics struggled during their early years, but 1950 marked a turning point for the organization when the team hired 33-year-old Arnold Jacob "Red" Auerbach as head coach. A three-year letterman at George Washington University and a navy veteran, Auerbach had coached professionally with the Washington Capitols of the BAA and the NBA's Tri-Cities Blackhawks before coming to Boston. The new coach soon would cement his position as one of the legendary figures in the history of American sports.

In 1950, the Celtics also acquired rookie Bob Cousy from the Chicago Stags and selected Charles "Chuck" Cooper of West Virginia State in the second round of the NBA draft. Cooper, the first African American player drafted by an NBA team, was a solid performer for four years. Cousy quickly established himself as a star and a master showman. Unlike any other player before him, the Celtics's new point guard routinely dribbled the ball behind his back and between his legs, dumbfounding opponents with quick fakes and no-look passes.

Over the next few years, Cousy and standout teammates Ed Macauley and Bill Sharman turned the Celtics into a perennial contender. In 1956, Auerbach acquired the rights to recently drafted center Bill Russell from the St. Louis Hawks by trading Macauley and rookie Cliff Hagan. That same year, he drafted Tom Heinsohn and K.C. Jones. While all three would contribute to the success of the franchise, Russell's presence transformed the Celtics into a dynasty and revolutionized professional basketball.

A two-time National Collegiate Athletic Association (NCAA) champion with the University of San Francisco, Russell took the NBA by storm with his shot blocking, rebounding, and outlet passes that started countless Celtics fast breaks. During his career, he would be selected to the NBA All-Star team 12 times and would win five NBA Most Valuable Player (MVP) trophies.

With all of the pieces in place, Auerbach's Celtics won their first NBA title during the 1956–1957 season. The following year, the St. Louis Hawks upset Boston in the finals—the last playoff series that the Celtics would lose for almost a decade. Beginning with the 1958–1959 season, the Celtics won eight consecutive NBA titles. In the process, Russell took his place as one of the greatest basketball players of all time and developed a legendary rivalry with the era's other dominant big man, Wilt Chamberlain.

Although Cousy retired at the end of the 1962–1963 season, Boston added future Hall of Famer John "Hondo" Havlicek to keep the string of championships alive. After the Celtics won their eighth consecutive title in 1967, Auerbach retired as head coach, but he remained with the team as general manager and, later, as president.

Russell succeeded Auerbach as player-coach, becoming the second African American to coach a major professional sports franchise in the United States. The aging Celtics's string of championships came to an end the year after Auerbach retired, but under Russell as player-coach, Boston won league titles in 1967–1968 and 1968–1969, giving the franchise 11 titles in 13 seasons. Russell retired in 1969.

Havlicek's Celtics

With the retirement of Russell, it seemed as if the Celtics's run as a dominant force in the NBA was coming to an end. However, with Auerbach at the helm in the front office, the team reestablished itself with an infusion of new blood in the 1970s.

Veteran Havlicek became the undisputed leader of the team, and he was surrounded by a talented supporting cast that included Jo Jo White, Paul Silas, Don Chaney, Paul Westphal, and a scrappy center named Dave Cowens. Drafted fourth overall out of Florida State University, Cowens was named NBA Rookie of the Year in 1971 (together with Geoff Petrie of the Portland Trail Blazers) and quickly emerged as one of the league's toughest stars. In 1973, he was recognized as the NBA's MVP.

The 1973–1974 season marked the return of the Celtics to championship form as they defeated the Milwaukee Bucks and that team's dominant young center, Kareem Abdul-Jabbar, for the title in seven games. Following the 1975–1976 season, Boston won their second and final championship of the 1970s, defeating the Phoenix Suns.

Larry Bird and the Rivalry with the Lakers

Havlicek retired in 1978, and the following year, the Celtics inaugurated yet another successful era when rookie Larry Bird from Indiana State University joined the club. The Celtics, with the multitalented Bird as their centerpiece, quickly built another championship-caliber team that included outstanding players such as Kevin McHale, Robert Parrish, Cedric Maxwell, Dennis Johnson, Nate Archibald, and Danny Ainge. During the 1980s, the Celtics had a heated rivalry with the Los Angeles Lakers, and Bird continued his personal rivalry with the Lakers's Earvin "Magic" Johnson, whom he had faced in the 1979 NCAA finals. During his career, Bird was named Rookie of the Year, collected three MVP awards, and was a ten-time All-Star.

Bird led the way to NBA titles in 1981, 1984, and 1986. However, a monumental tragedy befell the franchise in 1986 when first-round draft pick Len Bias of Maryland died of a drug overdose before playing a single game. Bias had been handpicked to revitalize a Celtics lineup that soon would begin to age, and his loss was a blow to the future of the franchise.

As the Bird era in Boston ended in the early 1990s, the Celtics began a steep decline and suffered another tragedy. In 1993, rising star Reggie Lewis, the new team captain after Bird's retirement the previous year, died of a heart ailment. Following the 1994–1995 season, the team moved from the storied Boston Garden into the newly constructed Fleet Center (renamed the TD Banknorth Garden in 2005). The original parquet floor was transferred to the new facility, but many fans lamented the move.

Boston suffered through several poor seasons, but in 1998, the team drafted Paul Pierce, a prolific scorer and playmaker from the University of Kansas, who eventually helped improve the franchise's fortunes. The era also saw the hiring of Rick Pitino as head coach, with great fanfare. A high-profile championship college coach, Pitino was unable recreate his success in the professional ranks and resigned after only three and a half years.

Pierce served as the catalyst of a rebuilding program, and in 2001–2002, Boston made the playoffs for the first time in years. But the team soon receded and went a dismal 24–58 in 2006–2007. However, General Manager Danny Ainge rebuilt the club in one year by adding Kevin Garnett and Ray Allen to the perennial All-Star Pierce. They went 66–16, and then 14–2 in the playoffs to capture the NBA championship.

The Celtics started the 2008–2008 season with a remarkable 27–2 mark, but injuries hurt them. They finished 62–20 and only advanced to the second round of the playoffs. In 2009–2010, the team went just 50–32 but went all the way to the seventh game of the NBA finals, losing to the Lakers, 83–79.

In the history of the franchise, the Celtics have won 17 NBA Championships and have contributed 33 players to the Naismith Memorial Basketball Hall of Fame in Springfield, Massachusetts. Fourteen former Celtics also were on the list of the NBA's Fifty Greatest Players that was announced in 1996 in conjunction with the league's fiftieth anniversary.

Ben Wynne

See also: Basketball, Professional, NBA Era; Russell, Bill.

Further Reading

Auerbach, Red, and John Feinstein. *Let Me Tell You a Story: A Lifetime in the Game.* New York: Little, Brown, 2004.

Bjarkman, Peter C. *Boston Celtics Encyclopedia.* Champaign, IL: Sports Publishing, 2000.

Nelson, Murry R. *Bill Russell: A Biography.* Westport, CT: Greenwood, 2005.

Reynolds, Bill. *Cousy: His Life, Career, and the Birth of Big-Time Basketball.* New York: Simon & Schuster, 2005.

Ryan, Bob. *Boston Celtics: The History, Legends, and Images of America's Most Celebrated Team.* Reading, MA: Addison-Wesley, 1989.

Shaughnessy, Dan. *Ever Green: The Boston Celtics: A History in the Words of Their Players, Coaches, Fans and Foes, from 1946 to the Present.* New York: St. Martin's, 1990.

Shaw, Mark. *Larry Legend.* Lincolnwood, IL: Masters, 1998.

Celtics, Original

The Original Celtics were the finest team in the early days of professional basketball. The club began in New York in 1914 with a squad of Irish American players. The team played in a variety of early professional leagues, and eventually they became a touring team that played at least 150 games a year across the country. In one season, the Celtics played more than 200 games, with a record of 193–11–1.

Frank McCormick organized the Celtics in 1914 as a team of Irish American youths to play in the junior division of New York City's Bureau of Recreation league. The team disbanded during World War I, but brothers James and Tom Furey reconstituted the squad and appropriated the name "Celtics." After a dispute arose over the rights to the name, the Fureys' team played as the Original Celtics of New York. They signed contracts with players, paying them by the season rather than by the game, and pioneered the zone defense.

The Celtics were a good team in 1918–1919, but the next season, they became an outstanding club with the addition of Ernie Reich, Mike Smolick, Joe Trippe, and Eddie White to holdovers Pete Barry and Johnny Whitty. The Celtics reportedly won 65 of 69 contests, played mostly in metropolitan New York. The Furey brothers sought to strengthen the team and expand its playing area, adding Johnny Beckman, Henry "Dutch" Dehnert, and Oscar "Swede" Grimstead for the 1920–1921 season.

The Celtics played as an independent team, traveling throughout the Northeast for games. In April 1921, the team, which claimed the title of world professional basketball champions, met the Whirlwinds of New York, another contender, splitting two games; the deciding third game was never played. Shortly thereafter, the Celtics signed two Whirlwinds stars, Nat Holman and Chris Leonard, and the latter team disbanded. The

Celtics also signed George "Horse" Haggerty, a burly center, for the 1921–1922 season.

The team was a powerhouse, dominating their opponents. In December 1921, they left the independent ranks and entered the Eastern Professional League, replacing a bankrupt franchise. They captured the second-half league title and then the league championship, defeating the first-half winner, the Trenton Tigers, in a three-game series. In February 1922, Ernie Reich, the Celtics captain, died of pneumonia, but the team still managed to win most of their contests. They left the Eastern League the next year (1922–1923) and began the following season in the Metropolitan League, where they went 12–0 before negotiating a return to the Eastern League, playing as Atlantic City, whose franchise they had replaced. Financial problems plagued the league, however, and it folded in January 1923.

For the next three and a half seasons, the Celtics played an independent schedule, traveling throughout the Northeast and making occasional trips to the South and Midwest. The team made one significant personnel change during this time, dropping "Horse" Haggerty and signing 23-year-old Joe Lapchick, a 6-foot, 5-inch (2-meter) center from Yonkers, New York, in 1923.

Often playing more than 100 games a season and winning 90 percent, the Celtics were the biggest draw in basketball with their creative passing and team play. As many as 10,000 fans attended Celtic games, often breaking arena attendance records. One of the team's biggest rivals was the New York Renaissance, known as the "Rens," the best all-black quintet. The Celtics were recognized as world champions in 1923–1924 and 1924–1925.

In 1925–1926, the new American Basketball League (ABL) was formed, the first truly national professional basketball league, with very good franchises from Boston to Chicago. The Celtics played several ABL clubs early in the season and suffered only one loss. Soon, however, the ABL teams became too busy with league play to schedule games against the Celtics, who had to travel farther and farther on their road trips. The Celtics suffered injuries to Lapchick and seemed to tire from their relentless traveling, leading to some unexpected losses.

Then, in April 1926, James Furey, the Celtics's owner, was indicted for stealing more than $100,000 from the Arnold Constable Corporation, where he was head cashier. The Celtics players' salaries had been among the highest in professional basketball, funded largely with cash from Furey's embezzlement. He subsequently pleaded guilty and served three years in prison.

The Celtics players took over the team as a cooperative enterprise and added Davey Banks, a star from the South Philadelphia Hebrew Association team, for the 1926–1927 season. They entered the new Metropolitan League, where they won 14 of 17 games before leaving the league in November.

The team had trouble finding top competition, largely because the ABL ordered its teams not to play the nonleague Celtics. In December, the Celtics relented and agreed to play as an ABL franchise, representing Brooklyn, whose team had dropped out for financial reasons. Taking on Brooklyn's 0–5 record, the Celtics finished the first half at 13–8. In January, Banks became a starter, and the team became almost unstoppable. They went 19–2 in the second half of the season and won the best-of-five championship against the first-half winner, the Cleveland Rosenblums, three games to none.

In 1927–1928, the ABL switched to a full season to determine playoff positions. The Celtics went 40–9, swept Philadelphia in two games for the Eastern Division title, and then defeated the Fort Wayne Hoosiers for the ABL title, three games to one. Unfortunately, the Celtics's success did not translate into financial success for the ABL, as only Celtics's games were well attended. As a result, the league decided to break up the team and redistribute their players throughout the league. Unfortunately, this plan to increase interest did not succeed. The ABL ceased operation amid the Great Depression in 1931; it began play again a few years later but remained a minor league in pro basketball.

Meanwhile, Joe Lapchick tried to revive the Celtics in 1932, mostly as a barnstorming team, with only Banks and Lapchick from the original squad. In later years, several other attempts were made to reconstitute the team, but none succeeded for more than a few years. The Original Celtics of the 1920s were enshrined in the Naismith Memorial Hall of Fame in 1959. Holman, Lapchick, and Dehnert later were enshrined for their individual accomplishments.

Murry R. Nelson

Further Reading

Bole, Robert D., and Alfred C. Lawrence. *From Peachbaskets to Slam Dunks: A History of Professional Basketball, 1891–1987.* Canaan, NH: B&L, 1987.

Meany, Tom. "The Original Celtics." In *Total Basketball: The Ultimate Basketball Encyclopedia,* ed. Ken Shouler, Bob Ryan, Sam Smith, Leonard Koppett, and Bob Belotti. Wilmington, DE: Sports Classics, 2003.

Nelson, Murry R. *The Originals: The New York Celtics Invent Modern Basketball.* Bowling Green, OH: Bowling Green State University Popular Press, 1999.

Peterson, Robert W. *Cages to Jump Shots: Pro Basketball's Early Years.* New York: Oxford University Press, 1990.

Central Park, New York City

Central Park, completed in New York City in 1858, was a product of the municipal park movement of the 1840s, which sought to improve the quality of urban life by setting aside public space for recreation. Central Park was not the first public park in North America, but during the post–Civil War period, it became the model for large suburban parks, places where city folk, primarily the middle class, could enjoy its fresh air and beauty and use the space for uplifting activities.

Today, Central Park is home to a wide array of sporting and recreational activities within its 843 acres (341 hectares) of woods, lakes, grass, and lanes. Yet the practice of competitive physical activities in New York City's largest park was long a subject of contention, especially in the decades following its construction. The project initially lacked the promised sporting facilities, as park designer Frederick Law Olmsted emphasized receptive recreation rather than active recreation. Eventually, everyone's wishes were accommodated, and today, the park includes a beautiful garden, wooded areas, and open spaces for sports.

Overcrowded New York City, the largest metropolis in North America, had a population of 312,710 in 1844. Urban life was deteriorating as a result of immigration, overcrowding, poverty, crime, and high rates of communicable diseases.

In 1844, journalist and poet William Cullen Bryant and landscape architect Andrew Jackson Downing suggested, as a respite from urban issues, that the city build a public park modeled after the Bois de Boulogne in Paris or Hyde Park in London. Such a park, they argued, would give New Yorkers a chance to get out into the fresh air and exercise to improve their health, enjoy the beauty of nature, and learn to emulate the behavior of their social betters. Property values would rise, and New York would gain recognition as a world-class city.

The state legislature in 1853 set up a fund exceeding $5 million to buy land for a park. In 1857, Mayor Fernando Wood sponsored a contest to select the best plan for the park, which was to include sporting areas. Local sports organizers had lobbied for sports fields for some time. The baseball fraternity, experiencing a dramatic increase in participation and spectatorship, bemoaned the curtailment of playing spaces, such as vacant lots, which were superseded by industrial sites.

Olmstead and Calvert Vaux submitted the winning proposal, called the Greensward Plan. Olmsted's high-minded vision of a *rus in urbe* (country in the city) struck a chord with the park's Board of Commissioners. The idealistic designer hoped for an uninterrupted unfolding of re-created nature with curvilinear ponds, delicate grassy hilltops, and awe-inspiring vistas. The plan also included a cricket field. Aside from the healthful benefits of such charms, Olmsted wanted the park to have a socializing mission—to soften the ruggedness of city life, provide a venue for people of different classes to mingle, and, by the enforcement of a strict code of conduct, encourage the lower ranks to emulate the virtues of the most educated. He would go on to design many of the finest large parks in the United States.

Olmsted superintended the construction of Central Park during the economic depression of 1857–1858. This challenging task required fighting the Tammany Hall political machine, which hoped to use the project for patronage jobs. During the planning stage, the park's board decided on an important departure from the original plans: excluding competitive sports from the list of legitimate uses. Their argument was that the social composition of ballgame crowds—essentially gamblers and rowdy characters—did not sit well with the park's dedication to tranquillity and receptive recreation. In their minds, the park's grass was for contemplation, not to be scuffed and marred by athletes. Their annual reports made it clear that no sport's "objectionable features" should "deface" the attractive "picture" of the park. Despite its initial claims of inclusiveness, the early park was more of a visual respite for the elite and middle classes.

Initially, President Andrew Haswell Green of the Board of Commissioners limited access to playing fields to pupils recommended by their teachers. On the other hand, Green tolerated and even encouraged sports that he considered "suitable" to the park's etiquette. Ice-skating was a big success as soon as the park opened, with 50,000 skaters for the 1859 Christmas Parade. Other commendable sporting activities were horseback riding and croquet, a popular pastime in the 1860s. There were no baseball fields until the 1880s, which were soon followed by tennis courts.

The uses of Central Park evolved considerably in the early twentieth century. Progressive reformers did not endorse the idea of a romantic park, but instead wanted to employ its open spaces to promote social and cultural programs such as drama, music, and sports for the well-being of all New Yorkers. Consequently, after the draining of the Lower Reservoir, it did not become a classical promenade, as originally envisioned, but instead was turned into a Great Lawn for space-demanding sports. In addition, in 1937, philanthropist August Heckscher, Sr., donated the first equipped playground.

Robert Moses continued this trend during his 27-year tenure as head of Mayor Fiorello La Guardia's newly founded Department of Parks and Recreations. He efficiently used New Deal funds to refurbish the decaying park with macadamized lanes, tennis and basketball courts, athletic fields in the North Meadow, and more recreational programs. The Great Lawn got permanent ball fields with backstops for corporate softball and neighborhood Little League teams. From the 1960s onward, Central Park welcomed a wider spectrum of social events, such as the annual Shakespeare Festival, open-air concerts (classical and popular), and political rallies.

In the 1980s, severe budget cuts necessitated that control of the park's future be handed over to the privately financed Central Park Conservancy. However, policies on sports remained sympathetic to the existing practices within New York's "breathing space."

In the 2000s, more than 40 sporting and leisure activities were available to a large public from most social classes and ethnic origins. They included common activities such as bicycling, rowing, jogging, handball, inline skating, yoga, and tai chi, as well as activities such as bird watching, cross country skiing, "catch and release" fishing, model sail boating or even rock climbing, all practiced without a permit at a low cost. On the other hand, the Parks Department demanded a paying registration for playing baseball, softball, touch or flag football, tennis, and soccer. The park also continues to host such events as the New York City Marathon. First run through Central Park in 1970, the race currently concludes in the park, and 44,829 people finished the marathon in 2010.

As the park's uses imitated changes taking place in the broader society, it has managed to make traditions coexist with the latest trends. Today, members of the wealthy New York Lawn Bowling club, founded in 1926, roll their balls just a few yards away from where instructors teach open-air fitness workshops.

Peter N. Marquis

See also: Class, Economic and Social; Parks, Municipal; Playgrounds and Playground Movement; Urbanization.

Further Reading

Miller, Sara Cedar. *Central Park, an American Masterpiece.* New York: Harry N. Abrams, 2003.

Riess, Steven A. *City Games: The Evolution of American Urban Society and the Rise of Sports.* Urbana: University of Illinois Press, 1989.

Rosenzweig, Roy, and Elizabeth Blackmar. *The Park and the People: A History of Central Park.* Ithaca, NY: Cornell University Press, 1992.

Chamberlain, Wilt (1936–1999)

From the late 1950s to the early 1970s, Wilt Chamberlain was a remarkable presence in professional basketball. Standing 7 feet, 1 inch (2.2 meters), and weighing 275 pounds (125 kilograms), he shattered basketball's standards for offensive production, scoring 31,419 career points (fourth all-time) and an average of 30.07 per game (second after Michael Jordan), and became his sport's first genuine celebrity. From his high school years in Philadelphia and college ball in Kansas through his professional career with the Harlem Globetrotters and the National Basketball Association (NBA), Chamberlain compelled admiration, awe, resentment, and frustration.

Born on August 21, 1936, in Philadelphia, Chamberlain stuck out from the crowd at an early age. A shy boy who stuttered, he grew defensive when people marveled at his height; he compensated by working at odd jobs and playing sports. A natural at track and field, he reluctantly tried basketball. By his senior year, Chamberlain had led Overbrook High School to two city championships, and *Sport* magazine featured him in an article titled "The High-School Kid Who Could Play Pro Now." Already 7 feet tall (2.1 meters), he possessed excellent coordination and surprising strength. More than 200 colleges recruited him. Never before had a high school basketball player garnered such national attention.

Chamberlain attended the University of Kansas, a longtime force in college basketball. Other schools, disappointed at losing him, prompted a National Collegiate Athletic Association (NCAA) investigation of illegal recruiting. In 1956–1957, Chamberlain's first varsity season, observers marveled at how his speed and power were reshaping the sport. "Can Basketball Survive Chamberlain?" asked an article in the *Saturday Evening Post*. Despite a promising start, Chamberlain left Kansas on bad terms. Although he led his team to the NCAA finals, the Jayhawks lost to the University of North Carolina, and some Kansas fans blamed

Chamberlain. The next season, his team failed to qualify for the NCAA tournament.

Chamberlain decided to forgo his senior year of college ball and signed a lucrative contract to tour with the Harlem Globetrotters, a barnstorming team that was not restrained by NBA recruiting rules. He thrived during his year with the Globetrotters, who focused on entertaining their customers and faced little pressure to win competitive games. He considered playing another full season with the Globetrotters, but chose to test himself in the NBA.

In 1959, the Philadelphia Warriors of the NBA drafted Chamberlain as a territorial pick (an option ended in 1966), because he had grown up and attended high school in Philadelphia. He was the only NBA territorial pick selected due to his high school location. In the fall of 1959, Chamberlain joined the Warriors to great anticipation, and he proceeded to awe basketball fans, drawing large audiences on the road. Chamberlain destroyed single-season records, averaging 37.6 points and 27 rebounds a game. At the same time, he set himself apart by sparring with Warriors Coach Neil Johnston, remaining aloof from his teammates, and announcing a brief retirement until he won a new contract.

In the following seasons, Chamberlain only increased his statistical output. In 1961–1962, he averaged more than 50 points a game. Against the New York Knicks on March 2, 1962, in Hershey, Pennsylvania, Chamberlain tallied 100 points in one game, an iconic and practically unbreakable record for points scored in one NBA game. Chamberlain also was a prodigious rebounder who averaged 22.9 per game over his career, and he picked off 55 in one game, both all-time records.

Chamberlain's celebrity transcended basketball. He cut a rhythm and blues single called "By the River," appeared on variety shows such as *The Ed Sullivan Show,* and purchased the legendary Harlem nightclub Small's Paradise. At a time when the NBA still was seen as a "bush league" by many sports fans, Chamberlain attracted attention like a Hollywood star.

In 1962, the Warriors moved to San Francisco. Throughout the early the 1960s, Chamberlain continued to lead the league in scoring, but the Warriors never won an NBA title. His rivalry with Boston Celtics center Bill Russell compelled media fascination. Although Chamberlain outshone Russell in terms of individual accomplishments, Russell earned greater respect from supporters for his defense, unselfishness, and leadership of championship teams. Chamberlain's detractors accused him of selfishness and mental frailty.

In January 1965, the Warriors traded Chamberlain to the Philadelphia 76ers, and he elevated the team to a title contender. In the playoffs, however, the Celtics beat the 76ers in the Eastern Conference Finals. In the midst of the series, Chamberlain weakened his team's cause by writing a critical two-part series for *Sports Illustrated* titled "My Life in a Bush League." The 76ers lost to the Celtics again in 1966. For all of Chamberlain's individual accomplishments, most public attention focused on his limitations.

In 1967, Chamberlain captured his first NBA title, leading the 76ers by adapting his game to focus more on passing and less on shooting. The 76ers might have become the new NBA dynasty, but they improbably lost to the Celtics again in the 1968 playoffs. Philadelphia then traded a disgruntled Chamberlain to the Los Angeles Lakers.

With Chamberlain teamed with superstars Jerry West and Elgin Baylor, the Lakers appeared to be the favorite for the NBA title. But Chamberlain feuded with new coach Butch van Breda Kolff, and Bill Russell outdueled his nemesis in the 1969 playoffs, capturing yet another championship for the Celtics at Chamberlain's expense. The next year, the Lakers lost in the NBA finals to the New York Knicks. In the decisive Game 7 of that series, he seemed unnerved by the heroic, dramatic play of his New York counterpart Willis Reed, who suffered from a torn thigh muscle that had kept him out of Game 6.

Chamberlain won his second NBA championship in 1972. Focusing on defense and rebounding, he spurred the Los Angeles fast-break attack. By this time, he mostly had recovered from his image as a villain or loser. Once many white fans had considered him a black threat, but after the rise of the radical Black Power movement, he was seen as less of a threat than as a charming and charismatic athlete. He still possessed a curious individuality; for instance, he was the rare black athlete who supported Richard Nixon in the 1968 presidential election. Chamberlain retired in 1974 holding virtually every major offensive record in the NBA, and he was the league's most recognizable face.

Even in retirement, Chamberlain compelled public fascination. During the 1973–1974 season, he coached the San Diego Conquistadors of the American Basketball Association with a humorous nonchalance. His custom-built home in Bel Air, near Hollywood, was the subject of numerous media features. In his two memoirs, he made controversial statements about basketball and sexuality. Most famously, he claimed in 1991 to have slept with 20,000 women, earning him another round of newspaper headlines.

Chamberlain died on October 12, 1999, of a heart attack. He left a dual legacy: as basketball's greatest individual offensive force, and as its first great celebrity.

Aram Goudsouzian

See also: American Basketball Association; Basketball, College; Basketball, Professional, NBA Era; Harlem Globetrotters; Lakers, Los Angeles/Minneapolis; 76ers, Philadelphia/Syracuse Nationals; Warriors, Golden State/San Francisco/Philadelphia.

Further Reading

Chamberlain, Wilt, and David Shaw. *Wilt: Just Like Any Other 7-Foot Black Millionaire Who Lives Next Door.* New York: Macmillan, 1973.

Cherry, Robert Allen. *Wilt: Larger Than Life.* Chicago: Triumph, 2004.

Pomerantz, Gary M. *Wilt, 1962: The Night of 100 Points and the Dawn of a New Era.* New York: Crown, 2005.

Taylor, John. *The Rivalry: Bill Russell, Wilt Chamberlain, and the Golden Age of Basketball.* New York: Random House, 2005.

Cheerleading

Cheerleaders use verbal commands and body motions to direct a crowd to cheer in unison in support of a sports team. Cheerleading, an American invention, has evolved from an accessory to competition to become a competitive sport in its own right. Beginning in the late 1800s, yell leaders and cheerleading squads sponsored by colleges and schools rallied enthusiasm for their teams during competition. In the twentieth century, professional football and basketball teams and youth sports leagues added cheerleading squads to their organizations. By the 1970s, squads sponsored by schools, colleges, and independent clubs began to participate in competitive cheerleading as an independent athletic event.

Cheerleading emerged in nineteenth-century New England to support athletic competitions at men's colleges such as Harvard and Princeton, and grew in the twentieth century to become a fixture of public school, college, and professional team sports throughout North America. The cheerleader's original function, to lead yells during football games, endured, and the sport expanded to include entertaining crowds with spectacular tumbling and acrobatic stunts for a variety of team sports. Spirit groups—pep squads, drill teams, and dance groups—later evolved to increase the pageantry of sporting contests.

The spontaneous yelling of early cheerleaders developed into stylized, physically demanding gymnastic routines performed by trained specialists. Elite practitioners now participate in competitive cheerleading against other peer squads. Organized cheerleading was fostered by educational theories that promoted the development of a school's identity, by businesses seeking new competitions to televise, and by others eager to equip and train cheerleaders. The institutionalization and commercialization of cheerleading determined who participated, defined cheerleaders' roles off the field, shaped performance style, and ultimately has entrenched it as a pervasive symbol in mass media and popular culture.

Origins of Cheerleading

The earliest cheerleader was a student who stood up and urged fellow spectators to yell encouragement to players during a game. By the 1890s, many colleges had a designated "yell leader" to direct cheering; he was chosen for his enthusiasm and charisma. One of the first was Johnny Campbell, the University of Minnesota's yell leader in 1898, who, as an alumnus, continued to lead cheers in the stands for 40 years.

Community and media interest in college games grew rapidly, and the trappings of big-time athletics—paid coaches, marching bands, and mass rallies—were in place by the early 1900s. Colleges such as Yale added multiple yell leaders who performed synchronized acrobatics and cheers to focus the attention of the fans.

Women were attending state-supported and land-grant institutions by the late 1880s. They later joined pep clubs that formed organized cheering sections in the stands. During the 1920s, coeducational pep clubs gave women the opportunity to serve as yell leaders. By the early 1930s, some women had made the transition to coed cheering squads. Nonetheless, fans still viewed collegiate cheerleading as an athletic, masculine role.

By this time, collegiate cheerleading had expanded from emotional support of the team to include crowd entertainment. Two types of spirit groups emerged: song girls and drill teams, each incorporating music and choreography, elements that would form the prototype for today's professional cheerleader dance troupes. Beginning in 1929, the University of California, Los Angeles, featured, in addition to male yell leaders, a small squad of song girls who led crowds in choruses of school songs. In the 1950s, the squad supplanted singing with dance routines.

Drill teams, composed of larger groups of women who performed precision marching and dance elements set to music, grew out of sports traditions of marching bands and synchronized dance routines in stage and film musical revues. Gussie Nell Davis, who organized the Kilgore College Rangerettes of Kilgore, Texas, in 1940, established this genre.

College drill teams became popular, and secondary schools widely adapted them as an activity for female participants. Dance and drill teams require space and time for routines, limiting their performances to breaks during games. Compared with the emotional support role of cheerleaders connected to game action, the entertainment function of dance and drill teams is a more formal and separate aspect of game-day pageantry.

Adults Take Control

Throughout the 1920s and 1930s, educators debated the appropriateness of female cheerleaders; they were both concerned about females' ability to perform athletic stunts and the erosion of ladylike behavior. In response, advocates argued that because most sports were restricted to boys, cheerleading was a valid activity for girls.

By the 1950s, organized athletics, cheerleading, and pep clubs had spread from colleges to high schools and to middle and elementary schools. Public school educators stressed school spirit and leadership as part of a broader curriculum of socialization and citizenship. They established cheerleaders as student role models, adding scholarship and character criteria to a formal selection process. At the same times, middle and secondary schools feminized cheerleading, making male cheerleaders the exception.

Cheerleading, like other sports, became professionalized under adult control. Educators added adult sponsors or coaches to train and supervise cheerleaders. In 1927, Frank Gradler published an instruction manual, *Psychology and Technique of Cheer-Leading*, and George M. York produced *Just Yells,* a national compilation of cheers. High schools offered clinics led by college cheerleaders to train and critique school cheerleaders. Lawrence Herkimer, head cheerleader at Southern Methodist University in 1947–1948, was one of the first entrepreneurs to offer cheer clinics and camps as a full-time business. Cheer entrepreneurs formed companies to teach clinics, publish manuals, and supply uniforms. (The business currently earns millions of dollars, serving hundreds of thousands of cheerleaders.)

In the 1970s, cheer entrepreneurs promoted their services by sponsoring competitions among squads who could qualify at their camps and advance through regional to national contests. These competitions played a major role in establishing cheerleading as a sport. In 1983, ESPN televised a high school competition sponsored by the Universal Cheerleading Association, followed in 1984 by a contest for college squads. Hundreds of private cheer clubs also developed to train cheerleaders to compete in events sponsored by cheerleading companies, providing an athletic outlet outside interscholastic competition.

Some school athletic associations field statewide championship cheerleading and drill team competitions, as they do for other sports. Where cheering is designated as a sport, schools provide coaches, athletic trainers, insurance, transportation, and uniforms. When college and high school girls joined early squads, they sometimes performed in the athletic tradition established by male cheerleaders. Today, many all-girl and coed squads perform physically demanding lifts, tosses, catches, and pyramids, which require year-round conditioning, weight training, and gymnastics. They incur injuries, like all athletes, ranging from sprains and broken bones to permanent vocal damage and catastrophic spinal cord trauma, making safety and liability issues prominent in the sport.

Title IX, the 1972 federal law that mandated equal opportunity for women in sports and other pursuits, had paradoxical implications for cheerleading. Because the law required that girls' and boys' teams receive comparable treatment, if cheer squads appeared at boys' games, they also had to appear at girls' games. At the same time, girls previously limited to cheerleading now could compete in other sports, reducing the appeal of cheerleading but also increasing the demand for cheerleaders.

Professional Cheerleading

Professional cheerleading, a creature of professional sports promotion and television exposure, is akin to the drill and dance groups that originated in collegiate athletics. Early on, professional football teams adopted aspects of college pomp and spirit. In the 1920s, the Chicago Bears had their own fight song. A decade later, the Washington Redskins had a 150-member marching band that performed for home and division title road games. During the 1960s, some teams used volunteer high school cheerleaders, such as the CowBelles & Beaux, who performed at Dallas Cowboys games from 1961 to 1971. The Miami Dolphins featured the Dolphin Dolls, a teenage precision dance group, from 1961 to 1978.

Dallas Cowboys Manager Tex Schramm established the prototype for glamorous dance teams accompanying professional games today. In 1971, he hired a choreographer to bring in Broadway-style dancers for games in the Cowboys's new stadium. Beginning in 1972, all of the Cowboys cheerleaders had to be at least 18 years old; in succeeding years, both choreography and costumes increasingly emphasized their sex appeal. The Dallas Cowboy Cheerleaders became a national sensation, appearing in several films and issuing their own swimsuit calendars. They set a trend, widely imitated by professional football and basketball organizations in the United States and Canada.

Cheerleading in Popular Culture

Positive and negative images of cheerleaders are pervasive in American media and culture. The cheerleader who appears in advertisements, television, movies, visual art, cartoons, tabloids, and fiction for adults and children usually is female. Cheerleaders are portrayed as wholesome "good girls," promiscuous "bad girls," social leaders, sexual trophies, the pinnacle of adolescent success, and the unfortunate girls who peaked too soon. The cheerleader appears as a victim in slasher horror movies and as a warrior-heroine in the movie *Buffy, the Vampire Slayer* (1992) and the television series *Heroes* (2006). These images convey mixed messages about cultural expectations for girls and ignore male cheerleaders altogether.

At its best, cheerleading gives youth the benefit of adult coaching and mentorship. At its worst, cheerleading is a vehicle for fanatical adult ambition that is harmful to young participants. An example of such an extreme is the behavior of Wanda Webb Holloway, the "Cheerleader Hit Mom," who in 1991 plotted to murder the mother of a rival competitor so that her daughter could claim a spot on the Channelview, Texas, junior high cheerleading squad.

Stereotypes portray the cheerleader as one of two feminine American icons: the popular high school goddess or the suggestive dancer on the sidelines at professional football games. This gendered identification reflects cheerleading's transition from a college boys' invention to a coeducational and promotional activity that permeates sports and culture. The feminized portrayal, however, does not reflect the continued participation of male cheerleaders at the school and college level or the athletically demanding sport of cheer competition.

Beyond cultural stereotypes, cheerleading means different things to those who cheer. Some benefit from

collegiate athletic scholarships and, after their own cheering stints, continue as coaches, instructors, competition judges, and entrepreneurs in the field. Female cheerleaders with dance training can join professional cheerleading troupes. Cheerleaders may seek development in leadership, dance, or athletic skills; the enjoyment of extracurricular activity; the camaraderie of training, performing, and competing in a squad; or the recognition and celebrity attached to athletics. For some, cheerleading is a relatively incidental activity in their lives; for others, cheering is significant enough to be mentioned in their obituaries.

Mary Ellen Hanson

See also: Cowboys, Dallas; Football, College; Football, Professional; Title IX; Women.

Further Reading

Adams, Natalie G., and Pamela Bettis. *Cheerleader! An American Icon.* New York: Palgrave Macmillan, 2003.

Chappell, Linda Rae. *Coaching Cheerleading Successfully.* Champaign, IL: Human Kinetics, 1997.

Gradler, Frank A. *Psychology and Technique of Cheer-leading: A Handbook for Cheer-leaders.* Menomonie, WI: Menomonie Athletic Book Supply, 1927.

Hanson, Mary Ellen. *Go! Fight! Win! Cheerleading in American Culture.* Bowling Green, OH: Bowling Green State University Popular Press, 1995.

Hawkins, John. *Texas Cheerleaders: The Spirit of America.* New York: St. Martin's, 1991.

Villarreal, Cindy. *The Cheerleader's Guide to Life.* New York: HarperPerennial, 1994.

Chinese Americans

Since the 1920s, Chinese American youth have participated in sports as a means to assimilate into American society, adopt dominant cultural values while rejecting those held by older generations, and negotiate between integrated and segregated sporting opportunities. References to Chinese prizefighters, baseball and football players, and cyclists were reported in the Los Angeles and Sacramento press by the 1880s, but it was not until the 1920s and 1930s that Chinese participation in American sports and other physical recreations increased dramatically.

The first era of Chinese immigration (1849–1882) culminated with a population of about 110,000, mostly male peasants working as laborers in the West. Thereafter, the Chinese Exclusion Act restricted immigration except for family. The Chinese were barred from naturalization, because they were considered inassimilable, a policy that did not change until 1942.

In the early twentieth century, the Chinese population in North America primarily lived on the Pacific Coast in neighborhoods known as "Chinatowns" in Los Angeles, San Francisco, and Seattle. Similar communities existed in Hawaii and in Vancouver, Canada. In general, first-generation Chinese Americans were uninterested in acculturating, and they did not participate in American sports. Ah Wing, a Sacramento porter, was a rare exception; he boxed in the early 1900s, challenging racist stereotypes related to manliness. Second-generation Chinese Americans, however, particularly in San Francisco's Chinatown, the largest Chinese community in North America, were increasingly Westernized and acculturated. They sought to create a middle ground for themselves, and this included involving themselves in traditional American sports.

By the 1910s, there were Chinese baseball teams on the mainland United States and in Hawaii. The Hawaii University Chinese team toured the mainland from 1910 through 1916, playing college, semiprofessional, and black professional baseball teams. In late 1914, Chinese Hawaiian Lang Akana signed with the Portland Beavers of the Pacific Coast League, but a threatened boycott led to his release. Then, in 1932, Lee Gum Hong of Oakland had a brief trial with the local Pacific Coast League team.

During the interwar years, Chinese American youth became involved in sports as a means of establishing their American identity and gaining respect from white society. Chinese American sports heroes often were celebrated in the local press. Yet the growing interest in sports also was a source of intergenerational conflict, as parents feared that their children were losing their cultural identity. This often led to such cautionary warnings by community elders as *fahn ball no fahn sic* (play ball, no rice to eat).

Despite this concern, Chinese American youth established sports and social clubs, primarily within their communities, as they encountered discrimination in many mainstream sports clubs and in public high schools. The Yoke Choy Club of San Francisco sponsored a football team in the 1920s, and members of the Lowa Club of Los Angeles played softball, tennis, volleyball, ping-pong, and basketball through the 1930s. Local leagues, such as the Pacific Athletic Association, sponsored basketball tournaments.

In smaller Chinese communities on the East Coast, there also were sporting programs, such as the North American Chinese Invitational Volleyball Tournament, begun in 1937, with a contest between teams from Boston and New York. One of the largest Chinese athletic organizations in the country by the 1930s was the 150-member Chinese Tennis Association.

While San Francisco was the center of Chinese American sports, there was a desperate need for outdoor recreational space for Chinatown's 5,000 children. This led to the construction in 1927 of the Chinese Playground, where attendance exceeded 124,000 in its first year. The growing popularity of badminton led to the founding in San Francisco of the Chinatown Badminton Club in 1937, which had an "open-door" policy allowing non-Chinese to participate, and competed against both Chinese and white clubs. In addition, several national sporting associations were rooted in Chinatowns, including the San Francisco–based Chinese Golfers Association of America.

In the early 1900s, Young Men's Christian Associations (YMCAs) in California provided Chinese Americans with opportunities to participate in soccer, track and field, softball, and table tennis tournaments. In 1936, when the Chinese Methodist Boy Scouts were established in San Francisco as the first Chinese Boy Scout troop in the United States, members gained additional competitive opportunities in basketball and track and field. Church missions also provided sporting activities for Chinatown youth, including the Catholic Youth Organization in the 1930s, an important locus for basketball tournaments. Basketball was very popular among Chinese boys, especially compared to white boys, who preferred baseball, football, and swimming.

The Chinese YWCA of San Francisco provided tap dance classes for Chinese girls throughout the 1920s, though attendance declined in 1930 when a fee was introduced. However, by the late 1930s, increasingly strong interest in tennis and basketball among Chinese girls led to competition for Chinatown's limited athletic facilities. The girls were not very interested in swimming, which may have been a result of discrimination at public swimming pools. Chinese girls in Los Angeles were more likely to play sports under ethnic auspices than school-based teams, which brought together players otherwise dispersed among the city's public schools.

In Portland, Oregon, one of the top basketball teams in the 1930s was the Chung Wah five, led by former high school star La Lun Chin. Such young women countered prevailing stereotypes about Chinese women. Their achievements in community basketball leagues, clubs, and recreational play often were documented in local newspapers as a matter of ethnic pride.

After 1947, with the easing of restrictive housing covenants, growing numbers of Chinese Americans moved away from Chinatowns, which opened up greater opportunities in recreation. Badminton, basketball, golf, tennis, bowling, and football were among the sports that either had been previously been discontinued and then were reinstated, or became newly available through expanded leagues and teams. The growing participation of Chinese Americans in sports was highlighted by sharpshooter Frank Chow, the first Chinese American Olympian at the 1948 London Games.

Chinese immigration resumed following the Immigration and Nationality Services Act of 1965. The newcomers included highly educated professionals, and unskilled laborers who became factory workers. Some of the newest immigrants were outstanding badminton and ping-pong players who soon represented the United States in international competition.

Most of the outstanding Chinese American athletes since the 1980s and 1990s have been second-generation Americans competing in upper-middle-class sports, a reflection of their high level of assimilation. Gymnast Amy Chow, a 1996 Olympic gold and silver medalist, is among the most outstanding. Also notable is tennis player Michael Chang, who won the French Open in 1986, becoming the youngest man ever to win a Grand Slam tournament, and ranked as high as number two in world tennis. Perhaps the most successful Chinese American athlete is figure skater Michelle Kwan, who won nine national championships, five world championships, and a silver medal at the 1998 Olympic Games, followed by Amy Chow, gold medal gymnast in 1996, and winner of three Olympic medals. In Canada, Lori Fung won a gold medal in rhythmic gymnastics in 1984.

Chinese American athletes have gained renown primarily in elite women's sports. They mostly have focused on traditional female sports, such as skating, tennis, and golf (Michelle Wie). Chinese American men have been less successful, although there are now Chinese and Taiwanese players in Major League Baseball and the National Basketball Association. In 2010, Jeremy Lin, a former star guard at Harvard University, joined the Golden State Warriors.

Susan G. Zieff

See also: Figure Skating; Lee, Bruce; Race and Race Relations; Young Men's Christian Association and Young Women's Christian Association.

Further Reading

Franks, Joel S. "Chinese Americans and American Sports, 1880–1940." *Chinese America: History and Perspectives* 10 (1996): 133–147.

King, C. Richard. *Asian Americans in Sport and Society.* London: Taylor & Francis, 2011.

Park, Roberta J. "Sport and Recreation Among Chinese American Communities of the Pacific Coast from Time of Arrival to the 'Quiet Decade' of the 1950s." *Journal of Sport History* 27:3 (Fall 2000): 445–480.

Takaki, Ronald. *Strangers from a Different Shore: A History of Asian Americans.* Boston: Little, Brown, 1989.

Yung, Judy. *Unbound Feet: A Social History of Chinese Women in San Francisco.* Berkeley: University of California Press, 1995.

Zieff, Susan G. "From Badminton to the Bolero: Sport and Recreation in San Francisco's Chinatown, 1895–1950." *Journal of Sport History* 27:1 (Spring 2000): 1–29.

Class, Economic and Social

The sporting experience of Americans has been heavily shaped by their position in the three-tiered social structure. A person's social class mainly is determined by wealth and occupation, although there are other contributing factors, such as education, religion, race, and ethnicity.

The wealthy, elite members of society traditionally had the widest choices in their athletic pastimes. They generally preferred expensive sports organized by restrictive clubs that enabled them to affirm or enhance their social prestige.

The middle class, composed mainly of white-collar workers, farm owners, and artisans, was at first more reticent about participating in sports because of moral qualms about gambling, blood sports, and idleness. However, they became avid fans and participants as a positive sports creed developed in the mid-nineteenth century that promoted sports as uplifting, and as pastimes such as baseball emerged that fit into the new ideology.

The experience of the lower class was more complicated. In the first half of the nineteenth century, when many lived in rural areas, they had ready access to traditional sports. Blue-collar workers in cities were often members of the bachelor subculture and enjoyed a robust sporting tradition that centered on gambling, blood sports, and other activities that violated Victorian-era decorum and values.

Bowling, brought to colonial America by the Dutch, was a predominantly urban, ethnic, working-class sport until the mid-twentieth century. After World War II, it gained widespread popularity among the middle class, including suburban housewives. *(Time & Life Pictures/Getty Images)*

However, working-class sporting options were curtailed in the second half of the nineteenth century by the rise of industrial capitalism, which took away free time; urbanization, which limited access to sporting sites; and immigration, which brought in newcomers from Eastern and Southern Europe with no sporting heritage. Nonetheless, lower-class youth saw professional sports, particularly boxing, as a vehicle for Americanization and social mobility. In the early 1900s, their opportunities improved as progressive reformers and educators promoted sports in the inner city to assimilate newcomers and to build character and health, and as employers financed sports at the workplace to exercise social control over their workers and show workers management's interest in their welfare and thus counter the appeal of labor unions.

Lower-class sporting options were enhanced by the prosperity of the 1920s, when North Americans enjoyed their highest standard of living to that time. Since the end of World War II, sporting opportunities have become far more democratic than ever before, although class has not disappeared entirely as a factor in the world of sports.

Sports and Social Class in the American Colonies

By the late seventeenth century, Virginia's great planters used sports to display their superior social standing. They raced horses and gambled with their peers in emulation of the English aristocracy.

By the 1730s, wealthy Southern planters and rich Northern merchants formed sports clubs, beginning in Philadelphia with the Schuylkill Fishing Company of Pennsylvania (1732), the first sports club in the Anglo-American world; jockey clubs in Charles Town, South Carolina (1734), Williamsburg, Virginia (1739), and Annapolis, Maryland (1745); and the Gloucester Fox Hunting Club of Philadelphia (1766). These voluntary associations were limited to the elite, and they represented communities of like-minded men who enjoyed sports and socialized with each other. The status of favorite upper-class sports suffered during the Revolutionary War, when those activities were identified with the British occupiers and were perceived as aristocratic and undemocratic.

Sports was less important among the middling sort in the eighteenth century, who participated at their favorite taverns in activities such as marksmanship contests or lawn bowling, or went hunting in the nearby woods, or fishing in local streams. In New England, however, there were long-standing legal restrictions on such pastimes as billiards, bowling, and shuffleboard, which were considered idle pastimes associated with gambling.

The lower classes also enjoyed sports at pubs that involved a lot of gambling, such as billiards, bowling, and cock fighting. While they engaged in such activities as hunting and fishing, for them, what were field sports for well-off people more often were about making money by killing vermin or harvesting furs, or about acquiring meat or fish to eat. Thus, such activities more often fell into the category of work than recreation.

Early Republic and Antebellum Eras

The elite continued to dominate the sports scene in the first half of the nineteenth century. Upper-class sportsmen made up a part of the sporting fraternity, an informal brotherhood of pleasure seekers who were particularly interested in gambling and violent sports, although they still participated in expensive sports and organized jockey, cricket, and yacht clubs to help define class boundaries.

The preeminent elite sportsman was industrialist John C. Stevens. He organized the famous horse race between Eclipse and Sir Henry in 1823 that helped revive Northern thoroughbred racing. Stevens also founded the New York Yacht Club in 1844, which became the continent's most prestigious sports club after his *America* captured the 1851 yacht race at the Isle of Wight associated with London's World's Fair.

The majority of men in the sporting fraternity belonged to the working class. They included relatively well-paid artisans, butchers, and other food tradesmen who worked unusual hours, giving them free time in the afternoons, as well as machine politicians and unskilled young men, often Irish immigrants, who hung out in saloons, fire stations, and dance halls. They were members of the bachelor subculture who enjoyed the company of other men. They drank excessively, chased women, gambled, fought, and were interested in sports. These "boys of pleasure" maintained a traditional lifestyle with a casual attitude toward discipline, and they took time off from work to gamble on blood sports, horse racing, and billiards. Their favorite spectator sports included boxing, ratting, and cockfighting, illegal sports that took place in their neighborhoods or in other secret locations.

In general, the antebellum middle class opposed sports that involved gambling or cruelty to animals, or that challenged Victorian standards of decorum. They were white-collar workers, farm owners, and future-oriented artisans who disdained the bachelor subculture. These men affirmed their masculine identity by working and supporting their families, not by betting or attending boxing matches.

The first urban middle-class sport was harness racing, which thrived, despite its connection to gambling. Riders displayed their prowess by driving their own horses in wagons (later sulkies) on city streets. Supporters emulated the elite by organizing the New York Trotting Club (1825) to help regulate the sport. Harness racing was considered an "American" and a democratic sport, in comparison to aristocratic thoroughbred racing, because it used inexpensive American standard-bred horses that were cheaper to maintain than thoroughbreds.

The middle class became more supportive of sports as social reformers in the 1830s and 1840s promoted a positive sports creed, which argued for the uplifting value of clean sports as a way to improve morality, health, and character and to make men better workers. The ideology emphasized the need for sedentary white-collar workers to get up from their desks and exercise.

The middle class also was influenced by the constructive role model of English and German sports clubs, and by the team sport of cricket. Professionals, merchants, clerks, and artisans joined cricket clubs in the 1840s to play a "manly" game that required courageous batters to stand up against fast bowlers, and fielders to catch balls on the fly. By the 1850s, however, cricket had been supplanted as the preeminent team ball game by the new sport of baseball, the rules of which were codified in 1845 by the Knickerbocker Club, an association of middle-class men in New York City. Baseball fit in better with the middle-class lifestyle of most Americans, because games required much less time to play than cricket, an important consideration for men whose leisure time was limited.

The first baseball players were mainly white-collar workers or artisans who played on teams that were organized by occupation, neighborhood, or political affiliation. Just a handful of players were drawn from the lowest classes. At first, white-collar teams did not play blue-collar squads, but by the late 1850s, teams became less exclusive; instead, they were composed of ambitious, forward-looking men who sought middle-class respectability.

There was even some support for middle-class women to participate in such physical activities as calisthenics and horseback riding to improve their health and beauty. In addition, women became interested in co-educational sports that encouraged socializing, notably ice-skating, which was enormously popular at New York's Central Park, and croquet and cycling, which were the focus of brief fads in the late 1860s.

Sports and Class in the Industrial Age, 1870–1920

The growth of industrial capitalism in the late nineteenth century had a major impact on sports. It enabled a few people to become extremely wealthy and improved the standard of living for the urban middle class.

However, the middle class underwent a transformation from independent producers and professionals to paid salary employees. Clerks were no longer budding businessmen, but working-class employees. The rise of industrialization and the factory system also weakened the situation of artisans, many of whom became semi-skilled machine operators. Such changes encouraged members of these groups to turn to sports as a means of demonstrating their manliness.

Industrialization also gave rise to an unskilled proletarian class that was employed in dangerous, insecure jobs for low wages and worked for long hours. This led to a decline in sports activities among such workers in the late nineteenth century.

Elite

The upper class lived a life of conspicuous consumption, with expensive mansions, lavish parties, exclusive men's clubs, and expensive sports. Vigorous sports gave them a chance to develop their leadership skills and to prove their manliness at a time when the size of families was declining, and culture and religion were becoming feminized. The elite sent their sons to boarding schools and private day schools where athletics, modeled after the English public schools, were compulsory, and to Eastern colleges, where they were encouraged to partake in strenuous sports, particularly football, which was considered the moral equivalent of war as a test of manhood.

The elite organized new sports clubs for track and field, golf, horse racing, polo, hunting, and yachting that were open only to the rich and well-born, and even those who were thus qualified had to be approved by older members. The clubs promoted competition by establishing eligibility rules, sponsoring contests, and securing playing sites. The more expensive sports organizations, such as the Westchester Polo Club, were the most prestigious. In addition, the prestige of clubs in the same sport depended on their home city. For example, Toronto's "Royal clubs" were more prestigious than other Canadian clubs, and elite clubs in New York City had the highest status of all American clubs.

The lowest-status clubs were downtown athletic clubs that emphasized track and field and provided a convenient escape from the pressures of work. The first was the New York Athletic Club, founded in 1868 to promote amateur competition among men from the same social backgrounds. It barred entrants (presumably of lower social status) who had competed for money, played against professionals (who had a competitive advantage, because they devoted themselves to sports fulltime), or taught athletics at schools or colleges.

Following the Civil War, upper-class sportsmen revived horse racing by establishing elite jockey clubs to operate lavish racetracks such as Jerome Park in New York and Washington Park in Chicago. Suburban country clubs were an important innovation, beginning in 1882 with the Country Club in Brookline, Massachusetts, where members could emulate English country life. Such clubs featured sumptuous clubhouses and expansive grounds used primarily for sports, such as tennis and golf, that were suitable for older men, wives, and daughters, whose social status enabled them to ignore standard conventions and participate in these sports. Young men and women also used the club to meet potential spouses.

Middle Class

The middle class continued to oppose gambling and immoral and violent sports through organizations such as the American Society for the Prevention of Cruelty to Animals (1866) and Anthony Comstock's Society for the Suppression of Vice (1874). But now they also were strong advocates of useful and moral sports. Middle-class men had sufficient money and discretionary time to enjoy themselves as spectators or participants, and they had ready access to parks in their neighborhoods or to ballparks that were an affordable streetcar ride away. Their sons could play competitive sports in public high schools, which developed sports teams in emulation of colleges.

Middle-class sportsmen formed voluntary associations that helped define their social status. These included upper-class games such as tennis and golf that they played at public courses. By 1878, they were forming bicycle clubs, and riding became a popular fad in the 1890s following the invention of the safety bicycle. Men enjoyed racing bicycles, while women appreciated the freedom they gained, enabling them to travel about on their own. Bicycling also encouraged women to wear sports clothing, which helped revolutionize fashion.

Baseball was especially popular with the middle class because it was considered good, clean fun, and presumably taught such traditional values as individualism, honesty, and respect for authority, as well as more modern priorities of industrial society, such as teamwork and cooperation. Most spectators were members of the middle class, and about two-thirds of major leaguers in the early 1900s were the sons of white-collar workers and farm owners.

In addition, most sports entrepreneurs and promoters belonged to the middle class. This business was disdained by the rich because owning a sports franchise at the time did not have the cachet that it would have in the future. Nearly all of the first professional baseball and hockey teams in North America were operated by middle-class businessmen.

Lower Class

Industrialization most affected the lives of the lower classes, who worked long hours—often 60 hours a week—at the hardest and most hazardous jobs and earned the lowest pay, leaving them little discretionary time or income. Workingmen also were limited by urbanization, as once-vacant lots and nearby wooded areas were developed, local bodies of water were polluted, and suburban parks became harder to reach. In addition, there was a huge influx of Polish, Italian, and Jewish immigrants who had little or no sporting heritage.

Workers were further restricted by Sunday blue laws, which barred sports on workers' only day off, especially in the East and the South. Sunday recreation was more common in newer Midwestern and Western states,

where traditional norms were harder to impose, and in cities and regions with a strong continental tradition, such as New Orleans.

Working-class sports generally were inexpensive, required little space, and took place in the participants' crowded residential neighborhoods; such activities often were sponsored by employers, unions, political bosses, ethnic societies, or saloon owners. Manual laborers played billiards in poolrooms and saloons and bowled in local taverns and bowling alleys, which became especially popular in the 1920s after Prohibition closed down workingmen's clubs (saloons).

At the turn of the century, immigrant youths were avid sports fans, despite parental opposition. They grew up playing stickball and other street games, and they received formal instruction in boxing, track and field, and basketball at neighborhood settlement houses, schools, community centers, and private gymnasiums.

Blue-collar fans kept up with sports through the penny press, or weeklies such as the *National Police Gazette,* which were available at male hangouts in saloons, cigar stores, and barbershops. Manual laborers attended boxing matches at their neighborhood gyms; they also enjoyed all-day events, such as six-day walking and bicycle races, as admission to such events cost just 25 cents, and they could stay for hours on end. But they were underrepresented at baseball games because the games were played in the afternoon, and because of the cost of tickets.

Those blue-color workers who attended baseball games mainly were artisans, city workers, and men with unusual work shifts. General admission to major league games was usually 50 cents, plus the cost of carfare, food, and beverages. In the 1880s, the American Association made a direct appeal to working-class fans by charging just 25 cents for admission, selling beer, and often staging Sunday games; however, it merged with the National League in 1892 and adopted the senior league's pricing policy. The absence of Sunday games severely limited attendance, a fact exemplified by the large crowds that came to New York games in 1919 (20,000–25,000), once Sunday games finally were allowed.

Working-class sports got a boost from the rise of welfare capitalism. This trend began in the town of Pullman, Illinois, established in 1881 by George Pullman, owner of the Palace Sleeping Car Company. In his company town, Pullman created the Pullman Athletic Association to promote sports in the community. The association emphasized high-level competition that advertised the company, and Pullman recruited Scottish and English artisans who also were expert rowers and cricketers to play on the company's nationally renowned squads.

Corporate sponsorship peaked in the 1920s as industrialists provided gymnasiums, swimming pools, and baseball diamonds at the workplace to promote Americanization, company loyalty, character building, and anti-unionism. Several major corporations emulated Pullman in recruiting athletes to play on company baseball and football teams that played the teams of other firms. In 1920, the National Football League was organized with industrial teams such as the Columbus Panhandles (originally sponsored by the Pennsylvania Railroad and named for one of its divisions) and the Decatur Staleys (sponsored by the A.E. Staley Starch Works).

Sports and Social Mobility

Sports were widely seen as a valuable avenue of social mobility for talented athletes, but for the most part, this was a myth. There were only a small number of jobs in professional sports. Professional athletes had very short careers, and those who rose from poverty often ended up indigent after retiring from sports, unless they used their prowess to gain an education.

Prizefighters, for instance, often came from the poorest backgrounds. The first prominent boxers were Irish Americans in the nineteenth century; they were succeeded in order by Jews, Italians, African Americans, and Latinos. Few fighters other than contenders and champions made much money, and even those men, such as heavyweight champion John L. Sullivan (1882–1892), spent their money on liquor, women, and gambling, and did not prepare for the future.

The situation was different in basketball, whose players also came from the inner city. Pro basketball was a minor sport until the National Basketball Association was founded in 1949. Players seldom made much money; however, by the 1920s, many of the best players leveraged their skills to get a college scholarship and graduate from college so that they had a profession to fall back on.

Baseball was the main professional sport. In the late nineteenth century, when the sport had little prestige, most players came from middle-class or high-level blue-collar backgrounds but not from the lowest levels of society. They earned more than $1,700 a season, but tenure was brief, and it was difficult for them to find a good job after baseball. The status of the game and its pay scale improved by the early 1900s, reaching an average of $3,000 by 1910, but only about one-third of the players were blue collar. Those men, in particular, struggled to succeed after retiring from baseball, unlike their better-educated colleagues in football and basketball.

Men in team sports did not earn large salaries until the latter part of the twentieth century. The average major leaguer made about $12,000 in 1950 and $46,000 in 1975, and the typical professional football player made $8,000 in 1949 and $42,000 in 1975. Thereafter, the pay scale increased rapidly as players organized and successfully challenged reserve clauses, which had given team owners almost complete control of their players' employment and salaries.

At the same time, the popularity of sports on television brought unprecedented income to the teams. In 2010, the average salaries were $5.85 million in the National Basketball Association, $3.3 million in Major League Baseball, $2.4 million in the National Football League, and $1.9 million (a median of $770,000) in the National Hockey League, enabling top professional athletes to go from rags to riches.

The Declining Role of Class

The higher standard of living in North America during the 1920s opened up opportunities for all sportsmen as fans and participants. People had more free time and access to parks and commercial recreation. Sporting equipment was relatively inexpensive, and admission prices were low. Radio broadcasts made events such as the World Series accessible to nearly everyone. Furthermore, nearly all young men attended high school, where gifted athletes could play varsity sports.

The Great Depression hurt everyone's sporting opportunities, as millions lost jobs and discretionary income and one-fourth of company sponsored programs were terminated. But the national government stepped in, and the Works Progress Administration spent billions to build parks, playgrounds, baseball fields, beaches, and swimming pools, which significantly increased working-class recreational opportunities.

Democratization accelerated after World War II, allowing people from all social classes to play a wide range of sports. In addition, the spread of television allowed anyone to watch virtually any broadcast sport. Working-class people skied, golfed, and played tennis at public or fee-based private courses. Bowling achieved enormous popularity among the middle class, particularly among suburban housewives, who played in large upscale facilities in shopping malls.

At the same time, there was some continuity with the past. There still were restrictive upper-class sports organizations, such as yacht clubs, polo clubs, and country clubs. And boxing and basketball still were dominated by inner-city youth.

By the start of the twenty-first century, the trend toward democratization of access to live spectator sports had reversed, as the cost of attending sporting events had skyrocketed, making it harder for many Americans to afford the expenditure. An average family of four attending a major league game in 2010 spent $194.98, including an average of $26.74 per ticket, plus the cost of parking, food, programs, and souvenirs. The best seats to go to wealthy celebrities or to corporations entertaining clients, and, as a result, crowds at sporting events are becoming less representative of a democratic society.

Steven A. Riess

See also: Athletic Clubs; Amateurism; Blue Laws; Country Clubs; Industrialization; Race and Race Relations; Urbanization.

Further Reading

Adelman, Melvin L. *A Sporting Time: New York City and the Rise of Modern Athletics, 1820–70.* Urbana: University of Illinois Press, 1986.

Breen, T.H. "Horses and Gentlemen: The Cultural Significance of Gambling Among the Gentry of Virginia." *William and Mary Quarterly* 34:2 (April 1977): 239–257.

Gorn, Elliott J. *The Manly Art: Bare-Knuckle Prize Fighting in America.* Ithaca, NY: Cornell University Press, 1986.

MacCambridge, Michael. *America's Game: The Epic Story of How Pro Football Captured a Nation.* New York: Random House, 2004.

Metcalfe, Alan. *Canada Learns to Play: The Emergence of Organized Sport, 1807–1914.* Toronto, Canada: McClellan & Stewart, 1987.

Morrow, Don, and Kevin B. Wamsley. *Sport in Canada: A History.* Don Mills, Canada: Oxford University Press, 2005.

Moss, Richard J. *Golf and the American Country Club.* Urbana: University of Illinois Press, 2001.

Nixon, Howard L., II. *Sport and the American Dream.* New York: Leisure, 1984.

Riess, Steven A. *City Games: The Evolution of American Urban Society and the Rise of Sports.* Urbana: University of Illinois Press, 1989.

———. "From Punters to Putters: The Recent Scholarship on Sport and Class, 1983–1992." *Journal of Sport History* 21:2 (Summer 1994): 138–184.

———. "Professional Sports as an Avenue of Social Mobility in America: Some Myths and Realities." In *Essays on Sport History and Sport Mythology,* ed. Donald G. Kyle and Gary D. Stark. College Station: Texas A&M University Press, 1990.

———. "A Social Profile of the Professional Football Player, 1920–1980." In *The Business of Professional Sports,* ed. Paul D. Staudohar and James A. Mangan. Urbana: University of Illinois Press, 1991.

———. *Touching Base: Professional Baseball and American Culture in the Progressive Era.* Rev. ed. Urbana: University of Illinois Press, 1999.

Sammons, Jeffrey T. *Beyond the Ring: The Role of Boxing in American Society.* Urbana: University of Illinois Press, 1988.

Vincent, Ted. *Mudville's Revenge: The Rise and Fall of American Sport.* New York: Seaview, 1981.

Clemente, Roberto (1934–1972)

Roberto Clemente, with 12 Golden Glove awards and a .317 lifetime batting average in 18 major league seasons (1955–1972), is considered one of the greatest outfielders and hitters in baseball history. Born in Puerto Rico, Clemente led the Pittsburgh Pirates to World Series titles in 1960 and 1971. He also was known as a humanitarian and an advocate for Latino players in Major League Baseball.

Clemente was born in Carolina, Puerto Rico, a suburb of San Juan, on August 18, 1934, the son of Melchor Clemente, a foreman at a local sugar mill, and his wife Luisa Walker Clemente. He grew up during a period of political, environmental, and economic instability on the island. The Clemente family was poor, but baseball was an important part of Clemente's childhood. Like others, he improvised equipment from whatever he could find as he learned the game and began to play on the sandlots of San Juan.

Roberto took a keen interest in the professional black ballplayers who competed in Puerto Rico. San Juan, like other Caribbean cities, was a hub for barnstorming teams composed mostly of players from the Negro Leagues in the United States, who sought extra income during the winter months. In Puerto Rico, unlike the United States, black and white players could compete on the same teams. Clemente most admired Monte Irvin, one of the first black players in the major leagues, who played the outfield for the New York Giants and later was elected to the Baseball Hall of Fame. The integrated baseball environment in his homeland made an impression on Clemente, who, throughout his life, viewed race as irrelevant in determining the quality of an individual player.

In 1952, five years after Jackie Robinson broke the color barrier in the major leagues, Clemente earned a tryout with the Brooklyn Dodgers. His skills caught the eye of Al Campanis, the team's chief scout in the

A revered figure in America's Latino community and its first member of the Baseball Hall of Fame, Puerto Rican–born Roberto Clemente won four batting titles in 18 years with the Pittsburgh Pirates. He was killed in a 1972 earthquake-relief mission to Nicaragua. *(Focus on Sport/Getty Images)*

region. Two years later, Clemente signed a contract with the Dodgers, and he was sent to the team's minor league affiliate in Montreal, Canada. At the end of the 1954 season, however, the Dodgers lost their claim on Clemente when they chose not to promote him to the majors.

The last-place Pittsburgh Pirates quickly drafted Clemente, and he moved up to the big leagues. During the next few seasons, he played well enough to be a starter, but he did not live up to his potential. He finally came into his own in 1960, when he batted .314 and drove in 94 runs to help Pittsburgh win the National League pennant and beat the New York Yankees in the World Series.

From 1960 to the end of his career, Clemente was among the top players and personalities in baseball. He won the National League Most Valuable Player

(MVP) award in 1966, captured four batting titles (in 1961, 1964, 1965, and 1967, when he hit a career best .357), and was widely considered the finest right fielder of his era, earning 12 straight Gold Glove awards (1961–1972). He also played in 14 All-Star Games, had base hits in all of his 14 World Series games, and was voted MVP of the 1971 World Series, when he batted an impressive .414 as the Pirates beat the Baltimore Orioles in seven games. At the end of the 1972 season, his eighteenth as a major leaguer, his lifetime batting average was .317 with 3,000 hits. However, his stellar play was only part of his story.

Clemente also was an outspoken advocate for Latinos in the major leagues. The proud Puerto Rican often criticized the English-speaking press for presenting inaccurate images of Latin Americans. He also urged major league teams to orient young Latino recruits before sending them to play in the mainland United States.

In Puerto Rico, Clemente created a foundation for the construction of a sports center that he called Ciudad Deportiva (Sports City), which was designed to advance the skills of young baseball hopefuls and train them to become better citizens. Always generous with his time and money, Clemente enjoyed tutoring young boys in the principles of baseball in his home commonwealth, throughout the Caribbean, in Central America, and in Pittsburgh. As a result, he developed a strong following of fans who saw him as a leader on the diamond and as a humanitarian off the field, even though sportswriters often found him difficult and uncooperative.

On December 23, 1972, a devastating earthquake hit Managua, the capital of Nicaragua in Central America. Thousands of people were killed, and hundreds of thousands were left homeless. Almost immediately, Clemente began to organize aid for the half-destroyed city. On December 31, he was on an airplane filled with relief supplies when the plane crashed into the sea shortly after taking off from Puerto Rico. His body was never recovered.

Throughout the baseball world, fans of Clemente expressed their grief with a vast array of testimonials. Thousands, including President Richard M. Nixon, donated large sums of money for the development of Clemente's Sports Center. Within months of Clemente's death, the Baseball Writers Association of America convened and voted to enshrine him in the Baseball Hall of Fame, making Clemente the first Puerto Rican and the first Latino inductee.

Since 1973, people in and out of baseball have supported measures to honor Clemente's legacy. Less than a year after his death, the Commissioner's Award, given to players in recognition of their humanitarian contributions, was renamed the Roberto Clemente Award. In the late 1980s, the Puerto Rican government began to allocate money on an annual basis for the upkeep of Clemente's Sports City. And in 1999, the Allegheny County Board of Supervisors voted to name one of Pittsburgh's bridges in honor of their fallen star.

Samuel O. Regalado

See also: Latinos and Latinas; Pirates, Pittsburgh.

Further Reading

Maraniss, David. *Clemente: The Passion and Grace of Baseball's Last Hero.* New York: Simon & Schuster, 2006.

Markusen, Bruce. *Roberto Clemente: The Great One.* Pittsburgh, PA: Sports Publishing, 2001.

Musick, Phil. *Who Was Roberto? A Biography of Roberto Clemente.* Garden City, NY: Doubleday, 1974.

Wagenheim, Kal. *Clemente.* New York: Praeger, 1973.

Clothing

Clothing for sports is a many-faceted subject that includes everything from athletic uniforms, protective clothing, and accessories to fan clothing. While the variety of sports clothing is great, the general purpose of such garb—at least today—is summarized more easily: sturdy, flexible, sensible dress that allows the body to move to its maximum efficiency while still maintaining decorum. The various forms of sports clothing are well adapted to their uses and usually are gender specific, although women's wear often takes its cues from men's wear.

The history of sports clothing is intertwined with the rise and evolution of modern sports, changes in social mores, and technological breakthroughs in the production of textiles. (It should be noted that sports clothing differs from sportswear, the latter encompassing simple and easy-to-wear separates, often inspired by sports clothes.)

Emergence of Sports Clothes

The ancients, notably the Greeks, competed nude; even Roman women stripped down to something like an early bikini for their athletic endeavors. Distinct sports clothing first appeared in modern times with the rise of upper-class athletic games. The inventories of England's Henry VIII, for example, included some suits specifically worn for tennis and others for hunting. Equestrian sports had a particularly significant influence during this time, shaping and simplifying contemporary fashion for both men and women. Men's sporting costume eliminated the lace and ruffles of their more formal dress. Women began copying male dress for riding, wearing masculine-style doublets along with full skirts. By the eighteenth century, simplified elegance for sports was standard wear for the upper classes.

For much of the nineteenth century, men's clothing for sports consisted of the casual clothing of the day, sometimes simplified to allow for greater freedom of movement. The earliest exception was formal gymnasium sports, in which men first wore leotards, and, from the end of the nineteenth century, shorts accompanied by sleeveless shirts that resembled today's tank tops. In most other cases, they wore straight trousers (called pantaloons) and removed their jackets, even their vests, to play sports—something that no self-respecting man would have done under normal circumstances.

Baseball was the first major sport to develop its own distinctive costume. The earliest baseball uniforms, usually colored blue and white, were worn by the renowned Knickerbocker Base Ball Club, a group of young middle-class New Yorkers who pioneered the game in the 1840s. Wearing a uniform identified a young man as part of the baseball fraternity.

The next major change came in the late 1860s, when the Cincinnati Reds, the first avowedly professional team, replaced the long, straight trousers of earlier baseball with knee-length wool garments that resembled seventeenth-century knee breeches, called "knickerbockers." These were matched with loose wool shirts and red stockings. Their opponents copied the new uniform, but wore different colors and patterns. The new knickerbockers, which became known as "knickers," remained the male sporting pants of choice—for bicycling, golf, hunting, football, and tennis, along with baseball—well into the twentieth century.

Early Women's Sports Clothing

Women's sports clothing prior to World War II was far more restricted than men's. Modesty and fashion limited women's options in sports clothing to versions of day wear for other uses. As women began participating in sports, such as croquet, in the 1860s, they shortened their wide, full, hooped skirts a bit to allow greater flexibility, although corsets, hats, and gloves remained a required part of the ensemble. In 1914, Tennis player Elizabeth Ryan lamented this state of affairs, describing the scene in one changing room: "It was not a pretty sight, as many of the [corsets] were blood-stained from the wounds they had inflicted."

It was the bicycling fad, which began with the invention of the easy-to-ride safety bike in the 1890s and was one of the few exertive sports permitted Victorian women, that led to the first significant changes in women's sports clothing. Women cyclists often discarded their corsets and floor-length dresses for bloomers—a type of loose trouser, gathered at the ankle, first developed by social reformer Amelia Bloomer in the 1850s—split skirts, and knickers, all of which increased mobility and safety.

Initially, bloomers—the first such garments promoted for women as daily wear—failed miserably in reforming women's clothing, as they were shunned by most women and ridiculed by men. However, within a decade or two, urban women and female students began wearing them in gymnasiums, though often under their skirts. As competitive games for women became popular, notably basketball in the 1890s, the skirt eventually was discarded, leaving wide, baggy, knee-length wool bloomers visible. Corsets, hats, and gloves likewise were eliminated.

Bloomers and the middy blouse—a light, loose-fitting top, sometimes cinched at the waist—formed a combination that became something of a uniform for sporting women by the early decades of the twentieth century. This process unfolded fairly quickly among the participants in indoor sports. The garments women wore while participating in outdoor and field sports—tennis, golf, and field hockey—were much slower to change.

Tennis and Golf

Tennis became a popular upper-middle-class game in the late 1880s and 1890s. By the end of the century, designers had begun to introduce sporty outfits for male participants, often with collars and trim echoing sailors' uniforms and generally incorporating the ubiquitous knickers. Wearing all white for tennis was customary by the turn of the century, made possible by improved laundry facilities.

Though there was some variance in casual tennis clothing at the turn of the century, the costume for formal tournaments was more circumscribed, with the All England Lawn Tennis and Croquet Club dictating etiquette on both sides of the Atlantic. Male players were expected to wear white button-down shirts and long white flannel trousers. In the 1930s, shorts slowly became an acceptable alternative to flannels.

Female players were expected to wear formal white dresses with gloves and corsets. By 1919, most women at Wimbledon wore white cotton skirts that were mid-calf length, hose, a short-sleeved middy blouse, and a wide-brimmed bonnet. Within a few years, French designer Jean Patou was designing tennis outfits for French star Suzanne Lenglen—sleeveless tops with skirts that started out knee length, and by 1922, were above the knee. Wimbledon featured its first shorts-wearing female player (Alice Marble) in 1932.

Tennis is a fairly conservative sport, and since the 1930s, its customs regarding fashion have changed relatively little. White still is considered the only "proper" color for many tennis tournaments—particularly Wimbledon—and those who disregard the convention (most notably Andre Agassi) are labeled by conservatives as rebellious freethinkers at best, and as disrespectful louts at worst. Similarly, skirts still are preferred for female tennis players, even if those skirts are far shorter than would have been acceptable a century ago.

As with tennis players, the golfers of the late nineteenth century adopted a fairly formal "uniform" that remained in place for many decades. From the 1870s and 1880s, male golfers wore knickerbocker pants accompanied by a sweater or a shirt and tie, and topped off the outfit with a soft, floppy golf cap. In the 1890s, when women began playing, they wore long skirts, jackets, hats, and sometimes even high-heeled shoes.

Golf retained its conservative air for many decades. In the 1950s and 1960s, however, male golfers began to abandon knickers in favor of more casual full-length pants, often made from cloth with garish bright patterns. Women's golf wear grew more relaxed as well, with shorter, more pliant skirts the norm by the 1940s, and shorts commonplace by the 1970s. Recent decades have seen some small movement back in the direction of more formal golf wear, particularly among professionals—notably Tiger Woods—who, for marketing purposes, look to project an image of sophistication and refinement.

Swimwear

Swimwear, which aims to improve performance while maintaining a modicum of modesty, represents the class of sports clothing most reliant on textile innovations, from early wool knits that appeared in the late 1800s through the synthetic Speedo LZR racer of the 2008 Olympics.

At the turn of the century, women wore two-piece suits that covered most of the body. These generally included a loose, thick blouse paired with some sort of trousers or leggings, sometimes covered by a skirt. Men wore sleeveless shirts and loose-fitting trunks that covered them down to the knee. Neither costume was particularly efficient for swimming; in fact, the women's version could be downright dangerous when saturated with water.

Leading the charge for better women's swimwear was long-distance swimmer Annette Kellerman of Australia, who had taken to wearing a one-piece bathing suit by 1907, when she was arrested for wearing the suit in public. The suit was a figure-hugging wool knit blend with a sleeveless tank that covered the body from the shoulders to the middle of the thigh, with hose covering her legs. Kellerman's willingness to flout the conventions of her day—she was the first woman ever to do a nude scene in a movie (*A Daughter of the Gods,* 1916)—meant that the one-piece suits, known as "Annette Kellermans," gained acceptance slowly. Such bathing suits eventually took off in the 1920s, when women were freer to express their sexuality, and more revealing clothing became the norm.

Thereafter, the size of women's bathing suits began to shrink, often through the influence of movies and images of movie stars in magazines and newsreels lounging around their California pools. In the 1930s, open-backed, form-fitting short trunks with lower necklines, as well as two-piece brassiere suits that exposed the midsection, began to appear. In the 1940s and 1950s, manufacturers developed corset-like suits to hide physical flaws.

In the 1960s, the bikini—a French import—became a popular bathing suit for young women. Since that time, such two-piece suits have dominated the market for casual swimwear, though designs have grown more revealing over time. Since 1964, this trend has been documented and encouraged by *Sports Illustrated* in its annual swimsuit issue. This has become the single best-selling sports-themed publication every year, with a circulation in excess of 1 million.

Men's swimwear also grew less modest over the course of the twentieth century. By the 1920s, males largely had stopped wearing shirts while swimming, and form-fitting shorts called "swim trunks" had become commonplace. The critics who denounced this new costume as indecent would have been left apoplectic by the 1956 Olympics, which witnessed the introduction of the now-famous water-resistant swim briefs made by the Australian company Speedo. There has been relatively little change in bathing suit styles since that time, and today, the casual male swimmer

chooses between waterproof shorts and brief-style swimwear not terribly different from the 1956 Speedos, except perhaps in terms of the material used.

Elite athletes, for their part, no longer use the clothing worn by casual swimmers, preferring instead high-tech, skintight bodysuits. The LZR Racer is the best known and most advanced of these. Crafted from polyurethanes, its designers spent years trying to improve on existing models, carefully studying the movement and skin texture of sharks, and also making liberal use of NASA wind tunnels. Speedo claims that the suit increases oxygen flow to the body, repels water, and helps maintain a proper posture for swimmers. The evidence seems to support these claims; since the LZR Racer was introduced, 33 of 36 Olympic medals have gone to athletes clad in the suit.

Winter Sports Clothing

Thanks to entrepreneurs in cold-weather European locales, particularly the Swiss town of St. Moritz, winter-only activities such as skating, skiing, and bobsledding emerged in the 1870s and 1880s as popular sporting activities. At that time, there was no specialized clothing for winter sports enthusiasts; they simply wore their regular clothing and added extra layers to compensate for the cold.

In the 1920s, amateur and professional skiers and sledders—in search of more aerodynamic clothes and thus greater speed—began to wear long Norwegian trousers with cuffed hems, along with short, tailored jackets. The jackets usually had shoulder pads and left room for a coat to be worn underneath. This ensemble certainly was less wind-resistant than previous alternatives, but winter sports enthusiasts still were simply adapting everyday clothing.

It was not until the 1950s, with the development of water-resistant synthetic fibers, that sportswear manufacturers began to make and market special clothes for winter sports. Flexible pants—cinched at both the knee and waist with elastic—were paired with jackets that featured a belt and a shirt-like collar. This outfit, which quickly became known as a ski suit (though it also was used for other winter sports), remained predominant among cold-weather athletes for decades. Quite often, the ski suit was paired with a knitted cap, or with a balaclava. The balaclava, known to Americans as a "ski mask," is a soft head covering with one or more holes in the front for the wearer's eyes (and sometimes mouth).

The 1970s and 1980s witnessed the introduction of an array of fabrics that could be fashioned into skintight clothing. The one-piece bodysuit, made from Spandex or similar material, supplanted the ski suit in some circles at this time. Bodysuits remain popular with elite winter athletes today (particularly bobsledders and speed skaters), but they have fallen out of favor with most amateurs. In part, this is because skintight clothing is unforgiving on less-sculpted bodies. It is also because bodysuits, while windproof, nonetheless make it more difficult to keep warm.

Another development that served to undermine the bodysuit—while also driving winter fashion forward—was the rise of snowboarding. As is the case with surfers and skateboarders, snowboarders are deeply concerned with both their sport and with maintaining a hip, rebellious image. Not only do they prefer two-piece outfits (which are better able to accommodate their acrobatic maneuvers), but they also demand very colorful, highly fashionable clothing that can be worn during their everyday lives. In a sense, then, winter sports clothing has come full circle. In the 1870s and 1880s, trendsetting participants wore fashionable everyday clothing, and today they do the same.

Sports and Fashion

As amateur and professional sports grew in popularity in the decades after the Civil War, they prompted the rise of the sportswear industry. In 1879, for example, George Wright and Henry Ditson formed the sporting goods company Wright & Ditson. The firm was bought out in 1892 by Albert G. Spalding & Brothers, which had started its own sports clothing line in Chicago in 1876. Munsingwear, a company that made the knitted shirts, sweaters, and underwear worn by players in various sports, opened in Minneapolis in 1886.

Indeed, the term "sweater" dates to this period. Originally, it was a knitted wool garment designed to keep players warm and to absorb sweat from their exertion. Images of heroic star players wearing their uniforms of knickers and sweaters appeared in countless magazines and newspapers at this time. And with the addition, by the turn of the century, of protective helmets (made out of leather and padded canvas), the image of the broad-shouldered, muscular ideal American was born.

Beyond introducing sweaters and a general conception of male attractiveness, the world of sports made other contributions to fashion in the early decades of the twentieth century. Baseball caps became a popular accessory among youths, and then eventually with adults. The invention of vulcanized rubber in the late 1890s led to the development of sneakers—soft-soled, sturdy shoes used for playing croquet and tennis. Soon, the new footwear was so thoroughly identified with the latter sport that the name "sneakers" was mostly supplanted by the slang term "tennis shoes." By the 1910s, tennis shoes, like Keds, were a staple of everyday casual wear, even among nonsporting Americans.

The 1920s witnessed a sea change in American notions of female beauty. Before that time, women's participation in sports was viewed with suspicion and often was dismissed as unfeminine. However, with the cultural changes that followed World War I, the youthful, slim, athletic female became the new ideal. While casual fashion continued to be shaped by athletic wear, as it had been for decades, this new development meant that the world of sports crossed paths with the world of high fashion for the first time. In particular, Jean Patou and Gabrielle "Coco" Chanel became famous for their sports-inspired haute couture. "Sports has more to do than anything else with the evolution of the modern fashion," declared *British Vogue* in 1926.

The Great Depression created a demand for cheap, efficient clothing options. The T-shirt first was developed for American sailors in the 1890s, and it became a common undergarment for athletes thereafter. In the 1930s, football players at the University of Southern California began to take their T-shirts from the locker room home with them. They wore them around campus as a comfortable and cheap substitute for more formal alternatives, and a national trend took hold.

It was also around this time that clothing designers began to look for more cost-effective alternatives to men's long underwear. Everlast founder Jacob Golomb turned to pugilists for inspiration, introducing "boxer" shorts in the late 1920s. They promptly became the nation's most popular male underwear. In 1935, Arthur Kneibler of Coopers, Inc., drew inspiration from the athletic supporters worn for bicycle and horse racing, creating the first pair of jockey shorts. They, too, found a ready audience, supplanting boxers as the top-selling men's undergarment by the end of the 1930s.

After the Great Depression, athletic clothing became much more muted. Two wars, along with a general culture of conformity, encouraged the development of utilitarian athletic apparel made in somber colors. In this context, the influence of sports on fashion diminished. There were a few designers following in the footsteps of Patou and Chanel—notably Teddy Tingling, known for his flared tennis dresses crafted from waffle pique fabric—but they were the exception to the general rule.

Athletics in the 1970s and 1980s once again began to have a noticeable impact on fashion. A national fitness craze took hold in the 1980s, and once again, the slim, athletic body was idealized, as it had been in the 1920s. In addition to sweaters and T-shirts, which had never gone out of style, Americans began to wear polo shirts, track shorts, sweat shirts and sweat pants, leggings or tights, leg warmers, and headbands. The shell suit—a two-piece, zippered nylon tracksuit in ocean-themed colors—was a particularly iconic manifestation of this new emphasis on being fit. So, too, was clothing made from Spandex and other skintight textiles, which quickly crossed over from sports to music (especially heavy metal), television, and hipster culture. These trends have never abated, and since that time, sports-inspired clothing has been integral to American casual wear.

The 1980s also saw sports reclaim an important place in the world of high fashion. Many designers—Calvin Klein, Ralph Lauren, Tommy Hilfiger, and Prada—introduced complete sportswear lines. Thanks to companies such as Adidas, Nike, and Reebok, tennis shoes—which, of course, had been popular for decades—emerged as an important and expensive part of the fashionable American's wardrobe. In 1970, there were 15 different models of tennis shoes on sale in the United States that cost less than $20 a pair. By 1990, there were more than 250 models, some of them selling for more than $300 a pair.

Today, the market for sports-related clothing is as strong as it ever has been. The amount of money spent by Americans on sportswear has doubled in the past decade. There are lines of sportswear targeted to specific segments of the populace—the National Football League, for example, has a collection of form-fitting pink-colored clothing for women, while companies such as FUBU and Sean John market themselves to African Americans. At the same time, the fashion-conscious public has come to place athletes on something of a pedestal. Jock-endorsed accessories—Air Jordan shoes, the yellow Livestrong bracelets of cyclist Lance Armstrong, Tiger Woods's TAG Heuer watches—sell millions of units. Further, in addition to baseball caps, fans now clamor for authentic jerseys bearing their favorite stars' names.

Distressingly, these seemingly benign developments have had some serious downsides. There have been, in recent decades, numerous cases of violence centered on athletic shoes and other expensive items of sports clothing. Further, some sports teams' apparel—notably that of the Oakland Raiders and the Los Angeles Kings—have been adopted as a quasi-uniform by urban gangs.

Technology

The demands placed on sportswear are greater, perhaps, than those imposed on any other class of clothing. Both athletes and casual wearers require durability, flexibility, protection from the elements and from injury, and some means of venting the heat and perspiration generated by a body in motion. Ever since the rise of major organized sports in the 1860s and 1870s, technological innovations—particularly new textiles—have been applied in an effort to meet these needs.

The sportsmen and women of the nineteenth century generally wore their everyday clothes. This was suitable—if not ideal—for more genteel sports such as croquet and golf. However, the cotton, silk, and linen textiles of the day did not stand up well to the demands of more rigorous sports, such as baseball and football. Those athletes generally were forced to turn to more durable wool or wool blends. These fabrics were sturdy, but they did not vent heat well, tended to weigh athletes down, and smelled bad when saturated with sweat.

The first textile deployed in an effort to solve these concerns was jersey, invented in Great Britain in 1882. A knitted fabric made of cotton (then) or synthetic fibers (now), jersey breathes well and also stretches, expanding by up to 25 percent when necessary. The fabric originally was intended for undergarments, but by 1900, it had been adopted by horsemen for use in their riding breeches. In 1916, Chanel created a stir when she introduced a line of sportswear built on jersey fabric, but the trend soon caught on, and the textile was in widespread use by sports enthusiasts by the 1920s.

The 1930s witnessed a pair of important technical innovations in the area of sports clothing. The first innovation was Lastex yarn, which features string made of cotton or other fabric wound around a thin rubber core. It is enormously flexible and is particularly useful for clasps or fasteners and when a tight fit is needed in sleeves and waistbands. The second innovation was nylon, a synthetic fiber invented by DuPont's Wallace Carothers in 1925. Nylon is lightweight, weather resistant, and durable. For decades, it remained the preferred material for athletes in sports such as rowing, skiing, and swimming.

The need to make flexible and durable clothing that protected soldiers from the elements had a profound impact on athletic apparel in the postwar era. Hoods were introduced that could be hidden inside collars with a snap when not in use, jackets were designed with deep pockets to hold snacks, and gloves were made with zippered compartments for ski tickets—all improvements borrowed from the military.

Plastics also were widely used in sports clothing, particularly in safety equipment, such as athletic supporters, goggles, helmets, shin guards, and shoes. In 1965, DuPont developed Kevlar, a lighter, more flexible, and more durable material than plastic that is used in all manner of sports apparel—belts, gloves, hats, helmets, cleats, and tennis shoes.

World War II also encouraged experimentation with different types of synthetic materials; for instance, nylon was improved, and polyester was invented in 1941. When blended with cotton, polyester replaced wool in the uniforms of most team sports.

Another new fiber was Spandex, which was invented in 1959 by chemist Joseph Shivers. Also known as elastane, Elaspan, or Lycra, spandex is stretchy and form fitting like rubber but stronger and more durable. It soon found its way into bicycle shorts, knee braces, leggings, socks, swimsuits, and wetsuits. Today, Under Armour and other purveyors of elastane-based sports clothing sell moisture-wicking (transferring moisture through capillary action) undergarments for athletes.

Breathable and moisture-resistant materials have been a particular focus of researchers in the past several decades. In 1969, Bob Gore, a leader in this field, invented Gore-Tex, an extruded polytetrafluoroethylene microporous material that allows water vapor from perspiration to evaporate but prevents water droplets from passing through, thus keeping the wearer dry. Gore-Tex and similar high-tech waterproof, breathable textiles are very popular, as are durable water repellent coatings, such as Nikwax or Scotchguard, which are applied to natural and manmade materials to add additional waterproofing. Garments made with these materials and coatings are used extensively in golf wear, hiking apparel, ski suits, and clothing designed for many other sports.

Similarly, today's athletes have access to materials that are extremely lightweight while still very warm. In 1979, Malden Mills created Polar Fleece (generically known simply as "fleece"), which offers the texture and insulation associated with wool but is not nearly as heavy or as prone to absorbing perspiration. The current generation of fleeces is known by a variety of names—Microfleece, Polartec, and Windbloc among them. In addition, modern synthetic fill materials—such as Polarguard, Primaloft, Thermolite, and Thinsulate—add lightweight insulation to outer garments.

Surely, the sportsmen and women of the nineteenth century would find the modern world of sports apparel truly remarkable. From the eclectic wool uniforms of the 1860s and 1870s, today's professional athletes wear light, flexible, moisture-resistant, wicking garments that do much to ensure their comfort and safeguard their well-being. Sports teams intimately are identified with those uniforms, many of which—the pinstripes of the New York Yankees, the starred helmet of the Dallas Cowboys, the blue of the University of North Carolina—have become iconic in American culture. At the same time, the amateur sports enthusiast has a dizzying array of efficient, cost-effective options to choose from, both in their daily and their sporting lives.

Christopher G. Bates and Patricia Campbell Warner

See also: Business of Sports; Endorsements, Athlete; Injuries, Protection Against and Remediation of; Technology.

Further Reading

Davis, Laurel R. *The Swimsuit Issue and Sport: Hegemonic Masculinity in Sports.* Albany: State University of New York Press, 1997.

Engleman, Larry. *The Goddess and the American Girl: The Story of Suzanne Lenglen and Helen Wills.* New York: Oxford Univ. Press, 1988.

Grundy, Pamela. "Bloomers and Beyond: North Carolina Women's Basketball Uniforms." *Southern Cultures* 3:3 (1997): 52–67.

Warner, Patricia Campbell. *When the Girls Came Out to Play: The Birth of American Sportswear.* Amherst: University of Massachusetts Press, 2006.

Wiltse, Jeff. *Contested Waters: A Social History of Swimming Pools in America.* Chapel Hill: University of North Carolina Press, 2007.

Cobb, Ty (1886–1961)

Few players in baseball history were as driven to succeed as Ty Cobb, the volatile outfielder whose personality and skills dominated the major leagues during his 24 years, mainly with the Detroit Tigers (1905–1926). Although his contemporaries regarded him as the greatest player in the game's history, his hostility toward teammates and foes alike also made him the most hated player of his generation. Cobb's win-at-all-costs attitude spilled over into his life off the field, provoking turbulence and controversy.

Family Background

Tyrus Raymond "Ty" Cobb was born on December 18, 1886, in an area of rural Georgia called the Narrows, and grew up in the town of Royston. His father, William, was a prominent educator, publisher, and state senator who raised his oldest son on the classics and expected him to become a doctor or a lawyer. But the youngster preferred playing ball and, like many baseball stars of his generation, had to fight his parents' belief that sports was an unsuitable career. He secured his first minor league job in nearby Augusta by bombarding the local newspaper with anonymous letters praising the talents of a prospect named Cobb.

When Cobb was 18, his mother shot and killed his father after he broke through her window, suspecting her of infidelity. At the 1906 trial, she claimed that she had believed the intruder was a burglar and was acquitted. However, biographers of Cobb say, a deep psychological wound was inflicted on their son. William Cobb had accepted his son's foray into baseball with the admonition, "Don't come home a failure." Ty dedicated himself to proving his worth to the man who would never see him play.

Soon after the family tragedy, Cobb found himself the target of hazing when he joined the Detroit Tigers, who purchased his contract in 1905, only three weeks after his father's death. Such treatment was standard for rookies, and Southerners were scarce in the major leagues, making them an easy target. The "Georgia Peach," as he came to be called, took the harsh treatment personally. In keeping with his naturally fiery temperament, he fought back, not caring about the resulting feuds and rifts with his teammates.

Cobb entered the American League during the "deadball era," so called because the baseballs used were too soft and irregular to be hit out of the park for home runs. Offensive strategy emphasized scoring one run at a time, using short hits, bunts, hit-and-run plays, and aggressive base running. Cobb soon proved his superiority at every one of those skills. Tall for his time at 6 feet, 1 inch (1.9 meters) and physically imposing, he had more extra-base power than most hitters. But he also was adept at choking up to place hits in open spots on the field, and he could bunt and chop grounders as well, using his great speed to leg out base hits.

"The Intimidator"

It was on the bases that Cobb raised the stakes. There are myriad stories of Cobb stealing second, third, and home in succession; racing from first to third base on a ground out; scoring from second on an infield hit; overrunning a base on purpose to draw a throw, then dashing safely to the next base; and terrorizing infielders by sharpening his spikes in public before the game, then sliding with his spikes flying high, ready to slash

a careless fielder. These tactics made him the most feared and loathed player in baseball but also gained him the most respect for his unprecedented run-scoring journeys around the bases. He was relentless in his search for new ways to take an extra base, consistently staying one step ahead of the opposition to ensure his team's success and his own glory.

The statistics demonstrate how thoroughly Cobb ran roughshod over the American League. He won 11 batting titles in 13 seasons, including five in a row. Three times he batted over .400, a feat matched only by Rogers Hornsby, including a career-best .420 average in 1911. He led the league in hits eight times, in slugging average eight times, in runs scored five times, in runs batted in four times, in stolen bases six times, in doubles three times, in triples four times, and even in home runs once, in 1909, when he won baseball's Triple Crown (the league leader in home runs, runs batted in, and batting average). Cobb despised the slugging trends of the 1920s, claiming that anybody could hit for power if he wanted to and backing up his boast by slamming three home runs in a game in 1925.

Cobb led the Tigers to consecutive American League pennants in his first three full seasons, but the team failed to win the World Series each year. In 1907, he struggled, hitting a paltry .200 as the Tigers were swept in four games by the Chicago Cubs. The Tigers repeated as American League champs in 1908 and faced the Cubs again in the World Series. Cobb led the Tigers with a .368 average and four runs driven in, but they fell to the Cubs in five games.

The 1909 Series brought a showdown with the Pittsburgh Pirates and Honus Wagner, the best player in the National League. This Series went a full seven games before the Pirates prevailed. Wagner won a personal duel, too, batting .333 to Cobb's .231, driving in more runs, and stealing six bases to Cobb's two.

Cobb never again played in the World Series. Mighty on offense but weak in pitching, the Tigers floundered in the middle of the pack for the next 25 years, not winning another pennant until 1934. Cobb took over as manager in 1921. He kept the team in the first division, finishing second once but never coming closer than six games behind the pennant winner. As a manager, he enjoyed mentoring young hitters such as future Hall of Famer Harry Heilmann, but he alienated many players with his unrealistic belief that everyone should perform as aggressively as he had on the field.

Cobb's career was marred by numerous incidents of violence. He fought often, including a postgame fight with umpire Billy Evans, several with teammates, and a celebrated brawl with Charles "Buck" Herzog of the New York Giants that began during a spring training exhibition game and continued in Cobb's hotel room that evening.

The most notorious incident occurred in 1912 in New York, when Cobb charged into the grandstand to attack a spectator who had heckled him, continuing to pummel the fan even after onlookers yelled to him that the man had no hands. Cobb drew an indefinite suspension for this assault, but his teammates felt that he had been provoked and called a strike on his behalf. When the regular players refused to play, the Tigers management recruited a team of semiprofessionals for a game against the Philadelphia Athletics, losing 24–2. Cobb's suspension soon was reduced to 10 games.

Scandal and Retirement

Cobb's tenure with the Tigers ended after the 1926 season, when he, Tristram "Tris" Speaker, and "Smoky Joe" Wood were accused of fixing a game between Detroit and Cleveland late in the 1919 season so that they could win money betting on it. Commissioner of Baseball Kenesaw Mountain Landis conducted an investigation, and there was documented evidence of a conspiracy. However, the accuser, former hurler Hubert "Dutch" Leonard, refused to travel from California for the formal hearing, which persuaded Landis to exonerate the players. The price for this whitewashing, however, was that Cobb and Speaker would give up their positions as managers.

In 1927, Cobb joined the Philadelphia Athletics as an outfielder. He played two productive seasons with them (he was joined by Speaker in 1928), batting .357 and .323, respectively, before retiring at the age of 42.

When Cobb retired, he held career records for hits (4,189), runs scored (2,245), stolen bases (892), and games played (3,034), and he was second in doubles and triples. Those marks all were surpassed eventually, but it is unlikely that any hitter ever will approach Cobb's lifetime batting average of .366. As of 2010, the highest lifetime average of any player who broke into the majors after 1945 was .338 (Tony Gwynn, 1982–2001).

Cobb also far outclassed his contemporaries in making money. He was an early investor in Coca-Cola, and he bought General Motors and other blue-chip stocks, becoming one of baseball's first millionaires. Following his playing career, he kept his competitive juices flowing by engaging in pastimes such as golf and gambling, but nothing slowed the increase in his fortune. Though his reputation has suffered from tales of his unabashed racism and violent tendencies (such as his unprovoked attack on a black waiter), the ledger is balanced somewhat by his considerable philanthropy. He endowed a hospital in his hometown and aided hospitals and charities elsewhere, usually without publicity.

In 1936, in the first balloting for the National Baseball Hall of Fame, Cobb received more votes than anyone, including Honus Wagner and Babe Ruth. He was inducted when the museum opened in 1939. He lived in California for many years, twice divorced and estranged from his five children, before returning to Georgia, where he died of cancer on July 17, 1961, at the age of 74.

Gabriel Schechter

See also: Baseball, Major League; Tigers, Detroit.

Further Reading

Alexander, Charles C. *Ty Cobb*. New York: Oxford University Press, 1984.

Bak, Richard. *Ty Cobb: His Tumultuous Life and Times*. Dallas, TX: Taylor, 1994.

Cobb, Ty, with Al Stump. *My Life in Baseball: The True Record*. Garden City, NY: Doubleday, 1961.

Ritter, Lawrence. *The Glory of Their Times*. New York: Macmillan, 1966.

Stump, Al. *Cobb: A Biography*. Chapel Hill, NC: Algonquin, 1994.

Cockfighting

Cockfighting is a traditional rural amusement that pits specially trained and bred roosters against one another in bouts, often leading to the death of one of the birds. Dating back several thousand years to the domestication of the chicken, cockfighting was one of the most popular sports in colonial North America, and it remained so among the sporting fraternity in antebellum America.

The violence of the sport—and the gambling associated with it—led to cockfighting being banned nearly everywhere by the middle of the twentieth century, though it continues to exist outside the law, mainly in the rural South and in Hispanic enclaves in urban areas. The sport has its own subculture that promotes a sense of male community and aggressive masculinity.

Spanish Origins

The sport is believed to have been brought to North America by Filipinos, who came to New Spain, including the American Southwest, via the Manila Galleons, and by Englishmen who brought the sport from their villages. The latter introduced gaff fighting, tying an instrument that resembles a rapier with a sharpened point and a round body to each leg of the cock. The Spanish, Filipinos, and eventually Mexicans brought a tradition of "slasher" or knife fights, in which a blade, resembling a curved, single-edged razor, was tied to the cock's leg. Slasher fights increased the risk to the combatants, reducing the effect of the birds' skill but enhancing the possibility for an upset.

By the 1700s, cock matches were common everywhere outside of New England, where strong Puritan beliefs against gambling and blood sports precluded matches through mid-century. Taverns became important centers of matches and, indeed, cockfighting may have been the most common sport at the tavern grounds, drawing people from all races and classes. Some taverns built formal pits for the sport; these ranged from simple holes dug in the ground to elaborate stage-like facilities, providing open spaces for matches or mains (a series of fights). Cockfighting was second only to horse racing among Southern sportsmen, drawing the largest crowds during "public times," when the county court or provincial legislature was in session and there were many out-of-town visitors. Matches also were staged on plantations.

Bird owners took great pride in breeding fowl for speed and ferocity and training them for fighting. The fight was simple—handlers placed the birds in the ring, or cockpit, and let them loose against one another—but the preparation took countless hours. The birds' wing feathers were clipped to prevent opponents from grabbing them, they were fed special diets, and they were trained to fight aggressively. Aficionados favored birds with small heads, strong backs and legs, quick and large eyes, and long and sharp spurs. Birds with an upright stance were considered proud and thus more courageous.

Matches were highly ritualized events that enabled observers to suspend ordinary social conventions and boundaries, providing a rare opportunity for different classes and races to comingle. Yet the rich often attended contests apart from the lesser sorts, on their own plantations or at high-status urban taverns such as the "Sign of the Fighting Cock" in New York City. Even such luminaries as George Washington and Thomas Jefferson are known to have attended cockfights.

Despite its popularity, cockfighting had many critics. During the First Great Awakening of evangelical Christianity in the 1730s and 1740s, religious leaders chastised participants in the sport for gambling and violence. Patriot leaders often associated cockfighting with decadent English culture, and thus opposed the sport at the time of the Revolutionary War. Nevertheless, cockfighting remained a popular urban sport in the postrevolutionary period.

In the North, cockfighting was a staple of the sporting fraternity in New York City and Philadelphia, even though newspapers refused to advertise matches. Instead, broadsides posted at public places and handbills distributed at major street corners informed the sporting crowd about the location of mains. Many Northern contests were private affairs, and fanciers were informed of matches by word of mouth. The sport also was popular in the South, where, in the early 1800s, there were state rivalries. In addition, the United States inherited the Mexican cockfighting tradition when it took possession of Mexico's northern territories in 1848.

Slaves, too, engaged in cockfighting among themselves on Sundays and holidays, and they attended public matches at which they could bet against white men. Plantations might employ a slave who was involved in poultry production to train fighting birds. This became a part of American memory through Alex Haley's *Roots* (1977), which introduced "Chicken George," an African American slave nicknamed for his cockfighting skills. Chicken George's adeptness at training his birds eventually won him his freedom.

Legal Status

Despite the widespread popularity of cockfighting in antebellum American, clergymen and other critics in the North saw the sport as promoting immorality, gambling, idleness, vulgarity, and a hardening of sentiment. In the 1820s and 1830s, many states began considering anti-cockfighting bills. The first law prohibiting cockfighting in the United States was an 1830 statute in Pennsylvania, followed by one in Massachusetts in 1836.

Despite the widening circle of laws banning the sport, it was so popular that during the Civil War, General Orlando Willcox of the Union army paused to conduct cockfights for his adjutants and soldiers. Legal cockfighting persisted, though in fewer and fewer jurisdictions, until well into the twentieth century.

All states currently allow the breeding of all types of chickens. Roosters may be raised for aggressive tendencies and exported to places where cockfighting is legal; however, every state prohibits cockfighting, on the grounds that such fights are inhumane and cruel to animals. The last state to impose such a ban was Louisiana in 2007, which had been home to more than 40 established back-road pits. Cockfights remain legal in several U.S. territories, including Puerto Rico, Guam, and the Virgin Islands. On May 3, 2007, President George W. Bush signed into law the Animal Fighting Prohibition Enforcement Act, which criminalized the transfer of cockfighting implements across state or national borders, and increased the penalty for violations of federal animal fighting laws to three years' imprisonment.

Meanwhile, immigrants from the Caribbean and Mexico, where cockfighting still thrives, increasingly have influenced the subterranean world of cockfighting in the United States in the late twentieth and early twenty-first centuries.

Jerry Garcia

See also: Gambling; Violence in Sports.

Further Reading

Dundes, Alan. *The Cockfight: A Casebook.* Madison: University of Wisconsin Press, 1994.

Garcia, Jerry. "The Measure of a Cock: Mexican Cockfighting, Culture, and Masculinity." In *I am Aztlan: The Personal Essay in Chicano Studies,* ed. Chon Noriega and Wendy Belcher. Los Angeles: University of California, Los Angeles, Chicano Research Center, 2004.

College All-Star Football Game

Professional football is the most popular spectator sport in the United States, measured by television ratings and average attendance at games. However, professional football did not always hold this exalted spot. From its earliest days in the 1890s, professional football was denigrated by university officials and football coaches as a threat to the spirit of amateurism and school loyalties. Ironically, the annual College All-Star Game, held between 1934 and 1976, was important in establishing the professional sport.

On July 6, 1934, the *Chicago Tribune* carried an announcement of a football game to be played on the evening of August 31 at Soldier Field, the city's lakefront stadium. The participants would be a professional team, the Chicago Bears of the National Football League (NFL), and a squad of collegiate All-Americans made up of players who had completed their eligibility during the 1933 season. The man in charge of the affair was Arch Ward, the sports editor of the *Tribune,* who had originated baseball's All-Star Game only a year earlier.

During summer 1933, other promoters had staged a college all-star football game at Soldier Field on August 24; it was attended by 45,000 enthusiastic fans as part of the festivities for the World's Fair. The game was a matchup between two squads of recently graduated college players. Ward recalled the excitement of that game when he was asked to organize another sporting attraction as the Century of Progress was extended into 1934. Matching a professional football team against a squad of collegians raised some serious concerns, but Ward decided to proceed.

In early summer 1934, the *Tribune* announced that the players and coaching staff for the College All-Star team would be selected by a national vote of college football fans. Many conferences threatened disciplinary action against coaches who agreed to participate. When Noble Kizer of Purdue University was elected as the head coach of the collegiate team, officials from the Big Ten Conference unsuccessfully attempted to prevent his involvement. The first game of the series produced a 0–0 tie between the All-Stars and the Bears, but it attracted 79,433 football fans and made sports pages around the country the next day.

Before the 1935 game, Ward and his sponsors, the Chicago Tribune Charities, were not convinced that the All-Star Game was going to be anything but a one-year phenomenon. To make sure they had a gate attraction, they invited the Chicago Bears again, despite the team's loss in the 1934 NFL title game. Beginning in 1936, however, the All-Star Game organizers decided that the designated NFL representative always would be the league champion of the previous fall.

Ward portrayed the games at first as a means to decide the on-field superiority of college versus professional football. The collegiate stars came up winless in the first three matchups of the series, yet many national sportswriters persisted in claiming that pro football lagged behind the college game in terms of overall talent. The All-Stars won their first game in 1937—a 6–0 victory over the Green Bay Packers. In fact, the early games, which were seen by many participants as a simple exhibition, proved to be fairly evenly matched.

The College All-Star Game soon became a summer institution. Large crowds flocked to the annual event—averaging nearly 80,000 fans, and increasing to well over 90,000 by 1941—and each year, Ward upped the publicity and game-night spectacle. As the game gained popularity, which was evidenced by the increasing attendance figures and the growing numbers of fans voting in the annual player poll, more than 300 sportswriters from newspapers across the country descended on Chicago each summer, and their accounts of the games were read from coast to coast.

The annual All-Star event was forced to make some adjustments during World War II, when the games of 1943 and 1944 were shifted to Dyche Stadium at Northwestern University. With the All-Stars wearing their star-studded uniforms of red, white, and blue, and their ranks bolstered by former college stars on leave from their military units, the games presented magnificent displays of patriotic spectacle. The All-Stars defeated the Washington Redskins in the 1943 game and lost a thriller to the Bears the following summer.

By 1948, professional football clearly had moved into the forefront in terms of overall on-field talent and organization. The problems of matching a college all-star team with only three weeks of practice together against a championship professional team became more difficult over the years. In the 1950s, the game's promoters responded to the growing dominance of the NFL teams by hiring a staff of experienced professional football coaches each year to prepare the collegians for their approaching showdown. The All-Stars continued to suffer mounting losses, yet the annual game retained its national popularity into the 1960s. Every summer, Chicago became the football capital of the country, as many gridiron groups held their annual meetings in the city during game week.

The All-Stars registered their last win in 1963 with a shocking 20–17 victory over the Green Bay Packers. However, by the late 1960s, the realities of modern professional sports were intruding into the game, bringing with them the problems of player agents and player unions. Increasingly, agents for the All-Stars barred their players from joining the All-Star squad if they had not already signed a professional contract, while team owners complained about having to risk their high-priced players in an exhibition. The game narrowly avoided cancellation in 1970 because of a dispute between the NFL Players Association and the team owners, and in 1974, the game was called off during another labor–management dispute.

In the last years of the series, with national television ratings declining, the NFL and the game's organizers searched for alternative formats that would allow the tradition-laden game to continue; however, high costs finally spelled the end of the series in 1976. Fittingly, the final game was called late in the third quarter because of heavy rain, with the Pittsburgh Steelers leading the All-Stars 24–0. In all, 42 games were played in the series, with the professionals winning by a count of 31–9–2.

Raymond Schmidt

See also: Bowl Games, College Football; Football, College.

Further Reading

Littlewood, Thomas B. *Arch: A Promoter, Not a Poet.* Ames: Iowa State University Press, 1990.

Schmidt, Raymond. *Football's Stars of Summer: A History of the College All-Star Football Game Series of 1934–1976.* Lanham, MD: Scarecrow, 2001.

College Basketball Scandal of 1951

The first great scandal implicating college athletes came to light in 1951, when it was learned that for several years, basketball players at a number of schools had been fixing the outcomes or final scores of games in return for payments from professional gamblers. Altogether, 32 players at seven schools admitted to fixing games or "shaving" points; though all faced prosecution, only four served jail time in a scandal that brought the relationship between college sports and gambling to the public's attention.

Prior to World War II, professional gamblers had developed a means of handicapping games known as the point spread, which projected the number of points by which a team was favored to win. Betters did not bet on one team to win, but rather on whether the favored team would win by more or less than the margin predicted by the point spread. Attempts to keep game scores within the point spread were known as point shaving; gamblers convinced players that point shaving did not require them to purposely lose, or "dump," games, but merely to influence the margin of victory—an easier sell.

Professional gamblers began approaching basketball players from colleges in the New York at least as early as the mid-1940s, although anecdotal evidence suggests that the practice may have started even earlier. Many of these contacts originated during summer exhibition games at family resorts in the Catskill Mountains. The resorts hired players as waiters and bellhops, and expected them to play exhibition games in the evening as entertainment for the guests. These exhibition games included heavy gambling on the part of both guests and professional bookmakers and acculturated

Basketball stars from City College of New York, along with accused bribers, are booked by police in February 1951. Players at seven schools, most of them from CCNY, were charged with fixing game scores in exchange for money. *(New York Daily News/Getty Images)*

players to the mind-set and process of shaving points. Back on campus during the academic term, older players generally recruited younger players, and in this way, a culture of point shaving or, in some instances, dumping games outright, might exist on a team for several years.

The popularity of college basketball rose during the 1930s, when promoter Ned Irish began sponsoring Saturday afternoon double-headers at New York's Madison Square Garden. New Yorkers' enthusiasm for basketball brought huge attendance, providing substantial profits and a higher profile to the teams playing. As a result, teams from around the country clamored to land a spot in Irish's Garden doubleheaders. This allowed Madison Square Garden to emerge as the epicenter of college basketball's gambling scene, providing gamblers with access to the best teams from around the country and large numbers of fans who were willing to put down a stake on either a favorite team or an alleged "sure thing."

The scope of the problem became apparent in January 1951, when Manhattan College player Junius Kellogg reported to authorities an offer from a teammate to shave points for an upcoming game. New York City District Attorney Frank Hogan initiated an investigation and, with the aid of Max Kase, the sports editor of the *New York Journal-American,* who had been conducting his own investigation, rapidly secured indictments and arrests of players from Manhattan College, City College of New York, Long Island University, and New York University.

Virtually every player caught in Hogan's dragnet readily admitted to taking cash payments in exchange for affecting the margin of victory or defeat. In addition to implicating the professional gamblers who paid them, many of the players also indicated that the fixes included players and schools from outside the New York area, who shaved points or dumped games at the behest of East Coast gamblers when they played in Madison Square Garden. The commission of such violations in the state of New York gave Hogan jurisdiction to investigate colleges and players across the country.

Hogan's investigations eventually implicated players at Bradley University in Illinois, Toledo University in Ohio, and the University of Kentucky in addition to the New Yorkers. In all, 32 players at seven schools faced criminal charges for allegedly fixing 86 games between 1947 and 1950. Rumors and circumstantial evidence suggested that many more players and schools had taken part, including St. John's University, a Catholic school.

The only major New York City–area basketball school not formally implicated, St. John's had long been identified with the gambling scene at Madison Square Garden, along with the other schools. Though no evidence ever has been produced to justify such claims, commentators at the time and writers since then have suggested that Hogan's Catholicism and the personal involvement of New York Bishop Francis Cardinal Spellman kept St. John's from facing similar scrutiny.

The players who were caught up in the scandals bore a heavy burden, both personally and professionally. The sentencing of the players took on larger implications when New York Judge Saul Streit used his decisions as an opportunity to inveigh against the corruption of college sports and to connect it to a larger threat to the national character of American youth. Streit damned the National Collegiate Athletic Association, the coaches, the schools, and the public for creating an environment that had facilitated the scandals.

However, the coaches of the schools involved all proclaimed their ignorance of the fixing schemes and largely avoided any sanctions. The schools placed most of the blame on the environment at Madison Square Garden and refused to schedule games there. Among the colleges located outside of New York City, only the University of Kentucky faced any serious sanctions when the university president cancelled its team's entire 1952 season. As a result, Streit's broad condemnation fell mostly on the players, who faced public vilification as well. In addition to fines, probation, and, in the case of four defendants, prison time, all were banned for life from the professional leagues.

The school worst hit by the scandal was the City College of New York, which had won both the National Invitational Tournament and National Collegiate Athletic Association tournaments in 1950. Four players admitted to shaving points, and two went to jail. Coach Nat Holman lost a year of coaching, and the team was reduced to having the sport deemphasized to a level comparable to that of small colleges. The financial loss

of revenue from the team not playing at Madison Square Garden resulted in several sports being dropped altogether from the school's program.

Although the scandals of 1951 exposed the complicity of gambling in college basketball's postwar rise to prominence and led to greater scrutiny of the sport, the fixes did not result in a solution to the problem. A larger scandal involving more players and more schools was revealed in 1961, and similar practices continue to plague college basketball to the present day.

Kurt Edward Kemper

See also: Basketball, College; Crime, Organized; Gambling; Madison Square Garden.

Further Reading

Rosen, Charley. *Scandals of '51: How the Gamblers Almost Killed College Basketball.* New York: Seven Stories, 1999.

Sperber, Murray. *Onward to Victory: The Crises That Shaped College Sports.* New York: Henry Holt, 1998.

Stanley, Cohen. *The Game They Played.* New York: Farrar, Straus and Giroux, 1977.

Colts, Indianapolis/ Baltimore

The Colts football team, first playing in Baltimore in 1947 and then in Indianapolis from 1984 to the present, are one of the most storied franchises in National Football League (NFL) history, enjoying three periods of on-field prominence, in the 1950s, 1960s, and 2000s. In Baltimore, the club was known for having some of the most devoted fans in the sport. In addition, the Colts competed in two of the most significant games in NFL history—the 1958 championship game against the New York Giants and the 1968 Super Bowl against the New York Jets.

Origins and Disappointment

In the 1940s, both large and small cities sought to secure professional football franchises in order to boost their stature. However, the NFL restricted new membership to large cities with Major League Baseball clubs (the Orioles did not begin playing in Baltimore until 1954). This policy did not dissuade boosters in Baltimore and a number of other cities from trying to buy into the league. In 1946, a group of investors organized their own league, the All-America Football

Conference (AAFC), but shaky financial backing and an inability to secure a stadium lease initially left Baltimore out of that league, too.

Baltimore finally received its first pro football franchise, the AAFC's Colts, in 1947, and the club quickly became a meaningful part of the city. During their three years in the AAFC, the Colts posted a meager 10–29–1 record, but fan support remained high, and thousands of boosters accompanied the team to away games. In 1948, when the 4–6–0 Colts returned home from a three-game losing road trip, they were greeted by 5,000 fans, as well as bands, songs, speeches, and a parade.

Despite such community support, the Colts did not turn a profit, and their future seemed uncertain. The competition between the AAFC and the more established NFL escalated player salaries and operating expenses in both leagues, and few pro football clubs were making money. Even though the team had played only one season, Colts owner Robert Rodenberg, a Washington, D.C.–based attorney, withdrew his support. Only after more than 200 Baltimore boosters pledged between $100 and $5,000 each to save the team and form a large ownership group did the franchise remain solvent.

In 1949, when the AAFC merged with the NFL, the Colts had to pay what the Baltimore *Sun* dubbed "a ransom" to Washington Redskins owner George Preston Marshall for territorial rights. Local businessman Abe Watner worked out an ownership agreement with the Colts's 200 stockholders, agreeing to pay Marshall $150,000 over three years and to run the team.

After the 1950 season, Watner, with a terrible team, a large debt to Marshall, and $80,000 in operating losses from the Colts's first NFL season, ignored pleas and donations from the community and returned the franchise to the league for $55,000 and the cancellation of his debt to Marshall. The Colts disbanded, leaving Baltimoreans without a team. Fans claimed that they had been "sold down the river" and immediately filed lawsuits against the NFL and Watner. Commissioner Bert Bell proclaimed that legal action was the "worst way possible for Baltimore to try to get back into the league."

A New Franchise

While boosters pursued legal action, some fans acted as if their Colts had never left—the Colts Marching Band even continued to perform. In 1953, the NFL saw an opportunity to stave off additional litigation

from Baltimore and to give the city another franchise when the Dallas Texans club was left without ownership and a city in which to play. As part of the deal, however, the Colts's 200 stockholders had to agree to relinquish any right to own the team and to drop all lawsuits against the NFL, and at least 15,000 season tickets had to be sold to local fans—a task easily accomplished. The new Baltimore Colts were born under the league's handpicked owner, millionaire Carroll Rosenbloom, who had been a friend of Commissioner Bell since they had played on the University of Pennsylvania football squad together in the 1920s.

Baltimore's support for the Colts was strong, and the "new" Colts were becoming a good team as well. After the club's first winning season in 1957, 38,000 season tickets were sold. After the Colts won their first championship in 1958, 30,000 Baltimoreans greeted the team at the airport—the start of a civic celebration that lasted for days. By end of the 1950s, every game was a sellout. Colts Corrals (fan clubs) were organized, and thousands of Baltimoreans regularly traveled to nearby road games.

Players such as Eugene "Big Daddy" Lipscomb, Gino Marchetti, Art Donovan, Jim Parker, Raymond Berry, Alan Ameche, Lenny Moore, and Johnny Unitas turned the Colts into the best team in pro football. For 15 years (1957–1971), the Colts posted no losing seasons, made five NFL title games, and won three NFL championships, including Super Bowl V in 1971 by a score of 16–13 over the Dallas Cowboys.

The team played in two of the best-remembered games in NFL history. In 1958, the Colts, under Coach Wilbur "Weeb" Ewbank, won the NFL championship game against the New York Giants. Late in the fourth quarter, the Colts trailed 17–14. Quarterback Johnny Unitas took charge as the clock ran down, taking the Colts from their own 14-yard line to the Giants's 11. With seven seconds left, the Colts kicked a field goal and sent the game into the first sudden-death overtime. The Giants received first possession in the overtime but were forced to punt. Once again, Unitas took charge, carrying the Colts downfield to the Giants's 1-yard line. From there, fullback Alan Ameche plunged into the end zone with the winning score, as the Colts won 23–17. The game was a watershed moment in NFL history, with a record 40 million television viewers, revealing pro football's growing popularity and the potential for television advertisers. The two teams played for the title again in 1959; the Colts also won that contest, 31–16.

The success of the 1958 game led to the formation of another rival league, the American Football League

(AFL), in 1960. The AFL grew slowly, helped immensely by television revenue. In 1966, the AFL merged with the NFL, and they agreed to play a championship game between the top-ranked AFL and NFL teams beginning in January of the following year. (The two leagues merged into a single entity for the 1970 season).

Few believed that the AFL could match the NFL on the field. In fact, the first two NFL-AFL World Championship Games (later renamed the Super Bowl) were won easily by the NFL's Green Bay Packers. Most believed that the third game in 1968, pitting Don Shula's Colts at 13–1–0 against the AFL's New York Jets, would be more of the same. However, quarterback Joe Namath and the Jets upset the Colts in Super Bowl III, 16–7, propelling pro football into its modern era. This time, the Colts were the goats (to NFL fans) rather than the heroes.

A Move to Indianapolis

For Baltimore, the turning point in Colts history came in 1972, when Carroll Rosenbloom and Robert Irsay, a Chicago-based businessman who had just purchased the Los Angeles Rams, traded franchises. Throughout the 1970s and early 1980s, the Colts languished in mediocrity, making just three playoff appearances and three first-round losses.

The biggest news to come from Baltimore during Irsay's ownership was the player who got away. In 1983, the Colts drafted John Elway with the first selection in the NFL draft, but the future NFL Hall of Famer refused to play for the team and was traded to the Denver Broncos, where he went on to a stunning career.

Meanwhile, Irsay, like so many other owners since, wanted the city of Baltimore and the state of Maryland to build the Colts a new stadium. When city and state officials hesitated, Irsay took matters into his own hands. Secretly, he signed a deal with Indianapolis, which gave him more than $16 million in incentives and a 20-year lease of the city's Hoosier Dome (later renamed the RCA Dome). He hired Mayflower moving trucks to pack the Colts's possessions under cover of darkness on the morning of March 28, 1984, and move them to Indianapolis. Baltimore had lost its football team for the second time.

Meanwhile, in April, 1984, 20,000 Indianapolis residents and Mayor William Hudnut threw a welcome rally for the Colts at the Hoosier Dome, an event Irsay called "the greatest thrill I've had in football." In their first 15 years, the Indianapolis Colts had little success on the field, and rumors persisted that Jim Irsay, son of

Robert Irsay and team owner after Robert's death in 1997, might move the franchise again.

Two factors prevented another move. First, the team drafted Peyton Manning, the star quarterback at the University of Tennessee in 1998. Manning's first seasons were uneven, as the team struggled to address other weaknesses, but in 2006, the Colts finally went all the way. They won their division title, came back from a 21-point deficit in the conference championship to defeat New England 38–34, and beat the Chicago Bears in Super Bowl XLI, 29–17.

Even as the Colts became Super Bowl victors, the team gained the commitment of local government to contribute $400 million to a new stadium. Lucas Oil Stadium opened in 2008, securing the Colts's future in the city for at least the next 30 years. The team returned to the Super Bowl in 2009, but they lost to the New Orleans Saints. Television viewership soared to more than 100 million for the first time.

Back in Baltimore, the city languished without an NFL team for 12 years. Finally, in 1996, the NFL gave permission to Cleveland Browns owner Art Modell to move his team to Baltimore. To avoid endless legal disputes with angry Cleveland supporters, the league decreed that the Browns's name and franchise records would remain in Cleveland (which would receive a new franchise in three years).

The new Baltimore team chose the name Ravens and began play (with the former Cleveland roster). Ironically, the Ravens reached the Super Bowl and won the championship in 2001, five years earlier than the Colts in Indianapolis.

Craig R. Coenen

See also: All-America Football Conference; Football, Professional.

Further Reading

Callahan, Tom. *Johnny U: The Life and Times of John Unitas.* New York: Crown, 2006.

Coenen, Craig R. *From Sandlots to the Super Bowl: The National Football League, 1920–1967.* Knoxville: University of Tennessee Press, 2005.

Euchner, Charles C. *Playing the Field: Why Sports Teams Move and Cities Fight to Keep Them.* Baltimore: Johns Hopkins University Press, 1993.

Gildea, William. *When the Colts Belonged to Baltimore: A Father and a Son, a Team and a Time.* New York: Ticknor & Fields, 1994.

MacCambridge, Michael. *America's Game: The Epic Story of How Pro Football Captured a Nation.* New York: Random House, 2004.

Steadman, John. *From Colts to Ravens: A Behind-the-Scenes Look at Baltimore Professional Football.* Centreville, MD: Tidewater, 1997.

Comiskey, Charles (1859–1931)

Charles Comiskey, one of the few former ballplayers to become a major league owner, was one of the most important executives in the history of the game. He was instrumental in founding the American League and in establishing the Chicago White Sox. He capably ran the team for more than 30 years, developing it into one of the top clubs on the field and at the box office. Unfortunately, in 1919, his team of star players, considered the finest squad in the majors, tarnished their reputations by taking money from gamblers and fixing the World Series.

Playing Career

Charles Albert Comiskey was born in Chicago on August 15, 1859. Of Irish descent, he was one of eight children of Mary "Annie" Kearns and John Comiskey, a building contractor and Democratic city ward boss who served four terms in the city council, was city council president in 1870, and was Clerk of the Cook County Board of Commissioners in 1875. Charles attended St. Ignatius College in Chicago and went on to St. Mary's College in Kansas.

In 1879, Comiskey launched his professional baseball career under the tutelage of Ted Sullivan, a baseball pioneer who founded the Northwestern League, playing first baseman for the Dubuque Rabbits, a team of the Northwestern League. In 1882, he made the majors with the St. Louis Browns of the American Association, hitting .270 over the course of his 13-year career. He is credited with revolutionizing the style of first-base play by playing off the bag, requiring the pitcher to cover first on ground balls to the right side of the infield.

He served as a player-manager briefly in 1883 and 1884, and then full time from 1885 to 1889. His Browns won four straight American Association titles (1885–1888), including an upset in 1886 over the powerful Chicago White Stockings in the forerunner to the modern World Series. In 1890, Comiskey abandoned his contract with the St. Louis team to lead the Chicago Pirates of the rebellious Players' League in its only season. He returned to the Browns as player-manager in

1891 and then managed the Cincinnati Reds from 1892 to 1894.

Becoming an Owner

In 1895, Comiskey used his life savings to purchase the struggling Sioux City team of the Western League; he transferred the franchise to St. Paul, Minnesota. League President Ban Johnson, a friend of Comiskey's, renamed the league the American League on October 11, 1899. The next year, Comiskey moved his St. Paul team to Chicago's South Side, where they became the Chicago White Stockings (formerly the nickname of Chicago's National League team), which was shortened to the White Sox in 1902. The new team won the American League pennant in its first year.

In 1901, the American League declared itself a second major league, sparking a bitter three-year war with the established National League. Comiskey and his fellow American League owners helped the cause of the new league by luring away National League stars with lucrative contracts.

The White Sox enjoyed early success, winning the league championship again in the American League's first season. The White Sox were particularly popular with Irish Americans and other immigrants living in the Bridgeport neighborhood adjacent to their ballpark, which was called South Side Park. Comiskey affectionately was nicknamed "The Old Roman" for his prominent Roman nose, and for his strong leadership and good deeds in the community. In 1910, he bolstered his reputation by building a durable brick-and-steel baseball stadium, soon to be known as Comiskey Park, which was used by the White Sox until 1990.

In 1907, a group of prominent citizens, including politicians, show people, and sportswriters, organized the White Sox Rooters Association, one of the earliest chartered fan groups. The organization became known as the Woodland Bards in 1912, commemorating annual all-expenses-paid hunting and fishing junkets to the North Woods to Comiskey's vacation compound in Mercer, Wisconsin, where, among other pastimes, they recited Shakespearean verses around the evening campfire. The members of this exclusive group repaid Comiskey's generosity by ensuring positive coverage of the White Sox in a two-team city where fan loyalties were split.

Comiskey's first great triumph came in 1906 when the Sox, known as the "hitless wonders," upset the powerful Cubs, who had won 116 games that season, in Chicago's only intercity World Series. Eight years later, he and his team embarked on a triumphant world tour with John McGraw's New York Giants, and Comiskey was hailed as one of America's most influential sportsmen. In 1917, his club, with the best pitching and offense in the American League, won the pennant (100–54) and went on to defeat McGraw's Giants in the World Series in six games.

Comiskey was at the apex of his public career when the White Sox captured the 1919 American League pennant, though they lost the World Series to the underdog Cincinnati Reds. During the 1920 season, however, investigators accused eight members of the White Sox of conspiring with powerful gamblers to lose the World Series to the Reds. Four players admitted their involvement to the press or the grand jury; however, the grand jury records mysteriously were lost before the trial, and the players were acquitted.

Major League owners, recognizing the threat of corruption, appointed former judge Kenesaw Mountain Landis as the first commissioner of baseball. Landis's first act as commissioner was to ban the eight White Sox players—who came to be known as the "Black Sox"—from organized baseball for life.

Many later accounts suggested that Comiskey's relationship with his players was less positive than his relationship with community leaders and sportswriters. He paid among the lowest salaries in the majors and humiliated players who objected to his offers. Several of the accused players expressed resentment of their employer.

In 1921, the White Sox sank to seventh place in the eight-team league; they never challenged for the pennant again during Comiskey's lifetime. Comiskey lost much of his zeal for the game. He tried to rebuild, but the team was a consistent loser.

Shattered by the betrayal of his players and the death of his wife Nancy in 1922, Comiskey went into a decade-long, self-imposed exile at his private estate in Eagle River, Wisconsin, where he died on October 26, 1931. He left ownership of the team to his only son. The Comiskey family maintained a controlling interest in the ball club until 1959 and sold the last of their shares three years later.

Comiskey was elected to the Baseball Hall of Fame in 1939. Despite the fact that the Black Sox scandal continue to tarnish his reputation, he was one of the key architects of Major League Baseball.

Richard C. Lindberg

See also: Baseball, Major League; Black Sox Scandal; Reds, Cincinnati; White Sox, Chicago.

Further Reading

Asinof, Eliot. *Eight Men Out.* New York: Holt, Rinehart and Winston, 1963.

Axelson, Gustaf W. *"Commy": The Life Story of Charles A. Comiskey.* Chicago: Reilly & Lee, 1919.

Carney, Gene. *Burying the Black Sox: How Baseball's Cover-Up of the 1919 World Series Fix Almost Succeeded.* Washington, DC: Potomac, 2006.

Lindberg, Richard C. *Total White Sox: The Definitive Encyclopedia of the World Champion Franchise.* Chicago: Triumph, 2006.

Nathan, Daniel A. *Saying It's So: A Cultural History of the Black Sox Scandal.* Urbana: University of Illinois Press, 2003.

Cosell, Howard (1918–1995)

One of the best-known and most controversial figures in the history of American sports broadcasting, Howard Cosell made a name for himself by "telling it like it is," as he put it, during the 1960s, 1970s, and 1980s. Cosell never shied away from the most difficult issues of the day, and as a result, he became a lightning rod for controversy. His friendship with heavyweight boxing champion Muhammad Ali was the stuff of legend, and his overbearing presence in the broadcasting booth helped establish ABC's *Monday Night Football* as a television institution. At the height of his career, Cosell's was probably the most mimicked vocal delivery in the United States.

He was born Howard William Cohen on March 25, 1918, in Winston-Salem, North Carolina, to Polish Jews Nellie and Isadore Cohen, who was an accountant. When he was three, his father moved the family to Brooklyn, New York. Howard intended to become a journalist, but his parents steered him toward the law. He graduated from New York University as an English major and went on to earn a juris doctorate from its law school, where he edited the law review. In 1940, he changed his name to Cosell (his grandfather's name was Kosell), and was admitted to the New York State Bar the following year.

After service as a major in the U.S. Army during World War II, he joined a Manhattan law firm that represented celebrities and high-profile sports figures. Among Cosell's clients was the New York Little League, and in 1953, the attorney got his start in broadcasting by hosting a local radio program for young baseball players.

Cosell soon abandoned his legal career for full-time broadcasting and began covering boxing matches during the 1950s for the American Broadcasting Company (ABC). First on radio, and then on television, the outspoken sportscaster would become a fixture at ABC for decades.

Cosell began attracting attention for his coverage of boxing on television, but he emerged as a national figure during the 1960s as a result of his friendship with Muhammad Ali, who won the heavyweight championship as Cassius Clay in 1964. Ali sparked controversy by joining the Nation of Islam, changing his name, and refusing to be inducted into military service during the Vietnam War on religious grounds. Cosell was one of Ali's few defenders and an outspoken advocate of the champion's right to due process after Ali was stripped of his title and banned from boxing.

By publicly chastising Ali's accusers, Cosell generated a great deal of publicity for himself, but he also endured a harsh backlash of criticism that polarized public opinion regarding the controversial sportscaster. Though many respected Cosell for defending Ali's antiwar stand, others would hate him forever for sympathizing with a draft dodger during the Vietnam era.

Ali eventually was vindicated by the U.S. Supreme Court and was reinstated by boxing authorities. He regained the heavyweight championship and established himself as a sports hero with a worldwide following. Throughout the ups and downs of the champion's career, Cosell went along for the ride, and the interviews that he conducted with Ali became some of the most famous and entertaining in the history of sports journalism.

In 1970, Cosell joined the broadcast team for the inaugural season of ABC's *Monday Night Football*, the program that would cement his place in broadcasting history. Cosell's impeccable vocabulary, long-winded diatribes, and oddly rhythmic nasal delivery made him a star, and arguably the most recognized television personality of the era. *Monday Night Football* reached its peak of popularity during the 1970s, with Cosell in the broadcast booth along with former players Frank Gifford and "Dandy" Don Meredith.

Viewers particularly enjoyed Cosell's exchanges with the homespun Meredith, former quarterback of the Dallas Cowboys. Both men were master showmen who were comfortable in front of the microphone and television cameras, despite their sharply contrasting personal styles. As a result, ABC did not have to worry about broadcasting the occasional lackluster game on Monday nights, as fans would continue to tune in, regardless of the teams playing or the score of the contest, just to hear Cosell and Meredith.

On *Monday Night Football*, Cosell continued to be a polarizing figure. Many of his comments drew the wrath of fans, and he routinely made unofficial lists as one of the "most hated men in America." Probably the most difficult, if not the most poignant, moment of Cosell's tenure on the program came on December 8, 1980, during a game between the New England Patriots and Miami Dolphins, when he stunned viewers by announcing that John Lennon of the Beatles had just been shot and killed in New York City.

While Cosell was best known for his 14 years with *Monday Night Football,* he made frequent appearances on other television programs and appeared in cameo roles in several movies. He was a major part of ABC's coverage of the Olympics, broadcast baseball games, and continued to be the network's voice of most major boxing events. In 1975, he launched his own short-lived weekly variety show, *Saturday Night Live with Howard Cosell.*

After Cosell left *Monday Night Football* in 1984, his television career began to decline, and he seemed to grow increasingly bitter. In 1985, he published an autobiography, *I Never Played the Game,* in which he blasted former colleagues and coined the phrase "jockocracy" to describe former athletes who, he believed, had landed broadcasting jobs that they did not deserve. He also denounced boxing, the sport that he had covered for so many years, for its brutality and vowed to never announce another match. Though he made occasional television appearances, he chose to work primarily in radio for the remainder of his career, doing daily sports programs and interview shows.

After treatment for cancer, Cosell retired in 1992 and shunned the spotlight for the rest of his life. He died on April 23, 1995, in New York City at the age of 77. Regardless of how they felt about Cosell personally, fans across the United States recognized his passing as the end of an era in the history of American sports.

Ben Wynne

See also: Monday Night Football; Television.

Further Reading

Arledge, Roone. *Roone: A Memoir.* New York: HarperCollins, 2003.

Cosell, Howard. *Cosell.* New York: Pocket Books, 1974.

Cosell, Howard, with Peter Bonventre. *I Never Played the Game.* New York: William Morrow, 1985.

Gunther, Marc, and Bill Carter. *Monday Night Mayhem: The Inside Story of ABC's* Monday Night Football. New York: Beech Tree, 1988.

Kindred, David. *Sound and Fury: Two Powerful Lives, One Fateful Friendship.* New York: Free Press, 2006.

Country Clubs

A country club is a private club that usually is owned and operated by its members. It typically provides access to athletic facilities such as a golf course, tennis courts, or swimming facilities, as well as rooms for dining and socializing. As the name suggests, country clubs usually are located outside major cities in suburban or exurban areas.

The first country clubs in the United States were organized in the late nineteenth century by wealthy and socially prominent city dwellers. Some early organizers were members of elite urban male-only sporting clubs who saw the country club as a temporary respite from city life and an opportunity to pursue sports such as golf that require more land. Early country clubs also involved a strong social aspect, offering their members opportunities to meet and socialize with others with similar backgrounds and interests. Businessmen soon saw that the clubs could be an ideal place for entertaining clients in a private setting.

The first country club was the Myopia Club, established in 1878 near Winchester, Massachusetts, 8 miles (13 kilometers) north of Boston, but it was not very accessible and could not attract enough members to succeed. Four years later, several members, led by James Murray Forbes, organized a new year-round facility, the Country Club, in the Boston suburb of Brookline to provide a private destination for weekend coach excursions and to include family members in club life. The Country Club was an enormous success, attracting more than 400 charter members, who paid an entrance fee of $25 and annual dues of $30. The club soon developed major commitments to golf, tennis, and other sports. In 1894, it was one of five founding clubs that organized the Amateur Golf Association of America (later renamed the United States Golf Association), and in 1913, it played host to the U.S. Open golf tournament.

Perhaps the most luxurious early country club was the Tuxedo Club in Orange County, New York, established in 1886 by Pierre Lorillard IV, with facilities for steeple chasing, pigeon shooting, and tobogganing. Over the next few years, the club also added a golf course, tennis courts, and a racquet house. The club had lavish ballrooms where socially prominent families came to attend formal dinners and dances. The formal attire for men known as a tuxedo gets its name from the Tuxedo Club, where it was introduced in 1887.

By the mid-1890s, country clubs embraced the growing sport of golf. The first U.S. facility was a six-hole course opened in 1888 at St. Andrew's Golf Club in Yonkers, New York. However, the model American course was at the Shinnecock Hills Golf Club. It was built in 1891 in Southampton, New York, for magnate William K. Vanderbilt and 43 rich friends, who each put up $100. Said to be the oldest formally organized golf club in the United States, Shinnecock Hills has the distinction that women played there from the beginning. In 1892, renowned architect Stanford White built the first American golf clubhouse on its grounds. The oldest Canadian club still located on its original site is the 1,150-member Victoria Country Club in Victoria, British Columbia, which was founded in 1893 by wealthy expatriates from Great Britain.

By 1895, the country club idea was spreading so rapidly that many older clubs that were devoted to the nineteenth-century pastimes of riding, hunting, and cricket built golf courses on their land to attract new members. By 1900, there were 1,040 country clubs across the United States, led by New York (165), Massachusetts (157), Pennsylvania (75), Illinois (57), and California (43).

As golf grew in popularity, its appeal extended to middle-class businessmen and families. Many public courses were built. Golfers who began playing on these course often joined less prominent country clubs to gain access to private courses. By 1927, there were about 5,500 American country clubs, ranging from the most extravagant to the very modest.

Jews, African Americans, and other racial and ethnic minorities traditionally were excluded from early country clubs. In response, wealthy German Jews near New York and Chicago established their own clubs. The first Jewish country clubs included the Inwood Country Club (1901) in New York and Chicago's $750,000 Lake Shore Country Club (1908). By the 1920s, there were 20 Jewish country clubs in metropolitan New York and 7 in Chicago. A few black clubs were founded, most notably the Shady Rest Golf and Tennis Club in New Jersey (1921), which previously had been a white-owned club. It became an important social center for the black elite in the 1920s but also welcomed less privileged African Americans on Saturdays for a 75-cent admission charge. The practice of excluding minorities from membership in private clubs did not become controversial until the 1940s and 1950s.

The Great Depression and World War II had a dramatic impact on country clubs. During the Depression, about 15 percent closed, and overall membership dropped by 78 percent. During the war, service in the armed forces and restricted travel at home continued to depress the clubs. Things began to look up in the late 1940s, as soldiers returned from the war and a new wave of suburban development began.

Between 1955 and 1960, the number of clubs increased from 2,807 to 3,236. At the same time, there was an even bigger boom in daily-fee and public golf courses, and by the 1970s, there were more public courses than private country clubs. By 1995, there were 4,324 private country clubs and 9,700 daily-fee and public golf courses.

Between 1950 and 2000, many clubs ended or greatly reduced discrimination against minorities and women. Some prominent clubs have been embarrassed by their restrictive policies when sponsoring major tournaments. In 1990, for instance, the Professional Golfers' Association (PGA) Championship was scheduled for the Shoal Creek Country Club in Birmingham, Alabama, which continued to discriminate against African Americans. Corporate sponsors successfully pressed the club to change. However, 11 other private clubs with antiblack policies passed up the opportunity to host PGA events rather than change.

Women still are barred from membership at about 25 clubs, most notably Augusta National in Georgia, host of the PGA Masters Tournament. Even where women are allowed to play golf at country clubs, however, they may be barred from voting on club matters, serving on important boards, eating at men's grills, or remaining members of the club if they divorce their husband.

Today, many private country clubs remain equity clubs owned by the members and governed by an elected board of directors, while others are owned by an individual or corporation, which then offers limited memberships.

Dan Drane

See also: Class, Economic and Social; Golf; Polo; Race and Race Relations; Tennis; Urbanization.

Further Reading

Kirsch, George B. *Golf in America.* Urbana: University of Illinois Press, 2009.

Mayo, James M. *The American Country Club: Its Origins and Development.* New Brunswick, NJ: Rutgers University Press, 1998.

Moss, Richard J. *Golf and the American Country Club.* Urbana: University of Illinois Press, 2001.

Peper, George. *The Story of Golf.* New York: TV Books, 1999.

Perdue, Joe, ed. *Contemporary Club Management.* Alexandria, VA: Club Managers Association of America, 1997.

Cowboys, Dallas

Although it is among the newer franchises in the National Football League (NFL), founded in 1960, the Dallas Cowboys are certainly one of the most successful teams in the league. As of 2010, the Cowboys held the NFL record for most playoff wins (33) and Super Bowl appearances (8). With five Super Bowl victories, the team is tied with the Pittsburgh Steelers and San Francisco 49ers for the most in league history. This winning tradition helped earn the Cowboys the nickname "America's Team."

The Cowboys originated in response to the rise of the American Football League in late 1959, which intended to establish as a competitor to the NFL with a franchise in Dallas. Afraid that the new league would dominate this valuable market, NFL owners hastily convened and awarded a franchise to Texas oil tycoon Clint Murchison, Jr. He hired Tex Schramm as the team's general manager, Gil Brandt as head of player scouting, and New York Giants assistant Tom Landry as head coach.

Like most expansion franchises, the Cowboys struggled in their early years. The team went 0–11–1 in its first season in 1960, losing more games than it won every year until 1965. But the losses also meant that the Cowboys received high selections in the NFL's annual draft of college seniors, which they turned into future Hall of Famers Bob Lilly at defensive tackle, Mel Renfro at defensive back, Roger Staubach at quarterback, and wide receiver Bob Hayes. Other high draft choices, such as linebacker Lee Roy Jordan and offensive lineman Ralph Neely, also had long and productive careers.

The turning point for the franchise came in 1965. After the Cowboys lost a game in Pittsburgh to drop their record to 2–5, Landry's job was in jeopardy. In the locker room after the game, Landry admitted that he might not be back the next season, and he broke down in front of the team. As told to Peter Golenbock in *Cowboys Have Always Been My Heroes* (1997), Lilly said, "We were touched. We had always taken coach Landry for granted, and this time we saw a real person and we wanted to fight for him."

The Cowboys rallied to make the playoffs that year, starting a string of 18 playoff appearances in 19 years. During the period from 1965 to 1983, Dallas won 20 playoff games, and Super Bowls in 1971 (24–3 over the Miami Dolphins) and 1978 (27–10 over the Denver Broncos). No team in NFL history has been as successful or as consistent over such a long period of

The Dallas Cowboys of the National Football League—dubbed "America's Team" in the 1970s for their frequent television appearances—got a colossal new stadium in 2010. The retractable-roof facility has the world's largest column-free interior. *(Sports Illustrated/Getty Images)*

time. Near the end of this streak, the Cowboys claimed the title "America's Team" in a promotional video. The nickname seemed so appropriate that it was taken up by broadcasters and journalists alike, becoming the most popular moniker in football.

Innovators

Part of the Cowboys's success was attributable to the team's stability. Murchison, Schramm, Brandt, and Landry ran the Cowboys for 24 years, until Murchison sold the team in 1983. Landry was considered one of the most creative coaches in NFL history, developing offensive and defensive schemes that remain in use today.

The Cowboys also were innovators in other areas. In 1971, they built Texas Stadium, the only NFL arena to have a roof over the stands but an opening over the playing field. The saying at the time was that the Cowboys had left the stadium open so that God could watch his favorite team play.

The Cowboys also pioneered the use of computers in drafting and evaluating players. This reinforced the popular opinion of the Cowboys as an impersonal, arrogant organization. Wide receiver Pete Gent, who played in the late 1960s, criticized this attitude in his best-selling novel *North Dallas Forty* (1973). The book was a fictionalized account of fun-loving players rebelling against an authoritarian coach and organization, but parallels to the real Cowboys were obvious. As Gent told Golenbock, "I wanted out of there. The minute they didn't need me, I was gone. And so from then on, that was my attitude toward Tom Landry, and the rest of the organization going all the way up to Tex Schramm."

Other teams in the NFL were quick to pick up on another innovation—the Dallas Cowboys Cheerleaders. In the early 1970s, the Cowboys dressed their cheerleaders in skimpy outfits, had them add intricate dance moves to their routine, and made them a focal point of the game-day experience. The Cowboys's cheerleaders soon became a national phenomenon, and they have appeared in several calendars as well as in movies. Almost every team in the league now has a similar cheerleading squad.

Murchison's sale of the team and poor draft picks led to a downward spiral in the 1980s. The team missed the playoffs in 1984, and by 1988, it had a record of 3–13. H.R. "Bum" Bright, one of the city's leading entrepreneurs, owned the team for five years, but sold it in February 1989 to Arkansas oil and gas tycoon Jerry Jones. One of Jones's first orders was to replace Landry with college coach Jimmy Johnson.

Even though the Cowboys were losing at the time, the move shocked and angered Dallas fans. Landry had become a local icon, and his 270 wins were the third highest in NFL history. On April 22, 1989, downtown Dallas hosted a "Hats off to Tom Landry Parade," which drew more than 50,000 people. Public sentiment was decidedly against Jones and Johnson, who were viewed as too inexperienced to rebuild the team.

Return to Glory

The franchise's low point came during Johnson's first season, when the Cowboys went 1–15, setting a team record for most losses in a season. But just as they had during the early 1960s, the Cowboys began to stock up on young talent through the draft. Running back Emmitt Smith came along in 1990, joining young stars Troy Aikman at quarterback and wide receiver Michael Irvin. The trade of star running back Herschel Walker to the Minnesota Vikings brought more draft picks, and by 1991, the Cowboys returned to the playoffs. Amazingly, just three years after winning only one game, Dallas won the Super Bowl in 1993, crushing the Buffalo Bills 52–17. They also won the Super Bowl the next season, beating Buffalo again, 30–13.

Whereas Tom Landry had been reserved and quiet, Jimmy Johnson was brash, outgoing, and arrogant. A clash of egos with Jones prompted Johnson's departure from the Cowboys in spring 1994, just two months after the team's second Super Bowl win. To replace him, Jones hired another college coach with no professional football experience, Barry Switzer. Many predicted that the team would suffer a decline without Johnson, but Switzer led the Cowboys to their third Super Bowl win in four years, a 27–17 defeat of Pittsburgh after the 1995 season.

As a college coach at the University of Oklahoma, Switzer had run into trouble because of his easygoing style and lack of discipline among his players. The same problems followed him to Dallas, where several players ran into trouble with the law. Some players frequented a private residence called the "White House" near the team's training facility, to take part in drugs and illicit sex. In March 1996, Irvin pleaded no contest to cocaine possession and received four years' probation. In 2001, lineman Nate Newton was arrested in possession of more than 200 pounds (91 kilograms) of marijuana, and he spent two years in prison. Newton later admitted, "It was all the fun the law would allow. And then some."

Off-field problems helped end the Cowboys's success in the late 1990s. The team had a losing record in 1997, which led to Switzer's departure and the hiring of Chan Gailey. Gailey coached only two seasons before he was replaced by assistant Dave Campo. After three losing seasons, Jones brought legendary coach Bill Parcells out of retirement. Parcells had won two Super Bowls with the New York Giants, but he could not duplicate his success in Dallas. In four seasons under Parcells, the Cowboys made two postseason appearances but did not win a playoff game. Parcells retired in 2007 and was replaced as head coach by Wade Phillips.

Despite recent struggles, the Cowboys remain one of the most successful franchises in the NFL and have played in some of the most famous games in NFL history, including the 1967 NFL Championship in Green Bay, Wisconsin, known as the "Ice Bowl," in which the temperatures reached -15 degrees Fahrenheit (-16 degrees Celsius), and the legendary "Hail Mary" playoff game in 1975, in which Roger Staubach threw a last-minute touchdown pass to beat the Vikings. As of 2010, 11 Cowboys were members of the Pro Football Hall of Fame: Staubach, Lilly, Renfro, Landry, Schramm, Aikman, Hayes, tackles Randy White and Rayfield Wright, and running backs Tony Dorsett and Emmitt Smith, the NFL's all-time leading rusher.

The franchise that Clint Murchison founded for $550,000 in 1959, and that Jerry Jones bought for $150 million in 1989, was worth $1.8 billion in 2010, making it the most valuable franchise in the league and the second most valuable in the world, after the Manchester United soccer team ($1.87 billion). The new Cowboys Stadium in Arlington, seating 100,000 fans, was completed in 2009 at a reported cost of $1.3 billion. It was the site of Super Bowl XLV in 2011.

Brad Schultz

See also: Cheerleading; Football, Professional; Television.

Further Reading

Dallas Cowboys. http://www.dallascowboys.com.

Golenbock, Peter. *Cowboys Have Always Been My Heroes: The Definitive Oral History of America's Team.* New York: Warner, 1997.

Guinn, Jeff. *Dallas Cowboys: The Authorized Pictorial History.* Arlington, TX: Summit, 1996.

Coyotes, Phoenix/ Winnipeg Jets

The history of the Phoenix Coyotes of the National Hockey League (NHL) is the story of the migration of the Canadian Winnipeg Jets to a larger-market U.S. city in 1996. It also is the tale of two leagues—the Winnipeg franchise began play in the World Hockey Association (WHA) in 1972, joining the NHL in 1979 when the latter league collapsed.

The Jets, who took their name from the local minor league hockey franchise, were a source of community pride in Winnipeg. Businessman Ben Hatskin, who established the franchise, made it a public company by 1974, one of the few in professional sports. The Jets's biggest early star was Bobby Hull, who signed an unprecedented ten-year, $1 million contract to leave the NHL, and became the WHA's Most Valuable Player in 1972–1973 and 1974–1975.

During the league's seven years, the Jets reached the championship finals five times, winning the title three times (1975–1976, 1977–1978, 1978–1979). Management's chief innovation was heavy reliance on European imports, whom North American teams previously had avoided.

In 1979, a syndicate headed by Barry Shenkarow bought the team when the WHA was dissolved, and the Jets became one of four franchises to join the NHL. The Jets were placed in the Norris (later Central) Division. The former WHA teams were allowed to retain only a few players, losing the rest of their rosters to a dispersion draft.

Whereas the Jets once had been consistently strong regular-season contenders, they turned in dismal showings, finishing in last place in 1979–1980 and in 1980–1981, compiling a dismal record of 9–57–14 (32 points), 24 points worse than any other team. The Jets became competitive again by the mid-1980s, but by then, they were playing in the same division as the powerful Edmonton Oilers and Calgary Flames. The Jets made nine first-round exits in 11 NHL playoff appearances, often being swept.

Meanwhile, the team had high operating costs and salaries, even as it played in the NHL's second-smallest market, and thus it had a hard time keeping top players. The governments of Winnipeg and the province of Manitoba agreed to cover the losses, which totaled several million dollars a year. The Jets continued losing money every year, and by 1994, their days in Winnipeg seemed numbered. The owners insisted that they needed a new, publicly built $140 million arena to replace the aging Winnipeg Arena (capacity 15,250) at a time when local governments were retrenching.

Local politicians, businessmen, and the media backed a campaign to "Save the Jets," raising $12 million in public contributions in a week. But it was too little, too late, and the franchise was sold to a syndicate from Phoenix in 1996. The Jets left a legacy of sorts, including a playoff tradition of fans dressing in all white clothing and spinning white towels in the air. But the loss of the team was a significant blow to Winnipeg and to Canada, demonstrating that larger and wealthier cities in the United States could outbid Canadian municipalities.

Businessmen Steven Gluckstern and Richard Burke led the Phoenix group, which nicknamed the team the Coyotes. The desert city of Phoenix did not seem a likely place for hockey, although it had supported the Roadrunners of the Western Hockey League for 30 years. Burke bought out Gluckstern in 1998, but he needed additional financial support. He sold the team to local developer Steve Ellman in 2000, with retired hockey superstar Wayne Gretzky as a partial owner and head of hockey operations.

By the 2000–2001 season, the Coyotes's financial burdens were nearing dangerous levels once again, forcing management to trade team captain Keith Tkachuk and release veteran Jeremy Roenick. As a result, the Coyotes missed the playoffs. However, the franchise's future was cemented in Phoenix with the approval of plans for a new arena to be built in the nearby suburb of Glendale.

The team did better than expected the following year, considering the impact of ongoing payroll cuts. In the absence of any high-profile offensive talent, goalie Sean Burke raised his game to a new level, with 2.29 goals against average, leading the team to a winning record of 40–27–9–6. However, the Coyotes made a first-round exit from the playoffs, falling to the San Jose Sharks in five games.

The Coyotes played eight seasons in America West Arena, the second-smallest facility in the NHL, with just over 16,000 seats. Then, in 2003, they moved into the $180 million, 17,799-seat Glendale Arena (now Jobing.com Arena). The team finished the season in last place.

The Coyotes have had just five playoff appearances since moving to Phoenix, all resulting in first-round eliminations. The teams' lack of postseason success inspired constant roster changes and numerous revisions to the coaching staff. In the eight seasons before the 2004–2005 players' strike, management already had burned through four different head coaches. In 2005, Gretzky became Phoenix's fifth head coach, and he struggled to turn the team's fortunes around. In 2006, stockholder Jerry Moyes, a local trucking company executive and partial owner of baseball's Arizona Diamondbacks, bought the team for $127 million; however, the franchise continued to lose money.

The team began to rely more heavily on its own young draft picks rather than expensive veterans and free agents, and its record improved. In 2007–2008, Phoenix finished with 83 points, just missing the playoffs, but the squad ranked twenty-ninth in average NHL home attendance (14,820) out of 30 teams. Things did not improve in 2008–2009, and before the next season began, Gretzky stepped down as coach, yielding to Dave Tippets. In 2009–2010, Tippets, who was named NHL Coach of the Year, led the Coyotes to the playoffs, but they lost in the first round to the Detroit Red Wings. In 2010–2011, the team was valved at $134 million, the lowest in the NHL.

Ron Reynolds

See also: Ice Hockey.

Further Reading

Currie, Roger. *The Winnipeg Jets: A Celebration of Hockey in Winnipeg.* 2nd ed. Winnipeg, Canada: Studio Publications, 2008.

Nauright, John, and Phil White. "'Save Our Jets': Professional Sport, Nostalgia, Community and Nation in Canada." *AVANTE* 2:4 (1996): 24–41.

Sherer, Jay. "Globalization and the Construction of Local Particularities: A Case Study of the Winnipeg Jets." *Sociology of Sports Journal* 18:2 (2001): 205–230.

Silver, Jim. *Thin Ice: Money, Politics and the Demise of an NHL Franchise.* Halifax, Canada: Fernwood, 1996.

Crawfords, Pittsburgh

The Pittsburgh Crawfords, one of the most talented baseball clubs ever assembled, in the opinion of many sports historians, began as a youth team on the streets and sandlots of Pittsburgh's Hill District in 1925. In 1930, Gus Greenlee, a nightclub owner and numbers baron, took charge of the team, and it became the leading squad in the Negro Leagues. In those days, no major or minor league teams in organized baseball employed a single African American player; however, a network of Negro Leagues stretched from coast to coast and gained extra strength from the countries of the Caribbean, which allowed integrated teams and winter play. The 1935 Crawfords, with several future Hall of Famers in the lineup, often have been compared to the legendary 1927 New York Yankees.

In 1925, Teenie Harris and Bill Harris, unrelated teenagers living on the Hill in Pittsburgh, combined the black players of their respective teams at Watt and McKelvey schools after the two interracial squads played against each other. In order to compete at a higher level, the players needed to segregate themselves. The resulting all-black team entered and won a city league championship under the sponsorship of the Crawford Bathhouse in 1926. They soon became the darlings of the Hill District, the city's principal black neighborhood. Most were the sons of migrants from the Deep South who had arrived in Pittsburgh during the Great Migration, which remade the black community during World War I and the 1920s.

William "Woogie" Harris, Johnny Moore, and the original Crawfords were joined in 1927 by Neal Harris, Charlie Hughes, Claude Johnson, William Kimbo, Ormsby Roy, and Harold Tinker from the Edgar Thomson Steel Works club. They, too, were mostly sons of migrants. Tinker, who had watched Pittsburgh's Homestead Grays play at Forbes Field as a boy, said, "I wanted to put together a team that would defeat them. And every team that I became a part of, I took that nucleus of players that I knew in my heart would be coming toward that aim."

In 1928, Tinker recruited 16-year-old Josh Gibson to the Crawfords. Gibson was the son of a migrant from Georgia who had found work in a Pittsburgh steel mill. With Gibson anchoring a fine squad of sandlot players, the Crawfords were ready to take on the Grays during the 1930 season.

Before that happened, though, Grays owner Cum Posey recruited Gibson to catch for his team. The Grays won the first few games against the Crawfords, but then a new force entered the scene. The Crawfords approached Greenlee for financial support. He agreed to put the players on salary, thus becoming the club's owner. Greenlee's cash also made it possible to attract legendary pitcher Leroy "Satchel" Paige and to bring Gibson back to the team. After that, the Crawfords finally beat the Grays.

Greenlee began to remake the team, recruiting center fielder James "Cool Papa" Bell, manager and first baseman Oscar Charleston, and third baseman Judy Johnson away from the Grays. Gibson led the Negro National League in home runs 1932, 1934, and 1936, and he developed into an outstanding catcher. Other Crawfords stars included Leroy Matlock, who won 18 games without a loss in 1935, Sam Bankhead, Jimmy Crutchfield, Vic Harris, and Ted Page. These men replaced most of the original Crawfords. Along with Gibson and Paige, Bell, Charleston, and Johnson were among the first Negro Leaguers elected to the National Baseball Hall of Fame.

Greenlee also helped re-form the Negro National League, which had collapsed in 1931 following the departure of founder Rube Foster. He based the league in Pittsburgh, with headquarters above the Crawford Grill. Greenlee also built the finest black-owned ballpark in the country on the Hill in 1932, calling it Greenlee Field.

The Crawfords won Negro National League titles in 1933, 1935, and 1936 (although the 1933 championship also was claimed by the Chicago American Giants). Along with the Homestead Grays, they made Pittsburgh the center of a black baseball universe that stretched across the nation and into the Caribbean. However, politics in the Caribbean intervened in 1937 and tore the club apart.

The best Negro Leaguers often played winter ball in the Caribbean, where they made more money, received greater respect, and played on integrated teams. In 1937, Satchel Paige went to the Dominican Republic to play for Ciudad Trujillo, a team in the Dominican capital named for the nation's dictator, Rafael Trujillo. Ciudad Trujillo was formed that season by combining the capital's two teams, Licey and Escogido, after a team from San Pedro de Macoris had won the island championship in 1936. Trujillo wanted to make sure that the capital city's team did not lose again. To maximize their success, the team went after Paige, and he persuaded other African American stars to play for Trujillo, including Bankhead, Bell, Gibson, Matlock, and several other Crawfords.

Ciudad Trujillo won the Dominican championship that summer, but the Crawfords were finished. Neither Paige nor Gibson, who was traded to the Grays, or the other players returned to the Crawfords. The club stumbled through two more seasons in Pittsburgh before leaving for Toledo and then oblivion. Greenlee abandoned baseball and turned his sporting interests to boxing. Greenlee Field was torn down and replaced by the Bedford Dwellings housing project.

Greenlee reformed the Crawfords in 1945 as part of the United States League. Branch Rickey backed the operation, largely using the league as his stalking horse for integration. United States League clubs rented Brooklyn Dodgers–owned ballparks and gave Rickey a better knowledge of black players. The league folded after the 1946 season, and the Crawfords, who won the title that season, disappeared along with it.

Rob Ruck

See also: African American Baseball, Negro League Era; Gibson, Josh; Greenlee, Gus; Paige, Satchel.

Further Reading

Youngling, Molly, dir. *Kings on the Hill: Baseball's Forgotten Men.* Pittsburgh, PA: San Pedro Productions, 1993.

Lanctot, Neil. *Negro League Baseball: The Rise and Ruin of a Black Institution.* Philadelphia: University of Pennsylvania Press, 2004.

Lester, Larry. *Black Baseball's National Showcase: The East-West All-Star Game, 1933–1953.* Lincoln: University of Nebraska Press, 2001.

Ruck, Rob. *Sandlot Seasons: Sport in Black Pittsburgh.* Urbana: University of Illinois Press, 1987.

Cricket

For most casual sports watchers around the world, North America is assumed to be a cricket wilderness, because it is currently such a minor pastime, yet the sport was played here 300 years ago, and the United States and Canada were major forces in the game during the first half of the nineteenth century. Even more surprisingly, the first international cricket match took place between the two countries on September 24–26, 1844, at the St. George's Cricket Club in New York. Today, however, North America holds only a minor place in cricket, while the sport enjoys great popularity in the home of the sport, Great Britain, as well as in the Caribbean, Australasia, several African nations, and especially the Indian Subcontinent.

The first mention of cricket in North America dates to 1709. Throughout the eighteenth century, the sport was played enthusiastically by British army officers and the American landed gentry. The *New York Post-Boy* of April 29, 1751, reports a game between

Londoners and New Yorkers, which the latter won 157–80. The coming of the American Revolution dampened enthusiasm for cricket, as Americans associated the sport with British colonial rule. John Adams, the nation's second president, was an early cricket fan. According to lore, he conceived of the country's highest office by declaring that if cricket clubs could have presidents, so could the United States.

By the 1830s, cricket had regained its popularity, and it was the most popular ball sport in North America for two decades. It was played extensively in Eastern factory towns and most major urban centers, mainly at first by immigrant English artisans and businessmen. The most prestigious club was New York's St. George's Cricket Club, founded in 1840 by first-generation English merchants, but other major clubs were founded in Toronto (1827), New York (1838), Newark (1845), San Francisco (1852), Philadelphia (1854), and Lowell, Massachusetts (1857). On September 7, 1859, an English team captained by George Parr departed for America on its first-ever international tour, playing a match against a U.S. team consisting of 22 players on October 3–5 at the Elysian Fields in Hoboken, New Jersey.

When the modern nation of Canada was formed in 1867, Prime Minister John A. McDonald declared cricket the national game. By then, England and Australia were making fairly regular tours of North America. However, baseball's rapid growth in popularity in the United States brought an irreversible decline for cricket.

Philadelphia and Toronto, where teams were composed of the well-to-do, were the last major bastions of cricket playing in North America. In 1878, Philadelphia drew a game against a talented Australian XI (teams are composed of 11 players, hence they are called "XIs") that included Fred Spofforth, Australia's finest bowler (similar to a pitcher in baseball) of the nineteenth century, and Charles Bannerman, the scorer of the first century in Test cricket (matches between national teams that can last up to five days). Canada toured England in 1887, playing Ireland, Scotland, and teams in the English counties, winning two games and drawing 12 others.

The Philadelphia Cricket Club also toured England ten years later, by which time the standard was so high that the games were awarded first-class status (still the benchmark of professional cricket), which recognizes the team's quality and includes the privilege of playing three-day matches. In the 1890s, touring teams from England and Australia again played Philadelphia.

These are isolated examples of cricket's continuing popularity, however. The future of the game in North America was sealed several decades earlier with the in-

vention of town ball and rounders and, later, baseball. Although related to cricket, these were simpler games that could be played in much smaller areas, in less time, and with less equipment. Perhaps more important, baseball lacked the colonial and aristocratic associations of cricket; it was identified as an "American" game and became the representative sport of the democracy, financed by local politicians and businessmen. Because the skills needed to play cricket and baseball were similar, baseball teams recruited many of their early professional players from the ranks of amateur cricket.

There were a few distinguished moments for North American cricket in the early twentieth century. In 1908, Brad King, America's greatest cricketer, topped the English first-class bowling averages—an impressive achievement in an era featuring rivals such as Englishman Wilfred Rhodes. Also that year, Philadelphia embarked on its final first-class tour of England. As late as 1912, Philadelphia beat Australia, but when the team toured England again in 1921, the games no longer were granted first-class status.

While other cricketing nations developed their professional systems, the United States and Canada clung to amateurism, a decision that resulted in an inevitable gap in playing standards. Australia made brief tours of North America in the 1920s, and on one occasion, the great Don Bradman announced that Stanley Park in Vancouver was his favorite cricket ground.

Cricket continued to be played as a minor sport in North America throughout the twentieth century, sustained almost entirely by immigrants from major cricket-playing countries, most recently Pakistan and India. In 1958, a Los Angeles television station covered a match between the Corinthian and Hollywood cricket clubs; despite its good ratings, it remained a onetime broadcast.

In 1961, the United States of America Cricket Association (USACA) was formed, and it joined the International Cricket Conference (ICC, the game's world governing body) in 1965. Although the United States qualified for the ICC Champions Trophy in 2004, the USACA has been notoriously dysfunctional, with elections shrouded in controversy and an inability to get its constitution and bureaucracy straightened out. It briefly was banned from official ICC tournaments in 2005 and 2007, but in both cases was reinstated roughly a year later. Meanwhile, the USACA has attempted to gain sponsors to finance league competition in the United States.

Cricket fared far better in Canada. Its national team qualified for the 1979 Cricket World Cup and played its first officially recognized One Day International tournament. The length of major matches was limited, since spectators no longer had the time or inclination to watch the old first-class matches, nor were the long matches conducive to television coverage. The team did not qualify again until 2003, when it won its first One Day International against Bangladesh. Playing against the West Indies team, Captain John Davison scored the fastest century in World Cup history, his hundred coming off just 67 balls. Canada qualified again for the 2007 World Cup, but the team lost all of its three first-round matches.

North American cricket currently is dominated by immigrants from South India and the Caribbean, but the sport is hampered by the lack of any real infrastructure and its unfamiliarity to mainstream sports fans raised on baseball. The future is far from certain, but North America holds an important place in the history of a game that still is avidly played and watched by millions of people around the world.

Mark Storey

See also: Baseball, to 1870; Wright, Harry.

Further Reading

Bowen, Rowland. *Cricket: A History of Its Growth and Development Throughout the World.* London: Eyre & Spottiswoode, 1970.

Kirsch, George B. *Baseball and Cricket: The Creation of American Team Sports, 1838–72.* Urbana: University of Illinois Press, 2007.

Sentance, P. David. *Cricket in America, 1710–2000.* Jefferson, NC: McFarland, 2006.

Crime, Organized

In the late nineteenth century, organized crime—a term that was not coined until the 1920s—developed as a network of highly coordinated syndicates, often ethnically based, that engaged in businesses providing clients with popular but illegal goods or services, including prostitution, gambling, and narcotics. These syndicates often operated with considerable impunity because of their close ties with and payoffs to urban machine politicians.

Sports were an important nexus between crime syndicates and machine politicians, who not only had political clout but also were prominent entrepreneurs in baseball, prizefighting, and horse racing. Underworld figures developed social and business relationships with sports promoters; owners of teams and horses; managers of professional boxers; operators of tracks, ballparks, and arenas; and even individual athletes.

The primary focus of organized crime always has been gambling, especially illegal off-track betting at poolrooms and through neighborhood bookmakers (known as "handbooks," or "bookies"), which became one of its most profitable ventures. Members of organized crime syndicates made money in a variety of ways. First, they operated as bookmakers themselves, taking a percentage of every bet, called the "vig," a term derived from the Yiddish word *vyigrysh,* or "winnings." They also took a cut of debts collected—through the threat or application of violence—on behalf of bookmakers. Underworld figures used their control over the telegraphic racing wire to secure rapid data about race results, allowing them to put down bets on sporting events before the results were reported. Organized criminals also were known to convince athletes to "throw" or "shave points" on contests, for example, by purposefully losing a boxing match or failing to score enough points to make the spread. Finally, organized crime figures made money in legitimate ways, by owning arenas or promoting boxing matches.

Aside from the financial opportunities of a cash-rich business, underworld figures became involved in professional sports, because they enjoyed the action and prestige of being associated with an exciting pastime and well-known athletic figures. Gangsters ran a few racetracks in the late 1880s, and after the sport experienced a revival in the 1920s, hoodlums took outright possession of some tracks. At the same time, the underworld moved into the newly legalized sport of prizefighting, maintaining a dominant role through the 1960s. Ultimately, organized crime has had a deleterious impact on sports because of the illegal gambling, the threat to the integrity of competition, and the mistreatment of athletes who were cheated, extorted, and even physically abused.

Mike McDonald and the Origins of Sporting Syndicates

One of the first kingpins of organized crime was Michael Cassius McDonald in Chicago, a city renowned for its vice districts, including "Gambler's Row." McDonald and two partners established "The Store" in 1873, a gambling emporium that became the center of the city's sporting life. By 1877, he was the city's gambling boss and head of organized crime, relying on his clout within the Democratic Party to protect his associates.

McDonald was involved in several sports. In 1876, he supported promoter Parson Davies's scheduling of boxing bouts and pedestrianism (long-distance foot-races). In 1881, the syndicate brought in aspiring heavy-weight contender John L. Sullivan to "spar" (prizefighting was illegal), and McDonald refereed some of his matches. Thereafter, McDonald's syndicate backed Sullivan's bid for a title bout until he broke with them. In 1889, McDonald refereed the Jack McAuliffe–Billy Myer light-weight championship fight in North Judson, Indiana. McDonald also was involved in baseball, and he alleg-edly tried to fix an 1877 game between the St. Louis Brown Stockings and the Chicago White Stockings by bribing two of the Browns through umpire L.W. Burtis. However, the team owners were tipped off to McDon-ald's plan and prevented the fix.

McDonald's most lucrative sport, however, was thoroughbred racing. By 1885, his syndicate had mo-nopolized illegal off-track betting in Chicago and domi-nated betting on the racetracks. Six years later, the organization opened up the highly profitable Garfield Park Race Track, an outlaw operation that was subject to no regulating body and attracted underworld-connected characters. However, the "bookmaker's track" did not enjoy the political protection it needed, and re-form mayor Hempstead Washburne closed the opera-tion in 1892. McDonald retired from his illegal businesses that year, but Chicago remained a major cen-ter for off-track gambling.

In the early 1900s, Chicago syndicates divided the action by geographic region. Aldermen Michael "Hinky Dink" Kenna and "Bathhouse John" Coughlin con-trolled downtown, Alderman Johnnie Rogers the West Side, James O'Leary the South Side, and Jacob "Mont" Tennes the North Side. Their syndicates received na-tionwide race results via Western Union, and clerks telephoned the information to affiliated poolrooms and bookmakers at saloons and cigar shops. In 1905, Illi-nois banned racing, and Western Union dropped the wire service under pressure from social reformers and stockholders. However, off-track betting continued to flourish, and Western Union still transmitted racing news as a common carrier for "information services." By 1911, Tennes had secured a national monopoly on the racing wire through his General News Bureau, after surviving a gang war with his rivals.

Organized Crime and the Turf in New York

Horse racing, which was virtually defunct in the North by the 1840s, boomed in metropolitan New York after the Civil War when the social elite established major tracks. During this time, the so-called sport of kings developed a strong relationship with organized crime.

The main figure behind the opening of the Sara-toga Race Track in 1863 was former heavyweight box-ing champion John Morrissey, the leading professional gambler in New York, who soon became a prominent Democratic politician. In 1866, the elite American Jockey Club opened in Westchester with a membership that included William "Boss" Tweed of Tammany Hall. Four years later, the prestigious Monmouth Park Racing Association opened at Long Branch, New Jersey. The track's president was Amos Robbins, president of the New Jersey state senate, and Jockey Club members in-cluded patricians such as Pierre Lorillard, as well as Tweed, robber barons Jay Gould and James "Diamond Jim" Fisk, Jr., and gamblers John Chamberlain and Price McGrath.

The elite tracks' success led to the construction of proprietary racetracks by entrepreneurs with political clout, such as Brighton Beach (1879) and Gravesend in Brooklyn (1886). New Jersey had two blatantly crooked tracks, Guttenberg (1885) and Gloucester (1890), which ran year-round. Their owners were politicians closely tied to the underworld. The gambling crowd gained increas-ing influence with the state legislature in 1893, but they lost control in a voter revolt at the following election, and the tracks closed.

New York's jockey clubs and other racing inter-ests, including agricultural societies, secured legisla-tion that permitted on-track gambling but opposed all off-track betting, which was legalized by New York State only in 1970. Illegal off-track betting was a ma-jor source of revenue for local crime syndicates. Many smaller bettors preferred off-track betting, because they did not have the time to travel to the racetracks or the ready money to make cash bets. They appreci-ated the convenience of betting near their home or place of employment, where they could bet on out-of-town races. Off-track betting operated through bookmakers, who took bets at saloons, cigar stores, candy stores, on the streets, and at poolrooms (the pop-ular term for a betting parlors) located primarily in downtown Manhattan.

The state tried to halt off-track betting with the Anti-Poolroom Act of 1877, and then the Sexton Act of 1893, which made operating a poolroom a felony. However, Tammany Hall judges and policemen pro-tected the Irish-dominated business. Poolrooms were controlled at the turn of the century by the Gambling Trust, which included "Big Tim" Sullivan, the number-two man in Tammany Hall; Mayor Robert Van Wyck; Frank Farrell, one of the city's leading gamblers; and

Police Chief Bill Devery. Farrell and Devery owned the New York Highlanders (later renamed the Yankees) from 1903 to 1915. The trust controlled 400 poolrooms, which paid up to $300 a month to operate. Any new poolroom going into business needed the trust's approval to open. The trust took in $3 million per year, half from horse race betting, and the rest from crap games, gambling houses, and policy.

Boxing and the Underworld

In 1920, New York legalized boxing under the State Athletic Commission, inaugurating a golden age of prizefighting. Machine politicians, who were the main promoters of illegal matches at the time, used their clout to temporarily legalize boxing in New York and San Francisco, but they soon lost control of the sport to the underworld, which encountered little interference from any boxing commission outside New York.

Organized crime figures were drawn to boxing because of the excitement, the opportunities to be seen ringside with celebrities, and the chance to make money by managing fighters and gambling on the outcomes of fights. Gangsters typically grew up alongside other tough inner-city youth who became boxers, and they were themselves an integral part of the boxing subculture.

One such boxer was Barney Ross, who held three world-boxing titles simultaneously in 1934 and grew up with future gangsters on Chicago's Near West Side. He had a rough childhood—his father was murdered when he was 13. Ross became a street thug and aspired to join a gang, ultimately becoming a messenger boy for Al Capone, who pushed him into a different career path.

Gangsters hung out in boxing gymnasiums, attended matches, and caroused with old pals in the fight game at nightclubs, racetracks, and baseball games. They admired fighters such as Abe Attell, the world featherweight champion (1904–1912), who, after retiring in 1917, worked as the "eyes and ears" of Arnold Rothstein, the leading gambler in New York, and a major strategist for organized crime, keeping track of what was going on in the boxing trade. In 1919, Attell was involved in the Black Sox scandal, a conspiracy between gamblers and players on the Chicago White Sox to fix the World Series.

Gangsters generally operated behind the scenes in prizefighting, because their criminal records barred them from getting a license to serve as a manager or promoter. They got close to promising fighters by wining and dining them and by giving them gifts. From

there, it was a short step for the mobster to take over the fighter's career by buying out or intimidating the manager. Boxers enjoyed the attention of mobsters, whom they thought could secure good matches for them and thereby advance their careers.

Waxey Gordon (Irving Wexler), who ran Rothstein's bootlegging (illegal alcohol) operations during Prohibition, was one of the better-known undercover managers. His top boxer was Reuven "Ruby" Goldstein, whom he had seen fight as an 18-year-old. Gordon was impressed with Goldstein and had an associate tell Goldstein's manager that he wanted to assume control of the boxer's career. The manager agreed. The undefeated "Jewel of the Ghetto" quickly became a contender, and in 1926, he fought tough Asa "Ace" Hudkins in preparation for a welterweight championship fight. Gordon bet $45,000 that Goldstein would win with a first-round knockout. Goldstein tried his best, and he did knock down Hudkins in the first round, but he tired himself out and ended up losing in the fourth round.

Chicago mobster Al Capone also was a boxing fan who bet heavily on bouts and socialized with fighters. In 1927, the night before the Jack Dempsey–Gene Tunney heavyweight championship rematch in Chicago, he took scheduled referee Davey Miller for a car ride and tried to influence him. Capone was a heavy backer of Dempsey, while Philadelphia numbers and bootlegging king Max "Boo Boo" Hoff, who operated the largest stable of boxers in the country and promoted fights in Philadelphia, bet on Tunney. The Illinois Athletic Commission found out about the visit, and replaced Miller with Dave Barry. The match became known as the "long-count" fight, because when Dempsey knocked down Tunney in the seventh round, Barry did not start the count until Dempsey had moved to the farthest neutral corner, allowing Tunney extra time to get up before the 10-count and, ultimately, to win the bout.

One of the most famous mob-controlled fighters was Primo Carnera, the world heavyweight champion in 1933 and 1934. The Italian giant—he stood 6 feet, 5.5 inches (2 meters) and weighed 284 pounds (129 kilograms)—actually was controlled by several underworld figures, primarily Owen "Owney" Madden, a prominent New York bootlegger and the owner of the Cotton Club. They helped promote his career by fixing several bouts, including his title fight against champion Jack Sharkey, whom he knocked out with a phantom upper cut. The underworld's control of boxing was an open secret, often depicted in popular movies such as *Golden Boy* (1939), *Body and Soul* (1947), a fictionalized biography of Barney Ross, and *Champion* (1949). When

Sports Illustrated began publication in 1954, it featured investigations of crime in boxing.

The acknowledged "Czar of Boxing" was Paul John "Frankie" Carbo, a former hit man for the Murder, Inc., syndicate, who virtually monopolized the middleweight division in the 1940s and influenced other divisions as well. Carbo used threats and violence to gain control of fighters, employing "front men" as managers of record. He had close ties to matchmakers, who often owed their jobs to him, and promoters needed him to arrange matches because he controlled so many fighters.

Sometimes, both boxers in championship fights were Carbo's men. Fighters who did not cooperate, such as Jake LaMotta, the top middleweight contender in the mid-1940s, could not get a title fight. In 1947, LaMotta finally agreed to throw a fight against light heavyweight contender Billy Fox in return for future championship bouts. LaMotta's admission to the fix opened a 1960 U.S. Senate investigation of organized crime's role in prizefighting under Senator Estes Kefauver of Tennessee.

Carbo was close to the International Boxing Club (IBC), established in 1949 by James D. Norris and Arthur Wirtz, the owners of New York's Madison Square Garden, Detroit's Olympia Stadium, and Chicago Stadium. Over the next seven years, the IBC promoted more than 90 percent of U.S. title bouts and prime-time televised matches from Madison Square Garden. However, in 1955, the U.S. Supreme Court dismantled the IBC monopoly. In the late 1950s, Carbo received a two-year jail sentence for working as an undercover manager; he subsequently was sentenced to 25 years in jail for extortion for trying to control the career of welterweight champion Don Jordan.

Among Carbo's top associates was Frank "Blinky" Palermo, the Philadelphia numbers king, who managed several prominent fighters, including undisputed lightweight champion Ike Williams (1947–1951) and future heavyweight champion Sonny Liston (1958–1960). While such organized crime lords lost their stranglehold on prizefighting, figures with connections to the underworld continued to play an important role in the sport. Among the most notable of these figures was Don King, a former bookmaker and convicted murderer, who became the leading boxing promoter from the 1960s to the 1980s and is best known for promoting the 1974 "Rumble in the Jungle," fought in Kinshasa, Zaire, between Muhammad Ali and George Foreman. A Federal Bureau of Investigation probe in the late 1990s found that King's business relied heavily on payoffs to secure high rankings for fighters and sanctioning of championship fights.

The Negro Leagues

During the Great Depression of the 1930s, when there was little capital in black America, teams in baseball's Negro National League (established in 1933) were owned mainly by men in the "numbers" business, an illegal lottery that was popular among the working class. The individual behind the league was Gus Greenlee, Pittsburgh's "numbers king," who owned the Pittsburgh Crawfords. He sought a legitimate outlet for his money, but he also wanted to provide a valuable service to the community. Other Negro League owners in the numbers racket were Cuban American Alejandro "Alex" Pompez, an associate of the notorious gangster Dutch Schultz (New York Cubans), Abe Manley (Newark Eagles), James "Soldier Boy" Semler (Baltimore Elite Giants), Ed Bolden (Philadelphia Stars), and Robert A. Cole, Sr. (Chicago American Giants).

Racetracks, 1920–1960

Horse racing enjoyed a revival after World War I, as purses doubled by 1920 and doubled again by 1926. Several states legalized on-track gambling to raise revenue. In Stickney, a Chicago suburb, the Hawthorne Race Course reopened in 1921, employing oral betting schemes that allowed for evasion of taxes. Five years later, the state legislature legalized pari-mutuel gambling at the tracks.

By 1929, 34 tracks were in operation in the United States, and more opened during the Great Depression as warm-weather states such as Florida (1931) and California (1933) sought new sources of money. The tracks were very profitable, earning money from admissions, betting fees, parking, and concession rights. This alone attracted the interest of the underworld, including Rothstein, a stockholder at Maryland's Havre de Grace track when it opened in 1912.

The glamour and prestige of racing attracted organized criminals, who also saw opportunities for laundering money from their illegal operations, extorting money from workers and contractors, skimming money from a cash-rich business, facilitating illegal gambling, and fixing races by drugging horses or paying off jockeys. They used bribery, jobs, and the sale of offers of underpriced stock shares to win influence with state racing commissions that controlled licensing applications and racing dates, as well as local politicians who controlled the municipal services their tracks needed.

In the late 1920s, gangsters also owned dog-racing tracks. In 1928, Capone initiated dog racing at the Hawthorne Kennel Club in Stickney under attorney Edward J. O'Hare, who controlled the patent for the mechanical rabbit that motivated the dogs to run. Capone's competitor in metropolitan Chicago was bootlegging rival George "Bugs" Moran, owner of the Fairview track. In fact, dog racing was illegal in Illinois, but court fights helped keep the sport operating there until 1932. That year, O'Hare redesigned the Hawthorne Kennel Club into a thoroughbred horse racing facility, and renamed Sportsman's Park. O'Hare also operated gangster-run dogs tracks in Miami and Tampa (legalized in 1932) and in Boston (1934).

Several bootleggers and former bootleggers began to take over racetracks in the early 1930s. In 1931, Canadian bootleggers converted Tropical Park near Coral Gables, Florida, from a dog track into a thoroughbred track managed by "Big Bill" Dwyer, a major New York bootlegger and partner of the infamous Frank Costello, known as the "Prime Minister of the Underworld." Dwyer owned several nightclubs, the New York Americans team of the National Hockey League, and racetracks in Montreal, Canada; Cincinnati, Ohio; and Jacksonville, Florida.

In 1934, a syndicate led by Meyer Lansky, the gambling king of organized crime, bought Tropical Park. Lansky also was involved in Florida's Gulfstream Park, along with Chicago bootleggers, and the nation's preeminent bookmaker Frank Erickson, who by the 1930s was a close associate of Costello. Schultz, the "Beer Baron" of the Prohibition era in the Bronx, owned the River Downs Race Track near Cincinnati, previously owned by Canadian bootleggers. Schultz used the easily manipulated betting results from pari-mutuel racing to determine the winning numbers for the Harlem bookmaking market, which he took over in the early 1930s.

Gangsters remained deeply involved in racing after World War II. Costello, for one, owned stock in New York harness-racing tracks along with Erickson's son and son-in-law. In West Virginia, Detroit mobsters Pete Licavoli and Joseph Zerelli ran Wheeling Downs from 1946 until a decade later, when they sold the operation to William Lias, an old bootlegger. Zerelli also ran Detroit's Hazel Park in the 1950s and early 1960s. Raymond Patriarca, the crime boss of New England in the early 1950s, controlled Scarborough Downs in Maine and Berkshire Downs in Massachusetts, the latter with Tony "Three-Finger Brown" Lucchese, head of his own New York underworld family.

Sports Gambling

Gambling on sports was a huge business for the underworld, especially in major cities such as Chicago, Detroit, New York, and Philadelphia. Bookmakers were taking bets on baseball by the 1870s, and 20 years later, they sold baseball pool cards at saloons and on street corners for as little as 10 cents. Clients bet on wins, but also on strikeouts and runs. The Keystone pool in New York is said to have sold 165,000 tickets a week, netting $50,000 (after one-third of the profits went toward police payoffs). Football pools also became popular in the 1930s. By that time, New York City fans were betting roughly $60 million on baseball, basketball, and football.

Still, horse racing remained the cornerstone of syndicate gambling for decades in major metropolitan areas and in regional gambling centers such as Covington, Kentucky; Hot Springs, Arkansas; and Las Vegas, Nevada, which legalized off-track betting in 1931. Gambling boss Mont Tennes, under pressure from the Capone mob, sold the General News Bureau wire service in 1927 to newspaper publisher Moe Annenberg and retired. Annenberg had been a newspaper circulation manager in early 1900s Chicago, a business notorious for its strong-arm tactics. Annenberg consolidated his far-flung racing news businesses, including the *Daily Racing Form* and the *Morning Telegraph,* and established the Nationwide News Service in 1934, which served about 15,000 bookmakers in 223 cities.

In 1939, Annenberg went to jail on charges of income tax evasion and sold the racing wire to protégé James Ragen and his partner Arthur "Mickey" McBride, who renamed it the Continental News Bureau. McBride was a founder of the All-America Football Conference in 1946 and the publisher of the *Cleveland News.* He once had employed Morris "Moe" Dalitz's gang to help him in circulation wars. Chicago mobsters Tony Accardo, Jake Guzik, and Murray "The Camel" Humphreys pressed Ragen to sell out, and when he would not, they formed the Trans-American Publishing and News Service in California, run by gangster Benjamin "Bugsy" Siegel, to undercut him. Later that year, they assassinated Ragen. The Continental News Bureau supposedly was the property of McBride's college-age son, but in fact, the syndicate had taken it over. However, the wire was on its last legs, as independent bookies had ample access to information by telephone, radio, and television, ran their own betting operations, and bought their own police protection.

Organized crime next moved into the sports book—that is, organized betting on games. In the 1940s, Erickson and Costello operated sports books out of Florida hotels. In 1947, Siegel unsuccessfully promoted legal sports betting at the ill-fated Flamingo Hotel. Eleven years later, Chicago gangster Sam Giancana pushed sports betting at Las Vegas's Stardust Hotel. However, the sports books did not flourish until 1974, when the federal government ended its 10 percent tax on sports gambling. Thereafter, sports betting flourished, particularly at the Stardust Hotel under Frank "Lefty" Rosenthal. Even more profitable, however, was illegal sports gambling, which increased from an estimated $20 billion business in the 1970s to more than $200 billion in the early 2000s. In terms of gambling on sports, the single biggest event remains the Super Bowl, when 30 million people bet some $3 billion, mostly illegally.

Big-time sports leagues long have kept alert to threats against the integrity of the games they promote. In 1963, the National Football League suspended star players Paul Hornung and Alex Karras for contacts with organized crime figures. Since the league was founded, 21 owners have been identified as connected, financially or socially, to organized crime figures, often because they shared an interest in gambling. They include shopping mall magnate Edward J. DeBartolo, Sr., who in 1977 bought the San Francisco 49ers, even though Major League Baseball rejected him as a team owner because of his alleged business ties to top organized crime figures.

While organized crime still makes large sums of money from its sports operations in the early twenty-first century, it has lost its influence because of the widespread legalization of gambling. With casinos and sports books operating in states across the country, the underworld no longer enjoys a monopoly on the lucrative business of betting on sporting events. Meanwhile, the government has broken up many of the organized crime syndicates, which once asserted undue control over the careers of leading professional boxers.

Steven A. Riess

See also: Black Sox Scandal; Boxing; Business of Sports; Canine Sports; College Basketball Scandal of 1951; Gambling; Government, Local; Horse Racing; Urbanization.

Further Reading

Davies, Richard O., and Richard G. Abram. *Betting the Line: Sports Wagering in American Life.* Columbus: Ohio State University Press, 2001.
Haller, Mark H. "Bootleggers and American Gambling, 1920–1950." In *Gambling in America: Appendix,* U.S. Commission on the Review of the National Policy Towards Gambling. Washington, DC: U.S. Government Printing Office, 1976.
———. "The Changing Structure of American Gambling in the Twentieth Century." *Journal of Social Issues* 35:3 (Summer 1979): 87–114.
———. "Organized Crime in Urban Society: Chicago in the Twentieth Century." *Journal of Social History* 5:2 (Winter 1971–1972): 210–234.
Johnson, David R. "A Sinful Business: The Origins of Gambling Syndicates in the United States, 1840–1887." In *Police and Society,* ed. David Bayley. Beverly Hills, CA: Sage, 1977.
LaMotta, Jake, with Joseph Carter and Peter Savage. *Raging Bull: My Story.* Englewood Cliffs, NJ: Prentice Hall, 1970.
Moldea, Dan E. *Interference: How Organized Crime Influences Professional Football.* New York: William Morrow, 1989.
Nagler, Barney. *James Norris and the Decline of Boxing.* Indianapolis, IN: Bobbs-Merrill, 1964.
Pietrusza, David. *Rothstein: The Life, Times and Murder of the Criminal Genius Who Fixed the 1919 World Series.* New York: Carroll & Graf, 2001.
Riess, Steven A. *City Games: The Evolution of American Society and the Rise of Sports.* Urbana: University of Illinois Press, 1989.
———. "Only the Ring Was Square: Frankie Carbo and the Underworld Control of American Boxing." *International Journal of the History of Sport* 5:1 (May 1988): 29–52.
———. "Sports and Machine Politics in New York City, 1890–1920." In *The Making of Urban America,* ed. Raymond A. Mohl. Wilmington, DE: Scholarly Resources, 1988.
Sammons, Jeffrey T. *Beyond the Ring: The Role of Boxing in American Society.* Urbana: University of Illinois Press, 1988.

Croquet

Croquet, a lawn sport in which players use long-handled mallets to hit hard wooden balls through wickets, became popular in the United States after the Civil War as a genteel pastime that was suitable for both sexes, allowing them to socialize and compete at the same time. While croquet can be a highly competitive game played on perfectly pitched greens by players decked out in white, it historically has been a family game played in backyards or public parks.

The term "croquet" derives from *croche,* an old northern French word meaning "shepherd's crook." The game may have originated in ancient times, when shepherds knocked around hardened sheep droppings with their crooks. In the fourteenth century, peasants in Brittany and southern France played a game called *paille maille,* in which crude mallets were used to knock balls through hoops made of bent willow branches. *Pele mele,* or pall mall, became popular at the English court of King Charles II in the late seventeenth century, but it subsequently lost favor and disappeared.

In the 1830s, the Irish began playing *crooky,* employing implements similar to modern croquet mallets. From there, the game was brought back to England in 1852 by Lord Lonsdale, and it soon became a craze. In the mid-1860s, interest in croquet spread from England to the United States, where it gained popularity among members of New York's high society. By the late 1860s, croquet had become an American fad.

Croquet owed its popularity to the fact that it was not an especially strenuous game, allowing Victorian-era women and children to compete. It bridged gender and age, stressing sportsmanship over gamesmanship, and provided a genteel activity that appealed to middle-class ideals of a refined lifestyle, in the process teaching patience, perseverance, amiability, and selflessness. Sociability and etiquette took precedence over competition. On balance, Mayne Reid, author of the one of the earliest and most influential guides to the sport, *Croquet: A Treatise and Commentary* (1863), viewed the sport as a healthy outlet for male aggression.

The game was well suited to suburban yards and did not need specially prepared surfaces. It often was played at social gatherings in the late nineteenth century. Adding to its availability, municipalities made croquet sets available at public parks. The game also was one of the first sports to be played in New York City's Central Park.

Organized croquet clubs also flourished, with newspapers reporting on matches. Ladies' magazines promoted the game as way for women to exercise, get fresh air, and meet romantic partners. Writers instructed how a woman could draw aside her skirt to show her ankle to the best advantage when striking the ball, while warning against wearing skirts that were too long and might interfere with play.

Meanwhile, the sport's development also owed to entrepreneur Milton Bradley, who manufactured croquet sets and published a manual of rules that became standard for the game. His manuals applauded the game for requiring physical coordination, mental alertness, and emotional control. In 1882, the National Croquet Association was formed to supervise the game, and the first national tournament was held at Norwich, Connecticut. Croquet was played at the 1900 Olympic Games in Paris, and a variant, called *roque,* played with short-handled mallets and with rigid walls bounding the court, was contested at the 1904 Games.

Despite such events, croquet's popularity began to wane, and by the 1890s, it had been supplanted by lawn tennis. Croquet's decline was attributable, in part, to the game's increasingly unsavory reputation. Angry passions were aroused by purposefully propelling an opponent's ball across the pitch, misdirecting play, and cheating; blows from mallets could cause serious physical injuries. Physicians warned that constant play would lead to a curvature of the spine and the shortening of one leg, and they advised young girls to avoid the sport. The game also became associated with gambling, drinking, and philandering to such an extent that it was banned in Boston in 1890.

Croquet enjoyed a revival after World War I. The ability of women and children to compete on relatively equal footing with adult males again made croquet popular as a family-oriented sport. During the 1920s and 1930s, the croquet craze struck Hollywood, giving the game some glamour after it was taken up by celebrities such as comedian Harpo Marx and producer Darryl Zanuck. Croquet also was an affordable game for families during the Great Depression, as the equipment did not cost much, and it could be played almost anywhere.

The game's popularity once again waned in the 1950s, as other outdoor games gained followers. In 1977, Jack Osborn organized the U.S. Croquet Association to promote the game, but it has never approached its earlier popularity.

Caryn E. Neumann

See also: Class, Economic and Social; Country Clubs.

Further Reading

Charlton, James, and William Thompson. *Croquet: The Complete Guide to History, Strategy, Rules, and Records.* New York: Turtle Press, 1977.

Lewis, R.M. "American Croquet in the 1860s: Playing the Game and Winning." *Journal of Sport History* 18:3 (Winter 1991): 365–386.

Sterngass, Jon. "Cheating, Gender Roles, and the Nineteenth-Century Croquet Craze." *Journal of Sport History* 25:3 (Fall 1998): 398–418.

Cross Country

Cross country is a long-distance off-track running sport. It is a team contest in which both individual finishers and teams are awarded placements, the latter based on the totals of each team's top-place winners (the number of team runners varies according to the sponsoring organization's rules). In the United States, cross country, generally a fall sport, was the dominant off-track racing event between the 1880s, when professional long-distance running and walking declined in popularity, and the late twentieth century, which saw a dramatic increase in marathons and road races.

Cross country began as the English sport of hare and hounds, which engaged public school youngsters as early as 1837 at Rugby School in Warwickshire. Replicating the chase of hare and hounds, one or two runners (the hares) would take a head start, followed by about five runners (the hounds). The hares would drop slips of paper to indicate their scent, prompting sportswriters to describe the race as a "paper chase." Runners came to be called "harriers," a name that came from the type of hounds that generally were used to hunt rabbits; the term subsequently was adopted by cross country runners.

The Westchester Hare and Hounds Club, which was established in 1878 near New York City, was the first cross country club in North America. Its initial race on Thanksgiving Day set a traditional date for such races in the United States. In 1879, Harvard University was the first American college to adopt the sport.

By the mid-1880s, the sport was known as "cross country," and it evolved into a more formal team sport with scoring, timing, and record keeping. The first national organization, the National Cross-Country Association of America, was formed and held its first national championship in 1887. The first intercollegiate cross country meet—involving City College of New York, Cornell University, and the University of Pennsylvania—was organized in 1890, the same year the Amateur Athletic Union (AAU) introduced its first national cross country meet.

Cross country spread rapidly after 1900, mostly in the Mid-Atlantic states, where colleges formed the Inter-Collegiate Cross Country Association (ICCA) in 1899 and conducted the first championship run. Cornell dominated, taking eight of nine ICCA championships; after sponsorship was taken over by the Intercollegiate Athletic Association of the United States in 1908, Cornell won seven more contests in nine years. The AAU national cross country championships produced some notable runners, including Frank Bellars (who won in 1907 and 1909–1910) and Abe Kiviat (who won in 1913).

The first secondary schools to conduct cross country meets were the private schools of the Interscholastic League of New York City during 1898–1899. Interest was sustained though the Public Schools Athletic League, which made cross country a varsity sport in 1906. Philadelphia was another hotbed of cross country running, where the University of Pennsylvania inaugurated a major meet for high schools in 1903. That same year, the International Cross Country Union was founded and staged its first championship.

Cross country debuted as an unofficial contest at the 1904 Olympics in St. Louis with just two club teams from New York and Chicago. It became a medal sport in 1912 and was added to the modern pentathlon, along with fencing, pistol shooting, swimming, and cross country riding. Cross country was dropped as an Olympic sport after the 1924 Games, when the United States came in second in team competition and Earle Johnson captured the bronze medal for his individual finish.

In the 1920s, the Columbia Interscholastic (established in 1911) emerged as the largest high school cross country meet in the United States, and in 1926, Newark Preparatory introduced a national scholastic championship. High schools from Schenectady, New York, dominated both competitions. Finnish-born Willi Ritola took five AAU national titles, while Don Lash won seven straight championships in the 1930s.

The Intercollegiate Association of Amateur Athletics of America sponsored a national championship for colleges during the 1920s and 1930s, dominated in the latter decade by Michigan State. The National Collegiate Athletic Association (NCAA) started its own national championship meet in 1938. The top programs were Drake University (in the 1940s), Michigan State (1950s), Villanova (1960s), the University of Texas at El Paso (1970s), and the University of Arkansas (1980s and 1990s). Three-time collegiate champions included Gerry Lindgren (Washington State in the 1960s), Steve Prefontaine (University of Oregon in the early 1970s), and Henry Rono (Washington State in the late 1970s). The first NCAA meet for women was held in 1981; Stanford University and Villanova University had the most successful women's programs.

In national competition, the most notable runners were Frank Shorter (AAU champion in 1970–1973) and Pat Porter (Athletics Congress champion in 1982–1989). The first national cross country meet for women was held in 1964, and has included such notable competitors as Doris Brown (champion in 1968–1970), Lynn Jennings (1985, 1987–1993, 1996), and Deena (Drossin) Kastor (1997, 1999–2003, 2007).

By this time, many top competitors, such as Shorter, had become better known as marathoners or Olympic long-distance runners, as cross country became less prominent, although the sport was sustained in schools and clubs organized by age group. The AAU, which ended its role as the sponsoring organization in the United States in 1979, continued to support an age-group program in cross country.

In international competition, the most outstanding performer was American Doris Brown, five-time International Cross Country Champion (1967–1971), who helped lead the United States to team titles in 1968 and 1969. Since the International Association of Athletics Federations took over international competition in 1973, the only American champions have been Craig Virgin (1980–1981), Julie Brown (1975), and Lynn Jennings (1990–1992). The U.S. women's team won in 1975 and four times in the 1980s. Since that time, cross country competition has been dominated by East African runners.

Robert Pruter

See also: Marathon; Running; Track and Field.

Further Reading

Shorter, Frank, with Marc Bloom. *Olympic Gold: A Runner's Life and Times.* Boston: Houghton Mifflin, 1984.

Simons, William M. "Abel Kiviat Interview." *Journal of Sport History* 13:3 (Winter 1986): 235–266.

Cubs, Chicago

The Chicago Cubs of the National League of Major League Baseball is the second oldest professional sports franchise in the United States, dating back to 1876. A top team in the early days of the National League, the Cubs won several titles in the 1880s and took the world championship in 1907 and 1908.

Since then, however, they have not won another championship, the longest title drought in U.S. professional sports history. In fact, they have not even reached the World Series since 1945. Despite frustration on the field, the Cubs remain among the most popular teams in the major leagues, consistently boasting one of the best game attendance records.

Chicago on Fire: 1871–1908

Chicago's first professional baseball team was the White Stockings, which was established in 1870. One year later, the team joined the National Association of Professional Base Ball Players in its inaugural season. The franchise was suspended after the Great Chicago Fire destroyed much of the city in 1871, but it was revived in 1874.

In 1875, coal merchant William Hulbert became president and chief owner of the franchise. He recruited several stars for the 1876 season, including pitcher-manager Al Spalding and first baseman Adrian "Cap" Anson, and then he helped establish the National League.

An ace pitcher, Spalding went 47–12 and pitched 528.7 innings in his first season, and he soon became a part owner of the team. He founded a sporting goods company and retired from the diamond, becoming the team's majority owner and baseball's most powerful force. Spalding left the team's management in the capable hands of future Hall of Famer Anson, who would become infamous for leading the exclusion of African Americans from professional baseball.

In its early years, the team was a powerhouse, with great players such as catcher Mike Kelly, pitcher John Clarkson, and shortstop Ned Williamson, who belted 27 homers in 1884, a major league record until it was broken by Babe Ruth in 1919. The White Stockings won six pennants between 1876 and 1886, generating big profits for Spalding. The club participated in the 1885 and 1886 postseason series against the St. Louis Browns of the American Association, tying in 1885 and losing in six games in 1886.

In 1890, several top White Stocking players jumped to the local franchise of the new Players' League, organized by the Brotherhood of Professional Baseball Players, the sport's first union. Anson recruited young replacements in their stead, whom he dubbed "colts" or "cubs." Soon, these nicknames were heard and seen in print more often than the White Stockings. By 1905, the team was known as the Cubs.

At the same time, the team was on its way to its glory years under manager Frank Selee and the famed double-play combination of shortstop Joe Tinker, second baseman Johnny Evers, and first baseman Frank Chance, who were immortalized in the poem "Tinker to Evers to Chance" (1910). (All three eventually would be elected to the Baseball Hall of Fame.) The team also had outstanding pitching, led by Hall of Famer Mordecai "Three Finger" Brown.

When Selee contracted tuberculosis, Chance became the Cubs's manager, leading the team to a 116–36 record in the 1906 season and a cross-town World Series against the White Sox (the American League team had adopted the Cubs's former nickname). The Sox, known as the "Hitless Wonders," upset the Cubs in six games. The next season, the Cubs won 107 games and beat the Detroit Tigers in the World Series (4–0–1).

In 1908, the team faced a tough pennant race. A key play came in a late-season game against the first-place New York Giants. In a tie game, the Giants came up in the bottom of the ninth inning. With two outs and runners on first and third, batter Al Bridwell hit a single, and the game appeared to be over; however, Cubs second baseman Evers noticed that the runner on first, a rookie named Fred Merkle, had neglected to touch second base. Evers screamed to the center fielder to throw the ball in. Already, thousands of Giants fans were mobbing the playing field.

Evers got the ball and touched the base. He made sure the umpire saw the action, and the Cubs claimed that the force-out nullified the apparent winning run. With the field covered with celebrating Giants fans, the game could not continue. Major League Baseball upheld the Cubs's protest and ordered the game replayed. On the second chance, the Cubs won, securing their third straight pennant by a single game—all because of "Merkle's bonehead play." The Cubs captured a second World Series, again besting the Tigers (4–1).

1909–1945: Seven World Series but No Wins

The Cubs remained one of the best teams in baseball for the next few years. They won 104 games in 1909, yet came in second, and 104 games in 1910, but lost the World Series to the Philadelphia Athletics. However, their parsimonious owner, Charley Murphy, who had bought the club from Spalding in 1905 for $105,000, allowed his profitable team to falter (the Cubs made $810,000 from 1906 to 1915), and he went through six managers.

In 1916, after the demise of the Federal League, the Cubs were sold to Charles Weeghman, owner of the Chicago Whales, the former Federal League team, and the team moved from their West Side Park into Weeghman Park on the up-and-coming North Side. The stadium was renamed Cubs Park in 1920.

In 1918, many players were serving in World War I, including Cubs star pitcher Grover C. "Pete" Alexander, or they were off doing war-related work. That year, the Cubs won the pennant but lost the World Series to the Boston Red Sox. Three years later, stockholder William Wrigley, Jr., owner of the Wrigley Chewing Gum Company, became the primary owner. The ballpark was renamed Wrigley Field in his honor in 1927, when a second deck was added to the stadium.

The team was a big draw in the late 1920s, setting a National League record with 1.1 million spectators in 1927. The Cubs put a terrific lineup on the field and finished no worse than third in the next 11 seasons, with pennants in 1929, 1932, 1935, and 1938, but no World Series championship.

The 1929 club, managed by Joe McCarthy, included Hall of Famers Lewis "Hack" Wilson at center field, Rogers Hornsby at second base, and Hazen "Kiki" Cuyler at right field, plus left fielder Riggs Stevenson, who had a lifetime .336 batting average. That year, the Cubs drew nearly 1.5 million fans, a major league record for many years. However, they were beaten in the World Series by one of the all-time great teams assembled by the Philadelphia Athletics. The following year, the team fired McCarthy and replaced him with Hornsby. Hack Wilson set a major league season runs-batted-in record of 191.

In 1932, "Jolly" Charlie Grimm replaced Hornsby as manager in mid-season and turned the Cubs around, leading them to the pennant. However, the squad was swept in the World Series by the New York Yankees, managed the ex-Cub McCarthy. This series was best known for Babe Ruth's "called shot" home run at Wrigley off Charlie Root in Game 3. In 1938, longtime Cubs star catcher Gabby Hartnett replaced Grimm and took the Cubs to the Series, but they were swept by the Yankees once again.

In 1945, with Grimm back as manager, and most stars still in uniform as World War II wound down, the Cubs appeared in their last World Series and broke their old attendance record. The Series highlight was Cub Claude Passeau's one-hitter in Game 3, but the Detroit Tigers prevailed in seven games.

The series also was famed for fostering one of baseball's great legends. When restaurateur Bill Sianis was not allowed to bring his pet goat into Wrigley Field, Sianis put a curse upon the Cubs, which superstitious fans have blamed for the Cubs's inability to make the World Series ever since.

1946–2002: No World Series at All

In 1947, the Cubs began 16 straight nonwinning seasons and, in terms of fan excitement, became the second team in the city, after the White Sox. Desperate for improvement, they instituted the so-called College of Coaches in 1961, in which eight coaches rotated through the minors and then up to the Cubs. The experiment lasted two seasons, with little effect, but the Cubs did hire the first African American major league coach, Negro Leagues great John "Buck" O'Neill, in 1962.

The Cubs's big star in the 1950s was Hall of Fame shortstop Ernie Banks, who became the first African American to play for the team in 1953. In the 1960s, the team added two Hall of Famers—left fielder Billy Williams and pitcher Ferguson Jenkins—as well as Hall of Fame–caliber third baseman Ron Santo, the late Cubs broadcaster, but had little success on the diamond.

In 1969, the Cubs finally seemed to be on their way to the pennant, but Manager Leo Durocher's fatigued team blew an eight-and-a-half game lead to New York's "Miracle" Mets late in the season, who went on to pull out an astonishing World Series upset over the heavily favored Baltimore Orioles. After Durocher left in 1972, Wrigley Field became a frustrating and short stop-over for managers, including Lee Elia, who, in 1983, famously blasted Cubs fans as jobless bums (in fact, his exact phrasing was filled with expletives), with ample time to attend their day-only home games.

In 1977, owner P.K. Wrigley died; four years later, his family sold the franchise to the Tribune Company, publisher of the *Chicago Tribune.* The new corporate owner broadcast games nationwide on WGN, recruiting Cubs faithful throughout North America. In 1981, revered announcer Jack Brickhouse, a 42-year veteran, was succeeded by the exuberant Harry Caray, who became the voice of the Cubs until his death in 1998.

The Cubs in the late 1970s and 1980s had their share of star players, including second baseman Ryne Sandberg and reliever Bruce Sutter, plus right fielder Andre Dawson and reliever Lee Smith, all future Hall of Famers. Like many Cubs hurlers, Smith and Sutter were underappreciated in hitter-friendly Wrigley Field, which has little foul territory, and where batters are aided by the winds that blow predominantly toward the outfield.

In 1984, manager Jim Frey led the Cubs to the Eastern Division title and their first postseason appearance in 39 years, losing the National League Championship Series to the San Diego Padres. At that time, attendance at Cubs's games was the second highest in the National League, and it has remained in the top half of teams ever since. Fans continued to turn out regardless of the team's success on the field, taking advantage of the park's convenient location in the heart of the city, its cozy ambience as the oldest field in the National League, and postgame festivities in the renovated neighborhood (now known as Wrigleyville).

In 1988, 53 years after the first major league night game, the Cubs became the last major league franchise to add lights for night contests. In 1989, Manager Don Zimmer led the Cubs to another division title but lost in the first round of the playoffs to the San Francisco Giants.

The team's star was pitcher Greg Maddux, but he became a free agent in 1993 and moved to the Atlanta Braves. Thereafter, energetic right fielder Sammy Sosa became the star of the mediocre Cubs teams. Sosa's dramatic home run race against Mark McGwire dominated headlines in 1998, and he helped lead the Cubs back to the playoffs, though they were swept in the first round by the Braves.

Since 2003: Hopes Unrealized

New manager Dusty Baker led the Cubs to postseason play in 2003. Early on, it looked as if this might be the season for the Cubs as they took the lead in the National League Championship Series against the Florida Marlins. But then, as fans say, another curse on the Cubs operated once more.

The Cubs were ahead three games to two and needed only five more outs to go to the World Series. Then, a foul ball curved toward the stands with Cubs left fielder Moises Alou in pursuit. Several fans were reaching out for the ball and one, Steve Bartman, deflected it from Alou's grasp. The batter got a hit, and the Marlins came back to win the game, then won the National League title the next day. There was so much anger in the city that Bartman was forced to go into hiding to avoid irate Cubs fans. Long-suffering Cubs rooters consider this the "Bartman curse," adding it to the vast lore of the "Lovable Losers."

Since that season, say close followers of the Cubs, the team has felt increasing pressure to win. In 2006, Chief Executive Office Andy McPhail left, the more aggressive Lou Piniella replaced easygoing Baker as manager, and investor Sam Zell took over the faltering Tribune Company. The team acquired expensive new talent in 2007, led by left fielder Alfonso Soriano. The Cubs captured division titles in 2007 and 2008, but they were swept out of the playoffs in both years. The failure in 2008 was especially disappointing, as it occurred on the centennial anniversary of the team's last World Series title.

Despite one of the best attendance records in baseball (3.3 million for the season, at near 100 percent capacity of 40,000-plus for every game), the financially troubled Zell sold the team prior to the 2009 season to the Ricketts family of discount stockbrokers for $900 million. It was the largest price ever paid for a North American sports franchise.

David Stevens

See also: Baseball, Major League; National Association of Professional Base Ball Players.

Further Reading

Claerbaut, David. *Durocher's Cubs: The Greatest Team That Didn't Win.* Dallas, TX: Taylor, 2000.

Gold, Eddie, and Art Ahrens. *The Golden Era Cubs.* Chicago: Bonus, 1985.

Golenbock, Peter. *Wrigleyville: A Magical History Tour of the Chicago Cubs.* New York: St. Martin's, 1996.

Holtzman, Jerome, and George Vass. *The Chicago Cubs Encyclopedia.* Philadelphia: Temple University Press, 1997.

Riess, Steven A. *Touching Base: Professional Baseball and American Culture in the Progressive Era.* Rev. ed. Urbana: University of Illinois Press, 1999.

Santo, Ron, with Randy Minkoff. *Ron Santo, for Love of Ivy.* Los Angeles: Bonus, 1994.

Shea, Stuart, with George Castle. *Wrigley Field: The Unauthorized Biography.* Washington, DC: Brassey's, 2004.

Curling

Curling is a popular winter sport played on ice that was introduced to North America by Scottish immigrants during the late eighteenth century. Curling is one of the oldest sports played today, evidenced by a curling stone dated to 1511 found in Stirling, Scotland. The term "curling" first appeared in Scotsman Henry Adamson's poetry in 1620. Canadian curlers organized many of the sport's earliest clubs, a reflection of the country's Scottish heritage, hosted its first tournaments (called "bonspiels"), and developed the game into its present form, in which Canadians are a world power. There are currently 1,200 Canadian and 140 American curling clubs.

Curling is a strategic game in which five-member teams—composed of a skip, vice, second, lead, and alternate—deliver stones down a sheet of ice into a "house," a series of rings resembling a bull's-eye painted on the ice. The object is to get the stone closest to the center ring.

The first recorded curling match in North America took place in 1760, when Quebec's 78th Highlanders curled on the frozen St. Charles River. The first North American curling club was the Royal Montreal, founded in 1807 by 20 merchants. It is the oldest active athletic club in North America. Another Quebec club was founded in 1821 in Quebec City. Scottish immigrants brought curling to English-speaking Ontario by establishing a Kingston curling club in 1820. By 1838, there were six clubs in Ontario, and the southern part of the province, which was accessible by rail travel, became the center of Canadian curling.

In the East, Nova Scotia's first curling club was established in Halifax during the winter of 1824–1825. Scottish immigrants organized Newfoundland's first curling club in St. John's in 1843. New Brunswick founded a curling club in Fredericton in 1854, and in 1887, Prince Edward Islanders began a curling club in Charlottetown.

In the West, the prairie's winter temperatures ensured a long curling season and allowed bonspiels to be planned in advance. Curling clubs sprouted up across Manitoba from Winnipeg (1876) to Emerson and Portage La Prairie (1880), Brandon (1883), and Stonewall (1884). In 1888, seven provincial clubs formed the Manitoba Branch of the Royal Caledonian Curling Club (later renamed the Manitoba Curling Branch), which one year later organized the Winnipeg Bonspiel. It was the most important Canadian curling competition until the "Brier" was established in 1927. Farther west, clubs were organized in Lethbridge (1887), Calgary (1888), and Edmonton (1888), Alberta; Regina, Saskatchewan (1889); and Kaslo, British Columbia (1905).

North American curlers, especially Canadians, have been at the forefront of developing the game's practical elements, such as stone refinements. During the late 1700s, Quebec curlers used irons, not rocks, that weighed from 45 to 65 pounds (20 to 29 kilograms) each—a practice that continued until 1955. However, round granite stones were the norm outside Quebec, and in 1879, Torontonian J.S. Turner developed a stone that suited most ice conditions. Based on his specifications, Andrew Kay of Ayrshire, Scotland, manufactured curling stones of equal weight and size, and the use of such stones became the universal practice.

Originally, straw sweepers were used to clear the snow off the frozen ponds and lakes on which the game was played. As brooms became part of the game, straw gave way to corn brooms and finally to brushes. The hacks—the fixed metal or rubber device from which the player's stone is delivered—also have undergone significant modifications to facilitate a more solid delivery of the stone. An early foothold was a piece of iron fixed into place with spikes dug into the ice. Another device, called a "crampit," fastened onto a player's boot. In the late 1800s, fixed hacks, originally made of wood or steel and then rubber, replaced the crampit and became universally employed.

A final major development in the game was the playing surface. Canadians constructed covered rinks in Montreal (1847), then in Toronto (1859), Hamilton (1860), Ottawa (1868), and Winnipeg (1876). These early rinks were 90 to 120 feet (27 to 37 meters) compared to the present-day standard of 146 feet (45 meters).

The presence of curling clubs throughout the nation led to the formation of the Canadian Curling Association in 1935. The association coordinates the major

Canadian curling championships, which include the national championship or the Brier (1927) for men and the Scotties Tournament of Hearts (1982) for women.

Curling became popular among Canadian women in the 1890s. In 1894, the Montreal Ladies Curling Club was established, probably the first women's curling club in the world. In 1900, there was a curling bonspiel between women from Montreal and Quebec. However, it was another dozen years before Ontario ladies' clubs were recognized by the Ontario Curling Association.

Curling was slower to penetrate the United States. The first American club was Michigan's Orchard Lake Club, formed in 1831. Later, curling clubs sprung up in Milwaukee (1845), Philadelphia and New York (1855), Boston (1856 and 1858), and Detroit (1865). In 1867, 12 clubs formed the Grand National Curling Club of America, which still exists today. The first U.S. national championship was held in 1957. The American sport is controlled by the U.S. Curling Association, formed in 1976 by the merger of the U.S. Women's Curling Association (1947) and the U.S. Men's Curling Association (1958).

The first curling match between Canada and the United States took place in 1865, when more than 50 Canadian and American curlers competed in Buffalo, New York. The first transatlantic curling games were played, appropriately, between Scottish and North American teams. Scottish curlers toured Canada and the United States from December 1902 to February 1903.

Canadians curlers toured Scotland in 1949 and again in 1959, this time as part of the World Curling Championship (originally called the Scotch Cup), which featured only Canadian and Scottish teams until 1962. Canadian men have won the gold medal 30 times and, since 1979, when women first competed, Canadian women have won 14 times. American men have captured the gold four times and the women once.

Curling debuted at the 1924 Olympic Games in Chamonix, France, but in 1932, 1988, and 1992, it was only a demonstration sport. Curling became an official medal sport at the 1998 Games in Nagano, Japan. Since then, Canadian men have taken home one gold medal in 2006 and two silver medals, and Canadian women captured the gold once in 1998 and the bronze twice. The United States has won only one bronze medal, in 2006.

Nathan Andrew Wilson

See also: Olympics, Winter.

Further Reading

Creelman, W.A. *Curling Past and Present*. Toronto, Canada: McClelland & Stewart, 1950.

Hansen, Warren. *Curling: The History, the Players, the Game*. Toronto, Canada: Key Porter, 1999.

Maxwell, Doug. *Canada Curls: The Illustrated History of Curling in Canada*. North Vancouver, Canada: Whitecap, 2002.

Mott, Morris, and John Allardyce. *Curling Capital: Winnipeg and the Roarin' Game, 1876 to 1988*. Winnipeg, Canada: University of Manitoba Press, 1989.

Pezer, Vera. *The Stone Age: A Social History of Curling on the Prairies*. Calgary, Canada: Fifth House, 2003.

Russell, Scott. *Open House: Canada and the Magic of Curling*. Toronto, Canada: Doubleday Canada, 2003.

Cycling

The history of bicycles and cycling in America—both for leisure and for competition—is marked by two great periods of enthusiasm separated by a long interlude of relative disinterest. The first period of enthusiasm began with the invention of the bicycle in the 1860s, intensified with the development of the easier-riding safety bike in the late 1880s, and continued into the early twentieth century. The second period began with the baby boom generation (born between 1945 and 1960), who rediscovered cycling in the 1960s and 1970s. Between those two periods, cycling lost its mass appeal to young adults, who turned to cars for transport, relegating the bicycle to the status of child's toy. Still, even during this period of lowered interest, a coterie of dedicated long-distance cyclists remained.

Origins and Technological Developments

The origins of the bicycle go back to German inventor Karl Drais's eponymous "draisine" of 1817, on which the rider sat and propelled himself or herself by pushing his or her feet along the ground, a kind of running cycle. In 1865, Frenchman Pierre Lallement attached pedals and cranks to the front wheel and created the velocipede, known as the "boneshaker." He obtained a patent, and the cycle enjoyed a brief fad in the late 1860s. Velocipede races attracted audiences of 5,000 and more to see riders compete indoors in races of up to a mile (1.6 kilometers) in length, reaching averaging speeds of 12 miles (19 kilometers) per hour.

Next came the hard-to-master high-wheel or ordinary bicycle, which held the stage in the 1870s and

High-wheel cyclists take the starting line for a race sponsored by the League of American Wheelmen in Niagara Falls, New York, in 1890. The advent of chain-driven safety bicycles at about that time led to a boom in cycling for both sport and recreation. *(Library of Congress)*

early 1880s. The $100 direct-drive bicycle had cranks and pedals connected right to the hub. But its design, with a very large front wheel to maximize speed and a tiny back wheel, made the vehicle inherently unstable, while the elevated seat made it difficult to mount.

Several inventions in the late 1880s contributed to the development of the so-called safety bicycle, including the chain wheel drive, which allowed for smaller wheels of equal size and a lower overall profile, and the pneumatic tire, which gave enthusiasts a more comfortable ride. The creation of this easier-to-ride cycle led to a hug fad, as upper- and middle-class riders took to parks, city streets, and country roads, both for leisure and for transportation.

With new bicycles in demand, manufacturers competed for brisk sales. Early bicycle makers soon would become prominent in the development of the automobile and the airplane, including Barney Oldfield and Henry Ford in auto building and the Wright brothers and Glenn Curtiss in aviation. Cycling also had an impact on social relations in the United States; access to bicycles gave women in particular new opportunities for

mobility, while the pastime provided a venue for young couples to court outside the purview of their parents.

Meanwhile, even before the safety bicycle came on the scene, enthusiasts were institutionalizing the sport of cycling, with the first club dedicated to the activity opening its doors in Boston in 1879 under the aegis of bicycle manufacturer Albert Pope. Like similar clubs that opened in the Northeast in those years, the Massachusetts Bicycle Club organized outings, exhibitions, and social events.

Pope was an evangelist for the new sport, publishing cycling magazines and helping to set up the first national organization, the League of American Wheelmen (LAW, now the League of American Bicyclists) in Newport, Rhode Island, in 1880. LAW not only tried to create enthusiasm for the sport but also fought for better roads and more access to those roads for cyclists. In addition, LAW published road maps for cyclists and evaluated routes and places to stay and eat, much as the American Automobile Association does today.

Early Competitive Cycling

The league also promoted competitive cycling. Although it became much more popular in Europe, bicycle racing has a long history in the United States. The first high-wheel bicycle race—a 50-mile (80-kilometer) endurance event won by English champion David Stanton—took place on an indoor track in New York City during the late 1860s. The development of the safety bicycle expanded the number of riders, including competitive ones, and led to an ever-expanding circuit of both indoor track and outdoor distance races.

By the early twentieth century, bicycle racers were among the highest-paid and best-known athletes in the country, with fans collecting trading cards of their favorites. Riders such as Charles "Mile-a-Minute" Murphy, who gained fame through stunts, such as racing against a train, followed a circuit of races that began in the Northeast in the late spring and continued on to events on the Pacific Coast in the late fall. Other well-known racers of the period included New Jersey's August Zimmerman, cycling's first world champion in 1893, who reportedly earned a total of $40,000 from events in the United States and Europe, and African American Marshall "Major" Taylor, who became the world champion sprint rider at a Montreal event in 1899.

Such events routinely brought out tens of thousands of fans to witness American riders beating out the best of Europe. With its first hosted Olympics—in St. Louis, Missouri, in 1904—America introduced cycling to the international sporting event. There, only Americans competed in the seven races, which ranged in length from 440 yards (402 meters) to 25 miles (40 kilometers).

So competitive for new records were some of the racers that they turned distant Salt Lake City, Utah, into a cycling mecca, as cyclists could ride slightly faster in the thinner air there. In 1901, John Chapman, known as the "Georgia Cyclone," joined with his major competitor, Iver Lawson, in Utah's capital to set a 5-mile (8-kilometer) tandem world record that stood for 50 years. Chapman became the undisputed "czar" of bicycle racing and a major supporter of the sport in Salt Lake City, drawing thousands of fans from around the country to watch races there.

Perhaps the most successful of American sprint bicycle champions was Frank Kramer, another New Jerseyan. Initially an amateur rider, Kramer won LAW's sprint championship in 1898 and the National Cycling Association title the following year. In 1900, taking Taylor's advice, Kramer turned professional, though he initially lost out to Taylor in their first competitive race. After that, however, Kramer seemed unbeatable, going on to win 16 straight sprint titles between 1901 and 1916. He also won the world championship in 1918 and 1921, earning an average of $20,000 a year, making him one of the highest-paid athletes in the world. But Kramer would be the last competitive American sprint racer. As his countrymen shifted their enthusiasm to automobile racing, Americans lost out to European riders in competitive cycling.

Six-Day Races

Long-distance racing, however, was another matter. Begun in England during the late 1870s, six-day bicycle races came to dominate American cycling from the 1890s to the 1930s, at least as far as public interest was concerned. In these contests, teams of two riders—one eating or resting while the other circled a steeply banked, one-sixth-mile (0.3-kilometer) wooden track inside a velodrome, or bicycle arena—pedaled continuously for six days, the winner being the team that covered the greatest distance in that time.

The six-day races combined the atmosphere of extravagant parties with a sporting venue, much like tailgating today. Men in suits and ladies in fancy dresses packed the stands. Singers performed and bands played day and night in the infield. The races at Madison Square Garden—the premier venue for six-day races in the country—attracted the entertainment and literary giants of the day.

Racers usually started out strong, often averaging 25 miles per hour. After a day's riding, however, saddle sores and stiffness in wrists, necks, arms, and legs began to take their toll. To keep the adrenalin flowing among the racers, and to maintain the interest and excitement for the spectators, promoters inserted designated sprints and prizes for teams that lapped the field. The spectators took part in the action by offering their own monetary prizes for sprints. Known as "premes," such prizes varied from several hundred dollars to several thousand dollars each, keeping the tempo up throughout the long days and nights of the race. Over the course of the six days, racers could cover more than 2,700 miles (4,345 kilometers), or only 300 miles less than the distance required to cross the country from coast to coast.

Newspapers reported the standings daily, including the number of miles ridden. Accidents were frequent, with most riders suffering minor injuries. Sometimes, however, the injuries were severe, with one rider dying after a splinter from the wooden track penetrated his chest following a crash.

Winners became national heroes. In 1925, Fred Spencer became the first racer to win both the national championship and a six-day race in one year. He and his partner, Bobby Walthour, Jr., journeyed to Washington, D.C., to meet President Calvin Coolidge. In the 1920s, racing promoter George "Tex" Rickard sponsored a banquet to honor the "Kings of Sport"; he gathered together baseball legend George Herman "Babe" Ruth, boxing's world champion Gene Tunney, tennis star Bill Tilden, golfing's Bobby Jones, hockey star Bill Cook, swimmer Johnny Weissmuller, and two cyclists—Spencer and Charley Winter.

The six-day race, however, soon went into decline. The Great Depression reduced attendance at the nation's velodromes, many of which seated 10,000 spectators or more. When fire destroyed the New York Velodrome and the wrecker's ball knocked down the decrepit Newark Velodrome, both in 1930, neither was replaced. The Grand Circuit ended, although six-day races continued at Madison Square Garden and in other venues around the country. The last race at Madison Square Garden, shortened to five days, took place in 1939.

Following World War II, promoters attempted to reestablish the multi-day races in New York and other North American cities, bringing over some of Europe's finest riders, including Hugo Koblet, the future 1951 Tour de France winner. However, the races never regained their popularity, and American cycling went into the doldrums.

Both amateur and professional racing suffered, making it difficult for Americans to compete internationally. Certainly a major obstacle to professional racing was the small prize; few racers could earn enough to live on. Still, there was the occasional breakthrough cyclist, such as Jack Heid, who won a bronze medal in the sprints at the 1949 world championship, the first for America since the early 1920s.

Long-distance racing, however, slowly was revived with the advent of the 4-mile (9-kilometer) Tour of Somerville in central New Jersey in 1940. Over subsequent decades, the tour became the most prestigious bicycle race in the country, drawing the biggest names in Olympic and professional cycling. Before he won his championships in the Tour de France during the late 1980s and early 1990s, Greg LeMond competed in the Tour of Somerville before thousands of spectators.

Indeed, by the 1980s, American racers also were beginning to compete again internationally in long-distance racing, though they remained largely unrepresented in Olympic style track racing. In 1981, Californian Jonathan Boyer became the first American to compete in the Tour de France, long-distance cycling's premier event, finishing thirty-second, though just five years later, LeMond became the first non-European to win the race. He would go on to win twice more at the Tour de France in 1989 and 1990. By far, the most successful long-distance American cyclist of the modern era was Texan Lance Armstrong, who won a record seven consecutive Tour de France titles from 1999 to 2005.

The modern era of competitive cycling also saw the development of ultra-long-distance races, most notably the Race Across America, begun in 1982 and dominated by American riders ever since. Riders in the ultra-marathon use lightweight, multigeared bicycles and travel with support crews who provide water, food, spare parts, and shelter. Unlike stage races, there are no designated rest periods. Riders begin in California, and the first one to cross the finish line at the Atlantic Ocean, approximately 3,000 miles (4,828 kilometers) away, wins. Riders are in the saddle up to 22 hours a day, completing the race in eight or nine days. In 1986, Pete Penseyres recorded the fastest men's time at 15.4 miles (27.8 kilometers) per hour over 3,107 miles (5,000 kilometers), with Seana Hogan recording the fastest woman's time in 1995, 13.23 miles (19.7 kilometers) per hour over 2,912 miles (4,686 kilometers).

Revival of Cycling

The growth in the popularity of competitive cycling since the 1980s owes much to the revival of adult recre-ational cycling since the late 1960s. As baby boomers came to value exercise, they looked for new forms of outdoor recreation. Cycling took off, aided by steeply higher gasoline prices in the 1970s, which encouraged people to abandon their cars for bicycles as daily transportation. The development of low-cost and lightweight aluminum-frame, ten-speed bicycles, which made climbing hills easier, added to the popularity of the sport. Between 1960 and 1975, the number of bicycles purchased in America quadrupled to more than 17 million units annually. Municipalities and states responded by developing bike lanes and dedicated bike paths in urban and rural areas.

The surge in cycling's popularity also spawned the invention of the mountain bike in 1981, which allowed riders to leave paved roads for wilderness trails. Inevitably, the spread of recreational off-road cycling led to a new form of competition, known as bicycle moto-cross (a somewhat nonsensical term adopted from off-road motorcycle racing), or BMX. First developed among young riders in California in the 1970s, the dirt track races have grown so much in popularity in the United States and worldwide that they became an official competition at the Beijing Olympic Games in 2008 with the U.S. team winning three medals.

Duncan R. Jamieson

See also: Armstrong, Lance; Taylor, Major.

Further Reading

Goddard, Stephen B. *Colonel Albert Pope and His American Dream Machines: The Life and Times of a Bicycle Tycoon Turned Automotive Pioneer.* Jefferson, NC: McFarland, 2000.

Harmond, Richard. "Progress and Flight: An Interpretation of the American Cycle Craze of the 1890s." *Journal of Social History* 5:2 (Winter 1971–1972): 235–257.

Herlihy, David V. *Bicycle: The History.* New Haven, CT: Yale University Press, 2004.

Nye, Peter. *Hearts of Lions: The History of American Bicycle Racing.* New York: W.W. Norton, 1988.

———. *The Six-Day Bicycle Race: America's Jazz Age Sport.* San Francisco: Cycling Publishing, 2006.

Ritchie, Andrew. "Amateur World Champion, 1893: The International Cycling Career of American Arthur Augustus Zimmerman, 1888–1896." *International Journal of the History of Sport* 22:4 (July 2005): 563–581.

———. *Major Taylor: The Extraordinary Career of a Champion Bicycle Racer.* Baltimore: Johns Hopkins University Press, 1996.

Strange, Lisa S., and Robert S. Brown. "The Bicycle, Women's Rights, and Elizabeth Cady Stanton." *Women's Studies* 31:5 (September–October 2002): 609–626.

Davis, Al (1929–)

Allen "Al" Davis was a self-made street kid from Brooklyn, New York, who worked his way up the coaching ladder to become chief executive and principal owner of the Oakland Raiders. He coached the American Football League (AFL) franchise and then became commissioner of the league until it negotiated a merger agreement with the National Football League (NFL) in 1966. He became the Raiders's coach in 1963, general manager in 1970, and managing general partner in 1972, wielding more hands-on authority than any other owner of his day. Davis helped produce one of the strongest teams in professional football, emphasizing the vertical game. He employed youthful, inexperienced coaches and often recruited players discarded by other teams. The formula worked. From 1967 to 1985, the Raiders won 13 division championships, made 15 playoff appearances, and won three Super Bowls (1977, 1981, and 1984), all the while burnishing a popular reputation as the "bad boys" of the NFL.

Davis was born on July 4, 1929, in Brockton, Massachusetts, to Louis and Rose Davis. Six years later, the family moved to Crown Heights in Brooklyn, where Louis Davis became a successful clothing manufacturer. From an early age, the younger Davis's goal was to manage and own a professional sports team. He got an early start at Erasmus Hall High School, where he managed the basketball team, before graduating from Syracuse University with a degree in English. Davis also played junior varsity football and basketball and attended varsity football practices to learn coaching techniques.

Davis was line coach at Adelphi College in 1950–1951. In 1952–1953, while serving in the U.S. Army, he coached the army team at Fort Belvoir, Virginia. Davis also worked briefly as a volunteer scout for the Baltimore Colts before becoming line coach at the Citadel in South Carolina. In 1957, he was named offensive end coach at the University of Southern California.

Davis started in the AFL in 1960 as the offensive end coach for the Los Angeles Chargers under the great head coach and offensive guru Sid Gillman. Three years later, co-owner Wayne Valley of the Oakland Raiders hired Davis as head coach and general manager, making him the youngest man to ever hold both positions simultaneously. The team improved from 1–13 in 1962 to 10–4 in 1963, and Davis was named AFL Coach of the Year. He coached for two more seasons, going 23–16–3 and creating a new image for the team as rough and intimidating. This was reflected in the team logo that he chose, which depicted crossed swords and a helmeted pirate with a patch over his eye. Davis's innovations included the "bump and run" tactic for his cornerbacks. His offenses mixed an aggressive running game with a liberal dose of long-distance passing.

Davis became AFL commissioner on April 8, 1966, and took an aggressive position against the NFL. His take-no-prisoners approach worried owners in both leagues, and the AFL owners finally went behind Davis's back to sign a merger agreement with the NFL. The junior league agreed to pay the NFL $26.75 million plus an additional indemnity of $2 million for the New York Jets and Oakland Raiders, both of which were located in NFL markets. Davis resigned as commissioner on July 25, 1966, soon after the agreement was announced.

He returned to the Raiders as head of football operations and bought a 10 percent interest in the franchise (then worth about $1 million) for $18,500. A great talent evaluator, he ran excellent drafts, made shrewd trades, and brought in veterans who were considered misfits or over the hill. In 1967, for instance, he traded for Buffalo Bills reserve quarterback Daryle Lamonica to run the passing game and brought in 39-year-old veteran quarterback George Blanda as placekicker and quarterback mentor.

In 1967, the Raiders, under head coach John Rauch, won the AFL championship, but they were crushed by the Green Bay Packers 33–14 in Super Bowl II. Rauch was tired of Davis's interference and quit to coach the Buffalo Bills. Davis then selected linebacker coach, 32-year-old John Madden as head coach. Madden led the Raiders to five American Football Conference title games in seven years, but the team lost them all. Finally, in 1976, the Raiders went 13–1 and won the 1977 Super Bowl, 32–14, over the Minnesota Vikings.

In the meantime, Davis went to Raiders co-founder E.W. McGah in 1972. McGah signed an agreement by which Davis became the managing general partner in place of Wayne Valley. Valley sued unsuccessfully to overturn the agreement and then sold his stock in 1976. Davis became the majority owner in 2005, buying out McGah's family and eventually gaining roughly two-thirds of the stock.

Madden retired after the 1978 season as the youngest NFL coach to win 100 games. Raiders assistant Tom Flores became the first Latino head coach in the NFL and led the team to Super Bowl victories in 1981 and 1984. He was succeeded by former Raiders star tackle and assistant coach Art Shell, the first African American head coach in the modern NFL. In 1997, Davis hired Amy Trask as the first woman chief executive officer of an NFL franchise.

Successful on the field, Davis courted controversy off it, doing whatever it took to enhance the commercial viability of his franchise, even when he ran foul of NFL Commissioner Pete Rozelle. Following the 1979 season, Davis tried unsuccessfully to increase revenues by getting the public Oakland–Alameda County Coliseum to build luxury suites in the stadium. When the public owners of the facility refused, Davis decided to move to Los Angeles, even though the Raiders had played 12 straight sellout seasons in Oakland. When other NFL owners blocked the move by a 22–0 vote, Davis filed an antitrust suit against the league and won a $35 million judgment, which he later settled for $18 million. In 1982, the Raiders moved to the Los Angeles Memorial Coliseum.

Already unpopular with his fellow owners, Davis angered them further when he alone supported the United States Football League's antitrust lawsuit against the NFL, instigated in 1984. The rival league won its case in 1986, but it was awarded just $1.

Meanwhile, Davis grew unhappy with the Los Angeles Memorial Coliseum, an ancient facility without luxury boxes and other amenities that was situated in a crime-ridden neighborhood—factors that made it difficult to earn money or sell out its 100,000-plus seats. Under NFL broadcast rules, this resulted in frequent blackouts of home games.

In 1987, Davis proposed moving to Irwindale, a tiny industrial suburb of Los Angeles, which agreed to a $155 million loan to construct a 65,000-seat stadium. The deal fell through, but Davis nevertheless managed to hold on to the first installment of $10 million. Next, Davis pursued a plan to build a stadium in Inglewood, near Los Angeles International Airport. Finally, in 1995, Davis moved the team back to Oakland and sued the NFL for sabotaging his effort to build the stadium in Inglewood. After a tortuous history in the courts, Davis's suit was rejected in 2007.

After the Raiders's return to Oakland, Davis seemed to lose his touch, employing inexperienced coaches whom he could intimidate, making poor choices in the NFL draft, and bringing in ineffective veterans. The team did not have a winning season until 2000, and then made it to the 2003 Super Bowl, losing 13–6 to the Tampa Bay Buccaneers. From 2003 through 2009, the club lost 11 games or more each season and then improved to 8–8 in 2010.

In 1992, Davis was inducted into the Pro Football Hall of Fame as an administrator. He received the first NFL Players Association's Retired Players Award of Excellence for his contributions, including his work toward a collective bargaining agreement while a member of the Executive Committee of the NFL Management Council in the late 1980s and early 1990s.

Steven A. Riess

See also: Football, Professional; Raiders, Oakland/Los Angeles.

Further Reading

Dickey, Glenn. *Just Win, Baby: Al Davis and His Raiders.* New York: Harcourt Brace Jovanovich, 1991.

Harris, David. *The League: The Rise and Decline of the NFL.* New York: Bantam, 1986.

MacCambridge, Michael. *America's Game: The Epic Story of How Pro Football Captured a Nation.* New York: Random House, 2004.

Ribowsky, Mark. *Slick: The Silver and Black Life of Al Davis.* New York: Macmillan, 1991.

Simmons, Ira. *Black Knight: Al Davis and His Raiders.* Rocklin, CA: Prima, 1990.

Davis Cup

The Davis Cup is the preeminent annual men's international team tennis tournament and the largest yearly sports competition in the world. It is run by the International Tennis Federation (formed in 1913), with competitors drawn from nations with a recognized tennis association or other such organization.

In 2010, 133 nations competed over a 12-month period, with the matches (called "ties") contested at numerous international sites. The competition began in the United States in 1900; U.S. teams have won 32 tournaments and have come in second 29 times, the best record of any nation. The women's equivalent of the Davis Cup is the Fed Cup, which began in 1963.

United States and the Davis Cup

The idea for the Davis Cup was conceived by Dwight Davis, a graduate of Harvard University, in 1899. An outstanding tennis player, he was the runner-up in the 1898 U.S. singles championship and won the 1899 national college men's singles title. Davis believed that an international team tennis championship would improve and promote goodwill among competing countries. The tournament initially was called the International Lawn Tennis Challenge.

After gaining support for the idea from the U.S. Lawn Tennis Association, Davis commissioned the design of a 13-inch (33-centimeter) sterling silver championship cup from the Boston firm of Shreve, Crump & Low. Davis devised the format for the team matches, which included four singles and one doubles contest. The defending champion nation was not required to play until the final, called the Challenge Round.

The first tournament was played in 1900, with only the United States and Great Britain as competitors. The U.S. team upset Great Britain, with Davis winning a singles match and playing as part of the winning doubles team, providing 2 of the 3 points needed to win the tie. There was no competition the following year, but in 1902, the United States again defeated Britain.

Beginning in 1904, more countries began to enter teams. The U.S. team did not win again until 1913, when it defeated Britain. The tournament was not held during World War I (1915–1918), and it resumed in 1919.

The greatest era for the United States was the 1920s. The U.S. squad was led by the world's top two players, Bill Tilden and Bill Johnston. The Americans captured the Davis Cup in 1920, and then repeated this success every year through 1926. During this time they won every Challenge Round by a score of 4–1 or 5–0. Tilden won 13 of his 14 singles matches, and Johnston won 11 of 12.

The only singles loss suffered by Tilden during the string of U.S. championships came in the final match of the 1926 Challenge Round, when he was upset in four sets by René Lacoste of France. This proved to be a sign of things to come. The next year, the French team defeated the United States 3–2 in the Challenge Round at Philadelphia.

After Johnston's retirement from tennis in 1927, Tilden could not carry the team. The United States lost the next three Challenge Rounds in Paris (1928–1930) to France. In 1931, Tilden turned professional, a bad sign for the Davis Cup, as it had been conceived as a tournament for amateur players only.

The U.S. team reached the Challenge Round in 1932, 1934, and 1935, only to lose each time. But in 1937, the Americans won the Davis Cup, led by the brilliant Don Budge, who was ranked number one in the world. Budge had emerged on the international stage in 1935, highlighted by a dramatic four-hour, five-set win over the number-two-ranked Jack Crawford of Australia in a Davis Cup preliminary match.

In the 1937 Inter-Zone Final (the tie prior to the Challenge Round), the U.S. team of Budge, Frank Parker, and Bitsy Grant came up against a powerful team from Germany that was led by Baron Gottfried von Cramm, the number two player in the world. The tie was deadlocked at 2–2 heading into the final match, between Budge and Von Cramm. Before the match, Von Cramm received a telephone call from German Chancellor Adolf Hitler, who urged him to win the match for the German Fatherland. The match that followed is considered one of the greatest ever.

The German came out fast and won the first two sets (6–8, 5–7). Budge rallied to take the next two sets (6–4, 6–2) to level the tally. In the final set, Von Cramm jumped out to 4–1, but Budge elevated his play, tying the set at 6-all, then winning 8–6 on his sixth match point. A week later in the anticlimactic Challenge Round, the United States won the Davis Cup from Great Britain. Budge returned in 1938 to lead the Americans to a successful defense of the Davis Cup against Australia before he turned professional.

Davis Cup competition was suspended during World War II (1940–1945), and when Dwight Davis died in November 1945, the tournament was renamed the Davis Cup in his honor. After the war, the United States captured the Davis Cup in four consecutive years (1946–1949) with teams that featured Pancho Gonzalez, Jack Kramer, and Ted Schroeder.

Australia dominated the competition from 1950 to 1967, winning the Davis Cup 15 times in 18 years.

The United States did surprise Australia in the Challenge Round at Sydney in 1954, as the team of Tony Trabert and Vic Seixas swept the first three matches to clinch the Davis Cup. In 1958, the Americans again upset the Aussies for a 3–2 win and the Davis Cup, behind the sensational play of Alex Olmedo, who was responsible for all 3 U.S. points.

The United States mounted an excellent team in 1963 that was led by Chuck McKinley (number two in the world) and Dennis Ralston. In a preliminary round against Venezuela, Arthur Ashe became the first African American to play for the United States in the Davis Cup tournament, capturing the last singles match. After wins over Mexico, England, and India, the U.S. team traveled to Australia for the Challenge Round, in which Ralston won a dramatic match in five sets over John Newcombe on the first day. After McKinley and Ralston won the doubles in an upset, McKinley clinched the Davis Cup for the Americans in the fifth and final match against Roy Emerson.

Davis Cup and Open Tennis

Tennis opened many of its tournaments to professional players in 1968, but the Davis Cup competition remained amateur. In 1972, the Davis Cup committee eliminated the Challenge Round format, requiring the previous year's champion to play through the entire tournament. The U.S. amateurs captured five straight Davis Cups (1968–1972) with teams led by Ashe and Stan Smith, who in 1972 swept all three of his dramatic final matches, leading the way to a 3–2 win over Romania before hostile crowds at Bucharest.

In 1973, the Davis Cup committee bowed to changes in the tennis world, opening the tournament to professionals. The United States did not win again until 1978 and 1979, with teams led by John McEnroe. After a loss in 1980, McEnroe and the Americans won twice more, in 1981 over Argentina and 1982 over France. McEnroe compiled an all-time U.S. record for singles play in Davis Cup competition with 41 wins and only eight losses.

Through the rest of the decade, U.S. teams lost; however, they attracted press attention because of the on-court antics and bad sportsmanship of McEnroe and Jimmy Connors. Also, as prize money increased in pro tennis, some top players refused invitations to play in the Davis Cup, which did not offer individual prize money.

The United States finally regained the Davis Cup in 1990 with a 3–2 win over Australia in the final that featured Andre Agassi and Michael Chang, each of whom won thrilling matches for a quick lead on the first day. After losing the 1991 final to France, the Americans regained the Davis Cup in 1992 with a win over Switzerland behind the play of Agassi and Jim Courier. The United States next won the Davis Cup title in 1995 with a 3–2 win over Russia, as Pete Sampras won all three of his matches in Moscow, including an exciting five-set contest on the first day and then a four-set win to clinch the Davis Cup on the final day.

After 11 winless years, the United States won its thirty-second Davis Cup championship in 2007 with a 4–1 victory over Russia in the final at Portland, Oregon. The Americans were led through the tournament by the brilliant singles play of Andy Roddick and James Blake. As of early 2011, the United States had not reached the final round since then.

Raymond Schmidt

See also: Gonzales, Pancho; Tennis; Tilden, Bill.

Further Reading

Collins, Bud, ed. *Total Tennis: The Ultimate Tennis Encyclopedia.* Kingston, NY: Sport Media, 2003.

Coombe, D.C. *A History of the Davis Cup: Being the Story of the International Lawn Tennis Championship, 1900–1948.* London: Hennel Locke, 1949.

Grimsley, Will. *Tennis: Its History, People and Events.* Englewood Cliffs, NJ: Prentice Hall, 1971.

Kendrick, Martyn. *Advantage Canada: A Tennis Centenary.* Toronto, Canada: McGraw-Hill Ryerson, 1990.

Trengrove, Alan. *The Story of the Davis Cup.* London: Stanley Paul, 1985.

De La Hoya, Oscar (1973–)

Nicknamed "Golden Boy" because of his good looks and his impressive string of victories, Oscar De La Hoya rose to prominence as a successful amateur boxer, demonstrating both devastating punching power and the skills of a complete boxer. While his professional career spanned most of the 1990s and the early 2000s, De La Hoya did not define himself only as a boxer. He also recorded albums, developed promotions and marketing interests through his Golden Boy Productions, and traded on his celebrity to become a bilingual spokesman for a variety of products and companies.

De La Hoya was born on February 4, 1973, in the Los Angeles suburb of Montebello to Mexican immigrants. He grew up in a tight-knit, working-class neighborhood in East Los Angeles. De La Hoya's father, Joel, Sr., worked as a warehouseman, and his mother, Cecilia, was a seamstress. Together, they raised De La Hoya and his older brother Joel, Jr., and younger sister Ceci.

In De La Hoya's youth, it was his brother who appeared to have inherited the boxing talent that was handed down through multiple generations of the De La Hoya family. His father fought professionally in the lightweight division, and his grandfather, Vicente, was an amateur featherweight boxer in the 1940s. At first, Oscar showed little aptitude or interest in boxing, but that soon changed. By his early teens, he began to evidence the boxing talent and punching prowess that would mark his amateur and professional years.

De La Hoya's amateur career culminated in a gold medal victory in the lightweight class at the 1992 Olympic Games in Barcelona—a victory he dedicated to his mother, who had died of breast cancer before the Games. By this time, his fans already expected excellence, as his amateur career was punctuated by many high points. De La Hoya won a national Golden Gloves title, a national amateur boxing championship, and a Goodwill Games title; he was named Boxer of the Year by the amateur governing body USA Boxing. Altogether, he won 223 fights, more than two-thirds by knockout, and had just five losses.

De La Hoya turned professional shortly after the Olympics and immediately began to tally victories over much more experienced fighters. A natural left-hander, he boxed flatfooted, staying primarily in the center of the ring, while looking for openings. He garnered derision in some quarters because of his boxing style and respect for his mounting number of victories over more classical-style Latino boxers, who try to maintain a distance from their opponents, using fast, long-range punches.

By November 1994, he had won two championships, the World Boxing Organization's super featherweight and junior lightweight titles. In 1995, *The Ring* magazine named De La Hoya Fighter of the Year and, in 1997, rated him the Best "Pound for Pound" Fighter in the world after he won the World Boxing Council's welterweight crown.

While De La Hoya's rise seemed uninterrupted to many observers, he had many setbacks and distractions. His personal life went through a period of turmoil that included sexual assault charges, palimony suits, and the birth of multiple children by three different women in 1998 and 1999. Throughout the 1990s, De La Hoya

changed managers and trainers, and he seemed to lose interest in the sport.

He also developed many interests outside boxing, including musical performance. In late 1999 and 2000, his boxing career seemed to stall with two high-profile defeats. At the same time, he released his first album, *Oscar,* which topped Billboard's Latin Dance charts for several weeks; "Ven a Mi," a single from the album, was nominated for a Grammy Award. In 2001, De La Hoya married Puerto Rican singer Millie Corretjer.

During the period from 1999 to 2004, De La Hoya fought a series of title bouts at varying weights, losing to welterweights Felix Trinidad once and Shane Moseley twice, both by decisions, and middleweight Bernard Hopkins in his only knockout loss. He earned respect from boxing fans even in his losses because of his willingness to challenge taller and faster boxers at higher weights. After a prolonged layoff, De La Hoya returned to the ring in 2006 to defeat Ricardo Mayorga and capture the World Boxing Council's light middleweight title.

De La Hoya was a controversial figure among Latino fight fans and commentators because of his boxing style and public persona, but he demonstrated the desire to test his skills against the best fighters of his era, including fabled Mexican welterweight champion Julio César Chávez. As a multiple world champion, De La Hoya surpassed the historic records of "Sugar" Ray Leonard and Thomas "Hit Man" Hearns by winning championship belts in six weight classes, from 130 to 160 pounds. This unprecedented achievement cemented De La Hoya's record in the annals of boxing. As a professional, he won 39 matches and lost six. His pay-per-view fights earned $700 million, the highest total of any fighter.

In early 2009, De La Hoya announced his retirement from the ring. Throughout his career, he had sought to strike a balance between his activities in the ring and his growing interests in media and sports promotion. Continuing in the latter field, he continues to be a notable sports figure and a celebrity of significant marketing and promotional value who can bridge the gap between mainstream and Latino audiences.

Fernando Delgado

See also: Boxing.

Further Reading

Delgado, Fernando. "Golden but Not Brown: Oscar De La Hoya and the Complications of Culture, Manhood, and

Boxing." *International Journal of the History of Sport* 22:2 (March 2005): 196–211.

Kawakami, Tim. *Golden Boy: The Fame, Money, and Mystery of Oscar De La Hoya.* Kansas City, MO: Andrews McMeel, 1999.

Rodríguez, Gregory S. "Boxing and Masculinity: The History and (Her)story of Oscar De La Hoya." In *Latino/a Popular Culture,* ed. Michelle Habell-Pallan and Mary Romero. New York: New York University Press, 2002.

———. "Saving Face, Place and Race: Oscar De La Hoya and the 'All-American' Dreams of U.S. Boxing." In *Sports Matters: Race, Recreation, and Culture,* ed. John Bloom and Michael Nevin Willard. New York: New York University Press, 2002.

Dempsey, Jack (1895–1983)

Jack Dempsey was the world heavyweight boxing champion from 1919 to 1926. Managed by Jack "Doc" Kearns and heavily promoted by George "Tex" Rickard, Dempsey's rise was a Roaring Twenties "rags to riches" story: He started as a relentless brawler from the Old West and became the richest boxer of his era. He was admired for his power, with early-round knockouts in 83 percent of his victories. Dempsey transformed the perception of professional boxing from a roughneck pastime to one cheered by sports fans nationwide.

He was born William Harrison Dempsey on June 24, 1895. His father, Hirum, had left West Virginia in 1880, heading west in search of a better life for his family. Hirum moved them from town to town in Colorado, including Manassa, a Mormon settlement, where "Harry" was born. The boy left home at 16 and roamed the region, working odd jobs by day, and seeking challengers for impromptu barroom fights for money at night. By 1914, he had settled in Salt Lake City to begin a career as a professional boxer and adopted the name Jack Dempsey, after an almost unbeatable Irish American middleweight champion who died in 1895.

Two years later, Dempsey moved to New York City. Encounters with crooked promoters left him physically depleted and broke, and he returned to Salt Lake City. While boxing throughout the West, Dempsey met manager John Leo McKernan, known as Doc Kearns, who took over Dempsey's career in 1917. Over the next two years, he guided the undersized heavyweight through a series of bouts that established Dempsey as the number one contender for the world championship, then held by Jess Willard.

Willard had won the championship title in 1915 by defeating the great Jack Johnson, but since then, he had defended his crown only once. After a lengthy search for a site (boxing was illegal in many states), Tex Rickard, the top promoter of the era, signed Willard and Dempsey to fight on July 4, 1919, in Toledo, Ohio. The champion outweighed Dempsey by more than 50 pounds (23 kilograms), but he was no match for the challenger's savage, lightning attack. After three punishing rounds, Willard did not answer the bell for the fourth round, and Dempsey was the new world champion.

Dempsey quickly became a national sports hero, overcoming a scandal over his draft exemption during World War I that was fueled by his ex-wife Maxine, who claimed that she could prove Dempsey was a draft dodger. He was exonerated, but the allegations of unpatriotic behavior would dog him for years. His first title defense took place a year after winning the championship, when he knocked out Billy Miske in three rounds, followed by a tough 12-round decision against Bill Brennan.

In Dempsey's first major title defense, on July 2, 1921, he faced French challenger Georges Carpentier in Jersey City, New Jersey. The fight produced boxing's first million-dollar gate, and the publicity before the fight swamped all other news stories. Carpentier, with his Continental charm and heroic war record, represented the European culture that had been devastated by World War I. Dempsey, by contrast, was the rough, undisciplined American—as untamed and strong as his homeland. In the lopsided fight, Dempsey was never threatened, and he knocked out Carpentier in the fourth round.

Dempsey did not defend his title again for two years. One reason was that the chief contender was African American Harry Wills, and the public opposed a title fight involving an African American challenger. Dempsey, or perhaps Rickard, drew the line against fighting Wills, although Dempsey later claimed that the real reason had been financial. Regardless of the reason, Wills never got the title shot that many, including the New York Boxing Commission, felt he deserved.

Another circumstance preventing a title bout was the fact that Rickard was mired in a legal battle involving charges of sex with underage girls. He was acquitted, but the trial occupied most of his attention in 1922.

For Dempsey's next title bout, a group of business leaders in Shelby, Montana, population 2,500, agreed to host a match with challenger Tommy Gibbons of St. Paul, Minnesota, on July 2, 1923, anticipating that the fight would draw spectators to the oil boomtown. They guaranteed Dempsey $300,000, but the organizers did not have the cash, and as fight day approached, it appeared that the contest might be called off. The uncertainty devastated attendance, and only about 8,000 to 12,000 spectators, including 4,000 gate-crashers, occupied the 40,208-seat arena.

Dempsey easily defeated Gibbons, but a number of Montana businessmen lost enormous amounts of money, creating the perception that Dempsey and his manager Doc Kearns, who both got their guarantees, had fleeced the organizers. In response, Doc Kearns and Dempsey sought a title defense that would restore the champion's reputation. Rickard signed Dempsey to defend his title against Luis Firpo of Argentina on September 14, 1923, at the Polo Grounds, home of baseball's New York Giants. The prefight publicity hyped the rivalry between the United States and South America.

The fight lasted less than two full rounds, but it created a raucous spectacle. Dempsey knocked Firpo down nine times in winning the bout, but he was knocked down twice himself—once landing in the first row of sportswriters. The scene was captured by artist George Bellows in his famous painting *Dempsey and Firpo* (1924). The furious action spread to the 80,000 spectators; amid the shouting, stomping, and collapsing benches, fans fought each other. Baseball star Babe Ruth reportedly punched welterweight boxing champion Mickey Walker.

The spectacle triggered two rule clarifications: First, a boxer knocked out of the ring had to return under his own power. Several critics felt that Dempsey had been boosted back into the ring by the sportswriters. Second, the knockout count would not begin until the standing fighter had moved to a neutral corner. Many spectators were horrified as Dempsey stood over Firpo after knockdowns and renewed his attack as soon as Firpo's knees were off the canvas.

From 1923 until 1926, Dempsey did not defend his title. Champions often remained inactive to build interest in the next title bout, but this was an unusually long period. During the hiatus, Dempsey married film actress Estelle Taylor Pencock on February 7, 1925. Their European honeymoon turned into a prolonged goodwill tour through which Dempsey earned the respect of the Continent's sports fans. He also gained fans and made money from appearances in films and on the vaudeville circuit.

Dempsey Versus Tunney: Two Classic Matches

By 1926, Dempsey was ready to defend his title against number one contender Gene Tunney, a former Marine and a skilled boxer from New York City. The fight, scheduled for September 23 in Philadelphia, matched boxers of contrasting styles. Tunney's defensive, intelligent style would challenge Dempsey's instinctive, relentless brawling. As Dempsey prepared for the fight, he did so without Doc Kearns's guidance; they had parted ways, mostly because of tension created by Dempsey's marriage. Tunney's style confounded Dempsey, and he easily defeated Dempsey in a ten-round decision to win the title.

Fans demanded a rematch, but at first, Dempsey was reluctant. When he relented, Rickard saw an opportunity for additional gate receipts. He matched Dempsey on July 21, 1927, against young challenger Jack Sharkey, with the winner to fight Tunney. Dempsey seemed to be repeatedly striking Sharkey with illegal blows below the belt. In the seventh round, Sharkey turned to the referee to complain, leaving himself defenseless, and Dempsey knocked him out with a left hook to the chin.

The Dempsey–Tunney rematch was set for Soldier Field in Chicago on September 22, 1927. More than 100,000 fans paid a total of $2,658,660 to attend—the largest gate for an event of any kind up until that time, and a record for a boxing match that stood for decades. After rumors that referee Davey Miller had promised gangster Al Capone that Dempsey would win, Miller was replaced by another official.

As in their first fight, Tunney skillfully avoided Dempsey's aggressive charges. Then, in the seventh round, Dempsey knocked the champion to the canvas. Rather than move to a neutral corner, as the rules required, Dempsey instinctively stood over Tunney, ready to press the attack. Referee Dave Barry had to shove Dempsey away to begin the count. Ringside observers estimated that this famed "long count" gave Tunney 14 to 17 seconds to recover. From there, Tunney avoided Dempsey for the rest of the round, and Tunney eventually won a second ten-round decision.

After the Tunney fight, Dempsey retired from professional boxing, even more popular after his first two defeats than before. In 1930, he and Estelle divorced. Dempsey appeared in countless boxing exhibitions and refereed professional wrestling matches. He enlisted in the U.S. Coast Guard during World War II and put to rest charges that he was a draft dodger by landing with U.S. troops on Okinawa, Japan, in 1945.

Dempsey opened a successful restaurant, Dempsey's, in New York City in 1935; it closed in 1974. He had two children by his third wife, Broadway singer Hannah Williams, whom he married in 1933. She died in 1943, and shortly afterward, he married Deanna Rudin Piatelli, who was at his side when he died in New York on May 31, 1983.

John Carvalho

See also: Boxing.

Further Reading

Dempsey, Jack, with Barbara Piatelli Dempsey. *Dempsey.* New York: Harper & Row, 1977.

Evensen, Bruce J. *When Dempsey Fought Tunney: Heroes, Hokum, and Storytelling in the Jazz Age.* Knoxville: University of Tennessee Press, 1996.

Kahn, Roger. *A Flame of Pure Fire: Jack Dempsey and the Roaring '20s.* New York: Harcourt Brace, 1999.

Kelly, Jason. *Shelby's Folly: Jack Dempsey, Doc Kearns, and the Shakedown of a Montana Boomtown.* Lincoln: University of Nebraska Press, 2010.

Rice, Grantland. *The Tumult and the Shouting: My Life in Sport.* New York: A.S. Barnes, 1954.

Roberts, Randy. *Jack Dempsey, the Manassa Mauler.* Baton Rouge: Louisiana State University Press, 1979.

Didrikson (Zaharias), Babe (1911–1956)

In 2000, the Associated Press and *Sports Illustrated* voted Babe Didrikson Zaharias the Outstanding Woman Athlete of the twentieth century. She was an Olympic champion, a multisport athlete, co-founder of the Ladies Professional Golf Association (LPGA), and a humanitarian. As a golfer, "Babe" won 82 tournaments over 18 years. She held and broke dozens of sports records and personified the fiercely competitive woman athlete.

Youth and High School

Mildred Ella Didriksen was born June 26, 1911, in Port Arthur, Texas, the sixth of seven children of Ole Didriksen, a seaman and cabinetmaker, and Hannah Marie Olson, who laundered clothes. An error in her school registration changed her name from Didriksen to Didrikson. The nickname "Babe" is said to have originated from the Norwegian word *baden* (baby), but Babe claimed that it was attributable to her Babe Ruth–like athletic skills. A 1917 hurricane forced the family's move inland to Beaumont, Texas. As a girl, Babe challenged boys at foot races, baseball, marble shooting, and jumping, shunning all girls' games. Her parents encouraged her athleticism with a backyard gym.

At David Crockett Junior High, she excelled in baseball, tennis, swimming, golf, diving, and basketball. The outstanding player on Beaumont High's Royal Purple basketball team, she was scouted by Colonel M.J. McCombs of the Employer's Casualty Insurance Company (ECIC) of Dallas for its Industrial League team. She was hired before graduating from high school and moved to Dallas. The insurance company paid her $75 a month, the bulk of which she sent home to help support her family.

At ECIC, she supposedly worked as a secretary, but actually she was a paid athlete for the company's Golden Cyclones team, which was composed of female employees who played basketball and softball and participated in track and field. Its roster had eight All-Americans, and the company's track and field team held two world records. Babe, at 5 feet, 6 inches and 140 pounds, was selected to the All-America team from 1930 to 1932. At the 1931 tournament, she scored 106 points in five games and led ECIC to a national championship. The team was renamed "Mildred Didrikson and Her Employers Casualty Girls." She returned briefly to Beaumont High to earn her diploma.

Babe also was a power-hitting softball star, played doubles tennis, and specialized in platform and springboard diving. Her multisport success was dazzling. At the 1930 national Amateur Athletic Union (AAU) championship meet in Dallas, she won the javelin, setting a U.S. record of 133 feet, 6 inches (40.69 meters). In 1931, she won the 80-meter (87-yard) hurdles in 12 seconds, an AAU record that stood for 18 years, and captured the broad jump championship with a distance of 17 feet, 11.75 inches (5.48 meters). She won the baseball throw in 1930 and 1931, the latter a world record at 296 feet (90.22 meters). She did not get along well with her teammates, however, who resented her grandstanding and the media coverage she received.

1932 Olympics and Beyond

Colonel McCombs entered Babe as a one-woman team in the 1932 national AAU championship in Evanston, Illinois, which doubled as the Olympic tryouts. She entered eight of ten events and won or tied six: shot put, 39 feet, 6.25 inches (12.05 meters), a U.S. record; baseball throw, 272 feet, 2 inches (82.96 meters); javelin, 133 feet, 5.5 inches (40.68 meters), breaking her own world record set in 1930; 80-meter hurdles, 12.1 seconds, having set a world record of 11.9 in a heat; broad jump, 17 feet, 6 inches (5.36 meters); high jump, 5 feet, 0.1875 inch (1.53 meters), tying for first place; and broad jump, 17 feet, 6 inches (5.36 meters). In three hours, she broke three world records and earned 30 points, beating the second-place Illinois Athletic Club's 22 points by herself.

She easily qualified for the 1932 Olympic Games in Los Angeles, but she was permitted to compete in only three events—an International Olympic Committee rule intended to protect women's "frail" physiology. She chose the javelin, 80-meter hurdles, and high jump. She emerged as the star of the Summer Games. Her javelin throw—143 feet, 4 inches (43.69 meters), an Olympic record—won the gold medal. She won the 80-meter hurdles in 11.7 seconds and set a world record. She also tied for first in the high jump against teammate Jean Shiley with a distance of 5 feet, 5.25 inches (1.66 meters); however, officials ruled that Babe had jumped head first over the bar rather than using the required "feet first" style. Shiley got the gold medal, and Babe received the only half-gold/half-silver medal in Olympic history. At the end of the year, the Associated Press selected her Woman Athlete of the Year the first of six times.

Didrikson, a heralded champion, garnered cruel press coverage that scorned her sexuality and her body. She was called the "Third Sex"—an accusation that pained her endlessly. After the Olympics, she barnstormed with the all-male House of David baseball team, pitched in exhibition games against major league greats, boxed against the middleweight champion's brother, and entertained on stage.

Pursuit of Golfing Excellence

Babe chose golf to elevate her social status, earn money, and regain her credibility as a legitimate athlete. She was tutored by golf pros, and in 1935, she toured with the renowned Gene Sarazen. She manipulated the press, kept her name in the headlines, and earned hundreds of dollars per match. However, she was not deemed a professional, as there was no women's professional golf organization at the time.

In 1935, Babe entered the Texas State Women's Golf Championship in Houston. She encountered hostile opposition from women golfers because of her

Widely regarded as the greatest woman athlete of the twentieth century, Mildred "Babe" Didrikson earned two gold medals at the 1932 Olympics (*above*), won a total of 55 professional golf tournaments, and excelled in basketball, swimming, and other sports. *(Getty Images)*

unpolished ways. Undeterred, she won the driving contest and the championship by one stroke. Shortly after, the United States Golf Association banned her from amateur competition because of the money she earned in baseball, basketball, and billiards.

Babe entered the Los Angeles Open—a men's Professional Golfers' Association (PGA) tournament—in 1938. She was paired with wrestler George Zaharias, who was known as the "Crying Greek from Cripple Creek." She missed the cut in the tournament, but Zaharias swept her off her feet. In January 1939, the two were married, and George became her manager, financial advisor, trainer, and traveling companion.

On tour in Australia, she came within one stroke of beating Charles Conners, the male Australian PGA champion. Back in America, George supported Babe and her family for three years, while she waited to regain amateur standing so that she could play golf against the leading amateur women. She studied tennis under Eleanor "Teach" Tennant and tried bowling, averaging 170 in Southern California league play. A crowd pleaser at golf exhibitions, she did trick shots and cavorted with the gallery.

After her amateur status was restored, Babe became a regular on the women's amateur circuit. In 1945, she won the Texas Women's Open by 13 strokes, the Western Open, and challenge matches in Los Angeles and San Antonio. She was honored as Woman Athlete of the Year. In 1946, she began a phenomenal streak of 13 consecutive tournament wins, including the U.S. women's amateur national championship. In 1947, she was the first American to win the British Ladies Amateur Championship.

Ladies Professional Golf Association

After her British Ladies Amateur Championship win, Babe turned professional. In 1948, she and several other female pros co-founded the Ladies Professional Golf Association, which was funded by Wilson Sporting Goods and Weathervane Clothing. In 1950, she won two-thirds of the LPGA tournaments, earning $14,800 in prize money. She also led the U.S. women to a 6–0 sweep in the Walker Cup against Great Britain. In 1951, she won 7 of 12 tournaments.

She was a relentlessly hard worker who practiced until her hands bled. Her drives were long, and her short game was precise. Babe's total earnings (including prize money, endorsements, sponsorships, movie and television shorts, and exhibition matches) surpassed $100,000, then a record for a woman athlete.

Babe began to distance herself from George, embarrassed by his domination, obesity, and loudness. At a San Antonio tournament in 1950, she met golfer Betty Dodd, who was 20 years younger and a rising star. They became inseparable and sexually intimate. George uneasily tolerated this arrangement, and the three lived together in the Zaharias' home in Tampa, Florida.

Babe was sidelined with a strangulated femoral hernia in 1952, but she stormed back to win the 1953 Texas Women's Open. She became so fatigued, however, that in April 1953 she sought medical help. Doctors diagnosed colon and rectal cancer. After surgery, she was told, falsely, that her cancer had been cured, a common practice among physicians at the time.

She regained her glory in 1954, winning five tournaments. (She won 41 LPGA tournaments in all.)

But in August 1955, Babe was hospitalized at the University of Texas Medical Branch in Galveston and underwent surgery for a herniated disk. Her pain actually was attributable to the spreading cancer. When she died on September 27, 1956, it was international front-page news. Her life was depicted in the 1975 movie *Babe,* which romanticized her stormy relationship with George, but made no mention of Betty.

Babe was not a self-conscious role model nor was she an advocate for women's advancement, but still she inspired countless women and broke ground for elite female athletes. She is the member of several halls of fame, including the National Track Hall of Fame (1974), the National Women's Hall of Fame (1976), the Texas Sports Hall of Fame (1954), the World Golf Hall of Fame (1951), and the World Sports Humanitarian Hall of Fame (2004). ESPN rated her tenth among all American athletes of the twentieth century.

Susan E. Cayleff

See also: Golf; Olympics, Summer; Track and Field; Women.

Further Reading

Cahn, Susan K. *Coming on Strong: Gender and Sexuality in Twentieth-Century Women's Sports.* New York: Free Press, 1994.

Cayleff, Susan E. *Babe: The Life and Legend of Babe Didrikson Zaharias.* Urbana: University of Illinois Press, 1995.

Johnson, William Oscar, and Nancy P. Williamson. *"Whatta-Gal": The Babe Didrikson Story.* Boston: Little, Brown, 1975.

Lenskyj, Helen. *Out of Bounds: Women, Sport, and Sexuality.* Toronto, Canada: Women's Press, 1986.

Zaharias, Babe Didrikson, as told to Harry Paxton. *This Life I've Led: My Autobiography.* New York: A.S. Barnes, 1955.

DiMaggio, Joe (1914–1999)

Joe DiMaggio, known as the "Yankee Clipper," was a major league baseball outfielder, considered by many the greatest center fielder of all time after his 13-year career with the New York Yankees (1936–1951). He was an outstanding hitter and fielder who starred on one of the most successful teams in baseball history, winning ten American League pennants and nine World Series. DiMaggio was renowned for his steady play, exemplified by a 56-game hitting streak in 1941, the longest in major league history to this day. After he retired, DiMaggio's renown continued to grow. He became an American cultural icon both for his consistent excellence on the field and his style off the field.

Giuseppe Paolo DiMaggio was born in Martinez, California, on November 25, 1914, the second-youngest of nine children of Italian immigrants Giuseppe DiMaggio, a commercial fisherman, and his wife Rosalie Mercurio. Quiet and moody as a youth, DiMaggio dropped out of Galileo High School in San Francisco in 1930 after just one year.

He was a natural athlete, and his older brother Vince already was playing minor league baseball. DiMaggio soon became a standout semiprofessional ballplayer in the San Francisco area. He hoped that his earnings would convince his father to set aside objections to having another baseball player in the family.

A superb natural hitter who needed little coaching, 17-year-old DiMaggio was signed by the San Francisco Seals of the Pacific Coast League near the end of the 1932 season, and he played the last three games of the year at shortstop. The next year, he became a full-time outfielder and compiled an amazing record for the season, batting .340 with 28 home runs and a league-leading 169 runs batted in (RBIs). Even more impressive was his streak of making a hit in 61 consecutive games—a new minor league record.

DiMaggio was scouted as a potential star by many major league clubs, but in 1934, he suffered a serious knee injury while stepping out of a taxi cab. He still hit 341 for the Seals, but his damaged knee prevented him from receiving any major league offers. Finally, the New York Yankees purchased his contract for $25,000 and five minor league players, and they agreed to let DiMaggio play in San Francisco for the Seals for one more year. DiMaggio responded by leading the Pacific Coast League in batting average (.398) and RBIs that

season, and he was named the league's Most Valuable Player (MVP).

When spring training opened for the 1936 season, DiMaggio reported to the Yankees, at a mature 21 years of age, standing 6 feet, 2 inches and weighing 193 pounds. The rookie joined an outstanding team that included future Hall of Famers Bill Dickey, Lou Gehrig, Vernon "Lefty" Gomez, Tony Lazzeri, and Charles "Red" Ruffing. He started in right field but soon moved to center field. DiMaggio quickly demonstrated outstanding natural instincts as a graceful outfielder, as well as uncanny batting skills, hitting for both power and average. In his rookie season, he posted a .323 batting average, slugged 29 home runs, and had 125 RBIs, as the team rolled to the American League pennant and a World Series win.

Yankee Stadium was a ballpark with deep center and left field fences, which usually hampered right-handed pull hitters such as DiMaggio. But in 1937, he convincingly demonstrated his power as he led the American League in home runs (46), slugging percentage (.673), runs (151), and total bases (418), while hitting .346 and driving in 167 runs. The Yankees won the pennant and defeated the Giants in the World Series.

With DiMaggio now recognized as a team leader, the Yankees extended their streak to four straight pennants and World Series wins in 1938 and 1939. The 1939 season was the first of several in which DiMaggio played while hampered by minor injuries, yet he still led the American League with a .381 batting average, was named the American League's MVP, and was selected as Player of the Year by *Sporting News*.

That year, DiMaggio married Dorothy Arnold, a Hollywood starlet whom he had met while appearing in a movie. They had one son during their five-and-a-half-year marriage.

In 1940, DiMaggio seized his second batting championship with an average of .352. That season, however, the Yankees finished third behind the pennant-winning Detroit Tigers.

The 1941 season was notable for the hitting duel staged throughout the summer by DiMaggio and Ted Williams of the Boston Red Sox. Williams won the batting crown with an incredible .406 average, yet DiMaggio posted an impressive .357 average while leading the league with 125 RBIs. The most compelling story of 1941, however, was DiMaggio's 56-game hitting streak. It began on May 15 and did not end until July 17 against the Cleveland Indians, when a pair of sensational defensive plays by third baseman Ken Keltner turned away DiMaggio's bid to extend the streak.

The next day, he started a new 17-game streak. During his record streak, a mark that rarely was threatened in the next 60 seasons, DiMaggio had 91 hits in 223 at bats for a .408 average. The Yankees captured the pennant. DiMaggio was voted the MVP and was named Male Athlete of the Year by the Associated Press.

The 1942 season was a disappointment: DiMaggio hit only .305, and the Yankees lost their only World Series during his tenure. Baseball was overshadowed that year by American involvement in World War II, and in 1943, DiMaggio enlisted in the U.S. Army, where he served as a physical education instructor. He missed three full seasons—as did many other major league players—returning to the Yankees for the 1946 season.

Through the remainder of his career, DiMaggio never matched the eye-popping statistics of his early years. In 1946, he hit only .290 with 25 home runs, and the Yankees finished well behind Boston in the American League pennant race. The Yankees bounced back in 1947, and DiMaggio hit .315 with 20 home runs, leading the team to another pennant and a World Series win over the Brooklyn Dodgers. That year, DiMaggio won his third MVP award.

The 1948 season was a rare disappointment for the Yankees, who finished two games behind in the pennant race. DiMaggio demonstrated that he still could hit with power, though, as he led the American League with 39 home runs and 155 RBIs. During the season, DiMaggio was bothered by a bone spur in his right heel and underwent surgery that fall. When he reported to spring training in 1949—having signed the first-ever $100,000 contract—the heel had not fully recovered, and his playing too soon likely shortened his career. DiMaggio was limited by injury to just 76 games in 1949, yet he posted a .346 batting average to help the Yankees to another pennant by just one game over the Red Sox.

DiMaggio bounced back in 1950 to hit 32 home runs and 122 RBIs, and he posted a league-leading .585 slugging percentage. The Yankees won another pennant and defeated the Philadelphia Phillies in the World Series in four straight games. It was DiMaggio's last big season.

In 1951, injuries kept him on the bench; he managed only 12 home runs and a .263 average. The Yankees, reinforced by great younger players, such as 19-year-old rookie Mickey Mantle, won still another pennant and defeated the New York Giants in the World Series. After these victories, DiMaggio announced his retirement. The next season, he was replaced in center field by Mantle.

DiMaggio posted some impressive statistics during his 13 seasons, including 2,214 career base hits and a .325 batting average. He also finished with 361 home runs, 389 doubles, 131 triples, and 1,537 RBIs. He started in nine All-Star games, selected to the team in every season in which he played. In ten World Series, he rapped out 54 hits, including 8 home runs, and drove in 30 runs. Experts agree that hitting in his home park hurt his power numbers more than any other ballplayer in history.

In 1952, DiMaggio met the glamorous Hollywood actress Marilyn Monroe, and the couple married on January 14, 1954. However, DiMaggio, who had been the center of attention for years, was uncomfortable with his new wife monopolizing the limelight. He also became upset over some of her movie scenes, which he considered a personal embarrassment, and they divorced in October. They remained lifelong friends, and DiMaggio always considered Marilyn his greatest love.

After some time out of the spotlight, DiMaggio returned to the sporting world with personal appearances at old-timers games and conventions, which by the 1980s expanded into lucrative autographing appearances at memorabilia shows. From 1968 to 1989, he served as a part-time coach and front office executive with the Oakland Athletics. In the 1970s, his renown grew as he appeared in a series of television commercials for the Bowery Bank (1972–1992) and as a representative for a new coffee maker called Mr. Coffee. He also was part owner for many years of a restaurant on San Francisco's Fisherman's Wharf known as DiMaggio's.

Despite a reputation for being moody and aloof, DiMaggio's legendary status continued to grow throughout his retirement years. Ernest Hemingway's protagonist Santiago (*The Old Man and the Sea,* 1952) idolized DiMaggio for his resilience and courage. In 1955, DiMaggio was inducted into the Baseball Hall of Fame, and in 1969, he was voted the Greatest Living Player in a poll of sportswriters and fans.

DiMaggio's place as an American cultural icon was cemented for all time in 1967, when he was featured in the lyrics of the song "Mrs. Robinson" by Paul Simon, who regarded him as a national hero who had consistently performed with skill and grace. After a lengthy illness, DiMaggio had surgery for a lung tumor in early 1999. He never fully recovered and died at his home in Hollywood, Florida, on March 8, 1999.

Raymond Schmidt

See also: Baseball, Major League; Yankees, New York.

Further Reading

Cramer, Richard Ben. *Joe DiMaggio: The Hero's Life.* New York: Simon & Schuster, 2000.

De Gregorio, George. *Joe DiMaggio: An Informal Biography.* New York: Stein and Day, 1981.

Fetter, Henry D. *Taking on the Yankees: Winning and Losing in the Business of Baseball, 1903–2003.* New York: W.W. Norton, 2003.

Moore, Jack B. *Joe DiMaggio: Baseball's Yankee Clipper.* New York: Praeger, 1987.

Sanford, William R., and Carl Green. *Joe DiMaggio.* New York: Crestwood House, 1993.

Seidel, Michael. *Streak: Joe DiMaggio and the Summer of '41.* New York: Penguin, 1989.

Disability Sports

Disability sports, referred to in the past as "sports for the disabled" or "sports for the handicapped," has expanded since World War II to become a global phenomenon. The highest level of competition, the Paralympic Games (now taken to mean "parallel to the Olympics"), is second only to the Olympic Games in the number of athletes who participate.

The United Kingdom, Canada, and the United States all have contributed significantly to the development of disability sports, and all currently produce a number of top-level athletes. In North America, national and regional sports organizations are devoted to people with a range of disabilities, including blind, deaf, amputee, wheelchair, and dwarf sports organizations. Organizations also support athletes with cerebral palsy, intellectual disabilities, as well as disabilities that do not fit into the other groups (known as *les autres,* or "the others"), such as polio or muscular dystrophy.

Origins of Disability Sports

It is almost impossible to untangle developments in disability sports in North America from the place of people with disabilities in society more generally, or from developments in disability sports on the international stage. Prior to the twentieth century, disabled people were not considered fully participating members of society. They depended on their families, lived in institutions, or were left to fend for themselves, often with limited prospects. There were few, if any, sporting or recreational options for people with disabilities.

During the mid- to late 1800s, forms of play, games, and sports were adopted in some of the more progressive institutions for children with visual and hearing impairments. Sports clubs for people with hearing impairments also arose in various European nations in the late nineteenth century, including Belgium and Germany.

There is evidence that sports were used as a form of medical therapy for disabled veterans during World War I. Sporting activities were included as part of more general programs of rehabilitation prescribed at leading institutions such as the Walter Reed Hospital in Washington, D.C., and Hart House in Toronto, Canada. The first International Silent Games for the deaf were held in Paris in 1924; however, major developments in disability sports beyond the deaf community would await the end of World War II.

Post–World War II Era

Disability sports expanded in the late 1940s as disabled veterans returned to their home countries. At the Stoke Mandeville Hospital in England, Ludwig Guttmann prescribed exercise, then wheelchair polo and wheelchair basketball for veterans with spinal cord injuries. The hospital organized a set of wheelchair games in 1948, which evolved into an annual international sports festival under the auspices of the International Stoke Mandeville Games in the 1950s. However, the focus of disability sports in Great Britain remained primarily on medical well-being into the 1970s.

Similar developments occurred in the United States and Canada, although veterans organized most of the initial effort themselves, leading to a greater focus on participation and competition rather than the therapeutic benefits of sports. Wheelchair basketball was organized in 1945 at the Corona Naval Station in California, and within three years, there were six touring teams. In 1949, Tim Nugent organized the first wheelchair basketball tournament at the University of Illinois, which gave birth to the National Wheelchair Basketball Association.

The 1950s and 1960s brought further organization and expansion of disability sports competition at the regional, national, and international levels. In 1957, the Paralyzed Veterans Association of the United States hosted the first national wheelchair games, capitalizing on the expansion of wheelchair sports beyond basketball. The National Wheelchair Sports Association was formed shortly thereafter. Three years later, the first "Paralympics" games were held in Rome following the

Eunice Kennedy Shriver (*right*), founder of the Special Olympics in 1968, encourages a long jumper at the 1983 competition. Special Olympics events attract millions of participants from more than 160 nations. *(Time & Life Pictures/Getty Images)*

Summer Olympics. Though the games offered only competition for wheelchair users, the events took place in the same facilities used for the Olympics.

Further examples of the expansion of disability sports include the 1964 establishment of the International Sports Organization for the Disabled, serving amputee, blind, and cerebral palsy athletes; the 1967 founding of the National Handicapped Sport and Recreation Association (now Disabled Sports USA), which focused on skiing for amputees and wheelchair users; and the first Pan-American Wheelchair Games in Winnipeg, Canada, in 1967. Much of the expansion of disability sports occurred in tandem with the burgeoning disability rights movement in the 1960s and increasing social advances for the disabled.

The creation of the Special Olympics was a milestone in disability sports. In the early 1960s, Canadian physician Frank Hayden developed fitness programs for people with intellectual disabilities. His work came to the attention of Eunice Kennedy Shriver, who was inspired to found an international athletic competition for people with intellectual disabilities. The first Spe-

cial Olympics Games, held at Soldier Field in Chicago in 1968, hosted 1,000 U.S. athletes and one Canadian floor hockey team. Currently, more than 1 million participants in 160 countries take part in Special Olympics competitions. It is a participatory movement, with awards for all athletes and for volunteer "huggers." The Special Olympics often are confused with the Paralympics, an elite-level sporting event that is intended primarily for people with physical rather than intellectual disabilities.

The Movement to Elite-Level Sports

Over the last three decades of the twentieth century, disability sports transitioned from a focus on medical therapy toward elite-level competition. One of the forces behind this change was the hiring of athletes with disabilities in significant organizational and administrative positions within national and international sports organizations.

The 1970s and 1980s was a period of both coming together and fragmentation within disability sports. As opposed to "mainstream" sports organizations, which generally focus on a single sport, disability sports associations tended to be formed on the basis of disability, overseeing athletes with particular disabilities in a variety of sports. The 1976 Paralympic Games in Toronto, also called the "Olympics for the Disabled" or the "Torontolympiad," brought together for the first time visually impaired and amputee athletes with wheelchair users.

This prompted calls for the creation of an umbrella organization, and the International Coordinating Committee of World Sports Organizations for the Disabled (ICC) was established in 1982. However, the ICC suffered from infighting and organizational difficulties, and in 1989, it was replaced by the International Paralympic Committee (IPC). Canadian university professor and sports administrator Robert Steadward was elected the IPC's first president. He served in that capacity until 2001, steering the movement through a period of substantial expansion and growing public awareness.

In 1988 (Seoul) and 1992 (Barcelona), the Paralympic Games were held shortly after the Olympic Games in the same facilities, thanks to the goodwill of the Olympic organizing committees. This became the organizational model, followed—sometimes with resistance, as in Atlanta (1996)—by every Olympic organizing committee since then. Agreements signed between the IPC and the International Olympic Committee in 2001 entrenched the organization of both sets of games in the host city until 2012. Hosting the Paralympics along with the Olympics is an integral part of the bid and planning process, evidenced by the Winter Games in Salt Lake City (2002) and Vancouver (2010).

Since the 1980s, athletes with disabilities increasingly have been integrated into able-bodied sports competitions. Wheelchair racing first appeared as a demonstration sport at the Summer Olympics in Los Angeles in 1984. The Commonwealth Games moved toward offering full medal status for athletes with disabilities in the 2000s. At the Commonwealth Games in Melbourne in 2006, highly decorated Canadian wheelchair racer Chantal Petitclerc became the first athlete with a disability to bear the flag for an integrated team.

The U.S. Olympic Committee and the U.S. Paralympic group are integrated, with athletes training side by side at high-performance centers, and there are strong connections between the Canadian Olympic Committee and the Canadian Paralympic Committee. Many of the national sports federations, such as those in swimming

and athletics, also have been integrated. Integration is a subject of some debate within the disability sports community: some argue that the focus should be on stronger disability sports, and that athletes with disabilities remain "second-class citizens" in integrated programs when it comes to funding and training opportunities.

As in able-bodied sports, there are a variety of recreational, mass participation, and elite-level sports organizations for people with disabilities in North America. And, as in able-bodied sports, the majority of funding goes to elite-level sports rather than grassroots organizations. Yet the public still sees disability sports as medically oriented or participatory. Public perceptions of athletes with disabilities, exacerbated by a lack of media coverage, remain a challenge for disability sports in North America at all levels.

Despite significant challenges and ongoing debates, disability sports in North America and globally stands alongside, and is becoming more integrated with, able-bodied sports from the grassroots to the elite. Currently, there are diverse opportunities in sports for people with disabilities at all levels, a possibility that would have been unimaginable just 30 years ago.

Fred Mason

See also: Government, U.S.

Further Reading

Bailey, Steve. *Athlete First: A History of the Paralympic Movement.* Chichester, UK: Wiley, 2008.

De Pauw, Karen P., and Susan J. Gavron. *Disability Sport.* 2nd ed. Champaign, IL: Human Kinetics, 2005.

Gregson, Ian. *Irresistible Force: Disability Sport in Canada.* Victoria, Canada: Polestar, 1999.

Howe, David. *The Cultural Politics of the Paralympic Movement.* New York: Routledge, 2008.

Joukowsky, Artemis A.W., and Larry Rothstein. *Raising the Bar: New Horizons in Disability Sport.* New York: Umbrage, 2002.

Mastandrea, Linda, and Donna Czubernat. *Sports and the Physically Challenged: An Encyclopedia of People, Events, and Organizations.* Westport, CT: Greenwood, 2006.

Diving

The modern sport of diving features athletes who jump from a springboard or platform, perform a series of acrobatic maneuvers, and then plunge headfirst or feetfirst into a pool of water. Diving first emerged as a serious athletic discipline in Europe during the nineteenth and early twentieth centuries, with the emphasis shifting fairly quickly from strength and power to skill and agility. In its modern form, it is an exceedingly difficult sport to master. As one sportswriter observed, diving "demands acrobatic ability, the grace of a ballet dancer, iron nerve, and a liking for heights." This is a sport the United States used to dominate in the Olympics, with 131 out of 320 medals awarded, including 48 out of 106 gold; however, the tide has turned, and the U.S. team has not won a single medal since 2000.

Diving has been practiced as a leisure activity for thousands of years. The Tomba del Tuffatore (Tomb of the Diver), for example, was constructed in modern-day Italy around 480 B.C.E. Its walls feature images of men diving from platforms. Greek and Roman literature from 500 B.C.E. to 500 C.E. also contains references to diving, and there are several civilizations in South America and the Polynesian Islands that have traditions of diving dating back many centuries. The modern version of the sport first developed in Germany and Sweden, where athletes would take pieces of gymnastic equipment to the beach and use them to perform stunts prior to entering the water. As early as 1843, German authors published books on the subject.

In 1883, the first organized diving competitions were held in Great Britain. These contests featured a style of diving known as "plunging." Participants would launch themselves forward with as much momentum as possible, landing in the water and remaining face down for one minute. The diver who traveled the longest distance during that minute was the winner; large, heavyset men were at a distinct advantage. Plunging competitions survived until the 1940s, and plunging was even an Olympic sport on one occasion (in 1904). Preeminent among all plungers was Briton Frank Parrington, whose 1933 record of 26.4 meters (28.9 yards) still stands.

Though plunging was popular, it did not take long for the German and Swedish style of diving—which featured somersaults, twists, and other graceful maneuvers—to assume preeminence on the world stage. Springboard diving, in which participants launch themselves from a flexible board that is mounted relatively close to the water—usually 3 or 5 meters (3.2 or 5.5 yards)—became an Olympic sport in 1904. Platform diving, in which participants jump from a rigid board that is mounted higher in the air, usually 10 meters (11 yards), was added to the Olympic program in 1906. Although diving bears more resemblance to gymnastics than it does to other water sports, it nonetheless was placed under the auspices of the International Federation of Aquatics, founded in 1908. Shortly after, in 1912,

women divers were allowed to participate in the Olympics for the first time.

Once diving was an official Olympic sport with a governing body, participants flocked to the sport, exploring the possibilities of what could be done while traveling through the air. In addition to the two different types of diving boards, many different types of dives emerged. Divers can begin their dive facing forward or backward, or even standing on their hands. They can rotate forward or backward, doing as many as three somersaults during one dive. They can twist laterally, again, doing so as many as three times during one dive. They can assume one of five different positions during the dive: straight, pike (bent in half at the waist), tuck (folded into a tight ball), free (some combination of pike, straight, and tuck during a twisting dive), or flying (shifting from straight to pike and tuck during a dive). Given this broad variety of options, there are more than 100 specific dives that are recognized formally in competition today, each of which is assigned a degree of difficulty.

Naturally, procedures for scoring dives vary from place to place and from era to era. Generally speaking, divers are evaluated by a panel of five to seven judges who award a score of 1 to 10—10 being highest—based on approach, takeoff, execution, and entry into the water. The highest and lowest scores are discarded, and the remainder are combined and then multiplied by the dive's degree of difficulty, which ranges from 1.2 to 3.5. The perfect score from a panel of seven judges, then, is 175, denoting perfect execution of the most difficult dive.

Given their role in developing the sport, it is not surprising that Swedes and Germans dominated diving in its early years. After World War I, however, Americans seized control, thanks in large part to the excellent diving programs at many of the nation's universities. Between 1920 and 1968, American men and women won 94 of the 120 Olympic medals awarded for diving, a staggering total. The best-known diver of this period is Pat McCormick, who won the women's springboard and platform competitions in both the 1952 and 1956 Olympics. She was the first diver to take home gold medals in consecutive Olympics.

The most famous of all American divers is Greg Louganis. Bursting onto the scene as a 16-year-old in 1976, he took home a silver medal in platform diving. As the United States boycotted the 1980 Olympic Games in Moscow, Louganis was unable to compete as a 20-year-old. However, he returned in both 1984 and 1988 to win gold medals in the men's springboard and platform competitions, leaving him with a career total of five medals. His medal-winning springboard performance in 1988 was particularly dramatic, as he had seriously injured himself by hitting his head on the board during a preliminary dive.

Since Louganis's time, the United States's iron grip on the sport of diving has weakened, with China taking over as the world's power. This has been particularly the case in synchronized diving, a newer form of the sport in which two divers jump concurrently from side-by-side platforms; they are judged on the degree to which they remain in sync with one another. The 10-meter and 3-meter synchronized diving events were added to Olympic competition in 2000; since that time, Americans have not claimed a single Olympic medal in the discipline.

Indeed, Americans have only claimed one Olympic diving medal of any sort since the introduction of synchronized diving—Laura Wilkinson's gold in the 10-meter platform dive at the 2000 Olympic Games. The trend seems unlikely to reverse itself anytime soon; cuts in funding for college athletics have led to the elimination of many collegiate diving programs, the training ground for most of the great American divers of the twentieth century. Without them, the United States has little hope of matching the significant investments being made by China and, to a lesser extent, Russia and Australia.

Christopher G. Bates

See also: Swimming.

Further Reading

Louganis, Greg. *Breaking the Surface.* New York: Random House, 1995.
O'Brien, Ronald. *Springboard and Platform Diving.* Champaign, IL: Human Kinetics, 2003.
Rackham, George. *Diving Complete.* London: Faber and Faber, 1975.

Dodgers, Los Angeles/ Brooklyn

The Dodgers are one of the oldest teams and most successful franchises in professional baseball history, beginning in 1883 in Brooklyn, New York, and moving in 1958 to Los Angeles as one of the first two major league teams west of St. Louis. In Brooklyn, the team struggled during its early years, with modest rosters sometimes better known for their eccentric players rather than for their skills. In the 1940s, the Dodgers became one of the finest clubs in the majors, dominating the National League from 1947 to 1955. They were the first team to play an African American in the modern era, when Jackie Robinson started for the club in 1947. After moving to Los Angeles, the Dodgers enjoyed some of the highest attendance in all of professional sports and mixed success on the field.

Origins

Beginning in the 1850s, the city of Brooklyn was a hotbed of baseball and home to several outstanding teams, including the Atlantics and the Excelsiors of the 1860s. The Dodgers were founded in 1883 by real estate magnate Charles Byrne as part of the Interstate League and became a major league team in 1884 when they joined the American Association. The team originally was known as the Atlantics, then the Grays in 1885, and the Bridegrooms in 1888 (when four players got married around the same time). In 1889, they won the American Association pennant, and one year later, they captured the National League (NL) pennant.

In 1891, the club moved to Eastern Park. There, they soon were nicknamed the "Trolley Dodgers," as fans had to avoid the nearby trolley lines on their way to the field. In 1898, architect and politician Charles Ebbets became president of the team. His co-owners also controlled the Baltimore Orioles, and they bolstered the Brooklyn team in 1899 by shifting the Orioles's best players to the Brooklyn squad, which became known as the Superbas. The team took the NL championships in 1899 and 1900.

In 1913, the team began play at Ebbets Field, one of the first steel-and-concrete stadiums in baseball. The team was renamed the "Robins" during the tenure of manager Wilbert Robinson (1914–1931), and then the name reverted to the Dodgers. The Robins captured the NL pennant in 1916 but lost the World Series to the Boston Red Sox in five games. They won a second pennant in 1920 but again lost the Series, this time to the Cleveland Indians, five games to two. Thereafter, they became a mediocre second-division squad. Sports cartoonist Willard Mullins depicted them as "Dem Bums," an epithet that stuck for decades.

In 1938, Larry McPhail was named general manager of the Dodgers. He implemented several key innovations, most notably remodeling cozy Ebbets Field and introducing night baseball to Brooklyn. He also hired

Members of the Los Angeles (formerly Brooklyn) Dodgers are introduced to the hometown crowd before their first game in L.A., on April 18, 1958. The Dodgers beat the San Francisco Giants, 6–5. *(Sports Illustrated/Getty Images)*

play-by-play announcer Walter "Red" Barber as the radio voice of the team. Barber stayed through 1953.

McPhail built up the Dodgers's farm system. In 1941, the team won its first NL pennant in two decades, but they lost the World Series in five games to its crosstown rival, the New York Yankees. McPhail joined the military in 1942, and he was succeeded as general manager by Branch Rickey, who had built the St. Louis Cardinals into a league powerhouse.

In October 1945, Rickey signed African American Jackie Robinson to a Dodgers contract. After one season with the team's farm club in Montreal, Robinson joined the Dodgers on April 15, 1947, becoming the first African American to play in the major leagues since 1884.

Rickey's decision to bring up Robinson was highly controversial with other team owners, some Dodgers players, and opposing teams. Though he faced insults and threats from fans and opponents, Robinson persevered, and he was named Rookie of the Year. He helped the team finish in first place; they lost the World Series to the Yankees in six games.

Robinson soon was joined on the Dodgers by other African Americans, including catcher Roy Campanella and pitcher Don Newcombe. Their examples helped persuade other major league teams to sign African Americans.

The Dodgers captured four pennants between 1947 and 1953 with an outstanding lineup that featured Robinson, Campanella, Harold "Pee Wee" Reese (shortstop), Gil Hodges (first baseman), Carl Furillo (right field), and Edwin "Duke" Snider (center field). However, each time, they lost the World Series to the Yankees (1947, 1949, 1952, and 1953). After each loss, the fans looked to the future. "Wait 'til next year" was their theme.

That "next year" finally came in 1955. The team easily won the NL pennant and split the first six games of the World Series with the Yanks. Then, in Yankee Stadium, they won the seventh game, 2–0. Dodgers fans in Brooklyn and across the country celebrated their achievement. The Dodgers returned to the World Series in 1956 and faced the Yankees yet again, but they lost in seven games.

Move to Los Angeles

During this run of regular-season success, Walter O'Malley, a real estate investor and attorney, became the team's majority owner in 1950, when he bought out Rickey's shares. O'Malley wanted to relocate to a new ballpark in downtown Brooklyn, where it could attract more spectators than the run-down Ebbets Field, but he received no support from the city of New York. In 1957, the Dodgers were the most profitable team in the NL.

After that season, O'Malley and Horace Stoneham, owner of the New York Giants, announced that they were relocating their teams to Los Angeles and San Francisco, respectively. Brooklyn fans were despondent over the loss of their team, probably the most beloved institution in the borough. But fans in California were eager to welcome their first major league teams.

The Dodgers played for three years at the cavernous Los Angeles Memorial Coliseum, beginning with a first-game victory on April 18, 1958, 6–5 over their new northern California rival, the Giants. The next season, the Dodgers won the pennant and defeated the Chicago White Sox in the World Series in six games. Southern Californians loved their new team, and the Dodgers led the NL in attendance from 1959 through 1966. In 1962, the team moved into Dodger Stadium, in the Chavez Ravine area of Los Angeles; it was the last ballpark built entirely with private funds for more than 40 years.

Throughout the 1960s, the Dodgers fielded a contending squad led by Cy Young Award–winning pitchers Sandy Koufax and Don Drysdale. In 1963, the Dodgers met their old New York rivals in the World Series. This time, there was no doubt—the Dodgers beat the Yankees in four straight games. Two years later, the Dodgers were back in the World Series, this time facing the Minnesota Twins. Koufax pitched shutouts in Games 5 and 7, earning the Series Most Valuable Player (MVP) title and leading the Dodgers to another championship. The Dodgers won another pennant in 1966 but were swept in the Series by the Baltimore Orioles. After the season, Koufax retired.

Over the next several years, the team was rebuilt, and Peter O'Malley took over the franchise from his father. The Dodgers were strong contenders in the early 1970s and won the pennant in 1974, but they fell in the World Series to the Oakland Athletics in five games.

Two years later, longtime skipper Walter Alston (1954–1976) was replaced by old Dodgers farmhand Tommy Lasorda, whose infield included Steve Garvey at first, Davey Lopes at second, Bill Russell at shortstop,

and Ron Cey at third. The team reached the World Series in 1977 and 1978, facing their longtime rival New York Yankees, but they lost both Series in six games.

In 1981, the Dodgers exacted their revenge on the Yankees, beating them in the World Series, four games to two, after a season shortened by a players' strike. They were led by Rookie of the Year and Cy Young Award winner, pitcher Fernando Valenzuela of Mexico, who became a great local hero.

The Dodgers earned trips to the postseason in 1983 and 1985, but they lost both years in the National League Championship Series. They returned to the World Series in 1988, led by season MVP Kirk Gibson and pitcher Orel Hershiser; however, they were the underdogs to the Oakland A's. In the first game, the Dodgers were behind in the bottom of the ninth, 4–3. With one man on, Dodgers slugger Gibson hobbled to the plate as a pinch hitter. With a count of three balls and two strikes, Gibson hit a home run to win the game 5–4. The Dodgers went on to win the Series in seven games.

The Dodgers's success was attributable to their excellent scouting system, which discovered great young talent, and to a top-notch farm system that nurtured prospects. Between 1992 and 1996, five Dodgers were named Rookie of the Year (Eric Karros at first base, Mike Piazza as catcher, Raul Mondesi in right field, Hideo Nomo on the mound, and Todd Hollandsworth in the outfield). Lasorda retired in 1996 and soon was elected to the Hall of Fame.

The team has remained competitive but has failed to return to the World Series. The O'Malley family sold the Dodgers in 1998 to Rupert Murdoch's News Corporation, the owner of the Fox Network and 20th Century Fox. Murdoch, in turn, sold the team six years later to real estate developer Frank McCourt. In 2011, *Forbes* magazine estimated the team's value at $800 million, the third highest in baseball.

The Dodgers returned to the National League Championship Series in 2008 and 2009, losing in both years to the Philadelphia Phillies in five games. In the meantime, the divorce proceedings of McCourt and his wife Jamie, which began in 2009 and remained unresolved as of early 2011, prompted Major League Baseball to assume control of the team's operations. Trial testimony had revealed that the couple had used over $100 million from team revenues to support their lavish lifestyle instead of focusing on the team's best interests.

Maureen Margaret Smith

See also: Baseball, Major League; Koufax, Sandy; O'Malley, Walter; Rickey, Branch; Robinson, Jackie.

Further Reading

Kahn, Roger. *The Boys of Summer.* New York: Harper & Row, 1972.

Stout, Glenn. *The Dodgers: 120 Years of Dodgers Baseball.* Boston: Houghton Mifflin, 2004.

Sullivan, Neil J. *The Dodgers Move West.* New York: Oxford University Press, 1987.

Tygiel, Jules. *Baseball's Great Experiment: Jackie Robinson and His Legacy.* New York: Vintage Books, 1984.

Dog Racing

See Canine Sports

Drugs, Performance-Enhancing

Recent decades have seen growing tension between individual athletes wishing to stretch the limits of human performance through pharmacological enhancement and athletic officials seeking to safeguard the health of their athletes and the fairness of their competitions. In some cases, athletes have been supported by national sports authorities whose primary interests were winning victories in international competition. For example, the former German Democratic Republic (East Germany) implemented state-sponsored doping regimes in order to increase their medals at international events. North American competitors were not so blatant in their drug use but also were connected to the drug culture. As John Hoberman put it in his pathbreaking book, *Mortal Engines* (1992), "For the past century high-performance sport has been a vast, loosely coordinated experiment upon the human organism."

The Early Twentieth Century

The first modern instance of doping by a North American athlete occurred at the 1904 Olympic Games in St. Louis, Missouri. U.S. runner Thomas Hicks ingested a dangerous concoction of strychnine, brandy, and raw eggs prior to the marathon. He won the race, but collapsed at the finish line. Charles Lucas, who was observing the event, described Hicks's weakened condition: "His eyes were dull, lusterless, the ashen color of his face and skin had deepened; his arms appeared as weights well tied down; he could scarcely lift his legs, while his knees were almost stiff."

The episode provoked little public reaction, however, as such practices were considered acceptable at the time. Hicks, without any sense of remorse, explained to reporters that he would rather have won the race than become president.

The Coming of the Russians

The Soviet Union's entry into Olympic competition at the 1952 Games in Helsinki, Finland, was a milestone in the use of performance-enhancing drugs. The Soviet weightlifting team surprisingly dominated the competition, winning seven medals in seven events (three gold, three silver, and one bronze). American coach Bob Hoffman believed that one reason was the athletes' use of performance-enhancing substances.

A subsequent encounter by U.S. team physician John Ziegler with his Soviet counterpart at the 1954 World Powerlifting Championships confirmed suspicions that the Soviets were using the male hormone testosterone to gain strength and power. Upon returning home, Ziegler began experiments that verified testosterone's performance-enhancing properties.

By the 1956 Olympic Games in Melbourne, Australia, rumors swirled that several U.S. track and field competitors were using the hormone in training. North American athletes secured greater access to the substance when the CIBA pharmaceutical company announced in 1958 that it had developed a synthetic version of the hormone, the anabolic steroid Dianabol. It quickly became a drug of choice for elite competitors.

Drugs in the Age of Aquarius

During the 1960s, widespread experimentation with drugs drew in many athletes. The dangerous potential of such experimentation struck sports administrators after Danish cyclist Knud Jensen collapsed and died at the 1960 Olympic Games in Rome while under the influence of Ronicol, a peripheral vasodilator known to stimulate blood circulation. In response, sports organizations began to develop antidoping policies to curb such use. The International Olympic Committee (IOC) was slow to enact comprehensive policy reforms, but it eventually created a medical commission to issue and enforce doping regulations.

The IOC conducted its first drug tests at the 1968 Games in Mexico City. However, the testing protocol utilized, which included a limited number of drugs, was designed primarily to control the use of amphetamines.

Although some athletes undoubtedly stopped using performance enhancers because of the new test, others found means to hide their drug use.

Asked about the new ban on amphetamines, for example, an anonymous American weightlifter expressed his contempt for the regulations. "What ban?" he asked, according to *Sports Illustrated* columnist Bil Gilbert in an influential 1969 article. "Everyone used a new one from West Germany. They couldn't pick it up in the test they were using." Further elaborating on how the rules could be avoided, he explained, "When they get a test for that one, we'll find something else. It's like cops and robbers."

Anabolic steroids were not included on the IOC's list of banned substances for the 1968 Games, because there was no reliable test to detect them. Physician and U.S. Olympian Tom Waddell, who placed sixth in the decathlon, estimated that one-third of his teammates on the track and field squad were using steroids at the team's high-altitude training camp in Lake Tahoe, Nevada.

Better Performance Through Biochemistry

Issues regarding performance-enhancing drugs continued to plague North American athletes during the 1970s. At the 1972 Olympic Games in Munich, Germany, U.S. swimmer Rick DeMont's prescribed asthma medication triggered a positive drug test, resulting in his disqualification. American athletes also saw Soviet and East German athletes—the latter aided by a state-sponsored doping regime—begin to dominate Olympic events. This created the perception that pharmacological agents were prerequisites for success in elite competitions.

After the 1972 competitions, United States Olympic Committee members, eager to keep up with the communist bloc, announced that the possible applications of anabolic steroids would be a topic for the organization's medical research. Four years later, the obvious employment of drugs by East German women, who won 11 out of a possible 13 gold medals in the swimming events, prompted North American swimmers to protest.

By the 1970s, drugs also had become common features of the domestic sports scene. Anabolic steroids were especially prevalent in "power" sports, such as football. Star National Football League defensive end Lyle Alzado, who began his gridiron career in 1971, was a notable steroid user; he blamed his use of anabolic drugs for the brain cancer that eventually took his life. Throughout the decade, other football players were equally forthcoming. In 1979, several members of the Washington Redskins informed a reporter that about one-third of their squad regularly took the field while "on" amphetamines.

The 1980s

At the 1980 Winter Olympic Games, held in Lake Placid, New York, a $1.4 million drug-testing program was implemented. Despite official claims that the doping protocols were the most rigorous in the history of international athletics, testing discovered not a single positive indication of drug use. Athletes learned to avoid the screens by replacing anabolic steroids right before competition with exogenous testosterone, which the IOC's tests could not detect, because the male hormone occurs normally in the bodies of both men and women.

The boycott of the 1980 Olympic Games in Moscow prevented U.S. and Canadian athletes from competing, but drugs remained staples in their training practices. By that time, German physician and IOC doping expert Manfred Donike had developed a procedure to detect testosterone; unofficial screens showed that 20 percent of the competitors in Moscow were using the hormone.

Officially employed for the first time at the 1983 Pan-American Games in Caracas, Venezuela, the new tests challenged American athletes who competed there. Fearing the potential negative consequences of the tests, 12 members of the track and field squad immediately withdrew. Several other athletes, including celebrated weightlifter Jeff Michaels, tested positive for drug use and were suspended.

At the 1988 Olympic Games in Seoul, South Korea, the sporting world was stunned when Canadian sprinter Ben Johnson failed an anabolic steroid screen after running the 100-meter (109-yard) sprint in a world-record time of 9.79 seconds. The episode so badly embarrassed the Canadian government that it appointed a commission chaired by Associate Chief Justice Charles W. Dubin of the Supreme Court of Ontario to investigate doping in elite sports. Dubin's report added weight to a growing sentiment in the Olympic community that its historically unintegrated doping control mechanisms should be coordinated through a central body.

As a first step in the intensification of doping regulations, American sports officials signed an agreement with their Soviet counterparts near the end of the 1988

Games that called for a cooperative effort to eliminate drugs in athletics. In November, the proposal was tentatively expanded to include an exchange program through which representatives from the superpowers would be allowed to test athletes from the other country.

Taking the concept a step farther, Soviet administrators hosted a United Nations Educational, Scientific and Cultural Organization (UNESCO) conference in Moscow that called for random, out-of-competition drug tests for Olympic athletes. However, the United States had withdrawn from UNESCO in 1984 because of the organization's anti-Western bias and politicization, and that hindered the effort. The Soviet Union's interest evaporated when the country disintegrated in 1991. Nevertheless, the agenda was set for expanding the Olympic drug-testing program.

Tightening Controls in the 1990s

The drive toward centralized policies continued in the 1990s as the North American public became increasingly sensitive to the drug crisis. The U.S. Congress adopted the Anabolic Steroids Control Act of 1990, which made synthetic anabolic hormones Schedule III controlled substances. Such drugs have less potential for abuse than Schedule I and II drugs, but abuse may lead to high psychological dependence and moderate or low physical dependence. Possessing synthetic anabolic steroids without a valid medical prescription became a federal crime subject to a substantial fine and up to a year's imprisonment. Subsequent violations would result in greater penalties.

Between 1991 and 1994, the U.S. Drug Enforcement Agency (DEA) initiated 185 investigations of steroid trafficking, resulting in 283 arrests. Among those detained was New York Giants offensive lineman Eric Moore. Moore told DEA agents that he had received prior notice of drug tests by team representatives so that he could substitute a clean urine specimen in place of his own. The report illustrates the mixed motives of professional leagues and teams in policing the use of performance-enhancing substances. Testing and enforcement remained halfhearted and inconsistent.

In international sports, on the other hand, leading sports officials sponsored a series of drug conferences as pressure built to control the proliferation of drugs at their competitions. In February 1999, the IOC hosted the World Conference on Doping in Sport in Lausanne, Switzerland, which resulted in a proposal for a new drug-testing authority. In the United States, Senator John McCain chaired a Commerce Committee hearing on drugs in October of that year. Barry McCaffrey, head of the White House Office of Drug Control, testified that only an independent doping control organization could adequately address the problem.

In the spirit of these suggestions, the World Anti-Doping Agency was created in November 1999. Conceived as a partnership between national governments, private sports bodies, and international organizations, the agency was set up as an autonomous doping authority that would regulate international sports.

The Current Situation

While problems related to drugs remain in the Olympics, the World Anti-Doping Agency's efforts have been reasonably successful in eliminating political and organizational impediments to an effective antidoping strategy. By contrast, professional sports leagues in North America have been slow to enact rigorous doping policies. One reason is that the leagues are required to confer with representatives of players' unions, who generally have opposed strong enforcement.

The antidoping regime of Major League Baseball did not include anabolic steroid screens until 2004. Dissatisfaction with the arrangement finally resulted in the creation of a tougher testing program in 2005. In March, the U.S. Senate began holding hearings on the issue. Several star ballplayers, including Sammy Sosa and Mark McGwire, who had competed to set a new season home run record in 1998, testified. Sosa denied allegations of prior anabolic steroid use. When Mark McGwire was asked, he tearfully replied that he had been advised by his lawyers not to answer questions regarding his rumored use of steroids.

Meanwhile, the Justice Department pursued a criminal case after discovering that the Bay Area Laboratory Co-operative (BALCO) was providing anabolic steroids and other performance-enhancing drugs to elite athletes. All-time home run champion Barry Bonds emerged as a central figure in the BALCO scandal. He allegedly used a variety of performance-enhancing drugs, including amphetamines, anabolic steroids, and a human growth hormone. Bonds was indicted in November 2007 on charges of lying to a federal grand jury and obstructing justice. He was convicted of a single charge of obstruction of justice in April 2011 and faced a possible 10-year jail sentence.

In December 2007, former U.S. Senator George Mitchell released the results of a comprehensive investigation of drugs in professional baseball. Authorized and funded by Major League Baseball, 89 major league players were named as having used performance-enhancing drugs, most prominently seven-time Cy Young Award winner Roger Clemens.

Clemens was so incensed by former trainer Brian McNamee's claim that he had injected the All-Star pitcher with an anabolic steroid that he filed a defamation lawsuit. In February 2008, Clemens and McNamee appeared before a U.S. congressional committee to discuss allegations. A subsequent federal investigation determined that Clemens had lied under oath; he was indicted on six counts of perjury.

The Future

Even as old issues remain unresolved, athletes and administrators are likely to face new concerns over doping. The mapping of the complete structure of human DNA has the potential to improve human life in many ways, but it also raises questions about legitimate uses of DNA testing and gene therapy. Some athletes already see the genetic revolution as a means to take the next step toward perfecting human performance. Others, however, worry that genetic testing might prove a handicap to their success.

For example, the Chicago Bulls traded Eddy Curry to the New York Knicks after he refused to take a DNA test that sought to establish whether he might have a potentially fatal heart condition. Such cases raise the possibility of conflict between players' privacy and the right of teams or other organizations to have sensitive information about athletes' present or future physical condition.

Thomas M. Hunt and Jan Todd

See also: Baseball, Major League; Business of Sports; Government, U.S.; Psychology, Sports.

Further Reading

Fainaru-Wada, Mark, and Lance Williams. *Game of Shadows: Barry Bonds, BALCO, and the Steroids Scandal that Rocked Professional Sports.* New York: Gotham, 2006.

Goldman, Bob, with Patricia Bush and Ronald Klatz. *Death in the Locker Room: Steroids, Cocaine and Sports.* Tucson, AZ: Body Press, 1987.

Guttmann, Allen. *The Olympics: A History of the Modern Games.* 2nd ed. Urbana: University of Illinois Press, 2002.

Hoberman, John M. *Mortal Engines: The Science of Performance and the Dehumanization of Sport.* New York: Free Press, 1992.

Kleinman, Carol Cole, and C.E. Petit. "Legal Aspects of Anabolic Steroid Use and Abuse." In *Anabolic Steroids in Sport and Exercise,* 2nd ed., ed. Charles E. Yesalis. Champaign, IL: Human Kinetics, 2000.

Pound, Richard W. *Inside the Olympics: A Behind-the-Scenes Look at the Politics, the Scandals, and the Glory of the Games.* Etobicoke, Canada: Wiley Canada, 2004.

Todd, Jan, and Terry Todd. "Significant Events in the History of Drug Testing and the Olympic Movement: 1960–1999." In *Doping in Elite Sport: The Politics of Drugs in the Olympic Movement,* ed. Wayne Wilson and Edward Derse. Champaign, IL: Human Kinetics, 2001.

Todd, Terry. "A History of the Use of Anabolic Steroids in Sport." In *Sport and Exercise Science: Essays in the History of Sports Medicine,* ed. Jack W. Berryman and Roberta J. Park. Urbana: University of Illinois Press, 1992.

World Anti-Doping Agency. http://www.wada-ama.org/en/.

Wrynn, Alison. "The Human Factor: Science, Medicine and the International Olympic Committee, 1900–70." *Sport in Society* 7:2 (Summer 2004): 211–231.

Yesalis, Charles E., Stephen P. Courson, and James E. Wright. "History of Anabolic Steroid Use in Sport and Exercise." In *Anabolic Steroids in Sport and Exercise,* 2nd ed., ed. Charles E. Yesalis. Champaign, IL: Human Kinetics, 2000.

Earnhardt, Dale (1951–2001)

Dale Earnhardt, Sr., was a legend in the sport of stock car racing from the 1970s through the 1990s and a key figure in the sport's transition from a small-time regional event to an international spectacle. Nicknamed "The Intimidator" for his hard-driving style, Earnhardt won seven Winston Cup titles and a total of 76 races. Although his win total makes him one of the most successful competitors in NASCAR (National Association of Stock Car Automobile Racing) history, Earnhardt's contributions to the sport transcended his competitive achievements. At the time of his tragic death in 2001, Earnhardt was one of the best-known and most beloved figures in sports. The outpouring of grief in the aftermath of his death was testament to his status as a hero and to the place NASCAR holds in American spectator sports.

Ralph Dale Earnhardt was born on April 29, 1951, in Kannapolis, North Carolina, the eldest son of Martha Coleman and Ralph Lee Earnhardt, a legendary stock car racer who had worked for Cannon Mills until he quit to race full time. The elder Earnhardt was a local legend who raced four times a week, primarily on the dirt tracks of the Carolina Piedmont. He compiled an impressive legacy of victories, including the 1956 Sportsman Championship.

Dale, like his father, decided to devote his life to full-time racing. His first race was a minor league affair at the Concord Speedway, a local dirt track where he drove a 1956 Ford Club Sedan that he and his friends had salvaged and modified. Earnhardt, a high school dropout, married for the first time in 1967, at age 17, and fathered his first son Kerry, who also would become a stock car driver. Earnhardt supported his wife and child by working in an automobile repair shop, but when his marriage ended in 1970, he began drifting from job to job, earning just enough to keep his racing career going.

Stock car racing was not an expensive sport in the 1960s and 1970s, as most drivers built their own cars out of salvaged and used parts. Nonetheless, Earnhardt's hard-driving style and tendency to crash kept him strapped for cash. He sometimes had to borrow money against future winnings in order to keep driving.

In 1971, Earnhardt married Brenda Gee, the daughter of renowned race car builder Robert Gee. The couple had two children, daughter Kelley in 1972 and son Dale, Jr., in 1974. Earnhardt's marriage to Brenda did not last either, but his father-in-law helped him build his first asphalt track race car. The transition to asphalt tracks introduced Earnhardt to NASCAR's Sportsman division (the equivalent of today's Busch Series) and set the stage for his first appearance in NASCAR's major league, the Grand National, or "Winston Cup" racing.

Ralph Earnhardt died of a heart attack in 1973. Without his father's unstinting support, Dale faced mounting pressure from his family to make a decent living at the sport or quit racing. In 1975, Earnhardt got his first big break in the Winston Cup races when Ed Negre picked him to drive a Dodge in the World 600 in Charlotte, North Carolina. Earnhardt finished twenty-second and drove for Negre eight more times over the next three years.

In 1978, Ed Osterlund offered Earnhardt the chance to drive his Chevrolet full time, replacing veteran driver Dave Marcis. Earnhardt responded by winning NASCAR's Rookie of the Year honor in 1979, scoring his first Winston Cup win at Bristol, Tennessee. One year later, Earnhardt won the first of seven Winston Cup championships, narrowly outpacing veteran Cale Yarborough.

When Osterlund sold his team to Jim Stacy midway through the 1981 season, Earnhardt left for a new team started by former driver Richard Childress. Childress's team was young and struggling to make its mark, however. Childress suggested to Earnhardt that he instead join Bud Moore's successful racing team, which had a big-time sponsor, Wrangler jeans.

Earnhardt spent two years driving the number 15 Wrangler Ford for Moore before rejoining Childress in 1984. At that time, stock car racing was controlled by a handful of powerful teams, and drivers for lesser teams had no chance of winning. Earnhardt and Childress were entrepreneurial pioneers—building their own cars, courting their own sponsors, and winning races for themselves. Such changes catapulted the sport into the big time. The reunion ultimately led to six Winston Cup titles (1986, 1987, 1990, 1991, 1993, and 1994), career earnings of more than $40 million, and finally a Daytona 500 victory in 1998, Earnhardt's twentieth attempt at the legendary race.

In 1980, Earnhardt established Dale Earnhardt, Incorporated (DEI), a racing and merchandizing enterprise. Over two decades, he built the corporation from a home-based business that he ran with his third wife, Teresa, into a multimillion-dollar a year enterprise that sponsored teams and drivers in each of NASCAR's top three circuits—the Winston Cup, the Busch series, and the Camping World Truck Series. The 70,000-square-foot (6,503-square-meter) DEI headquarters became known as the "Garage Mahal" for its sleek appearance and lavish accoutrements, including seven bays for work on team cars, a museum, a showroom, and other amenities for visitors.

Earnhardt died on February 18, 2001, after his car plowed head-on into the track's retaining wall during the final lap of the Daytona 500. For nearly 20 years, he had driven the black and red number 3 car, one of the most famous in racing. After his death, Earnhardt was widely rated as the second-greatest driver in stock car history, after Richard Petty.

Shocked by Earnhardt's death, fans clamored for more safety in racing. NASCAR complied by requiring the use of head and neck restraints, the construction of soft walls at the tracks, and the development of a roof-hatch escape system for race cars.

Darcy Plymire

See also: Automobile Racing; NASCAR.

Further Reading

Charlotte (North Carolina) *Observer. Dale Earnhardt: Rear View Mirror.* Charlotte, NC: Sports Publishing, 2001.

Montville, Leigh. *At the Altar of Speed: The Fast Life and Tragic Death of Dale Earnhardt.* New York: Broadway, 2003.

Rybacki, Karen Charles, and Donald Jay Rybacki. "The King, the Young Prince, and the Last Confederate Soldier: NASCAR on the Cusp." In *The Sporting World of the Modern South,* ed. Patrick B. Miller. Urbana: University of Illinois Press, 2002.

Eclipse

The racehorse Eclipse, also known as Long Island Eclipse, New York Eclipse, Northern Eclipse, and American Eclipse, was the United States's first national sports hero. The Great Match Race between the North and the South, held on May 27, 1823, was the first sporting event that fans across the continent followed with fervor. Nine years old at the time of the race, Eclipse, representing the North, won in spectacular fashion against a Southern opponent less than half his age.

In the 1820s, major thoroughbred races ran 4-mile (6.4-kilometer) heats, and winners in match races had to win two of three heats. After losing the first heat, Eclipse won the next two, running a total of 12 miles (19.3 kilometers). The distance made his victory even more impressive, as most thoroughbreds his age had long since been retired. He was a magnificent stallion whose triumph, coming at a moment of mounting sectional tension, seemed to Northerners to certify their superiority, having defeated the South at its own sport.

Eclipse was born on Long Island, New York, on May 25, 1814, bred by General Nathaniel Coles by Duroc, out of Miller's Damsel. He showed such promise as a foal that Coles named him Eclipse, after the legendary eighteenth-century English racehorse. He even resembled his illustrious namesake, with the same bright chestnut coat, white "sock" on his right hind leg, and white markings on his face, features that adorned a magnificent build.

Horse racing had been illegal in New York State since 1802. The sport was deemed immoral by the state legislature because of the drinking and gambling that generally accompanied it. Despite this prohibition, there was a core group of horsemen on Long Island who continued to breed racehorses and to race them illegally.

At the age of five, Eclipse already had won his first race, showing sufficient promise that Long Islander Cornelius van Ranst purchased him from Coles. No horse ever came close to beating Eclipse, and after two seasons of racing, when no one would run their horses against him, Van Ranst retired him to stud. Because there were so few racehorses in New York, Eclipse mainly was bred to utilitarian mares whose owners wanted good horses to pull their buggies or work their farms. The world ran on horsepower, and racehorses such as Eclipse made their contribution, helping to fuel the nation's economic growth.

In 1821, the New York State legislature legalized racing in Queens County. Van Ranst decided to bring Eclipse out of retirement and put him back into training in order to add legitimacy and introduce a quality horse to the new races. Though the prevailing wisdom among horsemen decreed that breeding ruined a stallion for racing, Eclipse defied all expectations and again proved a success. New York still had no horses his equal, and as his undefeated record continued, horsemen in the South began to take notice.

In the South, racing was very popular and always had been legal. Many Southern gentlemen were devoted to breeding and training the best horses possible. They believed that their top stallions, such as Sir Archie and his son Sir Charles, were the best in North America. They questioned Northern claims that Eclipse was just as good, even after his being retired to stud for two years. Southern turf men challenged Van Ranst to match Eclipse against Sir Charles in Washington, D.C., in November 1822, with each side putting up $5,000 in wagers.

Until this time, racing had been mainly a regional sport, with no single event drawing national interest. Now, however, politicians and private citizens poured into Washington to view the spectacle; however, on race day, Sir Charles turned up lame. Southerners were mortified by the infirmity of their hero, and his owner, James Junkin Harrison, decided to risk his horse and the South's racing reputation by running an abbreviated race of only one heat so that the crowds would not go home disappointed. Sir Charles's tendon lasted three turns of the track, but then gave way completely, allowing Eclipse to lope home unopposed.

Claiming that the race was not a true test of Southern horseflesh, Southern horsemen, led by William Ransom Johnson, known as the "Napoleon of the Turf," challenged Van Ranst to a rematch. Industrialist John C. Stevens posted a $3,000 forfeiture on behalf of several New York sportsmen. As it was clear that Sir Charles would never race again, the opponent in this race was to be any horse of the South's choosing. Because the South would be able to pick its best horse at the last minute, it seemed only fair to race on Eclipse's

home turf on Long Island. The odds favored the South because of Eclipse's advanced age and his years in the breeding shed, and because he had no understudy should he go lame in training. Nevertheless, Van Ranst accepted the offer, with the backers of each horse putting up $20,000, a sum that was unheard of at the time.

Johnson was so determined to prove Southern superiority on the turf that he auditioned horses from all over the South, before he finally narrowed the pool to four: Betsy Richards, John Richards, Henry (also known as Sir Henry), and Flying Childers (named after another legendary English racehorse). He trained all four in order to choose at the last minute, taking into account such factors as the condition of the track on race day.

Excitement before the race ran high. Washington papers even worried that passions over the race might undo the hard work of the Missouri Compromise of 1820, and rip the nation apart. A reported 50,000 people descended on the Union Course for the race, with many thousands coming from the South.

On race day, Eclipse faced the four-year-old Henry. In the first heat, jockey Billy Crafts could not control Eclipse, and his riding appeared to interfere with the big horse's stride. Crafts responded by whipping Eclipse mercilessly. To the horror of Northerners in attendance, Eclipse lost the first heat of his career. Henry set a record time of 7:37.

The Northern camp changed jockeys, replacing Crafts with the horse's regular jockey, the more experienced Samuel Purdy, who had been originally left off because he was 49—as old for a jockey as Eclipse was for a racehorse—and not in prime condition. The decision was made that, despite Purdy's infirmities, his experience made him the best man to ride Eclipse.

With a competent jockey on board, Eclipse evened the score in the second heat, with a time of 7:49. The jockeys knew that the third heat was a serious trial for their horses. Purdy decided that Eclipse's age would help him in the area of endurance and tried to outrun the younger horse from the start of the third heat. The technique worked, and Eclipse came home at 8:24, leaving Henry far behind. Eclipse was the clear champion of the American turf.

Despite Southern attempts to challenge Eclipse to one more race, Van Ranst decided that the horse had earned his retirement, with a perfect record of 8–0. Race mares were sent from all over the United States to be bred to him. His progeny quickly proved that he passed on his tough, fast genes—daughter Black Maria, for example, won 13 of 25 races, including one in which she raced 20 miles (32.2 kilometers).

By the time of Eclipse's death on July 10, 1847, his offspring were breeding with the outstanding stallions of the South to produce the foundation of the modern American thoroughbred. His descendents would include such greats as Man o'War and Secretariat.

Elizabeth Redkey

See also: Horse Racing; Stevens, John C.

Further Reading

Adelman, Melvin L. *A Sporting Time: New York City and the Rise of Modern Athletics, 1820–70.* Urbana: University of Illinois Press, 1986.

Eisenberg, John. *The Great Match Race: When North Met South in America's First Sports Spectacle.* Boston: Houghton Mifflin, 2006.

Robertson, William H.R. *The History of Thoroughbred Racing in America.* Englewood Cliffs, NJ: Prentice Hall, 1964.

Struna, Nancy L. "The North-South Races: American Thoroughbred Racing in Transition, 1823–1850." *Journal of Sport History* 8:2 (Summer 1981): 28–57.

Ederle, Gertrude (1906–2003)

No woman of the 1920s better captured the imaginations of newly enfranchised American women than Gertrude Ederle, one of the most heralded sportswomen of her day. Her record-setting swim across the English Channel was a triumph not only for Ederle, but also for the American nation and for a generation of women athletes who vied for credibility and acceptance in their sporting endeavors.

Ederle was born on October 23, 1906, to Henry Ederle, a butcher, and Gertrude Haverstroh Ederle, a housewife and caregiver to their six children. "Trudy," as her family called her, was raised in the German section of New York's West Side. She was a self-professed tomboy whose mother taught her how to swim at the family cottage in Atlantic Highlands, New Jersey, when she was nine years old.

Three years later, Mrs. Ederle took Trudy and her siblings to a swimming exhibition. There, Trudy first witnessed the technical skill required to swim competitively, and she decided that she would refine her skills and enter competitions. Ederle later claimed that she did not learn to swim correctly until she was a teenager,

when she mastered the crawl stroke that carried her across the English Channel.

A gifted athlete, Ederle won her first swimming competition at age 14. She dropped out of high school after one year and joined the Women's Swimming Association of New York. There, she received most of her formal coaching and training and was influenced by the association's founder, Charlotte Epstein, who had convinced the Amateur Athletic Union to register female swimmers and sponsor meets.

Between 1921 and 1925, Ederle set 29 freestyle amateur and world records. In 1924, she won a gold medal in the 4 x 100-meter (109-yard) relay at the Olympic Games in Paris, and individual bronze medals in the 100-meter and 400-meter (437-yard) freestyle. But her forte was long-distance swimming, and on June 15, 1925, she beat the men's record for the classic 21-mile (34-kilometer) race from Manhattan's Battery Park to Sandy Hook in New Jersey with a time of 7 hours, 11.5 minutes.

On August 18, 1925, Ederle made her first attempt to swim the English Channel, financed by the Women's Swimming Association. This was an extremely challenging feat—not just because of the distance (about 21 miles), but also because of the strong tides, crosscurrents, and choppy waves. A number of men and women previously had tried to conquer the Channel, but only five men had made it. After swimming for nearly nine hours and only 6 miles (9.7 kilometers) from her goal, a wave came over Ederle, forcing her to swallow a large amount of saltwater. When she stopped to spit it out, her coach, who thought she was nauseated, had a man swimming next to her reach out and pull her up, which immediately nullified her attempt. Ederle later insisted that she easily could have continued and vowed to attempt the Channel again.

A year later, on August 6, 1926, Ederle returned to Cape Gris-Nez on the coast of France for her second attempt. She was financed by Captain J.M. Paterson, publisher of the *New York Daily News* and the *Chicago Tribune,* who anticipated an exclusive story. She was paid a stipend and expenses, which made her a professional athlete. She entered the water at 7:05 A.M., wearing an outfit customized by her sister Margaret—red bathing cap, two-piece swimsuit, and wraparound goggles—and slathered with lanolin and lard to protect her against jellyfish and cold water during the crossing. High winds, driving rain, and shifting tides forced Ederle to swim an arduous extra 14 miles (22.5 kilometers). When her concerned father begged her to retreat into the accompanying boat, she replied "What for?" and kept on swimming until she saw welcoming bonfires off the coast of England.

A roaring crowd that had gathered to celebrate Ederle's accomplishment greeted her as she walked onto the shore at Dover at 9:35 P.M. She completed her quest in 14 hours, 31 minutes, breaking the previous record by 2 hours, 2 minutes. Overnight, she became the most famous woman athlete in the world. Ederle, feminists of the day argued, demonstrated that women were capable of even the most grueling of athletic endeavors.

Eschewing the spotlight, Ederle traveled to Germany to visit her father's family. She returned home to a massive celebration in her honor, first in New York Harbor to the din of swooping airplanes and steamship sirens, and then up Broadway to a ticker-tape parade attended by some 2 million people. At City Hall, Mayor James J. Walker compared her achievement to Moses crossing the Red Sea, Caesar crossing the Rubicon, and Washington crossing the Delaware.

The media was quick to size up the "Queen of the Waters" and "America's Best Girl" as the ideal American woman, while at the same time underscoring her sturdy German features and working-class origins. A telegram from the United German Societies of Americans of German Descent proclaimed their pride that the first woman conqueror of the Channel was a German American, a butcher's daughter who had grown up to be a "Queen."

The high point of Ederle's career was her reaching the Channel shore. In 1927, she played herself in the movie *Swim, Girl, Swim,* and she had a popular song and dance in her honor named the "Trudy"; however, her career was badly managed, and offers of lucrative theater and swimming engagements dissipated quickly. A red roadster promised by her father was one of the few tangible rewards she received for her swimming achievement. In the end, her biographers say, Ederle was traumatized by her triumph and celebrity, and she suffered a nervous breakdown at the age of 21.

In 1933, she injured her back when she fell down a flight of stairs, and she was forced to wear a plaster cast for four years. Although doctors told her that she likely would never walk or swim again, Ederle recovered and made a final swimming performance at Billy Rose's Aquacade at the 1939 World's Fair. She eventually lost her hearing, possibly as a result of the beating waves during her Channel swims, which exacerbated her growing shyness and lack of confidence.

During World War II, Ederle became an instrument technician for American Overseas Airlines at La Guardia Airport. She later taught children to swim at the Lexington School for the Deaf and earned appointment to President Dwight D. Eisenhower's Citizen's Advisory Committee on the Fitness of America's Youth. In 1965, she was one of the original inductees into the International Swimming Hall of Fame. Ederle died on November 30, 2003, at the age of 98.

Christiane Job

See also: Swimming; Women.

Further Reading

Gallico, Paul. *The Golden People.* Garden City, NY: Doubleday, 1965.

Mortimer, Gavin. *The Great Swim.* New York: Walker, 2008.

Severo, Richard. "Gertrude Ederle." *The New York Times,* December 1, 2003.

Ware, Susan. "Gertrude Ederle: 'America's Best Girl.'" In *Forgotten Heroes: Inspiring American Portraits from Our Leading Historians,* ed. Susan Ware. New York: Free Press, 1988.

Endorsements, Athlete

Companies have been using athletes to promote their products since the 1920s. In a medium that often glorifies youth, athletes are instantly recognizable paragons of virtue and health. Corporations perceive sports as a positive force that lends some of its wholesomeness to the products that athletes endorse. At the same time, endorsements and paid testimonials present athletes with a lucrative source of income to supplement their wages.

Finally, by using the same products as the athletes they admire, consumers may be led to believe that they will gain a likeness to that person. As a popular Gatorade commercial from the 1990s reminded viewers, it was necessary to drink Gatorade in order to be like basketball superstar Michael Jordan.

Magazine Advertising

Magazine advertising stretches back to the 1870s and 1880s, but it was not until shortly before World War I that the sort of endorsements that modern Americans would recognize began to appear in print. In the first decade of the twentieth century, companies used Dan Patch, a champion racehorse from Indiana, for advertising purposes. The celebrated horse served as the icon of the International Stock Food Company, and owner Marion Savage used his famous horse to promote a diverse line of products, including sleds, plug tobacco, gasoline, and automobiles.

Although especially prestigious athletes such as baseball star Ty Cobb might appear in ads for starched shirts, while Napoleon "Nap" Lajoie and George Edward "Rube" Waddell extolled the healing virtues of Coca-Cola, most early endorsements featuring athletes were only for sporting goods. Sports such as baseball or golf played a sort of metaphorical role in advertisements, symbolizing health, strength, and vigor. It was not until the consumer explosion of the 1920s that athlete endorsements and testimonials began to move beyond the realm of sporting goods.

Endorsements and Advertising

Endorsement advertising is perhaps the most common form that consumers recognize when sports are used to promote products. The 1920s were a golden age of sports, and the personalities available for advertising were extraordinary. Jack Dempsey (boxing), Bill Tilden (tennis), Harold "Red" Grange (football), and Babe Ruth (baseball) all were able to supplement their incomes with advertising dollars. Ruth got the first major promotion deal when he was paid $5 to describe each home run that he hit for United Press International. The Babe seemed to be everywhere, hawking almost everything from Red Rock Cola to candy bars to breakfast cereal.

Throughout the 1920s and 1930s, endorsement advertising became increasingly controversial, forcing the U.S. government to intervene. In order to combat the notion that endorsements were a form of fraud—because athletes were shilling for products that had nothing to do with their profession—the Federal Trade Commission established a set of codes in 1930 that ensured consumers of genuine endorsements.

According to the new codes, athletes could not endorse any product that they did not actually use. When New York Yankees slugger Mickey Mantle tried to endorse a brand of milk he did not actually drink in the 1950s, the commission promptly advised him to stop. Additionally, many states enacted privacy laws that protected individuals from the misuse of their name, forcing advertisers to obtain permission and offer compensation to any potential endorser. Such codes were a critical step in separating athletes from the snake oil salesmen and charlatans of the previous century.

Athletic endorsements, with a few exceptions, targeted a male audience and promoted masculine products. They included wholesome products such as the breakfast cereal Wheaties, which was endorsed by a wide range of athletes, including Ruth, Grange, Olympic skater Irving Jaffee, and hockey player Graham "Tiny" Teasdale, as well as female athlete Mildred "Babe" Didrikson. Jack Dempsey endorsed both DeSoto sedan automobiles and Gillette razor blades. Shaving cream, motor oil, and, after the repeal of Prohibition, alcoholic beverages, all featured celebrity athlete spokespersons. No product, however, was as closely associated with player endorsements as cigarettes.

Tobacco advertising increasingly utilized sports, radio, movie, and later television celebrities to glorify smoking and to attract young replacements for smokers who were quitting or dying. By the 1930s, athletes were the most prominent spokespeople for the tobacco industry, whose advertisements spanned the sporting world. Baseball, football, golf, basketball, and even rodeo stars helped lend smoking a glamorous, wholesome image. Baseball star Joe DiMaggio, footballer Frank Gifford, Boston Celtics point guard Bob Cousy, and golfer Arnold Palmer were just a few of the athletes who endorsed cigarette brands; DiMaggio endorsed both Chesterfields and Camels. Where advertisers practiced market segmentation, tobacco ads employed black athletes who could most effectively reach the segmented market, featuring endorsements by athletes such as Willie Mays in issues of the magazines *Jet* and *Ebony*.

Criticism of Athletic Endorsements of Tobacco Products

Money, of course, was the deciding factor in attaching an athlete's name to a certain product. There was, however, some tension in what was a generally lucrative financial partnership between baseball and the tobacco industry. Critics had long condemned sports for prostituting their images to sell tobacco and alcohol products.

Early in the twentieth century, Pittsburgh Pirates baseball star Honus Wagner asked that tobacco cards featuring his image be withdrawn from the market. Even though he personally enjoyed chewing tobacco and did smoke cigars, Wagner recognized that his endorsement did not provide a good example to one of baseball's most important audiences, America's youth.

Stances like Wagner's were rare. Endorsements eventually became a profitable fact of life in the sports universe. If a player was skilled enough on the field, if he looked the part and had the necessary charisma, he would prove an asset to marketers. Athletes were visible extensions of their game's virtues. Using an athlete's image in an advertisement was just one way of playing to a consumer's fantasies. As one executive of the J. Walter Thompson Advertising Agency suggested, people wanted to imitate those they felt possessed superior taste, knowledge, or physical skill. In the end, smoking the same cigarette, driving the same car, or eating the same cereal was an almost magical ritual that lent some of the endorser's attributes to the consumer.

Cigarette endorsements were so pervasive that it was almost second nature to associate a player's name with his cigarette brand. In some circles, players were more famous for the products they endorsed than for their prowess on the field. Longtime baseball owner Bill Veeck once opined that, later in his life, Joe DiMaggio was probably better known for Mr. Coffee commercials than for his baseball career.

In 1963, the tobacco industry adopted a code of advertising ethics that prohibited the use of celebrities and athletes to promote smoking, but the industry cleverly circumvented its own ban. In the 1970s, football star Walt Garrison and, later, baseball star George Brett appeared in ads for smokeless tobacco.

Endorsements, Marketability, and Big Money

Even after they were denied lucrative tobacco endorsement deals, athletes continued to supplement their salaries through advertising. The advent of television provided even more opportunities for sports stars to sign such deals. Super Bowl–winning quarterback Joe Namath lathered his beard with Noxzema shaving cream and even endorsed Lady Schick razors. Olympic swimmer Mark Spitz also approved of Schick, while Baltimore Orioles's ace pitcher Jim Palmer modeled Jockey underwear. Modern-day superstars such as international soccer icon David Beckham, retired boxer George Foreman, and golfer Tiger Woods parlayed fame into megamillion-dollar endorsement deals. With so much money wrapped up in endorsements—in 1977, New York Yankees slugger Reggie Jackson made almost three times his annual salary through endorsements—athletes' images increasingly were handled by powerful public relations firms.

No athlete's image proved as marketable as basketball star Michael Jordan's in the last decades of the twentieth century. Jordan's image initially was used to sell Nike products, specifically the Air Jordan brand of shoes, but in time, he practically became a brand in his own right. After he also appeared for Gatorade, Chevrolet, and Hanes, *Fortune* magazine estimated that Jordan had an almost $10 billion influence on the economy during his advertising prime.

Oddly enough, the advertising industry often has been conflicted when it comes to endorsements. Studies have demonstrated that, with a few exceptions such as Jordan, endorsements have almost no effect on buyers. Athletes enjoy a very small window of fame, and their favor with the public can prove fleeting. In addition, controversy can ruin the marketability of otherwise exceptional athletes. Los Angeles Lakers prodigy Kobe Bryant learned that lesson after facing inquiries into his sexual conduct in 2003. He subsequently was released from several endorsement deals. More recently, another athlete who lost product endorsements due to his sexual misconduct was Tiger Woods. In 2010, he lost $22 million in endorsements from companies such as AT&T and Gatorade but still made $70 million.

Research has concluded that an athlete's marketability depends less on athletic skill than on likeability; nevertheless, excellence on the field, court, or track remains the standard by which most celebrity athletes are judged. Athletes have continued to dominate the endorsement arena into the twenty-first century. It is estimated that companies spend close to $1 billion on athlete endorsements every year. In 2003, Nike set a new standard when the company signed basketball wunderkind LeBron James to a seven-year, $90 million deal.

Nathan M. Corzine

See also: Agents; Business of Sports; Jordan, Michael; Woods, Tiger.

Further Reading

Fox, Stephen. *The Mirror Makers: A History of American Advertising and Its Creators.* Urbana: University of Illinois Press, 1997.

Grover, Katherine, ed. *Fitness in American Culture: Images of Health, Sport, and the Body, 1830–1940.* Amherst: University of Massachusetts Press, 1989.

Lipsey, Richard A. *The Sporting Goods Industry: History, Practices and Products.* Jefferson, NC: McFarland, 2006.

Rielly, Edward J., ed. *Baseball and American Culture: Across the Diamond.* New York: Haworth, 2003.

Sleight, Steve. *Sponsorship: What Is It and How to Use It.* New York: McGraw-Hill, 1989.

Entertainment and Sports Programming Network

See ESPN

Epstein, Charlotte (1884–1938)

Charlotte Epstein is remembered as the "Mother of Women's Swimming in America" and a champion of women's participation in the Olympic Games in the 1920s. Through the New York Women's Swimming Association, which she founded in 1917, "Eppie," as she was known to friends, helped launch the careers of many early U.S. Olympic swimming champions, including Ethelda Bleibtrey, Gertrude Ederle, Eleanor Holm, Aileen Riggin, and Esther Williams. She also managed the U.S. women's swimming team in three Olympics.

Epstein, the daughter of Moritz H. and Sara Epstein, was born in 1884 in New York City. She was educated at the Ethical Culture School and became a court stenographer. Epstein enjoyed swimming for physical exercise and participated in competitions. She joined the National Women's Life-Saving League in 1911, and in 1913, she chaired its Athletic Branch. She and her life-saving teammates campaigned to reform gender constraints in aquatic sports in order to provide opportunities for women to swim for recreation and to swim and dive in competition.

In 1915, Epstein, along with fellow Jewish swimmers Lucy Freeman, Sophie Freitag, Rita Greenfield, Frances Ricker, and other avid women swimmers, strived to increase women's participation in swimming competitions. Epstein worked to get the Amateur Athletic Union (AAU) to recognize women's swimming, a sport that held promise for women to compete in the Olympics. In 1917, swimming officials appointed Epstein as the first woman on the Swimming Committee of the Metropolitan District of the AAU.

In addition to asserting women's right to swim, Epstein and her colleagues agitated for emancipation in aquatic sports, endorsing bathing-suit reform to allow women swimmers greater mobility and speed. Epstein urged that swimmers should have freedom of motion in swimming contests, and she urged women swimmers to forgo the stockings typically worn with bathing suits in an era when the public was concerned about female modesty. Competitive women swimmers asserted their right to wear one-piece bathing suits, which they draped with skirts when they were not in the water.

Epstein competed in the first intercity race between the New York Branch of the National Women's Life-Saving League and the Philadelphia Turnverein. The AAU-affiliated event drew keen interest in the 40-yard (37-meter) and 100-yard (91-meter) swims, the 4 × 160-yard (146-meter) relay, the plunge for distance (diving), and fancy diving (diving involving gymnastic moves such as somersaults and twists). Many other meets were held over the years.

Epstein espoused distance swimming for its health benefits, and she publicized its value for a woman's physical fitness. She recommended that more attention be given to long-distance swimming, in which several of her teammates excelled, particularly Lucy Freeman, one of the nation's best long-distance aquatic athletes.

In October 1917, Epstein founded the New York City Women's Swimming Association (WSA), a non-profit club that aimed to advance the sport of women's swimming. The WSA would dominate world-class swimming for decades. Epstein, the team manager, worked with Elsie Viet Jennings, an excellent organizer, and especially with volunteer coach Louis de Breda Handley (1904 Olympic gold medalist in swimming and a member of the International Swimming Hall of Fame), who worked at the club from 1917 until his death in 1952. He emphasized a stroke called the trudgen crawl (a sidestroke with a scissor kick).

Epstein battled the United States Olympic Committee to allow American female swimmers and divers to compete in the 1920 Olympic Games in Antwerp, Belgium. She chaperoned the U.S. women's swimming team, which was coached by Handley. The U.S. team dominated, winning four of five races and sweeping three events.

The team was led by Ethelda Bleibtrey, with her world-record victory in the 100-meter (109-yard) free-style event. She went on to win two more gold medals. Another star was Aileen Riggin, Olympic gold medalist in fancy diving at age 14. The team's success helped change American attitudes about women's participation in swimming and in sports in general, and it resulted in the expansion of the WSA.

At the 1924 Olympic Games in Paris, Epstein acted as a chaperone-manager, helping the team members in their workouts and arranging transportation to the competitions from their accommodations. One of her athletes was Gertrude Ederle, who became the first woman to swim the English Channel in 1926. Ederle had joined the WSA four years earlier when she was 15. Ederle starred at the 1924 Games, winning bronze medals in the 100-meter (109-yard) and 400-meter (437-yard) freestyle races, and a gold medal as part of the 400-meter freestyle relay team.

Epstein attended the 1928 Olympic Games in Amsterdam in an unofficial capacity. She became president of the WSA in 1929, and subsequently assistant manager of the 1932 U.S. Women's Olympic Swim Team, the first woman so named. She chaired the AAU Women's Sport Committee beginning in 1935 and in 1936–1937, as well as the national AAU Women's Swimming Committee.

Epstein not only maintained her Jewish identity, but she also served the Maccabiah movement, chairing the Swimming Committee at the 1935 Maccabiah Games. The "Jew Olympics," as the games were known, promoted athletics and Jewish culture in an international forum. One year later, Epstein was invited to coach the U.S. Women's Olympic Swimming Team, and she served on the U.S. Olympic Swimming Committee. However, Epstein refused to attend the 1936 Olympic Games in Berlin, Germany, where Adolf Hitler and the Nazi Party had taken power. She opposed American participation, because the Nazis were openly anti-Semitic and had begun to persecute Jews in Germany. One of Epstein's national swimming stars, Janice Lifson, a WSA member and a Maccabiah champion, followed her coach's lead and boycotted the Games as well.

Epstein's influence on swimming continued until her death on August 26, 1938. During her 22 years with the WSA, her swimmers set 51 world records, won 202 individual AAU Women's National Senior Championships in swimming and diving, and were awarded Olympic medals in swimming and diving. She was inducted into the International Swimming Hall of Fame and the International Jewish Sports Hall of Fame in recognition of her contributions to the development of U.S. women's swimming.

Linda J. Borish

See also: Olympics, Summer; Swimming; Women.

Further Reading

Borish, Linda, J. "'The Cradle of American Champions, Women Champions . . . Swim Champions': Charlotte Epstein, Gender and Jewish Identity, and the Physical Emancipation of Women in Aquatic Sports." *International Journal of the History of Sport* 21 (March 2004): 197–235.

Gems, Gerald R., Linda J. Borish, and Gertrud Pfister. *Sports in American History: From Colonization to Globalization.* Champaign, IL: Human Kinetics, 2008.

Slater, Robert. *Great Jews in Sports.* New York: Jonathan David, 2003.

ESPN

The self-proclaimed "Worldwide Leader in Sports," ESPN (Entertainment and Sports Programming Network) was the first 24-hour cable television network devoted entirely to sports and sports-related programming. Prior to the network's debut on American cable television in September 1979, sports television was limited to whatever live sporting events television networks broadcast, a few scattered sport-oriented programs, such as *ABC's Wide World of Sports,* and designated segments of local and national news programs.

The prospect of enjoying Australian rules football games in the middle of the night or getting minute-by-minute updates on the latest sports scandals was unimaginable before ESPN's emergence. It has become a globally recognizable symbol of the worldwide obsession with sports. Perhaps more important, ESPN has proven that a network devoted solely to sports programming could maintain viewer interest and generate significant profits, paving the way for more specialized sports-oriented cable and satellite channels.

Founding of ESPN

Bill Rasmussen, former communications director for the New England Whalers of the World Hockey Association, conceived and founded ESPN, planning a cable network focusing on Connecticut sports. He initially planned to purchase a regular block of time from a local network; however, he discovered that it would be cheaper to purchase a feed from a communications satellite. Suddenly, his local venture had the potential to become an international network.

Rasmussen initially named the fledgling network ESP-TV, or, Entertainment and Sports Programming Television; he changed the name to ESPN prior to its official debut in 1979. In *Sports Junkies Rejoice! The Birth of ESPN* (1983), Rasmussen explains, "What we're creating here is a network for sports junkies. This is not a network for the soft core sports fans who like to watch the NFL and then switch to news."

ESPN initially was funded by a $10 million investment from Getty Oil. In 1984, after the network established its popularity and profitability, the ABC network—famous for its imaginative sports programming—purchased a majority ownership. Two years later, ABC was purchased by Capital Cities Communications, a division of the Walt Disney Company.

As of late 2010, Disney owned 80 percent of ESPN, and media conglomerate Hearst Communications owned the rest. Though ESPN is now a global media institution, its corporate headquarters and broadcast studios still are located in Bristol, Connecticut, where Rasmussen founded the network.

Early Programming

In its early years, ESPN filled its 24-hour broadcast schedule primarily with sports whose broadcast rights were inexpensive, such as professional wrestling, drag racing, lacrosse, and even log rolling. After the network established its presence and proved its profitability to advertisers, it began televising mainstream professional sporting events, starting with the National Basketball Association in 1982.

Since that time, the network has held contracts with every major American sports organization, and it has featured live broadcasts of sporting events ranging from the Little League World Series to soccer's World Cup. It also has transformed seemingly banal sports-related events into popular media spectacles. For instance, ESPN was the first network to broadcast the annual National Football League and National Basketball Association drafts—now highly anticipated media events.

Sports Reporting and Investigative Journalism

In addition to broadcasting sports and sports-related events, ESPN produces its own sports programming, mostly with news-oriented and talk show formats. *SportsCenter* was the first program that ESPN televised, and it remains the network's flagship program. Since its debut in 1979, *SportsCenter* has become ESPN's most popular and influential sports program, and it is watched religiously—often multiple times daily—by fans and players alike. The show has aired more than 30,000 times, making it the most frequently broadcast program in the history of American television.

SportsCenter displays highlights from recent contests and features sports news. It currently is broadcast up to 12 times daily in either 60- or 90-minute segments, with a rotating cast of anchors. Its humorous style of reportage fuses sports and entertainment. Indeed, catchlines from its broadcasters, such as Chris Berman's "He could . . . go . . . all . . . the . . . way," Dan Patrick's

"Nothing but the bottom of the net," and Stuart Scott's "Boo-ya!" have gained currency far beyond the realm of sports.

In addition to *SportCenter,* the network has developed dozens of other long-standing programs, including *Baseball Tonight, Outside the Lines, Jim Rome Is Burning, Around the Horn,* and *Pardon the Interruption.* While these programs have adopted differing formats, they all build from *SportsCenter*'s commitment to providing commentary that both informs and entertains.

ESPN's programs are fueled by one of the world's most respected sports journalism teams. The network's staff have exposed significant and controversial stories, such as unfair labor practices in the Nike Corporation's Asian factories.

ESPN's commitment to investigative journalism is evidenced by *Outside the Lines,* which began in 1990. Hosted by Bob Ley and adopting a format similar to programs such as CBS's *60 Minutes, Outside the Lines* showcases human interest stories and examines politically charged topics in sports. For instance, in 2007, former NBA player John Amechi used *Outside the Lines* to come out publicly as gay and to speak out against discrimination against gay and lesbian athletes in professional sports.

Global Dimensions of ESPN

The company expanded its television operations in 1993 with ESPN2 to appeal to younger viewers. ESPN strove to capitalize on other niche audiences with the creation of ESPNEWS, a sports news–oriented network; ESPN Classic, a network devoted to replaying significant sporting events of the past and commenting on sports history; and ESPNU, which focuses on college sports. In 2003, ESPN formed ESPN HD, which broadcasts material from most of ESPN's channels in a high-definition television format.

While ESPN began as a cable channel, it is now a global media institution. The network developed ESPN Deportes to reach Spanish-speaking Americans, broadcasting entirely in Spanish. This multilingual service has further expanded to include programming in 20 languages.

ESPN and Non-Television Media

ESPN has ventured beyond the television medium. In 1992, the company staked a claim in audio broadcasting

ESPN opened a new broadcast set at its headquarters in Bristol, Connecticut, to launch its 3-D channel in time for the 2010 World Cup soccer tournament. The all-sports cable network, founded in 1979, markets itself as "the Worldwide Leader in Sports." *(Bloomberg/Getty Images)*

by launching ESPN Radio—a station nearly as pervasive on radio as ESPN is on television. ESPN.com, the company's Web site, offers continuously updated news, archived highlights, live-streamed footage of sporting events, and commentary from ESPN reporters. It also facilitates thousands of sports fan message boards and fantasy sports leagues.

In 1993, ESPN inaugurated the annual ESPY (Excellence in Sports Performance Yearly) Awards. The awards ceremony, with a format similar to the Academy Awards, honors the year's best athletes, teams, and performances. In 1998, ESPN began *ESPN: The Magazine,* a biweekly sports magazine geared toward a younger audience than *Sports Illustrated* and *Sporting News.* That year, ESPN opened the first ESPN Zone, an ESPN-themed restaurant and sports bar in Baltimore, Maryland, and it later opened eight other American sites. As these varied enterprises indicate, ESPN is not just a vehicle for sports broadcasting, it also marks a culture surrounding sports that includes award ceremonies, reading material, and restaurants.

ESPN is now the United States's largest cable network. In 2006, ABC's *Monday Night Football,* the longest-running sports program in the history of American network television, moved to ABC's sister channel ESPN. That same year, ABC changed the identity of its sports programming from "ABC Sports" to "ESPN on ABC." The decision of the parent company to use ESPN

as its sports programming brand reflects the network's profound influence.

Travis Vogan

See also: Television.

Further Reading

Evey, Stuart. *Creating an Empire: ESPN.* Chicago: Triumph, 2004.

Freeman, Michael. *ESPN: The Uncensored History.* New York: Taylor Trade, 2001.

Rader, Benjamin G. *American Sports: From the Age of Folk Games to the Age of Televised Sports.* 6th ed. Upper Saddle River, NJ: Prentice Hall, 2009.

Rasmussen, Bill. *Sports Junkies Rejoice! The Birth of ESPN.* Hartsdale, NY: QV, 1983.

Extreme Sports

Extreme sports, also known as "alternative," "lifestyle," "postmodern," "postindustrial," and "X" sports, were born out of the late-1960s counterculture in America. The preferred term, "extreme sports," was favored by corporate sponsors, most notably the apparel company North Face in the 1970s and ESPN in the late 1980s. Youthful practitioners have played a crucial role in the boom in extreme sports by inventing many contests and creating more and more difficult stunts.

These sports, by definition, evade description and defy precedent. ESPN's original Extreme Games—later rebranded the X Games, for the perceived mystique offered by the "X" moniker—featured nine events: inline skating, bicycle stunt riding, bungee jumping, adventure racing, skateboarding, skysurfing, snowboarding, sport climbing, street luge racing, and wakeboarding. The appellation since has widened to include BMX dirt-bike racing, mountain biking, motocross, whitewater kayaking, surfing, BASE (building, antenna, span earth) jumping, canyoning, free-climbing, kite surfing, bouldering, and speed biking. There have been nine winter and 13 summer sports at the X-Games.

Antecedents of Extreme Sports

Though they frequently are marketed as "new," extreme sports are not without precedent. Historically, they resemble Rome's gladiatorial contests and medieval Europe's jousting competitions.

Likewise, extreme sports' seemingly distinctive embrace of self-promotion, media documentation, and the search for athletic firsts may be traced to the pioneering athlete-journalists of the late nineteenth century. They participated in the sports they covered, devised their own gear, and charted their own courses while documenting their sporting adventures in text and images. They included British climber-illustrator Edward Whymper, Canadian sailor Joshua Slocum, and Scottish writer-adventurer Robert Louis Stevenson.

ESPN and the Origins of the Competitive X Games

The concept of competition among extreme athletes originated in ESPN's programming department in 1993. Two years later, ESPN organized the first Extreme Games, held June 24 to July 1, 1995, with events at Newport, Providence, Middletown, Rhode Island, and Mount Snow, Vermont. Contests in nine sports drew 198,000 spectators. The Games were televised in 198 countries, driven by corporate sponsors such as Mountain Dew, Taco Bell, Chevy Trucks, Nike, AT&T, and Miller Lite, which sought a youthful male audience.

The event was such a success that it was staged again a year later as the X Games. The first Winter X Games, held in January 1997 at Snow Summit Mountain Resort in Big Bear Lake, California, drew 38,000 spectators. The events included ice climbing, shovel racing, snowboarding, snow mountain bike racing, and a multisport

crossover. By 1999, attendance at a similar summer event had reached 275,000.

The Winter Games moved to Mount Snow, Vermont, and drew 83,500 spectators in 2000, but only about 50,000 in 2001. The Summer Games were staged in Philadelphia in 2001 and 2002, while the Winter Games moved to Buttermilk Mountain in Aspen, Colorado, for two years, beginning in 2003. Summer sports include barefoot water-ski jumping, bicycle stunt riding, snowboarding, BMX, in-line skating, motocross, rally car racing, skateboarding, skysurfing, and street luge.

ESPN also developed other extreme events, including the X Trials (qualifying events), the X Games Road Show (a two-day interactive traveling exposition), and the Xperience, a promotional tour. In 2004, the tenth-anniversary X Games were held in Los Angeles, telecast live, with 150 competitors, and drawing a crowd of 170,471 over four days for a finals-only format. However, the 2006 event drew just 138,000.

Extreme sports rapidly spread worldwide, thanks to ESPN's international following, corporate sponsorship, boosterism in local communities, and youthful, well-to-do fans. By 2002, skateboarding icon Tony Hawk was ranked by teens ahead of Michael Jordan and Tiger Woods as the "coolest big-time athlete." By then, participation in traditional team sports had fallen by 30 percent to 40 percent, a fact that helped lifestyle sports gain market share.

Star Power

Several charismatic athletes achieved renown in extreme sports. The most famous was Tony Hawk, the first skateboarder to land a 900 (a 2.5-rotation aerial spin). He ran several businesses after his retirement from competition, manufacturing skateboards; producing television, films, and video games; running a clothing line; and promoting skateboarding tours. Other extreme sports stars have included free skier Tanner Hall, who won a record seven Winter X Games gold medals; Danny Kass, who won silver medals in snowboarding at the 2002 and 2006 Winter Olympic Games; and Canadian freestyle skier Sarah Burke, who was named the Female Skier of the Year in 2001 and Best Female Action Sports Athlete in 2007.

In 2003, red-headed Shaun White, nicknamed the "Flying Tomato," became the first athlete to win medals in both the Winter X Games (snowboarding) and the Summer Games (skateboarding); he has captured ten X Games gold medals in all. He also won Olympic gold medals in 2006 and 2010 in the half-pipe. White won the 2008 Laureus Sports World Sports Award for the Best Action Sportsperson of the Year.

The almost overnight success of lifestyle sports put founding participants in an awkward situation. Free-spirited sports originally developed without big purses, and commercial promotion became program material for a international broadcasting power. Those who first reveled in the idea of "extreme" sports began to question the name. Skateboarder Tony Hawk, for instance, urged renaming the competitions "action sports."

This first-of-its-kind Action Sports and Music Awards was held on April 7, 2001, attended by 6,000 fans at the Universal Amphitheatre in Los Angeles. It brought together athletes, legends, musicians, and Hollywood celebrities. Most of the rising starts in extreme sports' were young white men. The activities seemed egalitarian in minimal start-up, equipment, and access costs, but participants needed a lot of free time to

A performer in the BMX Freestyle competition goes airborne at the 2010 X Games in Los Angeles. The X Games (originally "Extreme Games") is a televised action-sports festival held every summer and winter since 1995. *(Stephen Dunn/Getty Images)*

master their stunts. Extreme sports, which once seemed the antithesis of conventional team activities, now had suffered many of the same problems, including corporate co-option, divisive in-fighting, and race, class, and gender divisions.

Extreme Sports and Lifestyle

Despite their public growing pains, extreme sports have differentiated themselves positively and enduringly. Douglas Booth and Holly Thorpe identify four unique characteristics of extreme sports: participation, environment (often employing the outdoors as a "stadium"), values (embracing the "outlaw" and alternative), and presentation (discontinuous filming and broadcasts featuring prominent soundtracks, collage, and other forms of conspicuous cinematography to enhance the artistic presentation).

For the most part, enthusiasts have been more interested in exploring personal limits than in vanquishing opponents, more focused on skill acquisition, inventiveness, rigor, and collegiality than on wins and losses. The fellowship fostered by extreme sports has spilled over into the lives of its athletes, manifested in a renewed sense of sportsmanship, sociability, and fan accessibility, but also became linked to drugs, alternative music, and violence. The recklessness or courage of extreme sports enthusiasts prompted researchers to study the psychology of the participants. They found a strong hereditary component in risk-taking behavior as well as lessened receptivity to the elation-producing neurotransmitter dopamine among extreme athletes and other daredevils.

Extreme sports have been rapidly adopted by popular culture, but they face a number of problems in the future. In the most dangerous sports, there may be only a few dozen active competitors worldwide, making competitions seem more like stunt exhibitions than games. On the other hand, some early extreme sports, most notably bungee jumping, have become so regulated and limited that they run the risk of becoming humdrum leisure activities that are less likely to cause harm than conventional amusement park rides.

Extreme sports' most enduring legacy may turn out to be its contribution to the wider world of sports in the form of new types of athletic competition. For example, snowboarding, which was a marginal adventure sport in the early 1980s, became a sanctioned Winter Olympic event by 1998. More recently, BMX (off-road bicycle) racing was introduced at the 2008 Summer Games in Beijing. Other extreme sports, such as sky diving from the stratosphere, ostrich racing, and underwater golf, may not be.

Zachary Michael Jack

See also: Motorcycle Sports; Roller Sports; Skateboarding; Skiing, Freestyle; Snowboarding; Surfing; Triathlon; *Wide World of Sports, ABC's.*

Further Reading

Booth, Douglas, and Holly Thorpe, eds. *Berkshire Encyclopedia of Extreme Sports.* Great Barrington, MA: Berkshire, 2007.

Browne, David. *Amped: How Big Air, Big Dollars, and a New Generation Took Sports to the Extreme.* New York: Bloomsbury, 2004.

Olsen, Marilyn, ed. *Women Who Risk: Profiles of Women in Extreme Sports.* Long Island, NY: Hatherleigh, 2001.

Rinehart, Robert E., and Synthia Sydnor, eds. *To the Extreme: Alternative Sports Inside and Out.* Albany: State University of New York Press, 2003.

Todhunter, Andrew. *Dangerous Games: Ice-Climbing, Storm Kayaking, and Other Adventures from the Extreme Edge of Sports.* New York: Doubleday, 2000.

Wheaton, Belinda. *Understanding Lifestyle Sports: Consumption, Identity, and Difference.* New York: Routledge, 2004.

Zuckerman, Marvin. *Behavioral Expressions and Biosocial Bases of Sensation Seeking.* New York: Cambridge University Press, 1994.

Federal League

The short-lived Federal League of the 1910s was the last attempt at forming a third major league in professional baseball until the abortive Continental League in 1960. The Federal League rivaled the monopoly held by the National League and the American League, which merged in 1903. Entrepreneurs who aimed to profit from baseball's soaring revenues financed the independent circuit. Offering appealing salaries to major leaguers, the Federal League enticed them to "jump contracts" regardless of the reserve clause, which bound players to teams in perpetuity. The upstart league raised controversy both on and off the field during three hard-fought seasons, only to see the monopoly of "organized baseball," as the two major leagues were known, reaffirmed in 1922.

Origins

The Federal League had its origins in the Columbian League, which was formed in spring 1912 by John T. Powers, a Chicagoan who believed that baseball's increasing popularity gave independent circuits enough room to thrive without threatening the two major leagues. He planned a 60-game season, to be played mostly in six Midwestern cities, including Columbus and Cleveland; however, because of flagging interest, the Columbian League folded before the first game took place.

In May 1912, Powers regained the confidence of investors and launched the United States League, an eight-team circuit presided over by William Whitman, who owned the Richmond Rebels franchise. This league lasted just a few games, as financial troubles led too many teams to withdraw.

Adamant in his desire to offer a brand of baseball competitive enough to attract fans and break even financially, Powers gathered enough capital to establish the Federal League in 1913 as an independent minor league. Team owners were businessmen such as insurance magnate Marshall Henderson in Pittsburgh, brewery tycoon Otto Stifel in St. Louis, and James Gilmore, a leader in Chicago's heating industry.

Although an unrecognized circuit, the nascent Federal League tried to maintain good relations with organized baseball by vowing to respect the reserve clause and avoid schedule conflicts. It limited contract disputes by hiring mostly free agents or fading big league pitchers, such as former Pittsburgh Pirates ace Deacon Phillipe, who managed the Federal League's Pittsburgh Rebels. Baseball legend Cy Young gave credibility to the league as manager of the Cleveland Feds. The four other teams were the Chicago Whales, the Indianapolis Hoosiers, the St. Louis Terriers, and the Covington (Kentucky) Blue Sox, which relocated to Kansas City, Missouri, because of low attendance. The championship was won by Bill Phillips's Hoosiers, which ended the season 11 games ahead of Cleveland.

In 1914, Gilmore, owner of the Chicago team, emboldened by the Federal League's debut season, took over for Powers as president and brought in more wealthy entrepreneurs to enable the circuit to claim major league status. In preparation for the season, Fed owners erected four brand-new ballparks, including ones in Chicago and St. Louis, and refurbished three others, notably in Brooklyn, where the Tip-Tops, named after the leading product of millionaire baker and owner Robert B. Ward, played in Washington Park, the former home of Charles Ebbets's Brooklyn Dodgers. As part of the expansion eastward, the Buffalo Blues and the Baltimore Terrapins (replacing the Cleveland Feds) entered the Federal League. The rival league was now in head-to-head competition with organized baseball in four cities (Brooklyn, Chicago, Pittsburgh, and St. Louis).

Thanks to its solid financial backing, the Federal League went after proven performers. Gilmore favored the aggressive pursuit of major and minor leaguers by extending generous salary offers, prompting 221 players to jump contracts to join the Federal League. They included such well-known stars as future Hall of Famers Mordecai "Three Finger" Brown, who joined the St. Louis team as pitcher-manager, and the Cubs's star shortstop Joe Tinker, who was recruited by the Chicago Whales, as well as other capable players such as Benny Kauff and Ed Roush. Other major leaguers took advantage of the competition to secure larger, long-term salaries from their current teams. Pitcher Ray Fisher of the New York Yankees turned his $3,000 salary in 1913 into a three-year contract worth $20,000.

On opening day, 27,140 fans flocked to watch Buffalo take on Baltimore in Terrapin Park. The pennant race came down to the final day, with Indianapolis winning by just 1.5 games over Chicago.

The sporting press divided over their assessment of the independent league, with *Sporting News* (known to be close to the established leagues) depicting the "outlaw" Federal League as a joke, while *Sporting Life* and *Baseball Magazine* gave Federal League games fair coverage and took a neutral position in this "second baseball war." After the season, the Federal League sued baseball in federal court for antitrust violations by "conspiring to monopolize the business of baseball."

Tensions with organized baseball arose after the season, as the Federal League attempted to lure star major leaguers embroiled in salary disputes. In January 1915, organized baseball passed a law banishing for life any player who jumped to the rival league. Team owners also raised salaries by more than 100 percent to deter contract jumping, with the average salary increasing from $3,187 in 1913 to $7,327 in 1915. Superstar Ty Cobb boosted his salary to $20,000 a year.

In 1915, the Federal League had the closest pennant race in big league history to that time. On the final day of the season, 34,212 fans gathered at Weeghman Park (now Wrigley Field) for a two-day doubleheader between the Chicago Whales and Pittsburgh Feds to watch Chicago take the pennant by a mere .001 percentage point (86–66, .566) over St. Louis (87–67, .565).

Fan attendance rose by 20 percent, yet the Federal League ended the 1915 season in dire financial straits. It had sizable overhead with several new ballparks, paid handsome salaries, and had heavy legal fees because of numerous lawsuits with organized baseball over the validity of player contracts.

Termination

After the season, the leaders of organized baseball were worried about the Federal League's antitrust lawsuit, which languished in the court of Judge Kenesaw Mountain Landis, and fretted that the Federal League would invade other territorial markets, including the lucrative New York area. There were reports that the Federal League was planning to build a 55,000-seat stadium in Manhattan, although it was just a bluff. At the same time, the Federal League suffered a major blow when Tip-Tops owner Ward, one of its most ardent backers, suddenly died.

The situation encouraged the three leagues to negotiate a resolution. The settlement of December 22, sometimes known as the "buy-out truce," provided that organized baseball would pay an estimated $600,000 to six Federal League owners, who agreed to cease operations. Whales owner Charles Weeghman obtained control of the Chicago Cubs, and refrigerator magnate Phil Ball of the St. Louis Terriers purchased the bankrupt St. Louis Browns. As further compensation, the settlement banned the blacklisting of former Federal League players and provided amnesty for contract jumpers.

The Baltimore Terrapins, who received nothing in the proposed settlement, rejected the deal and continued the antitrust suit. The federal court ruled in April 1919 that organized baseball indeed had conspired to monopolize baseball, and awarded the plaintiffs $80,000, with damages tripled by the terms of the Clayton Antitrust Act. However, the major leagues appealed the ruling to the U.S. Supreme Court.

In 1922, Justice Oliver Wendell Holmes, Jr., ruled in *Federal Base Ball Club of Baltimore, Inc. v. National League of Professional Baseball Clubs, et al* (259 U.S. 200) that the business of baseball was "not an interference with commerce among the states" because "the transport of players [was] a mere incident" and that their "personal effort, which [was] not related to production, [was] not a subject of commerce." Therefore, baseball was exempt from the 1890 Sherman Antitrust Act, and the lower court's ruling was overturned. To date, the 1922 ruling—which gave the reserve clause its legal support—still holds, even though the reserve clause has been nullified by later arbitration and court decisions.

Peter N. Marquis

See also: Baseball, Major League; Landis, Kenesaw Mountain; Law.

Further Reading

Burk, Robert F. *Never Just a Game: Players, Owners, and American Baseball to 1920.* Chapel Hill: University of North Carolina Press, 1994.

Lindberg, Richard. "Chicago Whales and the Federal League of American Baseball, 1914–1915." *Chicago History* 10 (Spring 1981): 2–12.

Okkonen, Marc. *The Federal League of 1914–1915: Baseball's Third Major League.* Garrett Park, MD: Society for American Baseball Research, 1989.

Seymour, Harold. *Baseball.* 3 vols. New York: Oxford University Press, 1960–1989.

Feller, Bob
(1918–2010)

Bob Feller, an outstanding fastball pitcher for the Cleveland Indians, is considered the greatest hurler of his era, and one of the best right-handed pitchers in the history of baseball. A gifted player who never played in the minor leagues, he intimidated batters by throwing balls at speeds of nearly 100 miles per hour during his long career with the Cleveland Indians, from 1936 through 1956. Feller led the American League in strikeouts in seven seasons, in wins six times, and in innings pitched five times, despite losing several years in the prime of his career to military service during World War II.

Robert William Andrew Feller was born on November 3, 1918, outside Van Meter, Iowa, one of two children of William Feller, a farmer, and his wife Lena, a teacher and nurse. His father was a former semiprofessional baseball pitcher who taught Bob to play ball, even building a baseball diamond on their farm. At age 13, Feller already was playing shortstop and batting cleanup for the local American Legion team, and soon he was a star pitcher for Van Meter High School. As a junior in spring 1936, he pitched five no-hit games.

While still in high school, Feller secretly was signed to a minor league contract by the Cleveland Indians of the American League—a clear violation of major league rules. Shortly thereafter, the rights to Feller became the subject of a dispute between Cleveland and the Des Moines minor league club. Commissioner of Baseball Kenesaw Mountain Landis eventually awarded the pitcher to Cleveland but fined the Indians $7,500 for the illegal contract.

At just 17, Feller, 6 feet (1.8 meters) and 185 pounds (84 kilograms), made a few appearances as a relief pitcher for Cleveland in 1936. He had his first start on August 23, striking out 15 St. Louis Browns for a 4–1 victory. He soon was nicknamed "Rapid Robert" because of his blazing fastball, which was even more difficult to hit because he slightly turned his back to the hitter in his delivery, followed by a high leg kick. In September, he struck out 17 Philadelphia Athletics batters to tie the major league record. The teenager finished the 1936 season with a record of 5–3 in 14 appearances. Feller then returned to Van Meter for his last year of high school and graduated in June, 1937, shortly after he appeared on the cover of *Time* magazine.

During the 1937 season, Feller's effectiveness was restricted by arm trouble, although he compiled a 9–7 record. In 1938, he bounced back and achieved a 17–11 record. He led the league in strikeouts (240), though he had control problems, and in walks (208), still a major league record. The season was highlighted by a one-hitter, the first of 12 during his career, and a new strike-out record on the last day of the season, when he struck out 18 Detroit Tigers hitters. Feller was named an All-Star for the first of eight times.

Feller's career peaked in 1939, as he became the most dominant hurler in baseball for the next three seasons. He compiled an amazing string of records—finishing 1939 with a mark of 24–9, while leading the league with 246 strikeouts. Always possessing good entrepreneurial acumen, by the late 1930s, Feller led an all-star team on annual postseason exhibition tours against the famous Negro League pitcher Satchel Paige and his all-star squad. They resumed their rivalry after World War II and faced each other more than 20 times.

The 1940 season began with Feller throwing baseball's first opening day no-hitter, against the Chicago White Sox. He had added to his repertoire a sweeping curveball that was nearly as overpowering as his fastball. Feller went on to compile a record of 27–11 that season, while also leading the league with a 2.61 earned run average, 261 strikeouts, and most innings pitched (320.3). He followed up in 1941 with a record of 25–13 and again led the league with 260 strikeouts and 343 innings pitched.

Two days after the bombing of Pearl Harbor in December 1941, Feller became the first major league player to enlist in the military, joining the U.S. Navy on January 6, 1942. Feller lost nearly four full seasons to wartime duty. He was discharged in late 1945 after earning eight battle stars and five campaign ribbons as an antiaircraft gunnery officer in the Pacific. While in the service, he married Virginia Winther in January 1943; the couple would have three sons.

Feller returned to baseball in 1946 when he signed for $50,000, but he earned another $50,000 from incentives, endorsements, and profits from a barnstorming tour against Negro League stars. He pitched the second no-hitter of his career on April 30 against the New York Yankees. That season, *Life* magazine conducted a speed test of Feller's fastball that read 98.6 miles (159 kilometers) per hour. He went on to post a 26–15 record that included ten shutouts for the sixth-place Indians, while also racking up 348 strikeouts in

371.3 innings. In 1947, he signed a new contract for approximately $80,000 per year, earning an additional $70,000 from incentives and endorsements. That year, Feller led the American League with a mark of 20–11 with five shutouts and 196 strikeouts.

Beginning with the 1948 season, Feller was plagued by arm problems. Still, he posted a record of 19–15 that included six straight late-season victories as Cleveland finally won the American League pennant. He made two appearances during the Indians's victorious 1948 World Series against the Boston Braves, losing both games, including a 1–0 decision in the opening game. After two average seasons—by Feller's standards—he bounced back in 1951 to tally a 22–8 record that included the third no-hitter of his career on July 1 against the Detroit Tigers.

Thereafter, Feller was a "spot starter" on a Cleveland staff that was loaded with good pitchers. In 1954, he posted a 13–3 record, while the Indians won another pennant. He did not appear in the World Series that the Indians lost in four straight games to the New York Giants. Feller retired after the 1956 season, finishing with a career record of 266–162 in 570 game appearances, along with 2,581 strikeouts, 1,764 walks, and an earned run average of 3.25.

After his baseball days, Feller worked in insurance before becoming a member of the Cleveland Indians's public relations department, for which he traveled extensively. In 1962, Feller was elected to the National Baseball Hall of Fame in his first year of eligibility, and as part of professional baseball's centennial in 1969, he was named the greatest living right-handed pitcher.

Feller divorced Virginia Winther in 1971. Settling in Gates Mills, Ohio, he married his second wife, Anne, in October 1974. In his era baseball's biggest draw, Feller remained a hero in retirement, and he made numerous appearances at baseball memorabilia shows.

He died on December 15, 2010, in Cleveland. A statue of Feller stands outside the city's Progressive Field. He also is honored in the Bob Feller Museum in Van Meter.

Raymond Schmidt

See also: Baseball, Major League; Indians, Cleveland.

Further Reading

Feller, Bob, with Bill Gilbert. *Now Pitching, Bob Feller.* New York: Carol, 1990.

Schoor, Gene. *Bob Feller: Hall of Fame Strikeout Star.* Garden City, NY: Doubleday, 1962.

Sickels, John. *Bob Feller: Ace of the Greatest Generation.* Washington, DC: Brassey's, 2004.

Fencing

Fencing always has been a minor sport in North America, whereas in Europe, it was a martial art and long the preferred means for gentlemen to defend their honor. In the United States, the sport enjoyed some popularity among military officers, especially cavalrymen, who relied on the saber in combat, and among the elite, who wanted to emulate European aristocrats. Early competitive fencing, which began in the 1860s and 1870s, was centered in New York and a few other metropolises where there were well-known fencing schools directed by European masters.

By the late 1930s, fencing underwent a dramatic reorientation in the United States with the rising preeminence of upwardly mobile New York Jews who, following in the footsteps of their Central European counterparts, had learned the sport in the late nineteenth century to defend their honor against anti-Semites and to gain social acceptance. Since the 1980s, African Americans have achieved considerable success in fencing, both combating negative stereotypes and gaining personal recognition in the sport.

Origins in North America

The first fencing school in British North America opened in Boston in 1673. Virginia plantation owners who emulated the English gentry became interested in the sport during the eighteenth century, as gentlemen were expected to be familiar with swords. In 1734, Edwards Blackwell of Williamsburg, Virginia, wrote *A Complete System of Fencing or the Art of Defence,* the first sporting book published in British America.

Early fencing masters had a hard time finding students. John Rievers of Holland advertised in 1754 that he was prepared to teach fencing and dancing in New York City, but he did not get much business. His successor, W.C. Hulett, tried to support his fencing program by adding violin and flute lessons to the roster. At the turn of the century, New Orleans became the main site of fencing schools, run by French and Italian experts.

Certain preeminent Americans spoke positively about fencing, including lexicographer Noah Webster and General Andrew Jackson, who recommended that soldiers train with foils or sabers, because it shaped vision and taught coolness under pressure. Still, sword fights were rare among Americans, who mainly dueled with guns. Yet there was a fatal sword duel in Boston in

1728. By 1834, French-influenced New Orleans typically had ten duels a week at "The Dueling Oaks."

In the mid-nineteenth century, German immigrant Turners popularized the sport. They formed a fencing club in New York in 1850, where political émigré Franz Sigel, the future Civil War general, served as fencing master. The Boston Fencing Club opened in 1858 to give members access to fencing education in an environment that was free from the objections that public fencing schools were too democratic. After the Civil War, many colleges and athletic clubs adopted fencing under the instruction of Belgian, French, German, and Italian teachers.

One of the finest instructors was Régis Sénac, a French immigrant who established the Salle d'Armes in 1874, the first fencing school in New York. The U.S. fencing champion in 1876 and author of *The Art of Fencing* (1915), Sénac emphasized the style of the classical French school, featuring smooth, fluid moves. Another well-regarded instructor was the more popular Captain Hippolyte Nicholas, the preceptor of the New York Fencers' Club, formed in 1883, whose innovative system was based on the more aggressive Italian school of fencing.

In terms of equipment, American fencers preferred the saber, which makes a point in competition by striking any part of the body above the waist with either the point or the blade. Also popular was the foil, a thrusting weapon that scores torso hits with the tip of the blade.

The Amateur Athletic Union initiated national fencing championships in 1888, but disgruntled fencers formed the Amateur Fencers League of America (now the U.S. Fencing Association) in 1891, one year prior to the first national championships in Great Britain and France, and ten years before Canada. In 1894, Harvard and Columbia universities founded the Intercollegiate Fencing Association.

During this time, competitors wore dark suits, so that chalk marks from their sword tips could be easily detected. The uniform became white for foil in 1897 and for epee in 1911.

American fencers were less adept with the epee, a thrusting weapon derived from the rapier, which originally was popular in Europe as a dueling sword. It is stiffer and heavier than the foil and has a larger bell guard. Any strike on the body counts as a hit.

Women and Fencing

Fencing was considered a masculine sport, and women in New York did not receive instruction until the 1880s. Fitness experts advocated that women learn to use the lightweight foil, a graceful, healthful activity that was readily adaptable to a woman's strength. The sport was especially recommended for delicate urbanites who suffered many ailments because of their lack of exercise, as it would develop their chest and other muscles, quicken their blood, and promote flexibility, quickness of eye, delicacy of touch, and steadied nerves. The first women fencers often were actresses or students at Smith College, where the sport became part of the curriculum in 1895 under the direction of Senda Berenson.

Women's fencing organizations were formed in the early 1900s in New York and Philadelphia by wealthy women. The first women's college team was formed at the University of Pennsylvania in the early 1900s, and other prestigious schools such as Bryn Mawr, Mount Holyoke, and Vassar colleges, and the universities of Wisconsin and Michigan subsequently promoted the sport for physical training. In 1912, Adelaide Baylis of New York took the first national women's foil championship. Helene Mayer, the German Jewish Olympic star, won eight U.S. championships from 1934 to 1946.

Olympic Competition

The U.S. men's team has won 12 individual medals (one gold, five silver, and six bronze) and five team medals (two silver and three bronze) in fencing at the Olympic Games, a record skewed by the 1904 Olympics, when only Cuba and the United States competed. Albertson Van Zo Post alone took five medals at the St. Louis Games, including gold in the long-discontinued event of single sticks (cudgels). In 1912, Lieutenant George S. Patton competed in the modern pentathlon, finishing third in the fencing competition. The United States won few medals over the next decades, mainly team bronzes, though U.S. Navy Lieutenant George Calnan won a bronze medal in the epee in 1928 and Joseph Levis won a silver medal in foil in 1932. He was rated number one in the world prior to the 1936 Olympics.

In the 1930s and 1940s, fencing gained popularity, particularly among ethnic youth, who learned the sport at settlement houses. They saw fencing as wide open for quick and talented athletes, even though they remained barred from entry by the New York Athletic Club. New York Jews, trained at the city's outstanding fencing schools, were so successful that the entire men's foil team in 1956 was Jewish. The team was led by Albert Axelrod of the City College of New York, who won a bronze medal in 1960—the first U.S. medal since 1932. The next great American fencer was African

American Peter Westbrook of New York University (13-time U.S. champion and five-time Olympian), who took the bronze in saber in 1984. He became a role model and prominent supporter of inner-city fencing and developed several outstanding protégés, including saber star Keeth Smart, who in 2003 became the second American ever to be ranked number one in fencing.

Fencing became an Olympic sport for women in 1924, but U.S. women were not competitive at the Olympic level until 2004, when Americans Mariel Zagunis and Sada Jacobson came in first and third, respectively, in saber. Four years later, the United States captured six medals, a total in the sport second only to Italy. The U.S. men captured a team silver in saber, and the women took five medals, including a sweep in saber, led by repeat champion Mariel Zagunis and Sada Jacobson, who came in second. Between 2004 and 2008, American women captured five individual medals and two team world titles, all in saber. Since then, Zagunis won the world championship in 2009 and 2010.

Steven A. Riess

See also: Martial Arts; Olympics, Summer.

Further Reading

Cohen, Richard. *By the Sword: History of Gladiators, Musketeers, Samurai, Swashbucklers, and Olympic Champions.* New York: Random House, 2002.

Krout, John Allen. *Annals of American Sport.* New Haven, CT: Yale University Press, 1929.

Mondschein, Ken. "The Other Wild West: Fencing in New York in the 1880s and After." Association for Historical Fencing. http://www.ahfi.org.

Shaw, Andy. "The AFLA/USFA Story: In the Beginning: Our Sport Has Quite a Past in America." *American Fencing* 53:4 (2004): 28–30.

Field Hockey

Field hockey is a team sport whose forerunners date back more than 4,000 years to the Nile Valley in Egypt; the Greeks, Romans, Ethiopians, and Aztecs later played comparable games. North Americans played versions of field hockey known as "bandy" and "shinty" in the late eighteenth century. The British exported the modern game of field hockey to the United States at the beginning of the twentieth century, and it became a popular women's sport, especially at elite East Coast women's colleges. Field hockey did not become a men's sport until the 1920s. North American men never have achieved prominence in the sport, but American women are competitive in world-class play.

As its name implies, field hockey is played on a grassy field, known as a pitch, measuring 100 yards (91 meters) in length and 60 yards (55 meters) in width. At each end is a goal 7 feet (2.1 meters) high and 12 feet (3.7 meters) across. Two teams of 11 players, as well as five substitutes, use sticks—shaped like an elongated J—to hit a small ball into the goal. Players are allowed to hit the ball only with the stick. Bodily contact with the ball is permitted if it is unintentional and does not benefit the person touching the ball. Tackling of other players is permitted, as long as it done in pursuit of the ball and does not occur before the ball is hit. Field hockey matches are 70 minutes in length, divided into two 35-minute halves.

Englishmen played modern field hockey in the mid-nineteenth century, and in 1886, the Hockey Association was established. The military spread the game across the British Empire, and the 1908 Olympic Games in London featured field hockey. Originally considered too rough for women, changing attitudes about women's athletic abilities by the early 1900s made field hockey the only outdoor team sport widely considered acceptable for women. The first women's club was organized in England in 1887, and the All England Women's Hockey Association was set up two years later.

The game came to North America in 1896, when a match was played by girls in Vancouver, Canada. The Vancouver Ladies Club was formed, but no women's organization was established there until 1927. Men played at the turn of the century in Vancouver and Victoria, and a Vancouver League came into existence in 1902.

In 1901, British physical educator Constance Applebee was in the United States attending a seminar at Harvard University. She introduced the sport there, borrowing some sticks and a ball, and arranged a game behind the Harvard gymnasium. Harriet Ballintine, director of athletics at Vassar College, attended the demonstration and hired Applebee to teach field hockey there. The first hockey club in the United States was formed in Poughkeepsie, New York, in 1901. Later that year, the American Field Hockey Association (AFHA) was founded, with Applebee as president. One of its main accomplishments was the publication of standardized rules.

In 1904, Applebee moved to Bryn Mawr College as director of outdoor sports, staying there for 25 years. She actively and successfully promoted the game at Bryn Mawr and at a number of other elite women's colleges. Applebee also founded a field hockey camp at

Mount Pocono, Pennsylvania, and became editor and publisher of *The Sportswoman,* the first magazine aimed specifically at women athletes.

Other women's schools and public colleges in the East quickly adopted the sport. The uniforms included skirts of light wool materials with knickerbockers (baggy knee-length pants), but no petticoats, along with a flannel shirt or blouse. Goalkeepers and fullbacks often wore sweaters, or cots, for colder days. By 1923, there was no longer a dress code or any regulations of skirt length.

A second club was founded at the Merion Golf Club in Philadelphia. A club system was established in Philadelphia in 1904, and three years later, the first noncollegiate field hockey league was organized there. The game spread from Boston and Philadelphia (which both had secondary school leagues) to New York, Detroit, Chicago, Baltimore, Richmond, and Los Angeles. In 1915, Rosemary Hall in Greenwich, Connecticut, became the first boarding school to introduce field hockey.

Several colleges and clubs sponsored teams in the 1920s. In 1920, Applebee brought 15 all-stars from Philadelphia to Great Britain and went 2–8. There were a few tours afterward, and England toured the United States in 1928. In 1922, the women's U.S. Field Hockey Association (USFHA), which was separate from the AFHA of 20 years earlier, was founded with representatives from 15 states. The International Federation of Women's Hockey Associations (IFWHA) was founded in 1927 by representatives from eight countries, including the United States and six other English-speaking countries, along with Denmark.

Men's field hockey in the United States began in 1928 with a contest between the upper-class Germantown Cricket Club of Philadelphia and the Westchester Field Hockey Club. The Field Hockey Association of America (FHAA), dedicated to the men's sports, began that year, and it joined the Fédération Internationale de Hockey sur Gazon two years later. Henry Greer, president of the FHAA from 1930 to 1959 and a player-coach for the 1932 U.S. Olympic team, was the father of U.S. men's field hockey. At the 1932 Olympics in Los Angeles, the United States, one of only three teams competing, lost both of its games, including one match to India by a score of 24–1, but still got a bronze medal. The U.S. men's team competed in the 1936, 1948, 1956, 1984, and 1996 Summer Games. In 1993, the USFHA and FHAA merged into one national governing body. There currently are about 14,000 participants in men's field hockey.

Field hockey first became an intercollegiate sport in the United States in 1975 when the first Association for Intercollegiate Athletics for Women national championship was held. Since 1976, the game has been played largely on artificial turf, accentuating speed. Intercollegiate women's field hockey is dominated by Old Dominion University, with nine titles, followed by five each for the University of North Carolina and the University of Maryland. Currently, more than 100 colleges compete in field hockey.

The U.S. women's team competed in 1975 at the first IFWHA World Championship in Edinburgh, Scotland. Five years later, when women's hockey was added to the Olympic program, a U.S. women's team gained a slot, but the boycott of the Moscow Games precluded their participation. In 1984, under renowned coach Vonnie Gros, the United States captured the bronze medal. The team also appeared in the 1988 and 1996 Olympics and won a bronze medal at the 1994 world championships.

Steven A. Riess

See also: Lacrosse; Women.

Further Reading

Shillingford, Jenepher. *United States Field Hockey Association, 1922–1972.* N.p.: United States Field Hockey Association, 1972.

United States Olympic Committee. "Field Hockey History and Tradition." http:// usafieldhockey.com/usa-field-hockey/ history-and-tradition.

Wulf, Steve. "Who Are These Guys? And Why Aren't They Wearing Skirts?" *Sports Illustrated* 61:4 (July 18, 1984): 402–404, 406, 410, 412, 415, 418.

Figure Skating

Figure skating, a form of dancing on ice, either freestyle or following a series of prescribed patterns, stands at the intersection of sports, dance, and theater. A North American creation—long dominated in competitive circles by athletes from Canada and the United States—figure skating was one of the earliest sports to be considered appropriate for women athletes. Indeed, from its earliest years, women competitors have gained as large a fan following as males, perhaps larger. At first a strictly amateur sport, figure skating gained commercial appeal with the Norwegian skater Sonja Henie, who used her Olympic gold medal fame and blonde good looks to launch a lucrative career figure skating in live exhibitions and Hollywood movies.

Origins of Figure Skating

Skating on ice with steel runners dates to thirteenth- and fourteenth-century Northern Europe. American-born painter Benjamin West first exhibited his etchings of geometric ice drawings by ice-skating on London's artificially constructed Serpentine Pond in 1763.

The first figure skating club in North America began in St. John, New Brunswick, in 1833, just three years after the formation of the London Skating Club, and it had women members from the beginning. The first U.S. organization was the Philadelphia Skating Club in 1849. Members skated on river ice and were required to be attached to ropes in the event they fell through the ice. By the beginning of the Civil War, rinks devoted to skating had been built in a number of U.S. and Canadian cities.

The nineteenth-century public was awed by the exceptionally novel maneuvers they saw at informal ice shows on New York City's public ponds. These first great ice dancers entertained spectators by performing movements free from the repetitive monotony often seen on the ponds, as thousands of newcomers awkwardly attempted to learn the new rage in winter recreation.

In 1859, skating at New York City's new Central Park Pond gave male and female outdoor "ice artists," as they were called, the chance to astonish thousands of passersby. Skating at Central Park became one of the most popular recreations of the time, and the construction of city parks and ponds was central to the growth of ice-skating.

Among the first celebrities to perform on New York's outdoor stage were professional tinsmith "Jersey John" Engler, who set the standard for early ice dancing, also known as "open field skating," and New Yorker Jackson Haines, considered the father of modern figure skating. Haines combined his skills as a ballet dancer and added musical accompaniment to his performances to create what came to be known as the "international style," a major shift away from the rigid and formal English style. Engler, Haines, William Fuller, Carrie Augusta Moore (known as the first "Skatorial Queen"), Canadian Mabel Davidson, and other pioneers astonished a public who had never witnessed such novel movements on ice.

So popular were Haines and Moore that they were recruited by renowned showman P.T. Barnum in 1863 to perform on roller skates in stage pantomime acts, prompting Australian promoter George Coppin to recruit Fuller for a world tour of Asia, Australia, and Eu-

rope from 1865 until 1869. Haines achieved his greatest popularity in Europe during the mid-1860s, and his $20,000 annual earnings eventually attracted Chicagoan Callie Curtis, E.T. Goodrich, and Moore to join Haines on European tours of their own by 1873.

Nineteenth Century: Figure Skating as Performance

Scottish Canadian Robert Glasgow Hervey and his brother, Arthur Hervey, were major promoters of figure skating in its early years. In 1859, they began building the first of about 50 ice theaters (covered ice rinks) in such U.S. cities as Boston, Chicago, and Pittsburgh, and in Halifax and Montreal in Canada—all prior to the introduction of artificially refrigerated ice rinks in the late 1870s. When the Herveys first harnessed nature's freezing capabilities in their covered rinks, they vented warm air up and out through ceiling vents, allowing cold air to enter through ground-level windows, thereby freezing the water. Many Hervey covered rinks eventually were converted into rinks that produced ice by various chemical refrigeration processes, using miles of installed copper pipe undulating back and forth amid flooded water soon to be frozen. The Herveys also introduced artistic skating contests in 1867, the beginning of competitive figure skating.

By 1867, young skaters such as Curtis, Goodrich, and William Bishop (stage name Frank Swift) developed a partnership with the Hervey brothers and formed the short-lived American Skating Congress in 1869, which promoted the first touring ice shows and competitions—of dubious integrity—scheduled in Hervey rinks. It folded in 1873, and its major stars sought greater riches in Europe.

Figure skating's early history in North America essentially consisted of using Hervey's ice theater designs to showcase celebrity skating personalities who pioneered innovative and comedic dance choreography, all while shuffling back and forth between North America and Europe. At the same time, the Hervey brothers were caught in the business of promoting fraudulent skating contests and fooling the public by trying to pass off male skaters as female. After making a public apology, they immediately hired Canadian Maggie Elwood to compete on the traveling circuit against other female skaters. Still, these competitions—filled with monotonous routines—came to bore spectators. The Hervey ice shows went into a slow decline by the 1870s, and their competitors moved to Europe.

By the early 1880s, professional theatrical figure skating largely had disappeared from the North American scene. During the so-called amateur era of the 1890s and early 1900s, figure skating professionals tried to adapt by shifting to the new sport of figure roller-skating and stunt contests, such as roller derby, barrel jumping, and the Vaudeville roller stage.

Replacing the professional circuit of theatrical figure skating was amateur figure skating, dominated by set routines, which often satisfied athletes and competitors but did little to draw the public's interest. Still, there were local contests, and many figure skaters took part in speed skating competitions. In 1890, Canadian Louis Rubinstein—founder of the Amateur Skating Association of Canada—became the first North American to vie in international competition, winning the World Figure Skating Championship in Russia. Rubinstein's "closed figures" style contrasted with the "open field" style of the dominant Russian skaters, which incorporated long, flowing movements that had been the hallmark of the theatrical era in North American skating.

This tension between styles led to the creation of the International Skating Union in 1892, which tried to standardize the "science" of judging artistic ice-skating and ice dancing, along with strict standards for speed skating. Fifteen years later, the United States and Canada together formed the International Skating Union of America. The National Amateur Skating Association of the United States was formally established in 1903 and then supplanted in 1921 by the United States Figure Skating Association.

Still, North American figure skating between 1873 and 1909 was not particularly enjoyable for spectators and judges, who had to watch hours of tedious tracing of skate marks over previously etched lines. By 1909, amateur organizers recognized that their "sport" of figures was dying and, by 1915, returned to its dramatic and entertainment roots. That year, Rubenstein and others recruited 19-year-old German Charlotte Oelschlägel to perform on New York City's artificial ice stage at the Hippodrome theater; one year later, she appeared in movies, presaging the career of perhaps the most famous of figure skaters, Sonia Henie.

Elimination of Compulsory Figures: Skating's Shift from Art to Sport

In the early twentieth century, Europeans dominated competitive skating of all types. Swede Ulrich Salchow won ten world championships and created the salchow jump, which gave a more athletic dimension to the sport. Norwegian Sonja Henie reigned among women in the interwar years, winning ten straight world championships (1927–1936) and three Olympic gold medals. She brought elegance to skating and a certain sexiness to the sport with her short skirts. Henie moved to Hollywood in 1936, earning millions from her 15 films that focused on skating themes. She also went into business with Arthur Wirtz's Hollywood Ice Revue, making up to $2 million a year from skating exhibitions.

In the aftermath of World War II, Europe fell behind North America in figure skating as the emphasis of the sport shifted to speed, endurance, and energetic movements. Olympic gold medalists in this era included American Dick Button, who introduced the double axel jump, winning gold medals in 1948 and 1952, and later became the sport's preeminent television commentator. Canadian Donald Jackson won his nation's first male world championship in 1962, scoring seven 6.0 scores in the free skate, while Petra Burks, the 1963 world champion, took a bronze at the 1964 Olympics.

Canadians were particularly strong in pairs, winning seven world titles from 1954 to 1962, including four straight titles by Barbara Wagner and Robert Paul (1957–1960), and the Olympic gold medal at Squaw Valley, California, in 1960. The era of American dominance came to a tragic end in 1961 with an airplane crash that claimed the lives of the entire U.S. figure skating team.

Revival of North American Figure Skating

The successes of the so-called amateur Olympic figure skating contests of the 1950s, 1960s, and 1970s were based on the professional ice show models, which provided pleasing spectacles for audiences. The United States's resurgence in the sport began with Peggy Fleming, the national champion at age 16 in 1964 and winner of the Olympic gold medal in 1968. A superb artist, she was selected in 1976 to the first class of the World Figure Skating Hall of Fame. That year, Dorothy Hamill won a gold medal at the Olympics.

Male North Americans were even more dominant, winning 15 world championships from 1981 to 1997, including four for both Scott Hamilton and Canadian Kurt Browning. The American Olympic male champions were Scott Hamilton (1984) and Brian Boitano (1988), with Canadian Brian Orser winning a silver medal in both years.

A major development in elite figure skating was the end of compulsory figures in Olympic competition in 1990. More athletic triple and quad jumps and innovative dance choreography became the challenge for skaters, who had the difficult job of impressing judges with not only acrobatic athleticism but also with graceful dance art. Thus, in the late twentieth and early twenty-first centuries, figure skaters struggled to strike a balance between aesthetic appeal and the more athletic demands set by officials of the International Skating Union.

Despite the new rules, American women continued to have great success in international competition. Kristi Yamaguchi took a gold medal at the 1992 Olympics, as did Tara Lipinksi in 1998, and Sarah Hughes in 2002. The artistic Michelle Kwan, whose best Olympic finish was a silver medal in 1998, was nevertheless the dominant skater of the era, with five world championships between 1996 and 2003. Nancy Kerrigan won a silver medal at the 1994 Games in Lillehammer, Norway, after having been attacked at the U.S. Nationals by a man who struck her with a metal baton on the knee at the behest of rival Tonya Harding, who was stripped of her national title and banned from skating competitions.

American men were no longer at the top of the sport, although Canadian Elvis Stojko won silver medals in 1994 and 1998. At the 2002 Olympics in Salt Lake City, Utah, a scandal involving corrupted judges led the International Skating Union to award duplicate gold medals in pairs figure skating to Canada's Jamie Salé and David Pelletier, who originally had been given second place. In 2010, Evan Lysacek captured the gold.

The unfair judging resulted in the old scoring system being discarded in 2004. Under the old rules, skaters were rated on a 6.0 scale for technical merit, required elements in the short program, technical merit in the long program, and presentation in both, all in order to determine a preference ranking, or "ordinal" for each program. The combined placings then determined the overall winner. The new judging system awards technical marks for each skating element, which has a different value depending on difficulty. There are 12 judges, but only the scores of nine randomly selected judges are computed, with the highest and lowest ratings discounted.

By the twenty-first century, figure skating was once again declining in popularity. Many questioned its athleticism, along with that of its relative, ice dancing. With the acceptance of professionals in the Olympics, wealthy competitors jumped back and forth from Olympic skating to touring ice shows, once the exclusive arena of professionals.

Kristi Yamaguchi, a third-generation Japanese American (Sansei), glides to a gold medal in ladies' singles figure skating at the 1992 Winter Olympics in Albertville, France. The popular California native also won the world championship in 1991 and 1992. *(AFP/Getty Images)*

Meanwhile, professional and pro-am tournaments have enjoyed limited appeal. Television coverage has declined as a result of previous oversaturation, and touring ice shows have become less popular. Moreover, young athletes and their families have been discouraged by the expense of the sport and, in an increasingly multicultural America, the sport still has had limited appeal to nonwhites, though Asian American women continue to do well in competition.

Paul J. DeLoca

See also: Olympics, Winter; Speed Skating.

Further Reading

Bianchetti Garbato, Sonia. *Cracked Ice: Figure Skating's Inner World.* Milan, Italy: Libreria Dello Sport, 2004.

Brokaw, Irving. *The Art of Skating: Its History and Development.* New York: Scribner's, 1926.

Goodfellow, Arthur. *The Skating Scene: The Fact Book of Skating: Champions and Championships.* Phoenix: Goodfellow, 1981.

Hines, James R. *Figure Skating: A History*. Urbana: University of Illinois Press, 2006.

Whedon, Julia. *The Fine Art of Ice Skating*. New York: Harry N. Abrams, 1988.

Film

When Edweard Muybridge produced a series of photographs of Leland Stanford's champion racehorse Abe Eddington in 1873, he proved, once and for all, that when a horse gallops, all of its hooves leave the ground at the same time. Well documented at the time, with journalists covering it as both a sporting and a scientific landmark, the event also marked an important moment in the history of cinema. In fact, even though these photos were not "moving pictures," one still could call these images the prototype of the world's first sports film.

From this moment on, the worlds of sports and film became intimately connected. At first, the athletic motion of sports was a compelling subject for the new technology of moving pictures, but as the film industry developed into a studio-driven system dominated by narrative, the sports film began to develop a story structure all its own. Connected to sporting traditions that included both competitive sports and community-building athletic activities, the sports film genre developed around the theme of the level playing field. Underdogs worked hard to become champions as the genre fashioned an athletic masculine ideal. Through thousands of films from the late 1800s to the present, sports and cinema combined to produce and represent the athletic "American dream."

Sports and Early Cinema: 1890–1917

In its earliest period, the motion picture industry was unsettled, as was the exhibition space used for their display. In addition to more "traditional" movie theater exhibitions, audiences might see films at a walk-in Nickelodeon, where they would pay a nickel to peek into an individual viewer, or they might find the cinema at a vaudeville show in which a film screening was just one of the forms of entertainment offered. Similarly, the film form itself varied, with narrative and documentary offerings competing for prominence, and sporting activities quickly became some of the most popular subjects of early cinema.

The earliest sports films took the form of what historians call "actualities." These very short motion pictures did not offer narratives, but instead purported to offer a view of an "actual" slice of life. Sometimes, this was a recording of a real-life sporting event, but just as often, it was an exhibition specifically performed for the camera. Films such as *Newark Athlete* (1891), *Sandow: The Strong Man* (1894), and *Expert Bag Punching* (1903) were demonstrations of bodies in motion explicitly performed for the motion picture camera, while *Hockey Match on the Ice* (1894), *Harvard/Yale Football Game* (1903), *Basketball, Missouri Valley College* (1904), and others were typical of early attempts to record athletic events as they happened. Limited by technological and monetary constraints, these films used a single stationary camera shooting wide shots that captured the action, but not usually in a way that viewers could follow the flow of the game.

Working within the limitations of early cinema, however, some motion pictures were more successful in their display of sporting action. Boxing became the most popular cinematic sport, reflecting both the realities of cinema technology and the cultural moment of turn-of-the-century America. Even with the simple camera equipment of the era, early filmmakers were able to produce clear and compelling images that attracted enthusiastic audiences who were excited to view the popular yet somewhat disreputable sport of boxing, which was rendered more acceptable through the mediated lens of the movie camera. During this early period, there were filmed boxing exhibitions, such as *Glenroy Brothers* (1894) and *Dancing Boxing* (1907); re-creations of famous prizefights, such as *Leonard-Cushing Fight* (1894); and films depicting actual bouts, as was the case with the heavyweight championship *Corbett-Fitzsimmons Fight* (1897).

The business of boxing films influenced the course of fights such as the Jack Johnson–Stanley Ketchel heavyweight title bout of 1909, when Johnson agreed to "carry" his much smaller opponent so that they could make a movie. But in the twelfth round, Ketchel got too aggressive and knocked down Johnson, who retaliated with a one-punch knockout. Community leaders and their constituencies became so concerned about the imagery of a white man being beaten up by a black— Johnson was African American—that local governments often banned films of Johnson's fights. In 1912, it became a federal crime to transport fight films across state lines.

As movie palaces sprang up across the country and the film industry matured, motion pictures began to increase in length and audiences began to expect more than short actualities. By the 1920s, the look of the

American sports film solidified around conventions of display that were derived, for the most part, from the larger arena of sporting culture: playing fields, uniforms, demonstrations of athletic abilities, stock characters (coaches, trainers, gamblers, and so on), spectators, and scenes of training. In addition, camera positions habitually placed both the spectators within the movie and the film's audience in spectatorial positions reminiscent of traditional sporting events. At the same time, sports films (like most, if not all, Hollywood films) endeavored to have the audience identify with specific characters, often accomplished through point-of-view shots, such as the batter's view of the pitcher on the mound.

In addition to the look of the sports film, the narrative structure of the genre attained some consistency, too. Building on traditions established in youth fiction (as found in Frank Merriwell's series of dime novels) and newspaper sports pages, the narrative and social conventions of sports carried over into the sports film. The novice/natural becomes the expert/professional through hard work; individuals integrate themselves into social groups and forge "winning" communities; and the mind and body work together to form an integrated "winning" sports "hero." Although this basic storyline came in many variations, it was by and large a unique syntax that structured films featuring the spectacle of moving bodies and exploring the possibilities of the hero controlling his (or, much more rarely, her) own destiny.

The conventions of sports film established during the first decades of the twentieth century set a solid foundation for Hollywood to follow. In films such as *Strongheart* (1914), *The Heart Punch* (1915), *Brown of Harvard* (1917), *The Half Back* (1917), *The Pinch Hitter* (1917), and *The Busher* (1919), the viewer can find elements typical of the genre.

As the sports film moved forward, its level-playing-field ideology had appeal for poor and working-class Americans, particularly immigrants and their children who were looking for ways to assimilate and succeed themselves. Aligned with a rise in professionalism and the prospect of careers in sporting culture, the sports film represented stories of success for the common man.

Golden Age of Sports and Cinema: 1920s and 1930s

The "golden age of sports" in the 1920s made possible the emergence of sports superstars, complete with press agents and commercial endorsements. Baseball's George

Herman "Babe" Ruth, boxing's Jack Dempsey, and football's Harold "Red" Grange are shining examples of the new mass-mediated athletic icons of the era. These superstars were testaments to the new power of the media across print and radio, and all (and many more besides) appeared in both nonfiction and fiction films.

This was a period of maturity and growth for the film industry. The "Big Five"—MGM, Paramount, RKO, Fox, and Warner Brothers—and, to a lesser extent, the "Little Three"—Columbia, United Artists, and Universal—studios became well-integrated companies that controlled all the important elements of film production, distribution, and exhibition. The studios, with the advent of sound film in the late 1920s, made further gains in popularity and weathered the Great Depression, albeit with some difficulty. Hollywood became an assembly line of cinematic dreams. Producers annually released hundreds of films, made profitable by economies of scale.

The documentary impulse still was present at the intersection of sports and cinema, but re-creations or recordings of full events (such as prizefight films) gave way to shorter "news" stories featured in newsreel programs that emerged in the late 1920s. Sports reporting in newsreels such as *The March of Time, Movietone News,* and *Pathé News* became a regular part of the moviegoing experience.

Additionally, in the 1930s, athletes began to appear in instructional movies as well. Superstar golfer Bobby Jones, for example, starred in dozens of films with series titles such as *How I Play Golf* and *How to Break 90.* In 1938, one of the most influential sports documentaries of the twentieth century was released, *Olympia,* Leni Riefenstahl's artistic interpretation of the 1936 Olympic Games. In its emphasis on the beauty of athletic bodies in motion, this film brought forward the aesthetic qualities of sports and presaged the use of slow-motion effects and replays in future sports coverage. In its glorification of the Nazi Party and ideals of racial purity, however, it also exemplified the power of film as propaganda.

Fictional boxing films remained popular, including *Round One* (1921), *Dynamite Dan* (1924), *Battling Bunyan* (1925), *Battling Butler* (1926), *His People* (1926), *Celebrity* (1927), *The Champ* (1931), *Iron Man* (1931), *Prizefighter and the Lady* (1933), *Palooka* (1934), *Kid Galahad* (1937), and *Golden Boy* (1939), ensuring that boxing (the "sweet science") remained a vivid part of the cinematic landscape. In addition, the era witnessed the regular production of sporting films about baseball, basketball, hockey, wrestling, and other sports. Particularly noteworthy was the dramatic appearance of the college sports film.

In the interwar era, college football achieved widespread popularity among everyday Americans who had no direct connection to any university. With the apparent (if not fully realized) democratization of universities and the spread of automobiles and radio, which allowed greater numbers of fans to see and hear the games, it was not surprising that college athletics proved an enticing subject for the cinema.

The commercial and popular success of *The Freshman* in 1925 spurred interest in this subject. The movie chronicled the comic exploits of a hapless student who is taunted and spurned by his fellow classmates until he improbably becomes the campus hero by winning the big game. *The Freshman* was an athletic "coming-of-age" story in which a boy becomes a man by playing and succeeding at sports. It provided the rough narrative template followed by other college sports films.

For most of the 1920s and 1930s, the college campus was represented as a utopian setting in which anything was possible for athletically inclined men. Films such as *The Plastic Age* (1926), *College* (1927), *So This is College* (1929), *Touchdown* (1931), *Horse Feathers* (1932), *College Rhythm* (1934), *Rose Bowl* (1936), *Campus Confessions* (1938), and *A Yank at Oxford* (1938) showcased Hollywood stars and professional athletes as they created a cinematic university where men could succeed athletically and socially—academics typically were a low priority—regardless of their social class. This cycle of films came to a close in 1940, with the release of *Knute Rockne All American*.

War, Sports, and Cinema: 1940s and 1950s

Campus frolics seemed trivial to a country at war (both World War II and the early Cold War), and the college films of the previous two decades fell out of favor with the American public and Hollywood during the 1940s and 1950s. Instead, sports biopics—biographic films more accurately described as historical fiction—became more prominent during this patriotic era. These uplifting narratives of distinctively masculine achievement seemed to fit perfectly with an American culture that was looking to support soldiers overseas and then commemorate their victory afterward.

This celebratory impulse is evident in films such as *Gentlemen Jim* (1942), *The Babe Ruth Story* (1948), *The Great John L.* (1948), *Jim Thorpe, All-American* (1951),

Crazylegs (1953), and *Somebody Up There Likes Me* (1956). In perhaps the most famous sports biopic of the era, *The Pride of the Yankees* (1942), film historians have pointed out that the tragic life story of Lou Gehrig became a kind of "war movie," with the death of the baseball hero standing in for the death of American soldiers.

After the war, America coped with a landscape that was triumphant yet fearful, and, in addition to its usual escapist entertainment, American cinema showed its darker side with the motion pictures of film noir, a movement characterized by dark, shadowy lighting and stories of moral ambiguity. These dark elements were echoed in sporting cinema with films of moody, expressive boxers and wounded athletes taking center stage across the 1950s. In movies such as *Body and Soul* (1946), *Champion* (1949), *The Set-Up* (1949), *Iron Man* (1951), and *The Square Jungle* (1955), the violent and corrupt world of boxing becomes the venue in which athletes struggle to negotiate the fine line between appropriate and excessive violence. The heroes in these pictures have problems balancing the aggressive qualities necessary to remain competitive and the self-control necessary to remain socially acceptable.

For many returning veterans, physical and psychological injuries affected their transitions to a postwar society. The challenges they faced in overcoming such injuries became the subjects of sports film. For example, Monty Stratton returns to baseball after losing his leg in *The Stratton Story* (1949), Grover Cleveland Alexander battles vision problems and alcoholism in *The Winning Team* (1952). Similarly, Jimmy Piersall (who was not a veteran) overcomes mental illness in *Fear Strikes Out* (1957).

Rather than overcoming injuries, African American athletes typically faced other kinds of obstacles on the road to athletic success in America, though after World War II, that began to change. The integration of modern professional football (1946), baseball (1947), and basketball (1950) soon was followed by the release of films about African American star athletes, including *The Jackie Robinson Story* (1950), *The Harlem Globetrotters* (1951), *The Joe Louis Story* (1953) and *Go, Man, Go* (1954).

These movies' focus on African American sports heroes was innovative, but even with such releases, the sports films of the 1940s and 1950s largely were bleached of color, as the sporting cinema aligned itself with the rest of Hollywood and failed (for the most part) to produce films with nonwhite heroes. The specific parameters of the sports film made this deficiency increasingly problematic, as it was understandably difficult for the sporting cinema to thrive when its stories and images were further and further removed from the realities of sporting culture. A progressively more integrated sports world was harder to ignore as more African American athletes were appearing on television during the routine broadcasting of college and professional sports. Television, more than anything else, threatened sports films during the 1940s and 1950s.

In fact, the exploding popularity of television shook the foundations of sports and cinema. To begin with, the documentary traditions of sporting cinema relocated almost totally from film to television. Newsreels began to disappear, and the only significant nonfiction elements of sporting culture left to the cinema were popular biopics. Second, the movie studios were economically challenged when they lost control over their production, distribution, and exhibition monopoly in 1948 as a result of adverse court rulings.

As television became a major competitor, the entire moviemaking industry struggled to find its footing in a new media marketplace. Finally, and most significantly, sporting events became so plentiful on television that studios became reticent to produce sports films in what they believed was a sports-saturated marketplace. By the end of the 1950s, the sports film was in serious decline, and the cinematic genre of the athletic American dream was in danger of disappearing.

Fall and Rise of the Sports Film: 1960s and 1970s

During the 1960s, American cinema encountered upheaval both from within and without. Producers made just a handful of sports films in the 1960s, a mix of traditional uplifting sports stories such as *Safe at Home* (1962) and *Kid Galahad* (1962) and more cynical films such as *The Hustler* (1961) and *Requiem for a Heavyweight* (1962). Despite their varying moods, these films had much in common with prior sports films.

Later in the 1960s, however, moviegoers began to see the sports film genre branching out in new directions. Films such as *The Endless Summer* (1966) and *Downhill Racer* (1969) moved into relatively unexplored sporting territory (surfing and downhill skiing, respectively) and questioned what it meant to be an American and how sports might be involved (or implicated) in that defining process.

The Endless Summer is a documentary film that came along at a moment when nonfiction sports had fallen almost exclusively under the purview of television, but it was an economically successful and very visible film. It offered a vision of sports wrapped around 1960s-era notions of nonconformity, in which surfing and the laid-back culture that surrounds it challenged existing ideas of sports through an emphasis on noncompetitive athletics. The film provided a powerful alternative image of masculinity in the counterculture age.

The hero of *Downhill Racer,* on the other hand, is ultracompetitive but rejects the community-building aspects of sporting culture and refuses to submit to the government-sanctioned authority of his coach. He is an American antihero athlete. His struggles are not against outside competitors, internal vices, or even underworld influences. Instead, he battles the corporatization of the athletic American dream and challenges the notion that sports provide any sort of cultural benefit beyond individual achievement and personal fulfillment. In a 1960s moment, the very American sports film genre questioned the conventional tenets of patriotism and examined changes in American culture.

The 1970s began with the release of a handful of sports films such as *The Great White Hope* (1970), *Drive, He Said* (1971), *Bang the Drum Slowly* (1973), *The Longest Yard* (1974), and *Rollerball* (1975), all movies that questioned, some more pointedly than others, the values of professional sports. In this way, the films continued the trend of the 1960s.

Still, despite the success of some of these films, sports films appeared only sporadically to the mid-1970s. It was not until America's bicentennial celebration that the genre seemed to return to full health with a trio of movies that simultaneously redefined, condemned, and exalted sports in American culture. In 1976, Hollywood released *The Bingo Long Traveling All-Stars & Motor Kings, The Bad News Bears,* and *Rocky.*

Bingo Long was a critical film, as it presented somewhat ordinary African American athletes—as opposed to a film featuring stars—as leading characters in a sports film. It also was the first Hollywood production to focus on Negro League baseball.

Despite being a comedy about Little League, *The Bad News Bears* also broke new cinematic ground. Although companies had produced many family sports films—from *Shut Out in the Ninth* (1917) to *Angels in the Outfield* (1951)—most still featured single children in the midst of a host of adults. *The Bad News Bears,* on the other hand, not only focused on the child characters, but also created a rather "adult" movie in the process. The movie—with its abundance of cursing, an alcoholic coach, and a critical examination of parental overinvolvement in childhood athletics—was a critical look at America's competitive ethos.

Rocky was altogether different, a boxing film that focused less on the violence and corruption of the sport than on the Horatio Alger–type story of its underdog hero achieving success through determination and hard work, all the while presenting positive representations of American values. It is an optimistic and uplifting story of a bicentennial return to an unproblematic athletic American dream. *Rocky* won the Academy Award for best picture, and, along with the other two films of 1976, ushered in a return to prominence of the sports film, made evident with the release shortly thereafter of numerous films such as *One on One* (1977), *Heaven Can Wait* (1978), *Breaking Away* (1979), *North Dallas Forty* (1979), and *Rocky II* (1979).

It was not surprising that issues of nation would come to the forefront during these tumultuous two decades, but even as individual sports films questioned organized sports' role in the formation of American identity, the genre affirmed the value of "playing the game." Whether it was surfing or skiing, baseball or boxing, "playing" sports always is a good thing. It is only when outside forces—such as governments, corporations, or even over-zealous parents—get too involved that sports can become tainted.

Sports Films as an American Staple: 1980s to the Present

At the beginning of the 1980s, the sports film again had become a regular subject of Hollywood production. Filmmakers were poised to expand and change their vision as the world of sports and sporting media grew dramatically, and formerly marginalized groups took center stage in the American sports film.

However, in Ronald Reagan–era America, there first was a return to conservative values and unabashed America-first patriotism. In the 1980s, the athletic American dream prospered in this cultural and economic environment and propelled a succession of high-profile and commercially successful sports movies. Although this group of films includes the gritty and powerful *Raging Bull* (1980), the overwhelming majority of these films were far more positive in their outlook, often grounding their narratives in a comforting sporting nostalgia or gentle comedy. Memorable movies from this moment include *Caddyshack* (1980), *Chariots of Fire* (1981), *Rocky III* (1982), *All the Right Moves* (1983), *Karate Kid* (1984), *The Natural* (1984), *Bull Durham* (1988), *Hoosiers* (1988), *Eight Men Out* (1988), and *Field of Dreams* (1989).

The sports films of the 1980s provided a critical high point for the genre, and yet, for the most part,

Sylvester Stallone, who also wrote the screenplay, stars as Rocky Balboa, a small-time heavyweight who goes the distance in the 1976 boxing classic *Rocky*. The film won an Academy Award for Best Picture and was followed by five sequels. *(The Granger Collection, New York)*

they still ignored or relegated to supporting roles the nonwhite images and influences of sporting culture. This finally began to change at the end of the decade and into the 1990s, as the rise of hip-hop culture and an increase in nonwhite filmmakers brought forward African American and other minority athletic characters. With films such as *Major League* (1989), *Talent for the Game* (1991), *White Men Can't Jump* (1992), *Cool Runnings* (1993), *Above the Rim* (1994), *Space Jam* (1996), *He Got Game* (1998), *The Hurricane* (1999), *Remember the Titans* (2000), *Ali* (2001), *Undisputed* (2002), *Coach Carter* (2005), *Glory Road* (2006), and *Pride* (2007), the sports film's playing fields were no longer all—or mostly white—affairs. Although the stories were much the same, the look of the sports film changed because of the popularity of the African American aesthetic at the end of the twentieth century.

Sparked by the success of *The Mighty Ducks* (1992) and related to the development of a strong DVD market, the end of the century also bore witness to the growth of the family sports film. During this period, Hollywood released movies such as *The Sandlot* (1993), *Rookie of the Year* (1993), *Little Big League* (1994), *Little Giants* (1994), *Angels in the Outfield* (1994), *The Big Green* (1995), *Air Bud* (1997), *Angels in the Endzone* (1997), *Air Bud 2: Golden Retriever* (1998), *Championship Game* (2000), *Like Mike* (2002), *Rebound* (2005), and *Gridiron Gang* (2007). Focusing on youth sports, these films had storylines that resonated with the everyday experiences of children and the nostalgic experiences of adults. Family sports films in the 1990s and beyond presented multiethnic and multigendered child athletes who seem to make the athletic American dream available for all ages.

The athletic American dream was almost exclusively for men, except for the occasional foray into safe, noncontact sports such as tennis (*Hard Fast and Beautiful,* 1951), golf (*Pat and Mike,* 1952), or figure skating (*Ice Castles,* 1978). In the 1980s, there were two women athlete films of note, *Personal Best* (1982) and *A League of Their Own* (1987), and in the 1990s, the girl athlete emerged in family sports films. It was not until the twenty-first century, however, with films such as *Girlfight* (2000), *Love and Basketball* (2000), *Blue Crush* (2002), *Bend It Like Beckham* (2002), *Million Dollar Baby* (2004), and *Stick It* (2006) that mature female athletes began to appear in leading roles on a (somewhat) regular basis.

The end of the twentieth century and the beginning of the twenty-first was an era of dynamic transformation in sporting culture and cinema. To begin with, the expansion of cable programming, heralded by the birth of ESPN, helped push sports superstars to an unprecedented level of visibility and financial success. It also was an era of sports media supersaturation, a time when the documentary impulses attached to sporting culture expanded from television to the Internet, making sports images and information available all the time. In this marketplace, Hollywood tended to produce fictional sports films, but the emergence of American independent cinema in the 1990s also brought with it a surge of new documentary film production. Films such as *Hoop Dreams* (1994), *When We Were Kings* (1996), *The Life and Times of Hank Greenberg* (1998), *Dogtown and Z-Boys* (2001), *Riding Giants* (2004), and *Murderball* (2005) were among the acclaimed sports documentaries produced during this period.

Even with these recent changes, the themes of most sports film have remained recognizable to a moviegoer of decades past. Hollywood still is releasing films such as *Leatherheads* (2008), *Semi-Pro* (2008), *Never Back Down* (2008), and *The Longshots* (2008) on a regular basis, and these movies closely resemble the sports films that preceded them.

In a twenty-first-century America in which sports and sporting media have grown to vast proportions, the sports movie appears to be a healthy and vibrant part of the film industry, though it has not remained static. In 2009, ESPN ran an ambitious series, "30 For 30," documenting the prior 30 years of sports.

There have been specific cycles during particular moments in history, and in recent years, the genre has broadened to include a wider variety of race and gender representations. Still, with more than a century of production in its rear view mirror, the sports film genre persists in offering its own unique athletic American dream.

Andrew Miller

See also: Arts, Visual; Literature; Music; Television.

Further Reading

Baker, Aaron. *Contesting Identities: Sports in American Film.* Chicago: University of Illinois Press, 2003.

Baker, Aaron, and Todd Boyd, eds. *Out of Bounds: Sports, Media, and the Politics of Identity.* Bloomington: Indiana University Press, 1997.

Boyd, Todd, and Kenneth L. Shropshire, eds. *Basketball Jones: America Above the Rim.* New York: New York University Press, 2000.

Cohan, Steven. *Masked Men: Masculinity and the Movies in the Fifties.* Bloomington: Indiana University Press, 1997.

Gorn, Elliot J. *The Manly Art: Bare-Knuckle Prize Fighting in America.* Ithaca, NY: Cornell University Press, 1986.

Grindon, Leger. "Body and Soul: The Structure of Meaning in the Boxing Film Genre." *Cinema Journal* 35:4 (Summer 1996): 54–69.

Guerrero, Ed. *Framing Blackness: The African American Image in Film.* Philadelphia: Temple University Press, 1993.

McKernan, Luke. "Sport and the Silent Screen." *Griffithiana* 64 (October 1998): 81–141.

Miller, Andrew C. "Trotting Horses and Moving Pictures: A Sporting View of Early Cinema." In *Turning the Century: Essays in Media and Cultural Theory,* ed. Carol Stabile. Boulder, CO: Westview, 2000.

Oriard, Michael. *King Football: Sport and Spectacle in the Golden Age of Radio and Newsreels, Movies and Magazines, the Weekly and the Daily Press.* Chapel Hill: University of North Carolina Press, 2001.

———. *Reading Football: How the Popular Press Created an American Spectacle.* Chapel Hill: University of North Carolina Press, 1993.

Streible, Dan. *Fight Pictures: A History of Boxing and Early Cinema.* Berkeley: University of California Press, 2008.

Zucker, Harvey Marc, and Lawrence J. Babich, eds. *Sports Films: A Complete Reference.* Jefferson, NC: McFarland, 1987.

Fishing

Angling, or fishing with a hook, as a recreational activity in North America dates to colonial times, though, of course, fishing was practiced for subsistence by Native Americans long before that. Indeed, recreational fishing, although largely a solitary pleasure, was the first organized sport in North America. Many recreational fishermen formed clubs in the late nineteenth century to advance the interests of sportsmen against inland poachers and pot fishermen (subsistence fishing) by buying small lakes and streams or by lobbying for tougher fishing laws.

Periodicals such as *Forest and Stream* (1873) and *Field and Stream* (1897), training manuals, and the novels of Ernest Hemingway, especially *The Sun Also Rises* (1926) and *The Old Man and the Sea* (1952), further popularized the sport. More recently, fishing was promoted by the ABC program *The American Sportsman* (1965–1986), the film *A River Runs Through It* (1992), and professional angling competitions, including those of ice fishermen who compete for $170,000 in Minnesota's "Forest Lake VFW Fishapalooza." The sport also has been enhanced by technological innovation, including the development in the 1950s of cheap fiberglass fishing rods, synthetic lines, and monofilament leaders.

Rise of Recreational Fishing

Indigenous people and colonists in North America fished for sustenance, but European newcomers also fished for pleasure. The Puritans of New England supported fishing as a bonding experience for fathers and sons, while Pennsylvania founder William Penn's daughter cited fishing as her favorite summer amusement.

Colonial anglers enjoyed "still fishing" from a riverbank, boat, pier, or bridge, sometimes using a simple apparatus such as a pole with a line, sinker, and lure. The popularity of recreational fishing led to the formation of Philadelphia's Schuylkill Fishing Company of Pennsylvania in 1732, the first sports club in the American colonies, with membership limited to men of high status. The club promoted fishing, sociability, and fine dining.

Nineteenth-century Eastern fishermen were inspired by Izaak Walton's *Compleat Angler* (1653) and by fishing articles in contemporary periodicals such as the *American Turf Register and Sporting Magazine* (1829) and *The Spirit of the Times* (1831). They fished for trout using foreign-made rods, a landing net, and a basket in mountain streams, wooded rivers, creeks, and lakes in the beautiful Catskill and Adirondack mountains. Fishing also was popular along the Atlantic Coast in harbors, bays, and inlets, where men fished with spears and harpoons and trolled from small boats for grouper, sea bass, sea trout, snapper, and striped bass. The trans-Appalachian West was a popular region for sports fishing, especially black bass, which were considered equal to the brook trout in cunning and boldness.

Many anglers in the early nineteenth century made their own equipment, including artificial flies, but by the 1840s, fishermen could buy first-rate American-manufactured rods and line. Reel innovations included balanced crank handles and the first free-spool mechanism. Split cane rods, first made in the United States in the mid-1850s, were mass-produced by the 1870s.

Fishing After the Civil War

Game fishing declined as many Eastern waterways near cities became polluted. Good fishing sites became more remote, and by the 1870s, middle- and upper-class fishermen rode trains to distant sites, their travel often facilitated by excursion rates for club members. Bostonians engaged in weeklong outings to the Newfoundland banks in Canada, where they fished for cod, haddock, halibut, and mackerel.

Meanwhile, big game fishing began at the end of the nineteenth century, especially after news of the landing—with rod, reel, and an 18-tread line from an open skiff—of a 183-pound (83-kilogram) bluefin tuna off the coast of Southern California. This led to the formation of the world's first game fishing club, the Tuna Club of Avalon, which was based on Santa Catalina Island, off Los Angeles.

By the 1870s, angling clubs began proliferating to facilitate access to fishing sites, protect declining catches, and preserve the wilderness for recreational fishing. Clubs and protective associations blamed waning yields on overfishing by poor rural poachers and pot fishers, and also on pollution and the building of new dams due to the rising population and increasing industrialization. As a result, clubs pressured state and provincial governments to regulate fishing to prevent overfishing and to protect spawning fish, sometimes even hiring their own detectives and wardens. Upper-class clubs, which had membership fees of up to $450 a year, purchased small lakes and streams, which they controlled and protected for their private use. In 1922, the Izaak Walton League began as the first mass member conservation organization, and it had more than 100,000 supporters.

Fly-Fishing

Fly-fishing became popular in the mid-nineteenth century, mainly in the Catskills of New York. Few anglers bothered with fly-fishing, because they had access to large, well-stocked streams, and instead they used heavier tackles that required less skillful manipulation. When anglers overfished the popular brook trout, however, fishing agencies restocked rivers with brown and rainbow trout, which were harder to fool than the brook trout. To catch these trout, the preferred lure became a "fly," attached to a heavier line that is easier to cast than normal line. The skilled fly fisherman manipulates the lure so that it looks like an insect dancing on the water's surface.

Practitioners wrote about their experiences, helping to popularize the sport, beginning with Thaddeus Norris, known as the "Father of American Fly-Fishing," who wrote the *American Angler's Book* (1864); John L. Keene, who wrote *Fly-Fishing and Fly-Making* (1887); and Ted Gordon, who wrote for *Fishing Gazette* starting in 1890 and *Field and Stream* in 1903. Gordon lived in the Catskills, where he tied flies and fished in solitude. He founded the Catskill School of dry fly-fishing, designing lures to float and look like insects native to the Catskills, becoming best known for the Quill Gordon pattern. George LaBranche, author of *The Dry Fly and Fast Waters* (1914), made North American dry fly-fishing all the rage by developing flies whose size and bushy appearance made them float high and remain easily visible to fish.

The spread of fly-fishing was made possible by the development of new technologies. Vermont tackle shop owner Charles F. Orvis first helped popularize fly-fishing by designing the first fully modern fly reel in 1874. The Orvis Company helped institutionalize fly-fishing, selling angling equipment and accessories to millions. Tackle design evolved rapidly after the 1880s, when horsehair fishing line was replaced by silk, covered with coats of oxidized linseed oil for easy casting, enabling average anglers to cast three times farther than before, and facilitating both dry-fly and wet-fly fishing. In the new century, rods became shorter and lighter without sacrificing strength, as split bamboo largely was replaced by fiberglass and finally by carbon fiber. After World War II, North Americans began using fixed-spool reels along with nylon monofilament lines, creating a boom in spin casting. At the same time, plastic became the dominant material for artificial casting lures. And, in 1954, the Zero Hour Bomb Company (Zebco) introduced the first closed-face spin-casting reel, which made cast-and-retrieve fishing virtually foolproof.

Fly casting and bait casting anglers' tournaments were established to promote fly casting skills. In the 1880s, New York's Central Park and Van Cortlandt Park became prime sites of expert competition, with teams such as the Chicago Fly Casting Club and the Anglers' Club of New York. Events included both catching fish and casting purely for accuracy and distance.

Women were notable in the sport, and in 1932, the Woman's Flyfisher's Club was organized. Sara Jan McBride pioneered in fly-fishing, studying insect lifecycles from an angler's point of view, and she won a bronze medal at the 1876 Philadelphia Centennial Exposition for fly tying. Mary Orvis Marbury, daughter of Charles Orvis and head of his fly-tying department, wrote the 500-page *Favorite Flies and Their Histories* (1892). However, the first lady of fly-fishing was Cornelia "Fly Rod" Crosby, a national celebrity in the late 1890s for her salmon and trout fishing in Maine, nationally syndicated column "Fly Rod's Notebook," and public appearances at sportsmen's shows.

The most noted female fly fisher is Joan S. Wulff, who was inducted in 2007 into the International Fish Association's Hall of Fame. She won 17 casting championships between 1943 and 1960, with an unofficial best of 161 feet (49 meters), became a renowned columnist in *Outdoor Life* and *Rod & Reel,* and wrote the highly regarded *Fly Casting Techniques* (1997).

Bass Fishing in Post–World War II North America

Anglers in the early 1900s considered bass to be "trash fish," because they were not as tasty as trout. However, bass rapidly became one of the most popular sport fish, as they are attracted to natural bait, lures, and artificial flies. Interest in bass fishing developed after the creation of the Tennessee Valley Authority in 1932 and the construction of dams and establishment of reservoirs that were stocked with bass. Fishing equipment became increasingly sophisticated after 1948, when Skeeter Boats built a bass-fishing vessel; manufacturers soon added electronic fish finders.

The first bass fishing tournament was held in 1968, the same year in which *Bill Dance Outdoors,* the first bass fishing show, began airing on television in Memphis, Tennessee. Thirteen years later, Ray Scott created the Bass Anglers Sportsman Society (B.A.S.S.) to host competitions. By the 1990s, B.A.S.S. had more than 500,000 members worldwide. Larry Nixon was the most famous bass fisherman, earning $1 million from tournaments in 1992.

Bass fishing was so popular among women that in 1976, Sugar Ferris organized Bass 'N Gal, the first national fishing organization for women. By the 1990s, the organization had 33,000 members and held tournaments that drew 200 professional competitors; however, Bass 'N Gal went out of business in 1998. Nonetheless, by the early 2000s, 30 million people were bass fishing, mainly in warm southern waters, contributing $50 billion to the U.S. economy.

Sport fishing currently is the second most popular recreational activity in the United States, with nearly 40 million American anglers. The sport has an annual impact on the U.S. economy of more than $100 billion, and tourists spend $2.5 billion a year on fishing for such game fish as bass, northern pike, perch, salmon, trout, and walleye.

Steven A. Riess

See also: Canoeing; Hunting.

Further Reading

English Fly Fishing Shop. "The History of the Art of Fly Fishing." http://business.virgin.net/fly.shop/history.htm.

Foggia, Lyla. *Reel Women: The World of Women Who Fish.* Hillsboro, OR: Beyond Words, 1995.

Goodspeed, Charles Eliot. *Angling in America: Its Early History and Literature.* Boston: Houghton Mifflin, 1939.

Herd, Andrew A. "A Fly Fishing History." http://www.flyfishinghistory.com/news.htm.

Schullery, Paul. *American Fly Fishing: An Illustrated History.* New York: Lyons, 1999.

Waterman, Charles F. *A History of Angling.* Tulsa, OK: Winchester, 1981.

Flames, Calgary/Atlanta

The Calgary Flames originated in Atlanta, Georgia, in 1972–1973, an expansion team added to the National Hockey League (NHL) to balance the addition of the New York Islanders. The team remained in Atlanta through the 1979–1980 season, where it performed poorly on the ice and struggled to build fan support. At the end of the season, it was purchased by a syndicate headed by realtor Nelson Skalbania of Vancouver, and moved to Calgary, Alberta. The team captured the Stanley Cup in 1989.

The location of an NHL franchise in Atlanta was driven by the need to find an additional attraction, aside from the professional basketball team, the Hawks, for the Omni, the city's sports arena, which was built in 1971. A franchise was awarded to the Omni Sports Group Consortium that was led by real estate developer Tom Cousins, owner of the Hawks. The expansion was not well received, considering the dilution of NHL talent as a result of prior expansions and the coming of the rival World Hockey Association. In addition, Atlanta lacked any real hockey tradition.

The franchise derived its name, the Flames, from the fire that had destroyed Atlanta in 1864 and was famously featured in the epic Civil War film *Gone with the Wind* (1939). The team was led by General Manager Cliff Fletcher and Manager Bernie "Boom Boom" Geoffrion, who coached from 1972 to 1975. The team made the playoffs in six of eight seasons but managed only two playoff wins. Their best single-season mark came in 1978–1979, with a record of 41–31–8, but the team's 90 points failed to lift them out of last place in their division. The Flames also suffered from falling ticket sales, rising operating costs, and the lack of a major television deal.

Skalbania, who formerly had owned the Edmonton Oilers, bought the Flames in 1980 for $16 million, a record at the time, intending to move them from

Atlanta to Calgary. His venture was abetted by the sale of local television rights to Molson, a brewing company, for $6 million over ten years. But Skalbania, who owned 50 percent of the Flames, and his six Calgary partners, could not agree on how to run the club. In 1981, the Calgary stockholders bought out Skalbania.

The Flames were the third professional hockey team to represent Calgary, following the Tigers (1921–1926) of the Western Canadian Hockey League and the Cowboys (1975–1977) of the World Hockey Association. The city embraced the new club, which retained its nickname, buying 10,000 full- and half-season ticket packages in the 7,000-seat Stampede Corral, the Cowboys's old home. The players viewed the move as an opportunity for a fresh start. That year, the Flames came in third in the Patrick Division and went on to the semifinals in the playoffs, losing to the Minnesota North Stars in six games.

The Flames played in the Stampede Coral until a new arena opened in 1983, in preparation for the 1988 Winter Olympic Games. The $100 million (Canadian dollars) Olympic Saddledome—aptly named both for the inward curvature of the roof and for the city's famous rodeo events—was renamed the Canadian Airlines Saddledome (1995–2000), then the Pengrowth Saddledome (2000–2010), and finally the Scotiabank Saddledome. Since the team was acquired in 1980 by a group of seven Calgary businessmen, ownership of the franchise has fluctuated in number, but it has remained community based. As of early 2011, the team's ownership included N. Murray Edwards, Harley N. Hotchkiss, Alvin G. Libin, Allan P. Markin, Jeffrey J. McCaig, Byron J. Seaman, and Clayton H. Riddell.

Fletcher built the team using U.S. collegians and foreign stars, including Russians by 1989, making the Flames a top squad in the late 1980s. But they often were stymied in the Campbell Conference by the Edmonton Oilers. Fletcher's lineup eliminated the Oilers from the playoffs just once during the latter's dynasty years, in 1986. This marked the first time that Calgary had made the Stanley Cup finals since 1924. However, the Flames were no match for the Montreal Canadiens, who won the Cup thanks to the near-perfect performance of goalie Patrick Roy.

The Flames had their revenge three years later, capturing the Stanley Cup in 1989, defeating the Canadiens in six games. Montreal had taken a 2–1 series lead, but the Flames came back to win three straight. The final game was played at the Forum in Montreal on May 25. Until then, the Canadiens never had lost a championship on home ice while accumulating 23 Stanley Cups. Calgary's championship team included Theo Fleury, Doug Gilmour, Al MacInnis, Lanny McDonald, Joe Nieuwendyk, and Mike Vernon.

In 1991, Fletcher, who had been the franchise's only general manager since the 1972 Atlanta expansion, left to manage the Toronto Maple Leafs, and he traded for Doug Gilmour and several other key Flames player. As a result, the Flames plummeted in the standings, eventually posting a dismal 26–41–15 record (67 points) in 1997–1998, while the Maple Leafs began a new era of success.

It became increasingly difficult for the small-market Flames to keep their best players as a result of rising salaries and the declining value of the Canadian dollar. For instance, in 1999, Fleury, then the team's all-time leading scorer, was traded to the Colorado Avalanche. He was about to became an unrestricted free agent, and the Flames could not afford to keep him.

The team did not make the playoffs from 1996–1997 until 2003–2004. This decline in performance was accompanied by a drop in their normally high attendance. The fall was so sharp that in 1999, the owners warned fans that they might have to relocate the team to the United States, as had happened in Winnipeg and Quebec, unless more season tickets were bought. Calgarians responded by upping season ticket purchases from 8,700 to 14,000. Despite this show of support, the Flames still lost $14.5 million between 2001 and 2003.

A member of the Northwest Division of the NHL since 1998–1999, the Flames currently are led by Jarome Iginla, who has held the captaincy since 2003 (becoming the first black captain in NHL history). Iginla has won more major awards than any other player in franchise history, including two Maurice Richard trophies, an Art Ross Trophy, and a Lester B. Pearson Award. He and goalie Miikka Kiprusoff made up the foundation of the club's roster for the 2010–2011 season.

In 2004, the Flames made the Stanley Cup finals, getting there the hard way, having been the sixth-seeded team. Nonetheless, they captured the Western Conference championship by defeating the San Jose Sharks in six games. The squad went on to the Stanley Cup finals, falling in Game 7 to the Tampa Bay Lightning by a score of 2–1. From 2005 through 2010, the team made it to the playoffs four times but did not advance beyond the quarterfinals.

Ron Reynolds

See also: Ice Hockey.

Further Reading

MacKinnon, John. *Official NHL History.* New York: Whitecap, 1999.

Stewart, Monte. *Calgary Flames: Fire on Ice.* Canmore, Canada: Altitude, 2004.

Football, College

American football is derived from the English games of soccer and rugby. American colleges rejected soccer as their form of intercollegiate competition, and instead they adapted English rugby during the period from the 1870s to the early 1900s. Harvard University led the way in determining the type of football that was played, while Yale University and its coach, Walter Camp, helped transform the game of rugby into American football.

The brutality of the game, creeping commercialism, and the impact on the academic performance of student athletes led many, both inside and outside academia, to condemn the sport and to call for its banning, in spite of the formation of the National Collegiate Athletic Association (NCAA) in 1906 and other reform efforts. Nevertheless, football remained the dominant college spectator sport from the 1890s throughout the twentieth century. Major rivalries were established, including Harvard–Yale, Army–Navy, Ohio State–Michigan, Alabama–Auburn, Texas–Oklahoma, California–Stanford, and Notre Dame–Southern California.

After World War II, the NCAA began to legislate and execute policy for all of the major colleges, passing recruitment and subsidization rules and placing football telecasting under NCAA authority. By the second half of the twentieth century, college football functioned as a "minor league" for the National Football League, even as it became a huge moneymaking sport in its own right, followed by millions of sports fans.

By the late 2000s, there were four college stadiums seating more than 100,000 fans, led by the University of Michigan's Michigan Stadium (109,901). In 2010, NCAA Division I teams drew a record 49,670,895 fans to 1,475 games.

The First Game

Throughout the early and mid-nineteenth century, a number of Eastern colleges played a form of soccer that was contested between classes, often freshmen and sophomores. The contests functioned as a kind of initiation rite for the freshmen, rather than as organized sporting events. Kicking one's opponents appeared to be as common as kicking the ball. At Harvard University, for instance, on the first day of school from the 1830s to the 1850s, sophomores generally would beat the freshmen into submission in a contest that was called "Bloody Monday." The matches were so brutal that Harvard authorities banned this type of football in 1860. A number of other colleges continued these contests, including two New Jersey colleges, Princeton and Rutgers universities.

In 1866, Princeton beat Rutgers in their first intercollegiate baseball game, and soon Rutgers challenged Princeton to a game of soccer-style football. On November 6, 1869, the first American intercollegiate football game was played on the Rutgers campus. The two institutions agreed to common rules resembling those of English association football (soccer), although the 25 players on each side were allowed to bat the inflated rubber ball with their hands, fists, and feet. The goalposts were placed eight paces apart (about 20 feet/6 meters) at the ends of a 360-foot (110-meter) field. The first team to score six goals was the winner. Rutgers won 6–4; however, in a return match, played with rules more to Princeton's liking, Rutgers lost 8–0. This style of soccer-football, however, was short-lived.

Harvard and Rugby Football

The only important academic institution that was not playing some form of soccer was Harvard—a fact that was crucial to the development of American football. By the early 1870s, Harvard was playing a form of football, a pastime called the "Boston game." In this contest, a player could catch or pick up the ball, kick it, or even run with it, making this version of the game more like rugby than soccer. The opportunity to run with the ball was key to the development of football in America.

Yale University, Harvard's chief rival in the two most important college sports of the time, baseball and crew, played its first intercollegiate soccer match in 1872, beating Columbia University. Yale wanted to play its more influential rival in football, but their rules differed greatly. Yale called for a convention in 1873 to write common rules for league play. Harvard, however, refused to attend, protesting that soccer was inferior to its own game. Harvard's refusal to play soccer changed the history of American football. Yale, Princeton, Columbia, and Rutgers agreed to common soccer rules, while Harvard kept its own.

The showdown between the Army Black Knights and Navy Midshipmen, held annually since 1890, is a highlight of the college football season. The level of play is not of national championship caliber, but the rivalry between the academies is as fierce as any. *(Drew Hallowell/Getty Images)*

Rejecting its sister institutions, Harvard agreed to play McGill University from Montreal, Canada, in two matches in May 1874. Harvard beat McGill using Harvard rules and then tied McGill in a game of rugby football. Subsequently, Harvard decided that rugby was superior to its "Boston game." Harvard then played and lost to nearby Tufts College in the first intercollegiate rugby game between colleges in the United States.

Harvard's persistence led to the adoption of rugby football. Yale, desiring to play Harvard, agreed to "concessionary" rules, which resembled those of rugby more so than soccer. Harvard won as some Princeton students looked on; it became clear that if Princeton wanted to play, it would have to change to rugby rules. After Princeton chose rugby, a convention of the "Big Three," plus Columbia, met to adopt standard rugby rules and to form the Intercollegiate Football Association in fall

1876. This organization became the governing body for all American colleges playing rugby and initiated a championship game played each Thanksgiving Day in New York City.

Beginning in 1876, the Thanksgiving Day championship game was the most important collegiate contest in America, pitting the two best teams against one another, generally Yale and Princeton. By the 1890s, the contest marked the beginning of the social season for New York's elite, lending the game additional significance. As many as 40,000 spectators attended the contests at the Polo Grounds or at Manhattan Field. The Thanksgiving Day football tradition spread to the nation's colleges and later to high schools and professional football.

Rugby football did not last long, as the Americanization of the game soon took hold. The elite Eastern schools began to change the rules of rugby to suit

American needs. Walter Camp, often called the "Father of American Football," had played for Yale in the first Thanksgiving Day championship in 1876, and he remained an active participant in determining the direction the sport would take both during and after his playing days. Camp began attending the rulemaking group as a college sophomore; he continued until his death while attending a rules meeting in 1925, nearly 50 years later.

In 1880, Camp suggested what was likely the most radical rule in the development of American football—giving continuous possession of the ball to one team after a player was tackled. In rugby, when a player was downed, the ball was placed in a "scrummage." The ball might then go forward or backward, with possession in doubt. To Camp, this rule was irrational. Instead, he proposed a "scrimmage" to replace the "scrummage," so that the team in possession would snap or center the ball back to a quarterback, who would hand it to another runner. In this way, the team in possession could retain the ball until it scored, or the ball might be fumbled away or kicked to the opponent.

By the early 1880s, Camp suggested the notion of "downs," in which one team was given three attempts (downs) to advance 5 yards (4.5 meters) or else lose possession of the ball. The 5-yard chalk lines gave a "gridiron" effect, and a new nickname for the game. Gaining a short distance in a small number of attempts brought about a number of mass plays and the development of interference (blocking) for the ball carrier, which was illegal in rugby. These modifications essentially transformed rugby into the modern-day form of American football.

Brutality and the NCAA

Mass plays led to a more physical game and more player injuries. This provoked a backlash, as opponents claimed that the game was too violent. The change from rugby, in which there was more open running with no interference, to tight line smashes was intensified when a rule was implemented in 1887 to allow defenders to tackle the ball carrier below the waist.

The low tackle did much to reduce the effectiveness of open-field running and contributed to the creation of so-called mass formations such as the ingenious "flying wedge," an invention of Lorin F. Deland, a friend of Harvard, in 1892. While a number of colleges used V-shaped wedges to attack the defense, Deland suggested using war hero Napoleon's principle of the concentration of force in football. Deland's scheme had two groups of offensive players, about 25 yards (23 meters) from the ball, converge from different angles, forming a vortex at some point in the defense. The ball would be passed over the nine players, as they came together, to the runner, who would follow the flying wedge into the opponent's territory. The play was so successful in the season finale between Harvard and Yale that nearly every team adopted it the next season. After one year, however, it was banned as too dangerous even for American football.

Other mass plays continued, and games resulted in numerous injuries and even a few deaths. Because of injuries and poor sportsmanship, Harvard banned football for a time in the 1890s, and U.S. President Grover Cleveland banned the game at both the U.S. Army and U.S. Navy academies because of its brutality. At the same time, future president Theodore Roosevelt spoke for those who favored the manly game: "[I] would a hundred fold rather keep the game as it is now, with the brutality, than give it up." Despite such sentiments, by the early 1900s, the perceived institutional need for a sport that demonstrated the virility of college men was challenged by the Progressive Era spirit of reform.

College football had spread to all areas of the country by the early 1900s, and a great debate took place over its usefulness to colleges, or even whether it should be banned for its brutality and questionable ethics. The crisis year for American football came in 1905–1906. Prior to that season, several muckraking journalists had included football along with corporate corruption, political graft, labor racketeering, and adulterated foods as areas in need of reform. Magazines such as *McClure's, Outlook,* and *Collier's* clamored for the abolition or radical reform of football. The headmaster of the prestigious Groton preparatory school in Massachusetts, Endicott Peabody, called on Theodore Roosevelt, now president, to hold a meeting of leading colleges to do away with the most dangerous and unethical aspects of football.

Early during the football season, Roosevelt invited Harvard, Yale, and Princeton representatives to the White House so that they might agree on the means to clean up football, hoping that the leading schools would set the standards for other colleges to follow. While the Big Three agreed to lead honorable programs, the results on the playing field actually grew worse, and the final game of the season saw brutal play between Harvard and Yale, in which Harvard's Francis Butt was bloodied when he was smashed in the face on a fair catch. That same day, in a game between Union College and New York University (NYU), Union's halfback, Harold Moore, died in a pile-up of NYU players. NYU

Chancellor Henry MacCracken immediately telegraphed President Charles Eliot of Harvard, asking him to call a conference to reform or ban football. When Eliot declined, stating that college presidents did not have the authority to do so, MacCracken invited colleges that recently had played NYU to consider banning or reforming the game.

The MacCracken Conference, which was made up of lesser-known universities, prompted a call for a national conference to reform the rules of football. The meeting of 68 institutions at the end of December 1905 led to the establishment of the National Collegiate Athletic Association. The conference decided to create its own rules committee. If the old committee dominated by Harvard, Yale, and Princeton would not agree that the two rulemaking bodies should join together, the new committee would create its own rules. Only when Harvard's representative jumped from the old committee to the new group did the old board agree to consolidate the two committees and establish one set of reform rules.

A number of important rule changes resulted after numerous meetings. Runners were prohibited from hurdling the line to cut down on injuries. A ball-length neutral zone between the two teams was created to help curtail contact before the ball was centered. Six men were required on the offensive line of scrimmage to prevent mass formations. Tackling below the knees was prohibited to give incentive to more open field running. A 10-yard (9-meter), four-down rule was introduced to reduce the number of line smashes to gain a first down. Most important to the future of the game, the forward pass was introduced to open up play. The forward pass originally had a number of restrictions, but they were reduced after a few years, and passing became a major part of football.

While the NCAA introduced rules for football, and eventually for all of the sports played by the major colleges, the association had little control over other aspects of intercollegiate sports for nearly a half century. Individual institutions and conferences determined athletic policy rather than the NCAA. This was known as "home rule," similar to states' rights in national politics, and it continued until after World War II, when the NCAA formulated the first national rules for eligibility and financial aid and gained jurisdiction over televised football.

Meanwhile, regional conferences were forming in the 1890s, including the Southern Intercollegiate Athletic Association in 1894 and the Big Ten Conference in 1895. By the early twentieth century, conferences had been established in many other regions, including the Missouri Valley (1907), Rocky Mountain (1909), Southwest (1914), and Pacific 8 (1915). Conferences met the need to create a "level playing field" for all schools in the group. Thus, conferences passed rules to ensure that all athletes had uniform entrance requirements and were bona fide students; that athletes could participate only for a certain number of years; that freshmen, graduate students, or transfer students were either eligible or ineligible; that practice for certain sports could be held only at particular times; and that the rules of amateurism and financial aid would be enforced.

Pro Coaches, Bowl Games, and Stadium Building

While conferences were forming and football rules were being reformed, football coaching was becoming a professional endeavor, with winning coaches being paid ever-higher salaries. In the early years of football, the captain of the team also was the coach, determining who would play and what formations would be used. Soon, it was found that a former player might give more stability and expertise than a current player, and alumni coaches were used.

Eventually, a successful alumni coach might be hired away by another institution, and by the beginning of the twentieth century, this had become common. For example, Amos Alonzo Stagg, who played at Yale University, was hired at a salary of $2,500 by the University of Chicago to win football games and to give publicity to the John D. Rockefeller–financed university in 1892. A few years later, another former Yale player, George Sanford, was hired for $5,000 by Columbia University to lead its team in 1899. Fielding H. Yost was paid $2,000, the yearly salary of assistant professors, plus free room and living expenses for ten weeks of coaching at the University of Michigan in 1901. Three years later, John Heisman received $2,250 plus 30 percent of the net gate receipts at the Georgia Institute of Technology. Bill Reid was paid $7,000 in 1905 to coach football at Harvard, nearly as much as President Eliot was paid after having served in that position for more than three decades. Generally, the professional coach assumed the authority to run the team, diminishing the previously important role of the captain.

With the expansion of football near the turn of the century came postseason football games. The first postseason game was played in New Orleans in 1890 when the Southern Athletic Club invited players from various Northern teams to play on New Year's Day. Four years later, Stagg's University of Chicago team played the University of Notre Dame on New Year's Day in an indoor contest at Chicago's Tattersall's Riding Academy. Later that year, the Chicago team traveled to the West Coast and beat Stanford University on Christmas Day. The Carlisle Indian Industrial School in Pennsylvania beat the University of California in a West Coast game on Christmas Day in 1899.

All of these "bowl" games occurred before the University of Michigan trounced Stanford in the first Rose Bowl in Pasadena in 1902. Michigan negotiated a deal giving them first-class rail travel, meal money, hotel expenses, bus and car fare, and a return trip through New Orleans before accepting the postseason game. Some 8,000 spectators watched the 49–0 victory, while the Rose Bowl parade was viewed by about 50,000. The Rose Bowl was not a regular occurrence, however, until 1916, when Washington State University beat Brown University; ever since, the game has been an annual event.

By the 1920s, college football and professional baseball were the two most popular spectator sports in America. Giant stadiums were built across the nation to accommodate the thousands who wanted to see the action firsthand. Harvard initiated the building craze in 1903 when it opened the first reinforced-concrete stadium in the world. Yale and Princeton followed about a decade later.

After World War I, the stadium boom began in earnest. By the end of the 1920s, every Big Ten school had constructed a stadium, most seating more than 50,000. The University of California and Stanford built 60,000-seat stadiums soon after they reintroduced their American football rivalry in 1919. They had banned football after the 1905 season, replacing it with rugby football.

A second phenomenon accommodated far more spectators than increased seating at games—the invention of radio. The first broadcast of a football game came from an experimental station at the University of Minnesota in 1912, using a spark transmitter and telegraphic signals. Not until the 1920s could fans hear a broadcaster describe the game's activity. By 1922, the Princeton–University of Chicago football game was heard in New York via a long-distance telephone line from Chicago. Soon, major football teams had their games broadcast on radio, and in 1925, the Notre Dame–Stanford Rose Bowl game was carried from the West Coast to the East Coast.

Early in the next decade, during the Great Depression, colleges debated whether radio broadcasts would reduce attendance at games and income from admissions. Some universities banned radio broadcasts, but for the most part they continued, with colleges protecting their interests by charging broadcasters for the privilege of carrying the games. Not until the advent of television after World War II was there again a major concern for the impact of broadcasting on game attendance.

Commercialism, Television, and Critics

Radio was a major influence on the commercialization of college football, and it was commercialization that brought protests from a number of sources. The most visible protest came in a study by the Carnegie Foundation for the Advancement of Teaching, published in *American College Athletics* in 1929. The Carnegie report condemned the professionalism and commercialism that had developed over the previous eight decades, criticizing the recruitment and subsidization of athletes, the hiring of professional coaches, the abandonment of amateurism, and the lack of student involvement in athletic decision making. But the report's recommendations largely were ignored, as colleges continued to do whatever it took to fill their huge new stadiums and gain prestige from having winning teams.

Recruitment and subsidization of athletes remained an obstacle to amateurism in college football. Several conferences attempted to control the recruitment and subsidization of athletes before the NCAA took jurisdiction. In 1948, NCAA members voted overwhelmingly for the "Sanity Code," so called for its sane approach to the national control of financial aid and recruitment. The Sanity Code was based on the principle that "athletes shall be admitted to the institution on the same basis as any other student." Financial aid would be need based, it was not to exceed tuition and fees, and no recruiting was to be carried out by athletic interests. Large-scale violations resulted, and when a vote was taken to oust certain schools from the NCAA, it failed; along with it went the Sanity Code and the first NCAA effort to replace home rule with a national policy.

The NCAA did succeed in creating a national policy when the threat of television after World War II resulted in a restrictive policy for telecasting football games. The ability to carry television signals on coaxial cable from the Midwest to the East Coast in 1949 carried with it the potential of airing Notre Dame football contests to the largest American markets. Scheduling coverage of Notre Dame football, with its national fan base, each fall Saturday afternoon, as well as the telecasting of other college teams, was perceived as endangering stadium attendance and the financial welfare of college athletics. As a result, the NCAA presented a plan to limit the telecasts of college football games to no more than one each week. For 1951, the NCAA plan called for eight games.

Over the next three decades, this NCAA rule resulted in a tenuous balance between limiting television coverage to ensure stadium attendance and satisfying the public's desire to see their favorite teams on television. In the 1970s, however, some of the most powerful institutions in the NCAA challenged the organization's restrictive policy. These schools realized that if restrictions were lifted, they could earn large sums by broadcasting their own games. In addition, if the NCAA policy was not in force, these colleges would not have to share the income with smaller institutions.

The challengers, calling themselves the College Football Association (CFA), included five conferences—the Atlantic Coast, Big Eight, Southeastern, Southwest, and Western Athletic—and several powerful independent teams, including the University of Notre Dame and Pennsylvania State University. Only two major conferences, the Big Ten and Pacific 8, remained out of the CFA. The NCAA refused to budge, continuing its restrictive scheduling and threatening CFA schools and conferences with disciplinary action if they broke the ban on televising their own games.

In the early 1980s, the CFA sponsored a law suit by two member universities against the NCAA's television plan for the 1982–1985 seasons. In June 1984, the U.S. Supreme Court declared that the NCAA's restrictive television plan violated the Sherman Antitrust Act. This ruling allowed both conferences and independent universities to control their own television arrangements.

Minorities, Academics, and a Playoff

By the time of the 1984 Supreme Court decision, African Americans had been substantially integrated into American institutions of higher learning including athletics, first in the North and, by the 1970s and 1980s, in the South as well. The last conference to desegregate athletics was the Southeastern Conference, and by the early 1970s, all members of the conference had admitted black athletes.

While the level of competition was raised by allowing minorities to participate, the NCAA was faced with an academic dilemma. In 1965, the NCAA had passed an eligibility rule for incoming athletes based on a predicted 1.600 (C–/D+) grade point average, using high school grades and standardized test scores in the calculation. Those who did not meet this minimal standard could not participate in college athletics. However, this appeared prejudicial, especially to blacks, who often came from poorly performing secondary schools. African Americans were being recruited in the 1960s, when open admissions to universities were being emphasized at Northern institutions.

The ill-fated 1.600 rule ended in 1973, and until the mid-1980s, when new minimum eligibility requirements were legislated, there were no national entrance requirements for athletes. The breakdown of racial and academic barriers for college entrance helped institutions recruit far higher percentages of blacks for their football teams than before. This change is reflected in the Heisman Trophy winners: More than half of those selected from the mid-1960s to the mid-1980s were African Americans, whereas previously, only one had been chosen since the award's inception in the 1930s.

Football would continue to dominate the college scene into the twenty-first century, although basketball and its national championship tournament, known as March Madness, became a close challenger. The major football conferences never agreed on a national championship tournament, unlike every other sport among NCAA members. The sponsors of the historic bowl games and the presidents of major universities opposed a playoff system, preventing any agreement.

With or without a playoff, college football, like basketball, became a minor league for professional football. Professional football received a preponderance of its star players from the colleges as early as the 1920s. Unlike other universities throughout the world, American colleges developed a system of professionalized and commercialized football that fit well with the professional leagues formed in the twentieth century. This legacy has continued into the twenty-first century.

Ronald A. Smith

See also: Bowl Games, College Football; College All-Star Football Game; Football, Professional; Historically Black Colleges; Intercollegiate Athletic Associations and Conferences; Interscholastic Sports; Mascots, Names, and Symbols; Notre Dame, University of; Track and Field; Violence in Sports.

Further Reading

Bernstein, Mark F. *Football: The Ivy League Origins of an American Obsession.* Philadelphia: University of Pennsylvania Press, 2001.

Bowen, William C., and Sarah A. Levin. *Reclaiming the Game: College Sports and Educational Values.* Princeton, NJ: Princeton University Press, 2003.

Davis, Parke H. *Football, the American Intercollegiate Game.* New York: Charles Scribner's Sons, 1911.

Falla, Jack. *NCAA: The Voice of College Sports: A Diamond Anniversary History, 1906–1981.* Mission, KS: National Collegiate Athletic Association, 1981.

Lester, Robin. *Stagg's University: The Rise, Decline, and Fall of Big-Time Football at Chicago.* Urbana: University of Illinois Press, 1995.

Nelson, David M. *Anatomy of a Game: Football, the Rules, and the Men Who Made the Game.* Newark: University of Delaware Press, 1994.

Savage, Howard J. *American College Athletics.* New York: Carnegie Foundation for the Advancement of Teaching, 1929.

Schmidt, Raymond. *Shaping College Football: The Transformation of an American Sport, 1919–1930.* Syracuse, NY: Syracuse University Press, 2007.

Shulman, James L., and William G. Bowen. *The Game of Life: College Sports and Educational Values.* Princeton, NJ: Princeton University Press, 2001.

Smith, Ronald A. *Sports and Freedom: The Rise of Big-Time College Athletics.* New York: Oxford University Press, 1988.

Watterson, John Sayle. *College Football: History, Spectacle, Controversy.* Baltimore: Johns Hopkins University Press, 2000.

Football, Professional

Early professional football grew out of competition between workingmen's athletic clubs in the steel regions of Pennsylvania and Ohio. The professional game was seen by college administrators and football coaches as a corrupting enterprise. Early professional rivalries were local or regional, and the national press took little notice.

By the end of World War I, however, many former college players were attracted to the Sunday game. The formation in 1920 of what would become the National Football League (NFL) was a major step forward for professional football. Between 1920 and 1940, the NFL and other professional football leagues struggled first for survival and then for acceptance as a major sport in an era when baseball, horse racing, and boxing were America's top three professional sports.

During the prosperous post–World War II years, professional football experienced a boom, as did other major sports. By the early 1950s, television substantially bolstered the popularity of professional football, and the game spread across the country. By the final decades of the twentieth century, it had become America's favorite spectator sport, as measured by television ratings and average attendance at games. Professional football seemed to reflect the fast-paced, highly technical, and sometimes bruising nature of American society in the late twentieth and early twenty-first centuries.

The Early Years of Professional Football

The origins of professional football in the United States are difficult to determine precisely. American football, which evolved after the Civil War, was an offshoot of the British games of soccer and rugby. In England, these games were played at prep schools and universities, where the code of amateurism prevailed. American football also developed at institutions of higher education, but it was played at workingmen's athletic clubs as well.

The college game began as a contest between student-organized and student-controlled teams. By the 1890s, however, college administrators began to intervene, and, as the sport became more popular among alumni, its amateur ethic was strained. Colleges hired professional coaches, and teams fielded graduate students to play with undergraduates and even recruited nonstudents (known as "ringers"), who sometimes received jobs from the college or from football booster organizations. As a result, a small army of "tramp athletes" traveled around the country seeking employment as college football players.

At the same time, the football-playing athletic clubs formed rivalries that excited local fans, and they, too, bent or broke the amateur code. William "Pudge" Heffelfinger, a graduate of Yale University and an All-American lineman on its football team, often is identified as the first professional football player. In November 1892, he received $500 to play for the Allegheny Athletic Association against the Pittsburgh Athletic Club. It seems likely that other less notable players received pay for play before the Yale star.

The first fully professional football teams evolved out of the rivalries among these athletic clubs. The competition was particularly intense in the Pittsburgh area, which became known as the "Cradle of Professional Football." Club teams engaged in spirited competition, often attracting crowds of 3,000 or more and gate receipts in excess of $1,500. It was under these circumstances that Heffelfinger and other former college stars were recruited to play for local teams. Standing 6 feet, 3 inches (1.9 meters) and weighing 205 pounds (93 kilograms), Heffelfinger was a giant for his time, but he also was extremely agile. He originated the pulling guard play and was nimble enough to leap into a flying wedge formation and tackle the ball carrier.

Professional football soon spread throughout Pennsylvania and into neighboring states. In 1902, David Barry, a Latrobe newspaperman, established a professional league called the National Football League. Two of the teams, the Philadelphia Phillies and the Philadelphia Athletics, were managed by major league baseball skippers Bill Shettsline and Cornelius "Connie" Mack, who employed major league stars such as Christy Mathewson. The interest in professional football compared with major league baseball was negligible, however, and the first NFL lasted only one season. Professional football remained a popular autumn pastime in Pennsylvania, but gained a more avid following in eastern Ohio.

Professional football in Ohio developed along similar lines, with athletic clubs adding local outsiders to participate in critical games. These club rivalries were particularly intense in northeastern Ohio, where teams from Akron, Canton, Massillon, and Shelby, among others, vied for local supremacy. The Shelby Blues employed halfback Charles Follis in the early 1900s, making him the first known African American professional football player.

A scandal in 1906 concerning an alleged fixed game dampened interest in professional games for a time, but the sport made a comeback by 1910. By the 1910s, teams were bringing in enough in admissions to import players from outside the region. In 1914, George "Peggy" Parratt, player-manager of the Akron Indians, hired a group of linemen from the University of Notre Dame, including Knute Rockne (later Notre Dame's legendary coach), to play in an important game against Canton.

By the onset of World War I, this group of professional teams was known informally as the "Ohio League," and the finest professional football in the country was played there. In 1915, Jack Cusack, secretary-treasurer of the Canton Professionals (later the Canton Bulldogs) hired Native American sensation Jim Thorpe to play for $250 per game. An All-American halfback for the Carlisle Indian Industrial School and the winner of two gold medals in track and field at the 1912 Olympic Games, Thorpe attracted large crowds, especially at games between Canton and

Massillon. In 1915, more than 8,000 fans witnessed two Thorpe field goals carry Canton to a 6–0 victory over Massillon at the Bulldogs's League Park. The following season was Thorpe's finest in professional football, as he led Canton to a 10–0–1 record and the unofficial title of "Professional Football Champions of The World."

One of the better teams in the Ohio League was the Columbus Panhandles, named for a division of the Pennsylvania Railroad and made up of industrial workers. Between 1904 and 1926, seven Nesser brothers (none college men) played for the team, which received free train travel from the railroad. Al Nesser, a lineman, played 25 seasons in the Ohio League and later in the NFL, retiring in 1931.

After World War I ended, more former college players were recruited to play in Ohio. One of the featured match-ups was between Thorpe and the Akron Indians's African American star Fritz Pollard, a small but elusive former All-American halfback at Brown University. As the 1910s came to a close, professional football had become a major interest in coal and steel towns from Pittsburgh to the Mississippi River.

The Beginning of the National Football League

In September 1920, the owners of professional teams in five states met in Canton, Ohio, to organize a league. They convened at the Hupmobile automobile dealership run by Canton Bulldogs owner Ralph Hay. Because there were not enough chairs, many owners sat on the running boards and fenders of cars. The league was named the American Professional Football Association (APFA, renamed the National Football League in 1922), and Thorpe, the best-known professional player, was named president. In 1921, Thorpe was replaced by Joe Carr, a sportswriter from Columbus, Ohio, who headed the league for nearly two decades.

Each team in the league was assessed a membership fee of $100, although no team actually paid it; during the 1920s, teams joined and dropped out of the NFL in large numbers. The league was loosely organized: Teams made up their own schedules and often added games as the season went along in order to remain in contention for the championship. The league championship was awarded to the team with the highest percentage of wins (ties did not count), regardless of how many games they played. Players frequently "jumped" from one team to another during the season,

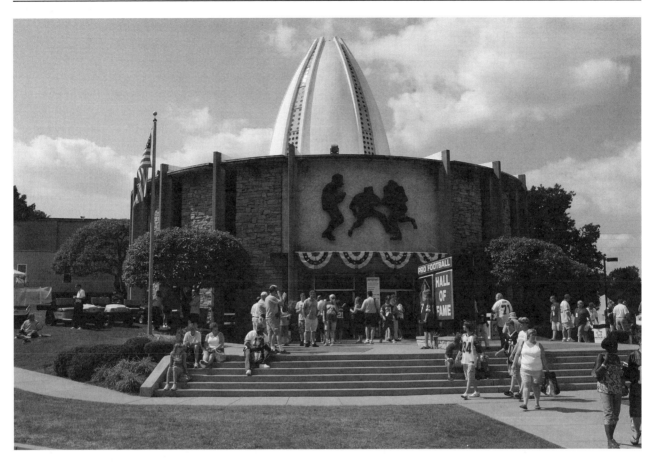

The Pro Football Hall of Fame is located in Canton, Ohio, where the predecessor of the National Football League was founded in 1920. Induction ceremonies for newly elected members are held in early August, with a preseason exhibition game played the following day. *(Scott Boehm/Getty Images)*

until Carr introduced a standard contract for players. Throughout the decade, the NFL included a number of "road teams," which played only a few league games, all of them at their opponent's field.

The professionals played by intercollegiate rules, but their games produced less scoring. Almost two-thirds of games in the 1920s were shutouts. Punting and field goal kicking were a large part of the game. The typical NFL player of the decade earned between $75 and $100 per game, with star performers receiving a few hundred dollars more. Playing fields varied from major league baseball parks such as Cubs Park (later renamed Wrigley Field) in Chicago to Minersville Park in Pottsville, Pennsylvania—according to the players, the surface of the latter park was mainly abrasive coal slag from coal-burning furnaces.

The new league's first year ended in controversy, as team records were not published during the season, and the method of selecting a champion had not yet been determined. Several months after the season, the Akron Pros (formerly the Indians) were awarded the championship cup for compiling an 8–0–3 record.

Akron was led by Fritz Pollard, one of two African American players in the league. Most major American sports were segregated, but the APFA included a few black players through the 1920s. Pollard played an important role in recruiting other African American players, including Rutgers University All-American Paul Robeson and Jay Mayo Williams. Pollard was the first black coach and quarterback in the NFL.

One of the most successful teams of this period was the Chicago Bears, which began as the Staleys, named for A.E. Staley, a starch manufacturer in Decatur, Illinois. In 1921, Staley allowed player-coaches George Halas and Ed "Dutch" Sternaman to take over the team and move it to Chicago, where they would play at Cubs Park, provided that they used the Staley name for a year. The team won the league championship, making a profit of $7. For the next season, Halas and Sternaman changed the team's name to the Chicago Bears, and they lost money. However, the franchise went on to become one of the most successful and stable teams in the NFL, winning nearly 70 percent of its games during the 1920s.

College officials and coaches continued to oppose professional football, charging that it was a sleazy game that corrupted young men. In 1925, professional football's integrity became a national issue when Harold "Red" Grange, a sensational three-time All-American halfback at the University of Illinois, turned pro after his last collegiate game. He hired an agent, C.C. "Cash and Carry" Pyle, and agreed to play for the Chicago Bears for the rest of their NFL season and a number of exhibition contests. Grange drew large crowds wherever he played. At New York's Polo Grounds, some 70,000 fans came out to see Grange and the Bears play the New York Giants. The Bears and their star went on a postseason tour that included 13 games in the South and on the West Coast.

After the season, Grange and Pyle asked the NFL to grant them a franchise to play in New York's Yankee Stadium in competition with the Giants. When the league refused, the two formed a new league of their own, the American Football League (AFL). In 1926, both leagues lost money because of the saturation of the market and extremely poor weather. The AFL folded after the season, but Grange's Yankees were allowed to join the NFL in 1927. Early that season, Grange suffered a severe knee injury and never was the same thrilling open-field runner, but he continued to play in the NFL until 1935.

Among the other stars of the late 1920s was quarterback Benny Friedman, who threw an oversized ball for 20 touchdowns in 1929, when six to eight scoring passes was considered a great accomplishment. One of the best runners of the decade was Ernie Nevers, who scored all of the Chicago Cardinals's points in a 40–7 victory over the Bears in 1929. Four days later, he scored all of Chicago's points in a 19–0 win over the Dayton Triangles.

From the Great Depression Through World War II

After the stock market crash of 1929 and the onset of the Great Depression, professional football, like other major sports, felt the economic impact of the downturn. By 1932, the NFL's membership had fallen to eight teams, the fewest in its history. However, paid admissions to NFL games increased throughout the decade, from around 7,000 per game in 1932 to nearly 20,000 in 1940. During these years, teams in small cities, many in industrial areas ravaged by unemployment, dropped out, leaving mainly big-city teams.

In 1932, the Chicago Bears and the Portsmouth (Ohio) Spartans tied for first place with identical 6–1–4 records, and the NFL held its first playoff. Freezing weather in Chicago forced the game to be played indoors at the Chicago Stadium, which the Bears won 9–0.

In 1933, the NFL was divided into two five-team divisions, with the winners of each division to meet in a championship game, similar to baseball's World Series. That season, the ball was further streamlined, making it more aerodynamic and easier to pass, resulting in higher scores. By the end of the 1930s, use of the new equipment helped quarterbacks, particularly Sammy Baugh and Sid Luckman, to become very accurate passers.

In 1934, African Americans disappeared from the ranks of the NFL. Team owners denied that they had made any sort of "gentlemen's agreement" to exclude black players, but no other explanation was convincing. Chicago Bears owner George Halas later speculated, "probably the game didn't appeal to black players at the time." Some football historians point to George Preston Marshall, owner of the Boston (later Washington) Redskins, as the likely instigator of the agreement to confine the league to white players. He resisted integrating his Washington team until the early 1960s, years after the rest of the league had done so. In other respects, however, Marshall was a pacesetter. He suggested the two-division format and popularized the halftime show, which became a staple at NFL games.

Another popular innovation during the 1930s was the College All-Star Game, first played in 1934. Each year, a College All-Star team was chosen with great fanfare in the early summer and met the NFL champion in Chicago late in August after a few weeks of practice. At first, the games were fairly evenly matched, but soon the NFL champs began to overwhelm the college stars. The NFL gained prestige from the series at the expense of the collegians. The annual event drew as many as 80,000 fans and continued until 1976.

A more permanent event, held for the first time in 1936, was the NFL's first college draft, instituted to distribute talent more equitably around the league. Player salaries were too low to attract many college stars, however. Jay Berwanger, the Heisman Trophy winner in 1935, was the first player to be drafted by professional football, but he declined the offer, becoming a businessman instead.

The professional game had prospered sufficiently by the late 1930s to inspire another big-time professional league in 1937, the American Football League. This second AFL, which included a West Coast team, lasted only one year.

Player salaries remained low during the Great Depression, averaging about $140 per game. Future U.S. Supreme Court Justice Byron "Whizzer" White of the Pittsburgh Pirates was the highest-paid performer of the decade, with a salary of nearly $16,000 in 1938. Other outstanding players of the 1930s were Baugh, end Don Hutson, and backs Bronko Nagurski and Clarence "Ace" Parker. The Green Bay Packers won four championships during the decade, while the New York Giants had the best overall record with a .661 winning average.

By the beginning of the 1940s, the Depression had ended and World War II had begun in Europe. The 1940 season saw the establishment of a third American Football League, which folded after the 1941 season. In the NFL, the T-formation replaced earlier offensive formations, partly as a result of the Chicago Bears's use of the T in their 73–0 rout of the Washington Redskins in the 1940 championship game. The following year, Elmer Layden, a member of the University of Notre Dame's famed "Four Horsemen," became the first commissioner of the NFL after Carr's death. Layden introduced playoff games to break ties in division races and a sudden-death overtime period to break ties in playoff games.

Following America's entrance into World War II in December 1941, player rosters and coaching staffs were ravaged by enlistments and the draft. In 1943, the NFL was reduced to two four-team divisions, because of a lack of quality players and wartime restrictions on travel. The Pittsburgh Steelers and the Philadelphia Eagles combined rosters and played as the Steagles. In 1944, the Steelers and the Chicago Cardinals merged and were known as the Car-Pitts.

Some veteran players who continued to be standout performers included Hutson, who caught 72 passes in 1942, and veteran quarterbacks Baugh, Luckman, and Cecil Isbell. In general, however, talented players were hard to find. Of the 330 players drafted by NFL teams in 1944, only 12 played in the league that season. Tackle Al Blozis played for the New York Giants in the 1944 NFL championship game while on military leave. He was killed while fighting in France one

month later. In all, 18 NFL players and former players were killed in World War II.

The Rise of the Modern Game, 1946–1966

In 1946, the NFL was challenged by a new professional league founded by *Chicago Tribune* sports editor Arch Ward. The All-America Football Conference (AAFC) consisted of eight teams, including two on the West Coast. In its four seasons, the new league was dominated by the Cleveland Browns under Coach Paul Brown. The Browns won the AAFC championship every year, posting a 15–0 record in 1948. In response to the upstart AAFC, NFL Commissioner Bert Bell authorized new NFL franchises in Los Angeles and San Francisco.

The NFL was under pressure to integrate black players, and their action was hastened by a city ordinance in Los Angeles, where the new Los Angeles Rams would play. The ordinance stated that no team could play in the Los Angeles Memorial Coliseum unless it was integrated. As a result, the Rams signed two African American players, running back Kenny Washington and end Woody Strode. The rival AAFC Cleveland Browns also employed two black players in 1946, guard Bill Willis and fullback Marion Motley, both of whom later were elected to the Pro Football Hall of Fame.

Integration was not easy for black players. They usually were underpaid, hired in pairs to avoid forcing a white player and a black player to room together. Blacks were "stacked" at one position so that the number of blacks playing at one time was kept to a minimum. Most African Americans were assigned to certain positions—those that coaches and managers believed did not require cooperation and leadership skills. It took years for this stereotyping to disappear. The league had only five African American players in 1949, and 52 (12 percent of all players) by 1960.

In 1946, the NFL also faced its first major gambling scandal. Players Merle Hapes and Frank Filchock of the New York Giants were suspended indefinitely by Commissioner Bell after reports that they had been approached by gamblers to throw the championship game against the Chicago Bears. Filchock denied any contact with gamblers and was allowed to play in the game, but Hapes, who admitted that he had been approached and had not reported the incident, was forbidden to play. Filchock played hard, but the Giants

366 Football, Professional

lost 24–14. Both players' suspensions later were lifted, but neither ever played another NFL game.

After the 1949 season, the NFL and the AAFC negotiated a merger agreement. Three AAFC franchises—Baltimore, Cleveland, and San Francisco—entered the NFL, while teams in Buffalo, Chicago, Los Angeles, and New York folded. Once again, the NFL operated unopposed by a rival league. During the 1950s, attendance at NFL games increased to 24 million. More important, the NFL became a regular fixture on Sunday afternoon television, bringing league games to untold millions of new fans. In 1956, the league negotiated its first television contract with CBS.

During most of the 1950s, the Cleveland Browns dominated the NFL, appearing in seven championships and winning three. The squad was led by quarterback Otto Graham, fullback Marion Motley, and the league's most reliable placekicker, Lou "The Toe" Groza. Later in the decade, the Browns featured power runner Jim Brown, whom many consider the greatest running back in NFL history.

The most memorable game of the decade was the 1958 championship contest between the New York Giants and the upstart Baltimore Colts. New York had won the championship in 1956 over the Chicago Bears, 47–7 and was heavily favored to dominate the Colts at Yankee Stadium. The Giants rallied from a 14–3 halftime deficit to lead 17–14 with minutes remaining. Baltimore quarterback Johnny Unitas coolly completed pass after pass to set up a field goal that tied the game with ten seconds to play. In the NFL's first sudden-death championship game, Unitas methodically moved the ball downfield to set up a goal-line plunge by Alan Ameche for a 23–17 Colts victory.

The 1956 championship game, seen in nearly 11 million homes on television, galvanized interest in NFL football. The increased coverage gave defense and defensive players far more attention than before. Defensive linemen and backs such as Gino Marchetti and Dick "Night Train" Lane became known to millions of fans. Despite the NFL's increased popularity, player salaries remained low, averaging between $7,000 and $10,000.

By the early 1960s, the NFL was increasingly popular and profitable. The 1961 championship game between the New York Giants and the Green Bay Packers produced the league's first million-dollar gate. Television and radio rights also reached an all-time high. These conditions encouraged the prospect of expansion, but the NFL was reluctant to add new teams. Taking advantage of the opportunity, Texas oilman Lamar

Hunt and other investors formed the rival American Football League (the third league with that name). The AFL began play in 1960 with eight teams in two divisions and a five-year, $10.6 million television contract with ABC.

In the NFL, the Green Bay Packers dominated the 1960s with five championships under Coach Vince Lombardi. Jim Brown remained the NFL's outstanding rusher and led Cleveland to a championship in 1964. The AFL, which many observers believed would be short-lived, proved to be more enduring. National television coverage helped the AFL gain a substantial following among fans who enjoyed the "run and gun"—high-scoring games that featured more passing and scoring than NFL contests.

The league rivalries also led to a bidding war for top college players and put upward pressure on player salaries. In 1965, for example, the AFL's New York Jets signed University of Alabama All-American quarterback Joe Namath to a contract for the unheard-of sum of $400,000.

The Beginning of the Super Bowl Era, 1967–1989

Under the leadership of Commissioner Pete Rozelle, who replaced Bell in 1960, the NFL prospered. During the 1960s, attendance nearly doubled over the previous decade, and teams played in eight new stadiums. On the other hand, the competition between the two leagues, especially the continuing salary wars, was an ongoing worry.

In 1966, officials from the two leagues began negotiations, and on June 8, they announced a merger agreement. Following the 1966 season, a championship game between the NFL and AFL champions would be played; at first called the AFL-NFL World Championship of Professional Football, the contest became known as the Super Bowl in 1969. The teams would continue to play as independent leagues until 1970, when they would merge operations. In the meantime, there would be only one college draft, ending the cutthroat competition.

In the game now known as Super Bowl I, the NFL champion Green Bay Packers routed the AFL's Kansas City Chiefs 35–10. The following season, Green Bay returned and defeated the Oakland Raiders. In Super Bowl III, the New York Jets, led by quarterback Joe Namath, faced the Baltimore Colts. Before the game, Namath, irritated by constant talk of the NFL's superiority, brashly "guaranteed" that the Jets would win.

When the clock ran out, the Jets had won 16–7, a sweet victory for AFL fans.

In the final part of the merger in 1970, the ten AFL teams made up the nucleus of the American Football Conference (AFC), which allowed old AFL rivalries to continue. To even the number of teams, three NFL franchises also joined the AFC: the Pittsburgh Steelers, Cleveland Browns, and Baltimore Colts. Altogether, the NFL would increase from 16 to 26 teams, promising continued huge television revenues.

The popularity of professional football continued in the 1970s, with attendance at NFL games increasing by nearly 70 percent over the 1960s, to 109 million. Polls conducted in 1972 indicated that football had surpassed baseball as America's favorite sport. More new stadiums were built, including the $175 million Louisiana Superdome, opened in 1975. Cheerleading took on a new dimension with the creation of the Dallas Cowboy Cheerleaders in 1972. The success of the NFL was reflected by ABC's *Monday Night Football,* which became one of the network's most popular shows, the second-longest-running show in prime time. The program debuted on CBS in the mid-1960s, but it became a fan favorite only after moving to ABC, where sportscaster Howard Cosell was joined by former NFL players Frank Gifford and Don Meredith.

Another indication of the interest in professional football was the founding of a new rival, the World Football League, in 1974, only three years after the NFL-AFL merger. The new league consisted of 12 teams, including one in Hawaii. It lasted only two seasons but gave another upward push to professional football players' salaries.

The Miami Dolphins, who under coach Don Shula won back-to-back Super Bowls in 1973 and 1974, lost key players to the World Football League, including star running back Larry Csonka. However, the team of the decade was Art Rooney's Pittsburgh Steelers, which won four Super Bowls. Rooney had owned an NFL franchise in Pittsburgh since 1933, but his team had never won a championship. The Steelers were anchored on defense by the "Steel Curtain," which featured fan favorite tackle

Joe Namath quarterbacked the New York Jets to a 16–7 upset victory over the Baltimore Colts in Super Bowl III in January 1969. The game helped pave the way for the full merger of the American Football League with the National Football League in 1970. *(Sports Illustrated/Getty Images)*

"Mean Joe" Greene and were led by their resilient quarterback Terry Bradshaw. Quarterback Roger Staubach of the Dallas Cowboys also led his team to two Super Bowl victories during the decade. Average player salaries climbed substantially from just $25,000 in 1967 to $79,000 in 1980.

During the 1980s, the NFL had continued success but also considerable turmoil. In 1983, the United States Football League (USFL) was organized, providing still another challenge to the established league, with a 12-team spring schedule. The league signed a number of outstanding college players—including Heisman Trophy–winning running back Herschel Walker to the biggest contract in professional football history, $4 million for four years—but the USFL folded in 1986.

At the same time, the NFL faced another challenge, this time from its own players. In 1982, the NFL Players Association called a strike over players' wages, which caused the NFL to cancel part of its schedule for the season. A second players' strike in 1987 focused on the issue of "free agency" for the NFL players. In a failed experiment, the owners used replacement players to continue the NFL schedule, but they eventually reached a settlement with the NFL players, who returned to finish the season.

Despite the turmoil, the NFL continued to prosper in the 1980s. Quarterback Joe Montana of the San Francisco 49ers led his team to four Super Bowl victories and was named Most Valuable Player in three of them. Super Bowl XVI between the 49ers and the Cincinnati Bengals in 1982 had the highest Nielsen television rating (49.1) of any sporting event in history. The Washington Redskins won two Super Bowls during the decade, its first NFL championships since 1942. The New York Giants, now playing home games at the Meadowlands in East Rutherford, New Jersey, won their first championship since 1956 by defeating the Denver Broncos in the 1987 Super Bowl. Giants linebacker Lawrence Taylor was one of the NFL's most intimidating players, piling up 104 quarterback sacks during the 1980s.

The most popular lineman was William "The Refrigerator" Perry, a 6-foot, 2-inch (1.9-meter), 340-pound (154-kilogram) defensive tackle for the Chicago Bears. In 1985, Bears coach Mike Ditka used Perry as an offensive back on plays when Chicago was near the goal line threatening to score. Fans watched in awe as the gigantic Perry handled the ball eight times, gaining 9 total yards (8 meters). He scored three touchdowns and passed for another. Dan Marino of the Miami Dolphins was one of the outstanding quarterbacks of the decade,

and Eric Dickerson, Walter Payton, and Tony Dorsett were among the top running backs.

Player salaries continued to rise during the 1980s, with Denver quarterback John Elway earning a record $2.117 million a year. Average salaries more than doubled in five years, to $194,000 in 1985, and rose to $352,000 in 1990. The NFL became more fully integrated during the decade: Doug Williams of the Washington Redskins became the first black quarterback to start a Super Bowl game in 1988, Johnny Grier was the first African American to referee an NFL game that year, and in 1989, Art Shell of the Oakland Raiders became the first black head coach in the modern NFL. By 2006, the NFL players were 64.1 percent African American.

America's Game, 1990–Present

In 1989, Paul Tagliabue replaced Rozelle as NFL commissioner. By the early 1990s, he was able to negotiate an agreement with the NFL Players Association that included a salary cap on all NFL teams and ended the bitter labor disputes of the 1980s. The NFL continued to expand and prosper during the 1990s and into the 2000s. One of the hallmarks of the period was the marketing of NFL football as a commercial product. The NFL licensed a wide range of products with the league logo. Tagliabue also hoped to expand the league to other countries with the establishment of the NFL Europe league in the 1990s. The new league was only a modest success, but it served as a training ground for NFL talent, along with the Arena League in the United States.

In the 1990s, the Dallas Cowboys, who suffered through a 1–15 season in 1989, made a resurgence. Behind the accurate passing of quarterback Troy Aikman and the power running of Emmitt Smith, Dallas won three Super Bowls during the decade. Team owner Jerry Jones aggressively marketed the team by signing sponsorship deals with corporate giants such as Pepsi, American Express, and Nike.

By the early 2000s, however, the center of the NFL power had shifted to the Northeast, where the New England Patriots under Coach Bill Belichick won three Super Bowls between 2002 and 2005. The Patriots returned to the Superbowl (XLII) in 2008 with an undefeated team, only to lose in the last seconds to the New York Giants, 17–14. During this stretch, Patriots quarterback Tom Brady established himself as one of the coolest and most accurate passers in the league.

Meanwhile, the Super Bowl became a national holiday, with weeks of coverage preceding the game and halftime shows more spectacular than George Preston Marshall ever could have imagined. Player salaries in 2000 averaged $1.1 million and rose to an average of $2.4 million by 2010. Professional football, played by 32 teams, had become America's game.

John M. Carroll

See also: All-America Football Conference; Football, College; *Monday Night Football*; National Football League Players Association; Stadiums and Arenas; Super Bowl; Violence in Sports.

Further Reading

Bennett, Tom, et al. *Illustrated History of Pro Football.* New York: Madison Square, 1990.

Brown, Paul, and Jack Clary. *PB: The Paul Brown Story.* New York: Atheneum, 1979.

Carroll, Bob. *When the Grass Was Real: Unitas, Brown, Lombardi, Sayers, Butkus, Namath, and All the Rest: The Best Ten Years of Pro Football.* New York: Simon & Shuster, 1993.

Carroll, John M. *Fritz Pollard: A Pioneer in Racial Advancement.* Urbana: University of Illinois Press, 1992.

———. *Red Grange and the Rise of Modern Football.* Urbana: University of Illinois Press, 1999.

Coenen, Craig R. *From Sandlots to the Super Bowl: The National Football League, 1920–1967.* Knoxville: University of Tennessee Press, 2005.

Daly, Dan, and Bob O'Donnell. *The Pro Football Chronicle.* New York: Macmillan, 1990.

Herskowitz, Mickey. *The Golden Age of Pro Football: NFL Football in the 1950s.* Dallas, TX: Taylor, 1990.

Jable, J. Thomas. "The Birth of Professional Football: Pittsburgh Athletic Clubs Ring in Professionals in 1892." *Western Pennsylvania Historical Magazine* 62:2 (April 1979): 131–147.

MacCambridge, Michael. *America's Game: The Epic Story of How Pro Football Captured a Nation.* New York: Random House, 2004.

Maltby, Marc S. *The Origins and Development of Professional Football, 1890–1920.* New York: Routledge, 1997.

McClellan, Keith. *The Sunday Game: At the Dawn of Professional Football.* Akron, OH: University of Akron Press, 1998.

Oriard, Michael. *Brand NFL: Making and Selling America's Favorite Sport.* Chapel Hill: University of North Carolina Press, 2007.

Peterson, Robert W. *Pigskin: The Early Years of Pro Football.* New York: Oxford University Press, 1997.

Ruck, Rob, Maggie Jones Patterson, and Michael P. Weber. *Rooney: A Sporting Life.* Lincoln: University of Nebraska Press, 2010.

Smith, Robert. *Illustrated History of Pro Football.* New York: Madison Square, 1970.

49ers, San Francisco

The San Francisco 49ers were an original franchise in the All-America Football Conference (AAFC) in 1946, a rival league that tried to break the monopoly of the National Football League (NFL) on professional football. The 49ers were among the first major league sports franchises on the West Coast. They joined the NFL in 1950 but for years were no better than mediocre. The franchise was rejuvenated by Coach Bill Walsh, who made them the team of the 1980s and the first squad to win five Super Bowls.

Origins

The 49ers originally were owned by trucking magnate Tony Morabito, who previously had tried to get an NFL franchise. His new team was composed mostly of local athletes and played at the publicly owned Kezar Stadium. The 49ers were the second-best team in the AAFC, behind the Cleveland Browns. After the AAFC broke up in 1949, the 49ers joined the NFL along with the Browns and the Baltimore Colts.

In the 1950s, the 49ers were a mediocre team. They had one of their best seasons in 1957, when they competed for the West Division title with the Detroit Lions, but lost in a playoff game. Nonetheless, they were innovative, employing the shotgun formation in 1960, featuring quarterback John Brodie, who played his entire career (1957–1973) with San Francisco.

The 49ers won their first division title (10–3–1) in 1970 under Mike Nolan, who was named NFL Coach of the Year, and went on to win the National Football Conference playoff, 17–14, over the Minnesota Vikings; however, they lost the NFL title game to the Dallas Cowboys, 17–10. After the season, the team moved to the more modern and accessible Candlestick Park. They won the West Division for the next two years and advanced to the title game each year against Dallas but lost both games. Thereafter, the team struggled for several years.

In 1977, Edward DeBartolo, the father of the American shopping mall, purchased 90 percent of the 49ers franchise for $17.5 million, and gave it to his son, Edward, Jr., who became active in the management of the team. In 1979, Bill Walsh, the former offensive coordinator for the Cincinnati Bengals and former Stanford University head coach, became the 49ers coach.

In Walsh's first season, the team went 2–14, repeating the dismal record of the two prior years. In 1981, the 49ers went on to the Super Bowl, the fastest turnaround in NFL history. They would become a dominant force in the NFL for the next two decades.

Walsh Era

Walsh employed the West Coast offense, which relied on giving the quarterback many options for short passes and required receivers to adjust their routes to take advantage of coverage weaknesses. The system needed a bright quarterback with patience, poise, and vision, who could make instant reads and adjust to pressure with dump-offs to outlet receivers. The 49ers found these qualities in former University of Notre Dame quarterback Joe Montana, whom other NFL teams considered too small, too slow, and lacking in arm strength.

In 1981, San Francisco took the conference 13–3 and toppled the New York Giants in the division playoffs, 38–24. They went on to defeat the Dallas Cowboys 28–27 in the league championship, when Dwight Clark made "The Catch," leaping high to snare a desperation pass from Montana deep in the end zone with less than a minute left to play. In Super Bowl XVI, the 49ers beat the Cincinnati Bengals, 26–21.

The strike-shortened 1982 season saw poor performance, as the team went 3–6. The following year, they achieved a 10–6 record and beat the Detroit Lions in the division playoffs, but they lost to the Washington Redskins in the conference championship game, 24–21.

In 1984, the 49ers went 15–1, then a record for regular-season wins. They took the next two playoff games and captured Super Bowl XIX over Dan Marino's Miami Dolphins, 38–16. The total season mark of 18–1 was the second best in NFL history to that time, after Miami's undefeated 1972 season.

In 1985, the team went 10–6, led by Roger Craig, the first NFL player to have 1,000 yards (914 meters) rushing and receiving in the same season. In 1986, the 49ers advanced to the NFL championship game, where they were devastated by the New York Giants, 49–3. They followed up with a 13–2 season, leading the NFL in offense and defense, but were upset in the first round of the playoffs by the Minnesota Vikings, 36–24.

The team struggled in 1988, going 10–6, but easily beat the Vikings in the playoffs and then upset the Chicago Bears 28–3 in the NFL championship at Soldier Field, playing in a wind chill of -26 degrees. They advanced to Super Bowl XXIII against the Bengals, who led by 3 points late in the game; however, Mon-tana drove his club 92 yards (84 meters), ending with a touchdown pass to John Taylor to win the championship 20–16.

Walsh retired in 1989, and defensive coordinator George Seifert replaced him. The club went 14–2 and swept through the playoffs, clobbering the Denver Broncos 55–10 in Super Bowl XXIV. Montana earned his third Super Bowl Most Valuable Player (MVP) award. The next season, the 49ers again went 14–2 and advanced to the NFL championship, losing to the New York Giants 15–13 after a last-minute fumble by Craig. From 1988 through 1990, the 49ers won 18 consecutive road victories, a league record.

In 1991, Montana injured his elbow, and he was replaced by Steve Young. The team went 10–6, but missed the postseason for the first time since 1982. The following year, the squad went 14–2, and Young was named MVP. But the Dallas Cowboys prevailed in the NFL title game, 30–20. The 1993 season ended with a similar result, as the Cowboys again bested the 49ers in the NFL championship, 38–21.

In 1994, the team owner invested heavily in star free agents, including Deion Sanders. The club went 13–3 for the season and returned to the NFL title game, finally defeating the Cowboys, 38–28. The 49ers went on to the Super Bowl and slammed the San Diego Chargers, 49–26. Young tossed a record six touchdown passes and was the MVP once again. The 49ers made the playoffs the next four years but failed to advance to the Super Bowl. At this time, they had a great passing attack led by Young and Jerry Rice, the NFL's all-time leading receiver and touchdown maker, who made 186 touchdowns with the 49ers.

A scandal off the field hurt the team's image. In 1997, DeBartolo was wiretapped and caught paying $400,000 to Louisiana Governor Edwin Edwards to secure a New Orleans casino license. He turned state's evidence and pled guilty. The owner was suspended from active control of the 49ers for one year, and his sister, Denise DeBartolo York, and her husband, Dr. John York, ran the team. DeBartolo subsequently was involved in family lawsuits that led to him to relinquish control of the team to his sister and brother-in-law.

Since then, the team's only playoff appearance came in 2002, when quarterback Jeff Garcia led the team to make up a 24-point deficit to beat the New York Giants, 39–30. They subsequently were ousted by the Tampa Bay Buccaneers. The 49ers did not have a winning season through 2010, while going through four coaches.

Steven A. Riess

See also: All-America Football Conference; Football, Professional.

Further Reading

Dickey, Glenn. *Glenn Dickey's 49ers: The Rise, Fall, and Rebirth of the NFL's Greatest Dynasty.* Roseville, CA: Prima, 2000.

Harris, David. *The Genius: How Bill Walsh Reinvented Football and Created an NFL Dynasty.* New York: Random House, 2008.

Silver, Michael. "The '80s: Walsh's West Coast Offense Reigns." *Sports Illustrated* 91:8 (August 30, 1999): 84–86.

Tuckman, Michael W., and Jeff Schultz. *The San Francisco 49ers: Team of the Decade.* Rocklin, CA: Prima, 1990.

Foster, Andrew "Rube" (1879–1930)

Andrew "Rube" Foster was a star pitcher in the Negro Leagues who later became manager and owner of the Chicago American Giants. An outstanding entrepreneur, he founded the Negro National League in 1920, serving as its president until 1926. Foster viewed the league as a means to promote black capitalism, advance the race, and promote community pride. He was recognized for his accomplishments by election to the National Baseball Hall of Fame in 1981.

Foster was born on September 17, 1879, in Calvert, Texas, to Andrew Foster, Sr., an elder of Calvert's Methodist Church, and his wife Sarah. Although he was asthmatic as a child, the younger Foster frequently played baseball. He reportedly organized and operated a team while still in grade school. After Foster's mother died, his father remarried and moved the family to southwest Texas.

Foster left school after the eighth grade and ran away to Fort Worth to pursue a baseball career. At the age of 17, he began playing for the Fort Worth Yellow Jackets, an independent black team that barnstormed throughout Texas and bordering states.

He also began to pitch batting practice to Major League Baseball teams that held spring training in Texas. In 1901, the 21-year-old Foster pitched against Cornelius "Connie" Mack's Philadelphia Athletics, which led to an offer to pitch for Frank Leland's Chicago Union Giants, a black semiprofessional team in 1902. However, his performance was unsatisfactory, and he was released. He pitched that summer for a white semiprofessional team, Bardeen's Otsego (Michigan) Independents.

Then in 1903, Foster moved to Philadelphia, where he would play for the next several years, beginning with the Cuban X-Giants (founded by a contingent of former Cuban Giants), for whom he reportedly won 44 straight games (accurate statistics for the Negro Leagues do not exist), leading the team to victory in the eastern Black championship. The following year, Foster switched teams yet again, moving to the Philadelphia Giants. Again, Foster led his squad to the eastern Black championship, helping the Giants defeat his former team. The Giants won again in 1905, and in 1906, they captured the International League of Independent Professional Ball Players pennant. The league was comprised of all-black and all-white teams in metropolitan Philadelphia.

In 1907, Foster returned to Chicago, where he joined the Leland Giants as player-manager and also booked games, strengthening the team by bringing with him some of his former teammates. Foster led the Leland Giants to the Chicago semipro City League title. They went 110–10 and had a 48-game winning streak. In 1908, the team changed its name to the Giants. One year later, Foster and the team's investors broke with Leland, and the court awarded Foster control of the team. After the major league season, they played the major league Chicago Cubs in a competitive three-game series.

In 1911, Foster established his own team, called the American Giants, in partnership with white baseball executive John M. Schorling. The team won the City League title in 1911 and 1912. The American Giants played at the site of the original White Sox park at 39th Street and Shields, just a few blocks from the growing "black belt," an area of Chicago's South Side that became home to many African American migrants from the South, often playing white teams during the week.

The American Giants attracted a growing following among baseball fans, both for their winning ways and their showmanship, and on some Sundays, they outdrew the city's two major league teams. The Giants attracted high-quality players with high salaries, the prestige of playing for a successful team, and the opportunity to travel the country on comfortable Pullman cars. They took or shared Negro League titles in 1914, 1915, and 1917. Beginning in 1912, Foster took his team on successful winter barnstorming tours to California, and in 1915, they won the California Winter League championship.

In 1919, Foster proposed the formation of the Negro National League to provide entertainment for the black

Former star pitcher Rube Foster organized the first successful black baseball league, the Negro National League, in 1920. The Chicago American Giants, of which Foster was owner and manager, dominated black baseball in the 1920s. *(Diamond Images/Getty Images)*

community, create new black businesses, and generate jobs for black athletes, umpires, and office clerks. He chose the right moment, as the "Great Migration" of African Americans from the rural South was in progress, dramatically increasing the population of blacks in Northern cities, who would make up the needed fan base. Foster hoped to limit or end white ownership of black baseball teams and to eliminate much of the infighting among black owners. Of course, he also intended to control and profit from the new league.

Several black team owners met in Kansas City, Missouri, in February 1920 to draw up the league's constitution. They created an eight-team league, located mainly in the Midwest, with Foster as president. The Negro National League prospered, leading to the creation of the Eastern Colored League in 1923. The two leagues contested the Black World Series from 1924 to 1927. The American Giants fared well in the league,

winning the first three league titles from 1920 to 1922, and then again in 1926–1927. Foster was criticized for favoring his team as league president. To his credit, however, he often offered other teams and even players financial assistance to keep the league stable.

In May 1925, a gas leak in his Indianapolis hotel room left Foster unconscious. Although he was rescued and survived, thereafter, he became prone to illnesses, and his behavior became increasingly erratic. In 1926, when he became dangerous and violent, a judge ruled Foster insane and had him placed in the state mental asylum in Kankakee, Illinois, where he died on December 9, 1930, from a heart attack. He was so respected in Chicago's African American community that mourners lined up around the block to pay their respects as Foster's body lay in state for three days. Some 3,000 people braved the cold and snow of the Chicago winter to attend the funeral.

Both the American Giants and the Negro National League declined without Foster's leadership, and with waning fan support, the Black World Series ended in 1927. While Foster was institutionalized, his partner Schorling ran the team for several years before selling out to white businessman William Trimble in 1928. In the early 1930s, some of Chicago's African American business leaders attempted to revive the team, but without Foster, they had little success. The Negro National League was forced to cease operations in 1931, an economic victim of the Great Depression.

Ronald Young

See also: African American Baseball, Before 1920; African American Baseball, Negro League Era.

Further Reading

Cottrell, Robert C. *The Best Pitcher in Baseball: The Life of Rube Foster, Negro League Giant.* New York: New York University Press, 2001.

Debono, Paul. *The Chicago American Giants.* Jefferson, NC: McFarland, 2007.

Heaphy, Leslie A. *The Negro Leagues, 1869–1960.* Jefferson, NC: McFarland, 2003.

Lomax, Michael E. "Black Entrepreneurship in the National Pastime: The Rise of Semiprofessional Baseball in Black Chicago, 1890–1915." *Journal of Sport History* 25:1 (Spring 1998): 43–64.